MASTERING™

MICROSOFT® OFFICE 2000
PROFESSIONAL EDITION

Gini Courter
Annette Marquis

SYBEX®

San Francisco • Paris • Düsseldorf • Soest • London

Associate Publisher: Amy Romanoff
Contracts and Licensing Manager: Kristine
O'Callaghan
Acquisitions & Developmental Editor: Sherry Bonelli
Editors: James A. Compton, Sally Englefried,
Kris Vanberg-Wolff, Kari Brooks, Tory McLearn
Technical Editors: Keith Giddeon, Pamela Rice Hahn,
Russ Jacobs
Book Designers: Patrick Dintino, Catalin Dulfu,
Franz Baumhackl
Graphic Illustrator: Tony Jonick
Electronic Publishing Specialists: Cyndy Johnsen,
Adrian Woolhouse
Project Team Leader: Shannon Murphy
Proofreaders: Judy Weiss, Shannon Murphy,
Bronwyn Erickson
Indexer: Ted Laux
Cover Designer: Design Site
Cover Illustrator/Photographer: Sergie Loobkoff

SYBEX is a registered trademark of SYBEX Inc.

Mastering is a trademark of SYBEX Inc.

Screen reproductions produced with Collage Complete.
Collage Complete is a trademark of Inner Media Inc.

TRADEMARKS: SYBEX has attempted throughout this
book to distinguish proprietary trademarks from
descriptive terms by following the capitalization style
used by the manufacturer.

Library of Congress Card Number: 98-88950
ISBN: 0-7821-2313-9

Manufactured in the United States of America

10 9 8 7 6 5 4 3 2 1

This book is dedicated to the staff of TRIAD Consulting, LLC, who have already become Office 2000 troubleshooters extraordinaire: Karla Browning, James Howe, Kim Keener, Sharon Roberts, and Richard Steinhoff.

ACKNOWLEDGMENTS

Sybex continues to amaze us with the quality of the people that they bring together to create a book. At times, this book felt like a family reunion; other moments felt like driving in rush hour. So, first, we'd like to acknowledge the family. Our special thanks go to Sherry Bonelli, our acquisitions and developmental editor, who acquired us with gusto, and associate publisher Amy Romanoff. Sherry and Amy have helped to guide the overall direction of this book and the whole Mastering series. We hadn't worked with our editor, Jim Compton, in a while. Jim works diligently at his craft and has kept the many pieces of this book in superb order. He sends gentle reminders and truly sees the book from the point of view of the reader—all of which he describes as "just doing my job." It's been a pleasure to work with Jim on this book.

Writing a volume this large, covering a huge, full-featured product like Office 2000, is a Herculean task. Three other authors were willing to work with us and had much to do with the quality of this book. We'd like to thank Karla Browning (who wrote the Publisher and PowerPoint chapters), Shiela Dienes (Word), and Claudia Willen (Excel) for their careful attention to this endeavor.

We appreciate the additional editorial support from Sally Engelfried, Kris Vanberg-Wolff, Kari Brooks, and Tory McLearn and the help of our technical editors, Keith Giddeon, Pamela Rice Hahn, and Russ Jacobs.

We also thank our Sybex production team: Shannon Murphy, project team leader; Cyndy Johnsen and Adrian Woolhouse, desktop publishers; and Judy Weiss and Bronwyn Erickson, proofreaders. We write words—they make them attractive and get the pages out to the printer on time. We appreciate the incredibly fast turnaround and all the hard work by our production team.

CONTENTS AT A GLANCE

APPENDICES

TABLE OF CONTENTS

PART II • CREATING DAZZLING DOCUMENTS IN WORD

PART III • AND NOW, PRESENTING POWERPOINT!

PART V • NUMBER CRUNCHING WITH EXCEL

22 Creating and Printing Excel Worksheets   541

APPENDICES

INTRODUCTION

Microsoft Office 2000 is the most feature-packed version of Office to be released to date. Office 2000 has everything you need to produce print and online documents that will put you at the head of the class.

Beyond the traditional word-processing, spreadsheet, and database tools, Office 2000 includes a massive array of Web creation and collaboration tools, data analysis and reporting tools, and graphic design features that gives everyone the ability to create any type of publication and manage any type of data imaginable. If you are a previous Office user, you'll be thrilled with the addition of Microsoft Publisher to this incredible suite. If you are new to Microsoft Office, you are in for a treat as you experience the power that has made Office the dominant office suite on the market.

Microsoft offers several editions of its Office suite to address the different needs of individuals, small business users, and large corporations. The Office applications are bundled together as follows:

Edition	Applications
Standard	Word, Excel, Outlook, and PowerPoint
Small Business	Word, Excel, Outlook, and Publisher
Professional	Word, Excel, PowerPoint, Outlook, Publisher, and Access
Premium	Word, Excel, PowerPoint, Outlook, Publisher, Access, FrontPage, and PhotoDraw
Developer's	Word, Excel, PowerPoint, Outlook, Publisher, Access, FrontPage, PhotoDraw, Visual Basic for Applications (VBA) 6 development system, and other programming support

All of the editions include Microsoft Internet Explorer and a number of smaller applets, such as the Microsoft Clip Gallery and Microsoft Chart. If the edition you have is missing an application you want, you can buy many of the applications separately. Once installed, the program will integrate with the other applications seamlessly.

As the title suggests, this book focuses on the applications in the Professional edition of Office 2000. For information about applications included only in the Premium or Developer's edition, please see *Mastering Office 2000 Premium Edition* (available in mid-1999) instead.

Using This Book

Mastering Office 2000 was written to help you put Office to work with a minimum of frustration. It would take a book five times as large as this one to cover every Office 2000 feature with the attention it deserves. We have chosen to include the most commonly used and the most useful features of each of the Office 2000 applications. You will find in-depth coverage of all of the major Office 2000 topics and most of the minor ones.

 NOTE Sybex also publishes a *Mastering* book nearly the size of this book for each major Office 2000 application. If you need additional information about an Office 2000 feature, we suggest you consult the *Mastering* book for the application you want to know more about.

Throughout the chapters, you will find sidebars, brief boxed discussions that call your attention to related topics. In general, these sidebars provide additional information about a topic or more detailed explanations of issues presented in the text. "Mastering the Opportunities" sidebars describe helpful techniques you can use to get the most out of Office 2000 in your setting. "Mastering Troubleshooting" sidebars focus on common mistakes or problems that users develop and show how to get around them. You'll also find Tips, Notes, and Warnings scattered throughout the book to highlight additional useful information.

 To focus on features introduced or greatly improved in Office 2000, look for the symbol shown here.

This book is divided into nine parts, each of which focuses on specific skills related to an application or group of applications.

Part I: Working in Office 2000

Chapters 1 and 2 provide an overview of Office 2000 and show you essential skills that cross over all the applications. Here you'll learn more about the Office 2000 family and see highlights of some of the exciting new features. You'll also be introduced to the brand-new look for Clippit, the helpful Office Assistant.

Part II: Creating Dazzling Documents in Word

Part II gives you a complete view of Word, from basic editing and formatting to advanced collaboration features. Chapters 3–6 teach how to apply paragraph formatting, such as borders and bullets or numbers, and how to use language tools such as the Spelling and Grammar Checker. You'll also learn to create newspaper-type columns and to display data in columns and rows using Word's powerful Tables features.

Once you've mastered the fundamentals, Chapters 7–12 take you deeper into Word's powerful high-level skills. You'll learn all about inserting and positioning graphics and how to streamline your work with styles, outlines and templates. Other power features you'll explore include mail merge, Word forms, working with large documents, referencing documents, and collaborating with others.

Part III: And Now, Presenting PowerPoint!

Part III takes you on a tour of PowerPoint. You'll learn how to create a basic presentation, how to add formatting and animation, and how to make a PowerPoint presentation. Although PowerPoint offers a more modest feature set than the other applications, there is still plenty you can do here. Chapters 13–16 take you through all the operations to make you a PowerPoint expert in no time.

Part IV: Getting Organized with Outlook

There is no better way to keep your life organized and your communications in order than with Outlook 2000. In Part IV, you'll learn how to keep contact information, manage your time and tasks, and track e-mail correspondence. If you have access to Microsoft Exchange Server, you'll also learn how to work with others across the Exchange Server network, sharing calendars and assigning tasks, among other things.

Part V: Number Crunching with Excel

Part V takes you through the major tools in the premier spreadsheet application, Excel 2000. Excel has always been a strong application, and the enhancements and additions in Excel 2000 only make it better. In this part, you'll learn how to enter and format spreadsheets, create formulas, design charts, and manage and analyze data. You also explore how to share workbooks and even merge workbook changes. You find out even more about Excel's new features in Parts VII, VIII, and IX.

Part VI: Access for the Nonprogrammer

Access is a powerful program that anyone who understands their data can use to create useful database applications, even without programming skills. In Part VI, you'll have a chance to create a database from scratch after obtaining a good background in database design and structure. You'll learn how to design tables, create forms for data entry, and write reports and queries to extract data from the database. When you've mastered these skills, you'll have a solid foundation to learn about macros and Visual Basic in Part VIII and Data Access Pages for the Web in Part IX.

Part VII: Using the Office Data Analysis Tools

Part VII is a mix of the old and the new. Microsoft Query, covered in Chapter 34, has been around for a while to help you query data in Excel and Access. But Office 2000 also introduces a whole new type of data analysis tool. In Chapter 35, you'll learn about creating three-dimensional OLAP cubes to examine your data from all sides. When combined with ODBC and Excel data sources, OLAP cubes allow you to dig into data in ways never before possible.

Part VIII: Integration and Automation

Part VIII takes you deep behind the scenes in Office 2000 to learn how to use Object Linking and Embedding and how to work with Office 2000's new online features. You'll also learn how to customize the Office environment and use macros and VBA to automate repetitive tasks. You'll learn about Web folders and Web discussions, conducting online meetings, adding toolbars and changing command bar options, and finally how to write the code you need to help you get your work done.

Part IX: Publishing with Office

If you still think of publishing as something that only happens in a big skyscraper in New York City, you're definitely behind the times. Publishing has taken on many new forms and Office 2000 offers a slew of tools to help you create online and print publications that rival Madison Avenue. Whether you're creating a Web site or a party invitation, Office 2000 has a tool for you. In Part IX you'll learn all about publishing in Office 2000. We start with an overview of desktop and online publishing and then move quickly into the newest member of the Office family, Publisher 2000. After Publisher, you'll have a chance to experience the exciting new Web design tools in Word, Excel, and Access and see how to create an online presentation with PowerPoint. By the time you're finished with Part IX, you'll know enough about publishing to make even the boss look good!

Appendix A: Installing Microsoft Office

This appendix walks you through the process of installing and reinstalling Microsoft Office 2000 on a stand-alone computer. By becoming familiar with the completely revised installation process and the choices available to you, you can maintain control over the installation process and use only the hard drive space that you need. Microsoft's new Install On First Use feature, for example, makes it easier to add functionality on the fly, and the Detect and Repair feature foresees problems with the Office program files before they affect your system.

Conventions Used in This Book

Throughout this book, you will find references to the Standard and Formatting toolbars and to the new Personal (or Personalized) toolbar. The Standard and Formatting toolbars are the two toolbars most commonly displayed in previous versions of Office applications as shown here.

The Personal toolbar is a new feature of Office 2000 that, by default, displays the buttons you use most commonly on one toolbar row. As you work with additional buttons, Office adds them to the toolbar, and less frequently used buttons are removed.

Buttons displayed on the Personal toolbar still "belong" to either the Standard or Formatting toolbar. In this book, you will see figures and graphics that display the Personal toolbar option and others that show the more traditional two-toolbar display. In either case, the text refers to the native location of the button, that is, the Standard or Formatting toolbar. To learn how you can turn Personal toolbars off, refer to Chapter 38.

We've also used a couple of typographic variations you've probably seen in other computer books: **boldface type** shows any text you would type into Office dialog boxes; and `this font` shows any kind of programming instructions, such as URLs, Excel formulas, and HTML or Visual Basic code.

We'd Love to Hear from You!

We hope this book provides you with the skills you need to master Microsoft Office 2000. We would love to hear what you think. We always enjoy hearing from our readers and are especially interested in hearing about your experiences and accomplishments with Office 2000.

Gini Courter and Annette Marquis
c/o Sybex, Inc.
1151 Marina Village Parkway
Alameda, CA 94501
E-mail: triad@kode.net

PART I

Working in Office 2000

LEARN TO:

- **Use the Office 2000 interface**

- **Create new documents in Office 2000**

- **Edit existing documents**

- **Manage files**

- **Preview and print documents**

CHAPTER <u>1</u>

How Office 2000 Works for You

Every release of Microsoft Office brings us closer to a fully integrated environment where each tool works seamlessly with every other tool. Microsoft Office 2000 is no exception. In fact, simplifying the user experience and increasing the integration between Office components were two of the key objectives Microsoft had in developing this product. Office 2000 is a powerful application even on a stand-alone computer, but it is designed as a workgroup tool, and that is where it really shines. If you are a single user, don't fret; Office 2000 will do most everything you ask of it, and more. And if you want to share your work with others, you can use Office 2000 to communicate with other users around the world through the Internet. However, if you want to truly experience the muscle contained in Office 2000, there is no substitute for a workgroup environment. Microsoft has gone all out to make Office 2000 the ultimate platform for the business user.

With Office 2000, you can produce impressive proposals, manage your busy calendar, track important contacts, make sound financial projections, create dynamite presentations, and establish and maintain a sensational presence on your corporate intranet or the World Wide Web.

There are several editions of Office 2000, including the Small Business Edition with Word, PowerPoint, Publisher, Excel, and Outlook, and the Premium Edition, which includes Word, Access, Excel, FrontPage, Outlook, PhotoDraw, PowerPoint, and Publisher. Microsoft Office Professional 2000, the version we cover in this book, features some of the most popular and powerful software programs around. The suite includes 32-bit versions of six applications:

Word: The most popular Windows word processor

Excel: A powerful and easy-to-use spreadsheet application

Access: A true relational database for the Windows platform

PowerPoint: A presentation tool that allows anyone to create slide shows

Outlook: A convenient desktop information manager

Publisher: A highly accessible desktop publishing system

These applications are the latest, most powerful versions of Microsoft's award-winning office productivity tools. If you have worked with prior releases of these products, you'll want to learn some new techniques for the Office 2000 version. Office 2000 programs support better integration: between applications, between yourself and other users, and with the Internet and intranets. All applications include the greatly improved Office Assistant, shown in Figure 1.1, an active help feature that offers timesaving advice to help you work more efficiently.

FIGURE 1.1

*Clippit, the newly
refurbished Office
Assistant, is ready and
able to come to
your aid.*

Office Professional 2000 also includes a number of smaller tools or applets:

Internet Explorer 5.0:   The latest release of the popular Internet browser

OfficeArt: A line-drawing and art manipulation program

WordArt: A text graphics program

Chart: A charting program

Clip Gallery: A program that helps you organize all your clip art and other multimedia objects, such as sound and video files

The applets are available from within all the major applications, so you can add line art, clip art, graphic representations of numeric data, or a text-based logo to any Office document.

What's New in Office 2000

The most significant improvements to Office 2000 center around its seamless integration with the Web. Microsoft has adopted HTML (hypertext markup language), the Internet standard, as an Office 2000 standard format. Quite simply, this means that documents you create in Office no longer have to be converted before you can post them to the Web, and you no longer have to wonder if the person you are sending e-mail to can open your documents. Word documents can be saved directly in HTML and reopened in Office without losing any functionality. Your colleague across the continent with a Macintosh can still open fully formatted Office documents you send her as long as she has a Web browser on her system. If you've ever been frustrated trying to open an important e-mail attachment (or if someone else has been unable to open something you've sent), you can appreciate how valuable this innovation alone is.

The adoption of HTML also means that corporate intranets just got a whole lot richer. Users around the enterprise can now create documents in Office and (with appropriate permissions) post them to the Web without any special training in Web document creation. Internet Explorer 5.0, which is included in Office 2000, can open documents in HTML and the standard Office 2000 file format. Accessing a Web server is as easy as saving a file to your hard drive with the new Open and Save As dialog boxes, shown in Figure 1.2.

FIGURE 1.2

The newly designed Save As dialog box makes it as easy to save documents to a Web server as to a file server.

Collaborating Across the Web

Microsoft is working to improve the functionality of Web pages you create in Office by providing tools that turn them from repositories of static data into living, breathing information animals. Office 2000 offers tools to make collaboration easier and provides data analysis and reporting tools that can be used on active data accessible on the Web. Office 2000 Web collaborations features include:

Web Discussions: Use Web Discussions to hold threaded discussions within Office documents.

Web Subscriptions and Notifications: When you are working on a team project, Office 2000 will notify you via e-mail when new documents are posted or changes made to existing documents.

Presentation Broadcast: Viewing a PowerPoint presentation across the Web can now be a communal affair with real-time chat and live information sharing about the presentation's content.

Online Meetings: Using Microsoft NetMeeting, users can activate a meeting across a network from any of the Office applications. Participants can use options for real-time collaboration on documents, including chat and white-board windows.

For teams that want to analyze live data across a network, Office 2000 offers three exciting new tools:

Office Web Components let you work interactively with real-time data across an intranet using PivotTables, spreadsheets, and charts.

Web Query Wizard takes data from any site on the Web and brings it into Excel for your analysis. Data can be refreshed on request or can be set up to automatically refresh at specified intervals.

Data Access Pages make developing live Web databases a practical possibility. If you've ever tried to create active server pages from your database, you know that it is no easy task—until now. Data Access Pages provide front-end forms in HTML format that are linked to data housed in Access. When users make changes on the forms from their browsers, the changes are immediately reflected in the database.

Simplifying the Office Environment

The Office Advisory Council is a group of Microsoft's corporate customers who participated in design reviews during the development of Office 2000. When this group put together their wish list for Office 2000, Microsoft found that over 25 percent of the requested features were already included in Office—people simply didn't know where to look for them. This prompted Microsoft to look for ways to make the product easier to use and its features more accessible. One result is that you'll find a personalized interface that adjusts to the way you work. Features you use most often are readily available on the toolbars and menu bars, and those you use less frequently are hidden from view. You'll also find it much easier to customize toolbars by checking the buttons you want to see and unchecking those you never use. Figure 1.3 shows the buttons available on the Formatting toolbar.

	Style:	
	Font:	
	Font Size:	
B	Bold	Ctrl+B
I	Italic	Ctrl+I
	Program Font	
	Bulleted List	
	NumberedList	
U	Underline	Ctrl+U
	Align Left	Ctrl+L
	Center	Ctrl+E
	Align Right	Ctrl+R
	Justify	Ctrl+J
	Numbering	
	Bullets	
	Decrease Indent	
	Increase Indent	
	Borders	
	Highlight	
A	Font Color	
	Single Spacing	Ctrl+1
	1.5 Spacing	Ctrl+5
	Double Spacing	Ctrl+2
x^2	Superscript	Ctrl++
x_2	Subscript	Ctrl+=
	Language	
	Reset Toolbar	
	Customize...	

Layout and design are becoming more important aspects of any document you produce. New views in Word, PowerPoint, and Outlook make it easy to see your work from different angles and work between views. Word's Print Layout and Web Layout views let you see how your documents will look in both forms. PowerPoint's Tri-Pane view, shown in Figure 1.4, allows you to see and work with slides, outlines, and presentation notes in one convenient view. In Outlook's Web view, you can review your schedule, explore a Web page, or preview your e-mail all within one simple interface.

FIGURE 1.4

*PowerPoint's Tri-Pane
view lets you work
between views with a
click of the mouse.*

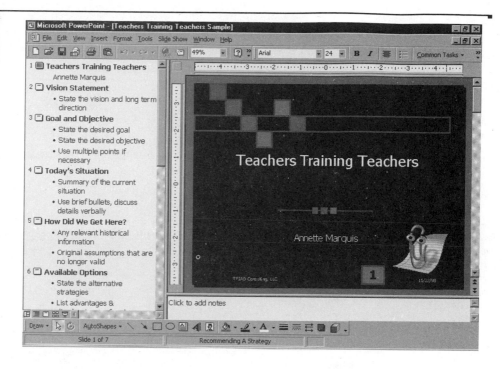

Improving on the Basics

Two long-awaited features of Office 2000 may make you wonder how you ever did
without them: Collect-and-Paste and Click-and-Type. In an earlier version of Office,
we were introduced to the spike, a well-hidden feature that let you cut multiple items
and paste them all together in one place—kind of like gathering the kids up and
putting them in the car. The problem with the spike is that you couldn't see what was
being held there and could only cut items, not copy them. Office 2000's new Collect-
and-Paste toolbar, shown in Figure 1.5, lets you cut and copy up to 12 items and then
paste them individually or as a group. You can point to any item on the Collect and
Paste toolbar to get a tip telling you what the item is.

FIGURE 1.5

*The new Collect and
Paste toolbar*

The second long-awaited feature, Click-and-Type, is designed specifically for Word and works only in Print Layout and Web Layout views. No more moving to the center of a page with hard returns and tabs before you can type on it. With Click-and-Type you click the cursor into place anywhere on the page and start typing. Word automatically inserts all the necessary hard return and tab codes you need to get to where you want to be.

Another feature designed to make life easier is Microsoft Office E-Mail. E-mail functionality has been extended in the applications so that you no longer need to send documents as attachments—the documents, including spreadsheets, become the body of the e-mail. All you have to do is click on the E-Mail button on the Standard toolbar, and a message header is added to the document, as shown in Figure 1.6.

FIGURE 1.6

In Office 2000 you can send any Word document or Excel spreadsheet as an e-mail message.

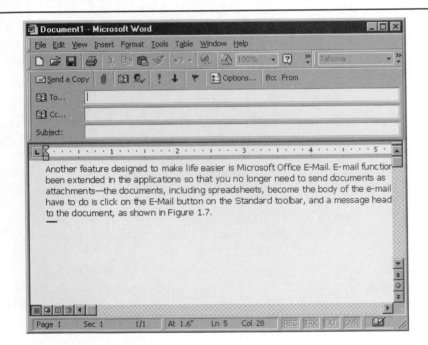

¿Habla Usted Ingles?

To respond to the growing demands of the global marketplace, Office 2000 includes incredible new features that can automatically detect languages in a document and apply the appropriate proofing tools. Although not every world language is available, Microsoft has amassed an amazing number of dictionaries that can be installed using the Microsoft Language Pack, which comes with Office 2000. As the Spelling and Grammar tool is checking your document, it switches languages and dictionaries on the fly. Even synonyms are available in your chosen language from the Office Thesaurus.

For languages with different characters sets and word-breaking rules, such as Japanese, Office 2000 provides additional formatting tools and custom options. Figure 1.7 shows some of the options available when the Japanese language is installed.

FIGURE 1.7

The Microsoft Language Pack builds options for different languages into the Microsoft Office applications.

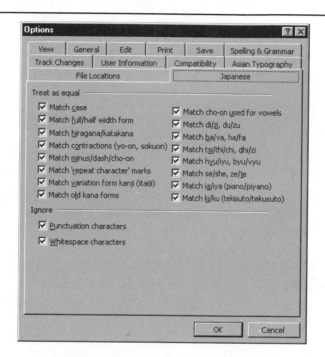

Of Special Interest to System Administrators

Office 2000 was designed with corporate-wide adoption in mind. In fact, Microsoft calls Office 2000 the first version of Office that is truly an enterprise application. Office 2000 integrates with Microsoft NT, Internet Explorer, Microsoft SQL Server, Microsoft Exchange Server, and development tools such as Visual Basic. It has been designed to improve communication, collaboration, and application development across networks in large and small organizations alike. With the addition of the Microsoft Office Developer's Edition, administrators have all the tools they need to effectively roll out Office throughout the enterprise. The Developer's Edition includes

Visual Basic for Applications source code control integration, a Package and Deploy Wizard for application distribution, tools to design and support dynamic Web content, and other features that assist with database connectivity.

Greater Ease of Administration

Besides ease of use, Microsoft made ease of administration a major Office 2000 objective. From its newly designed installation process to its self-repairing applications, Office 2000 is designed to reduce the cost of PC ownership by giving greater IT control over deployment, administration, and maintenance across the enterprise.

One of the most obvious enhancements to Office 2000 is the flexible and controllable installation process, which includes an Install on Demand feature and a Network Installation Wizard. Install on Demand means that you don't have to be concerned if you don't install all the right options the first time around. If there is a feature you need that isn't installed, Office prompts you to install it on the fly, as shown in Figure 1.8.

FIGURE 1.8

Office 2000's Install on Demand feature prompts you when you want to use a feature that is not installed.

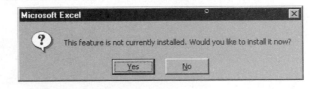

The administrator can set up where the Office files will be located, on a server or a CD, and then the user can decide whether to install the feature. This means that unnecessary features do not have to be installed until and unless they are needed.

Office 2000 can run from the desktop, from a network file server, or from a terminal server depending on the degree of control and flexibility that is required. Office 2000 reduces the need for a high-powered server because even with the Run from Server option, processing occurs on the users' desktops.

Office 2000 also includes these helpful installation features:

- Microsoft Office Custom Installation Wizard allows administrators to customize installations down to the level of individual features, toolbars and menus. Administrators can create custom profiles that determine what options and features are available to individual users.

- Intelligent Install determines the user's previous setup and migrates existing preferences and settings.

Reduced End-User Support Requirements

When do your users most often call the help desk? Usually, it's when a critical application won't run. Office 2000 has the ability to repair itself when it develops a problem with a missing or corrupted file. When an Office 2000 application boots, it automatically checks to make sure all the required files—including core executables, the registry, and key DLLs—are present and in good repair. If it discovers a problem, it fixes itself without even notifying the user there was a problem to begin with.

When users do experience a problem with an application, they can make use of the Detect and Repair option that is part of the installation program. Detect and Repair verifies all of the files that were installed and reinstalls any files that are inconsistent with the original install. In most cases, this should solve the problem without having to involve IT support directly.

Ever since Office 95, Microsoft has been actively improving the online user assistance available in Office products, and Office 2000 takes this to new ground. Thanks to a customizable office assistant and increased use of interactive help, users can find many of the answers to their everyday questions without calling for support. In an intranet, administrators can customize Help to give users instructions for completing company-specific forms or spreadsheets. Similarly, administrators can customize alerts and dialog boxes to direct users to company resources to help them solve problems and find the information they need. Although users may have to be encouraged to make use of these online resources, more often help desk personnel will be able to rely on the old grade school adage, "Look it up yourself!"

The Office 2000 Interface

Although Office 2000 looks and feels much like previous versions of Office, experienced users will immediately notice that only one row of toolbars is displayed when they open Word, Excel, or PowerPoint. In reality, the Standard and Formatting toolbars are both there; they've just been displayed side by side to increase the display space for the document window. You'll also be immediately introduced to the Office Assistant. The default Office Assistant is a restyled Clippit, but you can right-click on Clippit and choose another assistant. The Office Assistant is there to answer all your Office 2000 questions and entertain you while you work. Later in this section, you'll learn how to tone down your assistant or even turn it off completely, if you'd prefer.

For now, let's take a tour of the Office 2000 interface. If you've never worked in the Windows environment before, this will be a good introduction. If you're an experienced user, you can skim this section, focusing on what's new.

The Application and Document Windows

The Office 2000 applications share a common user interface. This means, for example, that once you get familiar with the *application window* in Excel (Figure 1.9), getting around in the application window in Word will be a piece of cake. Likewise, you'll notice a lot of other similarities between the applications.

FIGURE 1.9

Most elements of the Excel application window are common to all Office applications.

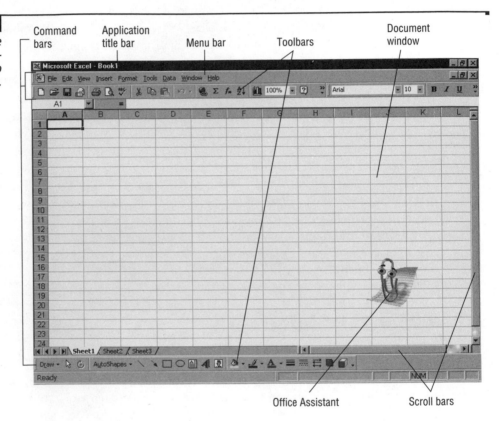

At the top of each application window is a *title bar* that contains three buttons: Minimize, Maximize or Restore, and Close. Use these buttons to change the size of your window or to close the window itself. When you're working in an application, you'll usually want to maximize it. Before you switch to something else, minimizing the first application will free up system resources, making more memory available to the active application. When a window is maximized, the Restore button is displayed.

When a window is restored to partial size, the Maximize button is displayed.

Office 2000 employs a new paradigm for managing open windows, called SDI or *Single Document Interface*. First introduced in Outlook 97, SDI essentially means that each document window operates independently of the application. The biggest advantage of SDI is that every open document appears on the Windows Taskbar; each appears with the appropriate application icon. This makes it much easier to switch between documents without having to access the Window menu to see what's open. The downside is that having two open documents looks the same as having more than one session of an application running.

When you only have one document open in an application, a document Close button appears at the right end of the menu bar beneath the application Close button on the title bar. Clicking the document Close button closes the document but leaves the application running. With SDI, when you have multiple documents open in the same application, there is no document Close button. Clicking the Close button on the title bar does not close the application—it only closes the active document, leaving the application running for the other open documents. SDI is on by default in Word and off by default in Excel. To turn it on in Excel, choose Tools ➤ Options ➤ View and check the Windows In Taskbar box.

The Document Window

In each application, your work area is known as the *document window*. Here you're surrounded by the tools you need to get the job done: *scroll bars* to move the display, a status bar to keep you informed of an operation's progress, and the *command bars* at the top of the screen to access all the program's features. There are two types of command bars: menu bars and toolbars. The menu bar organizes the features into categories: File, Edit, Help, etc. Clicking on any of the categories opens up a list (a *menu*) of related features for you to choose from. Many of the menu bar options open dialog boxes that allow you to set several options at once related to the feature you choose—all the print options, all the font settings, etc. Ellipsis characters (...) identify a menu option that displays a dialog box. The keystrokes listed to the right of a menu item are for shortcut keys; see "Accessing Commands in Other Ways" later in this chapter for information on shortcut keys.

Toolbars are the command bars with graphical buttons located below the menu bar. Toolbars make many of the most commonly used features only one click away. In Office 2000 the menu bar displays little buttons to identify those features that are also located on a toolbar. You'll use toolbars when you want a shortcut to a common feature and the menu bar when you want to see all the options related to a feature.

Personalized Toolbars and Menu Bars Adapt to Your Work Habits

Menu bars and toolbars are now designed to adapt to the way you use the Office applications. Menus, such as the one shown in Figure 1.10, collapse to display only commonly used commands until you choose to expand them to see the full list of options.

FIGURE 1.10

Menus expand to show all of the available commands.

Some buttons that were previously available on the Standard and Formatting tool-bars are not displayed, so that both toolbars can occupy a single row. To access a button that is not visible, click the More Buttons button located on the right end of each of the two toolbars. This opens a menu, shown in Figure 1.11, with additional button choices. When you find the button you are looking for, click it to activate the command and move the button to the active toolbar. Most often, this will replace some other button you haven't used in a while. There are approximately 20 buttons visible at any given time, but this number varies depending on the width of the buttons you have selected. You'll find buttons that were replaced on the More Buttons menu the next time you need them. Although this may take a little getting used to, after a while, you'll find most of the buttons you use regularly displayed on your toolbars.

FIGURE 1.11

Clicking any of the but-tons on the More Buttons menu moves the button to the active toolbar.

Adding Toolbar Buttons Is a Snap

If you find there is a button you are looking for that isn't available on the toolbar or the More Buttons menu, click the More Buttons button and click Add or Remove Buttons. Any button that is checked is currently displayed on either the toolbar or the More Buttons menu. Check any button to move it to the active toolbar.

For more about customizing toolbars and menu bars, refer to Chapter 38.

Accessing Commands in Other Ways

If toolbars and menu bars aren't enough, you can also execute commands from context-sensitive shortcut menus (sometimes informally called *context menus*) or by using short-cut keys. For example, to copy selected text in any application, you can use any of these techniques:

- Click the Copy button on the Standard toolbar (if it's visible) or choose the Copy button from More Buttons if it is not.
- Choose Edit ➢ Copy from the menu bar (see Figure 1.10).
- Right-click on the selected text and then choose Copy from the menu that appears.

- Hold Alt and press E to open the Edit menu, then press C to select the Copy command.

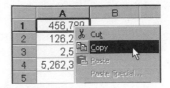

- Hold Ctrl and press C.

Notice that the Copy button and the keyboard shortcut are both shown on the Copy menu selection, so you can use the menu bar to help you identify quicker ways to access features you commonly use. *ToolTips* provide additional help with commands. If you're uncertain which toolbar button to use, point to the button and hover for a moment; a ToolTip will appear, showing the button's name. *ScreenTips* are a similar feature, appearing with other screen elements; for example, when you scroll through a PowerPoint presentation, a ScreenTip shows your current slide number.

 TIP To access different shortcut menus, right-click on various parts of the document or application window. The menu options vary depending on where you are clicking.

Even though there is usually more than one way to complete a task, no single method is always more efficient than another. If, for example, you're completing a series of tasks that use the mouse, it's most efficient to use the toolbar or context menu rather than take your hand off the mouse, hold Ctrl, and press a letter. To be a proficient user, you'll want to learn different methods that support the way you create documents in Office 2000. If you don't have prior experience with the newer Windows applications, experiment with the context menu—it's a speedy shortcut in many situations.

The Office Assistant

The *Office Assistant* is Microsoft's "social help interface" for Office 2000. Modified significantly from Office 97, the Office Assistant is now a separate application called an agent, which, like SDI windows, operates independently of the open application. The Office Assistant crosses all applications, and provides help for specific features of each application. You can choose from several Assistants from the Assistant Options. Each has its own "personality." The Assistant will offer help the first time you work with a feature or if you have difficulty with a task. Sometimes the offer is subtle; in Figure 1.12, the light bulb over Clippit, one of the characters you can select, means that you can click the Assistant to receive a tip that could save you time and energy.

FIGURE 1.12

The light bulb is a clue that the Assistant has something to say.

Working in
Office 2000

Other offers of help are a bit more intrusive. If, for example, you open a wizard, the Office Assistant pops up to ask if you'd like help with the feature.

After you've worked with Office 2000 for a few days, you might decide that you'd like a little less help from your eager Assistant. To change the Assistant's options, click on the Assistant, choose Options to open the Office Assistant dialog box, and then click the Options tab to display the Options page, shown in Figure 1.13.

FIGURE 1.13

The Office Assistant dialog box lets you adjust the amount of support you get from the Assistant.

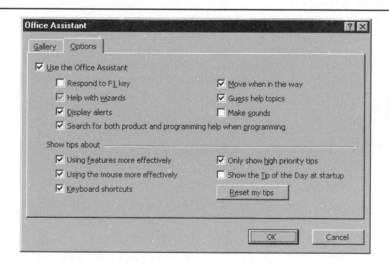

The Office Assistant is shared by all the Office 2000 programs. Any options you change affect the Assistant in all the Office programs, so if you request an increased level of assistance with Excel, you get the same increased level of assistance with Word.

When you're ready to go it alone, you can hide the Assistant by right clicking on the Assistant and choosing Hide. If you choose Hide often enough, you may be given the option shown in Figure 1.14.

FIGURE 1.14

Hiding the Office Assistant may make it feel unwanted.

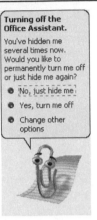

Turning off the Office Assistant.

You've hidden me several times now. Would you like to permanently turn me off or just hide me again?

● No, just hide me

● Yes, turn me off

● Change other options

If you start to get lonely, choose Help ➤ Microsoft Word Help to invite the Assistant back into your office.

 TIP For help with any dialog box in Office 2000, click the dialog box Help button (the button with the question mark), and then click on the item you want help with.

What's Next

Now that you have a feel for what Office 2000 is all about, Chapter 2 will show you everything you need to know to get started creating Office 2000 documents. You'll see how to save documents, edit documents and print. Best of all, you'll learn how to use some of Office 2000's exciting new features such as Collect-and-Paste and the Places view.

CHAPTER <u>2</u>

Getting Started with Office 2000

FEATURING:

Launching applications

Working with files

Entering and editing text

Selecting, moving, and copying text

Enhancing text with fonts and colors

There are plenty of differences between the Office 2000 applications, but there are basic strategies that work in several or all of the applications. For example, you save a file the same way in Word, Excel, and PowerPoint; so if you know how to save a file in one of these programs, you're home free in the other two. In this chapter, you'll find out about the common features that cross several or all of the Office 2000 applications. If you've used Office 95 or 97 applications, much of this will be familiar territory, but there are also some valuable new enhancements.

Launching Office 2000 Applications

In Microsoft applications there is always more than one way to get a job done. There are actually four ways to start an Office 2000 application to create a new document. You can launch Office applications from:

- the Office Shortcut bar
- the Start menu
- the Programs menu
- nearly anywhere on the Windows desktop

Using the Shortcut Bar

The Microsoft Office Shortcut bar is an icon bar that sits on the Windows desktop to help you navigate through your files and launch applications. Although the Shortcut bar is installed in a typical Office 2000 installation, it may not be running on your computer. To turn it on, choose Start ➢ Programs ➢ Office Tools and click Microsoft Office Shortcut bar. You will be asked whether you want the Shortcut bar to start every time you start Windows. If you do, it will be added to the Windows Startup group so that it is always available to you. You can drag the Shortcut bar to the edges of the desktop so that it runs vertically down one side of the desktop or horizontally across the top or the bottom.

To use the Shortcut bar to launch applications, click the Programs icon located at the beginning or the end of the bar and click the icon for the application you want to run.

NOTE   If the Programs icon is not visible, or if it does not include all the applications you wish to use, refer to Chapter 38 to learn how to customize the Shortcut bar.

Using the Start Menu or Programs Menu

If the Shortcut bar is missing from your desktop, try one of the other ways to launch an application. Anywhere in Windows, click the Start button to open the Start menu:

Choose New Office Document from the Start menu to open the New Office Document dialog box, shown in Figure 2.1. The page tabs at the top of the dialog box represent folders with different types of document templates. The General page includes new, blank documents for each application. Select a document type, and then click

PART

I

Working in
Office 2000

OK (or double-click the document icon) to open the application and begin creating a new document.

 NOTE As you can see, Office uses the term *document* for almost any type of file you can create with an application, including Excel worksheets and Access databases, as well as text-based documents. In this book we'll do the same.

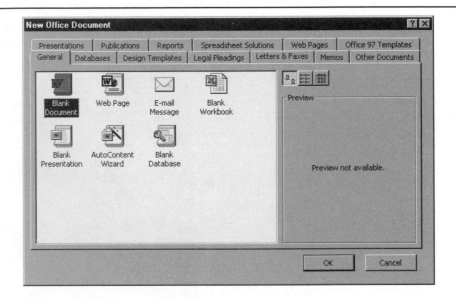

If you prefer to launch the application without immediately creating a new document (perhaps because you want to open an existing document), choose Programs from the Start menu. The Office 2000 applications are listed on the Programs menu. Choose the application you want to launch it.

Using the Windows Shortcut Menu

New Office 2000 documents are only a click away from the Windows desktop. Right-click on an empty area of the desktop (or in the right pane of the Explorer) and choose New from the shortcut menu. After a moment, the New menu opens, displaying the documents and items you can create from the menu:

Select the type of new document you want to create, and it will appear on the desktop. If, for example, you choose Microsoft Excel Worksheet, an icon for a worksheet named New Microsoft Excel Worksheet.xls is placed on the desktop with the filename selected. To rename the worksheet, type a name and press Enter.

To launch the application and open the new document, double-click on the document's icon.

Creating and Working with Documents

One of the great things about Office 2000 is that the dialog boxes used for common file functions are similar in all the applications. In this section, we'll look at the common features of the dialog boxes; features specific to an application are covered in the chapters related to that application.

Creating Something New

You've already seen how easy it is to create new documents from the Windows Start menu. Selecting New Office Document opens the New Office Document dialog box, shown in Figure 2.1. Each tab contains *templates* for a number of similar documents. Some of the templates (for example, the Fax templates) include text, graphics, or other content. Blank document templates for all the applications—a blank template for an Access database, Word document, Excel worksheet, PowerPoint presentation, and a blank binder—are found on the General page of the New Office Document dialog box. To open an application, simply double-click any document in the dialog box.

 NOTE *Binders* are collections of other documents. You use binders to hold all the documents for one project so you can switch between the documents quickly or print them all at one time.

 If you're already in an application, there are two ways to create a new document. Click the New button on the Standard toolbar to open a new, blank document in the active application. If you want a new template instead of a blank, choose File ➤ New from the menu bar to open the New Office Document dialog box with templates appropriate for the active application.

 NOTE With Office 2000's new personalized toolbars, some buttons may not be available where you would expect them. See Chapters 1 and 38 for more information about working with personalized toolbars.

Saving a File

 When you're finished working with a document or just want to store what you're working on before continuing, save the file. Either choose File ➤ Save from the menu bar or click the Save button on the Standard toolbar to open the Save As dialog box, shown in Figure 2.2.

FIGURE 2.2

*The Save As dialog box
in Excel*

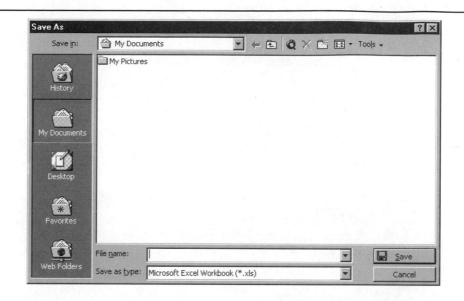

The dialog box opens to your default folder (directory), but clicking in the Save In text box opens a drop-down list of accessible drives, as shown in Figure 2.3. (Of course, your computer will have a different list of available drives.) Select a drive, and the folders on the drive are displayed in the pane below the list.

FIGURE 2.3

*Use the Save In drop-
down list to choose a
location for saving
a file.*

Double-clicking any folder opens it so you can view the files and folders it contains. When you have located the proper drive and folder, enter a file name in the File Name text box at the bottom of the dialog box. With Windows 95/98, file names can be up to 256 characters long, use upper- and lowercase letters, and contain spaces. They cannot contain punctuation other than underscores, hyphens, and exclamation points. And unlike file names on Apple computers, they are not case sensitive: *MY FILE* and *My File* are the same file name. Make sure the name of the current drive or folder appears in the Save In text box, and then click the Save button to save the file.

File Naming and File Management

Always name files and folders in a way that makes them easy to find when you need to open them. Here are some guidelines for naming files and folders:

- A file or folder's name should clearly identify its contents.
- While Windows 95/98/NT supports file names with up to 256 characters, twenty to thirty characters should be sufficient if you have a well-designed folder structure.
- Find out if your organization has naming conventions (for example, incorporating project numbers), and be sure to follow those conventions carefully.
- Be aware that older DOS and Windows 3.*x* applications can't use long file names, so they truncate everything after the first six characters. If you or other users need to access your Office 2000 files with older applications, choose a filename that will easily identify a file with the first six characters. For example, choose 99-00 Budget rather than Budget 99-00 for files in a Budgets folder.

The Save As and Open dialog boxes have a new Places bar, shown in Figure 2.4, that lets you easily navigate to common file locations and recently used files. Click History to see a list of your recently used files and folders. The other buttons—My Documents, Favorites, and Desktop—open their respective folders. Web Folders is a new location that lets you post documents directly to your corporate intranet if your company is running the Microsoft Office Web server extensions. See Part IX for information about publishing to a Web.

FIGURE 2.4

*The Places bar helps
you find common file
locations and recently
used files*

WARNING All the Office 2000 program dialog boxes locate documents based on file *extension*—the three characters following a period in a file name. For example, Word documents have the DOC extension. Don't create your own extensions or change the extensions of existing documents. If you do, the Office 2000 applications will have trouble finding your files—and so will you!

Creating Folders

If you're the organized type and want to save your document in a new folder, you can create the folder in the Save As dialog box before saving the file. Make sure the name of the drive or folder that should contain the new folder is in the Save In text box, and then click the Create New Folder button. A New Folder dialog box will open, prompting you for a folder name. Enter the name, click OK, and the new folder will appear in the open pane below the Save In text box. Double-click on the new folder to open it before saving the file.

TIP You can also create folders using Windows Explorer or My Computer. This approach may be more efficient if you need to create several folders at once, perhaps because a new project requires a standard folder organization.

Using Save As

After you've saved a file once, clicking the Save button on the Standard toolbar or choosing File ➤ Save saves the file without opening the dialog box. If you want to save a previously saved file with a new name, a different format, or in another location, choose File ➤ Save As from the menu bar to open the Save As dialog box. The Save As feature is particularly useful if you are using an existing document to create a new document and you want to keep both the original *and* the revised document.

If you share files with people using other programs, or older versions of Office programs, they may not be able to open your Office 2000 files. You can, however, save your file in a format they can open. In the Save As dialog box, scroll through the Save As Type drop-down list and select an appropriate file format. Figure 2.5 shows the Save As Type drop-down list from Word.

FIGURE 2.5

The Save As Type drop-down list

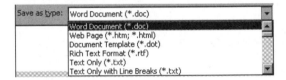

Closing a File

To remove a document from the document window, choose File ➤ Close or click the Close button on the document window. If you close a document that has been changed since it was last saved, you will be prompted to save your changes.

Opening an Existing File

In keeping with the Windows philosophy of giving the user as much flexibility as possible, there are four ways to open an existing Office 2000 document:

- If the document was created recently, click the Windows Start button and open the Documents menu. If the document appears there, you're in luck—you can open it directly from the menu.

- If the document doesn't appear on the Documents menu, choose Open Office Document from the Start menu to open an Open Office Document dialog box. Use the Look In drop-down list to locate the folder that contains the file.

- If you're already working in, for example, PowerPoint and want to open an existing presentation, click the Open button on the Standard toolbar to open the Open dialog box, shown in Figure 2.6. This Open dialog box is just like the Open Existing Document dialog box, but it is filtered to show only PowerPoint files. Use the Look In drop-down list to locate the proper folder and file.

- Open My Computer or the Explorer. Locate the document and double-click on it to open it in the appropriate application.

FIGURE 2.6

PowerPoint's Open dialog box shows files of PowerPoint presentation types; those in other Office applications are similarly filtered.

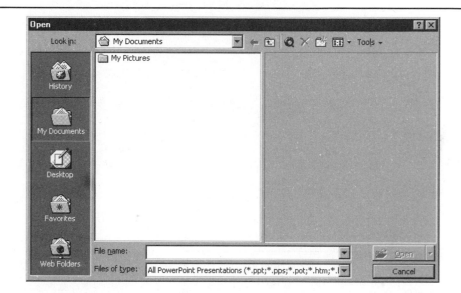

Converting Files from Other Formats

The Office 2000 applications will open files created in other applications and earlier versions of Office. However, to open a document created in a different file format, Office 2000 must first create a converted copy of the file. With the exception of Access and Publisher, Office 2000 applications share the same file format as Office 97 documents, so documents should open interchangeably between the two.

The file format for Access 2000 has changed, however, to comply with the new international character standard called Unicode. As a result of this and other changes in Access, when Access 2000 opens a database created in Access 2 or Access 97, it prompts you to convert the database, as shown in Figure 2.7. If you choose not to convert the database, you will be able to use it, but you won't be able to change its structure. Once the database file is converted, you cannot reopen it in the original application. Publisher 98 cannot open files created in Publisher 2000; to share a Publisher 2000 document, save it in the Publisher 98 format using Save As on the File menu.

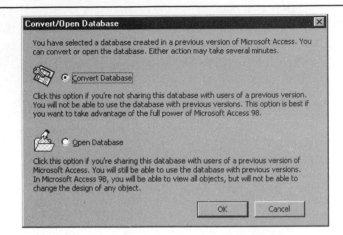

Word, on the other hand, automatically converts documents to the Word 2000 format. However, when you save the document, Word prompts you to let you know the document was created in a version prior to 97 and asks which version you want to save in, as shown in Figure 2.8. The prompt comes from the Office Assistant if it is in use, and no dialog box appears.

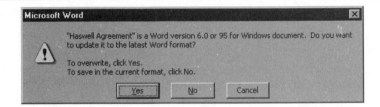

If you click Yes, the document is saved as a Word 97 file. If you click No, the document is saved in its original format, but any changes (particularly formatting changes) that the prior version doesn't support will be lost. Clicking Cancel cancels the Save and returns you to the document. If you have co-workers who are using Word 6 or 7 and need to access this document in its original format, be sure to choose No.

Renaming and Deleting Documents

You can rename or delete documents in either the Save As or Open dialog boxes. Select the document you want to delete or rename, and then right-click to open the shortcut menu. Choose Delete, and you will be prompted to confirm the deletion. Choose Rename, and the document's name will open for editing so you can enter a new name. If the document's name includes a file extension, the name you enter should also include the extension. If it does not, you will be warned that changing the extension may make the file unusable:

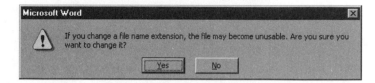

Cancel the change and enter the new file name, including the extension.

 TIP File extensions in all Office 2000 dialog boxes are displayed or hidden based on the View ➢ Options settings in the Windows Explorer. When extensions are hidden, you don't have to type extensions when renaming files.

Print Preview and Printing

 Access, Excel, Outlook, and PowerPoint allow you to preview a document before printing. (You'll see in Part III that PowerPoint has plenty of other viewing capabilities; and Publisher, covered in Part IX, is always in Preview view.) Click the Print Preview button on the Standard toolbar to open the preview window. Exactly what you'll see in the preview window depends on the application, but in general, it displays the document with all the elements that will appear when printed, including headers and footers.

There are two ways to print a document, depending on how much control you need:

- If you need to specify print settings, choose File ➢ Print from the menu bar to open the Print dialog box, shown in Figure 2.9. While each application's Print dialog box is slightly different, all allow you to select a printer, choose a number of copies, and specify what should be printed. Clicking the Options button at the bottom of the dialog box opens an Options page where you select print quality and other settings. Application-specific Print settings are discussed in the chapters related to each Office application.

FIGURE 2.9

Word's Print dialog box. Those in other Office applications are very similar.

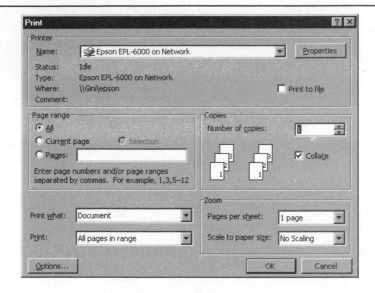

- To send a document to the printer immediately, using the default print options (and without opening a dialog box), click the Print button on the Standard toolbar. This can be convenient in most of the applications, but is problematic in PowerPoint, where the default print settings are full-page pictures of each slide in a presentation. What a way to tie up a printer!

Editing in Office 2000

Many editing features are shared among the Office 2000 applications. Some applications may have more precise ways of editing in particular circumstances, but in this section, you'll learn the editing features that work no matter where you are or what you're doing.

The Insertion Point

The insertion point, or cursor, is the flashing vertical bar that shows where the next character you type will be placed. You'll see the blinking insertion point, shown in the example below, as soon as you open a document or form. The only exception is Excel, where the insertion point only appears after you begin typing.

When you move the mouse pointer into an area where you can enter or edit text, the pointer changes to an I-beam. To edit existing text, move the insertion point by moving the I-beam to the text you want to edit. When you click, the insertion point will jump to the new position. Then you can type new text or delete existing text at the insertion point.

Correcting Mistakes

Helping you correct mistakes is one of the many things Office 2000 does exceptionally well. In its simplest form, Office will let you erase existing text manually. At its most powerful, Office automatically corrects the words you most commonly misspell.

Backspace and Delete

Most people are familiar with using the Backspace and Delete keys on the keyboard to delete text, but you're not alone if you are confused about when to use which one:

- Backspace (represented by a left-pointed arrow on some keyboards) erases one character to the *left* of the insertion point.

- Delete erases one character to the *right* of the insertion point.

Use whichever is more convenient based on where your insertion point is.

Undo and Redo

Office 2000 is exceptionally forgiving. The Undo button on the Standard toolbar lets you reverse an action or a whole series of actions you have taken. The Undo button will dim when you have reached the last action you can undo. Click the drop-down arrow next to the Undo button and scroll down the history to reverse multiple actions in one step.

If you change your mind again, clicking the Redo button reverses the last Undo. You can now use the Undo and Redo histories to reverse multiple actions in all the applications. Each application, though, has its own rules about how far you can undo, so it's not a good idea to count on them to get you out of every mess. File operations can never be undone; if you close a file and choose not to save your changes, Undo will not bring back the document.

TIP Always save your documents before you make any drastic changes to them, such as sorting an Excel spreadsheet or AutoFormatting a Word document. If the changes don't work out, you can close the document without saving changes and reopen the saved copy.

Overtype and Insert Modes

The default editing mode in Office 2000 is Insert: if you enter new text in the middle of existing text, the original text will move to the right to accommodate it. Overtype (OVR) mode replaces existing text with the newly entered text. To toggle between Insert and Overtype modes, press the Insert key on the keyboard.

 TIP If you look at your document and some of your text is missing, check to see if you are in Overtype mode (OVR on the Status bar in Word and Excel). You may have pressed the Insert key and accidentally overwritten the existing text.

A Quick Look at Spelling

No matter how many spelling tests you may have failed in elementary school, you can still produce documents that are free from spelling errors. The Spelling feature is available in all the Office 2000 applications. Word and PowerPoint will flag possibly misspelled words as you type by placing a wavy red line underneath them. All you have to do is right-click on a flagged word to open the Spell It shortcut menu, which lists suggestions for the proper spelling:

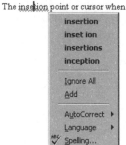

You can click on the correct spelling, choose to Ignore the word, or Add the spelling to your custom dictionary—a good idea with names you use a lot, so Spelling won't flag the name the next time you use it.

Outlook can check spelling in outgoing e-mail messages. To have Outlook automatically check your spelling when you click Send, choose Tools ➤ Options, click the View tab, and check the Always Check Spelling Before Sending box. In Excel and Access, you'll have to ask Office to check your spelling by clicking the Spelling button on the Standard toolbar. Office reviews your document, flags possible misspelled words, and opens the Spelling dialog box.

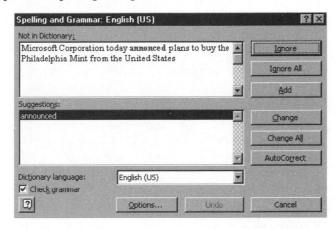

The Spelling dialog box gives you more options than the Spell It shortcut menu. You can choose to Ignore All occurrences of the word or Change All occurrences to the correct spelling. You can also enter the correct spelling in the Change To text box. All the Office applications share a custom dictionary, so words you add in one application aren't flagged in others.

Automatic Fixes for Common Errors

All Office 2000 applications access a shared feature called AutoCorrect. With Auto-Correct you can build your own list of common misspellings. When Office encounters one of those words, it automatically fixes it for you. Some words, such as "adn" and "teh" are already in the list. As you correct misspelled words, you can add them to the AutoCorrect list. AutoCorrect is one of the options in both the Spell It shortcut menu and the Spelling dialog box. You can also access it from Tools ➤ AutoCorrect. For more information about AutoCorrect, see Chapter 5.

Selecting, Moving, and Copying

Whether you are correcting mistakes or shuffling your whole document around, the first step is knowing how to select text, whether the text is in a cell, a database form or table, or a story in Publisher. Once text is selected, it can be moved, copied, deleted, aligned, or resized.

Each application has its own shortcuts to selecting text. You'll find more information about how to select text in the chapters related to each application. However, no matter what application you are working in, you can always drag to select—even in a dialog box. To select by dragging, move the insertion point to the beginning or the end of the desired text string, hold down the mouse button and move in the desired direction. Selected text typically changes to reverse video—the opposite color from the rest of the text. To unselect text, click anywhere in the document.

 WARNING Selected text is automatically deleted if you press any key on the keyboard. If you accidentally delete text in a document, click Undo. Undo won't work in dialog boxes.

Moving and Copying Text

Once you know how to select text, you can move and copy text in any of the Office applications; for example, you would move text to rearrange sentences in a Word document or topics in a PowerPoint presentation. When you *move* a selection, the original is deleted and placed in the new location. *Copying* text leaves the original in place and creates a copy in the new location.

You can also move text by cutting it from its current location and pasting it in a new location. When you cut a block of text, it is deleted from your document and copied to the Clipboard.

Information from the Clipboard can then be pasted into a document. By using the Clipboard as a staging area, you can move text from one spot to another within a document or between documents, even when the documents are created in different Office 2000 applications. For example, you can move part of an Excel worksheet to Word, or Publisher text to PowerPoint. (In fact, you can use the Clipboard with any Windows application, even if it's not part of the Office suite. For example, you could copy an e-mail address from a Lotus Notes message into an Access database.)

Copying text moves a copy of the text to the Clipboard without deleting the original. You can then paste the copied text once, twice, or many times in other locations. The text will only be removed from the Clipboard when you cut or copy something else or shut down the computer.

TIP Cut, Copy, and Paste are standard Windows functions, and as a result they have corresponding shortcut keys that you can use even if menu and toolbar options are not available. Select the text or object and press Ctrl+X to cut, Ctrl+C to copy, or Ctrl+V to paste.

Ever since Windows 3.1 took over the personal computer world in the early 1990s, Windows users have learned the hard way that if you don't apply Paste before you click Copy a second time, the first item you copied is gone from the Clipboard. The Windows Clipboard, that mysterious place that holds text and objects that are in transition, only holds the last thing you move or copy to it, but Office 2000 breathes new life into the old Cut, Copy, and Paste standby by adding an Office Clipboard. Now you can cut or copy up to 12 items to the Office Clipboard at a time. You can choose to paste them all in one location or position them one at a time in twelve different documents.

To access this new feature, also called Collect-and-Paste, select some text and click Cut or Copy. Before Pasting the first selection, select some more text and click Cut or Copy again. The Clipboard shown in Figure 2.10 should appear on the screen. If it doesn't, click View ➤ Toolbars and click on Clipboard to activate it.

FIGURE 2.10

The Collect and Paste toolbar lets you gather up to 12 items before pasting them.

Point to any of the items on the Clipboard to receive a tip telling you what it is:

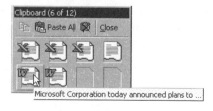

When you locate the item you want, click the clip to insert the text into the document.

If you would like to insert all the clips in one location, position the insertion point and click the Paste All button.

If you want to empty the Clipboard, click the Clear All button. To close the Clipboard, click the Close button.

> **TIP** All the moving and copying techniques work with pictures or other objects, including Collect and Paste, just as they do with text. Collect and Paste does not work in non-Office applications, which rely on the Windows Clipboard.

Adding Pizzazz with Fonts and Font Styles

One of the primary benefits of using Windows applications is the ease with which you can give your documents a professional appearance. The right combination of fonts, font styles, sizes, and attributes can make your words or numbers jump right off the page.

Fonts and Font Styles

Selecting the right font can be the difference between a professional-looking document and an amateur effort that's tedious to read. Fonts are managed by Windows, which means that a font available in one application is available in all Windows applications. You can access fonts and many of their font attributes right from the Formatting toolbar. Word's Formatting toolbar looks like this:

> **NOTE** Your Formatting toolbar may contain different toolbar buttons because of the new personalized toolbar features of Office. To focus on font formatting, click the More Buttons button and add the Font, Font Size, Bold, Italics, Underline, and Font Color buttons to the active toolbar. For more about working with personalized toolbars, see Chapters 1 and 38.

To change the font, click the drop-down arrow next to the font name. The default font is either Times New Roman or Arial, depending on the application. All Windows TrueType fonts (designated by the TT in front of them) are scalable, which means that you can make them any size by typing the desired size in the Font Size text box. Of course, you can also select from the sizes listed in the drop-down list.

To turn on Bold, Italics, or Underline, click the corresponding button on the toolbar. Click the down arrow on the Font Color button to choose from the color palette.

 TIP   Remember that you must select existing text before you can change its font or font style.

For all of the available font options, click Format ➤ Font, or in Excel choose Format ➤ Cells and click the Font tab, to open the Font dialog box.

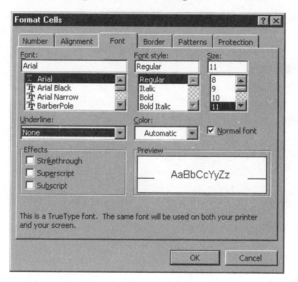

The actual font is displayed in the Preview window as it is in the toolbar drop-down Font list. You can also choose from several underline options, depending on the application. For example, you can choose a Wave underline style in Word and a Double Accounting underline style in Excel. You can also apply a number of different effects to your text such as Strikethrough, Superscript, and Subscript. Word and PowerPoint also have some fancy effects such as Shadow and Emboss.

Copying Existing Formats

Once you have formatted text just the way you like it, there is no need to re-create the format for other text that you want to treat the same way. You can easily copy a format to other text in your document using the Format Painter.

Select the text whose format you want to copy and click the Format Painter button on the Standard toolbar. Your mouse pointer changes shape to an I-beam with a paintbrush next to it.

Drag the Format Painter I-beam over some existing text, and it will be reformatted to look just like the text you copied the format from. Once you've applied the format, the Format Painter will turn off automatically. If you need to copy the formatting more than once, select the text you want to copy and double-click (instead of single-clicking) the Format Painter button. When you are finished, click the Format Painter button again to turn it off.

The Format Painter not only copies fonts and font attributes but other formatting such as line spacing, bullets and numbering, borders and shading, and indents.

What's Next

Now that you are familiar with the features that are common to all the Office 2000 applications, we'll start to look at all the applications in depth. Chapter 3 takes you on a tour of creating documents with Word. You'll see how to select and edit text in Word and how to print everything from standard documents to envelopes and labels.

PART II

Creating Dazzling Documents in Word

LEARN TO:

- *Enter and edit text in Word*

- *Format text and paragraphs*

- *Create tables and columns*

- *Use styles, outlines, and templates*

- *Merge documents to create letters and labels*

- *Add graphics to documents*

- *Add footnotes, endnotes, and reference tables*

- *Share documents with colleagues*

CHAPTER **3**

Getting Started with Word

FEATURING:

Navigating through a document

Viewing a document in different ways

Entering text using Click and Type

Moving and copying text

Applying print options

n this world of lightning-speed technological advances, the written word still serves as one of the most essential forms of communication in our society. If you know how to produce high-quality written documents, you can make the right impression even before anyone reads a single word. In this chapter, you'll learn the essentials of creating documents using Word 2000. We'll also show how to produce good-looking printed documents by taking advantage of some new printing options. Whether you are new to Microsoft Word or are stepping up to the latest version, knowing these fundamentals is guaranteed to enhance your personal or corporate image.

Although the Word application window is similar to those of other Office 2000 applications (introduced in Chapter 2), there are a few differences you should know about. The document window, contained within the application window, includes a ruler bar that you can use to set tabs and columns. You'll find View buttons at the left end of the horizontal scroll bar and Browse buttons at the bottom of the vertical scroll bar. The Browse buttons help you review your documents page by page or by any other identifiable object. Figure 3.1 identifies features of the Word application window that differ from those in the other Office 2000 applications.

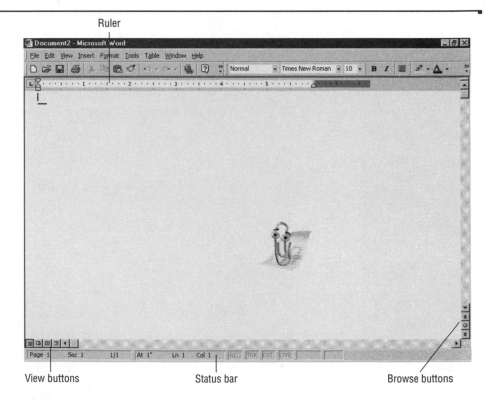

FIGURE 3.1

Word's application and document windows

Ruler

View buttons

Status bar

Browse buttons

Getting Around

You probably already know how to use scroll bars to move around in a document. You'll be happy to know that Word 2000 has a number of other tools that make it easy to navigate documents of any length. Rather than using the vertical arrows at the top and bottom of the scroll bar, you can drag the scroll box to make a ScrollTip appear, showing the page number you are scrolling past. If the document has headings, the heading will also appear in the tip:

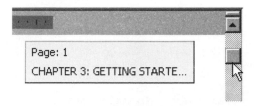

Browsing can be a quick way to review specific features of a lengthy document. On the bottom of the vertical scroll bar is a set of Browse buttons: Previous Page, Select Browse Object, and Next Page.

Click the Select Browse Object button to display a toolbar; then select the object type you'd like to browse:

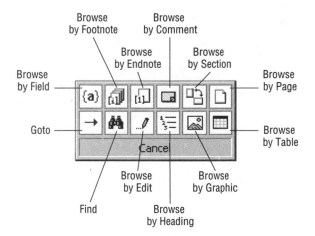

Objects are files or documents created in another application and inserted into a document: for example, pictures, line art, or an Excel worksheet placed in a Word document. In this menu the term also includes other document landmarks you might want to browse: Fields, Endnotes, Footnotes, Sections, Comments, Pages, Edits, Graphics, Headings, and Tables. If you choose the Go To or Find button, a dialog box asks you where you want to go or what you want to find.

  When you decide which object you want to browse, select the object's icon from the toolbar, then use the Previous and Next scrollbar buttons to move to the previous or next object of that type. If you choose to browse by any object type other than Page, the Previous and Next buttons turn blue to remind you that another choice is active. To return to "normal" browsing, open the Select Browse Object menu and choose Browse By Page.

Getting a Different Perspective

Word 2000 gives you several ways to view documents, depending on whether you are writing, outlining, preparing to print, or just reading a document. To the left of the horizontal scroll bar are the View buttons:

 Normal view: Best used for entering, editing, and formatting text. Headers, footers, graphics, and columns are not visible in this view.

 Web Layout view: Shown in Figure 3.2, this replaces Online view from Word 97. It's designed to be used when reading documents on the screen. There are no visible margins or page breaks in Web Layout view, making it easier to scroll through a document without interruption.

 Print Layout view: This allows you to work with your document exactly as it will look when it is printed.

 Outline view: This is useful when you are developing a document's structure and content and want to create a preliminary outline or review the outline as you are working.

In addition to the four standard views, the Document Map gives you the ultimate in navigational control. To use the Document Map, you must apply styles to your document's headings. (For more about applying heading styles, see Chapter 8.) Each heading appears in the Document Map as a hyperlink, as shown in Figure 3.3. Click on a heading to move immediately to that section of your document.

FIGURE 3.2

A document in Web Layout view

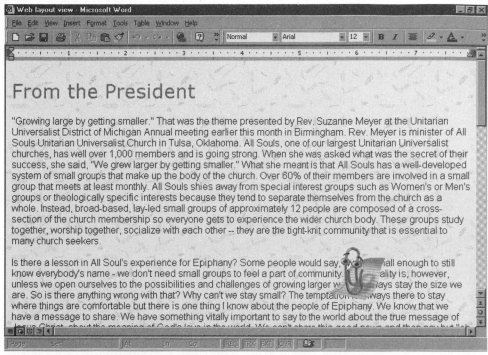

FIGURE 3.3

The Document Map provides an easy way to jump directly to the part of a document that interests you.

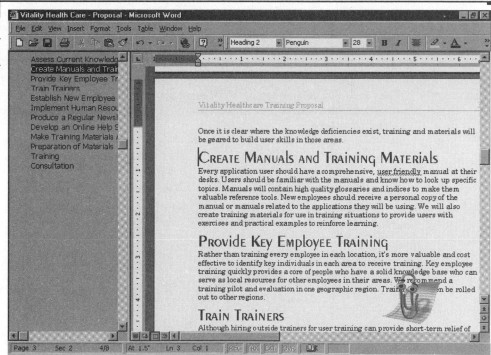

This is a good time to open any Word document and spend a few moments examining any features described above that are unfamiliar. If you don't have a Word 2000 document, open any WordPerfect or Word document and Word 2000 will automatically convert it.

 NOTE Word 2000 documents have the same file format as Word 97 documents. You can open both types of documents in either version of Word without the need to convert them first.

Entering Text

Word 2000 tries to make your life easier right from the first letter you type by watching what you're doing and figuring out how it can be most helpful. As you enter text, Word does several things behind the scenes (see Figure 3.4):

1. The Office Assistant evaluates what you are doing to see if it has any suggestions to offer.

2. The AutoCorrect feature automatically corrects misspelled words that are in its dictionary, such as "teh" and "adn".

3. The Spelling and Grammar feature reviews your text to determine if there are other possible misspellings or grammatical errors.

 TIP The accuracy of the Grammar feature is significantly improved when compared to Word 97. However, be careful about accepting its advice without verifying the accuracy of the suggestions. It still makes more than its fair share of errors. See Chapter 5 for more about Grammar.

To enter text in Word, begin typing in the document window. Text you type is entered at the flashing insertion point or cursor. The insertion point will move over to accommodate the new text. You can also overtype existing text, using overtype mode, as discussed in Chapter 2.

Text will automatically wrap to the next line when you reach the right margin. Within a paragraph, just let text wrap automatically to the next line. Pressing Enter at the end of a line inserts a hard return to create a new paragraph or a blank line.

In Normal view, you will see a black horizontal line at the left margin:

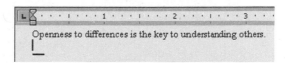

PART

II

Creating Dazzling
Documents in Word

FIGURE 3.4

*Office Assistant,
Spelling, and Grammar
features in action*

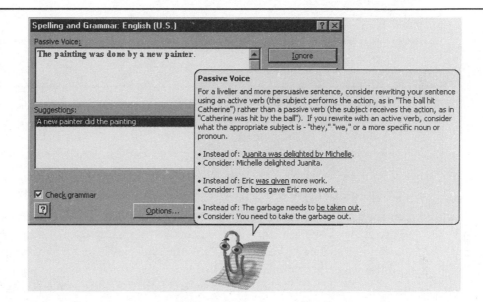

This represents the end of your document. In Normal or Outline view, you cannot move the insertion point or insert text or objects below the marker.

Moving the Insertion Point

Word provides several ways to move the insertion point using the keyboard. You can use the arrow keys to move the cursor up a line, down a line, and one character to the left or right, or use the special keys listed in Table 3.1.

TABLE 3.1: NAVIGATION KEYS

Key	Action
Home	The beginning of the current line
End	The end of the current line
Ctrl+Home	The beginning of the document
Ctrl+End	The end of the document
Page Up	Up one screen
Page Down	Down one screen
Ctrl+Left Arrow	One word to the left
Ctrl+Right Arrow	One word to the right

 TIP Ctrl+Page Up and Ctrl+Page Down move the insertion point to the previous or next Browse object. If Browse by Page is the object selected, Ctrl+Page Up/Page Down is the same as Page Up/Page Down.

Click-and-Type Lets You Type Anywhere You Want

 In addition to providing more graphically realistic displays, Print Layout and Web Layout views offer one incredible advantage over Normal and Outline views. With the addition of a new feature called Click-and-Type, you are now free to type anywhere on the screen without regard to where you last left the insertion point.

 Move the I-beam around the screen and notice that the icon changes to an I-beam with an alignment indicator (left, center, or right). Wherever you click, Word will automatically insert the additional hard returns and tabs to place the insertion point there. Click in the center of the page to type centered text; click near the right margin for right alignment.

 TIP Click-and-Type is an optional feature that is turned off by default. To activate it, choose Tools ➤ Options ➤ Edit and click the Enable Click and Type check box.

Click and Type is especially useful when you want use two different alignments in the same line, like those shown here:

TRIAD Consulting, LLC   1 Triad Towers   Flint, MI 48503

Just double-click on the right side of the screen and start typing. To see how Word manages this new trick, click the Show/Hide Paragraph Marks button to see the hard returns and tabs that Word adds to your document.

Editing Document Text

You can spot a Word power user because they use the minimum number of steps to complete a task. They're not just proficient; they're efficient, particularly with skills that are used frequently in Word. Knowing several ways to select and replace text will let you streamline many of the other tasks you'll be doing with your documents.

Selecting Text

Although you can always drag to select text, Word offers you a number of other options. Any of these methods can be used, but some methods are easier to use in certain situations. For example, if you've ever tried to drag to select text over multiple pages, you have already experienced the wonders of an out-of-control accelerated mouse pointer. But if you choose another method, such as Shift-select (see Table 3.2 below), you can select text smoothly without getting any new gray hairs.

TABLE 3.2: SELECTING TEXT WITH THE MOUSE

To Select	Do This
A word	Double-click anywhere in the word.
A sentence	Hold Ctrl and click anywhere in the sentence.
A paragraph	Triple-click anywhere in the paragraph.

Continued ▶

Creating Dazzling
Documents in Word

TABLE 3.2: SELECTING TEXT WITH THE MOUSE (CONTINUED)

To Select	Do This
Single line	Move pointer into the left margin. When the pointer changes to a right-pointing arrow, point to the desired line and click.
Entire document	Choose Edit ➤ Select All from the menu bar, or hold Ctrl and click in the left margin.
Multiple lines	Move the pointer to the left margin. With the right-pointing arrow, point to the first desired line, hold down the mouse button, and drag to select additional lines.
Multiple words, lines, or sentences	Move the I-beam into the first word, hold the mouse button, drag to the last word, and release.
Multiple words, lines, or sentences using Shift-select	Click on the first word, move to the last word (with mouse button released), hold Shift and click. Everything between the two clicks is selected.

If you begin entering text when other text is selected, the selected text will be deleted and the text you enter will replace it. This is an easy way to replace one word or phrase with another. It also works when you don't want it to—for example, when you forget you still have text selected from a previous action. When you are finished working with selected text, remember to click somewhere in the document to "deselect."

 TIP Hold Shift and use any of the navigation keys to select text. For example, hold Shift and press Home to select from the current word to the beginning of the line. Hold Shift and press the down arrow to select down a line.

Correcting Mistakes

The easiest way to correct mistakes is to select the troublesome text (using any of the methods listed in Table 3.2) and just start typing. Pressing any key will immediately delete the selected text. To correct mistakes that you make while typing:

- use the Backspace or Delete keys
- click the Undo button on the Standard toolbar
- press Ctrl+Backspace and Ctrl+Del to delete whole words at a time

Copying and Moving Text

The most commonly used method of moving and copying text is through the use of the Cut, Copy, and Paste features on the toolbar and menu bar (see "Selecting, Moving, and Copying" in Chapter 2). You'll find it easy to move and copy text short distances using a method called *drag-and-drop*. Drag-and-drop works best when you can see both the *source* (the location of original text) and the *destination* (the place you want the moved or copied text to appear). Select the text you want to move or copy, hold down the right mouse button, and drag the insertion point to where you want to paste the text. Select Move Here or Copy Here from the shortcut menu.

You can also use the left mouse button to drag-and-drop text, but you don't get the shortcut menu. Instead, the text is moved to the new location with no questions asked. If you want to copy text with the left mouse button, you must hold down the Ctrl key while dropping the text. It's easy to forget to hold down Ctrl or accidentally release Ctrl before the text is dropped, so it is good to get in the habit of dragging with the right mouse button.

If you want to use drag and drop in a large document, you can split the screen, as shown in Figure 3.5, so you can see different pages of the document at the same time.

PART

II

Creating Dazzling
Documents in Word

FIGURE 3.5

By splitting a Word document, you can see different parts of the same document at one time.

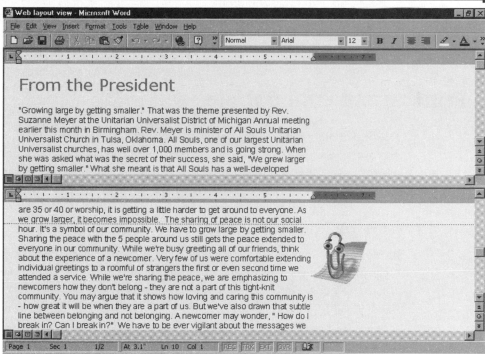

To split a document, point to the Resize tool at the top of the vertical scroll bar. When the pointer changes to a double-headed arrow, drag down to create a second window. You can also choose Window ➢ Split and position the divider where you would like it by clicking it into place:

To return to a full window, drag the Resize control back to the top of the document or choose Window ➢ Remove Split.

If you want to work with more than one document, open both documents, and choose Window ➢ Arrange All to see both documents. (When you want to work on just one of the documents again, click the Maximize button on the document's title bar.)

 TIP All of the drag-and-drop techniques described in this chapter work with other Office 2000 and Windows applications like the Windows Explorer.

Printing and Print Options

The dream of a paperless office may not be a long way from reality. In the meantime, however, we are still expected to generate a hard copy of most documents we write. A few tricks can make all the difference in producing a printed document that reflects the professional appearance you want to convey.

Previewing Your Document

Previewing your document before printing it gives you the chance to see how the pages break and whether there are any layout problems that will make the document look less than its best. Word 2000 offers you two ways to see how your document will look when it is printed:

- Print Layout view (View ➢ Print Layout) replaces Page Layout view in previous versions of Word. In this view, you are able to enter text, insert graphics, and work in columns while seeing how your printed document will turn out.

- Print Preview allows you to view multiple pages of the document at once, zoom in and out of pages easily, adjust margins, and shrink the document by one page to prevent a small carryover from appearing on a page by itself.

To open Print Preview, click the Print Preview button on the Standard toolbar or choose File ➢ Print Preview. Your screen will look like Figure 3.6.

FIGURE 3.6

Use Print Preview to see how your document will appear on paper.

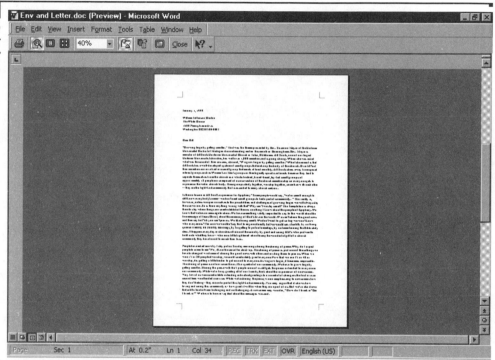

The following options are available on the Print Preview toolbar:

TABLE 3.3: OPTIONS IN PRINT PREVIEW

Button	Button Name	Placeholder
	Print	Prints the document.
	Magnify	When pressed, click on the document to zoom in or out. Inactivate to edit the document.

Continued ▶

PART

II

Creating Dazzling Documents in Word

TABLE 3.3: OPTIONS IN PRINT PREVIEW (CONTINUED)		
Button	Button Name	Placeholder
	One Page	Shows only one page of the document.
	Multiple Page	Shows up to six pages at one time.
 33%	Zoom	Changes the magnification level.
	View Ruler	Turns the vertical and horizontal rulers on and off.
	Shrink to Fit	Reduces the document by one page to prevent spill-over.
	Full Screen	Turns full-screen mode on.
 Close	Close	Closes Print Preview.
	Context-Sensitive Help	Activates Help about the next button you click.
	More Buttons	Opens the More Buttons menu to customize the Print Preview toolbar.

Inserting Page Breaks

Word paginates documents automatically—when text exceeds the length of a page, Word moves to the next page by inserting a soft page break. After you've previewed your document, you might decide you want a page to break earlier: at the end of a cover page, or just before a new topic. To insert a *hard page break* that forces the page to break at the insertion point's current location, press Ctrl+Enter.

Changing Page Orientation and Paper Size

If you think that your document would look better in *landscape* orientation (11×8.5) than *portrait* (8.5×11), you can change the orientation in Page Setup. Choose File ➤ Page Setup ➤ Paper Size or double-click on the gray frame at the top of the ruler bar to open the dialog box shown in Figure 3.7.

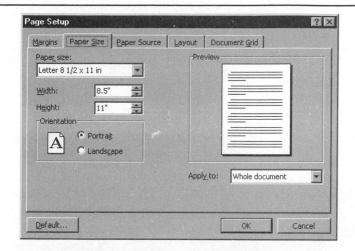

You can also change to another paper size entirely, including a custom size for non-standard forms like note cards or half-sheets. If you choose custom size, enter the dimensions for height and width. If you want to apply a page-size change to only part of your document, position the insertion point at the beginning of the page you want to change, go to Page Setup, change the page size, and choose This Point Forward in the Apply To control. To apply the change to a single page and not all the pages that follow it, move the insertion point to the end of the last page with this formatting, select This Point Forward, and change back to the original paper size.

Aligning Text Vertically

After you have the page orientation and paper size set, you may want to create a title page for your document. One easy way to do this is to enter the text you want on the title page and then center text vertically on the page between the top and bottom margins. To activate this feature, position the insertion point on the page you want to align. Choose File ➤ Page Setup and click the Layout tab. Under Vertical Alignment, you will find three options:

Top: The default setting; text lines up with the top margin.

Center: Text on the page is centered between the top and bottom margins.

Justify: Text is spread out so that lines are the same distance apart with the top line at the top margin and the bottom line at the bottom margin.

PART

II

Creating Dazzling
Documents in Word

Setting Margins

Word's default *margins*, the white space between text and the edge of the paper the text will be printed on, are 1.0 inch on the top and bottom and 1.25 inches on the left and right sides of the page. To change margins, use the Margins page of the Page Setup dialog box, shown in Figure 3.8.

FIGURE 3.8

Use the Margins tab of the Page Setup dialog box to set margins, header and footer placement, and a gutter size for two-sided printing.

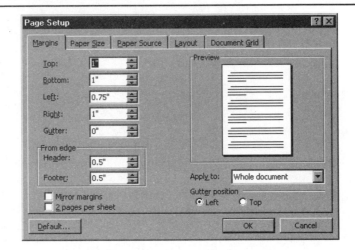

To change a document's margins, take these steps:

1. Position the insertion point where you want the margin changes to take effect.

2. Choose File ➤ Page Setup to open the Page Setup dialog box, and click the Margins tab.

3. Use the Top, Bottom, Left, and Right spin box controls to set the amount of white space on the top, bottom, left and right of the document.

4. Use the Gutter spin box control if you want to add additional space to a document that will be bound. If the binding material takes up a half inch, adding a 0.5" gutter will maintain equal white space on the portion of the document that extends past the binding. (You could, of course, set the left margin to 1.5" instead.) The default gutter position is on the left of the page. Click the Top Gutter Position option button for documents that will be top-bound.

5. Use the Header and Footer spin box controls if you want to adjust the size of the header and footer from the top or bottom edge of the page.

6. Click the Mirror Margins check box if you want to activate mirror margins for back-to-back printing. Clicking the Mirror Margin check box changes the preview to a two-page document and replaces the Left and Right margin controls

with Inside and Outside margin controls. Setting the outside margin changes the two margins that will be back to back: the left margin of the left page, and the right margin of the right page in the preview. The inside margins are the right margin of the left page and the left margin of the right page.

7. Click the 2 Pages Per Sheet check box if you want to divide each page so that two pages display on a page. Pages that have a portrait orientation are divided in half horizontally. Landscape pages are divided vertically.

8. Set the Apply To option to Whole Document or This Point Forward. The default for the Apply To control is Whole Document. This Point Forward applies margin settings from the insertion point to the end of a document.

9. Click OK to return to the document.

If you prefer, you can change margins using the vertical and horizontal rulers in Print Layout view. Point to the margin line on the ruler, and the pointer changes to a double-headed arrow:

When you hold down the mouse button, a dotted line extends through the document showing the location of the margin. Drag the dotted line in the desired direction to adjust the margin.

 MASTERING THE OPPORTUNITIES

Printing a Booklet in Word

Producing a booklet using Word takes planning and patience, but it is possible. Word does not have a way to produce 5.5" × 8.5" booklets where pages are automatically numbered and printed in the correct order. With the addition of the 2 Pages per Sheet option in Page Setup (click the Margins tab), it is possible to print two pages on a single 8.5" × 11" sheet and insert alternating page numbers on inside and outside margins (mirror margins) for booklet printing.

When creating a booklet, focus on writing the text of the booklet first and then worry about layout later. Once you have the contents in pretty good shape, change Page Setup options as follows:

1. Click File ➢ Page Setup.
2. Click the Margins tab and click the 2 Pages per Sheet check box.
3. Click the Paper Size tab and change to Landscape orientation.

Continued

4. Set other Page Setup options as desired.

5. Click OK to exit Page setup.

Now it's time to consider the cover page. Many booklets have a cover page that is blank on the inside. Take the following steps to prepare a cover page:

1. Move to the top of the document (Ctrl+Home).

2. Enter the text for the back cover.

3. Insert a page break (Ctrl+Enter or Insert ➢ Break ➢ Page Break).

4. Enter the text for the front cover.

5. Enter two additional page breaks after the front cover page so the first page appears on the right hand page after the cover and the left inside page is blank.

6. A booklet works best when the number of total pages is a multiple of 4. Add additional pages to the document as needed.

If you want to insert page numbers starting with the first page of text (excluding the cover pages), take these steps:

1. Insert the second page break in Step 5 above using Insert ➢ Break ➢ Next Page (Section break).

2. Choose View ➢ Header and Footer and make sure you are on the Section 2 Header (click the Show Next button if you are on the Section 1 Header) and the Same as Previous button is not pressed.

3. Enter the Header text and click the Insert Page Number button on the Header and Footer toolbar.

4. Click Format Page Number on the Header and Footer toolbar and make sure the numbering starts with 1. Click OK to save the format settings.

5. Click Close to exit the Header and Footer view.

You are now ready to print the document. Click the Print button or select File ➢ Print.

Once you have printed the document, it's time to resort to old-fashioned cutting and pasting. Assemble the pages by cutting them in half and taping the appropriate sides together. The cover page should be all set but the other pages will need to be rearranged. For example, in a four-page booklet with a cover, tape together 1 & 4 and 2 & 3. In an eight-page booklet, tape together 1 & 8, 2 & 7, 3 & 6 and 4 & 5.

Copy each page and then use the first copy as the master to produce additional copies. Set the copy machine to 1-side-to-2-side duplex and enter the number of copies you need. Staple the booklet in the center and you are all set.

Printing Options

If you click the Print button on the Standard toolbar, Word will use the current print options. By default, one copy of the document is sent to the Windows default printer. If you want to change the print settings, choose File ➤ Print to open the Print dialog box, shown in Figure 3.9.

FIGURE 3.9

The Print dialog box lets you choose a printer, a range of pages to print, and other options.

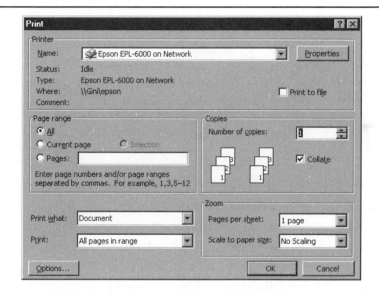

In the Print dialog box you can:

- Choose another printer.
- Print only designated pages of a document, including current page, a range of pages, or selected text.
- Choose to print the document properties (who created it, when it was created, how many words, characters, etc.) or other lists such as AutoText entries.
- Indicate in the Print text box whether to print just even pages, just odd pages, or both.
- Print to a file so that as long as you have the correct printer drivers, someone without Word 2000 can print your document.
- Increase the number of copies and have them collated (pages 1, 2, 3 for each copy rather than all copies of page 1, then all copies of page 2, and so on).
- Print multiple pages per sheet and scale the document to fit a different paper size.

Set the print options the way you want them and click Print to send the document to the printer.

PART

II

Creating Dazzling
Documents in Word

Creating and Printing Envelopes and Labels

One of the timesaving features of Office 2000 is its ability to maintain address books that are shared between the applications. (See Chapters 18 and 19 for information about Outlook address books.) Combine that with Word's Envelopes and Labels feature, and it has never been easier to prepare documents for mailing.

To print an envelope, take these steps:

1. If you are writing a letter, enter the name and address you want on the envelope as the inside address in the letter.

2. Choose Tools ➤ Envelopes and Labels and choose the Envelopes tab, shown in Figure 3.10.

3. The name and address you entered should appear in the Delivery address box. If not, close the dialog box, copy the name and address, reopen the dialog box, and use Ctrl+V or Shift+Ins to paste it.

4. Choose to enter or omit a return address.

5. Click the Options button to open the Envelope and Printing Options dialog box.

6. Click the Envelopes tab to set envelope options such as envelope size, delivery point bar code, and fonts.

7. Click the Printing Options tab to set printing options such as feed method and the printer tray that contains the envelope.

8. Click the Print button to send the envelope to the printer.

9. Click the Add to Document button to add an envelope page to your document. Figure 3.11 shows the document in Print Preview.

FIGURE 3.10

The Envelopes page of the Envelopes and Labels dialog box

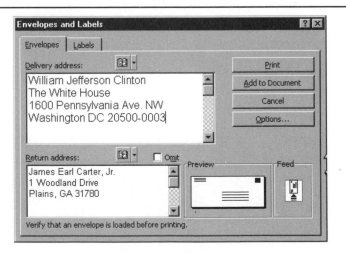

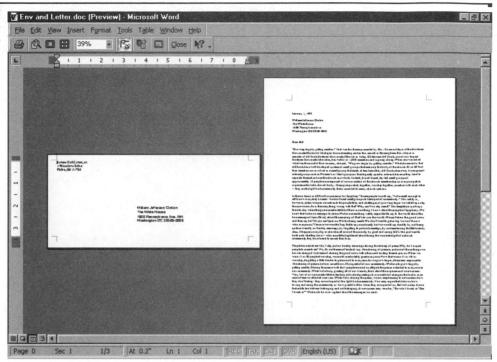

FIGURE 3.11

An envelope and letter
in Print Preview

TIP To have your return address appear as the default in the Envelopes and Labels dialog box, choose Tools ➢ Options ➢ User Information and enter your mailing address.

The Labels feature gives you the option to print one label or a full page of the same label. (See Chapter 9 for information about creating individualized labels for different people.) To create and print labels, do the following:

1. Click the Labels tab of the Envelopes and Labels dialog box (Tools ➢ Envelopes and Labels), as shown in Figure 3.12.

2. Choose whether you would like a Full Page Of The Same Label or a Single Label. You can even specify which row and column to print on, to use up those partial sheets of labels left over from other printing jobs.

3. If you want to print a full page of return address labels, click the Use Return Address check box.

4. Click the Options buttons to select a label style other than the default label, Avery standard, 2160 Mini Address labels.

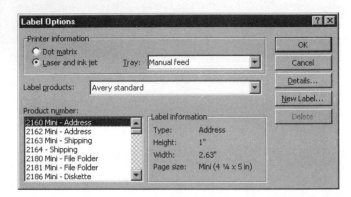

5. Choose the Product and Product number you want to use from the list provided. Click the Details button to see the actual measurements and layout of the labels you have selected or the New Label button to design a custom label size.

6. Click OK to close either page and OK again to return to the Envelopes and Labels dialog box.

7. Click the Print button on the Envelopes and Labels dialog box to print the labels.

FIGURE 3.12

Use the Labels tab to create and print labels.

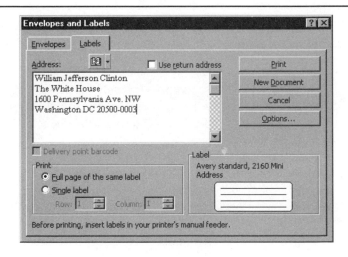

If you are creating return address labels or labels that you want to save, click the New Document button on the Labels tab to paste the labels into a new document. Save the document before sending the labels to the printer. In the future, to print more of the same labels without having to re-create them, open the saved label document and send it to the printer.

What's Next

Windows users have long enjoyed the ability to choose from a wide variety of fonts and font styles. But very few people really know how to use fonts to help them communicate their message. In the next chapter, we'll explore the use of fonts, aligning and formatting paragraphs, and creating bulleted and numbered lists. Word 2000 offers some exciting enhancements in these areas.

PART

II

Creating Dazzling
Documents in Word

CHAPTER <u>4</u>

Formatting Text and Paragraphs

FEATURING:

Using fonts and font styles for extra impact

Managing indents and tabs

Automatically numbering lists

Creating automatically bulleted lists

Applying multilevel bullets and numbering

Inserting special characters

S aying what you want to say in a document is only half the battle. Making it look good improves the odds that people will actually pick it up and read it. Chapter 2 provides a general overview of how to apply fonts and font styles to text in Office 2000. In this chapter, we'll focus on the font features that are specific to Word and also how to use tabs and indents without pulling your hair out. In addition, Word 2000 includes a couple of significant enhancements to bullets and numbering that even veteran Word users will find useful.

Making Fonts Work for You

All the fonts used by Windows programs are managed by Windows, so fonts available in one Office 2000 application are available in all the others. Unless you want to apply unique formatting like a double underline, you'll be able to make most of your font formatting changes using the Formatting toolbar. The toolbar includes buttons and drop-down menus that let you choose a font, font size, effects (such as bold, italics, and underline), and font color. If you need font options that are not available on the toolbar, open the Font dialog box (Figure 4.1) by choosing Format ➤ Font.

FIGURE 4.1

The Font dialog box offers Word's complete range of character formatting effects.

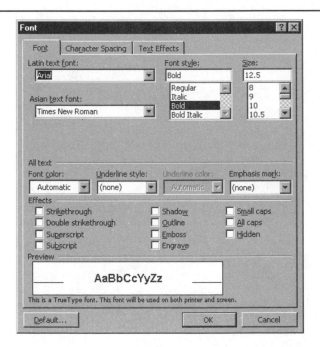

Word's Font dialog box has three page tabs: Font, Character Spacing, and Text Effects. On the Font page you can select font attributes and see how a font will look by noting the changes in the preview as you apply desired Styles, Sizes, Underlining, Colors, and Effects. Word 2000 provides nine different underline options.

Special Text Effects

There are 11 effects that you can apply from the Font dialog box. You can use Strike-through and Double Strikethrough to show proposed deletions in a contract or bylaws. Use Superscript and Subscript to place special characters in formulas (H_2O or πr^2). Shadow, Outline, Emboss, and Engrave stylize the text so that it stands out, as shown in Figure 4.2.

FIGURE 4.2
Text effects in Word

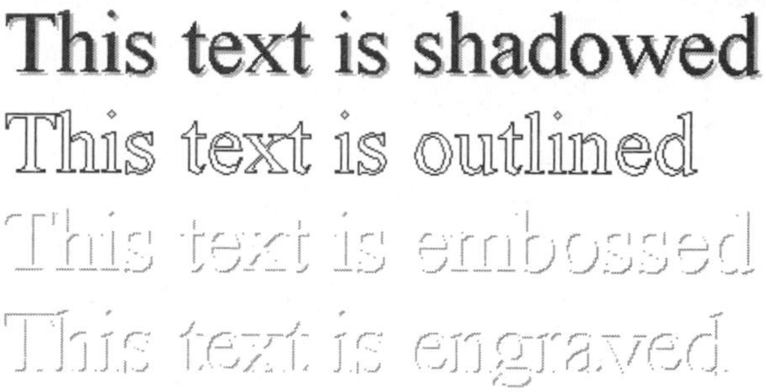

This text is shadowed
This text is outlined
This text is embossed
This text is engraved

Small Caps and All Caps are typically used in documents like letterheads or business cards. The Small Caps effect converts lowercase letters to smaller versions of the capital letters. To use Small Caps, enter all the text in lowercase or mixed case and then apply the Small Caps effect.

Hidden text doesn't print and can only be seen when Show/Hide is enabled. This effect was much more commonly used when there weren't more effective ways like Comments (see Chapter 12) to include nonprinting, invisible document notes.

TIP If you are circulating a document and marking revised text for review, you don't need to apply Strikethrough manually. Instead, you can use Word 2000's powerful Track Changes feature (see Chapter 12).

PART
II

Creating Dazzling
Documents in Word

Character Spacing

Use character spacing to adjust the distance between characters. For example, you can spread a title like *MEMORANDUM* across a page without having to space two or three times between characters:

M E M O R A N D U M

Character spacing is commonly used in advanced desktop publishing when you want to size and scale characters precisely.

Animation

Animation is a cute text enhancement designed for documents that will be read on-screen. There are six animation options that cause your text to blink, sparkle, or shimmer: Blinking Background, Las Vegas Lights, Marching Black Ants, Marching Red Ants, Shimmer, and Sparkle Text. To apply animation, select the text you want to animate, choose Format ➤ Font ➤ Text Effects, and select one of the six options. To turn it off, select the text again, and select None from the list of options.

 TIP A word of advice: Apply animation sparingly, and don't apply it until you are done editing document text. Overdone, it is pretty annoying, and animated documents use more computer resources, slowing down your system.

Highlighting Text for a Distinct Look

If you want to call someone's attention to a particular part of your text, you can *highlight* it so that it stands out for review. This is the computer equivalent of using a highlighter pen on the printout: if you have a color printer, the text will appear highlighted when printed. (Don't overlook the value of highlighting sections of text as a self-reminder.)

Select the text you want to highlight and click the drop-down arrow next to the Highlight button to choose and apply a highlight color. The button will save the last chosen pen color, so if you want to use the same color again just click directly on the

Highlight button. To turn highlighting off, select the highlighted text and choose None from the Highlight button drop-down list.

 If you prefer, you can choose a color to apply and highlight several sections of text. With no text selected, choose a highlight color and drag the pen over the text you want to highlight. The highlight pointer will remain active until you click the Highlight button again to turn it off.

Aligning and Formatting Paragraphs

In addition to formatting text or characters, skilled Word users must know how to format lines and paragraphs of text. In this section, you'll learn how to use indents and tabs and to control how text flows on the page.

Aligning Text

Word provides four options, illustrated in Figure 4.3, for aligning paragraph text: left, center, right, and full (justify).

FIGURE 4.3

Aligning paragraph text

The paragraph is **left-aligned**. Left Alignment is the most common alignment. It means that text lines up with the left margin and leaves a ragged edge at the right margin. Left-aligned test is the easiest to read.

The paragraph is **centered**. Centering is generally used for headings and desktop publishing creations. Centered text is equally positioned between the left and right margins.

This paragraph is **right-aligned**. Right alignment is used in headers and footers and other text that you intend to be put off to the side. It means that test lines up with the right margin and leaves a ragged edge at the left margin. Right-aligned text is the hardest to read.

This paragraph is **justified** or fully aligned. Justified test appears formal because text lines up evenly with the left and right margins. It is often used in documents with columns of text. Sometimes the paragraph looks unbalanced because too many spaces have to be inserted between characters.

To align text, position the insertion point anywhere in the paragraph and click on one of the alignment buttons on the Formatting toolbar:

PART

II

Creating Dazzling Documents in Word

Indenting Paragraphs

Word 2000 offers three ways to access paragraph-indenting features: the Formatting toolbar, the ruler, and the Paragraph dialog box.

You'll find the easiest method to change indents on the Formatting toolbar. Click anywhere in the paragraph you want to indent or select multiple paragraphs; then click the Decrease Indent button to reduce the left indent by a quarter-inch. Click the Increase Indent button to extend the indent.

Creating Indents Using the Ruler

The second method of indenting paragraphs—using the ruler—can take a little work to master, but it's a visual way to set left, right, hanging, and dual indents. You can use the ruler to set tabs as well as indents, and left and right margins in Page Layout view.

TIP If you prefer to do most of your work without the ruler, turn the ruler off by choosing View ➢ Ruler to remove the check. To make the ruler temporarily visible, point to the narrow gray line under the command bars and the ruler will reappear. As soon as the pointer moves back to your document, the ruler will slide back under the command bars.

There are four indent markers on the ruler, shown here:

First-line indent works the same as pressing Tab on the keyboard.

Hanging indent (sometimes called an outdent) "hangs" the remaining lines in a paragraph to the right of the first line when this marker is positioned to the right of the first-line indent marker.

Left indent sets a paragraph off from the rest of the text by moving all lines in from the left margin.

Right indent moves text in from the right margin and is typically combined with a left indent to make a *dual indent*. Dual indents are used most commonly to set off block quotations.

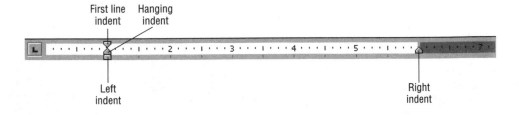

To change the indents for existing text, select the paragraph or paragraphs you want to indent and drag the indent marker on the ruler to the desired location. Moving the first line or the hanging indent marker indents or outdents the first line of each paragraph. Moving the left or right indent marker indents all lines of each paragraph.

If you forget which marker is which, point to any of them for a moment and view the ScreenTip. You can use the ruler to set indents before entering text. Position the insertion point where you plan to enter the new text before dragging the indent marker to the new location. The indents will apply to all newly entered text until you change the indent settings.

> **TIP** If you select paragraphs that do not share the same indent settings, one or all of the indent markers on the ruler will be dimmed. Click the dimmed marker(s) to make the indent settings the same for all the selected paragraphs.

Indenting Using the Paragraph Dialog Box

The third way to set indents is by using the Paragraph dialog box, shown in Figure 4.4. To access the dialog box, choose Format ➤ Paragraph or right-click and choose Paragraph from the shortcut menu.

FIGURE 4.4

The Paragraph dialog box

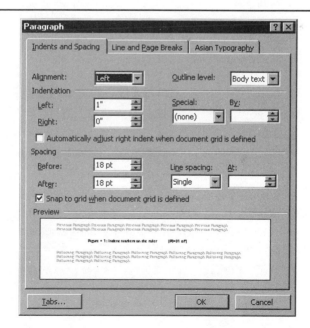

Follow these steps to indent using the Indents And Spacing page of the Paragraph dialog box:

1. Select the text you want to indent and open the Paragraph dialog box (Format ➤ Paragraph or right-click and choose Paragraph).

2. Click the Indents And Spacing tab if it is not already selected.

3. Click the spin arrows next to the Left and Right text boxes or enter decimal numbers directly in the text boxes.

4. Click the Special drop-down arrow to select First Line or Hanging indent. If you want the indent to be more or less than 0.5 inches, enter the special indent value in the By control.

5. Click OK to close the Paragraph dialog box and see your changes.

Setting Line Spacing Options

Word 2000 provides a number of options for adjusting *line spacing*, the vertical distance between lines of text:

Single provides enough room to comfortably display the largest character on a line.

1.5 lines gives you one-and-a-half single lines.

Double provides twice as much room as single spacing.

At Least lets you enter a minimum line spacing for the selection.

Exactly makes all lines evenly spaced regardless of the size of the fonts or graphics included in those lines.

Multiple is used to enter line spacing other than single, 1.5, and double.

To change the line spacing for existing text:

1. Select the text whose line spacing you want to change.

2. Choose Format ➤ Paragraph from the menu bar to open the Paragraph dialog box. Click the Indents And Spacing tab if the page is not visible.

3. Click the Line Spacing drop-down list to select the desired line spacing.

4. If you are choosing At least, Exactly, or Multiple, enter a number in the At control. For example, you can triple-space selected paragraphs by choosing Multiple and entering **3** in the At control.

5. Click OK to return to the document and review the changes.

To see all the formatting that is applied to a paragraph, choose Help ➤ What's This? and click on the paragraph. You'll get an information box that displays paragraph and font formatting related to the paragraph. Choose Help ➤ What's This? again to turn it off.

Using Tabs

Tab stops are markers set by default at half-inch intervals across the width of the document. Pressing the Tab key moves the cursor from one tab stop to the next. One of the most common uses of a tab is to indent the first line of a paragraph.

Tabs are also used to create *parallel columns*, vertically aligning text within a document. The tab-stop settings can be changed by using the ruler or the Tabs dialog box. You'll need to choose both the alignment type and the location for each tab stop you want to use. There are five basic types of tab stops, shown in Figure 4.5:

Left: The default type; text appears to the right of the tab stop.

Center: Text is centered under the tab stop.

Right: Text appears to the left of the tab stop.

Decimal: Used for numeric entries. Text lines up with the decimal point.

Bar: Used to create vertical line between columns of tabbed data.

PART

II

Creating Dazzling
Documents in Word

FIGURE 4.5

The five types of tab stops are all used in this document.

Tuesday's Schedule

Employee	Assignment	Hours	Rate
Seneca Sojourn	Create user interface	15	22.50
Sean Callan	Test table relationships	6	21.75
Jessica Beecham	Design queries	14	23.35
Jeff Morse	Draft reports	25	19.65

Setting Tab Stops Using the Ruler

Left Tab

At the left end of the ruler is a Tab Selection button that allows you to select the type of tab you want to set. By default it is set on Left Tab. Click the button to toggle through the four tab choices.

Once you have chosen the type of tab you want to set, click on the ruler to set a tab. The tab-stop marker appears, and all the tabs to the left of the marker are deleted. If you want to move the tab stop, click on the marker and drag it to a new location on the ruler.

NOTE You may notice two additional stops on the Tab Selection tool after the five tab choices. These are First-Line Indent and Hanging Indent. Use them to make it easier to select the indent markers on the ruler. When either tool is selected, you can click anywhere on the ruler (avoid the top gray bar) to move the corresponding indent marker to that position.

If you want the tab stops to apply to existing text, be sure to select the text first— before clicking the ruler. Unless you select the entire document or the last paragraph in the document, the tab stops will only apply to the selected paragraph(s). You can, however, set the tab stops for a blank document before you start entering text, and then the tab stops can be used throughout the document. To clear a tab stop, simply drag it off the ruler.

 TIP In most situations, it is easier to create parallel columns using Word 2000's Tables feature than it is to use tabs. See Chapter 6 for information about creating tables.

Setting Tab Stops and Leaders Using the Tabs Dialog Box

You can also create tab stops using the Tabs dialog box. Make sure the insertion point is located where you want the new tab stops to begin. (If the text you want to format is already entered, select it.) Access the Tabs dialog box, shown in Figure 4.6, by choosing Format ➤Tabs from the menu bar.

FIGURE 4.6

The Tabs dialog box

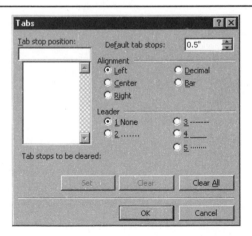

In the Tab Stop Position text box, type the location for the tab stop you want to create. In the Alignment control, choose how you want text to align at the tab stop. The Leader control lets you select a *leader* to lead the reader's eye across the text. The leader (see Figure 4.7) precedes the tabbed text.

FIGURE 4.7

Text with tab stops and leaders

TELEPHONE LIST

RIANNE ANDERSON 517-555-5623
CHARLOTTE COWTAN 810-555-3623
TISHA DEEGHAN...810-555-9562
BONNIE JOHN-MURRAY..517-555-9696
MAYA CAMPBELL 248-555-8956
SENECA JEAN SOJOURN 517-555-7585

When you have set the position, type, and leader (if you wish) for the tab stop, click the Set button. The new tab stop will be added to the list. Repeat these steps to set any other tab stops. Some users find the Tabs dialog box an easier way of changing tab stops than dragging arrows around the ruler:

1. Select the tab stop from the list below the Tab Stop Position control.

2. Change the Alignment and Leader options.

3. Click Set to apply your changes.

To remove an existing tab stop, select it from the list and click the Clear button. Clicking Clear All removes all the tab stops you added, reverting to the default tab settings. When you are finished setting tab stops, click OK to close the Tabs dialog box.

To see where tabs have been typed in existing text, click the Show/Hide Paragraph Marks button on the Standard toolbar. You'll see a right-pointed arrow to indicate a tab:

Tuesday's·Schedule¶
¶

Employee	→	Assignment	→	Hours	→	Rate¶
Seneca·Sojourn	→	Create·user·interface	→	15	→	22.50¶
Sean·Callan	→	Test·table·relationships	→	6	→	21.75¶
Jessica·Beecham	→	Design·queries	→	14	→	23.35¶
Jeff·Morse	→	Draft·reports	→	25	→	19.65¶

Creating Lists, Numbers, and Symbols

Word 2000 makes it easy to create bulleted and numbered lists. If you begin a list with a number, Word will automatically number following paragraphs when you press Enter. Begin with an asterisk, and Word will bullet each paragraph.

PART

II

Creating Dazzling
Documents in Word

To apply numbers to existing text, select the paragraphs and click the Numbering button on the Formatting toolbar.

Use the Bullets button to bullet existing paragraphs of text. To automatically number or bullet text as you type:

1. Type the number **1** and a period, space once, then enter your text for the item. For bullets, begin with an asterisk and a space.

2. Press Enter. Word will automatically number the next item 2 and depress the Numbering button on the Formatting toolbar, or it will bullet the next item and depress the Bullets button.

3. Continue entering text and pressing the Enter key to create numbered or bulleted points.

4. When you are finished creating the list, press Enter twice to turn automatic numbering or bullets off.

You can also begin numbering by clicking the Numbering button before you type your first paragraph. If you want to use letters rather than numbers in automatic numbering, type **A.** rather than **1.** to begin. Word will number the second and succeeding paragraphs B, C, D, and so on. If you number your first paragraph **I.**, Word will use Roman numerals to number your paragraphs.

TIP If automatic numbering or bullets do not work when you follow the steps above, choose Tools ➤ Options ➤ AutoCorrect to open the AutoCorrect dialog box. Make sure that Automatic Bulleted Lists is checked under AutoFormat and that Automatic Bulleted Lists and Automatic Numbered Lists are checked under AutoFormat As You Type.

Modifying the Bullet or Number Format

When you use the Bullets and Numbering features, Word supplies a standard, round bullet and leaves a default amount of space between the bullet or number and the text that follows. You can choose a different bullet character, number format, or spacing before entering your list, or you can modify the format of an existing list. If the bulleted or numbered list has already been entered, select the paragraphs you want to change. To change formats, choose Format ➤ Bullets And Numbering from the menu bar to open the Bullets And Numbering dialog box, shown in Figure 4.8.

PART

II

Creating Dazzling
Documents in Word

FIGURE 4.8

*The Bullets and
Numbering dialog box*

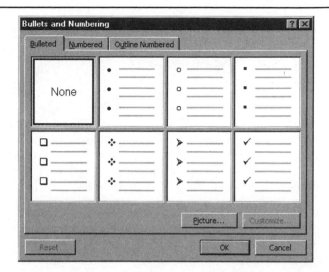

Click the tab for either Bulleted or Numbered. The dialog box displays eight styles
for bulleted text and eight styles for numbered. You can simply select any of the styles
shown.

If you really feel creative, click the Customize button to open the Customize Bulleted or Numbered List dialog box. (The Customize button will be dimmed if None is
selected.) We'll let you explore these options on your own.

Here's a review of the steps to applying custom number and bullet formats:

1. Select the list whose numbering or bullet style you want to change.

2. Choose Format ➤ Bullets and Numbering from the menu bar.

3. Make sure the tab you want (Numbered or Bulleted) is displayed.

4. Click a number, letter, or bullet format. To choose a different format, click
   Customize.

5. Enter a number format by choosing a number style and then adding any text
   before or after the field code, or choose to change the bullet character by clicking
   the Bullet button. If numbering, enter the starting number if it is other than 1.

6. Adjust the Bullet or Number position and the Text position as desired.

7. Click OK to save your changes and return to your document.

To remove numbers and bullets from text, select the bulleted or numbered list,
then click the Bullets or Numbering button on the toolbar to turn bullets or numbering off.

MASTERING TROUBLESHOOTING

Troubleshooting Bullets and Numbering

When you are creating a document with bullets and numbers, you may find that they are behaving differently than you expect. For example, you may find that the font is different for the number than for the text following the number or the bullet character is different than what you expect. Here are a few solutions to common problems that you may experience using bullets and numbers in your documents.

The font format of the bullet or number is different than the format of the text.

This occurs when you turn on bullets and numbering before turning on text formatting. To make the bullet or number match, select the bulleted or numbered list, open the Bullets and Numbering dialog box, choose Customize and click the Font button. Change the font formatting to match the text.

Numbers continue from the previous list rather than starting over at 1.

When the two lists follow each other with no text between them, the numbering continues from the previous list. To restart or continue numbering, select the list, open the Bullets and Numbering dialog box and click Restart Numbering or Continue Previous List. If you want to start numbering at a number other than 1, click Customize and enter the number in the Start At text box.

The bullet character used in a document does not appear the same from one computer to another.

If the bullet you choose is from a font that is not installed on both computers, Word will substitute a bullet from another font. Either install the font on the second computer or change the bullet to one that comes from a font available on both computers such as Symbol.

Applying Multilevel Numbering

If multilevel numbering brings back memories of tediously outlining ninth grade social studies papers, then you are in for a treat. With Word 2000 you can create multilevel bullets and numbering as easily as pressing a key.

To create a multilevel bulleted or numbered list, like the list shown in Figure 4.9, follow these steps:

1. Begin just as you would for a single-level list.
2. Press Enter and to move in one level (demote) press Tab. Type the second-level text.

3. Press Enter again and continue entering second-level points.

4. To move in another level, press Tab again.

5. To return to a higher level (promote), press Shift+Tab.

6. When you have entered all the points, press Enter twice to turn off Automatic Bullets and Numbering.

1) Hiring process
  a) Develop job description
    1) Get feedback from committee
    2) Talk with Board
  b) Determine the number of hours required
  c) Make proposal to the board
  d) Develop recruitment plan
    1) Set up interview committee
    2) Identify ad placements
    3) Contact resources
  e) Implement recruitment plan
2) Supervision Process

Customizing multilevel lists is similar to customizing single-level lists, except that you have to make decisions regarding bullet or number style and positioning for each level in the list. Open the Customize Outline Numbered List dialog box by selecting the list and choosing Format ➤ Bullets And Numbering and click the Outline Numbered tab (use this tab regardless of whether you are using bullets or numbers).

TIP If you would like the numbering scheme to start at a number other than 1, use the spin box controls on the Outline Numbered Tab to change the Start At number.

Inserting Special Characters

Many symbols used regularly in business documents aren't on the standard keyboard—the copyright sign (©), for example. Word 2000 makes many of these common symbols available to you with simple keystrokes, and others through the Insert ➤ Symbol option on the menu.

Choose Insert ➤ Symbol to open the symbol character map, shown in Figure 4.10, and the Special Characters page, shown in Figure 4.11.

Creating Dazzling Documents in Word

PART II

FIGURE 4.10

The symbol
character map

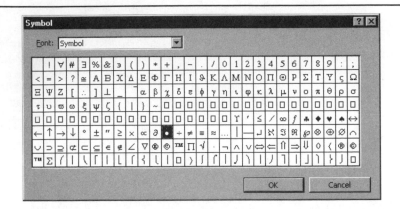

FIGURE 4.11

The Special
Characters page

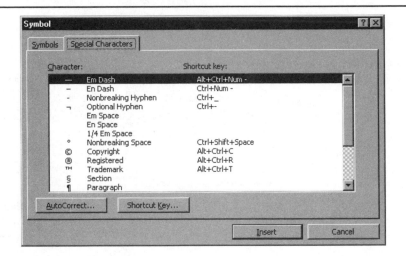

Choose from the symbol font sets or special characters shown; then click the Insert button to insert the symbol into your document. If you need the symbol more than once, copy and paste it to the other locations.

Word also lets you streamline access to symbols that you need to use frequently. From either page of the Symbol window you can click a button to define a shortcut key for the selected character, and from the Special Characters page you can also define an AutoCorrect entry (the AutoCorrect tool is discussed in Chapter 5). Enter a character string that will automatically be replaced with the desired symbol—enter **(p)** for ¶, for example. Make sure it is a character string you don't use in other situations, or you will find it replaced with the symbol every time you type it.

TIP To automatically insert en dashes (–) and em (—) dashes in your documents, make sure that the Symbol Characters (--) With Symbols check box is selected on both the Auto-Format As You Type and the AutoFormat tabs (Tools ➤ Options ➤ AutoFormat). To insert an en dash, insert a space after a word, type one or two hyphens, and then follow the dashes with more text. For example, 1 - 2 becomes 1–2. To insert an em dash, enter two hyphens between two words without inserting any spaces. In this case, 1--2 becomes 1—2.

Inserting Date and Time

Word 2000 provides 17 different formats you can use when inserting the current date and/or time, so the format you want is probably among them. Choose Insert ➤ Date and Time to open the Date and Time dialog box:

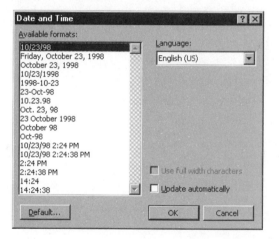

Select a format from the list. If you would like to automatically update the field to the current date and time every time you open the document, click the Update Automatically check box. This inserts the date and time as a field rather than as text. A Date and Time field is most useful when a document is in draft form and you want to know when it was last worked on, or when a memo or notice is regularly printed and mailed and should always have the current date. The Date and Time field is only updated when you print the document or right-click on the field and choose Update Field. Go to Print Preview to see the changed date and time. When you return to the document, the date and time will be updated.

WARNING Don't click the Update Automatically check box on the Date and Time dialog box when the date on a document is important to maintain a paper trail.

To change the default date and time settings, used whenever you insert a Date field code into a document, select the format you prefer from the Data and Time dialog box and click Default. Word will ask you to confirm that you want to change the default format to the selected one. Click Yes to confirm your choice.

What's Next

The Office language tools—Spelling, Grammar, Thesaurus, AutoText, and AutoCorrect— keep getting better and better. Office 2000 doesn't even limit itself to one language. It automatically detects other languages and if the appropriate proofing tools are loaded from the Office 2000 Language Pack, Office 2000 will even give you synonyms for German or Japanese words. Whether your needs are for improved English or well-spoken Spanish, Chapter 5 will help you make the best use of these powerful tools.

CHAPTER **5**

Applying Text and Language Tools

Creating and applying frequently used text

Checking spelling

Improving grammar

Finding the right word with the thesaurus

Finding and replacing text and formats

Professional typists know that minimizing the number of keystrokes is the key to high-powered efficiency. For those of us who don't type at lightning speed, every keystroke eliminated can result in a noticeable time saving. Word 2000 has tools to help you streamline your work and check your text—including your grammar—efficiently. There's even a thesaurus to help you find that perfectly descriptive word or phrase.

Creating and Applying Frequently Used Text

Word has two features that let you easily insert frequently used text and graphics. The first option—AutoCorrect—is introduced in Chapter 2 because it is common to Office 2000 applications. In this chapter, you'll find a little more in-depth information about AutoCorrect. The second feature, AutoText, is unique to Word and allows you to store formatted text or graphics, even entire paragraphs, and then recall them with a couple of keystrokes.

AutoCorrect is the feature that changes "teh" into "the" and "adn" into "and" without a bat of the eye. AutoCorrect maintains a dictionary of commonly mistyped words and when you mistype one, AutoCorrect fixes it automatically. AutoCorrect is also the feature discussed in Chapter 4 that changes the keystrokes **:)** into smiley faces ☺ and **(c)** into the copyright symbol ©.

Because some of the AutoCorrect changes can be a bit disconcerting, you have the option of turning these features on and off as desired. Figure 5.1 shows the AutoCorrect dialog box; you can access it by clicking Tools ➤ AutoCorrect.

To add a word or phrase to the AutoCorrect dictionary, you can either select the text in the document or enter the words in the Replace and With text boxes in the Auto-Correct dialog box. If you select text in your document and open the AutoCorrect dialog box, the text will appear in the With text box. You have the option of saving this AutoCorrect entry as plain or formatted text. Text that you enter directly in the Replace and With text boxes can only appear as plain text.

 NOTE AutoCorrect is case-sensitive. If text appears in the Replace column in uppercase, it must be typed in uppercase for AutoCorrect to replace it.

FIGURE 5.1

*AutoCorrect options
automatically correct
common typing
mistakes.*

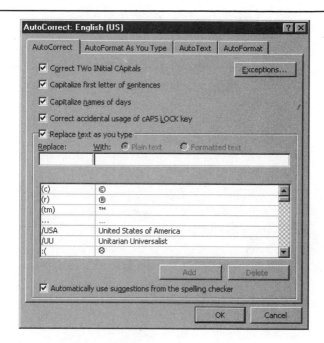

Although AutoCorrect is typically used to correct single words, you can use it to insert entire paragraphs or even longer segments of formatted text. Just be careful to use a "Replace" word that you don't typically type. Every time you type this word, the text will be replaced with the AutoCorrect entry.

AutoCorrect is designed to prevent typing and spelling errors, but it is also valuable as a shortcut tool. You can enter words that you type regularly into your AutoCorrect list to save yourself time and keystrokes—long company names, for example, or legal or medical terminology. Just enter a code that you will recognize, such as **USA**, and AutoCorrect will expand it for you into United States of America. However, if you think you will ever want to use the abbreviation without expanding it, enter a slash (/) or some other character in front of the abbreviation (/**USA**). Then you can choose whether to have AutoCorrect supply the long form (by typing /**USA**) or use the abbreviation (by typing **USA** without the slash).

TIP If you want the actual characters to appear in your document rather than the Auto-Correct symbol, type the characters—for example, type **(c)**—and as soon as the symbol appears (in this case, ©), press the Backspace key. This will replace the symbol with the original characters. This only works on symbols, however. It won't work to change text back to the typed text.

Using AutoText and AutoComplete

AutoText is similar to AutoCorrect, with two significant differences:

- AutoCorrect works automatically; AutoText has to be invoked.

- AutoText entries display an AutoComplete tip that completes the text without having to type the entire entry.

To create an AutoText entry:

1. Select the text you want to store as AutoText. To include the text's format such as font and font style, click the Show/Hide Paragraph Marks button on the Standard toolbar and make sure you include the paragraph mark in the selection.

2. Choose Insert ➢ AutoText ➢ New to create the entry (see Figure 5.2). You will be prompted to give the entry a name—make it short and easy to remember.

3. To insert the AutoText in a document, type the name you assigned to the entry and press the F3 key.

Creating AutoText

As Figure 5.3 shows, Word provides a number of canned AutoText entries that you can access from the Insert ➢ AutoText menu. Just choose a category, then select the entry you want to insert into your document. Most of the entries in the AutoText list will AutoComplete if you start typing them. To accept the AutoComplete tip, press Enter.

TIP If you're inserting a lot of AutoText into a document, you can turn on the AutoText toolbar by choosing View ➢ Toolbars ➢ AutoText or choosing Insert ➢ AutoText and dragging the narrow gray bar at the top of the menu to make it float. The toolbar's All Entries drop-down menu is the same as the menu bar's AutoText menu.

FIGURE 5.3

The AutoText menu
offers categories for
standard entries you
can define.

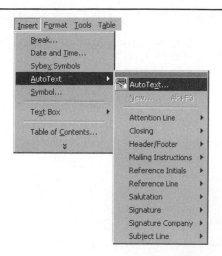

Delete AutoText entries in the AutoText dialog box (shown in Figure 5.4; choose
Insert ➤ AutoText ➤ AutoText) by selecting the entry you want to delete and clicking
the Delete button.

FIGURE 5.4

Use the AutoText page
to define AutoText
entries.

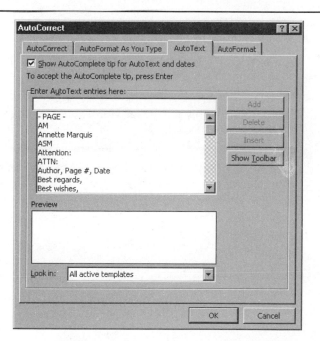

More about Spelling and Grammar

Spell-checking software has been around for a long time but if you really want it to work for you, it helps to understand how the Spelling tool works and the custom options available to you. Office comes with an extensive English dictionary and, if you install the Language Pack, dictionaries for other languages (see "Mastering Multilingual Editing" later in this section). When you run Spelling and Grammar or have the Check Spelling As You Type option turned on, Office checks each word against these dictionaries. When it doesn't find a word, it flags it for you to verify. You have a number of ways of dealing with a word that isn't in the Office dictionary:

Ignore this occurrence of the word.

Ignore All occurrences of the word in this document.

Add the word to the Custom dictionary so Office will recognize it the next time you use it.

Change the word by choosing one of the suggested corrections or editing the word manually.

Change All occurrences of the word in this document by choosing one of the suggested corrections or editing the word manually.

AutoCorrect the word (after choosing or entering a correction) and add it to the AutoCorrect dictionary.

Right-clicking on a red-underlined word gives you options to select a word from a list of choices, Ignore All, Add, or choose from a list of AutoCorrect entries. To get the full set of options listed here, run Spelling and Grammar from the toolbar; when Spelling finds a possibly misspelled word, you'll see the window shown in Figure 5.5.

 WARNING AutoCorrect and Spelling use two different dictionaries. When you add a word to the Spelling dictionary, it is not added to the AutoCorrect dictionary and vice versa.

FIGURE 5.5

Choose the correct spelling of a word from the list of choices offered by Office in the Spelling and Grammar dialog box.

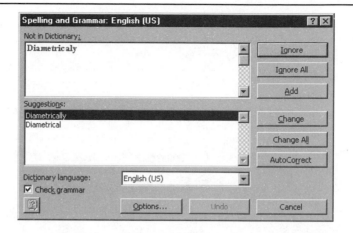

Working with Custom Dictionaries

When you choose Add from the list of Spelling choices, the identified word is added to the default Custom dictionary. The next time you type that word, Office recognizes it and ignores it. If you work in a field with lots of specialized terminology, you can save time and trouble by editing the dictionary directly. To access the dictionary and add new words or edit existing words, follow these steps:

1. Choose Tools ➤ Options and click the Spelling and Grammar tab.

2. Click Dictionaries to open the Custom Dictionaries dialog box.

3. Select the dictionary you want to open and choose Edit. This opens a document that contains any words already in the dictionary. If none have been added, the document is blank.

4. Type individual words, pressing Enter after each word.

5. Edit or delete misspelled words.

6. When you have finished adding or editing words, close and save the document in `*.dic` format. You will be prompted twice about file formats; click Yes both times.

All of the words you entered should now pass a spelling check with flying colors.

NOTE Office turns off Automatic Spell Checking each time you open a dictionary. To turn it back on, choose Tools ➣ Options, click the Spelling and Grammar tab and check the Check Spelling As You Type check box.

MASTERING THE OPPORTUNITIES

Making Custom Dictionaries Available across the Enterprise

If you work in a specialized business with its own nomenclature (that's just about every business today), making a custom dictionary available will save everyone in the organization time and energy. With Office 2000, you can house the dictionary on the server and give every user access to it. Because processing happens locally, there is no need to distribute it to every user. See Appendix A for more information about installation options.

To create a custom dictionary, follow these steps:

1. Choose Tools ➣ Options and click the Spelling and Grammar tab.
2. Click Dictionaries to open the Custom Dictionaries dialog box.
3. Click New to create a new Custom Dictionary.
4. Enter a name and file location for the dictionary. The default location is \\Windows\Application Data\Microsoft\Proof\ but you can choose any other location. Click Save.
5. The dictionary appears in the list of available dictionaries. Select the new dictionary and click Edit to open it.
6. Add words to the dictionary, pressing Enter after each word.
7. Close and save the file.

To gain access to the custom dictionary:

1. Choose Tools ➣ Options and click the Spelling and Grammar tab.
2. Click Dictionaries to open the Custom Dictionaries dialog box.
3. Click Add and locate the custom dictionary file. Click OK to add the dictionary to the list of active dictionaries.

Continued ▌▶

> ## MASTERING THE OPPORTUNITIES CONTINUED
>
> Office will use each of the active dictionaries when it checks spelling. You can deactivate a dictionary by clearing the check box in the Dictionaries dialog box. To remove a dictionary from the list of available dictionaries, select the dictionary from the list and choose Remove. Removing a dictionary does not delete it. You must actually delete the file directly to delete an entire dictionary.

Improving Your Grammar

Word's Grammar Checker uses "natural language processing" to evaluate sentence structure and word usage to determine if you may be making grammatical errors. If you have used other grammar checkers in the past, including those in previous versions of Word, you'll see some real differences here. Word 2000 not only identifies possible errors on the fly but will actually make suggestions about how to rewrite the text to make it grammatically correct. In Figure 5.6, the Grammar Checker identifies a sentence written in passive voice and makes a suggestion about how the sentence could be reworded to give it more punch.

FIGURE 5.6

The Grammar Checker can suggest improvements when it identifies a problem.

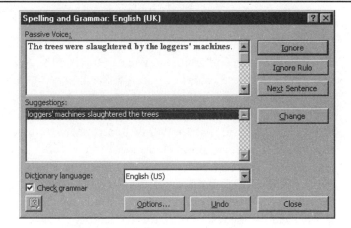

To use Grammar Checker, right-click on any word or phrase that has a wavy green line under it. Grammar Checker gives you three options:

- Make one or more suggested corrections.
- Leave the text alone.
- Open the Grammar dialog box.

By opening the Grammar dialog box, you can learn why the text was flagged. Click the Office Assistant button in the lower-right corner of the dialog box to receive some reference information about this particular grammar problem:

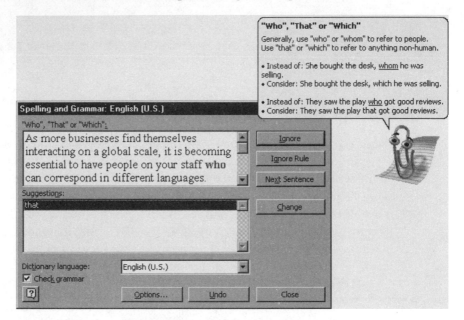

If you would prefer to wait until you have finished entering and editing text to check the spelling and grammar, you can turn off the Automatic Spelling and Grammar option. Choose Tools ➢ Options ➢ Spelling and Grammar and click in the Check Spelling As You Type and the Check Grammar As You Type check boxes.

 When you are ready to check your document, click the Spelling and Grammar button on the Standard toolbar. Word will review the entire document and stop at any misspelled words or grammar questions. You can choose to accept or ignore the suggestions. If you would rather not be challenged every time you write a sentence in passive voice (for example), click Ignore Rule in the Spelling and Grammar dialog box the first time Word encounters a passive voice sentence in your document. You'll be in the clear for the rest of the current document. Click Next Sentence to resume the process. If you would prefer not to check the grammar, clear the Check Grammar check box.

  The status bar includes an icon that shows you the status of Spelling and Grammar in your document. A red X means that there are flagged words or phrases in the document. A green check mark means that the document has been checked. If there are flagged words, you can double-click the icon to advance through them one by one, but it's generally easier to use the Spelling and Grammar button on the toolbar.

 WARNING Although Word 2000's Grammar Checker is a dramatic step forward in electronic proofreading, it regularly makes recommendations to fix text that is already correct or misses sentences that are obviously wrong. If you are uncertain, check another grammar reference.

 MASTERING THE OPPORTUNITIES

Mastering Multilingual Editing

As more businesses find themselves interacting on a global scale, it is becoming essential to have people on your staff who can correspond in different languages. Office 2000 lets you edit text in about sixty different languages or language variations (all languages may not be available in your copy of Office 2000. Updates to the Language Pack are available on the Microsoft web site, www.Microsoft.com).

No, Office won't translate it for you; you have to know enough of the language to create the text yourself (or use a language translation program). But Office will let you check the spelling and grammar, use AutoCorrect, and apply hyphenation and word-breaking rules. You can even read Help files and display menus and dialog boxes in some languages. To install and enable the multilingual features of Office 2000:

1. Install the Language Pack (it is found on its own CD-ROM). The Language Pack works with the Windows installer and makes it easy to install different languages as the need arises. Go to Add/Remove Programs in the Control Panel and choose Install. The Language Pack has its own setup files separate from the Office 2000 setup.

2. Click Start ➢ Programs ➢ Office Tools ➢ Microsoft Office Language Settings.

3. Select the languages that you want to use for menus and dialog boxes and for Help.

4. Click the Enabled Languages tab and select the languages you would like to be able to edit. You can choose to enable as many languages as you choose.

5. When you click OK or Apply, you'll be told that you must quit and restart all open Office applications. If you click Yes, Office will take care of this for you, prompting you to save if you have any unsaved documents.

Continued

PART

II

Creating Dazzling
Documents in Word

After you have installed the languages you want, return to Word and start entering text in the new language. Although Word may initially mark words with a wavy red underline indicating they are misspelled, it soon figures out that you are working in another language and removes the marks.

If Office recognizes the language but you haven't installed the spelling and grammar dictionaries, it asks if you'd like to install them now. Once the appropriate dictionaries are installed, you can run Spelling and Grammar on a document with multiple languages and Office will switch automatically to the correct language when it gets to that section.

When you enable some languages, you also get additional formatting options and language tools. For example, when you enable Japanese, you get a Format menu option called Asian Layout and a Tools ➤ Language menu option called Japanese Consistency Checker. Depending on the language, you also may find additional options available in the Options dialog box (Tools ➤ Options).

To set another language as the default language, choose Tools ➤ Language ➤ Set Language. In the Set Language dialog box, you can also indicate if you want to turn off Language AutoDetect and if you don't want to check spelling and grammar automatically.

Using the Thesaurus Command

Rather than highlighting errors that you may have made, the Thesaurus offers help only when called upon. It's there to help you find more descriptive, entertaining, or precise words to liven up your text.

To use the Thesaurus, take these steps:

1. Right-click on any word and choose Synonyms to see a quick list of synonyms.

2. Click on the word you want to use or choose Thesaurus from the shortcut menu to open the Thesaurus dialog box shown in Figure 5.7.

3. Click on words in the Meanings column that best represent your context to see synonyms for them. Double-click to get a list of words that have the same or similar meaning.

4. Enter a new word to look up in the Replace With Synonym text box.

5. To review previously looked-up words, select from the drop-down list under Looked Up.

6. When you find the word you want, select it and click Replace.

FIGURE 5.7

The Thesaurus
dialog box

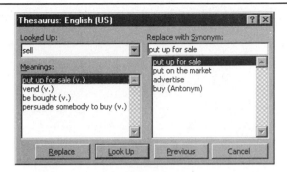

Customizing the Spelling and Grammar Options

Word gives you a lot of freedom to determine how intrusive you would like Spelling and Grammar to be in checking your work. Click Tools ➤ Options and click the Spelling & Grammar tab to access a set of options like that shown in Figure 5.8 (notice that the options may reflect other languages for which you've enabled spell-checking).

FIGURE 5.8

Spelling & Grammar
options give you a lot
of control over how
Word reviews your
documents.

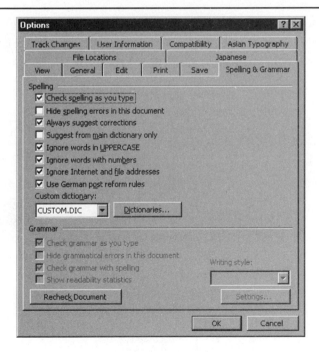

Use the Spelling and Grammar options to control what words get checked and how aggressive Word is in checking them. Clear the Check Spelling As You Type and the Check Grammar As You Type check boxes to avoid getting distracted by the wavy red and green lines under all the purported misspelled words and grammatical errors. Alternatively, if you'd like Word to check your spelling and grammar in the background but not tell you about it, check the Hide Spelling Errors In This Document and Hide Grammatical Errors In This Document check boxes. (You can then go back and view the errors later.) To skip over words that may be just an annoyance, make sure that the Ignore Words in UPPERCASE, Ignore Words With Numbers and Ignore Internet And File Addresses check boxes are checked.

 TIP Consider adding not-quite-words like Internet addresses to a custom dictionary so that Spelling can check them and flag any typos for you.

Word includes options for five typical writing styles or usage levels: Casual, Standard, Formal, Technical, and Custom. Each of these five styles has unique grammar and style rules Word will check for in your documents. For example, it may be acceptable to use contractions in casual writing, but doing that would raise eyebrows in a very formal document.

Choose the writing style you prefer on the Spelling and Grammar page of the Options dialog box and click Settings to review the specific grammar and style options for that style, shown in Figure 5.9. Word will flag violations of any of the categories of rules checked in this dialog box.

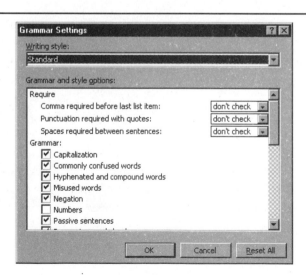

TIP When Word is checking spelling and grammar, watch the label on top of the text box in the Spelling & Grammar dialog box. It will identify the reason the text was flagged, such as Fragment, Use of I, Contraction, etc. so you're not left trying to figure it out yourself.

Finding and Replacing Text

One of the fastest ways to make repetitive changes throughout a long document is to use Find and Replace. Find helps you locate a text string and Replace substitutes new text for the existing string.

 Follow these steps to use Find and Replace:

1. Click the Select Browse Object button and the Find button to open the Find and Replace dialog box, shown in Figure 5.10.

2. Enter the characters you want to search for in the Find What text box. Click Find Next.

3. Close the Find dialog box and click the Next Find/GoTo button at the bottom of the vertical scroll bar. Browse through each of the occurrences of the text string.

FIGURE 5.10

*The Find and Replace
dialog box*

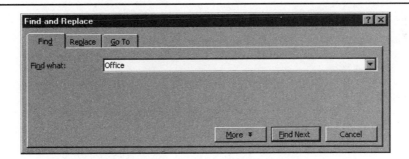

The More button in the Find and Replace dialog box provides you with additional searching options. You can have Word search the entire document (All), or for faster searching, just choose to search above (Up) or below (Down) the insertion point. You can also have it search for words that are in the same case as you entered (Match Case).

When Word searches, it will search for all occurrences of the text string—even if it does not form a whole word. For example, if you are searching for *will*, you will find

William, *wills*, and *willful*, unless you click Find Whole Words Only. If you would like all forms of the word, turn on the Find All Word Forms check box. Wildcards are characters that stand for any character. If you enter **j***, you will locate all words that start with *j*; ***ing** will bring you all words that end with *ing*. The Sounds Like option gives you words that start with the same sound—entering **kind** will find *cannot*; **boy** will return *by*.

You can also look for text formatted a certain way using the list that opens when you click the Format button. Use the Special button to find codes such as column breaks and paragraph marks; Figure 5.11 shows the complete list. For example, if you want to tighten up a document that contains two paragraph marks at the end of every paragraph resulting in a blank line between paragraphs, use the Special button to look for two paragraph marks and replace them with one.

FIGURE 5.11

You can find and replace any of these special characters or objects.

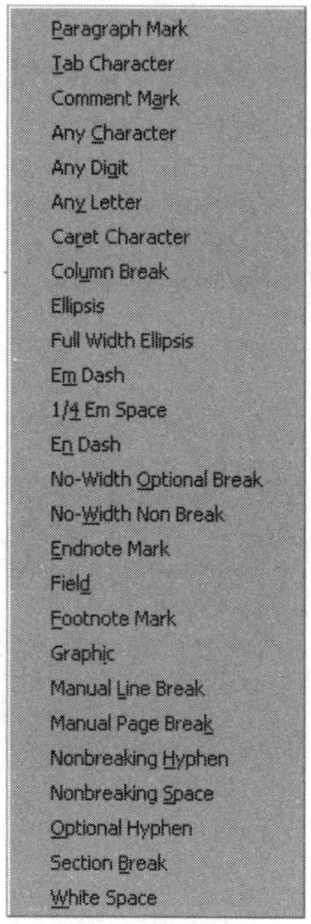

Paragraph Mark
Tab Character
Comment Mark
Any Character
Any Digit
Any Letter
Caret Character
Column Break
Ellipsis
Full Width Ellipsis
Em Dash
1/4 Em Space
En Dash
No-Width Optional Break
No-Width Non Break
Endnote Mark
Field
Footnote Mark
Graphic
Manual Line Break
Manual Page Break
Nonbreaking Hyphen
Nonbreaking Space
Optional Hyphen
Section Break
White Space

Using Replace

To replace text, open the Find dialog box and click the Replace tab. Enter the text you want to find in the Find What text box and the text you want to replace it with in the Replace With text box. You can choose to replace one occurrence at a time by clicking Find Next and then Replace. Or, if you're very sure of what you are doing, choose Replace All to complete the replacements in one step. When Word is finished, it opens a dialog box that tells you how many replacements it made.

Navigating through a Long Document with Go To

Find and Replace also gives you the option to Go To a specific type of text or object such as a page, footnote, or graphic. Click the Go To tab and select the type and the name or number of the item you would like to go to:

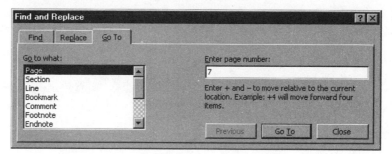

Go To is most useful in very long documents when you want to review all the occurrences of a specific type of text.

What's Next

Word can do a lot more than present neatly formatted paragraphs of text on a page. Using Word's Columns and Tables features, you can produce professional-quality published documents such a newsletters and reports that could be mistaken as coming from the best desktop publishing programs. In Chapter 6, you'll see how to put polish on your documents with headers and footers, page numbers and section breaks, and columns and tables.

CHAPTER 6

Designing Pages with Columns and Tables

FEATURING:

- *Understanding sections*
- *Creating and modifying page numbers*
- *Creating headers and footers*
- *Working with columns*
- *Entering and editing text in columns*
- *Revising column structure*
- *Creating and revising tables*
- *Formatting tables*
- *Changing the table properties*
- *Adding calculations to tables*

The document formatting features available in Word 2000 help you create highly professional-looking documents. For example, designing your company's newsletter with two or three columns on each page is a snap using Word's columns feature. If you are writing a financial report, tables make it easy to display and even calculate financial data.

Headers and footers that contain page numbers and other relevant information make a lengthy document easier to follow. Word can help you with everything from automatically numbering the pages for you to inserting different headers and footers on odd and even pages. You can also adjust hyphenation and other text flow options to make sure your final document looks its best.

Understanding Sections

Word uses sections to organize documents for formatting purposes. A *section* is a part of a document that has a specified number of columns and uses a common set of margins, page orientation, headers and footers, and sequence of page numbers. Word automatically inserts section breaks when you:

- Format text as columns.
- Change Page Setup options and indicate that you want the changes to apply from This Point Forward.

You will want to manually insert a section break to apply different page size or header and footer formatting within a document. For example, if you want a different header in each chapter in a document, put section breaks between the chapters before you create the headers.

To manually insert a section break:

1. Position the insertion point where you want the break to begin and choose Insert ➤ Break. The Break dialog box appears, as shown in Figure 6.1.

2. In the Section Break Types area, select one of the following options to specify where you want the new section to begin:

   Next Page: Inserts a section break and starts the new section at the beginning of the next page.

   Continuous: Inserts a section break without inserting a page break. Any subsequent text you type directly follows the existing text.

Even Page: Inserts a section break and starts the new section at the beginning of the next even-numbered page in the document. If the section break is inserted on an even-numbered page, Word leaves the intervening page (an odd-numbered page) blank.

Odd Page: Inserts a section break and starts the new section at the beginning of the next odd-numbered page in the document. If the section break is inserted on an odd-numbered page, Word leaves the intervening page (an even-numbered page) blank.

3. Choose OK to insert the section break.

FIGURE 6.1

The options in the Break dialog box allow you to specify what type of break to insert in a document.

Section break marks can be seen in both Normal and Outline views by default. You can also see section break marks in both Web Page and Print Layout views when you display nonprinting characters in your document. To do so, use either of the following procedures:

- Click on the Show/Hide ¶ button on the Standard toolbar.
- Choose Tools ➢ Options ➢ View, check the Hidden Text check box in the Formatting Marks area, and then choose OK.

Section break marks appear as double-dotted lines with the words *Section Break* and the type of break in them, as shown below:

Section Break (Continuous)

To delete a section break, select the break at the left margin or place the insertion point anywhere on the break, and then press the Delete key.

Creating and Modifying Page Numbers

Whether or not you have inserted section breaks, you may want a simple way to automatically number the pages. Nothing could be more effortless than Word's Page Numbering feature.

1. Choose Insert ➢ Page Numbers to open the Page Numbers dialog box, shown in Figure 6.2.

2. In the Position drop-down list, select Bottom Of Page (Footer) or Top Of Page (Header) as the location for your page numbers.

3. In the Alignment drop-down list, select Left, Center, Right, Inside, or Outside to specify the location of the page number within the header or footer.

4. To prevent the page number from appearing on the first page of your document, click the Show Number On First Page check box to remove the check from it.

5. When the page numbers appear with both the position and alignment you want in the Preview area, choose OK to have Word number the pages in your document.

FIGURE 6.2

Use the options in the Page Numbers dialog box to place sequential page numbers in your document.

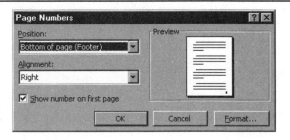

Page numbers appear on your screen in both Print Layout view and Print Preview, and they are automatically updated as you edit your document.

NOTE You can disable Word's automatic repagination feature in both Normal and Outline views by removing the check mark in the Background Repagination check box on the General tab in the Options dialog box. When you do, the number of the page that contains the insertion point is not displayed on Word's status line. In Web Layout view, Print Layout view, and Print Preview, you cannot disable background repagination.

Using Mirror Margins

The Inside and Outside page number alignment options are useful when combined with the Mirror Margins option (on the Margins tab in the Page Setup dialog box), for printing a document on both sides of the paper.

Mirror Margins automatically make the margins on facing pages "mirror" each other, so that the inside margins (the right margin on the left page and the left margin on the right page) are equal to each other, and so are the outside margins (the left margin on the left page and the right margin on the right page). Usually, you will want the inside margins to be larger than the outside margins to allow space for binding the document. You can specify the amount of space to add to the inside margin by adjusting the value in the Gutter text box on the Margins tab. This feature is useful for creating professional-looking business reports, contracts, proposals, or any document you want to bind along its left edge.

If you select Inside as the page number alignment, the page numbers appear on the right side of the left page and on the left side of the right page. When you select Outside as the alignment, the page numbers appear on the left side of the left page and on the right side of the right page. Each selection you make appears in the Preview area of the Page Numbers dialog box.

You can also change the format that is applied to the page numbers by applying a different numbering style and by having Word automatically insert the chapter number in front of the page number. For example, in a long document such as a proposal, it's common to number the pages of the Table of Contents using lowercase roman numerals and the pages containing the text of the proposal using Arabic numerals.

To change the format of the page numbers in your document:

1. Choose Insert ➤ Page Numbers to display the Page Numbers dialog box shown in Figure 6.2.

2. Click on Format to display the Page Number Format dialog box, shown in Figure 6.3.

3. Select the format for the page numbers in the Number Format drop-down list.

4. To have Word automatically place the chapter number in front of the page number, click the Include Chapter Number check box and then specify how you want the chapter number to appear using the following options:

   • In the Chapter Starts With Style drop-down list, select the Heading style that you are using for each chapter in your document.

- In the Use Separator drop-down list, select the character you want to appear between the chapter number and the page number.

5. To specify the number at which you want to start numbering for the document, choose either of the following options in the Page Numbering area:

Continue From Previous Section: Starts the page numbering in the current document section with the number next to the last number in the previous section. If this is the first section in the document, the number starts with 1.

Start At: Allows you to specify the number you want for the first page of your document. Choose this option if you want to start the page numbering at a number other than 1.

6. Choose OK in the Page Number Format dialog box, and again in the Page Numbers dialog box.

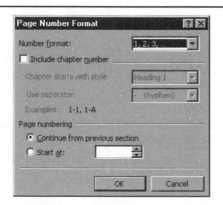

FIGURE 6.3

Display the Page Number Format dialog box to change the formatting applied to page numbers in your document.

If your document has more than one section, such as the proposal mentioned above, you can set up different page numbering for each section. Position the insertion point on the first page of the document (in this case, the Table of Contents, which is the beginning of the first section of the proposal), choose Insert ➤ Page Numbers to add page numbering, and then click Format to set up the formatting for this section's numbering. Then move the insertion point to the first page of the *second* section (the proposal's chapters) and repeat the process. You will probably want to select the Start At option in the Page Numbering area of the Page Number Format dialog box to specify that the text of the proposal start on page 1.

Repeat the process for any additional sections. If you want the page numbering to continue from the previous section, choose that option in the Page Number Format dialog box. If you want to remove page numbers, you need to edit the header or footer where the page number appears. See "Creating Headers and Footers" below to learn how to edit the headers and footers in your documents.

Creating Headers and Footers

Page numbers are certainly useful, but you'll probably also want to include other information on each page. For example, the current date, your name, and the name of your company are additional pieces of information that often appear on each page of a document. For this type of information, use Word's headers and footers. Headers are placed in the top margin and footers in the bottom margin on each page in the current section of the document.

To place a header or footer in your document, choose View ➢ Header And Footer. The existing document text is immediately dimmed and the Header text box at the top of your document opens. A floating Header And Footer toolbar, like the one shown in Figure 6.4, also appears.

PART

II

Creating Dazzling
Documents in Word

FIGURE 6.4

When you view your document's header or footer, the Header And Footer toolbar appears.

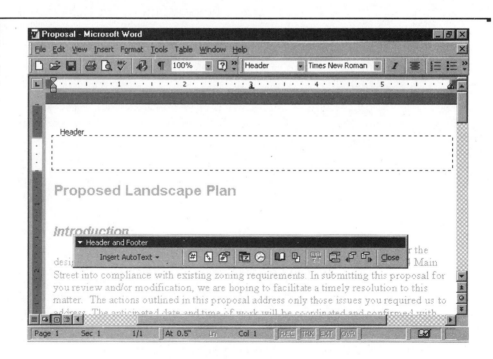

Enter the text you want to appear in the Header text box. Use the Header And Footer toolbar buttons, shown in Figure 6.5, to help you edit the headers and footers.

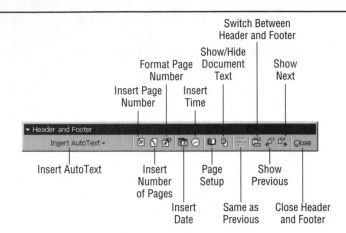

Whether you are creating headers, footers, or both, the process is the same:

1. Choose View ➢ Header and Footer to display the Header text box in the active section of the document.

2. Make any necessary changes to the header, including typing text and using the Insert Date and Insert Time buttons to place those field codes at the insertion point in the header.

3. If necessary, click the Switch Between Header And Footer button on the Header And Footer toolbar to move the insertion point to the footer, and then add any necessary text or field codes.

4. If necessary, click the Show Previous or Show Next button to activate the footer in the previous or next section of the document, and then make any necessary changes to that footer. Click the Switch Between Header And Footer button on the Header And Footer toolbar to activate that section's header, and then edit it as necessary.

5. When you are finished editing your document's header(s) and footer(s), click the Close button to close the Header And Footer toolbar and return to your document.

Unless you change the header and footer in a section of a document with multiple sections, all of the headers and footers will be the same in every section.

Creating Alternate Headers and Footers

Word contains two options that allow you to further edit the position of your document's header and footer. You can choose not to display the header or footer on the first page; and you can display different headers and footers on odd and even pages. These features are particularly useful for long documents, which may contain a cover page and may be bound.

For example, you would not want the document's header and footer to appear on the title page of the sample proposal mentioned above. In addition, you might want one header and footer to appear on the left pages of the proposal, and a different header and footer to appear on the right pages. To change the positions of your document's header and footer:

1. Click the Page Setup button on the Header And Footer toolbar to display the Layout page in the Page Setup dialog box, shown in Figure 6.6.

2. Choose from the following options:

   • Select the Different Odd And Even check box to create different headers and footers for even- and odd-numbered pages.

   • Select the Different First Page check box to create a different header and footer for the first page.

3. Choose OK in the Page Setup dialog box.

FIGURE 6.6

Display the Layout page in the Page Setup dialog box if you want to create alternate headers and footers.

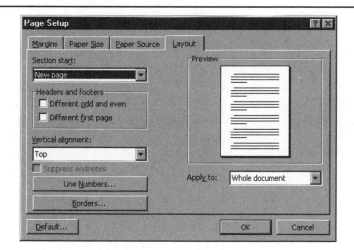

If you check the Different First Page box on the Layout page in the Page Setup dialog box, Word will provide a new text box titled First Page Header. Just leave the header and footer blank on the first page to suppress its display.

If you want to create different headers or footers for odd and even pages, check the appropriate box in the Page Setup dialog box. Word will provide two new text boxes titled Odd Page Header on the odd-numbered pages and Even Page Header on the even-numbered pages. Enter the first header or footer, and then click the Show Next button on the Header and Footer toolbar to enter the opposite page header or footer.

Taking Care of Loose Ends

Before you print the final version of a document, you should clean up dangling words, bad line and page breaks, and extra spaces that detract from the appearance of your document. There are three ways to clean up these loose ends:

- Are there spaces at the ends of lines because long words wrap to the beginning of the next line? If so, use hyphenation.

- Does the document have text strings that should be kept together but are broken over two lines? If so, use nonbreaking spaces.

- Are there paragraphs or lines of paragraphs that should be kept together but currently break across two pages? If so, use Line And Page Breaks options to specify how you want the text to flow within the document.

 TIP Make sure you have done all of your editing and formatting before attempting any of this final cleanup. When you add, delete, or reformat text, you have to clean up the document all over again.

Handling Line Breaks

Word 2000 includes options for either automatically or manually hyphenating your documents. With hyphenation, you can prohibit Word from hyphenating words in caps. You can also indicate the size of the *hyphenation zone*, the distance from the right margin that Word scrutinizes for words to hyphenate. Increase the area if you want more words hyphenated; decrease it if you don't mind ragged edges.

 TIP Your document may contain blocks of text that you don't want Word to hyphenate. To prevent automatic hyphenation, select each text block, choose Format ➢ Paragraph ➢ Line And Page Breaks, and turn on the Don't Hyphenate option.

When you have Word automatically hyphenate your document, hyphens are added as you type in the document. If you would like more control over how Word hyphenates your documents, you can choose to manually hyphenate your document. When you do, Word will review your document and locate candidates for hyphenation, and then recommend a location for the hyphen.

To hyphenate your document:

1. Choose Tools ➢ Language ➢ Hyphenation to display the Hyphenation dialog box shown in Figure 6.7.

2. To allow hyphens to be placed in words that consist of all capital letters, check the Hyphenate Words In CAPS box. Clear the check box to prevent Word from inserting a hyphen in words that appear in all capital letters.

3. If necessary, adjust the value in the Hyphenation Zone text box to specify the distance from the right margin in which Word will check for words to be hyphenated.

4. If necessary, adjust the value in the Limit Consecutive Hyphens To text box to specify the number of consecutive lines that can end in a hyphen.

5. To insert hyphens in your document, choose either of the following options:

- To have Word automatically insert hyphens in your document as you type, check the Automatically Hyphenate Document check box, and then choose OK.

- Click the Manual button to display the Manual Hyphenation dialog box shown in Figure 6.8, click in a different location for the hyphen if necessary, and then choose Yes to insert the hyphen in the document. To prevent hyphenating the selected word, choose No. Word automatically displays the next word in the document for which hyphenation is recommended.

When Word makes a recommendation, it is more concerned about spacing than about proper hyphenation. It will leave two characters at the end of a line or recommend some other awkward place for the hyphenation. Use your own judgment, and if you're not sure, refer to a dictionary or hyphenation guide.

 TIP If you are creating a document, such as a newsletter, in which the right edge should be even rather than ragged, click the Justify button on the Formatting toolbar to apply that format to each paragraph.

PART

II

Creating Dazzling
Documents in Word

FIGURE 6.7

Display the Hyphenation dialog box when you want to place hyphens in the current document.

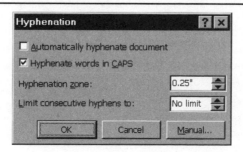

FIGURE 6.8

The Manual Hyphenation dialog box allows you to specify where you want the hyphen to appear in a recommended word.

 TIP To prevent a word or phrase that contains a hyphen (like a phone number) from breaking at the end of a line, insert a *nonbreaking hyphen* by holding down Ctrl+Shift when you type the hyphen. To enter an *optional hyphen*, a hyphen that breaks a word or a phrase at the designated place if it occurs at the end of a line, hold down Ctrl when you type the hyphen.

Nonbreaking Spaces

Occasionally, you might have a text string, such as an address, that should not be separated at the end of a line. You can protect this string by inserting *nonbreaking spaces* instead of regular spaces within the text string. These are similar to nonbreaking hyphens; text connected with nonbreaking spaces will move to the next line rather than breaking between lines. To insert a nonbreaking space, hold down Ctrl+Shift when you press the spacebar.

Handling Page Breaks

Word 2000 offers a number of other ways to keep text together so your document looks professionally printed. One of these options, called Widow/Orphan control, is on by default. This feature prevents the first line of a paragraph from being left alone at the bottom of the page (an orphan) or the last line of a paragraph from appearing by itself at the top of a new page (a widow).

You can also keep selected lines of text or entire paragraphs together. In addition, you can have Word insert a page break before the paragraph that contains the insertion point when you want the entire paragraph to be placed at the top of a page.

To specify how to break document text:

1. Select the text, then choose Format ➢ Paragraph ➢ Line And Page Breaks to display the Line And Page Breaks page in the Paragraph dialog box, shown in Figure 6.9.

2. Choose any of the following options in the Pagination area:

- Clear the Widow/Orphan Control check box to remove that feature. You can use this for drafting documents, but it is easier to leave this feature on.
- Check the Keep Lines Together box to prevent lines of the selected paragraph from being separated by a page break. The entire paragraph moves to the top of the next page.
- Check the Keep With Next box to keep the selected paragraph from being separated from the following paragraph by a page break (used, for example, to keep a heading with the first paragraph of text that follows).
- Check the Page Break Before box to insert a manual page break before the paragraph that contains the insertion point.

3. Choose OK in the Paragraph dialog box.

 TIP You can also insert a manual page break before a specific paragraph by positioning the insertion point where you want to place the page break and then pressing Ctrl+Enter.

FIGURE 6.9

Choose the appropriate line or page break option for selected text on the Line And Page Breaks page in the Paragraph dialog box.

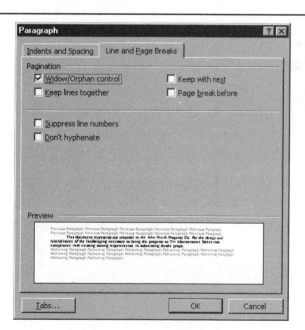

PART

II

Creating Dazzling
Documents in Word

Working with Columns

Some information is most effectively presented in *newspaper columns*, in which text flows from the bottom of one column to the top of the next. All Word documents consist of at least one column. If you create newsletters, flyers, reports, announcements, or other publications that contain multiple text columns, you'll probably use Word's newspaper columns feature quite a bit.

Entering and Editing Text in Columns

Working with newspaper columns requires a little advance design work. You'll find that it is often easier to enter document text into a single column, and then convert the text into multiple columns. Because of the space between the columns, one page of text takes up more than a page when poured into two or more columns. As a result, you may have to go back and edit text to get it to fit on a prescribed number of pages. However, by first focusing on your writing and then switching your attention to the design issues, you'll very likely end up with a better product in the long run.

When you are ready to work with columns, switch to Print Layout view so you can actually see the columns as they will appear on the page. Then follow these steps:

1. Select the text you want to place in columns.

2. Perform either of the following actions to create columns of equal width:

 Click the Columns button on the Standard toolbar to open the menu, and then drag to select the number of columns you want.

Choose Format ➤ Columns to display the Columns dialog box shown in Figure 6.10, adjust the value in the Number Of Columns text box, and then choose OK.

FIGURE 6.10

You can create columns using the options in the Columns dialog box.

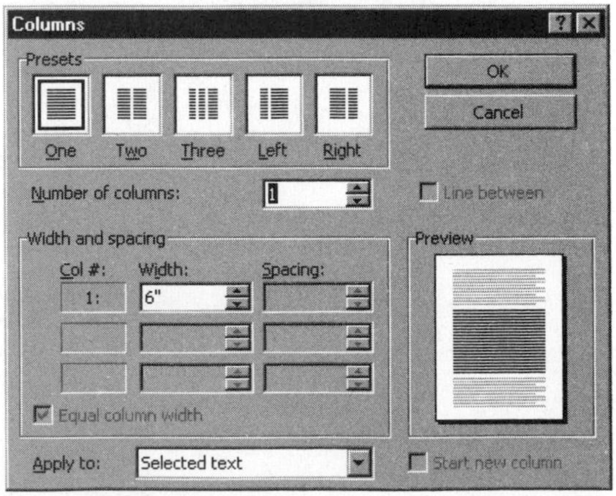

The selected text will be rearranged into columns, and column markers will be visible on the horizontal ruler.

Balancing Column Length

You can create *balanced* columns, or columns of equal length, for some documents. For example, a newsletter is a type of document that often contains multiple columns of the same length.

To create balanced columns, move the insertion point to the end of the text, choose Insert ➤ Break ➤ Continuous, and then choose OK to insert a continuous section break.

 TIP If you want to begin a new page after the balanced columns, position the insertion point after the continuous page break and either press Ctrl+Enter or choose Insert ➤ Break ➤ Page Break, and then choose OK to enter a manual page break.

Revising Column Structure

While you are creating a document with multiple newspaper columns, you may decide to change the appearance of your document by changing the number of columns in it.

To change the number of columns in a document with multiple columns, position the insertion point anywhere in the columns section and then either:

- Click the Columns button on the Standard toolbar, and then drag to select a new number of columns.

- Choose Format ➤ Columns, adjust the number in the Number Of Columns text box, and then choose OK.

 TIP To revert to a single column, choose one column or switch to Normal or Outline view and delete the section markers.

When you create columns with the Columns button, Word makes all the columns the same width. If you want columns of differing widths, such as those on a résumé, drag the Move Column marker on the horizontal ruler:

To change the amount of white space between the columns (the *gutter*), drag the Right and Left Margin markers on the Move Column marker.

Using the Columns Dialog Box

As you have already seen, you can use the options in the Columns dialog box, shown above in Figure 6.10, to create multiple newspaper columns and to change the number of columns in your document. Several other options in the Columns dialog box allow you to further change the appearance of columns. For example, you can use some of the options to establish columns of a specific width or to lock columns so that they will remain equally wide.

To specify exactly how your columns should appear, choose Format ➤ Columns, choose any of the following options in the Columns dialog box, and then choose OK:

- Choose any of the configurations in the Presets area to specify the number and position of the columns. If you choose One, Two, or Three, the Equal Column Width check box is automatically selected, so when you change the width of one column, the width of each column is automatically changed. When you choose Left, the left column is narrower than the right column. When you choose Right, the left column is wider than the right column.

- Create up to nine columns by adjusting the value in the Number Of Columns text box.

- Specify the exact width and spacing between each column by adjusting the values for each column in the appropriate Width and Spacing text boxes.

- Click on the Line Between check box to have Word insert vertical lines between each of the columns.

Keeping Text Together in Columns

All the tools that you use to keep page text together, including nonbreaking spaces, nonbreaking hyphens, and the Line And Page Breaks options, also work within columns. Word's Columns dialog box provides you with one other option for controlling where text breaks between columns:

1. Move the insertion point to the beginning of the text you want to reposition in the next column, and then choose Format ➤ Columns to open the Columns dialog box shown above in Figure 6.10.

2. Change the Apply To control to This Point Forward.

3. Click on the Start New Column check box.

4. Choose OK to insert an End Of Section mark and move the text to the next column.

Creating and Revising Tables

Parallel columns, such as the names and numbers in a phone book, display corresponding text in columns. Although tabs can be used to present information in parallel columns, it is far easier to use Word 2000's powerful Tables feature. With tables, every block of text can be easily formatted, edited, deleted, and moved around without affecting the remainder of the text. Tables are one of the most versatile tools in the Word toolkit.

There are three ways to create tables in Word, two of them quite handy:

 Click the Insert Table button on the Standard toolbar, and then drag to highlight the number of columns and rows you want in your table. As you drag, the number of rows and columns is displayed at the bottom of the buttons menu. When the number of rows and columns is correct, release the mouse button to insert the table in your document.

  Click the Tables and Borders button on the Standard toolbar to display the Tables and Borders toolbar. The Draw Table button is selected by default, and the mouse pointer appears as a pencil. Drag the pencil to create a rectangle about the size of the table you want. When you release the mouse button, the outside border of the table appears in your document. Drag with the pencil again to draw in column and row borders.

 You can easily move your table on the active page. To do so, position the mouse over the table until a small cross appears in a box at the upper-left corner of the table. Position the mouse pointer over the box until it appears as a move arrow (a cross with an arrowhead pointing in each direction), and then drag the table. An outline of the table appears as you drag. When the outline is in the position you want, release the mouse button to drop the table on the page.

If you want to specify exact measurements and formatting for the table when you create it, you can use the third method, in the Insert Table dialog box:

1. Choose Table ➤ Insert ➤ Table or click the Insert Table button on the Tables And Borders toolbar to display the Insert Table dialog box shown in Figure 6.11.

2. Adjust the value in the Number Of Columns text box to specify the number of columns in your table.

3. Adjust the value in the Number Of Rows text box to specify the number of rows in your table.

4. Choose one of the following options in the AutoFit Behavior area:

   Fixed Column Width: Allows you to specify the exact width of each column in the table by adjusting the value in the adjacent text box.

PART

II

Creating Dazzling
Documents in Word

Alternatively, choose Auto to have Word adjust the width of each column equally so the table spans from the left to the right margin.

AutoFit To Contents: Automatically adjusts the width of each column in the table to fit the longest cell contents in that column.

AutoFit To Window: Automatically adjusts the size of the table to fit in the window of a Web browser, even if the size of the browser window changes.

5. To save the settings you specified in the Insert Table dialog box so that Word will display them each time the dialog box is displayed, click the Set As Default For New Tables check box.

6. Choose OK to insert the table in your document.

 NOTE See "Formatting Tables" below to learn how to use Word's Table AutoFormat option, which is also available in the Insert Table dialog box.

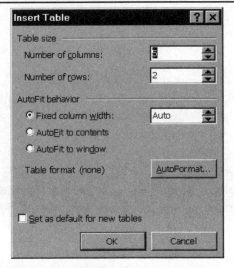

One of Word's new features is that you can now insert a table in an existing table *cell*, the rectangle at the intersection of a column and row. To do so, click in the cell where you want to insert a table, and then use any of the methods above to insert the table.

WARNING When you delete a table, any data in the table is also deleted.

To delete a table, click in any cell in the table, and then choose Table ➤ Delete ➤ Table.

Entering and Editing Text

Once you have created a table, you can enter text by clicking in any cell and then typing the characters you want in that cell. You can also use any of the following keys to activate a cell so you can enter text:

- Press the Tab key or the → key on the keyboard to move to the next cell to the right.
- Hold down Shift+Tab or press the ← key to move one cell to the left.
- Press the ↑ or ↓ key to move the insertion point to the cell above or below the current cell.

If you created your table by drawing it, click the Draw Table button on the Tables And Borders toolbar or close the toolbar to change the pointer from a pencil back to an I-beam. Then click in the cell and begin typing.

Table 6.1 shows how to select portions of a table.

TABLE 6.1: SELECTING IN TABLES

To Select	Action
A cell	Triple-click in the cell.
A row	Move the mouse to the left margin, point to the row, and click.
Multiple rows	Select the first row, hold down the mouse button, and drag down the desired number of rows.
A column	Move the mouse pointer above the column until it changes to a downward arrow and click; or hold down the Alt key and click in the column.
Multiple contiguous columns	Select the first column, hold down the mouse button, and drag through the desired number of columns; or use any method to select the first column and then hold down Shift and use any method to select the last column.
Entire Table	Choose Table ➤ Select ➤ Table; or click the table's Move icon.

PART

II

Creating Dazzling
Documents in Word

Formatting Text in Tables

Each table cell can be formatted separately. You can center text in the first column, left-align it in the second column, and right-align in the third column. You can apply boldface formatting to the *header row*, the row with the column names, and italicize other rows. Whatever you can do to a paragraph, you can do to the text within a cell. Use the buttons on the Formatting toolbar or the commands on the Format menu to apply fonts, font effects, alignment, bullets and numbering, and indents and spacing to the text in a table.

 You can also change the alignment of the text in the active table cell. To do so, click on the Align *Position* drop-down button on the Tables and Borders toolbar or right-click on the table, highlight Cell Alignment, and then click one of the text alignment options that appear.

The alignment assigned to the active cell appears on the Align *Position* button on the toolbar.

Rotating Text in Tables

Occasionally, the best (or only) way to fit table text into the available space is to rotate it so that it is no longer running in the traditional direction across the page. For example, you may need to do this if a table has many columns that require longish headings. With Word's Change Text Direction feature, you can rotate text in a table so that it runs vertically, facing either right or left. To do so:

1. Select the cell or group of cells that contain the text you want to rotate.

2. Choose one of the following methods to change the text direction:

 Click the Change Text Direction button on the Tables And Borders toolbar. The first click rotates the text so that it is facing right, the second click flips it to face left, and the third click returns it to horizontal.

Right-click on the table, and then choose Text Direction in the shortcut menu to display the Text Direction dialog box shown in Figure 6.12. Choose the rotation you want for the text in the Orientation area. The change appears in the Preview area. Choose OK to define the direction of the text in the selected cell.

As the text rotates, so do some of the buttons on the Formatting toolbar. The alignment buttons, Numbering, Bullets, Decrease Indent and Increase Indent buttons all rotate in the same direction as the text in the cell, as shown in Figure 6.13. The Columns button on the Standard toolbar also rotates. The Change Text Direction button on the Tables And Borders toolbar changes to display the rotation that will take place when you next click on that button.

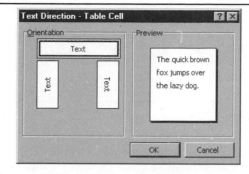

When you rotate text, even the insertion point rotates, so editing can be a little disconcerting at first. The main thing to remember is that you have to drag the mouse vertically to select text. Once you've gotten the hang of that, you're all set.

Modifying Table Structure

One of the best reasons to use tables instead of tabs in your documents is that tables are easily modified. You can add or delete rows and columns, change column and row widths, and merge and split cells without upsetting the rest of the table text.

In Word 2000, you can also set the table alignment and specify how you want document text to wrap around the table by changing the table's properties. In addition, tables can now be indented a specified distance from the left margin of the page.

Adding and Deleting Rows, Columns, and Cells

You can easily adjust the number of rows in an existing table by either adding new rows or deleting existing rows. Use one of the following methods to place new rows exactly where you want them in a table:

- To add a row at the end of a table, simply move to the last cell in the table and press Tab. Word will add a new row with the same formatting as the current row.

- If you want to insert rows in the middle of the table, select the number of rows you want to insert and choose Table ➢ Insert ➢ Rows Above or Table ➢ Insert ➢ Rows Below to have Word insert rows above or below the selection. Alternatively, click on the Insert Table drop-down list on the Tables And Borders toolbar, and choose Insert Rows Above or Insert Rows Below.

- To insert rows above the selected rows, right-click on the table and choose Insert Rows in the shortcut menu.

 NOTE As you change the table structure, the Insert Table button on the Tables And Borders toolbar changes to reflect your last action. For example, if you recently inserted rows in your table, the Insert Table button changes to the Insert Row button.

To delete selected rows, either choose Table ➤ Delete ➤ Rows or right-click and choose Delete Rows from the shortcut menu.

 WARNING When you delete a table row, all the data in that row is also deleted.

Inserting columns works in a similar way to inserting rows. New columns created in a table with fixed column width are the same width as the ones you select to create them, so you may have to adjust column widths if the table no longer fits into the width of the page.

Use one of the following methods to place new columns exactly where you want them in a table:

- To insert a column at the end of a table, click the Show/Hide ¶ button on the Standard toolbar, select the marks to the right of the last column, right-click on the table, and then choose Insert Columns.

- Select the number of columns you want to insert and choose Table ➤ Insert ➤ Columns To The Left or Table ➤ Insert ➤ Columns To The Right to have Word insert columns to the left or right of the selection. Alternatively, click on the Insert Table drop-down list on the Tables And Borders toolbar, and choose Insert Columns To The Left or Insert Columns To The Right.

To delete selected columns, either choose Table ➤ Delete ➤ Columns, or right-click on the table, and then choose Delete Columns.

 WARNING When you delete columns in a table, all the data in those columns is also deleted.

You can also insert new cells, rows, or columns into a table using the following steps:

1. Select the cells in the position in which you want to insert new cells.

2. Choose Table ➢ Insert ➢ Cells or click on the Insert Table drop-down list button on the Tables And Borders toolbar and choose Insert Cells to display the Insert Cells dialog box shown in Figure 6.14.

3. Choose one of the following options to tell Word where you want the new cells to be placed in your table:

Shift Cells Right: Inserts the new cells in the position of the selected cells, and then moves the selected cells to the right.

Shift Cells Down: Inserts the new cells in the position of the selected cells and then moves the selected cells, and every cell below the selected cells, to the next row.

Insert Entire Row: Inserts new rows above the selected cells.

Insert Entire Column: Inserts new columns to the left of the selected cells.

4. Choose OK to insert the specified cells.

PART

II

Creating Dazzling
Documents in Word

FIGURE 6.14

Display the Insert Cells dialog box when you want to insert cells in a specific location in a table.

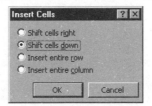

You can also delete selected cells, rows, and columns. To do so:

1. Select the cells you want to delete, and then choose Table ➢ Delete ➢ Cells or right-click on the table and choose Delete Cells to display the Delete Cells dialog box shown in Figure 6.15.

2. Choose one of the following options:

Shift Cells Left: Deletes the cells and their contents, and shifts any cells to the right of the selection to the left to replace the cells that were deleted.

Shift Cells Up: Deletes the cells and their contents, and shifts any cells below the selection up to replace the cells that were deleted.

Delete Entire Row: Deletes the row that contains the insertion point, including all the data in that row.

Delete Entire Column: Deletes the column that contains the insertion point, including all the data in that column.

3. Choose OK in the Delete Cells dialog box.

 WARNING When you delete selected cells, rows, and columns, all the data in the selection is also deleted.

FIGURE 6.15

You can use the options in the Delete Cells dialog box to delete cells, rows, and columns.

Changing the Column and Cell Width, and the Row Height

The easiest way to make adjustments to both columns and rows is to drag their borders. To do so, just move the mouse pointer to the border between the row or column until it changes to a double-headed arrow, and then drag that border in either direction. Column borders can be dragged left (to decrease the width of the column) or right (to increase the column width). Row borders can be dragged up (to decrease the row height) or down (to increase the height of the row). Hold down the Alt key while you drag either border to display the measurement of the row or column in the Ruler. Column sizes are displayed in the horizontal Ruler above the columns; row sizes appear in the vertical Ruler when you are in Print Layout view.

 NOTE To increase the width of a column while simultaneously decreasing the widths of each column to its right, hold down the Ctrl key while dragging the column's right border. Each column's width is changed proportionately.

There may be times when you want to make all the columns the same width or all rows the same height (for example, when creating a calendar). You can have Word do the work for you. To do so:

 Select the columns you want to be the same width and click on the Distribute Columns Evenly button on the Tables And Borders toolbar or choose Table ➢ AutoFit ➢ Distribute Columns Evenly.

 Select the rows you want to be the same height, and then click on the Distribute Rows Evenly button on the Tables And Borders toolbar or choose Table ➢ AutoFit ➢ Distribute Rows Evenly.

There are several other ways to quickly change the row height and column width of an entire table after you have entered your data in the table. You can select the table, or click in any cell in the table, and then perform one of the following actions:

- To change the row height and column width simultaneously to fit the contents of each cell, choose Table ➢ AutoFit ➢ AutoFit To Contents or click the Insert Table button on the Tables And Border toolbar and then choose AutoFit To Contents. The height of each row is adjusted to fit the cell with the tallest contents. The width of each column is adjusted to fit the widest contents.

- To adjust the width of the table to fit the window in Web Layout view, choose Table ➢ AutoFit ➢ AutoFit To Window or click the Insert Table button on the Tables And Borders toolbar and then choose AutoFit to Window.

 You can also specify an exact row height, column width, and cell width, and the vertical alignment in selected cells, using Word's Table Properties dialog box. In addition, you have some row options for tables that span more than one page.

To change the properties of selected rows:

1. Select the row or rows whose properties you want to change.

2. Choose Table ➢ Table Properties or right-click the table and choose Table Properties to display the Row page in the Table Properties dialog box, shown in Figure 6.16.

3. To change the height of the selected rows, click in the Specify Height check box to place a check in it, adjust the value in the text box to the height you want, and then select either At Least or Exactly in the Row Height Is drop-down list.

4. To specify how you want Word to display a table that spans multiple pages, choose either of the following options:

    Allow Row To Break Across Pages: Permits a selected row that contains multiple lines of text to be continued on the next page. This may be harder to read but allows you to fit more text into the available space.

Repeat As Header Row At The Top Of Each Page: Duplicates the contents of the selected top row or rows of the table on subsequent pages of the table. The top row(s) of a table that contain the title, column headings, and other information that for clarity should appear on each page, are called the *header* row(s), so this is a handy option.

5. If necessary, click Previous Row or Next Row to select that row, and then apply any necessary properties to that row as indicated in steps 2 through 4.

6. Choose OK to apply the row properties you selected.

You can change the properties of the selected row on the Row page in the Table Properties dialog box.

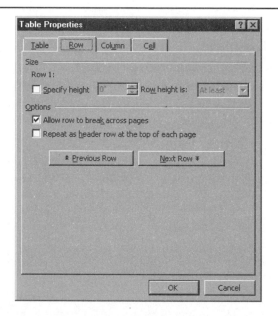

When you choose At Least in the Row Height Is drop-down list, you've specified that the rows will maintain a minimum height regardless of what is in them. Use Exactly when you want to designate a row height that doesn't change. This is useful when you are creating calendars, for example, where you want the row height to stay the same regardless of the contents.

 TIP If you want to break a table across two pages, you can enter a page break in the table. Select the row you want to appear on the next page, and then press Ctrl+Enter to create a manual page break.

Use the options on the Column page in the Table Properties dialog box to specify how the width of the selected column is determined:

1. Select the column or columns whose widths you want to change.

2. Choose Table ➤ Table Properties or right-click the table and choose Table Properties to display the Column page in the Table Properties dialog box, shown in Figure 6.17.

3. Choose from the following options in the Size area to adjust the width of the selected column:

   • Check the Preferred Width check box and then adjust the value in the related text box to the width you want for the column.

   • In the Measure In drop-down list, choose Inches to specify an exact column width, or Percent to have Word automatically adjust the column when other columns are resized.

4. Click either Previous Column or Next Column to select that column, and then choose the property options you want for that column.

5. When you have selected the options you want for each column, choose OK in the Table Properties dialog box.

PART

II

Creating Dazzling
Documents in Word

FIGURE 6.17

*You can change the
width of a column
using the options on
the Column page in
the Table Properties
dialog box.*

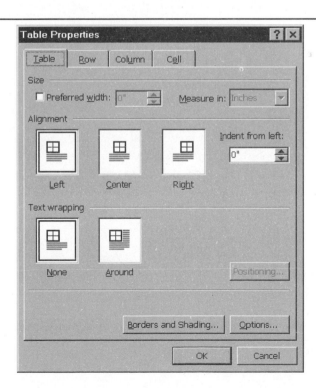

You can also choose specific properties for selected cells, such as the width of a cell, the cell's text alignment, and even the cell's margins.

1. Select the cell whose properties you want to change.

2. Choose Table ➤ Table Properties or right-click the table and choose Table Properties to display the Cell page in the Table Properties dialog box, shown in Figure 6.18.

3. To change the width of the selected cell, use the following options in the Size area when appropriate:

   • Check the Preferred Width check box, and then adjust the value in the related text box to specify the width of the cell.

   • In the Measure In drop-down list, choose Inches to define an exact cell width, or Percent to define the width of the cell relative to the width of the table.

4. Choose Top, Center, or Bottom to specify the vertical alignment of the text in the cell.

5. If necessary, choose Options to display the Cell Options dialog box shown in Figure 6.19, and then choose any of the following options:

   • Clear the Same As The Whole Table check box, and then adjust the appropriate values in the Top, Bottom, Left, and Right text boxes to specify the corresponding margin for the selected cell. Alternatively, check this box to apply the same margins in each cell in the table.

   • Select the Wrap Text check box to have Word automatically wrap text to the next line in the cell when the insertion point reaches the right margin.

   • Select the Fit Text check box to have Word reduce the font on your screen so that all the text you type appears in the cell. The font size is not changed, only its appearance.

   • Choose OK to return to the Cell page in the Table Properties dialog box.

6. Choose OK in the Table Properties dialog box.

FIGURE 6.18

Use the options on the
Cell page in the Table
Properties dialog box
to change the width or
alignment assigned to
the selected cell.

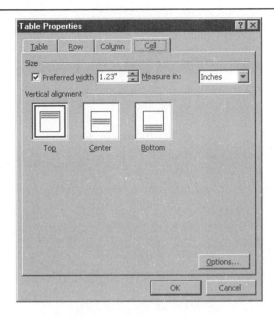

FIGURE 6.19

You can change the
selected cell's margins
using the options avail-
able in the Cell
Options dialog box.

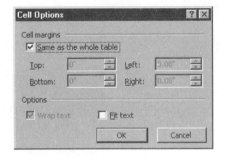

Merging and Splitting Cells

It doesn't take long when working with tables to discover that you don't always want
the same number of cells in every row or column. You might want to put a title in a
single cell that spans the top of the table. Or you might be creating a form, and want

fewer columns for the totals. When you want to make one cell from two or more cells, you *merge* the cells. *Split* cells to separate a single cell into multiple cells.

Use any of the following methods to merge selected cells:

Select the cells you want to merge and Choose Table ➤ Merge Cells.

Right-click on the table and choose Merge Cells in the shortcut menu.

 Click on the Merge Cells button on the Tables and Borders toolbar.

 If you prefer the visual approach, you can use the Eraser on the Tables And Borders toolbar to erase the border between cells you want to merge. Just click the Eraser button, and then click on the border you want to remove.

Follow these steps to split a selected cell:

1. Choose Table ➤ Split Cells, right-click the table and choose Split Cells, or click on the Split Cells button on the Tables And Borders toolbar to display the Split Cells dialog box shown in Figure 6.20.

2. Adjust the value in the Number Of Columns text box to specify the number of columns into which to split the cell.

3. Adjust the value in the Number Of Rows text box to specify the number of rows into which to split the cell.

4. Check the Merge Cells Before Split box if you want to merge more than one selected cell before you perform the split. This check box is not available if only one cell is selected.

5. Choose OK to split the cells.

FIGURE 6.20

The Split Cells dialog box contains options that allow you to specify how you want selected cells to be split.

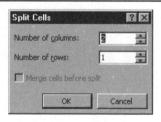

You can also click on the Draw Table button on the Tables And Borders toolbar, and then use the pencil to draw cell borders where you want to split cells.

The ability to define exactly how you want the cells, rows, and columns to appear in a table makes working in tables both useful and practical. You can, for example, create a table for use as an order form for your company, such as the one shown in Figure 6.21.

You can create a sample order form using Word's table and text formatting features.

Order·Form¤				¤
Item¤	**Price**¤	**Quantity**¤	**Total**¤	¤
¤	¤	¤	¤	¤
¤	¤	¤	¤	¤
¤	¤	¤	¤	¤
¤	¤	¤	¤	¤
Subtotal¤ ¤		¤	¤	¤
Sales·Tax¤			¤	¤
Total¤			¤	¤

The Order Form table was created by inserting a table with four columns and nine rows, merging some cells, and changing the formatting applied to text entered in the cells in the first two rows. Then, the widths of the four columns were adjusted, and the alignment of the text entered in the cells was changed. You can use any combination of these procedures to create a table to your own specifications.

Formatting Tables

Before you print your table, you might want to put some finishing touches on it to give it that polished, professional look. Word offers both automatic and manual table formatting options to add and remove borders, change border types, and add colors and shading. Word also lets you specify some properties for your tables.

Using AutoFormat

Word's Table AutoFormat feature provides you with a number of different formats that you can apply in one easy step. Table AutoFormat applies borders, shading, fonts, and colors that are stored in a named format. In addition, you can choose AutoFit to have Word resize the table to fit its contents. Most of the formats include special formatting for the header row, last row, and first and last columns since these often contain titles or summary information.

Follow these steps to have Word automatically format your table:

1. Click anywhere in your table and choose Table ➤ Table AutoFormat or click on the AutoFormat button on the Tables And Borders toolbar to open the Table AutoFormat dialog box shown in Figure 6.22.

2. Choose the name of the format to apply to the table in the Formats list box. A sample of the selected format appears in the Preview area.

3. If necessary, choose the Borders, Shading, Font, Color, and AutoFit check boxes, found in the Formats To Apply area, to apply each of those options to the table. Each time you check or clear an option, the changes to the table's format appear in the Preview area.

4. If necessary, choose the Heading Rows, First Column, Last Row, and Last Column check boxes, found in the Apply Special Formats To area, to apply each of those formats to the table.

5. When the table in the Preview area looks the way you want your table to appear, choose OK in the Table AutoFormat dialog box.

FIGURE 6.22

Display the Table AutoFormat dialog box when you want Word to apply a saved set of formatting to your table.

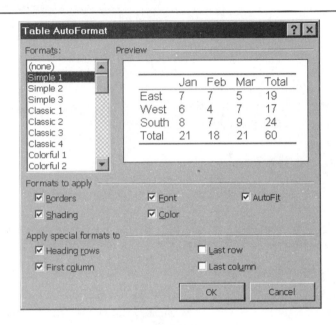

If you're not satisfied, click the Undo button on the Standard toolbar, or choose Table AutoFormat again and select a different format.

Adding Your Own Borders and Shading

You don't have to settle for Word's predesigned table AutoFormats. You can adjust the Table AutoFormats manually or start from scratch, whichever you prefer. Either way, you'll want to display the Tables And Borders toolbar before you begin formatting your table, so you can use the buttons and drop-down list options on the toolbar to apply formatting to selected cells.

The Line Style, Line Weight, and Border Color buttons each allow you to select the formatting you want to apply to the borders of selected cells. All three buttons are dynamic, which means that your most recent choice appears on the button.

Click the Line Style drop-down list arrow, and then select the style of the cell's border.

Click the Line Weight drop-down list arrow, and then select the size of the cell's border.

Click the Border color button to display a color menu, and then select the color for the border.

 TIP You can use the pencil pointer to draw over borders that you want to color. Make sure you draw over the entire length of the border, or the color will not be applied.

Once you have selected the style, weight, and color for the border, you can then apply the border to selected cells. To do so:

1. Select the cells to which to apply the border you chose.

 2. Click the *Location of* Border drop-down list button on the Tables And Borders toolbar to open a menu containing 13 border choices.

3. Click the type of border you want to apply.

 NOTE Inside Border can only be applied to two or more cells. Outside Border will affect the border around a single cell or a group of cells; typically, you will apply outside borders to the entire table.

You can also change the background color of selected cells, or of the cell that contains the insertion point. To apply a background color:

1. Click in the cell to which you want to apply a background color, or select all the cells to be formatted with the same background color.

 2. Click the Shading Color drop-down list button on the Tables And Borders toolbar, and then select the background color in the color palette that appears.

The Shading Color palette contains many different shading colors, including various shades of gray. One word of warning: if you plan to make photocopies of your printed table, be aware that some shades of gray do not copy well.

If you are applying a lot of different borders and shading to your table, you can pull both the menus off the toolbar so they float on the surface of your document. You can then apply as many borders or shades as you want without having to open the menus each time.

To float the Borders or Shading Color menu:

1. Click on the drop-down arrow to open the menu.

2. Point to the gray bar at the top of the menu, and the bar will turn the same color as your Windows title bars.

PART

II

Creating Dazzling
Documents in Word

3. Drag the menu into the document, so it appears similar to Figure 6.23.

4. Apply any borders and shading you want to your table.

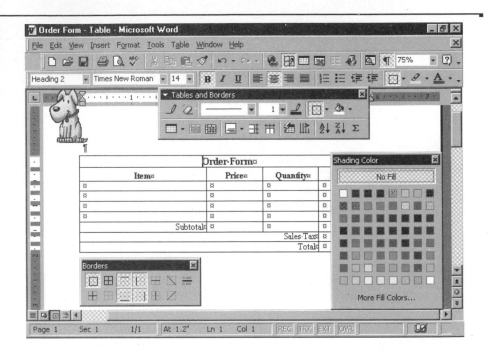

Floating menus appear on top of the table or other document text. You can drag them to a different location on the page if they cover the table you want to format.

 NOTE Borders and shading are not limited to use in tables. You can apply the same skills you just learned to any paragraph of text. Just select one or more paragraphs and click the Borders button or choose Format ➤ Borders And Shading.

You can also apply formatting to your table using the options in the Borders And Shading dialog box. To display it, choose Format ➤ Borders And Shading. The options for table and cell borders appear on the Borders page, and the options for shading cells appear on the Shading page. However, you cannot switch between the dialog box and your table, so it is usually easier to apply formatting using the Tables And Borders toolbar.

Centering Tables Horizontally

If you've adjusted the column widths in your table, then it may no longer extend across the entire width of the page. If you moved your table, it may no longer be centered horizontally on the page. In Word 2000, you can center the table between the left and right margins, so it appears nicely positioned when you print your document.

To center the table horizontally on the page, follow these steps:

1. Use either of the following methods to select the entire table:

   • Choose Table ➢ Select ➢ Table.

   • Click on the Move icon that appears at the top-left corner of the table when you move your mouse pointer over the table.

2. Click on the Center button on the Formatting toolbar.

Changing the Table Properties

Word 2000's new Table Properties feature allows you to specify the width and position of a table in your document precisely. You can have regular document text wrap around a narrow table and you can specify the distance between the table and the text.

To change the properties of a table:

1. Click in any cell in the table whose properties are to be changed.

2. Choose Table ➢ Table Properties to display the Table page in the Table Properties dialog box, shown in Figure 6.24.

3. To specify an exact width for the table, check the Preferred Width check box in the Size area, and then do the following:

   • Adjust the value in the Preferred Width text box to specify the table's width.

   • In the Measure In drop-down list, choose either Inches, to have the value in the Preferred Width text box appear in inches, or Percent, to change the value to percent. If you choose Inches, the table width will be as wide as the value. If you choose Percent, the table width will be proportioned to the specified percentage in relation to the width of the page between the left and right margins.

4. Choose Left, Center, or Right in the Alignment area to specify the position of the table between the left and right margins.

5. If necessary, adjust the value in the Indent From Left text box to specify how far the table is to be indented from the left page margin.

6. Choose either of the following options in the Text Wrapping area to specify how you want the regular document text to wrap around the table:

None: Places the table above the document text.

Around: Places the table in the document text.

7. If you chose Around in step 6, click on the Positioning button to display the Table Positioning dialog box shown in Figure 6.25, and then choose any of the following options:

- In the Horizontal area, the distance from the edge of the page to the left edge of the table is displayed. If necessary, type a different measurement or select Left, Right, Center, Inside, or Outside to specify the horizontal position of the table. Then choose Margin, Page, or Column in the Relative To drop-down list to specify what the Position is related to.

- In the Vertical area, the table's current distance from the previous paragraph appears in the Position drop-down list. Type a different distance, or choose Top, Bottom, Center, Inside, or Outside to specify the table's vertical position. Then choose Margin, Page, or Paragraph in the Relative To drop-down list.

- In the Distance From Surrounding Text area, adjust the values in the Top, Bottom, Left, and Right text boxes to specify the distance between the table's borders and surrounding document text.

- Check the Move With Text check box in the Options area so the table can move vertically in the document when you move the paragraphs surrounding it.

- Check the Allow Overlap check box in the Options area to allow the table to be partly covered with text or pictures when you are viewing it in a Web browser.

- Choose OK in the Table Positioning dialog box.

8. Choose OK in the Table Properties dialog box.

FIGURE 6.24

Display the Table page in the Table Properties dialog box to change the size, alignment, or text wrapping properties of the active table.

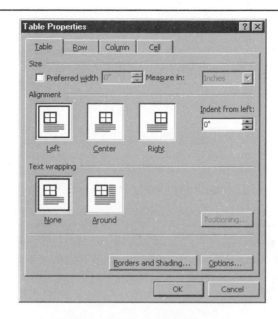

FIGURE 6.25

When document text wraps around the active table, display the Table Positioning dialog box to specify the position of the table in the document text.

Adding Calculations to Tables

As long as you only need an occasional sum now and then and don't anticipate a lot of revisions, you can safely enter calculations directly in your Word table, and save Excel worksheets for the more complex calculations. Word's Formula feature is useful for performing simple calculations in a table.

The order form created earlier (Figure 6.21) is an example of a table that could use some calculations. If you fill in some of the cells in the table with some sample items and prices, you can enter a formula in the cells in the Total column, and then have Word add up the totals of the items to calculate the Subtotal.

Rather than digging in your desk for a calculator, click in the cell where you want the calculation to appear. Then you can either enter a formula or use Word's AutoSum feature.

You can use AutoSum to quickly add the values in contiguous cells above the active cell. All you have to do is to click on the AutoSum button on the Tables And Borders toolbar to perform the calculation. If AutoSum doesn't find any numbers above the active cell, it will check in the cells to its left.

NOTE Word's AutoSum does not recalculate on its own. If you change any of the numbers in cells included in the formula, select the cell with the AutoSum results and click on AutoSum again.

If you are entering a formula, you need to know the cell addresses of the numbers you want to include in your formula. A *cell address* is the reference to a cell composed of the column letter and row number. In the filled-in Order Form table shown below, the Total cell for the Greeting cards item is D3; it is in column D and row 3. The Price cell for the Mailing labels item is B5.

Order·Form¤				¤
Item¤	**Price**¤	**Quantity**¤	**Total**¤	¤
Greeting·cards¤	$2.50¤	10¤	$··25.00¤	¤
Stationary¤	$4.80¤	6¤	$··28.80¤	¤
Mailing·labels¤	$9.89¤	3¤	$··29.67¤	¤
¤	¤	¤	¤	¤
Subtotal¤	¤	¤	¤	¤
		Sales·Tax¤	¤	¤
		Total¤	¤	¤

To place a formula in the Total cell for each item:

1. Place the insertion point in the cell into which you want the formula, and then choose Table ➢ Formula to display the Formula dialog box shown in Figure 6.26.

2. Word will automatically suggest a formula, based on what it sees around the insertion point, in the Formula text box. If necessary, delete the current formula and enter a new formula in the text box using one of the following methods:

   • Type in a new formula.

   • Select the appropriate function in the Paste Function drop-down list.

- Select the appropriate bookmark in the Paste Bookmark drop-down list. A bookmark in your document may contain a value that you want to use in your formula.

3. Choose the format for the results of the formula in the Number Format drop-down list. You can select whole number, decimal, currency, or percent format for the value that will appear as the result of the formula.

4. Choose OK in the Formula dialog box.

PART

II

Creating Dazzling
Documents in Word

FIGURE 6.26

You must display the Formula dialog box if you want to enter a formula in a table cell.

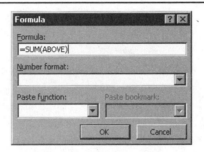

There are several things to consider when you place a formula in a table cell:

- You cannot type the formula directly in the cell. Instead, you must display the Formula dialog box, and enter it in the Formula text box.

- Formulas must begin with an equal sign (=).

- Use cell addresses to enter your formula, especially if the values in those cells might change.

- You can use the following common operators: + (addition); – (subtraction); / (division); and * (multiplication). For example, if you wanted to multiply the Price of the greeting cards purchased by the Quantity in the sample order form, the formula would be =B3*C3.

In addition to common operations such as addition and subtraction, you can also choose from a list of *functions*, or predesigned formulas such as Average, Minimum, Maximum, and Count. To use a function, enter = in the Formula text box, and then choose the function you want to use in the Paste Function list.

Click between the parentheses and enter the *range* of cells, a group of cells that are adjacent to each other in the table, to include in the function. You can use the Product function to multiply the values in the Price and Quantity cells for the Greeting cards item. To do so, you would enter **=PRODUCT(B3:C3)**. The colon indicates the first and last cells in the range of cells that are included in the calculation.

Because we want the results to appear in a specific format, in this case currency, you can choose that format in the Number Format drop-down list. Each zero (0) represents a required number, and the number symbol (#) represents an optional number. So the format #,##0.00 could represent, for example, 12,300.00 or 5.00.

 TIP You can make up your own number formats for displaying the results of a formula, but you must follow the same convention for indicating required and optional numbers.

Word's formulas are field codes. Once you've entered a formula in a cell, you can delete it, but you will also delete the field code that contains the formula. If you change any of the numbers the formula is based on, you must have Word recalculate the results because they are not automatically updated.

When you click in a cell that contains a formula, the results of the formula appear with a shaded background. By default, the results of field codes in Word documents appear with a shaded background when they are selected. This is helpful, because you know immediately that the cell contains a field code—in this case a formula.

 NOTE If your formula does not appear with a shaded background when you click in the cell, choose Tools ➢ Options, display the View page, and then choose When Selected in the Field Shading drop-down list. Choose OK in the Options dialog box.

To have Word recalculate the results of a formula, click in the cell that contains the formula, and then press the F9 key, or right-click the cell and then choose Update Field in the shortcut menu.

 TIP If you know how to use Excel (covered in Part V), embedding all or part of a worksheet is often easier than using formulas in a Word table.

 In the sample Order Form table, you can enter a multiplication formula in the Total column in each of the three cells adjacent to the items ordered. Then click in the Subtotal cell in the Total column and click on the AutoSum button on the Tables and Borders toolbar to quickly enter the SUM function in that cell. By entering **=D7*.06**

in the Sales Tax cell, you can have Word calculate the sales tax for the merchandise, assuming that the sales tax rate is 6 percent. Then, click in the Total cell and click on the AutoSum button again to calculate the total amount of this order. The Order Form table appears as shown in Figure 6.27.

FIGURE 6.27

You can use formulas to calculate the total amount of the order in the sample Order Form table.

Order Form			
Item	Price	Quantity	Total
Greeting cards	$2.50	10	$ 25.00
Stationary	$4.80	6	$ 28.80
Mailing labels	$9.89	3	$ 29.67
Subtotal			$83.47
Sales Tax			$ 5.01
Total			$88.48

What's Next

In the first four chapters of Part II, you've learned how to use Word's basic features to create a document. In addition, you've experienced some fairly advanced features, such as applying different formatting to sections of a document and creating and formatting tables. Now you are ready to learn how to use more of Word's advanced features. In the following chapters, you will learn how to use Microsoft Drawing to create your own clip art pictures, create and use styles to quickly format document text, and create an outline. You will also discover how to merge documents with a data source, create a form to be filled in online, and explore some of Word's features that are helpful in very long documents. Finally, you'll learn how to create multiple versions of a document and track changes that you and other reviewers have made.

PART

II

Creating Dazzling
Documents in Word

CHAPTER **7**

Using Graphics for Extra Impact

The old saying "A picture is worth a thousand words" is true—pictures, or *graphics*, can really enhance your message. Pictures also add visual interest to a document. Some documents, such as newsletters, almost require graphics. Graphics can enhance almost every document, making them more interesting and often more inviting.

Graphics can illustrate a concept, serve as a corporate logo, or simply make your document look better. Graphics can consist of charts, line art, text, clip art, or photos. You can either use existing images stored in a file or create your own graphic objects.

Using Microsoft Draw

If you want to design your own graphic objects, use Microsoft Draw. You can unleash your creativity or just have fun drawing your own graphics using the drawing tools, located on Office 2000's Drawing toolbar. Drawing is available in Word, Excel, and PowerPoint, and the drawing tools are available in the Access Toolbox. You use the same methods to create a drawing with the drawing tools, no matter which application you are using.

 NOTE You can also create a drawing in Word, Excel, or PowerPoint and paste it into an Access form or report or into another document.

The Drawing toolbar is displayed by default in PowerPoint. To display it in Word or Excel, use either of these methods:

Click on the Drawing button on the Standard toolbar.

Right-click on any toolbar or choose View ➤ Toolbars, and then select Drawing in the toolbar list.

When you display the Drawing toolbar, your Word document automatically changes to Print Layout view if it is not already in that view. As with any other toolbar, you can drag the Drawing toolbar away from its docked position above the status bar so that it becomes a floating toolbar, as shown here:

The Drawing toolbar includes two broad categories of menus and buttons. The first set, beginning with the AutoShapes drop-down list button and ending with the Insert Clip Art button, is used to create drawing objects. The remaining buttons are used to format existing objects.

Inserting AutoShapes

When you click the AutoShapes button, a drop-down menu appears with a list of AutoShape categories. AutoShapes consist of lines; basic shapes such as triangles, cylinders, hearts, and braces; block arrows; flowchart shapes; and many more. Choose the More AutoShapes option to see the complete list.

The easiest way to insert AutoShapes into your document is to display the AutoShapes toolbar, click on the category that contains the shape you want, and then click on the shape to select it. Use either of the following methods to display the AutoShapes toolbar:

- Click on the AutoShapes button on the Drawing toolbar, point to the AutoShapes menu's title bar, and then drag it off the menu.

- Choose Insert ➤ Picture ➤ AutoShapes.

To insert an AutoShape (other than a Curve, Freeform, or Scribble line, discussed below) in your document:

1. Click on the AutoShapes drop-down list button on the Drawing toolbar, and then highlight a category to display its menu of AutoShapes. Alternatively, display the AutoShapes toolbar and click on the button of the category you want to use.

2. Click on an AutoShape, position the insertion point where you want to place the AutoShape, and then click in your document to insert it.

When you first insert the selected AutoShape, it is created in its default size. As you position your insertion point in your document after selecting an AutoShape, notice that the mouse pointer appears as a crosshair. This means that you can also drag diagonally (from the top left to the bottom right) to insert an AutoShape in a custom size. Alternatively, you can drag one of the AutoShape's corner *handles*, the small squares that surround a selected AutoShape, to increase or decrease its size proportionally.

If you intend to add a lot of AutoShapes in the same category, you can drag the title bar at the top of the menu and place the menu in the document as a floating toolbar. For example, when creating a flow chart, you can drag that menu's title bar so the AutoShapes on it are easily available while you work, as shown in Figure 7.1.

Callout AutoShapes are text boxes used for annotating other objects or elements, so when you insert a callout in your document, the insertion point will automatically appear inside the callout. To place text in any closed AutoShape except those created using the Lines category, right-click on the AutoShape and choose Add Text in the shortcut menu. When you do, the insertion point appears in the object, and the Text Box toolbar appears.

Creating Dazzling
Documents in Word

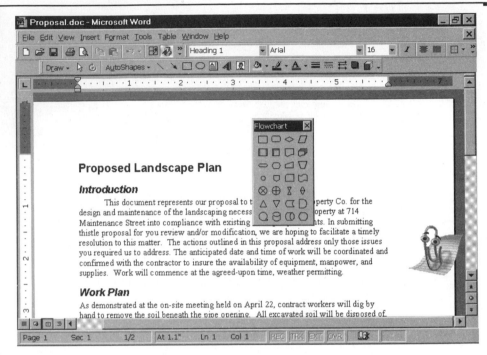

 NOTE See the explanation on using text boxes in "Inserting Line Art Objects" for additional information on using the Text Box toolbar.

Curve, Freeform, and Scribble objects are AutoShape line objects that consist of multiple line segments you create individually. The line segments are extremely small in Curve and Scribble objects; in fact, they are so small that the lines appear to be curved. You can easily see the various line segments in a Freeform object. To create a Curve, Freeform, or Scribble AutoShape, follow these steps:

1. Click on the AutoShapes drop-down list button, and then highlight Lines to display its menu of AutoShapes.

2. In the menu, click on Curve, Freeform, or Scribble.

3. Position the mouse pointer where you want to begin the line, and then click to start it. Gradually move your mouse to a different location and click again to form the first segment of the line. Continue until the line appears as you want, and then double-click to form the end of the line.

If your object is a closed Freeform, double-click near the beginning of the line to close it. Alternatively, right-click on the selected freeform, and then choose Close Curve in the shortcut menu that appears.

Inserting Line Art Objects

Line art objects include AutoShapes, lines, arrows, rectangles, ovals, and text boxes. You can easily insert any of the latter objects in your document by using the appropriate tool on the Drawing toolbar. To draw a line or arrow, follow these steps:

1. Click on the Line button or the Arrow button.
2. Move the pointer, which now appears as a crosshair, to one end of the line you want to draw.
3. Hold down the left mouse button and drag to draw the line.
4. Release the button to create the line, and then click on the Line or Arrow button to turn off that tool.

When you use the Arrow tool, an arrowhead appears at the end of the line where you released the mouse button.

 TIP If you want a line or arrow that is absolutely horizontal or vertical in relation to the page, hold down the Shift key while dragging.

The Line and other object buttons work like the Format Painter button: When you have more than one object to draw, begin by double-clicking on its button. The button will stay pressed, allowing you to draw more objects, until you click on any other drawing object's button. If you don't want to draw any more objects, just click on the button that is depressed on the Drawing toolbar to change your mouse pointer back into an I beam. To draw a rectangle or oval:

1. Click on the Rectangle or Oval button.
2. Move the pointer, which now appears as a crosshair, to the top-left corner or edge of the object you want to draw.
3. Hold down the left mouse button and drag down and to the right to draw the object.
4. Release the button to create the rectangle or oval and turn off the Drawing tool.

 TIP When you hold down the Shift key while dragging, an exact square or circle is created.

Because both the rectangle and oval are closed objects, you can add text in them just as you can in the closed AutoShapes. Right-click on the object, and then choose Add Text in the shortcut menu to position the insertion point inside the object and display the Text Box toolbar.

TIP If you need a series of identical objects, create one object and then paste as many copies of that object in the locations you want.

Use the Text Box tool to create text that floats on a layer above standard document text. Draw the text box as you would a rectangle. When you release the mouse button, the text box is active—an insertion point appears in it, and a lined border appears around it. You can type the text you want in the active text box.

You can also create a text box around existing text. For example, if you are creating a newsletter, it may be easier to type the text and then change the way it is laid out. Text boxes are particularly useful in documents that contain graphics, because they allow you to move text to any position, including within the margins. To create a text box around existing text:

1. Select the text you want to place in a text box.

2. Click on the Text Box button on the Drawing toolbar.

When you create a text box this way, the text box is selected—a shaded border with handles appears around the text box, but the insertion point is not in it. When the text box is selected, you can drag it to a different location on the page. You can also use the handles surrounding the selected text box to change it size. This is important, because text boxes do not automatically conform to the size of their contents—in other words, they don't grow as you add text or shrink when you delete text.

To activate a text box (place the insertion point in it) when you want to edit or format the text, just click inside the text box. You can then select the text and apply formatting to it using the options and buttons on the Formatting toolbar and the commands on the Format menu.

WARNING To delete a text box, select it and then press the Delete key. When you delete a text box, all the text in it is also deleted.

The Text Box toolbar appears when you draw a text box in your document. Use the buttons on the toolbar to perform the following actions:

 Activate or select a text box, click on the Create Text Box Link button on the Text Box toolbar, and then click on an empty text box to link the two text boxes in your document. Any text that does not fit in the first text box will automatically flow into the next linked text box. For example, your company newsletter may contain a story that is continued on another page. If you place the beginning of the story in a text box, you can link it to the text box that will contain the rest of the story.

 TIP Create and store the text for linked text boxes in a separate file, and make any formatting and editing changes there. Then copy the text into the first text box. Text that will not fit is automatically poured into the next linked text box.

 Activate the text box that contains the link (the one that was selected or active when you created the link), and then click on the Break Forward Link button to break a link between two text boxes.

  Click on the Previous Text Box button or on the Next Text Box button to select the previous or next linked text box. This is helpful because you can see where each linked text box falls in line.

 Click on the Change Text Direction button to rotate all the text in the active text box. The first time you click on the button, the text turns to the right. When you click again, the text turns so that it is facing left. The third time you click on the button, the text returns to its normal position. You can use rotated text in a text box to provide visual interest in a document.

 NOTE The same thing happens when you rotate text in a table cell. See "Creating and Revising Tables" in Chapter 6 for additional information.

You can delete a linked text box without deleting its contents. The contents will spill into the other text boxes to which the deleted text box was linked. You may need to resize those text boxes to accommodate the additional text.

Designing WordArt

WordArt is used to create a text graphic object. You'll use WordArt to create text logos, emphasize titles, and add excitement to a document. For example, you can create a vibrantly colored title page for a proposal or report. To create WordArt:

1. Place the insertion point where you want the graphic, and click on the Insert WordArt button on the Drawing toolbar to open the WordArt Gallery dialog box, shown in Figure 7.2. Alternatively, choose Insert ➤ Picture ➤ WordArt to open the WordArt Gallery dialog box.

2. Click on the style in which you want your text graphic to appear in the Select A WordArt Style area.

3. Choose OK to display the Edit WordArt Text dialog box, shown in Figure 7.3.

4. Type the text in the Text area of the dialog box.

5. If necessary, apply the following formatting to the text in the Text area:

   • Select a different font in the Font drop-down list.

   • Select a different font size in the Size drop-down list.

   • Click on the Bold and/or Italics button to apply that formatting.

6. Choose OK to place the WordArt object in your document and open the floating WordArt toolbar.

FIGURE 7.2

You can choose a style for you text graphic in the WordArt Gallery dialog box.

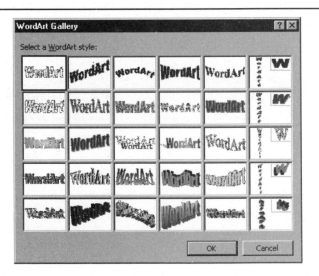

FIGURE 7.3

*Type the text for your
WordArt graphic in the
Edit WordArt text box.*

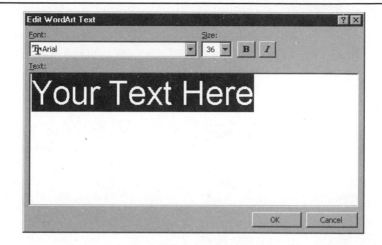

When the WordArt object is placed in your document, it is selected, and the small, square sizing handles appear around it. The WordArt toolbar is only displayed when a WordArt object is selected in your document. You can use the buttons on the WordArt toolbar to edit and apply formatting to your WordArt object. The toolbar buttons are described in Table 7.1.

 TIP To deselect an object, just click anywhere in the document. Deselected objects appear just as they will when the document is printed.

TABLE 7.1: WORDART TOOLBAR BUTTONS

Button	Name	Use
	Insert WordArt	Displays the WordArt Gallery dialog box to create a new WordArt object.
Edit Text...	Edit Text	Displays the Edit WordArt Text dialog box to edit text.
	WordArt Gallery	Opens the WordArt Gallery dialog box to change the WordArt style.

Continued

TABLE 7.1: WORDART TOOLBAR BUTTONS CONTINUED

	Format WordArt	Opens the Format WordArt dialog box so you can format colors, size, position, and wrap properties.
	WordArt Shape	Opens a shape menu so you can select the basic shape into which the text will be poured.
	Free Rotate	Changes the object handles to rotation handles so you can rotate the text. Click again to turn off.
	Text Wrapping	Displays a menu so you can select how text wraps around the WordArt object.
	WordArt Same Letter Heights	Makes all letters the same height, irrespective of case.
	WordArt Vertical Text	Changes the WordArt orientation from horizontal to vertical. Click again to reverse.
	WordArt Alignment	Opens an alignment menu with standard options and unique WordArt options.
	WordArt Character Spacing	Opens an adjustment menu so you can change space between characters.

Formatting Objects

Use the Drawing toolbar's formatting buttons to format selected objects quickly. You can even apply some formatting to selected WordArt objects, although it is easier to use the WordArt toolbar to change the appearance of a WordArt object. You can also use Drawing's shortcut menu, or some options on the Draw menu to change the appearance of a selected object.

To select a single object, just click on it. To select multiple objects, either hold down the Shift key while clicking on each object, or click on the Select Objects tool and drag a rectangle around the objects you want to select.

Use the following tools to format a selected object:

Click on the Fill Color drop-down list button to display a palette of colors. If you want an object without any color, choose No Fill. The Fill Color palette can be dragged onto your screen as a floating menu, which is useful if you have several objects to which to apply different fill colors. You can also choose More Fill Colors on the menu to create a custom color, and Fill Effect to apply a gradient, texture, pattern, or a picture as the fill for an object.

Click on the Line Color drop-down list button to display the Line Color palette, and then choose a color to apply to the lines in and around the selected object. Like the Fill Color palette, the Line Color palette can be dragged onto your document so it becomes a floating menu. You can create a custom color for the line or apply a pattern to it for different effects.

 Click on the Font Color drop-down list button to display its palette, and then choose a color for the text in a selected object such as a text box or callout. The Font Color palette can be dragged so it becomes a floating menu, and you can create custom colors to apply to the text in selected objects.

 TIP Click the Fill Color, Line Color, or Font Color button to apply its current color to a selected object.

 Click on the Line Style button to display a menu that contains various line styles, and then click on the style you want for the lines in and around a selected object. Alternatively, select More Lines from the menu to open the Format AutoShape dialog box and display the Colors and Lines page. You can change the line style, color, and weight, as well as many other attributes of the selected object.

The Format Text Box and Format AutoShape Dialog Boxes

The Format Text Box dialog box, which appears when you double-click on the border of a text box, contains options similar to those of the Format AutoShape dialog box. Each dialog box allows you to change the fill color, line style, line weight, size, scale, and text wrapping style for a selected object. The Format Text Box dialog box also allows you to change the text box's internal margins and convert it to a frame. If the text box is a callout, you can also change the style of the callout.

 Click on the Dash Style button to display its menu, and then click on one of the dashed line styles to apply that style to all of the lines in the selected object. You can change the weight of the line by selecting it in the Line Style menu. To change the lines back to a solid line, select that style in the Dash Style menu.

Creating Dazzling Documents in Word

Click on the Arrow Style button, and then select the style in the resulting menu to apply to the ends of the selected line. You can choose an arrowhead or one of various other line terminators. If the combination of line endings you want isn't in the menu, choose More Arrows to display the Format AutoShape dialog box, set a beginning and ending style for the line, and then choose OK. Arrow styles can be applied only to lines, arrows, and open AutoShapes.

The Draw menu, which appears when you click on the Draw button on the Drawing toolbar, also contains some commands that allow you to change the appearance of a selected object:

- Choose Text Wrapping, and then select how you want the regular document text to appear in relation to the selected object.

- Choose Edit Points to change the appearance of a Curve, Freeform, or Scribble AutoShape. When you do, each position in which you clicked your mouse while drawing the AutoShape appears with a small, black move handle. Drag the handle to change its position, thereby changing the appearance of the AutoShape.

- Choose Change AutoShape when you want to replace the current AutoShape with a different one. When you do, the AutoShapes menu appears. Choose the category that contains the AutoShape, and then choose the replacement. Any text in the AutoShape remains in the new shape.

NOTE You cannot use the Change AutoShape command to change the shape of a Line AutoShape. Instead, you must use the Edit Points command, and then drag the endpoints to different positions. Alternatively, you can delete a Line AutoShape and insert an AutoShape in a different category.

- To insert subsequent AutoShapes of the kind selected with the same formatting applied, choose Set AutoShape Defaults. Every new AutoShape of that type will appear in the same size, color, etc., until you specify a different default.

Special Shadow and 3-D Effects

Shadow and 3-D effects are designed to give a selected drawing object more depth. You cannot apply both shadow and 3-D formatting to an object. If you apply a 3-D effect to a shadowed object, the shadow is removed. If you apply a shadow to an object that has 3-D formatting, the 3-D effect is removed. Any drawing object can have either a shadow or a 3-D effect applied to it.

Click on the Shadow button to display a menu of various shadow styles, and then click on the style you want for the selected object. To change the format of the shadow, click on the Shadow button again, and then choose Shadow Settings to display the Shadow Settings toolbar. The toolbar buttons and their uses are described in Table 7.2.

TABLE 7.2: THE SHADOW SETTINGS TOOLBAR BUTTONS

Button	Name	Use
	Shadow On/Off	Displays or removes the object's shadow.
	Nudge Shadow Up	Pushes the shadow up.
	Nudge Shadow Down	Pushes the shadow down.
	Nudge Shadow Left	Pushes the shadow to the left.
	Nudge Shadow Right	Pushes the shadow to the right.
	Shadow Color	Displays a palette so you can select the color for the shadow.

 To choose the three-dimensional effect to apply to a selected object, click the 3-D button on the Drawing toolbar, and then click in the menu that appears. To change the formatting applied to the 3-D effect, click on the 3-D button again, and then choose 3-D Settings to display the 3-D Settings toolbar. Table 7.3 shows how to use the buttons on the toolbar to quickly change the format of the 3-D effect.

TABLE 7.3: THE 3-D SETTINGS TOOLBAR BUTTONS

Button	Name	Use
	3-D On/Off	Hides or displays the 3-D effect applied to the object.
	Tilt Down	Tilts the 3-D effect toward the object.

Continued ▶

PART

II

Creating Dazzling
Documents in Word

TABLE 7.3: THE 3-D SETTINGS TOOLBAR BUTTONS CONTINUED

	Tilt Up	Tilts the 3-D effect away from the object.
	Tilt Left	Rotates the 3-D effect to the left.
	Tilt Right	Rotates the 3-D effect to the right.
	Depth	Allows you to select or specify a different depth for the 3-D effect.
	Direction	Allows you to select a direction in which the 3-D effect points, and to specify whether the direction is Perspective (extends all sides of the effect to a single point) or Parallel (extends all sides of the effect parallel to one another).
	Lighting	Adjusts the position and intensity of the "light" shining on the 3-D effect to present a different appearance.
	Surface	Allows you to select the appearance of the composition of the 3-D effect.
	3-D Color	Displays a palette so you can select the color for the 3-D effect.

Arranging Objects

The Draw menu on the Drawing toolbar includes other options for manipulating objects. For example, you can change the position of a selected object on the page, display a grid to help you position an object precisely, and even group objects in order to move or edit them simultaneously.

Drawing objects are placed in separate layers on top of the text in a document, in the order in which they were created. To move objects from layer to layer:

1. Select the object you want to reposition.

2. Click on the Draw button, and then choose Order to display the Order menu. If necessary, drag the menu by its title bar to display the Order toolbar.

3. Choose one of the following options to change the order of the selected drawing object:

   • Choose Bring To Front to place the selection above (on the top layer of) other graphic objects. Choose Send To Back to place the selection below (on the bottom layer of) other graphic objects.

   • Choose Bring Forward or Send Backward to move the selected object one layer at a time.

- Choose Send Behind Text to place a selected object behind (below) the text layer of your document. Choose Bring In Front Of Text to place selected objects in front of the text layer.

 NOTE Use the Send Behind Text command to create a watermark for a single page. (Place the watermark in a header or footer to have it appear on every page of a document.)

You can see how objects are layered, and how each command works by creating three different drawing objects, such as a rectangle, triangle, and oval stacked on top of each other.

If you select the object on the top layer and then choose Send To Back, the object appears at the bottom of the stack of objects. When you choose Bring Forward, its position moves to the middle of the stack. You can choose either Bring Forward or Bring To Front to return the object to its original position in this example.

You can also send the object behind the text layer by choosing Send Behind Text. When you do, the text flows over the selected object but disappears behind the other objects. To place the selected object in its previous position above the text layer, choose Bring In Front Of Text.

If you're doing detailed work, consider turning on a grid of invisible horizontal and vertical lines to help you precisely align various objects in the drawing. The grid works by automatically pulling each object you draw into alignment with the nearest intersection of gridlines. You can display the gridlines, and you can adjust the distance between them to help you as you draw. To turn on the grid:

1. Click on the Draw button on the Drawing toolbar.

2. Choose Grid to display the Drawing Grid dialog box shown in Figure 7.4, choose the appropriate options (described below) to define the specifications for the grid, and then choose OK.

   - Check the Snap Objects To Grid box to turn on the grid.
   - Check the Snap Objects To Other Objects box to automatically align drawing objects with both the horizontal and vertical edges of other drawing objects.
   - Adjust the value in the Horizontal Spacing text box to specify the distance between the horizontal gridlines.
   - Adjust the value in the Vertical Spacing text box to specify the distance between the vertical gridlines.
   - Adjust the value in the Horizontal Origin and Vertical Origin text boxes to specify the beginning point for the gridlines, relative to the edges of the

page. Alternatively, check the Use Margins box to specify the margins as the beginning point for the gridlines.

- Check the Display Gridlines On Screen box to turn on the display of gridlines, check the Vertical Every box, and then adjust the value in the Vertical Every and Horizontal Every text boxes to a number greater than zero to display both sets of gridlines.

- To save the gridline settings you specified so they become the default, click on the Default button, and then choose Yes in the message box that appears asking if you want to change the default gridline settings. The default gridline settings are stored in the Normal template and will be used each time you turn on a grid.

FIGURE 7.4

You can display a grid to help you align objects within a drawing.

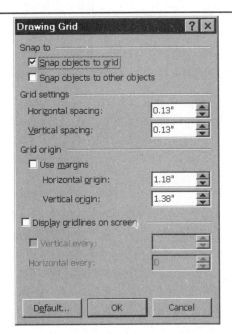

There are several other ways to adjust the positions of selected objects in a drawing. Click the Draw button on the Drawing toolbar and then choose from the following:

Highlight Nudge. You can choose Up, Down, Left, or Right on the Nudge menu to push the selection in the corresponding direction.

Highlight Align Or Distribute, and then drag its title bar to display the floating Align Or Distribute toolbar. If one object is selected, click Relative To Page to make the alignment options available. If multiple objects are selected, Relative To Page aligns the selection in relation to the edge of the page. If you do not select Relative To Page when multiple objects are selected, the objects are aligned in relation to each other. Then choose one of the following options to specify the alignment:

 Align Left aligns the selection along the left edge of the page but in the same horizontal position, or it aligns selected objects along the leftmost edge of the selection.

 Align Center aligns the selection in the center of the page in the same horizontal position, or it centers selected objects within each other.

 Align Right aligns the selection along the right edge of the page in the same horizontal position, or it aligns selected objects along the rightmost edge of the selection.

 Align Top aligns the selection vertically along the top edge of the page, or it aligns selected objects along the top edge of the selection.

 Align Middle aligns the selection vertically in the center of the page, or it centers selected objects within the selection.

 Align Bottom aligns the selection vertically along the bottom edge of the page, or it aligns selected objects along the bottom edge of the selection.

 Distribute Horizontally positions selected objects an equal horizontal distance from each other relative to the edges of the page, or it spaces each selected object equally in relation to the selection.

 Distribute Vertically positions selected objects an equal vertical distance from each other relative to the edges of the page, or it spaces each object in a multiple selection equally in relation to the selection.

Highlight Rotate Or Flip, and then drag its menu bar to display the Rotate Or Flip toolbar. Click any of the following buttons to perform the corresponding action to change the position of the selection:

 Free Rotate places small green diamonds on the corners of the selected object(s). Drag a corner in the direction you want to rotate the object. When the object appears in the position you want, click anywhere outside the selection to place the object in that position. The Free Rotate button is also available on the Drawing toolbar.

 TIP To confine the rotation to 15 degrees, hold down the Shift key while you drag one of the corner rotation handles. To rotate the object more than 180 degrees, hold down the Ctrl key while you drag the rotation handle.

Each time you click on the Rotate Left button, the selection is rotated 90 degrees to the left.

 Each time you click on the Rotate Right button, the selection is rotated 90 degrees to the right.

 Flip Horizontal repositions the object horizontally so that it appears as a mirror image of itself in the same location.

 Flip Vertical repositions the object vertically so that it appears as a mirror image of itself in the same location.

Grouping and Ungrouping Objects

When your drawing is complete, you can group all the drawing objects so that they are treated as a single object. When objects are grouped, all are selected when you select any one object in the group. Any formatting you apply is applied to every object in the group. For example, if you have selected a group of AutoShapes and you choose a Shadow to apply, each object in the group will have the same shadow.

You can also use the Nudge, Align Or Distribute, and Rotate Or Flip commands to manipulate the position of the group, or you can simply drag the group to a new location on the page to move every object in the group. To combine several objects into a group:

1. Hold down the Shift key while you click on each object to select it.

2. Click on the Draw button on the Drawing toolbar, and then choose Group.

The handles on the multiple selected objects will be replaced with one set of handles that can be used to size or move the entire object.

If you want to move, resize, format, or delete an individual element in a group, you can ungroup the grouped object, thereby changing the group back into separate objects. Each object can then be edited independently of the group. To ungroup a grouped object:

1. Click on the group to select it.

2. Click on the Draw button on the Drawing toolbar, and then choose Ungroup. Alternatively, right-click on the group, and then choose Grouping ➤ Ungroup.

 NOTE Usually, Clip Art images are composed of a grouped set of objects. To change the appearance of a Clip Art object, ungroup it and then edit individual objects as necessary.

When you have finished editing, select one of the objects and regroup them so you can move or size the entire image.

To regroup an ungrouped set of objects:

1. Select any object that was previously in the group.

2. Click on the Draw button on the Drawing toolbar, and then choose Regroup. Alternatively, right-click on the object, and then choose Grouping ➢ Regroup.

Adding Illustrations from the Clip Gallery

The newly revised Microsoft Clip Gallery, included with Office 2000, contains a broad selection of pictures. You can collect media clips including pictures, sounds, and motion clips, and import them into the Clip Gallery, where they will be available when you are ready to use them. To insert a media clip into your document:

1. Position the insertion point where you want to insert the clip.

2. Click on the Insert Clip Art button on the Drawing toolbar, or choose Insert ➢ Picture ➢ Clip Art to display the Insert ClipArt dialog box shown in Figure 7.5.

3. Click on the Pictures, Sounds, or Motion Clips tab to display the categories of files available for that type of clip.

4. Click on the category that contains the clip you want. If necessary, scroll through the list to find the category, or type a keyword describing the category in the Search For Clips text box to display the clips that match the keyword.

FIGURE 7.5

The Insert ClipArt dialog box contains the Clip Gallery with Pictures, Sounds, and Motion Clips available.

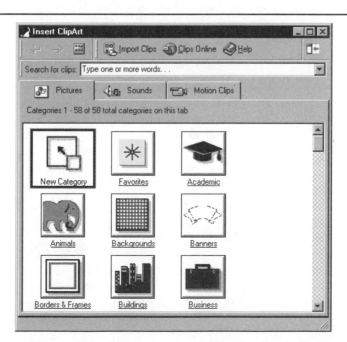

5. Click on the thumbnail of the clip you want, and then click on the Insert Clip button on the clip's toolbar that appears.

6. If necessary, click on the Change To Small Window button on the Insert ClipArt dialog box's toolbar to reduce the size of the dialog box, reposition the insertion point, and then repeat steps 3–5 to insert another media file into your document.

7. Click on the Insert ClipArt dialog box's Close button to return to your document.

NOTE Use the Insert ClipArt dialog box's toolbar to help you display the categories. Click on the Back button to return to the previous clips or category. Click on the Forward button to display the next clips or category in the dialog box. Click on the All Categories button to return to the list of categories that appears when you first display the dialog box.

You can also use the clip's toolbar options to preview the selected clip, to add the clip to your Favorites folder, or to display the thumbnails of clips that closely match either the selected clip or all clips with specific keywords.

Click on the Preview Clip button to display the clip in a Preview window so you can see the size and details of a picture, play a sound clip so you can hear it, or run a motion clip so you can see how it will appear in your document. Click on the Preview window's Close button to remove it from your screen.

Click on the Add Clip To Favorites Or Other Category button to display a dialog box containing a drop-down list in which you can choose Favorites or any other category to place the selected clip. Choose OK to add the clip to that category. Or, to close the drop-down list without placing the clip in a category, click on the Hide Pane button in the top-right corner of the dialog box.

Click on the Find Similar Clips button to display a dialog box that allows you to search either for the best matching clips or for similar clips by keyword. Click on the Artistic Style or Color & Shape button to find the closest matches for the selected clip. Alternatively, click on the hyperlink to the keyword that contains the clips you want. To close the dialog box without selecting a hyperlink, click on the Hide Pane button.

The Insert ClipArt dialog box also contains two other options:

• Click on the Import Clips button to display the Add Clip To Clip Gallery dialog box, shown in Figure 7.6. Highlight the name of the file that contains the clip, and then select Copy Into Clip Gallery, Move Into Clip Gallery, or Let Clip Gallery Find This Clip In Its Current Folder Or Volume as the Clip Import option. Choose Import to import the clip into the Clip Gallery.

• Click on the Clips Online button to take you to the Microsoft Clip Gallery Live web page, where you can choose from clip art, pictures, sounds, and motion clips to either preview or download. You can also search for additional clips by entering a keyword for that category of clips.

FIGURE 7.6

Display the Add Clip To Clip Gallery dialog box when you want to import another media clip into the Clip Gallery.

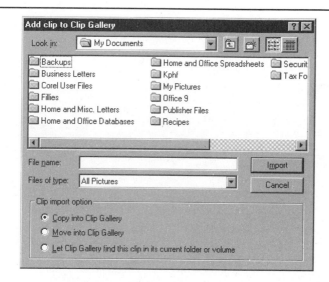

If the media clip you insert in your document is a picture, the Picture toolbar, containing buttons that allow you to format the picture, appears when it is selected. Table 7.4 describes the toolbar buttons.

TABLE 7.4: THE PICTURE TOOLBAR BUTTONS

Button	Name	Use
	Insert Picture	Inserts a picture from a file.
	Image Control	Determines the format of the picture; choose Automatic (applies the most appropriate format, usually the defaults), Grayscale (converts each color to a shade of gray), Black & White (changes each color to black or white, converting the image to line art), or Watermark (changes the picture to a bright, low-contrast format that can be placed behind document text).

Continued ▶

TABLE 7.4: THE PICTURE TOOLBAR BUTTONS CONTINUED

	More Contrast	Increases color intensity.
	Less Contrast	Decreases color intensity.
	More Brightness	Adds white to lighten the colors.
	Less Brightness	Adds black to darken the colors.
	Crop	Trims rectangular areas from the image.
	Line Style	Formats the border that surrounds the picture.
	Text Wrapping	Determines the way document text wraps around the picture.
	Format Object	Displays the Picture page in the Format Object dialog box so you can change the format to exact specifications.
	Set Transparent Color	Used like an eyedropper to make areas of the picture transparent. Used extensively for Web graphics.
	Reset Picture	Returns the picture to its original format.

The Crop and Set Transparent buttons are used with areas of the picture. All other buttons affect the entire picture.

 NOTE The Set Transparent button is only available for some imported pictures, such as bitmaps and GIF and JPEG files. When the button is available, no transparent options have been set for the selected picture. Use the Set Transparent button to make one color in the picture, usually the background, transparent.

You cannot move a picture while it's in the default layout position, In Line With Text. When you change the clip's layout to Square, Tight, Behind Text, or In Front Of

Text, the Horizontal Alignment options on the Layout page in the Format Picture dialog box become available. Choose Other if you want to reposition the picture by dragging it with your mouse. To change the layout position of a clip:

1. Right-click on the clip, and then choose Format Picture in the shortcut menu to display the Picture page in the Format Picture dialog box. Alternatively, click on the Format Picture button on the Picture toolbar.

2. Click on the Layout tab to display its page, shown in Figure 7.7.

3. Choose Square, Tight, Behind Text, or In Front Of Text in the Wrapping Style area.

4. Choose Other in the Horizontal Alignment area.

5. Choose OK in the Format Picture dialog box.

FIGURE 7.7

Display the Layout page in the Format Picture dialog box if you want to change the layout of the selected picture.

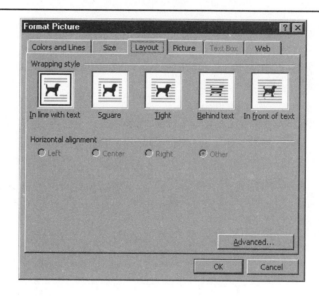

PART

II

Creating Dazzling
Documents in Word

You can now reposition the picture by dragging it to a different location on the page. The text wrapping style you chose in step 3 above will be in effect for the picture.

NOTE When you click on the Advanced button on the Layout page in the Format Picture dialog box, you can change the position of the text that wraps around the selected picture, and also its distance from the picture. The options that are available depend on which text wrapping style you select.

Inserting Other Pictures

Besides using the Clip Gallery as a source of art, you can insert pictures into your document from any file to which you have access. You can also format pictures inserted from a file using the buttons on the Picture toolbar. To insert a picture that isn't in the Clip Gallery, use the following steps:

1. Choose Insert ➤ Picture ➤ From File, or display the Picture toolbar and click on the Insert Picture button to open the Insert Picture dialog box, shown in Figure 7.8.

2. Select the name of the file that contains the picture. A preview of the picture appears in the right pane.

3. Click the Insert button to insert the selected picture in your document.

FIGURE 7.8

You can also insert a picture that is not in the Clip Gallery into your document.

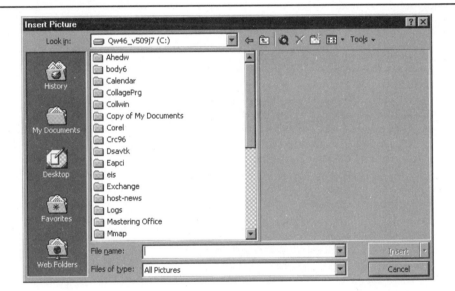

What's Next

In this chapter you've seen how to insert graphic objects in your document, whether you created them or they were stored in a file. One use of graphics is as logos, to provide related documents with a uniform look. Chapter 8 continues the discussion of Word's advanced features, including some that are essential tools for achieving visual consistency (and streamlining your work). You will learn how to create and apply styles to document text, and also how to save as a template a set of styles and page layouts you often use. Chapter 8 also discusses how to create an outline, which can be a helpful tool when planning and writing a long document such as a report.

CHAPTER 8

Using Styles, Outlines, and Templates

FEATURING:

Sparing us from repetitive work is one of the benefits of using computers, and Word 2000 has a number of features designed with this objective in mind. Learning to use styles and templates may take a bit of practice, but once they become part of your routine, you'll wonder how you lived without them. Outlines are particularly helpful for organizing your thoughts before you actually create a document. These features will make your work so much easier, you'll be glad that you took the time to learn how to use them.

Getting to Know the Styles

Word 2000's Styles feature lets you save existing formats and apply them to other text. Styles can include fonts, sizes, font attributes, alignment, character spacing, paragraph spacing, bullets and numbering, borders, indenting, and just about any other formatting you can think of. Word comes with many built-in styles stored in the Normal.dot template.

NOTE Every new, blank document you create is based on the Normal template, so all of the styles stored in that template are available in those documents. See "Using Templates" later in this chapter for more information about templates and how to use them.

There are two types of styles: character and paragraph styles. Character styles define formatting that applies only to text characters, such as fonts and font styles; paragraph styles include character formatting but also define formatting that applies to the entire paragraph, such as indents and alignment. You'll find that you mostly use paragraph styles in your documents. In fact, every paragraph in a new document is created by default using the Normal paragraph style, which consists of Times New Roman 10-point type, English language, single line spacing, left paragraph alignment, and widow/orphan control.

Once you've created a new style, all you have to do to apply the style is select it from a list. But the major benefit of styles is that if you change a style, all the text using that style is automatically changed, too—much easier than adjusting the font size on 25 subheadings.

Normal ▾

When you open a new Word document, you'll find the default list of paragraph and character styles available for your use in the Style drop-down list on the Formatting toolbar. To apply one of the default styles, click on the drop-down arrow next to Normal and select the style. You can either apply a style prior to entering text or apply it to selected text. If you select an entire paragraph and its paragraph mark, all of the formatting will be applied to the paragraph. If you select only text, the character formatting in that style will be applied to the selection.

 NOTE Each item in the drop-down list is formatted to show the characteristics of the corresponding style. For example, Heading 2 appears with both bold and italic formatting. When you look at the gray box to the right of the heading, you can see that Heading 2 is a left-aligned paragraph, and the font size is 14 points.

A Style All Your Own

Once you start working with styles, it won't be long before you're dissatisfied with the basic selection of paragraph styles and want to create your own. There are several ways to do so.

To quickly create a new paragraph style based on an existing style, follow these steps:

1. Apply the formatting to the paragraph until it appears the way you want.

2. Click in the Style text box on the Formatting toolbar to highlight the name of the current style.

3. Type the name of your new style, and then press Enter.

As an example, look at the newly created paragraph style in Figure 8.1. The characters appear in 26-point Comic Sans MS font with bold and italic formatting applied. The paragraph is centered and has a shadow border. When you click on Normal in the Style drop-down list, type **My Great Style**, and then press Enter, you've created a new style named My Great Style.

The new style name appears in the Style box on the Formatting toolbar. When you click on the drop-down list button, the new paragraph style name both appears in the list and illustrates what it looks like:

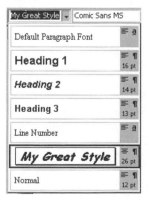

FIGURE 8.1

*You can quickly create
a new paragraph style
by renaming the style
of the paragraph
that contains the
insertion point.*

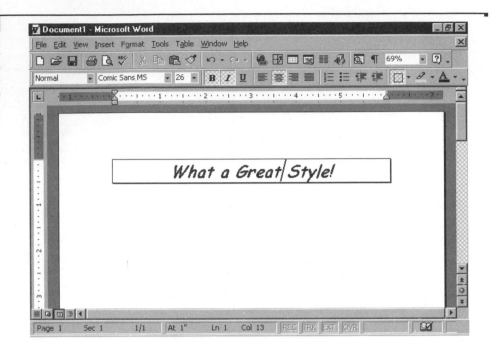

NOTE To apply the new style to other text, use the same technique as with built-in styles: select the text and then select the style from the list.

The next new paragraph you type after the paragraph with the newly created style will have the same style applied to it. If you want to apply a different style to it, just select the name of the style in the Style drop-down list on the Formatting toolbar.

MASTERING THE OPPORTUNITIES

Defining Styles Based on the Formatting You Apply

Word's AutoCorrect feature automatically creates new paragraph styles when you manually apply formatting to text in a heading or other paragraph. The Define Styles Based On Your Formatting option, which is found on the AutoFormat As You Type page in the AutoCorrect dialog box, is turned on by default.

Continued

For example, if you type a short line of text without ending punctuation in the Normal paragraph style, center the text, and then apply bold formatting to it, Word automatically changes the paragraph style to Heading 1. This also redefines the Heading 1 style. In addition, when you change the line spacing or font type in a paragraph whose text wraps to the next line and has ending punctuation, Word creates the Body Text paragraph style with those characteristics.

This feature is available as a toggle switch. To turn it off or on:

1. Choose Tools ➢ AutoCorrect to display the AutoCorrect dialog box.
2. Click on the AutoFormat As You Type tab to display that page.
3. Click in the Define Styles Based On Your Formatting check box.
4. Choose OK in the AutoCorrect dialog box.

You can also create a new character or paragraph style using the options in the New Style dialog box. To do so, follow these steps:

1. Position the insertion point in the paragraph to which you want to apply a new style or select the text to which to apply a new character style.

2. Choose Format ➢ Style to display the Style dialog box shown in Figure 8.2.

3. Click on the New button to display the New Style dialog box shown in Figure 8.3.

4. Change any of the following options as necessary:

   • Type a descriptive name for the new style in the Name text box.

   • Select either Paragraph or Character in the Style Type drop-down list.

   • Select the name of an existing style on which to base the new style. Most new paragraph styles are based on the Normal paragraph style, and most character styles are based on the character formatting contained in the Normal paragraph style.

   • Select the name of the style you want to apply to the new paragraph you create immediately after the paragraph to which the new style is applied in the Style For Following Paragraph drop-down list. All of the paragraph styles contained in the document appear in the drop-down list. If you are creating a Character style, this option is not available.

5. To choose the formatting for the paragraph, click on the Format button to display the formatting options, and then choose Font, Paragraph, Tabs, Border, Language, Frame, or Numbering to display the dialog box for that feature. Then select any options you want in that dialog box to apply that format.

6. If necessary, repeat step 5 until the format you want appears in the Preview and Description areas of the New Style dialog box.

7. If necessary, choose either of the following options:

> **Add To Template:** Stores the new style in the template on which the document is based. If you do not check this box, the new style is stored only in the active document.

> **Automatically Update:** Redefines the new style with formatting you apply manually to the paragraph in your document. Every paragraph in the document to which this style is applied will also be updated to contain the new formats.

8. Choose OK in the New Style dialog box.

9. Choose Apply in the Style dialog box to apply the style to the paragraph that contains the insertion point.

 WARNING Word does not inform you when you make changes to a paragraph style for which you've chosen Automatically Update. It is safer to keep this option turned off, because the formatting of every paragraph to which the style is applied will also be changed, perhaps giving you some unexpected results.

FIGURE 8.2

The Style dialog box allows you to manage styles in your document.

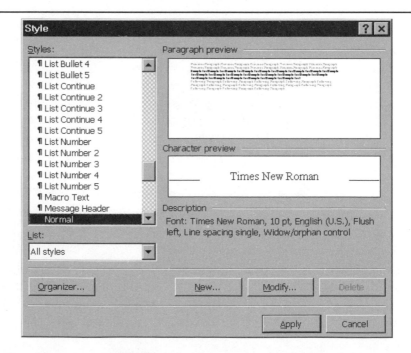

PART

II

Creating Dazzling
Documents in Word

FIGURE 8.3

*Use the New Style
dialog box to define
the characteristics of
your new style.*

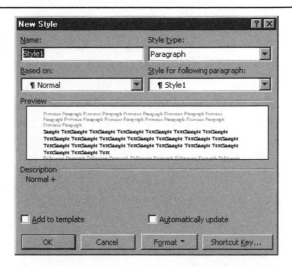

By default, only the basic styles in your document, along with any new styles you
create, appear in the Style box on the Formatting toolbar. You can control which styles
appear in the Style box for the current document:

1. Choose Format ➤ Style to display the Style dialog box shown in Figure 8.2.

2. Choose one of the following in the List drop-down list:

Styles In Use: Displays Word's basic built-in paragraph and character
styles, any styles you applied or modified, and any new styles you create.

All Styles: Displays all of Word's built-in styles, as well as any new styles
you create.

User-Defined Styles: Displays only the styles you created or modified.

3. Choose Apply in the Styles dialog box.

When you no longer need a style you created, you can delete it. When you do, Word
automatically applies the Normal paragraph style to all paragraphs in the document to
which the deleted style was applied. You cannot delete any of Word's built-in styles
from the template in which they are stored from within the Styles dialog box, but you
can delete some of those styles from the document in which they have been applied.

NOTE   Although you cannot delete Word's built-in styles from the document template
using the Styles dialog box, you can modify them to meet your needs. See the next section,
"Redefining Styles," to learn how to change an existing style in the current document.

For example, if you've applied Word's Normal Indent style to a paragraph in a document and then delete the style from the document, Word automatically applies the Normal style to every paragraph that has the Normal Indent style.

To delete a style from the current document:

1. Choose Format ➤ Style to display the Style dialog box shown in Figure 8.2.

2. Choose either of the following options in the List drop-down list:

    Styles In Use: Displays all the styles currently being used in the document. Choose this option if you want to remove some of Word's built-in styles from the document.

    User-Defined Styles: Displays all the styles in the document that you created or modified.

3. Highlight the name of the style to be deleted in the Styles list box.

4. Click the Delete button.

5. In the message box that appears, choose Yes to confirm that you want to delete the style.

6. Choose Apply to delete the style and return to your document.

If you want to use a built-in style that you've deleted in the document, display the Style dialog box again and choose All Styles in the List drop-down list, and then choose Apply. The Style drop-down list on the Formatting toolbar will again display all of the styles stored in the template.

Redefining Styles

After you've created and applied a paragraph style, you may decide that you don't like the font or you need some extra spacing between paragraphs. It's in situations like this that styles really shine. You can redefine the style, and it will automatically change all the text formatted in that style throughout the entire document.

There are several ways to redefine an existing style. To quickly change a style:

1. Select a paragraph or some text to which the style is applied and make the desired changes.

2. While the paragraph or text is still selected, click in the Styles text box on the Formatting toolbar, and then press Enter to display the Modify Style dialog box, shown in Figure 8.4.

3. Choose one of the following options:

> **Update The Style To Reflect Recent Changes:** Redefines the style using the formatting that is currently applied to the selection.

> **Reapply The Formatting Of The Style To The Selection:** Returns the selection to the formatting stored in the style.

4. To have Word automatically change the style definition to contain the formatting in the current selection in each paragraph or to every instance of text to which the style is applied, without first displaying the Modify Style dialog box, check the Automatically Update The Style From Now On check box.

5. Choose OK in the Modify Style dialog box.

FIGURE 8.4

Display the Modify Style dialog box when you want to quickly redefine the style applied to the current selection.

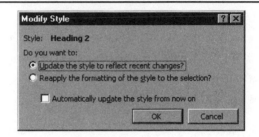

 WARNING It's safer to leave the Automatically Update The Style From Now On box unchecked, because you're not warned when additional formatting changes will affect a style.

You can also redefine a character or paragraph style using the options in the Modify Style dialog box, available from within the Style dialog box shown in Figure 8.2. The Modify Style dialog box is similar to the New Style dialog box, shown in Figure 8.3. Using the Modify Style options, you can change the entire definition of an existing style except for its type. In other words, you cannot change a paragraph style into a character style, or a character style into a paragraph style.

To modify an existing style:

1. Position the insertion point in the paragraph or select the text whose style is to be modified.

2. Choose Format ➤ Style to display the Style dialog box shown in Figure 8.2.

PART

II

Creating Dazzling Documents in Word

3. Click on the Modify button to display the Modify Style dialog box shown in Figure 8.5.

4. Change any of the following options as necessary:

Name: The name of the style is displayed in the Name text box. Type a different name in the Name text box if you want to create a new style.

Based On: Select the name of an existing style on which to base the new style. Most paragraph styles are based on the Normal paragraph style, and most character styles are based on the character formatting contained in the Normal paragraph style.

Style For Following Paragraph: Select a style to be applied to paragraphs that follow those in the style you are redefining. For example, you may want the Body Text style applied to paragraphs that follow headings. All of the paragraph styles contained in the document appear in the drop-down list. If you are creating a Character style, this option is not available.

5. To choose the formatting for the paragraph, click on the Format button to display the formatting options, and then choose Font, Paragraph, Tabs, Border, Language, Frame, or Numbering to display the dialog box for that feature. Then select any options you want in that dialog box to apply that format.

6. If necessary, repeat step 5 until the format you want appears in the Preview and Description areas of the New Style dialog box.

7. If necessary, choose either of the following options:

Add To Template: Stores the new style in the template on which the document is based. If you do not check the box, the new style is stored only in the active document.

Automatically Update: Redefines the new style with formatting you apply manually to the paragraph in your document. Every paragraph in the document to which this style is applied will also be updated to contain the new formats.

8. Choose OK in the Modify Style dialog box.

9. Choose Apply in the Style dialog box to apply the style to the selection.

 WARNING As explained earlier, it's safer to leave the Automatically Update option turned off.

FIGURE 8.5

Display the Modify Style dialog box from within the Style dialog box when you want to simultaneously modify a style and apply the redefined style to the selection.

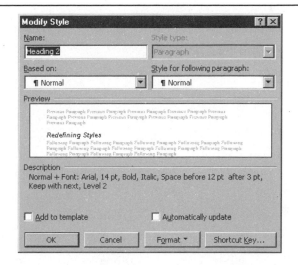

Creating an Outline

Outlining lets you make use of Word's built-in heading styles to view the major topics covered in your document—without having to scroll through pages and pages of text. You can collapse and expand heading levels to see more or less of your document at one time, making it easier to ensure you've covered the essential subject matter. You can even print a collapsed outline of your completed document to use as a summary.

 TIP Word's Outline feature is particularly helpful for planning long documents such as reports. With outlining, you can type the points you want to include in a document, and then arrange them in a logical sequence. In other words, you can move an idea to a different location in the document instead of creating the document around the location of the idea.

When you create an outline in Word 2000, you create the document's headings and subheadings in Outline view. After the outline is finished, you enter body text in Normal or Print Layout view. To create an outline in a new document:

1. Click on the Outline View button beside the Horizontal scroll bar, or choose View ➢ Outline to change to Outline view. The Outlining toolbar appears below the Standard and Formatting toolbars, as shown in Figure 8.6, and the default style is set to Heading 1.

PART

II

Creating Dazzling
Documents in Word

2. To begin the outline, type the text of your first heading and press Enter.

3. Repeat step 2 for each heading you want to enter in your outline.

FIGURE 8.6

The Outlining toolbar appears when you change to Outline view.

You can choose to enter all your first-level headings and then go back and enter lower-level headings, or you can switch back and forth between levels. The Heading 1 style does not refer to only the first heading, but to the first *level* of headings, each of which is formatted with that style. You can have several first-level headings in your document. For example, when you are creating an outline for a document that contains chapters, each chapter is a first-level heading, formatted in the Heading 1 style.

You can also have multiple headings of the same level below any other level of heading in an outline. To change an outline heading to a lower-level heading (or *demote* it), press Tab while the insertion point is anywhere in the paragraph. The second-level headings are formatted with the Heading 2 style. There are nine outlining levels you can use, as shown in Figure 8.7. If you want to change to a higher heading level (or *promote* the heading), press Shift+Tab.

FIGURE 8.7

Word 2000 contains nine built-in heading styles to use as your outline levels.

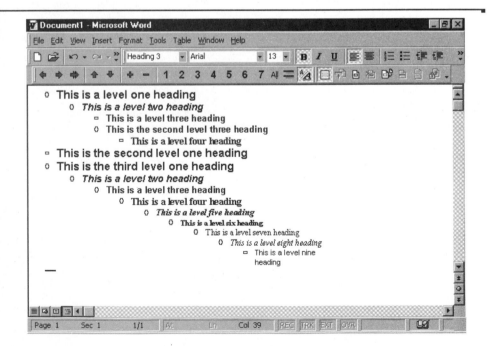

Promoting and Demoting Headings

You have already seen that you can press the Tab key to demote or Shift+Tab to promote the paragraph that contains the insertion point while you are in Outline view. There are several other ways to promote and demote selected outline headings.

Use one of the following methods to select the outline headings:

- Click to the left of the *outline symbol* (the plus or minus icon) before a single outline heading to select it.

- To select a heading and its *subheadings* (all of the headings following that heading at a lower level), point to the outline symbol in front of the heading. When the mouse pointer appears as a four-headed arrow, click on the symbol.

- To select multiple headings at the same level and any subheadings between them, drag to the left of the outline symbol before each heading.

 NOTE The plus outline icon indicates that the heading contains at least one subheading. The minus icon indicates that the heading has no subheadings.

To promote or demote selected headings, do any of the following:

Position the mouse pointer over the first outline symbol beside the selection, and then drag to the left to promote or to the right to demote that heading and its subheadings.

 Click on the Promote or Demote button on the Outlining toolbar.

 To demote headings to body text, which is the document text below a heading in an outline, click on the Demote To Body Text button on the Outlining toolbar. Body text appears with a small square icon as its outline symbol.

Numbering Your Outline Headings

By default, Word's outline headings are not numbered. Instead, the headings rely on indentation and character formatting to show their correlation to each other. Technical publications, contracts, and other documents sometimes need section numbering, and

Continued

Creating Dazzling Documents in Word

PART

II

CONTINUED

Outline view provides a convenient way to do that accurately. You can also add bullets to headings for visual emphasis. Follow these steps:

1. Click on the Outline View button next to the horizontal scroll bar, or choose View ➤ Outline to change the document to Outline view.

2. Choose Format ➤ Bullets And Numbering and click on the Outline Numbered tab to display that page.

3. Choose one of the bulleted or numbered styles for the outline. A preview of each appears on the Outline Numbered page.

4. Alternatively, choose one of the styles, and then choose Customize to edit the style to suit your needs exactly. Choose OK in the Customize Outline Numbered List dialog box to save the formatting changes to the selected style.

5. Choose OK in the Bullets And Numbering dialog box to return to the document. A number or bullet in the first-level style you've chosen (for example, *I.* or *1.*) will appear automatically.

6. Enter your first heading and press Enter. Word will supply *II.*, and you can enter your next heading.

7. To demote a level, press Tab. To promote a level, press Shift+Tab.

If you revise your outline (and document) by moving headings, Word will renumber them for you.

Viewing and Printing Selected Levels

Once you have created your outline, you can display as many levels as you would like at one time. This is useful for several reasons: You may want to show the bare bones of the outline to the rest of your workgroup for their input; also, it can help simplify or focus your thoughts when you write the body text in the outline.

To hide, or *collapse*, everything below a given level, click on any of the seven Show Heading buttons on the Outlining toolbar. For example, if you click on the Show Heading 3 button, only levels 1, 2, and 3 will be displayed. All headings 4 through 9 and body text will be hidden.

There are two ways to tell when some outline headings are collapsed, as shown in Figure 8.8:

- If you collapsed all of the outline headings below a level by using a Show Heading button, the numbered button appears depressed on the Outlining toolbar.

- A squiggly line appears below the lowest heading that is displayed.

FIGURE 8.8

When outline headings are hidden, a squiggly line appears below the lowest heading that is displayed.

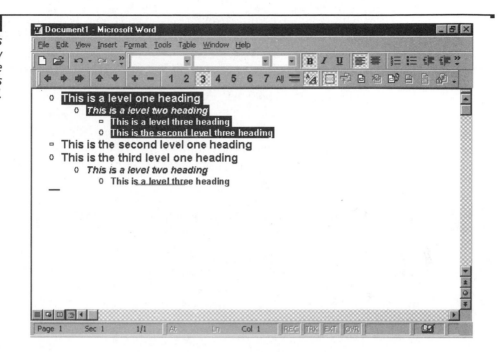

 When you are ready to redisplay, or *expand*, all the outline headings, click on the Show All Headings button on the Outlining toolbar.

If you want to focus on a particular point, you can collapse all the lower levels and then expand just the subheadings (and any accompanying body text) at the level you want to see. To do so:

 1. Click on the Show Heading 1 button to collapse the outline.

2. Move the mouse pointer to the left margin and select the heading you want to expand.

3. Perform either of the following as necessary:

 Click on the Expand button to expand one level at a time, or double-click on the plus icon to the left of the heading to expand all levels in the section.

 Click on the Collapse button to collapse one level at a time, or double-click on the minus icon to the left of the heading to collapse all levels in the section.

After you've created your outline, you can enter body text in one of the following ways:

 Type the body text as a heading in the outline, and then click on the Demote To Body Text button on the Outlining toolbar.

Switch to Normal or Print Layout view and enter body text under each heading. Just click to the right of the heading you want to write about, press Enter to begin a new paragraph, and type the text. If you decide you are not satisfied with the outline, you can switch back to Outline view at any time and rearrange it.

Once you have entered body text in your outline, you can collapse or expand it using the same methods described above to collapse or expand outline headings. You can also choose to display only the first line of each paragraph of body text. The remainder of each paragraph is represented by an ellipsis (...) at the end of the line. To display only the first line of each paragraph of body text in the outline, click on the Show First Line Only button on the Outlining toolbar.

Finally, you can toggle the default Show Formatting feature off, to display the outline without the formatting applied to the heading styles. This can save quite a bit of space. You will still see the headings' indentation, and if you switch to Normal or Print Layout view all the character and paragraph formatting will again be visible. Click the Show Formatting button on the Outlining toolbar to turn this feature off (or back on).

One of the great things about Outline view is that you can print the entire outline or any portion of it. Collapse or expand the outline so it shows just what you want to print, and then click on the Print button on the Standard toolbar. Print Preview will still show the entire outline. Don't worry about it. Only the expanded sections and headings will actually print.

TIP Heading styles are directly supported in Outline view. Even if you didn't originally create a document in Outline view, as long as you used heading styles, you can use the outlining features.

Modifying an Outline

Not only can you collapse and expand an outline, you can select a section of the outline and move it to another location. This is a convenient way to restructure your document. To do so, use either of the following methods while you display the outline in Outline view:

Click on the plus icon in front of the section, or the square icon in front of a paragraph of body text, then drag it toward its new location. As you drag, the mouse pointer changes into a double-headed arrow, and a horizontal line appears. Drop the section when the line is in the correct location.

Select the level, body text, or outline section to be relocated, and then click on the Move Up or Move Down button on the Outlining toolbar. Click as often as necessary to move the selection to the correct location.

 TIP It's easy to rearrange your document in ways that you didn't anticipate. It's always a good idea to save your document before any major restructuring.

Using Templates

Every document is based on a *template*, a collection of document formatting options, styles, and content that is available when you create a new document. By default, each new, blank document you create is based on the Normal template. You saw above that when you create or modify a style you would like to have available every time you create a new document, you need only check the Add To Template check box in the New Style or Modify Style dialog box.

 NOTE The Normal template also includes your AutoText entries, macros, toolbars, custom menu settings, and shortcut keys.

To help make your work easier, Word 2000 comes with templates for preformatted documents and template *wizards*, small programs that walk you through a series of steps to customize a preformatted document. Word includes additional templates and wizards for legal pleadings, letters and faxes, memos, publications, reports, and Web pages, as well as several other miscellaneous documents.

 To create a document based on the Normal.dot template, just click on the New Blank Document button on Word's Standard toolbar. When you do, a new, blank document appears on your screen.

Follow these steps to create a document based on a different template or wizard:

1. Choose File ➤ New to display the New dialog box, shown in Figure 8.9.

2. Click on the appropriate tab to display the page containing the template and wizard icons for that category.

3. Select the template or wizard icon you want to use to create a new document. A sample of the contents and formatting contained in the template appears in the Preview area.

PART
II

Creating Dazzling
Documents in Word

4. Choose Document in the Create New area.

5. Choose OK to open the new document.

Word's built-in templates usually include placeholders where you can insert your text. They also generally include instructions to help you use the template. After you have entered any text or made any other changes to the document, you must save it just as you save a document based on the Normal template.

Using the Fax Template and Wizard

One of the conveniences of today's world is the ability to send a fax without getting up from your desk. Of course, you first have to have a fax modem connected to your computer and an analog telephone line. Analog lines are the lines we typically have in our houses. Business telephone lines may be analog or digital, and you can't use a fax modem on a digital line.

NOTE To send faxes from your computer, you must also have fax software installed, such as Microsoft Fax or WinFax. If you are running Microsoft Outlook as your mail client, the software you use depends on whether you have the Corporate/Workgroup or Internet Only version of Outlook. See Chapter 19 for more information about sending faxes.

If you are connected by a fax modem to the outside world, then sending a fax using the Fax Wizard is as easy as printing. First you create the document to fax, and then you use the Fax Wizard to send it. Word 2000 comes with three fax templates that can be used to create a cover sheet—Contemporary Fax, Elegant Fax, and Professional Fax. Follow the steps in "Using a Template" above to create a cover sheet based on one of the fax templates, and then fill in the blanks as necessary. Alternatively, you can have the Fax Wizard create a cover sheet to send with another open document, or you can send only a cover sheet.

 NOTE If you create your cover sheet using one of Word's fax templates, the recipients' names and fax numbers will already be entered so the Fax Wizard can use them to send the fax.

To send a fax with the Fax Wizard:

1. Choose File ➤ New to display the New dialog box, shown above in Figure 8.9, click on the Letters And Faxes tab to display its page, and then double-click on the Fax Wizard icon to display the Fax Wizard starting page, shown in Figure 8.10. Alternatively, choose File ➤ Send To ➤ Fax Recipient.

2. Choose Next, and then choose one of the following options to specify what to send:

    The Following Document: Lets you select which open document to fax. Choose either With A Cover Sheet, if you want the Fax Wizard to create a cover sheet for you, or Without A Cover Sheet, if you used one of the fax templates to create the cover sheet document. If you choose this option, skip steps 4 through 6 below.

    Just A Cover Sheet With A Note: Lets the Fax Wizard create a cover sheet for you to send.

3. Choose Next, and then choose one of the following options to specify how to send the document:

    Microsoft Fax: Sends the fax using that program.

    A Different Fax Program Which Is Installed On This System: Lets you choose the name of your fax software in the drop-down list. If you choose Other, you can change the default printer for Word and for all your Windows programs.

    I Want To Print My Document So I Can Send It From A Separate Fax Machine: Allows you to print the document to your default printer.

PART

II

Creating Dazzling
Documents in Word

4. Choose Next, and then type the name(s) and fax number(s) of the person(s) to whom the fax will be sent in the appropriate text boxes. If the names and fax numbers are stored in your Address Book, click on the Address Book button, and then select the names.

5. Choose Next, and then choose the style you want for your cover sheet.

6. Choose Next, and then, if necessary, type in the sender's information. Alternatively, click on the Address Book and select the sender's information.

7. Choose Finish to display the cover sheet. Enter any additional text as necessary.

8. Click on Send Fax Now on the Fax Wizard toolbar to send the fax.

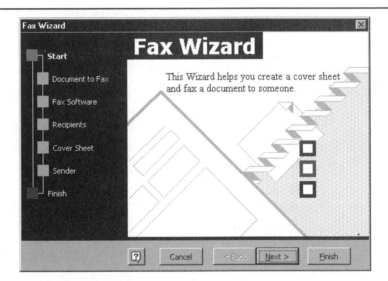

FIGURE 8.10

The Fax Wizard helps you prepare your document to be faxed.

Make sure when you enter the Fax Recipient that you enter the correct telephone number and any prefix numbers, such as the area code, that you would ordinarily need to dial. Some areas of the United States now require you to dial the area code, even if the number is not long distance.

Creating Your Own Templates

Templates allow you to store the layout and formatting for an entire document, along with any necessary styles, AutoText entries, macros, and toolbars, so you don't have to spend time re-creating them the next time you create a similar document. You can either customize Word's templates for your own use or create new templates from scratch.

For example, you can open a document based on the Contemporary Letter template, fill in the information that is the same for all your business letters, such as your company name and return address, your name and job title, and even a logo or other graphic, and then save the document as a customized template. Using custom templates saves you the time and energy required to perform these same actions over and over again. When you want to write another letter, just open a document based on your customized template and fill in the body of the letter.

There are times when you may want to create a template completely from scratch. In that case, you can use the Normal template, which appears as the Blank Document template on the General tab in the New dialog box.

You can edit a template directly or open a document based on the template and then save the document to a template file. When you save a customized template, you must give it a name with the .DOT file extension. You'll also need to specify where to store the template file. If you store it in the Templates folder, it will appear on the General page in the New dialog box. You can store it with similar templates by choosing the folder that contains those template files. Alternatively, you can create a new folder in the Templates folder in which to store the template file. When you do, a tab with the name of the new folder will also appear in the New dialog box.

 WARNING If you edit the template directly and then choose Save, you will overwrite the original template. Instead, choose Save As and assign the template file a different name. This is particularly important when you are basing your new template on the Normal.dot template.

Follow these steps to create a template:

1. Choose File ➤ New to display the New dialog box shown in Figure 8.9.

2. To create a template from scratch, select the Blank Document icon on the General page. To create a template based on any other template, click on the tab of the category that contains the template, and then highlight its icon on the displayed page.

3. Choose either of the following options in the Create New area, and then choose OK:

Document: Opens a new document based on the selected template.

Template: Opens the selected template.

4. Fill in any information that would be repeated, and enter any necessary text in the document or template.

5. Choose File ➤ Save As to display the Save As dialog box.

6. In the Save As Type drop-down list, choose Document Template (*.dot). The Templates folder is automatically selected as the storage location for the file in the Save In drop-down list.

7. Choose one of the following options to specify where to store the template file:

- Leave Templates as the location in the Save In drop-down list to have the new template appear on the General page in the New dialog box if you chose Template in step 3.

- To have the template file appear on a category page other than General in the New dialog box, highlight the name of the folder in that category.

- Create a new folder in the Templates folder in which to store the file. Each subfolder in the Templates folder appears as a category tab in the New dialog box.

8. If necessary, type a different name for the new template in the File Name text box.

9. Choose Save to save the new template file.

 WARNING If you are saving a regular document and the Save As dialog box forces you to save the document as a template, you may have a version of a Word macro virus on your system. You should immediately run a virus scan using virus protection software that can detect the Word Concept and other macro viruses. Visit the Microsoft Web site at `http://www.microsoft.com` for more information about macro viruses.

 MASTERING THE OPPORTUNITIES

Managing Your Templates with Organizer

If you create any styles, AutoText entries, toolbars, or macros in a document or template, you can use Organizer to copy them to another template to be used in any document to which that template is applied. You can also rename a style, or even delete a style from a template, including the Blank Document (Normal) template. (A word of caution: Many documents use the styles stored in the Normal template. If you delete a style in the Normal template, it will be deleted from existing documents based on the Normal template.)

Continued

Take these steps to copy a style you've created in your current document into the Normal template:

1. Choose Format ➤ Style, and choose Organizer, or choose Tools ➤ Templates And Add-ins, and then choose Organizer. Either method will display the Organizer dialog box.

2. On the left is a list box displaying the styles in the current document; on the right is a list of styles in the Normal template. Highlight the style (or styles) you want to save in the template, and then click the Copy button. The new style will appear in the right-hand list.

3. Choose Close when you have made all the necessary changes.

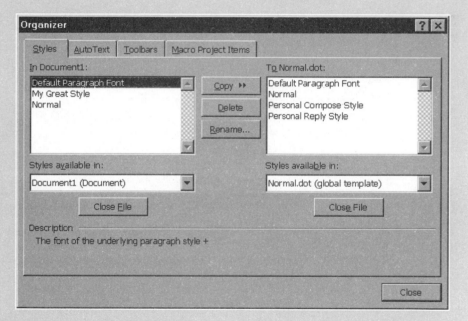

You can change the document or template that is named in either list box by choosing Close File below the appropriate list box, and then choosing Open File to open a different document or template file. When you do, the styles, AutoText, toolbars, and macros in that file appear in the list box on the corresponding page.

Use Organizer in a similar manner to copy, delete, or rename AutoText entries, custom toolbars, and macro projects to a different document or template.

PART

II

Creating Dazzling
Documents in Word

What's Next

Merging—generating form letters from merge documents and mailing lists or other data sources—has been around since the earliest word processors, but it's still one of the most powerful capabilities. Chapter 9 discusses how to create both a merge document and a merge data source. You will learn how to create a form letter, catalog or other list, and envelopes and labels as merge documents. You'll also learn how to create a data source and how to specify which data source and which records of data to use as the data to merge. Finally, you'll see how to perform the merge.

CHAPTER 9

Creating Merge Documents in Word

FEATURING:

Understanding mail merge

Creating a new data source in Word

Entering and editing records

Managing fields

Sorting lists, paragraphs, and tables

Creating a main document

Creating catalogs and lists

Creating envelopes and labels

Merging documents

Specifying records to merge

ncreasing your Word 2000 expertise is a sure way to know you're making the best use of your precious time and resources. One way to save time is by effectively using mail merge, one of Word's advanced features. Mail merge allows you to use Word for more than just word processing. Using Word, you can enter, sort, and search through lists of data: names, addresses, and items in an inventory. You can merge data lists with other Word documents and print labels, envelopes, and form letters. Word's mail merge feature is an excellent tool for managing information.

Mail merge also allows you to import data stored in an Excel spreadsheet or an Access database into a Word document, or even to import the entire database into Word. Word's mail merge feature is one way you can use the Office 2000 applications to organize your data and then place it in a useful format.

Understanding Mail Merge

Whether you want to send a form letter to five people or 500, you can use Word to personalize each one and create mailing labels or envelopes. You've heard about mail merge and you may even have used it, but it's never been more foolproof than it is in Word 2000. Don't let the term *mail merge* limit your thinking: you can use mail merge to create telephone directories, birthday lists, name tags, or any type of list you can imagine.

A mail merge requires two documents: a *data source* in which the individual records are stored and a *main document* that refers to the fields in the data source. These two documents then come together to create the final *merge document*, a document that uses the text and layout in the main document and the information in each record of the data source.

There are four types of main documents:

Form Letters: The letters or reports you want to personalize

Mailing Labels: Address labels or any other kind of label, such as name tags, video tape or disk labels, and file folder labels

Envelopes: Envelopes fed directly into your printer

Catalogs: Lists of data, such as phone lists or membership directories

A data source contains the *record* of each individual item. A record consists of all the information gathered about the item. For example, a record about a person may contain his/her name, address, telephone number, and date of birth. Each record consists of *fields*; a field is the smallest amount of data collected. A record about a person probably will contain quite a few fields. The person's name might consist of four fields in the record—SocialTitle, FirstName, MiddleInitial, and LastName. The address might contain a separate field for the StreetAddress, City, State, and PostalCode. Any item you might need to work with individually—whether as a *key* for sorting the records in a list or simply as a detail to be included or omitted depending on the purpose of the merge document—should have its own field. A data source contains multiple records, so you can enter information about many different people.

You can easily sort the information in the data source. The ability to store data such as your personal or business contacts, product catalog information, or purchasing records puts extra power in your hands. Using Word, you can access the data stored in any of the following:

- A data source file created using Word

- A file created with other Microsoft Office products such as an Excel spreadsheet (list) or an Access database

- A database file created using software distributed by other companies

Creating or Specifying the Main Document

The Mail Merge Helper helps you create a main document, create or select a data source, and then produce merged documents. You must create, or at least specify, which document is the main document before you create or select a data source. Your main document can be any document, including a new, blank document.

Follow these steps to create a main document:

1. If necessary, open an existing document or create a new document to serve as the main document. You can also create a new main document after you've started the Mail Merge Helper.

2. Choose Tools ➤ Mail Merge to display the Mail Merge Helper dialog box shown in Figure 9.1.

3. In the Main Document area (labeled 1 in the Mail Merge Helper), choose Create, and then choose Form Letters, Mailing Labels, Envelopes, or Catalog as the type of main document to create.

4. In the Microsoft Word dialog box that appears, choose either of the following options to specify which document will be the new main document:

   Active Window: Specifies that the document in the active window is to be the main document. Choose this option if you opened or created the document in step 1 above.

   New Main Document: Opens a new, blank document and then specifies that it is the main document. Choose this option if you want to create a document to serve as the main document.

5. If necessary, choose Edit in the Main Document area, and then select the main document in the drop-down list to close the Mail Merge Helper and activate the document on your screen. Alternatively, choose Close, and then edit the active document on your screen.

6. Save the main document to a descriptive file name.

FIGURE 9.1

Display the Mail Merge Helper when you want to create either a main document or a new Word data source file.

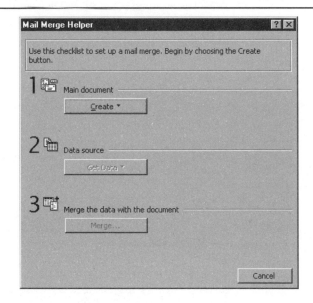

TIP When you save a merge document, it's a good idea to indicate the type of document somewhere in the file name. We suggest that you begin main documents with the word Main and when appropriate, the name of the data source it is linked to (*Main–Acknowledgment Letter to Customers*), so that you can identify your main documents easily.

Once the main document is specified, the Mail Merge toolbar appears on your screen below the Standard and Formatting toolbars while the document is active. You can make any edits you want in the active document, or none at all. Although you specified the type of document for your main document in step 3 above, you can change your mind and choose a different type of main document later.

NOTE You must specify a main document before you can create a Word data source.

Creating a New Data Source in Word

The next step is to create or specify the data source for your main document. Your data source can be used over and over again, with more than one main document. For example, if you want to send a form letter to your company's customers, you can use the same data source file for both the main form letter document and the main mailing labels document.

If you are using the data stored in an Excel spreadsheet or an Access database as the data source for the main document, see "Opening an Existing Data Source," below, for additional information.

 TIP When you save a data source file, it's a good idea to name the document so that it is easily identifiable as a data source file. You might want to begin all of your data source file names with Data; for example, *Data-Customers*.

A data source file consists of a table with a *header row*, the first row in the table that contains the names of the fields for which you will enter data. Each field name is in a separate cell in the row. The records, which contain the data, are entered in subsequent rows in the table. For example, each cell in the column below the cell that contains the LastName field will contain the last name of an individual.

Word comes with a list of suggested field names for a new data source. You can either insert new field names or delete existing field names to create a data source that exactly meets your needs.

Field names must follow these rules:

- A field name can be up to 40 characters long, but shorter is better for easy reference.

- Each field name must be unique—no two fields in a data source can have the same name.

- Field names can't contain spaces and must begin with a letter rather than a number. You can use the underline (_) character to separate words, but it is

PART

II

Creating Dazzling
Documents in Word

easier to omit spaces and underlines, and simply capitalize the first letter of each word in a name, such as StreetAddress or DateOfBirth.

- Field names cannot contain periods, commas, colons, semicolons, slashes, or backslashes.

This is a good time to think about how you will use your data source. If you use only one field, Name, for both first and last names, you can't open a letter with "Dear Joe." By separating names into FirstName and LastName fields, you have more options for how you use the name in your main document. If you're feeling formal and might want to use "Dear Mr. Smith" as the salutation, you will want to include a Title field for Mr., Mrs., Ms., and other social titles.

Addresses should be separated into StreetAddress or Address; City; State (or Province); and ZipCode or PostalCode. Later, you can choose to print labels that are sorted by Zip-Code, or only print envelopes and letters for clients in Arkansas.

If you are creating several different data source files, it's helpful to use the same field names in each data source. For example, if you use "FirstName" in one data source, don't use "FNAME" or "First" in other source files. When you use the Mail Merge Helper to create your data source, you can select many commonly used field names from a built-in list to help you keep your field names consistent. If you use the same field names, you'll often be able to use the same main documents with different data source files, rather than creating new main documents.

To create a Word data source:

1. If you exited the Mail Merge Helper to edit the main document in step 5 above, click the Mail Merge Helper button on the Mail Merge toolbar to display the Helper again.

2. Click the Get Data button in the Data Source area (labeled 2), and then choose Create Data Source. The Create Data Source dialog box, shown in Figure 9.2, appears.

3. A list of common field names appears in the Field Names In Header Row list box. By default, all the field names in the list will be included in the data source. Choose any of the following options to customize the field names in your Word data source:

   - Type a field name in the Field Name text box, and then click Add Field Name to insert the new field name at the bottom of the Field Names In Header Row list box.

   - Highlight the name of the field you want to delete in the Field Names In Header Row list box, and then click Remove Field Name.

   - Highlight the name of a field you want to relocate within the list in the Field Names In Header Row list box, and then click the ↑ or ↓ Move button beside the list box. The order in which the field names appear in the list is the order in which they will appear on the data form, which is used to enter the data in the data source.

4. When the field names in the Field Names In Header Row list box are in the order you want, choose OK to display the Save As dialog box. Then save the data source file to a descriptive name.

5. Choose either of the following options in the Microsoft Word dialog box that appears:

> **Edit Data Source:** Displays the Data Form dialog box, similar to the one in Figure 9.3, so you can enter data in your new data source file.

> **Edit Main Document:** Returns you to the main document that is attached to the new data source. If you choose this option, you can edit the data source file later.

PART

II

Creating Dazzling
Documents in Word

FIGURE 9.2

The Create Data Source dialog box contains a list of possible field names for your Word data source.

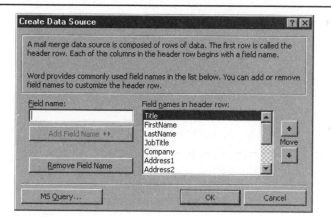

FIGURE 9.3

In the Data Form, you can fill in the field information for each record in a Word data source.

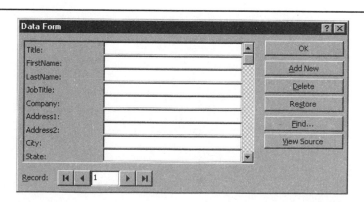

TIP If you will be entering records from an existing form or handwritten list, include the field names in the data source in the same order as they appear on the form or list. You can enter data more efficiently if you don't have to skip around on a page.

Entering Records

The easiest way to enter the records for your new data source is by using the Data Form, such as the one shown above in Figure 9.3. You can also open up the data source file, and enter the records directly in the data source's table, but that is more difficult. The advantage to using the Data Form is that it displays only one record at a time. If you open the data source file, all the records are displayed, which can make it difficult to keep track of the field for which you are entering data.

Follow these steps to enter data in a Word data source:

1. If you chose Edit Main Document in step 5 above, click the Edit Data Source button on the Mail Merge toolbar to display the Data Form.

2. Type the information for the first field in the text box beside its name, and then press Tab to move the insertion point to the next field's text box.

3. Repeat step 2 until you've entered data for each field in the first record, and then choose Add New or press Enter to place the current data in the data source and display the next empty record.

4. When you are finished entering data in the records, choose OK to return to the main document.

Use either of the following methods to view all the records:

Click the Edit Data Source button on the Mail Merge toolbar to redisplay the Data Form dialog box and then choose View Source.

Click the data source's button on the Windows Taskbar to activate the file.

 NOTE When you are finished entering records, be sure to save the data source file. If you forget, you will be prompted to save the file when you close it or when you close Word.

Editing Records and Managing Fields

Your data source records can be edited within the Data Form dialog box or directly within the data source file. Word automatically displays the Database toolbar when a data source file is active. The tools you will use to manage the data source are on the Database toolbar. You can enter new records, edit, or delete records in a Word data source just as you would in any table.

 To add a new row at the end of your data source in order to enter the data in a new record, click the Add New Record button on the Database toolbar. Alternatively, press Tab while the insertion point is in the last cell in the table to add a new row.

 To delete a record, click in any cell in the row to position the insertion point within the record you want to delete; and then click the Delete Record button on the Database toolbar.

WARNING   Be careful not to delete the first row, which contains the field names. If you do, you will have to re-create it to use this file as a data source.

 To add, remove, or rename fields in your data source, click the Manage Fields button to open the Manage Fields dialog box, shown in Figure 9.4. Perform any of the following, and then choose OK:

- To create a new field in the data source, type a name in the Field Name text box, and then choose Add. The new field name appears at the end of the list in the Field Names In Header Row list box, and a new column is created beside the last column in the data source.

- To remove a field from the data source, highlight its name in the Field Names In Header Row list box, and then choose Remove. Choose Yes to confirm that you want to remove the field, along with the data stored in it.

WARNING   When you remove a field from the data source, the data in that field is also removed. Be certain that the data is not needed for any other purpose before removing a field.

- To rename a field, highlight its name in the Field Names In Header Row list box, choose Rename to display the Rename Field dialog box, type a new name for the field in the New Field Name text box, and then choose OK.

 If you prefer to enter or view records using the data form, click the Data Form button on the toolbar to reopen the Data Form.

TIP You can convert an existing table to a data source by deleting text that precedes the table in the document, deleting any blank rows in the table itself, and renaming column headers so that they follow field name conventions. Word will recognize a document that meets these requirements as a data source. To use other database options with a table other than a data source, choose View ≻ Toolbars and then select Database to display the Database toolbar. The toolbar will be displayed until you toggle off its display.

To find a record in a data source that contains specified text in order to edit the record, follow these steps:

1. Click the Find Record button on the Database toolbar to display the Find In Field dialog box, shown in Figure 9.5.

2. Type the text you want to find in the Find What text box.

3. Select the field in which the text is stored in the In Field drop-down list.

4. Choose Find First to have Word highlight the first record in the data source that contains that text in the field. Make any edits as necessary.

5. Choose Find Next to have Word highlight the next record that contains the specified text, and make any necessary edits.

6. Repeat step 5 as necessary.

7. Choose Close to return to the data source.

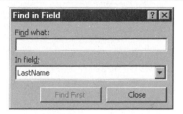

 When you are finished editing your data source, click the Mail Merge Document button on the Database toolbar to return to your main document. You can switch back and forth between the main document and the data source using the buttons available on the Mail Merge and Database toolbars.

Sorting the Data Source

You can organize your data source by sorting it on any field that you find useful. For example, you may want to see a list of the names of your customers in alphabetical order by their last names. Records can be sorted in *ascending order* (A to Z, or 0 to 9) or in *descending order* (Z to A or 9 to 0).

If you want to sort the records in a data source by only one field, you can use the sorting buttons on the Database toolbar. To sort the records in a data source, place the insertion point anywhere in the column you want to sort by, and then:

 Click the Sort Ascending button to sort the records in the data source in ascending order according to the data in that field. For example, place the insertion point anywhere in the LastName field before you click the Sort Ascending button to place the records in alphabetical order according to the last name entered for each record.

 Click the Sort Descending button on the Database toolbar to sort the records from highest to lowest or Z to A order. For example, to sort the data in the WorkPhone field so that the records with the highest area codes appear at the top and the lowest appear at the bottom of the list, place the insertion point anywhere in the WorkPhone column, and then click the Sort Descending button.

To sort the data source by more than one field—for example, to sort an alphabetized customer list by last name and then by first name—you'll need to use the Sort dialog box:

1. Place the insertion point anywhere in the table you want to sort.

2. Choose Table ➤ Sort to display the Sort dialog box, shown in Figure 9.6.

3. Choose from the following options to define the sort:

- In the Sort By area, select the field name on which to sort first, and then select what the data is—Text, Number, or Date—in the Type drop-down list. Choose Ascending or Descending to specify the order in which to sort.

- In the first Then By area, select a second field to use if there are duplicate entries in the Sort By field. Select what the data is in the Type drop-down list, and then choose Ascending or Descending sort order.

- If you need to define a third field to sort by, use the second Then By area.

4. In the My List Has area, choose Header Row to indicate that the data is in a table with field names in the first row.

5. The Sort dialog box also has an Options button. In sorting a mail-merge data source, you probably won't need to use the Sort Options dialog box, but if you're taking advantage of Office 2000's multiple-language features, you might want to select another language whose sorting rules you want to use in the Sorting Language drop-down list.

6. Choose OK in the Sort dialog box to sort the data.

FIGURE 9.6

Use the Sort dialog box to sort data by more than one field.

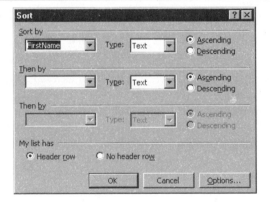

 WARNING It's a good idea to save your document before you sort, and always check your data immediately after a sort to make sure it sorted correctly. If it did not sort correctly, click Undo, or close the document without saving and reopen your saved copy.

Sorting Any Table or List

The Sort dialog box is Word's tool for sorting any kind of table or list, not just mail merge data sources. You can even sort a series of ordinary text paragraphs by first word. (You could use this technique to create an alphabetized glossary for a training manual, for example.) The procedure is generally the same as described above, particularly if you are sorting a table with a header row, but there are a few variations:

- If you're sorting anything other than a table, begin by selecting all the list items or paragraphs before choosing Table ➢ Sort.
- When you're sorting a table, the Sort By drop-down list shows you a list of field names or descriptive text in each cell in the header row of the table. You can indicate up to three sort levels when sorting data in a table or data source. You should also check whether or not your table has a header row.
- If you selected several columns in a document that has multiple columns of text, the Sort by drop-down list contains a list of the columns by number, such as Column 1, Column 2, and Column 3. You can sort by up to three columns, and you should make sure that No Header Row is selected for the list.
- If you've selected a bulleted list or several paragraphs of text, the Sort By list only gives you two options: Paragraphs and Field 1. Choose Paragraphs to sort by the first word in each paragraph, or Field 1 to sort by the first field or tabular column.

PART

II

Creating Dazzling Documents in Word

Opening an Existing Data Source

If you already have data in an Excel worksheet, an Access database, an Outlook address book or another type of database, there is no need to re-create that data in Word. Follow these steps to open an existing data source:

1. When you get to Step 2 of the Mail Merge Helper and click Get Data, choose Open Data Source for a database or Use Address Book for an Outlook address book.
2. Locate the data source in the Open Data Source dialog box (be sure to change Files Of Type to the correct file type).
3. Specify the table, query, or worksheet that contains the data in the dialog box that appears. Click OK.

You are now ready to add merge fields from the data source to the main document.

Using an Excel Worksheet as a Data Source

Excel worksheets are also tables, which, as you've seen, can be used to create a data source. An Excel data source is called a *list*. In Excel, each column is described with a label (the field name) and each row contains an individual record.

There are several things to keep in mind when you are using an Excel worksheet as your data source:

- The list cannot contain any blank rows or columns. Excel considers a blank row or column to indicate the end of the list.
- The column labels (field names) must be in the first row of the list. You can add special formatting to the column labels to differentiate them from the data entered in each record.
- Items in the list can be sorted on multiple fields.

There are certain restrictions that are unique to an Excel list you want to merge with a Word main document: You must use all the data in the first worksheet in the workbook, or the data in a named range in the first worksheet. No other data in the file is available when you choose a data source to attach to your main document.

To move a worksheet to the first tab position in the workbook, use either of the following methods:

- Click on the tab of the worksheet so the mouse pointer appears with a sheet icon beside it, and then drag the tab to the left. When the small black triangle points before the first tab in the workbook, release the mouse button to drop the worksheet in the new location.
- Click on the tab of the worksheet you want to use as the data source to activate it, and then choose Edit ➢ Move Or Copy Sheet to display the Move Or Copy dialog box. Highlight the name of the first worksheet in the Before Sheet list box, and then choose OK.

If you want to use only some of the data in the first worksheet as the data source, select the range of cells that contains the list items, including the column labels in the first row of the list, and then assign it a range name. Make sure you include the column labels as the first row in the named range because Excel uses the data in the first row as the merge field names. Use one of the following methods to create a range name:

- Select the range of cells, and then type the name you want for that range in the Name box at the left of the formula bar.

Continued ▮▶

- Select the range of cells, and then choose Insert ➤ Name ➤ Define to display the Define Name dialog box. Type the name in the Names In Workbook text box, and then choose Add. Choose OK when you are finished entering range names.

Once you have placed the worksheet in the first position in the workbook and saved the file, you are ready to attach it to the Word main document. To do so, follow these steps:

1. Open the main document and display the Mail Merge Helper.

2. Choose Get Data, and then select Open Data Source. Select the name of the Excel workbook file that contains the data to be merged, and then choose Open.

3. The Microsoft Excel dialog box appears. Choose Entire Spreadsheet, or one of the named ranges that appears in the Named Or Cell Range list box, and then choose OK.

4. Choose Edit Main Document in the Microsoft Word dialog box that appears.

Insert each merge field in the main document in the usual way—by positioning the insertion point where you want to place the data, clicking on the Insert Merge Field drop-down list button, and then selecting the field.

Adding Merge Fields to a Main Document

After you have created or identified the data source, you are ready to add *merge fields* to the main document. Return to the Mail Merge Helper (Tools ➤ Mail Merge or click Mail Merge Helper on the Mail Merge toolbar).

There are two kinds of text in a main document. *Regular text* will be the same in each version of the merged document, such as the body text in a form letter. *Variable text*, which will be different in each merged document, is represented by a merge field. Merge fields have the same names as the field names in the data source. For example, the recipient's name and address is variable text in the main document.

You can edit the regular text in your main document as necessary, using the same methods as those you use to edit any other document. Insert a merge field where you want text from the data source to appear in your final, merged document.

 NOTE Merge field codes must be entered using the Insert Merge Field drop-down list on the Mail Merge toolbar. You cannot type "<<" before the field name and ">>" after it.

Follow these steps to edit your main document:

1. Open the main document, and then type any regular text in the document. For example, type the date, salutation, body, and closing of a form letter.

2. To attach a data source to the main document, click the Mail Merge Helper button on the Mail Merge toolbar to display the Mail Merge Helper, choose Get Data, and then choose Open Data Source to display the Open Data Source dialog box. Highlight the name of the data source file, and then choose Open.

3. Choose Edit Main Document in the Microsoft Word dialog box that appears to return to the main document.

4. Place the insertion point where you want to enter the first merge field, click the Insert Merge Field button on the Mail Merge toolbar, and select the merge field to insert. For example, position the insertion point beside "Dear" in the salutation, press the spacebar to insert a space, and then select FirstName in the Insert Merge Field drop-down list. Type a colon after the field code.

5. Repeat step 4 for each merge field you want to include in the main document.

6. Save the main document.

As soon as you've set up the main document the way you want it, you'll want to save it for use in future merges. Figure 9.7 shows an example of a completely set-up main document. The merge fields appear in the document with double arrows (<< >>) around the field names.

NOTE By default, merge fields appear with gray shading when the insertion point is anywhere in the field. To have them always appear with gray shading in your main document, choose Tools ➤ Options ➤ View. In the Show area, choose Always in the Field Shading drop-down list and choose OK.

Once you have saved the main document, you can attach a different data source to it. Just follow steps 1 and 2 above to attach a different data source to your main document. Only one data source can be attached at a time. Now you can see the advantage of using consistent field names in your data source files!

FIGURE 9.7

A main document contains merge fields that access the data stored in the data source.

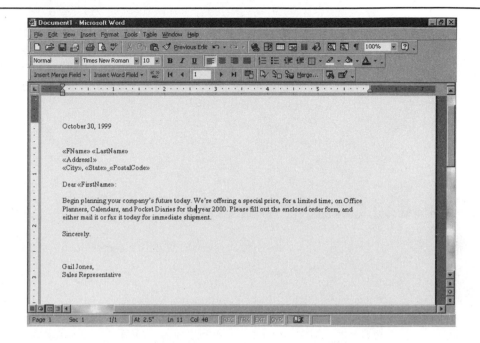

```
Document1 - Microsoft Word

File  Edit  View  Insert  Format  Tools  Table  Window  Help

Normal        Times New Roman    10    B  I  U

Insert Merge Field ▾   Insert Word Field ▾        1        Merge...


October 30, 1999


«FName» «LastName»
«Address1»
«City», «State»_«PostalCode»

Dear «FirstName»:

Begin planning your company's future today. We're offering a special price, for a limited time, on Office
Planners, Calendars, and Pocket Diaries for the year 2000. Please fill out the enclosed order form, and
either mail it or fax it today for immediate shipment.

Sincerely,



Gail Jones,
Sales Representative


Page 1    Sec 1        1/1    At 2.5"    Ln 11   Col 48    REC  TRK  EXT  OVR
```

 NOTE A main document can be attached to only one data source at a time, but a data source can be attached simultaneously to multiple main documents.

Previewing the Merged Document

When the main document and data source are merged, Word will generate a separate document or listing (if you are setting up a catalog) for each record in the data source, based on the layout of the main document. Before you perform the merge, it is a good idea to see a sample of how the merged document will appear.

 To see what the first record in the merge document will look like, click the View Merged Data button on the Mail Merge toolbar. Word inserts the data in the first record directly in the main document. If necessary, you can make any additional edits to the main document. For example, if you did not place a colon or other punctuation after the salutation, you can insert it now.

The Mail Merge toolbar includes a set of navigation buttons that you can use to move to the first record, previous record, next record, or last record. You can also type the number of the record you want to preview in the Go To Record text box in the center of the navigation buttons, and then press Enter to see its sample. You can preview, one at a time, all the merge documents using the navigation tools.

Click again on the View Merged Data button to return to the main document. If you made any changes to it, save it again.

Creating Catalogs and Lists

A catalog main document is used to create lists; each record is listed directly under the previous record on the same page. Word's Mail Merge tool doesn't shine its brightest with catalogs. However, if you know how to work around the awkwardness of Word's catalog merge, it's still a convenient way to present a list of the records in a data source. You can sort the records before performing the merge to make it easier to read the catalog. (See the accompanying Mastering the Opportunities box if you need to create something more ambitious.)

In a catalog main document, you can either create a table to hold the merge field codes or use tabs to separate the codes. Using a table produces consistent results with the least amount of hassle. Enter any text you want to appear with each record of the data source, but don't include other surrounding text. If, for example, you want a heading to appear above the records in the list, don't enter it now, or your merged document will include a heading, a record, another heading, another record, and so forth.

 TIP You can use View Merged Data to see each individual record as it will appear in the merged document. This is a good time to make any adjustments to the table width or to the width of any column in the main document.

After you have merged the data source and main document, you can add titles, column headings, and any other information to the merged document before you print it, as shown in Figure 9.8. You probably won't want to save the results of merged catalogs. If you have to add a lot of heading and title information after the merge, you may want to save it for future reference.

FIGURE 9.8

Insert titles, column headings, and any other general information in a catalog after you have merged the main document and the data source.

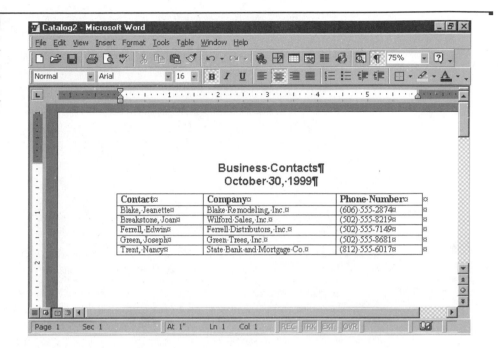

MASTERING THE OPPORTUNITIES

Inserting an External Database into a Word Document

As an alternative to using Mail Merge to create catalogs, Word lets you easily insert data from an external data source, such as an Excel or Access table, into a Word document. Using this feature, you can create a catalog where the data is linked directly to the data source; this way, you can update data without merging again. And unlike the Catalog Mail Merge feature, Insert Database allows you to insert data into a document that already contains existing text.

Follow these steps to insert an external database into a Word document:

1. Open a new, blank document, or open a document that contains the data source you want to replace.

2. If necessary, display the Database toolbar.

 3. Click the Insert Database button on the Database toolbar to display the Database dialog box.

Continued

MASTERING THE OPPORTUNITIES CONTINUED

4. Choose Get Data to display the Open Data Source dialog box, and then select the name of the folder that contains the database in the Look In list box.

5. Select the file extension of the database file in the Files Of Type drop-down list, highlight the name of the database file that contains the records you want to insert into Word, and then choose Open. (If you would like to create a database query before selecting the data source, click the MS Query button before choosing Open. For more about MS Query, see Chapter 35.)

6. Specify the table, query, or worksheet that contains the data in the dialog box that appears.

7. To filter or sort the data or to select specific fields, click the Query Options button and enter the criteria. Click OK to return to the Insert Data dialog box.

8. Choose Insert Data in the Database dialog box to display the Insert Data dialog box. Then choose any of the following options, and choose OK:

   • In the Insert Records area, choose All to insert all of the specified records, or choose From to insert a range of records, and then type the number of the first record in the adjoining text box and the number of the last record in the range in the To text box.

   • To have Word automatically update the data in the Word document each time the data in the original database changes, choose Insert Data As Field.

9. If you are inserting a database into an existing data source, choose Yes to confirm that you want to replace the current data source with the records in the database.

 If you chose Insert Data As Field in step 8, click the Update Field button on the Database toolbar to have Word update the data source with any edits made in the database that you used to create it.

Creating Envelopes and Labels

Labels and envelopes are two other types of main documents. Specialty labels are available at office supply stores, allowing you to create labels for any use. Word can merge to various sizes of envelopes, including standard, business, note card, and other sizes. If your printer can print on envelopes and labels, you can create them in Word. (You must also know how to load the envelopes and labels. If you're not sure, consult your printer manual.)

Follow these steps to create labels:

1. Display the Mail Merge Helper, and then choose Mailing Labels in the Create Main Document drop-down list.

2. Choose Get Data, and then choose Open Data Source to select a data source.

3. Choose Set Up Main Document in the Microsoft Word dialog box that appears to display the Label Options dialog box, shown in Figure 9.9.

4. Choose any of the following options:

   • Choose either Dot Matrix or Laser And Ink Jet in the Printer Information area. If you chose Laser And Ink Jet, select the tray that contains the labels in the Tray drop-down list.

   • Select the manufacturer of your labels in the Label Products drop-down list. (If the manufacturer of the labels you have is not listed, look on the box for the Avery equivalent. If there is one, choose Avery. If there isn't an Avery equivalent listed, get different labels, if at all possible. It's a lot of work to enter all the measurements manually.)

   • Select the product number (or Avery equivalent) that appears on your label package in the Product number list box. The items that appear in the list box depend on the selections you made in the two options above. A description of the selected label appears in the Label Information area, so you can see that it matches the label specifications on the package.

5. Choose OK to open the Create Labels dialog box, shown in Figure 9.10.

6. Click the Insert Merge Field button, and then select the first merge field to place in the label.

7. Enter any other text from the keyboard. For example, press the spacebar to insert spaces between the Title, FirstName, and LastName fields.

8. If you want to print a delivery point bar code, click the Insert Postal Bar Code button and identify which field holds the zip code and which is the street address field, and then choose OK in the Insert Postal Bar Code dialog box. Word will use this information to generate the bar code.

9. Choose OK to return to the Mail Merge Helper, and choose Close to return to the main document.

PART

II

Creating Dazzling
Documents in Word

FIGURE 9.9

Display the Label Options dialog box when you are creating a mailing label main document.

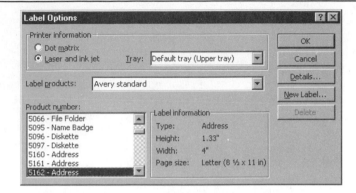

FIGURE 9.10

Create the layout of your label in the Create Labels dialog box.

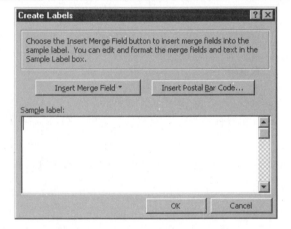

Preview your labels before printing them. If you don't see all the needed text, it's easier to re-create the labels from scratch than to edit them in the main document.

 TIP If you want to save the Label main document, include the word *Labels* (instead of *Main*) at the beginning of the filename.

Preparing an Envelope

Creating an Envelope main document is similar to creating a Label main document. Follow these steps:

1. Display the Mail Merge Helper, choose Envelopes in the Create Main Document drop-down list, and then choose either Active Document or New Main Document to specify which document is the Envelope main document.

2. Choose Get Data, and then choose Open Data Source to select a data source.

3. Choose Set Up Main Document in the Microsoft Word dialog box that appears to display the Envelope Options dialog box, shown in Figure 9.11.

4. Select the size of the envelope in the Envelope Size drop-down list, and then choose OK to display the Envelope Address dialog box.

5. Click the Insert Merge Field button, and then select the first merge field to place on the envelope.

6. Enter any other text from the keyboard. For example, press the spacebar to insert spaces between the Title, FirstName, and LastName fields.

7. If you want to print a delivery point bar code, click the Insert Postal Bar Code button and identify which field holds the zip code and which is the street address field, and then choose OK in the Insert Postal Bar Code dialog box.

8. Choose OK to return to the Mail Merge Helper, and choose Close to return to the main document.

9. If the envelope appears as you wish, save it to a file that begins with "Envelopes."

FIGURE 9.11

Choose the size of your envelopes in the Envelope Options dialog box.

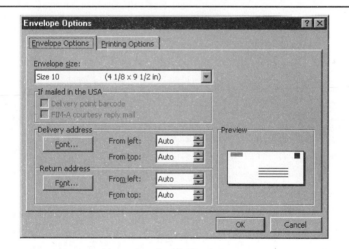

Envelopes appear with the return address specified as the mailing address on the User Information page in the Options dialog box. An Envelope main document is easy to edit once you have set it up. You can use the usual method to insert field codes. To remove the return address for preprinted envelopes, just select it and press the Delete key.

TIP To change the return address on your envelope main document, choose Tools ➤ Options, and then display the User Information page. Type a different name and address in the Mailing address text box, and then choose OK.

Merging Documents

Now you are ready for the actual merge. If necessary, activate the main document window so you can use the merge tools on the Mail Merge toolbar.

 Click the Merge To New Document button to have Word conduct the merge and create a new document with the results. Labels will appear in columns, form letters and envelopes will be separated by page breaks, and catalogs will display each record. You can review the results of the merge before sending the merge document to the printer. Once the merge is printed, there is no reason to save the merge results. If you need to print it again at a later date, you'll want to do the merge again, in case you've updated any of the records in the data source.

 Click the Merge To Printer button to send the results of the merge directly to the printer. If anything is wrong, the error is multiplied by the total number of records you have in your data source. Choose this option only if you have previewed your merge and everything is in perfect order (check that nobody has left purple and green paper in the printer!).

 If you need to make further choices, click the Start Mail Merge button to display the Merge dialog box, shown in Figure 9.12. Alternatively, choose Merge in the Mail Merge Helper to display the Merge dialog box. Choose any of the following options to specify how you want the main document and the data source to be merged, and then choose Merge:

- In the Merge To drop-down list, choose New Document, Printer, Electronic Mail, or Electronic Fax. If you chose Electronic Mail or Electronic Fax, choose Setup, specify the data field that contains the e-mail or fax address, and then type a subject in the Mail Message Subject Line text box. If necessary, check the Send Document As An Attachment box to send the person's portion of the merged document as a file. Choose OK when you are ready to send the merge.

- Choose All or From in the Records To Be Merged area. If you chose From, type the starting record number in the adjacent text box, and the ending record number in the To text box.

- To tell Word how to display the results of the merge, choose either Don't Print Blank Lines When Data Fields Are Empty or Print Blank Lines When Data Fields Are Empty in the When Merging Records area.

The Merge dialog box allows you to specify how and where to merge the main document and the data source.

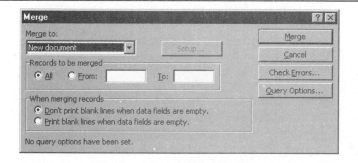

PART

II

Creating Dazzling
Documents in Word

Specifying Records to Merge

Suppose you have a list of names and addresses and only want to send letters to people in a certain zip code or state. You can *filter*, or separate, records based on criteria that you establish. In the database world, a *query* is a tool used to select a group of records that meet specific criteria.

 TIP If your data source is a database table you've developed in Access, you can use that tool to define more complex queries than Word allows. See Chapter 33 for details.

To use a query to filter the records before you merge the main document and the data source, follow these steps:

 1. Click the Start Mail Merge button on the Mail Merge toolbar to open the Merge dialog box, and then choose Query Options. Alternatively, choose Query Options in the Mail Merge Helper to display the Filter Records page of the Query Options dialog box shown in Figure 9.13.

2. In the Field drop-down list, select the field you want to use to select records. If, for example, you want to merge records with zip code 48439, choose the Zip-Code field.

3. Select one of the comparison operators in the Comparison drop-down list. Table 9.1 indicates what records each comparison will select if you compare to a ZipCode of 48439.

4. In the Compare To text box (at the far right of the dialog box), enter the text string you are looking for in the selected field. For example, to use only the records with the zip code 48439, type that zip code in the text box.

5. Choose OK to filter the records with one criterion.

6. Choose Merge to merge the filtered records with the main document.

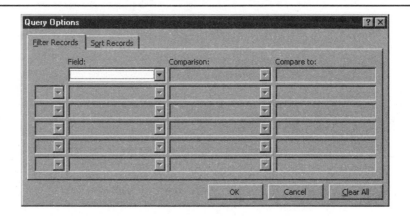

FIGURE 9.13

The Query Options dialog box allows you to specify the criteria necessary to merge only the records you want.

TABLE 9.1: EFFECT OF COMPARISON OPERATORS

Comparison	Selects Records
Equal To (the default)	With the ZipCode 48439
Not Equal To	With any ZipCode that is not 48439
Less Than	With a ZipCode in the range 00000–48438
Greater Than	With ZipCodes in the range 48440–99999
Less Than Or Equal	With a ZipCode 00000–48439
Greater Than Or Equal	With a ZipCode 48439–99999
Is Blank	Where there is no value in the ZipCode field
Is Not Blank	Where any ZipCode is included

Using And and Or

Once you enter a Compare To text string, the word And appears in the drop-down list to the left of the second row of the Query Options dialog box. You can enter multiple query criteria and select, for example, the records for people in California where the data source doesn't list a zip code. The single most confusing thing about writing queries is knowing when to use And and when to use Or.

Choosing And means both comparisons must be true for a match. If you enter the Field, Comparison, and Compare To information in the example given above, choosing And will select all records where the State is California *and* the ZipCode field in the data source is blank. Records for people from Arkansas, Oregon, or Massachusetts will not be selected. Records for people living in California with a zip code will not be selected. Choosing Or means a match will be found if either comparison is true. In this case, all Californians will be selected, as well as anyone from any other state who doesn't have a zip code listed in the data source.

Use Or when you want to select two different possible values for the same field. For example, when you want to send a mailing to all your customers in California and Nevada, you should select records where State is equal to California Or State is equal to Nevada. Don't select And, because no single record includes both states.

There is one time you use And when making two comparisons in the same field: when you want to select records within a numeric range. For example, you might want to send an advertisement to all families with annual incomes between $25,000 and $40,000. In this example, you would select Income greater than $25,000 And Income less than $40,000. If you used Or, all records would be selected, as every level of income is either less than $40,000 or more than $25,000.

 TIP Here's a general rule for troubleshooting queries: If you expected some records to be selected but none were, you probably used And when you should have used Or. If you got a lot more records than you expected, you probably used Or when you should have used And.

Sorting Records

After you select your merge criteria, you can also choose how you want your data sorted by clicking the Sort Records tab on the Query Options dialog box. See "Sorting Lists, Paragraphs, and Tables," above, for more information about sorting.

MASTERING TROUBLESHOOTING

Troubleshooting Merge Problems

There are three basic reasons for merge problems:

- document incompatibility
- problems with the data source
- problems with the main document

Document incompatibility means that either the data source or the main document isn't a valid Word mail merge file. A dialog box will appear, telling you that the main document has no merge codes or that the data source is invalid. Examine the file in question. If it is a data file, make sure it has field names, that there is no extra text at the beginning of the file, and that the data is in a table. If the problem is the main document, open it and check to make sure you have selected the correct data source file and that it has merge field codes. Even if both files seem to be OK, structural problems with individual records (like missing fields) can cause Word to stop in the middle of a merge.

 You can have Word check the data source for omission errors before merging. With the main document active, click the Check For Errors button on the Mail Merge toolbar to open the Checking And Reporting Errors dialog box, shown below. Using this tool is much like checking spelling before printing.

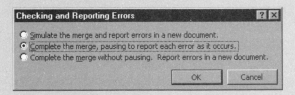

Choose one of the following options, and then choose OK:

- Have Word simulate a merge and report errors in a new document.
- Merge the two documents and report errors while the merge is taking place.
- Merge the two documents and report errors in a new document.

Continued

MASTERING TROUBLESHOOTING CONTINUED

If you expect errors, simulation is best. If you don't think there will be errors (always our hope), go ahead and have Word merge, stopping along the way to report any errors it finds. When Word finds an error, a dialog box will open. Depending on the kind of error, you may be allowed to fix the error and then continue merging. If you cannot, note the information provided, and click the OK button to continue finding errors. When Error Checking is complete, close the merged document and fix the data source and/or main document files before merging the documents again.

Even if Word finds no errors and your documents merge, you may still find mistakes in your merged document. There is an easy way to decide if a mistake is in the main document or in the data source. If the mistake appears in every merged document, look for the problem in the main document. For example, if there is no space between the first and last names in your merged form letters, you need to put a space between the merge codes for FirstName and LastName in the main document. Spelling errors in every merged document should lead you to suspect that you forgot to check the spelling in the main document before merging.

If a mistake appears in some but not all merged documents, the problem is in the data source. If a merged first name is spelled incorrectly in one of the merged letters, it's misspelled in the data source. Close the merged file, open the data source file and correct the error, and then merge the documents again.

What's Next

The next chapter shows how to use some of Word 2000's advanced features to create online forms. You will see how to create a form template, and use tables and frames in the form. You can add several types of controls to a form, which allow you to select specific information, much like the controls in a dialog box. You will also see how to add online help—an invaluable tool for the person who fills out an online form.

CHAPTER 10

Creating and Distributing Word Forms

FEATURING:

Designing a form

Creating a template for a form

Using frames and text boxes

Adding field controls

Modifying forms

Protecting and using forms

Sending a form online

As more people have computers on their desktops and more computers are networked together, the paperless office is becoming a reality. One way that's happening is through the creation and use of online forms, which are forms that are viewed and completed in Word. Online forms are distributed via e-mail or network sharing.

For example, if you need to create a vacation request form for your company, why go to the trouble of creating the form, printing it, making copies, and filing them? Each employee has to fill one out and submit it, and the boss has to sign it and return it to an assistant, who then copies it, returns one copy to the employee, and files the other one: endless paperwork enclosed in countless interoffice envelopes. By the time the form jumps through all its hoops, the vacation date has come and gone. With an online form, the employee opens the form online, fills it out, and sends it by e-mail to the boss, who approves (or disapproves) it and returns the e-mail. It's all over in a matter of minutes—no copies, no lost forms, no missed vacations.

 NOTE Two other types of forms can be created in Word: a printed form, which is filled out by hand directly on the page; and a Web form, which is distributed on the Web and viewed using a browser. The information filled in by the user is sent to a database on an HTTP server.

Designing a Form

The most difficult part of creating an online form is designing it to meet your needs. Before you start creating your online form, sketch it on paper or use an existing printed form as a model. This will give your form a better ultimate design and will save you the time and frustration of trying to design the form while you're creating it.

Creating a Template for a Form

Because you'll want to use the online form over and over again, you need to create your form as a template. As soon as you open a new, blank template in which to create your form, go ahead and save it. That way, you can just click the Save button each time you make a change that you want to keep.

To have the template available when creating a new document, save the template in one of the existing template folders. If you create many online-form templates, create a new folder in the Templates folder in which to store them. When you do, an Online Forms tab will appear in the New dialog box. This feature makes it easy for users to locate the templates when they want to create a form based on one of them.

To create a new template file, follow these steps:

1. Choose File ➤ New, highlight Blank Document on the General page, select Template in the Create New area, and then choose OK in the New dialog box.

2. Click on the Save button on the Standard toolbar to display the Save As dialog box.

3. Choose the folder in the Templates folder in which to store the template. Alternatively, create a new folder in the Templates folder.

4. Save the template to a named file with a .DOT file extension.

 NOTE If you forget to choose Template as the type of file to open in step 1 above, you can still save the document as a template file by selecting Document Template (*.dot) in the Save As Type drop-down list in the Save As dialog box.

Now that you have a new, blank template, you are ready to begin inserting the text and other objects that will be used repeatedly in the form. The easiest way to lay out the form is by using a table. Tables allow you to place text on different parts of the screen without worrying about user-entered text wrapping to a new line. Tables also make it easy for the user to enter text in the appropriate location. The user can press Tab to move from one cell to another.

Word 2000 comes with the Forms toolbar, a set of tools used to create online forms. The Forms toolbar includes buttons to insert form fields, to create tables and frames, to position questions and prompts on the page, to turn form-field shading on or off, and to protect the text and other objects on the form so that users can enter data only where you have placed form fields.

  To display the Forms toolbar, right-click on any toolbar and choose Forms. Click on the Draw Table or Insert Table button on the Forms toolbar to create a table in the new template.

 NOTE See "Creating and Revising Tables" in Chapter 6 for additional information about creating and formatting tables.

Figure 10.1 shows an example of an online form that was created using a table. The borders have been turned off except for some of the bottom cell borders, which form the lines for users' responses. As you can see, rows and columns aren't evenly distributed, and extra cells have been inserted to provide the appropriate spacing for items on the form.

PART

II

Creating Dazzling
Documents in Word

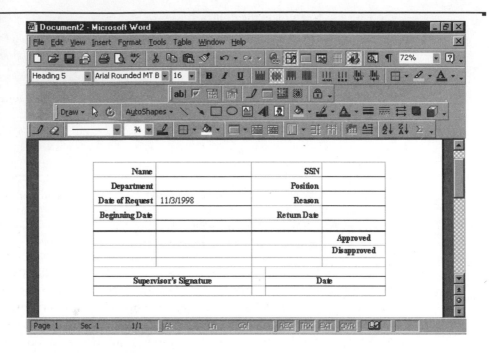

After you enter descriptive labels and prompts in the table, you can split cells, merge cells, change borders, and adjust column and row widths as needed. Because the form is to be viewed online, don't forget to add colors, shading, and graphics to really make an impression.

Using Frames and Text Boxes

The Forms toolbar has an option for frames that allows you to place an item precisely at any position on a form. For example, you may want to jazz up your form by placing its title in a frame or text box and then changing the direction of the title text. Both frames and text boxes can be formatted by adding or removing visible borders, backgrounds, and even shadows.

In Word 2000, if you want text to wrap around a graphic, it is not necessary to insert the graphic in a text box or frame. However, to help you position objects on a page, you can place either text or graphics in a frame.

NOTE Don't confuse the object frames discussed here with HTML frames, which are used to coordinate the content and layout of Web pages, as discussed in Chapter 44.

NOTE Some types of text, such as comment marks and certain fields, must be placed in a frame. See "Generating a Table of Contents" in Chapter 11 and "Inserting Comments" in Chapter 12 for additional information.

To insert a frame, click on the Insert Frame button, and then drag to create a rectangle the approximate size of the text or object you want to place in the frame. By default, a frame appears with a black border in the size and location in which you created it. A newly created frame is active—the insertion point is placed inside it, and a shaded border appears around the outside of its regular border. You can immediately begin to type text in a frame.

Unlike text boxes, frames expand to accommodate their contents. For example, if you type text in a frame, it will automatically grow so that all the text you type is inside the frame. To manually resize a frame, click on the shaded border of an active frame to select it, and then drag one of the black handles that appear around its borders. The mouse pointer changes to a two-headed resize arrow when you position it over a handle on the frame's border.

To manually reposition a frame, select it, and when the mouse pointer changes into a four-headed move arrow, drag the frame to a new position.

To change the size or position of the frame to an exact specification and to change the way text wraps around the frame, follow these steps:

1. Right-click on the frame and choose Format Frame, or select the frame and choose Format ➤ Frame to display the Frame dialog box shown in Figure 10.2.

2. To change the way text wraps around the frame, choose one of the following options in the Text Wrapping area:

None: Places text above and below the frame, but no text appears on either the right or left side of it.

Around: The default, this places text above and below the frame and on both the right and left sides.

3. To change the size of the frame, specify any of the following options in the Size area:

- In the Width drop-down list, choose Exactly, and then adjust the value in the adjacent At text box to specify the exact width of the frame. Alternatively, choose Auto to allow the frame's width to conform to a size that holds its contents.

- In the Height text box, choose At Least, and then adjust the value in the adjacent At text box to specify the minimum height for the frame; choose

Exactly, and then adjust the value in the At text box to specify the exact height for the frame; or choose Auto to allow the frame's height to conform to the size that holds its contents.

4. To define the horizontal position of the frame, specify any of the following options in the Horizontal area:

- In the Position drop-down list, choose Left, Right, Center, Inside, or Outside to define the position of the frame in relation to the Page, Margin, or Column, which is selected in the Relative To drop-down list. If the frame is in the margin of the page, type the distance from the edge of the page in the Position drop-down list.

- Adjust the value in the Distance From Text box to specify the amount of space between the edges of the frame and the text on the left and right side of the frame.

5. To define the vertical position of the frame, specify any of the following options in the Vertical area:

- In the Position drop-down list, choose Top, Bottom, Center, Inside, or Outside to define the position of the frame in relation to the Margin, Page, or Paragraph, which is selected in the Relative To drop-down list. Alternatively, type a measurement in the Position drop-down list to specify the position of the frame in relation to the margin, page, or paragraph.

- Adjust the value in the Distance From Text box to specify the amount of space between the edges of the frame and the text above and below it.

- Check the Move With Text box to allow the frame to move its vertical position up or down on the page when the paragraph to which it is anchored moves.

- Check the Lock Anchor box to lock the frame's anchor to the paragraph that currently contains it. For example, check the Lock Anchor box to lock the frame that contains a caption to the graphic the caption describes.

6. Choose OK to apply the selected options to the frame.

If you decide that you no longer want a frame in your form, you can delete it. Use either of the following methods:

- Select the frame, and then choose Format ➤ Frame to display the Frame dialog box shown in Figure 10.2. Choose Remove Frame to remove the frame without removing its contents.

- Select the frame, and then press Delete to remove both the frame and its contents.

FIGURE 10.2

The Frame dialog box contains options that allow you to specify the exact size and position of a selected frame.

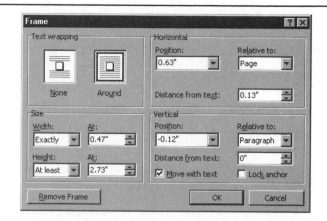

You can use the options available in the Borders And Shading dialog box to change the appearance of the frame's borders and shading:

1. Right-click on a frame, and then choose Borders And Shading to display the Borders And Shading dialog box.

2. Choose the border for the frame on the Borders page and the shading or fill color for the inside of the frame on the Shading page.

3. Choose OK when you have applied the border and shading you want.

 TIP The tools on both the Drawing and the Tables And Borders toolbars can also be used to apply some formatting to frames. For example, you can change the text direction in a selected frame using the Change Text Direction button on the Tables And Borders toolbar. Use the Shadow and 3D buttons on the Drawing toolbar to apply a shadow or three-dimensional effect to a frame. See "Creating and Revising Tables" in Chapter 6 and "Formatting Objects" in Chapter 7 for additional information about the Drawing and the Tables And Borders toolbars.

If it's text you want to position, Word 2000's text boxes, found on the Drawing toolbar, are also an option. With text boxes you can apply 3-D effects, shadows, fills, and background. In addition, you can both change the orientation of the text and flip and rotate the text boxes themselves. For more information about text boxes and other graphic tools, see Chapter 7.

Creating Dazzling Documents in Word

Adding Field Controls

Once your form is laid out, you must add *form fields,* or placeholders, that other people can use to submit their information. There are three types of form fields you can access from buttons on the Forms toolbar:

- Text form fields are open fields of any length where users can enter text.
- Check box form fields are check boxes that a user can check or clear to indicate yes or no answers.
- Drop-down form fields allow users to choose a response from a list of choices you provide.

The form fields are controls just like those you find in dialog boxes. When your form is completed and you turn on protection, users will be able only to enter text, add or remove check marks, or select one of the choices in the fields. The rest of the document will be off-limits to them.

 To insert a form field, position the insertion point where you would like the field to appear, and then click on the Text Form Field, Check Box Form Field, or Drop-Down Form Field button on the Forms toolbar.

It's helpful to have the Form Field Shading feature turned on while you are creating the form so that you can see where the fields are, especially Text form fields. Form Field Shading is a toggle, which is turned on by default when you first display the Forms toolbar.

 To toggle the display of shading for form fields, click on the Form Field Shading button on the Forms toolbar.

 After you have entered a field in the form, you'll need to specify the options you want to apply to the field. To do so, either select the field and click on the Form Field Options button on the Forms toolbar, or double-click on the field to open its Form Field Options dialog box.

When you display the Text Form Field dialog box, shown in Figure 10.3, you can choose any of the following options for the selected field and then choose OK:

- Select Regular Text, Number, Date, Current Date, Current Time, or Calculation in the Type drop-down list to specify what type of information the user can enter in the field. The field will not accept input that is not the correct type of information. For example, the user cannot enter a name in a field that is specified as a date field.
- Type the choice that users would most commonly give in the Default Text box. The user must type any different choice in the text box.
- Adjust the value in the Maximum Length text box either to Unlimited or to a specified number of characters, which limits the length of user entries.

- Choose Uppercase, Lowercase, First Capital, or Title Case in the Text Format drop-down list to specify how the text will appear in the form field.

- In the Run Macro On area, select the name of the macro to run whenever the insertion point enters or leaves the field.

NOTE See Chapter 37 for additional information on creating and using macros, and on using the VBA macro programming language. Any macros you want to run when entering or exiting the form field must be stored in the form's template.

- In the Field Settings area, type the name of a bookmark in the Bookmark text box to have a macro reference the contents of this field. Check the Calculate On Exit check box to have Word update and calculate all the fields after any exit macros run when the insertion point leaves this field. Check the Fill-In Enabled box to allow users to enter text in this field.

FIGURE 10.3

The Text Form Field Options dialog box contains options to specify what type of text can be entered in the field.

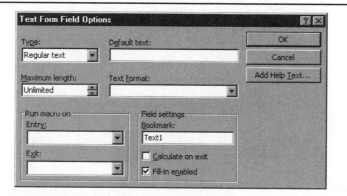

NOTE See "Using Bookmarks" in Chapter 11 for information on creating and using bookmarks in your documents.

When you display the Check Box Form Field dialog box, shown in Figure 10.4, you can choose any of the options for the selected field and then choose OK. These options are unique to check box form fields:

- In the Check Box Size area, choose Auto to make the check box the size of the text. Alternatively, choose Exactly, and then adjust the value in the adjacent text box to specify the exact size in points for the check box.

- Choose either Not Checked or Checked as the default value for the field when the form is opened.

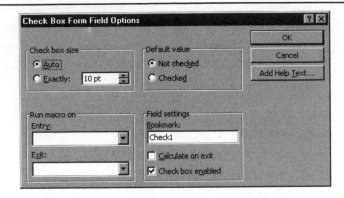

When you display the Drop-Down Form Field Options dialog box, shown in Figure 10.5, you can choose any of the options for the selected field and then choose OK. These options are unique to drop-down form fields:

- Type an item to include in the drop-down list in the Drop-Down Item text box, and then choose Add to place it in the Items In Drop-Down List box.

- Click either the ↑ or ↓ Move button to move the item highlighted in the Items In Drop-Down List box to a different position in the list. The items will appear in the drop-down list on the form in the order in which they appear in the Items In Drop-Down List box.

- To edit an item in the drop-down list, select it in the Items In Drop-Down List box, and then choose Remove to remove it from the list box and return it to the Drop-Down Item text box. Press Delete to delete the item, or edit the item and then choose Add to return it to the list.

FIGURE 10.5

Enter the items for a drop-down list in the Drop-Down Form Field Options dialog box.

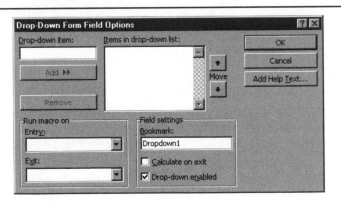

The first item in the list box appears on the form as the default. You may want to enter a blank item (press the spacebar several times before you choose Add) as the first choice. Alternatively, you can enter instructional text as the first item ("Select your department"). However, if you provide one of these options, you cannot prevent users from selecting it as their choice. Another consideration is that the length of the text string for the first item determines the width of the drop-down list field on the form. Think carefully about this before deciding which way you want to go.

Each of the three dialog boxes also has an option that allows you to add online Help to the form field. The Add Help Text option will endear you forever to your users.

To add Help text to the form field:

1. If necessary, display the form field's Options dialog box, and then choose Add Help Text to display the Form Field Help Text dialog box shown in Figure 10.6.

2. On the Status Bar page, choose one of the following options to specify what Help text will appear on the status bar when the field is selected:

    None: Provides no Help text on the status bar for the form field.

    AutoText Entry: Allows you to use a previously created AutoText entry as the Help text that appears on the status bar. Select the AutoText entry in the adjacent drop-down list.

    Type Your Own: Allows you to type up to 138 characters of Help text in the text box.

3. On the Help Key (F1) page, choose one of the following options to specify what Help text will appear in a message box when the field is selected:

    None: Provides no Help text for the form field when the F1 key is pressed.

    AutoText Entry: Allows you to use a previously created AutoText entry as the Help text that appears when you press F1. Select the AutoText entry in the adjacent drop-down list.

    Type Your Own: Allows you to type up to 255 characters of Help text in the text box.

4. Choose OK in the Form Field Help Text dialog box.

PART

II

Creating Dazzling
Documents in Word

FIGURE 10.6

Add online Help for a form field by choosing the location of the Help text in the Form Field Help Text dialog box.

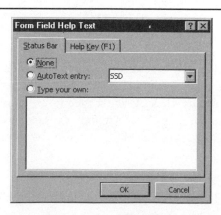

Protecting and Using the Form

 Your form is almost ready to distribute. You'll want to make the form appear just as it will when the user opens a document based on your form's template. For example, you'll probably want to turn off form field shading because it presents a neater appearance. In addition, the form field shading doesn't accurately reflect the length of the form field, so it may be confusing to the users. You may also wish to hide the gridlines if you used a table to create your form. When you do, only the descriptive labels and any cell borders you displayed appear on the form. This new feature in Word 2000 means that when you open a document based on the form template, the gridlines will not have to be turned off again, as was true in previous versions of Word.

After you're sure that everything is exactly the way you want it, you'll want to protect the form so the user can only enter data in the form fields. When you protect the form, the descriptive labels, formatting, and layout of the form cannot be changed. In addition, you will no longer have access to most toolbar and menu options.

 To protect the form, click the Protect Form button on the Forms toolbar.

The last step before distributing the form to users is to save the form template. Although many of the toolbar buttons and menu commands are no longer available, you can still save the template by clicking on the Save button.

After protecting your form, it's always smart to test the form by filling it out to check that the *tab order*, the order in which the fields are activated when you press Tab, is correct. Depending on how you created the table and positioned the items in it, it may not tab logically through the fields. To correct this, you may have to insert blank cells or reposition items on the form. You may also find that you made a field's length too short or that you didn't include all the options in a drop-down list. Use the form as if you were one of your potential users; if possible, ask a colleague to test the form for you. It's amazing how easy it is to overlook something when you already know what data is expected in a field.

If you need to edit the form, be sure to open the form's template (and not a document based on the template, a copy of the form). You can then turn on the Forms toolbar and click the Protect Form button. You will again have free rein to do whatever you want to the form (within reason, of course!).

When users open a protected-form document, such as the one shown in Figure 10.7, they will be able to select only a field control. Press Tab and Shift+Tab to move forward and backward through the fields. Users will have limited access to toolbar buttons and menu options. They can enter their information and then save or print the document so they have a copy of it. The form can also be e-mailed to a supervisor using the File ➤ Send To ➤ Mail Recipient (as Attachment) command.

FIGURE 10.7

When you open a protected form, the first field is selected so the user can enter the appropriate information.

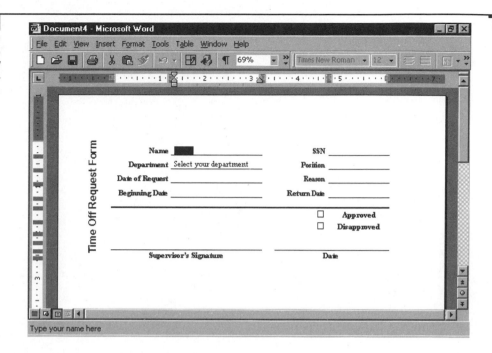

 NOTE See Chapter 19 to learn how you can use Outlook to send your online form as a file attached to an e-mail message.

What's Next

Now that you've had fun learning how to use tables and templates to create online forms, the discussion in Chapter 11 moves on to working in long documents. You'll learn how to use some of Word's features to automate the creation of a table of contents and an index. Chapter 11 also shows how to create footnotes and endnotes, and how to insert cross-references in a document. You'll learn how to insert hyperlinks, which can be used to move to a specific location in a document or to open another document. Finally, you'll see how to use Word's Master Document feature to manage your long documents.

PART

II

Creating Dazzling Documents in Word

CHAPTER 11

Making Documents Easy to Use

Although some of your documents, such as letters and memos, will be relatively short, many documents, such as reports and procedural manuals, may be very long. Word 2000 comes with several features to help you work in lengthy documents. For example, adding footnotes, endnotes, tables of contents, indexes, hyperlinks, and cross-references makes your documents easy to follow and helps your readers find what they are looking for. Using master documents helps you organize your work. When you plan ahead, Word 2000 takes the headache out of these additional touches, providing one more way for your work to stand out.

Adding Footnotes and Endnotes

When you want to provide readers with more information about your topic or a reference to the source of your information, Word 2000 gives you options for inserting both *footnotes,* which appear at the bottom of the page, and *endnotes,* which appear at the end of the document. Word automatically numbers the notes for you and calculates how much space footnotes will need at the bottom on the page. Where was this feature when we were typing term papers?

 NOTE You can insert both footnotes and endnotes in the same document. For example, you may want to insert footnotes to add comments to the text of a page and endnotes to add source information, such as a bibliography, at the end of a report.

Each time you insert a footnote or endnote, Word automatically inserts a *note reference mark* (a character in the text of the document that tells the reader to look for additional information) in your document at the location where you inserted the note. The reference mark can be automatically numbered using Arabic numerals (1, 2, 3, …) or using the consecutive numbers or symbols you specify in a different format. You can also choose to insert a custom mark or symbol to use as the note reference mark in your document. Automatic numbering is, of course, the easiest because Word knows what the next reference mark number should be. If you choose a custom mark, you must select the symbol each time you insert a new note, even if you are using the same symbol for every note.

Use either Normal view or Print Layout view when you are working in a document that includes footnotes or endnotes. When you insert a note in a document, Word inserts the note reference mark you specified and then:

- In Normal view, the notes pane opens. Type the text of your note beside the note reference mark. You can then press F6 to move the insertion point into the document pane in the position where you inserted the note. In this way, both the notes pane and the document pane appear on your screen at the same time. You can work in either pane by repositioning the insertion point either with the mouse or by pressing the F6 key. You can also choose Close to hide the notes pane and return to your document. Insert another note or choose View ➤ Footnotes to redisplay the notes pane.

- In Print Layout view, the insertion point moves to the actual location where the note will appear in your document. Type the text of the note, and then press Shift+F5 to return to the location where you inserted the note reference mark in your document.

 TIP Use Shift+F5 to return the insertion point to the last three locations in the document where you edited text.

You can decide which view is easier to use when working with notes. In either view, when you want to review your note, all you have to do is point to the reference mark. The mouse pointer will change to an I-beam with a note attached to it, and a second later, the note will appear. Just move the mouse pointer away, and the note disappears.

To insert a footnote or an endnote, follow these steps:

1. Position the insertion point where you'd like the note reference mark to appear, and then choose Insert ➤ Footnote to display the Footnote And Endnote dialog box shown in Figure 11.1.

2. Select Footnote or Endnote in the Insert area to specify what type of note you want to insert.

3. To specify the type of numbering to use as the note reference mark in your document, choose one of the following options:

   - Choose AutoNumber to have Word insert consecutive numbers or symbols in the numbering format selected.

   - Choose Custom Mark, and then click the Symbol button to display the Symbol dialog box. Choose one of the characters or symbols to use as the reference mark for this note only, and then choose OK in the Symbol dialog box.

4. Choose OK in the Footnote And Endnote dialog box.

FIGURE 11.1

Display the Footnote And Endnote dialog box each time you insert a note reference mark in your document.

There are some changes you can make to the location of the notes, the note reference marks, and the way the notes are numbered. For example, you can change the format of automatically numbered notes (Arabic numerals such as 1, 2, 3) to uppercase or lowercase letters, Roman numerals, or a list of symbols, which Word uses in a set pattern. You can also specify a position for the location of the notes in your document. Any changes you make to the way the notes appear are applied to all the footnotes or endnotes in the document.

To change the way footnotes and endnotes appear, use the following steps:

1. Position the insertion point where you'd like the note reference mark to appear, and then choose Insert ➤ Footnote to display the Footnote And Endnote dialog box shown in Figure 11.1.

2. Choose Options to display the Note Options dialog box shown in Figure 11.2.

3. Choose any of the following options on the All Footnotes page to specify how footnotes will appear in the document:

    Place At: Choose Bottom Of Page to place footnotes just above the bottom margin on the page that includes the note reference mark, or Beneath Text to place the footnotes below the last line of text on a short page of text.

    Number Format: Choose one of the options listed to change the automatic numbering format for notes.

    Start At: Adjust the value to assign the number or character you want to use for the first automatically numbered note.

    Numbering: Choose Continuous to have Word number every note consecutively; choose Restart At Each Section to have Word start the numbering for each document section with the character specified in the Start At text box; or choose Restart Each Page to have Word start the numbering on each page with the character specified in the Start At text box.

4. Choose any of the following unique options on the All Endnotes page to specify how endnotes will appear in the document:

Place At: Choose End Of Document to place endnotes after the last line of text in the document, or End Of Section to place the endnotes at the end of the section in which they occur.

Numbering: Choose Continuous to have Word number every note consecutively, or choose Restart Each Section to have Word start the numbering for each document section with the character specified in the Start At text box.

5. Choose OK in the Note Options dialog box to return to the Footnote and Endnote dialog box.

6. Choose OK in the Footnote And Endnote dialog box to both insert a note in the new format and change all existing notes to the new format.

FIGURE 11.2

Change the appearance, location, and number format for all notes in a document using the options in the Note Options dialog box.

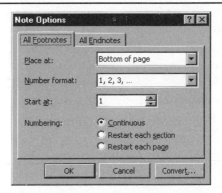

Revising Footnotes and Endnotes

Now that you have footnotes and endnotes scattered throughout your text, you may need to edit one of the notes. There are several ways to activate a note so you can edit it:

• Double-click any reference mark in Normal view to open the notes pane at the bottom of the screen. All notes of the same type appear in the pane—just scroll to the one you want to edit, make your changes, and click Close.

• If you are looking for a specific note in Normal view, click the Select Browse Object button on the vertical scroll bar, choose Go To, select Footnote or Endnote, enter the reference mark number you are looking for, and choose Go To. The insertion point automatically moves to the note in the notes pane.

• Move the insertion point into the notes area in Print Layout view, and then select the text you want to edit. Type the new text to replace the selected text.

You cannot edit the note reference mark in the document by selecting it and then replacing it with a different character. Instead, you must delete the note, choose Insert ➤ Footnotes so you can change the numbering or custom mark symbol, and then retype the text of the note.

Deleting Notes

When you want to delete a note entirely, click before or after the reference mark and press the Backspace or Delete key twice—the first time will select the reference mark, and the second time will delete both the mark and the note. Deleting the text inside the note pane or at the bottom or end of the document will not delete the reference mark in your document.

Converting Notes

After you've entered notes in your document, you may find that you want each note to be a different type. For example, if you indicated sources in footnotes and added comments as endnotes, you may decide that the notes would be better in opposite formats, or you may decide that you want only footnotes or only endnotes in the document. Word allows you to convert your footnotes to endnotes and your endnotes to footnotes.

To convert notes, use the following steps:

1. Choose Insert ➤ Footnote to display the Footnote And Endnote dialog box shown in Figure 11.1.
2. Choose Options to display the Note Options dialog box shown in Figure 11.2.
3. Choose Convert to display the Convert Notes dialog box.
4. Choose one of the following options, and then choose OK:

Convert All Footnotes To Endnotes: Changes all footnotes into endnotes.

Convert All Endnotes To Footnotes: Changes all endnotes to footnotes.

Swap Footnotes And Endnotes: Simultaneously changes all footnotes to endnotes and all endnotes to footnotes.

Using Bookmarks

Bookmarks are named locations in a document. Especially when you are working with long documents, it's useful to be able to mark an item or a location in the text that you want to return to later. This could be a place where you need to insert some additional information before finishing the final draft or a location in the document that contains information pertinent to the current topic. Whatever the reason, by inserting bookmarks you can easily move to specific text or objects in a document without having to scroll.

Bookmark names can include both numbers and letters, but they must begin with a letter. Although you cannot include spaces in a bookmark name, you can include the underline character to use instead of a space in names that consist of multiple words.

To insert a bookmark, use the following steps:

1. Select the text, graphic, table, or other object you want to mark. Alternatively, position the insertion point in the location you want to mark.

2. Choose Insert ➤ Bookmark to display the Bookmark dialog box, shown in Figure 11.3.

3. Type a name in the Bookmark Name text box.

4. Choose Add to create the bookmark and return to your document.

PART

II

FIGURE 11.3

Display the Bookmark dialog box when you want to insert a bookmark in a document.

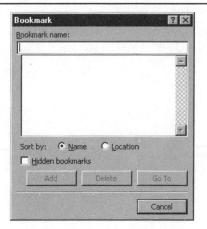

By default, you cannot see bookmarks in your document. To display bookmarks, you can do the following:

1. Choose Tools ➤ Options and display the View page in the Options dialog box.

2. Check the Bookmarks check box in the Show area.

3. Choose OK in the Options dialog box.

Large, gray brackets ([ ]) surround text or graphics to which bookmarks were added. A gray I-beam appears in the location in which a bookmark was inserted where no item was selected. The brackets are nonprinting characters, so if you're working a lot with bookmarks, it's handy just to leave them turned on.

Creating Dazzling Documents in Word

Use the options available in the Bookmark dialog box to delete existing bookmarks, to display hidden bookmarks, such as cross-references, or to move to a different document location that was marked. To manage your bookmarks, use the following steps:

1. Choose Insert ≻ Bookmark to display the Bookmark dialog box, shown in Figure 11.3.

2. To edit or move to bookmarks in a document, use one of the following options:

   • To delete a bookmark, highlight its name in the Bookmark Name list box, and then choose Delete.

   • To change the order in which the bookmark names are displayed in the Bookmark Name list box, choose an option in the Sort By area. Choose Name to display the bookmark names alphabetically. Alternatively, choose Location to display the bookmark names in the order in which they are located in the document.

   • To select the document location or item that is marked, highlight the name of the bookmark in the Bookmark Name list box, and then choose Go To.

3. When you are finished making changes or have found the location you want, choose Close to return to your document.

Another way to move to and select a bookmark in your document is to use Word's Go To feature:

1. Click the Select Browse Object button at the bottom of the vertical scroll bar.

2. Select Go To in the menu that appears to display the Find And Replace dialog box.

3. Choose Bookmarks in the Go To What list box, and then select the name of the bookmark in the Enter Bookmark Name drop-down list.

4. Choose Close to return to your document.

When you close the Go To dialog box, you can use the Previous Find/Go To and Next Find/Go To browse buttons, located above and below the Select Browse Object button on the vertical scroll bar, to move to and select each of your bookmarks.

Creating Cross-References

Use *cross-references* to refer to text or objects elsewhere in a document. Cross-references are used to automatically keep references within a document up-to-date throughout editing. For example, you might direct a reader to see a paragraph in a different chapter: "See 'Employee Benefits' in Chapter 5 for more information." If the Employee Benefits section is later moved to Chapter 4, you can rest assured that the reader will still look in the right place, because the cross-reference will be updated when the Employee Benefits section is moved.

 NOTE To insert cross-references to more than one document, change the documents into subdocuments of a master document. See "Managing Large Documents," later in this chapter, for additional information.

Cross-references can be linked to bookmarks, headings, numbered items, footnotes, endnotes, equations, figures, and tables—and you can choose how the reference will appear in the document. For example, if you want to refer to a heading, you can have the cross-reference indicate the actual text of the heading, the page number where the text is found, or just the word "above" or "below."

If your document is intended for use online or on-screen, leave the Insert As Hyperlink check box checked to create a more active kind of cross-reference. When a user points to a hyperlinked cross-reference, the mouse pointer changes to a hand shape, and a ScreenTip appears telling the user they will go to a location in the current document if they click the hyperlink. Click once to simultaneously move to the location in the document to which the hyperlink cross-reference refers and to display the Web toolbar.

 NOTE See "Adding Hyperlinks to Make Navigation Easy," later in this chapter, for information about inserting hyperlinks to a different document, Web site, or intranet page.

  You cannot click the hyperlink cross-reference again to return to that position in the document or to select it because it will always return you to the position linked to the cross-reference. Instead, click the Back button on the Web toolbar to return to the point of origin, the hyperlink cross-reference. Click the Forward button to jump once again to the position to which the hyperlinked cross-reference refers.

To insert a cross-reference in a document, use the following steps:

1. For a text cross-reference, type any optional text before the position in which you want to insert the cross-reference. For example, type **See page** and then press the spacebar to insert a space. For a hyperlinked cross-reference, position the insertion point where you want the hyperlink.

2. Choose Insert ➤ Cross-Reference to display the Cross-Reference dialog box shown in Figure 11.4.

3. Select the type of item to which the reference will refer in the Reference Type drop-down list. A list of the items of that type in the document appears in the list box.

4. Select the item in the For Which *Item* list box to which the cross-reference will refer.

5. Choose what you want to include in the reference in the Insert Reference To drop-down list. This item will be inserted in the position of the insertion point in the document. For example, select Page Number to have the page number of the item selected in step 4 appear beside your optional text.

6. Choose Insert to insert the cross-reference.

7. Repeat the steps above to insert as many cross-references as necessary, and then choose Close to return to your document.

FIGURE 11.4

The Cross-Reference dialog box allows you to insert a reference to information in another location in the same document.

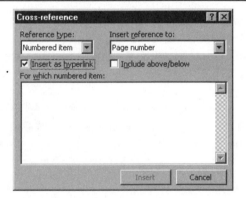

Cross-references are inserted as fields in the document. By default, the results of the field codes appear. If you want to see the actual field code, right-click the field, and then choose Toggle Field Codes. To display the results of the field code, right-click the field again, and then choose Toggle Field Codes.

NOTE The Field Code commands do not appear on the shortcut menu if the field codes contain a grammatical error, such as no space between the field code and the period of the previous sentence. You must correct the grammatical error before Word will display the shortcut menu with the Field Code commands.

Field Codes

Field codes are used in documents as placeholders for data that may change. Fields help you automatically enter some types of information. Some fields that are commonly used in documents include the PAGE field, which automatically updates the page numbers, and the DATE field, which automatically inserts today's date according to your computer.

By default, the results of field codes appear in your documents rather than the field codes themselves. When field codes are displayed, they appear in curly brackets ({ }). To change the view so that the field codes, rather than the results, are displayed, follow these steps:

1. Choose Tools ➢ Options, and display the View page in the Options dialog box.
2. Click the Field Codes check box to remove the check mark from it.
3. Choose OK in the Options dialog box.

Fields are inserted when you use specific commands, some of which are located on the Insert menu. For example, to insert page numbering (the PAGE field code), choose Insert ➢ Page Numbers, choose the position and alignment, and then choose OK. If you want to manually insert field codes, do not type the curly brackets. Instead, press Ctrl+F9 to have Word insert the field-code brackets, and then type the appropriate data between the braces.

The list of and information for Word's field codes can be found in the Field dialog box, which is displayed when you choose Insert ➢ Field.

If you make any changes to the document, you should manually update the results of the field codes. To do so, follow these steps:

1. Choose Edit ➢ Select All to select the entire document.
2. Press F9, or right-click the selection, and then choose Update Field in the short-cut menu.

 TIP To have Word automatically update all the field codes in a document before you print it, choose Tools ➢ Options, display the Print page, check the Update Fields check box in the Printing Options area, and then choose OK.

PART

II

Creating Dazzling
Documents in Word

Be careful not to delete an item that is referenced, or the link will be broken. If the cross-reference is a hyperlink, Word will take your readers to another location that contains similar text. Users clicking the See Employee Benefits hyperlink could find themselves, for example, on the Termination of Employment page—probably not the message you want to convey.

Indexing for Easy Reference

You can make lengthy documents more user-friendly by creating an index of key words and phrases. Index entries can consist of individual words, phrases, or symbols that you select in your document; a topic that extends through several pages that you have named as a bookmark; or a topic that references another index entry.

MASTERING THE OPPORTUNITIES

Marking Index Entries Using a Concordance File

A *concordance file* is a regular Word file that Word uses to automatically mark index entries in your document. A concordance file contains a two-column table. The exact text to be marked in the document is typed or pasted into the first column, and the text that is to appear in the index for that entry is typed in the second column. When you are ready, Word searches through the document for the text in the first column and marks it with an index entry field that includes the text in the second column.

You must first set up the concordance file. To do so, follow these steps:

1. Open a new, blank document.
2. Create a two-column table.
3. Type (or paste) the text you want Word to mark for the index entry in the first column. The text must be entered exactly as it appears in the document.
4. Press Tab to move the insertion point to the next cell, and then type the index entry for the text that appears in the first column.
5. Repeat steps 3 and 4 for every index entry.
6. Save the file.

Once you've created the concordance file, follow these steps to have Word mark the index entries in the document:

1. Choose Insert ➢ Index And Tables to display the Index page in the Index And Tables dialog box.
2. Choose AutoMark to display the Open Index AutoMark File dialog box, select the name of the concordance file, and then choose Open.

Although marking index entries is a manual process, Word 2000 automates the creation of the index and will update it on request. Word automatically inserts the XE (Index Entry) field code for each marked entry. You can either mark the entries individually or have Word mark every instance of the same entry.

To mark the first index entry, follow these steps:

1. Select the text you want to include in the index, and then press Alt+Shift+X to display the Mark Index Entry dialog box shown in Figure 11.5.

2. The selected text appears in the Main Entry text box. If necessary, edit the text so it appears as you want it in the index.

3. To place subentries below the main index entry when the index is generated, type up to two additional entries, separated by a colon, in the Subentry text box. For example, when the main entry is "Graphics," type **text box:AutoShape** to include both of those topics below the Graphics topic in the index.

4. Choose one of the following options in the Options area to specify what type of index entry you want the marked text to be:

   Cross-Reference: Adds the cross-reference text you type to the index entry instead of the page number. When you select this option, type the name of another index entry after "See" in the corresponding text box. For example, if the main entry is "text box," type **graphics** after "See."

   Current Page: Automatically adds the page number after the marked entry.

   Page Range: Allows you to select a previously named bookmark, which defines text that spans multiple pages, in the adjacent drop-down list.

5. To add bold or italic formatting to the entry's page number, check the Bold or Italic check box in the Page Number Format area.

6. Choose one of the following to mark the index entry:

   Mark: Labels only the selected text in your document as an index entry.

   Mark All: Labels every occurrence of the selected text in your document.

 NOTE   You can also display the Mark Index Entry dialog box by choosing Insert ➢ Index And Tables, and then choosing Mark Entry.

The Mark Index Entry dialog box will stay open while you return to your document and select the next text you want to appear in the index. When you click back in the dialog box, the selected text will appear in the Main Entry text box.

PART

II

Creating Dazzling
Documents in Word

Use the Mark Index Entry dialog box to create several different types of entries for an index in the current document.

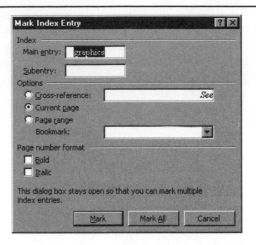

 NOTE A cross-reference index entry will only occur once in the index, so you can Mark but not Mark All cross-references.

When you are finished marking entries, get up from your chair and stretch for a minute. It's a tedious process but well worth it because Word will use the marked index entries to automatically generate the index.

When you're ready to generate the index, follow these steps:

1. Press Ctrl+End to move the insertion point to the last page of your document, and then enter a heading for the index. Press Enter a couple of times to leave some space after the heading.

2. Choose Insert ➤ Index And Tables to display the Index And Tables dialog box shown in Figure 11.6.

3. Choose any of the following options to specify how you'd like to format the index:

   • To specify how all subentries will appear below main entries, select one of the options in the Type area. Indented places subentries below main entries; Run-In places subentries on the same line as main entries.

   • Adjust the value in the Columns text box to specify the number of columns that will appear in the index. Choose Auto to have the index appear with the same number of columns as the document.

   • Select the language for the index in the Language drop-down list.

   • Check the Right Align Page Numbers box to have Word place the entries' page numbers along the right margin of the page or column. Then select dots, dashes, underline, or (none) as the character that appears before the right-aligned page numbers.

- Select the styles to apply to the index in the Formats drop-down list. If you choose From Template, choose Modify to display the Style dialog box, and then make any necessary changes to the selected index style.

4. When the sample index in the Print Preview area appears with the formatting you want for your index, choose OK to generate the index in the position of the insertion point.

FIGURE 11.6

Display the Index page in the Index And Tables dialog box when you are ready to generate the index.

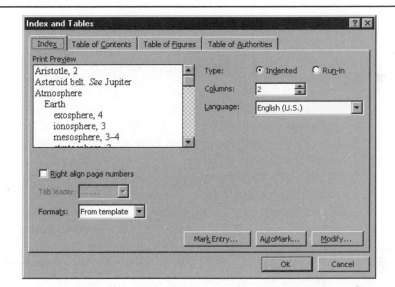

NOTE Apply a heading style to the index heading if you want to include it in your table of contents later. See "Generating a Table of Contents," later in this chapter, to learn about creating a table of contents.

Word gathers the marked index entries and then uses them to create the index. A continuous section break mark is automatically inserted before and after the index. Go through each entry in the index to make sure it says what you want it to say and that the references are accurate. If you find any errors, you can fix them in the index, but any changes made to the index itself will be lost if you regenerate the index. Instead, make any necessary changes in the Index Entry (XE) fields inserted in the document, and then regenerate the index.

PART

II

Creating Dazzling
Documents in Word

To regenerate the index after making changes, follow these steps:

1. Choose Insert ➤ Index And Tables, and then choose OK to regenerate the index.

2. Word will select the existing index and display a dialog box asking whether you want to replace it. Choose Yes.

If you edit the document after you generate the index, some of the page numbers in the index may no longer be correct. You can update the index without regenerating it because the entire index is a field. (The index that appears is the result of entering the INDEX field code at the insertion point.) To update the index, click anywhere in it, and then press F9. Any edits or formatting you've applied directly to the index will be replaced when you update it.

Adding Hyperlinks to Make Navigation Easy

A *hyperlink,* a connection between two areas of a document or two different documents, is commonly used in Internet sites and other documents that are to be viewed online. When they click a hyperlink, users move to a different location in the same document, a different file, or even an address on the World Wide Web. For example, you can insert a hyperlink in a Word document that opens a PowerPoint presentation.

Hyperlinks are underlined and appear in a different font color. (If they don't stand out, no one knows to click them!) By default, hyperlinks appear in a blue font on your screen. Once the user clicks on the hyperlink, it changes to magenta.

 TIP Type the e-mail or Web page address directly in a Word document to have Word automatically insert the address as a hyperlink. If the address does not appear as a hyperlink, check the Internet And Network Paths With Hyperlinks check box on the AutoFormat As You Type and AutoFormat pages in the AutoCorrect dialog box.

There are several ways to create hyperlinks in your documents. The easiest way is to drag selected text or graphics from a Word document or PowerPoint slide, an Excel spreadsheet range, or an Access database object into your Word document. The document that contains the selection must be saved to a named file.

 When you drag the selection, Word automatically knows the location of the object you dragged. It is not necessary to create bookmarks in the destination document or to name ranges in the destination worksheet before you drag a selection.

To create a hyperlink by dragging selected text or a selected object, use the following steps:

1. Open the file that contains the text or other object, and also open the Word document in which a hyperlink is to be inserted.

2. Display both files on your screen.

3. Select the object to which the hyperlink will jump in the destination file.

4. Hold down the right mouse button and drag the selection into the position you want for the hyperlink in your Word file.

5. Choose Create Hyperlink Here.

If the two files are both Word files, use the Window ➢ Arrange All command to have the two open documents arranged horizontally on your screen. If the destination file is an Access, Excel, or PowerPoint file, open the file and display the location to which the hyperlink will jump, and then resize both applications' windows so you can see them on your screen.

 TIP You can also use the Clipboard to create a hyperlink. Copy the data or object to the Clipboard, and then position the insertion point where you want to create the hyperlink. Choose Edit ➢ Paste As Hyperlink to create the hyperlink in your Word document.

When you point to the hyperlink, the path to its destination file appears in a ScreenTip. If you position the insertion point within the hyperlink text, you can then edit it. Use the arrow keys to position the insertion point. If you use your mouse, selecting the hyperlink text can be a little tricky because you'll often jump to the destination file.

You can also insert a hyperlink to an e-mail or Web page address, specify descriptive text for the hyperlink in a ScreenTip, or browse for the exact path of a hyperlink's destination file using the options available in the Insert Hyperlink dialog box.

To use the Insert Hyperlink dialog box to insert a hyperlink, follow these steps:

1. Position the insertion point where you want to insert the hyperlink, and then choose Insert ➢ Hyperlink to display the Insert Hyperlink dialog box, similar to the one shown in Figure 11.7.

2. Click Existing File Or Web Page in the Link To area.

3. Specify the following options for the destination:

   • Type the path to the file or the address of the Web page in the Type The File Or Web Page Name text box. Alternatively, select one of the files or Web pages that appear in the Or Select From List box. The addresses in the list box change depending on whether Recent Files, Browsed Pages, or Inserted Links is selected to the left of the list box.

- Choose File to display the Link To File dialog box when you want to browse for a file. Then select the name of the file, and choose OK to place its exact path in the Type The File Or Web Page Name text box.

- Choose Web Page to open your default browser. Then select one of the Web addresses in the Address drop-down list, and press Enter to place that address in the Type The File Or Web Page Name text box. If necessary, close or minimize your browser to return to the Insert Hyperlink dialog box.

- Choose Bookmark to display the Select Place In Document dialog box. Then select the name of a heading or a bookmark or one of the locations listed in the Select An Existing Place In The Document list box, and choose OK to place that location's address in the Type The File Or Web Page Name text box.

4. The address that is placed in the Type The File Or Web Page Name list box appears in the Text To Display text box. To have descriptive text appear as the hyperlink in your document, type it in the Text To Display text box.

5. By default, the address in the Type The File Or Web page Name text box appears as the ScreenTip for the hyperlink. Choose ScreenTip to display the Set Hyperlink ScreenTip dialog box, type the descriptive text that will appear in the ScreenTip when you point to the hyperlink in the ScreenTip Text box, and then choose OK.

6. Choose OK to insert the hyperlink in your document.

FIGURE 11.7

Use the options in the Insert Hyperlink dialog box to insert a hyperlink to a file or a Web page, an e-mail address, or a location in the current document, or to create a new document as the hyperlink's destination.

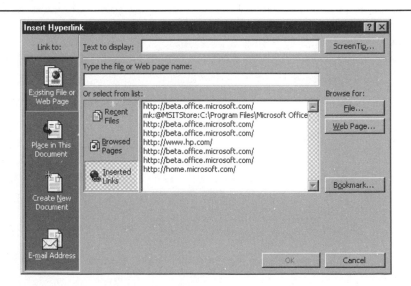

The following options are unique to the other destinations available in the Link To area in the Insert Hyperlink dialog box:

Place In This Document: The Select A Place In This Document list box appears in the Insert Hyperlink dialog box. Select a heading, bookmark, or Top Of The Document as the hyperlink's destination within the active document.

Create New Document: Type a name for the new document in the Name Of New Document text box. Alternatively, choose Change to display the Create New Document dialog box, select the folder for the new document, type its name in the File Name text box, and then choose OK. Choose Edit The New Document Later or Edit The New Document Now in the When To Edit area.

E-mail Address: Type the e-mail address in the E-mail Address text box, and then type the subject of the e-mail message in the Subject text box. Alternatively, select one of the e-mail addresses listed in the Recently Used E-mail Addresses box to enter it in the E-mail Address text box.

Creating Dazzling Documents in Word

Generating a Table of Contents

Creating a table of contents (TOC) is similar to creating an index. Instead of marking entries into the table of contents, you apply Word's built-in heading styles to the text that is to appear in the TOC. Word automatically selects the document's headings to list in the table of contents. If you did not apply heading styles when you created the document, you can go through the document and apply them before you create the table of contents.

One of Word 2000's new features is that the document headings are entered as hyperlinks in the table of contents. You can point to one of the headings to move immediately to that position in the document. If the document is to be printed, display it in Print Layout view so the page numbers appear along with the headings. If the document is to be viewed online, display it in Web Layout view so that the headings are displayed as hyperlinks.

To create the table of contents, follow these steps:

1. Position the insertion point at the beginning of the document, and then choose Insert ➤ Index And Tables to display the Index And Tables dialog box, shown in Figure 11.6.

2. Click the Table Of Contents tab to display its page in the Index And Tables dialog box, shown in Figure 11.8.

3. Choose any of the following formats for your TOC:

- Check the Show Page Numbers box to have page numbers appear when the document is viewed in Print Layout view or when the document is printed.

- Check the Right Align Page Numbers box to have displayed or printed page numbers aligned along the right margin of the page. Select (none), dots, dashes, or underline as the character to appear before the page number.

- Select the formatting you want for the table of contents in the Formats drop-down list. If you choose From Template, choose Modify to display the Style dialog box, and then make any necessary changes to the TOC headings.

- Adjust the value in the Show Levels text box to display the number of heading levels you want to appear in the table of contents.

4. Choose OK to generate the table of contents.

FIGURE 11.8

The Table Of Contents page in the Index And Tables dialog box shows you samples of the table of contents in both Print Layout and Web Layout views.

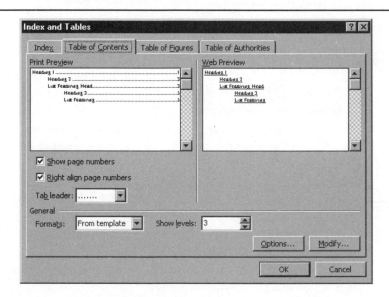

When you generate the table of contents, a page break is inserted above the insertion point, and Word enters the TOC field code on the new page.

MASTERING THE OPPORTUNITIES

Using Other Options to Create a Table of Contents

You can also create a table of contents using existing styles (other than heading styles) in the document or TC (table of contents entry) fields or both. If you want to use other styles, simply assign each style a TOC level, which replaces the heading styles' TOC levels when the table is generated. To create table of contents entries exactly as you want them to appear in the table of contents, insert TC field codes in your document.

Follow these steps to use either option to create a table of contents:

1. Choose Insert ➢ Index And Tables ➢ Options to display the Table Of Contents Options dialog box.
2. Check the Styles check box to have Word build the table from available styles in your document, and then assign each style the appropriate TOC level by typing the level in the adjacent TOC Level text box.
3. Check the Table Entry Fields check box if you inserted TC field codes in the document.
4. Choose OK to return to the Index And Tables dialog box.
5. Choose the formatting for the table of contents from any of the available options.
6. Choose OK to generate the table.

Modifying a TOC

Although you can directly edit the text in the table of contents, any changes you make will be lost if you regenerate the table or update the TOC field code. In addition, you need to use the arrow keys to move to the text you want to edit because each table of contents entry is a hyperlink.

Generally, it's a good idea to update the entire table of contents instead of editing it. For example, if you edit the text of the document, the page numbers in the table of contents may be incorrect. When you want to update the table, move the insertion point into it and press F9. If the page numbers still don't seem to be correct, check the following:

Index entry fields are formatted as hidden text. To hide them and other hidden text so they do not appear in the document (and increase its onscreen length), click the Show/Hide ¶ button on the Standard toolbar. Then update the table of contents.

Remove any hidden section or page breaks from the document, and then update the table of contents.

If you decide that you want fewer (or additional) heading levels to appear in your TOC, choose Insert ➤ Index And Tables ➤ Table Of Contents, and adjust the number of heading levels. You can also change the tab leader by selecting a different one from the Tab Leader list. When you click OK, the TOC will regenerate with the requested number of levels. In some documents you may even want two TOCs—one with all heading levels and one with only the first-level headings.

Managing Large Documents

As a policy manual, personnel handbook, report, contract, or similar document gets longer, it uses more resources to open, save, or print. It takes forever to scroll down a couple of pages and editing becomes a nightmare. With a little foresight, you can avoid this dilemma by starting with an outline and then dividing the entire document, called the *master document,* up into various related documents, called *subdocuments*. You—and others in your work group—can then work with subdocuments as autonomous entities. However, at any point, you can work with the entire master document, so you can have continuous page numbering, add headers and footers, create a table of contents, attach an index, and insert cross-references—all those things you cannot do with individual, unrelated documents.

What if you're already 10 chapters into a large document? Don't despair—those kind people at Microsoft thought ahead for you. Word 2000 can combine separate documents into one master document and divide one long document into several subdocuments. So there's no excuse for working with a document that's out of control—the remedy is right at your fingertips.

Creating Master Documents and Subdocuments

To create a new master document from scratch, open a new document, and then display it in Outline view. To change to Outline view, choose View ➤ Outline, or click the Outline View button next to the horizontal scroll bar.

In Word 2000, the Master Document tools appear on the Outlining toolbar. Create an outline just as you normally would (see "Creating an Outline" in Chapter 8), using the same heading level for each section that you want subdivided into its own document.

When you have finished creating the outline, select the headings and text you want to split into subdocuments. Click the Create Subdocument button on the Outlining toolbar, and Word will create individual subdocuments using the highest level heading text you selected as the subdocument name.

The master document will show each subdocument in a box with a small subdocument icon in the upper left corner when displayed in Master Document view (the default). Click the Master Document View button on the Outlining toolbar to display the master document in Outline view. When you do, the subdocument icon and box no longer appear, and the display shows the section break marks that Word inserted before each selected heading when you created subdocuments.

When you save the master document, each subdocument is automatically saved in a separate file in the same folder as the master document, using the first part of the heading text as the filename. In addition, each subdocument automatically becomes a hyperlink in the master document. When the master document is open, you can simply click the hyperlink of a subdocument to open it for editing. In addition, you can open a subdocument when the master document is not open, using the same methods you would use to open any other file.

 NOTE To open a subdocument before you save the master document, double-click its subdocument icon.

 The primary purpose of creating a master document is to be able to work with discrete sections of the document. It makes sense, then, to collapse the master document so that just the document names are visible. Word automatically displays the master document with collapsed subdocuments when you open the master document file. If you want to see all the text in the entire document, click the Expand Subdocuments button on the Outlining toolbar. The button is a toggle switch—clicking the Collapse Subdocuments button on the Outlining toolbar will collapse the subdocuments again.

 The subdocuments of a master document can be *locked,* which means that they are read-only files. Read-only files can be viewed, but no changes can be saved to them. To lock a subdocument, click the Lock Document button on the Outlining toolbar. Click the Lock Document button again to unlock a locked subdocument.

 NOTE In Master Document view, subdocuments are collapsed by default and always appear to be locked—the subdocument icons have padlocks—even if they are not. To see whether the subdocuments in a master document actually are locked, click the Expand Subdocuments button on the Outlining toolbar.

Word automatically locks an open subdocument. If someone opens a subdocument that is already open, it opens as a read-only document. In addition, subdocuments that are shared as read-only are locked, as are subdocuments stored on a read-only file share.

When the master document is expanded, you can work with it as if it were one document by switching to Normal or Print Layout view. You can apply page numbering, insert headers and footers, a table of contents, index, cross-references, and adjust styles just as you would in a normal document. The styles in the master document's template are used for all the subdocuments when the document is printed. If you want to use different formatting for a subdocument, change the formatting in the master document section that contains the subdocument. The page numbers, borders, headers, margins, and number of newspaper columns can be changed in individual sections of a master document.

You can use a different template in a subdocument. To do so and then print the subdocument with different styles from those in the master document, open the subdocument in its own window and print it from there.

NOTE You can also change the section's formatting by opening the subdocument in its own window and then making the changes.

Converting Existing Documents

For a document to be converted to a master document, you must apply Word's built-in heading styles to some of the text so you can work with it in Outline view. After you have applied heading styles, you can switch to Master Document view and follow the same steps you would to create a new master document.

If you have several documents that you want to combine into one master document, follow these steps:

1. Open a new, blank document or a document based on the template you want to use for the master document.

2. Position the insertion point where you want to insert an existing document, and then click the Insert Subdocument button on the Master Document toolbar to display the Open dialog box.

3. Select the name of the file to insert, and then choose Open.

Click a subdocument's icon to select it. Hold down the Shift key while you click to simultaneously select another subdocument. Hold down the Ctrl key while you click the subdocument icon to select all of the subdocuments in the master document. Once you've selected files, you can merge two subdocuments into one, split one subdocument into two, delete a subdocument, or convert a subdocument into master document text:

 To merge two subdocuments, select both files and click the Merge Subdocuments button on the toolbar.

 To split one subdocument into two, place the insertion point where you want to split and click the Split One Subdocument button.

To delete a subdocument, select it and press the Delete key.

 To convert a subdocument to master document text, select it and click the Remove Subdocument button.

Printing Master Documents

When all the text is entered in the subdocuments and all the formatting is applied to the master document along with a table of contents, index, and any other document items, you are ready to print the master document. Word 2000 allows you to print the entire master document or only specified details, depending on the heading levels and text displayed on your screen.

To print the entire master document, do the following:

 1. Click the Expand Subdocuments button on the Outlining toolbar to expand the subdocuments.

2. Change the display to Normal or Print Layout view.

3. Print as you would any other document.

To print only some of the details of the master document, follow these steps:

 1. Click the Expand Subdocuments button on the Outlining toolbar to expand the subdocuments.

2. Use the Show Heading *No.* buttons and the Expand and Collapse buttons on the Outlining toolbar to specify the amount of detail you want to print.

3. Print the document as you would any other document.

What's Next

In the final chapter about Word, you will learn how to work in a workgroup. Chapter 12 discusses saving multiple versions of the same document and tracking the changes made to it. You will learn how to accept or reject changes, highlight text, and insert comments in an online document. You will also see how to protect your document from unauthorized use and how to route the document to others in your workgroup.

PART

II

Creating Dazzling
Documents in Word

CHAPTER 12

Using Word in a Workgroup

Many companies today use a team approach to completing word processing projects. For example, several people may create and edit your company's benefits manual. Working together online saves, time, money, energy, and paper. Although two (or more) heads are better than one, mistakes can occur when many people access a single document file. Word 2000, along with the other Office components, is designed to be used online by workgroups.

Using the Reviewing Tools

Word's Reviewing tools, including versioning, tracking changes, comments, and the highlighter, allow you to keep your online documents intact while permitting others' input. In addition, Word allows you to protect a document so that the tracked changes and comments cannot be edited. The Reviewing tools can be found on the Reviewing toolbar. To display it, right-click any displayed toolbar, and then choose Reviewing.

Saving Multiple Versions of a Document

One of Word's most useful features for working with others is its ability to save multiple versions of a document. For example, if you are sending an online document to be reviewed by others, you can save the original version, and then save the version that includes the changes suggested by reviewers.

In times past, if you wanted to change an existing document and keep the original intact, you had to remember to save the revised document using a different name. If you're like most people, there were those inevitable times when you saved without thinking and, with one click of the mouse, wiped out any vestige of the original document. Word's versioning feature allows you to save multiple versions of a document within the document itself and open a different version to edit.

NOTE Word saves only the changes that were made to the document, not the entire document, when you save a version.

To save a version of the active document, follow these steps:

   1. Click the Save Version button on the Reviewing toolbar to display the Save Version dialog box, shown in Figure 12.1. The date, time, and name of the person creating this version are displayed at the top of the dialog box.

2. Type any comments you want to make about this version of the document in the Comments On Version text box.

3. Choose OK. The Versions icon appears on the right side of the status bar to let users know that this document contains a version.

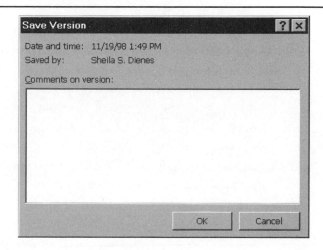

Save Version

Date and time: 11/19/98 1:49 PM
Saved by: Sheila S. Dienes

Comments on version:

OK   Cancel

PART

II

Creating Dazzling
Documents in Word

You can also have Word automatically save a version of the document each time it is closed, which is especially useful if you need to keep track of who made changes to the document and when they were made. The most recently saved version of the document will open by default the next time you open the file.

Word also allows you to manage the versions in other ways. For example, you can see how many versions of the document have been saved, the date and time each was saved, and the name of the person who created each version. The most recent version appears highlighted at the top of the list.

Any existing version can be saved to a separate file. When the version is in a separate file, you can make sure that the reviewers are evaluating the most recent version (by circulating only that version), or you can compare it to another file to find changes that were made with Track Changes turned off. You can also delete a saved version, which is useful when your file becomes large and seems to work slower.

TIP When you save a document as a Web page (Chapter 44), any versions it contains will be lost. Save the file as a regular document before you save it as a Web page, and use the document file to create any subsequent versions.

Use the following options to manage your versions and the size of the file:

1. Choose File ➤ Versions to display the Versions In *Document* dialog box, shown in Figure 12.2.

2. Check the Automatically Save A Version On Close box to have Word save the document each time the file is closed.

3. Choose Save Now to display the Save Version dialog box (shown in Figure 12.1) if you want to save the current version of the file. Alternatively, highlight the version you want to manage, and then use any of the following options:

    • Choose Open to open the selected version in another window on your screen. (The document is also open and appears in its own window.) Save the open version to a named file on your disk.

    • Choose Delete to delete the selected version when you no longer need it, and then choose Yes in the message box that appears to confirm the deletion.

    • Choose View Comments to display a message box containing all of the comments that were entered by the reviewer when the selected version was saved.

4. If necessary, choose Close to return to your document.

 NOTE If you deleted a version of the document, you must save the document before the version is actually deleted.

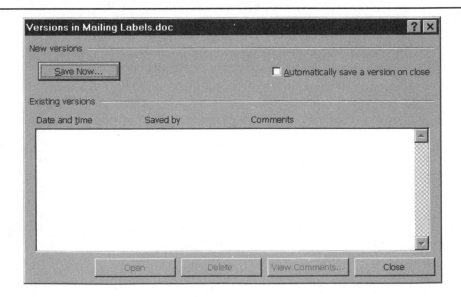

FIGURE 12.2

Use the Versions In Document dialog box to request automatic version-saving and to manage versions in other ways.

Tracking Changes to a Document

Although saving each version of a document is helpful, it's still difficult to identify where all the changes were made. To make that easier, Word can track each change to a document and allow you to accept or reject individual revisions or all revisions in one fell swoop.

To begin tracking changes, use one of the following methods to turn on the feature:

 Click the Track Changes button on the Reviewing toolbar. The button is a toggle switch, so you can click it again to turn off the Track Changes feature.

 Right-click the dimmed TRK option on the status bar and select Highlight Changes. This option is also a toggle switch, so you use the same method to turn off Track Changes when you are finished editing the document.

By default, when Word's Track Changes feature is turned on, any changes to the document are indicated on your screen and will be printed when you print the document. Word formats inserted text so that it appears both underlined and in a different color; deleted text appears with a strikethrough character through it and in a different color; and a vertical line in the outside margin indicates each line in the document where text has been changed. You can have Word continue to track changes in these ways, or you can modify the feature so that changes are not indicated either on the screen or in the printed document. To do so, follow these steps:

1. Choose Tools ➢ Track Changes ➢ Highlight Changes or right-click the TRK icon on the status bar and choose Highlight Changes to display the Highlight Changes dialog box, shown in Figure 12.3.

2. If necessary, check the Track Changes While Editing check box to turn on Word's Track Changes feature.

3. To specify how Word indicates changed text, do any of the following:

   • Clear the Highlight Changes On Screen check box to remove the on-screen color and underline from the font as changes are made to the document.

   • Clear the Highlight Changes In Printed Document box to remove the color and underline from the font when the document is printed.

   • Clear both check boxes to have Word show no visible signs in the document that the Track Changes feature is on. The TRK icon on the status bar is active, indicating the changes are being tracked.

4. Choose OK to have Word track changes in the manner indicated.

FIGURE 12.3

Specify how you want Word to indicate changes to a document in the Highlight Changes dialog box.

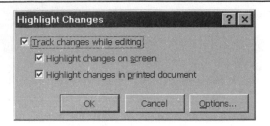

As other people open the document, changes they make will appear in different colors (up to eight authors can work on one document before colors repeat). If you would prefer that all inserted text appear in one color and all deleted text in another, you can select a color for each. In addition, you can change the way Word indicates inserted and deleted text, changed formatting, or changed lines of text in the document.

Follow these steps to specify the formats and characters you want Word to use when tracking changes:

1. Right-click the TRK icon on the status bar and then choose Options, or choose Tools ➢ Options and display the Track Changes page, shown in Figure 12.4.

2. Choose any of the following options in the corresponding Mark drop-down list to specify the formatting or character applied to any changes in the document:

- In the Inserted Text area, select (none), Bold, Italic, Underline, or Double Underline as the format to apply to inserted text.

- In the Deleted Text area, select either Hidden or Strikethrough as the format to apply to text that is deleted from the document. Alternatively, choose ^ or # to replace the characters that are deleted if you want to prevent others from reading deleted text.

- In the Changed Formatting area, select (none), Bold, Italic, Underline, or Double Underline as the format to apply to text when the actual formatting has been changed.

- In the Changed Lines area, select (none), Left Border, Right Border, or Outside Border as the location for Word to insert a vertical line in the margin when any changes have been made to a line of text.

3. To change the color for any of the editing changes listed above, choose one of the following options in the corresponding Color drop-down list:

- Select the color in which all inserted text, deleted text, and text whose formatting is changed appears, and select the color for the vertical line that appears in the margin beside a line where text was changed. Or choose Auto to display all text changes in the default font color (usually black).

- Choose the By Author option to have Word assign a different color to the first eight reviewers who insert text, delete text, or change the formatting applied to the document text.

4. When the Preview area for each change appears with the formatting and characters you want, choose OK.

FIGURE 12.4

Display the Track Changes tab when you want to modify the way changes to the document appear on your screen and in printed copies.

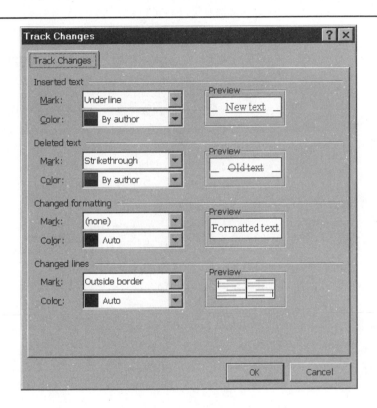

To display information about a change, just point to the marked text to see a Screen-Tip that indicates the type of change, who made it, and the time and date it was made.

Accepting or Rejecting Changes

After a document has been edited by all reviewers, you can accept or reject the changes. The easiest way to accept or reject changes is to use the following buttons on the Reviewing toolbar:

  Click the Previous Change button to select the change preceding the position of the insertion point, or the Next Change button to select the change following the position of the insertion point.

Click the Accept Change button to agree to the selected change, or on the Reject Change button to remove the proposed change and return the document to its original text in this instance.

 TIP Click the Undo button on the Standard toolbar immediately after accepting or rejecting a change to return it to the original edit.

Another way to accept or reject changes is to use the options available in the Accept Or Reject Changes dialog box. You can either scroll through and accept or reject each proposed change, or accept or reject all of the proposed changes simultaneously.

To use the Accept Or Reject Changes dialog box to accept or reject proposed changes:

1. Right-click the status bar TRK icon and then choose Accept Or Reject Changes, or choose Tools ➢ Track Changes ➢ Accept Or Reject Changes to display the Accept Or Reject Changes dialog box, shown in Figure 12.5.

2. Choose one of the following options in the View area:

   Changes With Highlighting: Displays the document with the proposed changes highlighted according to the highlighting options you specified.

   Changes Without Highlighting: Displays the document as it would look if you accepted all the proposed changes.

   Original: Displays the document as it would look if you rejected all the proposed changes.

3. Click the ←Find or →Find button to select the previous or next proposed change.

4. Choose one of the following options:

   Accept: Changes the selection so that it becomes regular document text.

   Reject: Removes the proposed change and returns the document to its original text.

   Accept All: Alters every proposed change into regular document text.

   Reject All: Removes every proposed change and returns the document to its original text.

   Undo: Reverses the last of the above actions you performed.

Or click →Find to move to the next revision or ←Find to move to the previous revision without either accepting or rejecting the current one.

5. When you have reached the end of the document, choose OK to begin searching for changes at the beginning of the document, or Cancel to remove the message box.

6. Choose Close to return to your document.

7. If you don't want any more marked revisions, turn off the Track Changes feature.

FIGURE 12.5

Display the Accept Or Reject Changes dialog box to accept or reject individual changes or to simultaneously accept or reject all proposed changes.

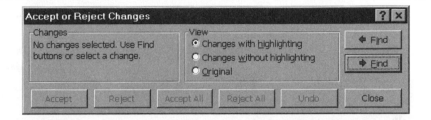

 TIP Change the view of the document to Changes Without Highlighting to see how the document will look before you choose Accept All. Change the view to Original to see how the document will look before you choose Reject All.

Inserting Comments

When you're creating or editing a document with others, it's often valuable to be able to make comments that aren't part of the printed document but can be viewed on-screen. Word 2000's Comments feature fits the bill. You can insert comments, view comments from one or all reviewers, and print the comments.

When you insert a comment, the word immediately preceding the insertion point is highlighted and your initials and a comment number appear in the text. The comment pane opens at the bottom of the screen with the insertion point beside the corresponding comment number so you can enter the text of your comment.

To insert a comment, follow these steps:

1. Position the insertion point where you want to place the comment, and then either click the Insert Comment button on the Reviewing toolbar or choose Insert ➤ Comment.

2. Type the text of your comment.

3. Press F6 or click in the document pane, and then repeat steps 1 and 2 to insert another comment.

4. Choose Close to remove the comment pane.

PART

II

Creating Dazzling
Documents in Word

To view the comment, just position the mouse pointer over the highlighted word for a moment—the insertion point will change to an I-beam with a note attached, and a second later the comment will appear in a box above the text.

Use the following buttons on the Reviewing toolbar to edit your comments:

 Click the Edit Comment button to display the comment pane to review comments or edit the text of a comment. Click the button again to close the comment pane.

 Click the Previous Comment button to move the insertion point to the preceding comment. If you continue pointing at the Previous Comment button, the comment will be displayed.

 Click the Next Comment button to move the insertion point to the following comment. If you continue pointing at the Next Comment button, the comment will be displayed.

 Click the Delete Comment button to delete the comment that contains the insertion point.

If you want to print the comments in a document, choose File ➤ Print to display the Print dialog box, choose Comments in the Print What drop-down list, and then choose OK. The comments will be printed consecutively along with the number of the page on which the comment is located.

Highlighting Text

Word 2000's highlighter is one of the easiest tools to use when you want to make sure that anyone reviewing an online document notices a particular section of text. Imagine using a highlighter pen, and you know almost everything you need to know to use this formatting feature.

To begin highlighting:

 1. If necessary, click the Highlight button drop-down arrow and select one of the fifteen colors in the palette. (Skip this step to accept the default highlight color.)

2. Click the Highlight button. The pointer will change into a highlighter pen with an I-beam attached.

3. Drag the pen over the text you want to highlight.

Because the highlighter includes an I-beam, you can highlight text as you select it. For example, double-click to highlight a word, and triple-click to highlight a paragraph.

When you are finished highlighting in your document, click the Highlight button again to turn off highlighting. If you need to remove highlighting from selected text, change the highlight color to None, and then select the text.

TIP Some highlighting colors obscure the underlying text. Use a light color if you intend to print a document with highlighting on a monochrome or dot matrix printer.

Adding Comments Using Document Summary Information

Every Windows file has a Properties sheet that saves information about the file—when it was created, who created it, when it was last modified, and so on. File properties help you to identify, locate, and organize your files. Word 2000 takes properties one step further by letting you enter detailed information about the document that others can view from the Open dialog box without actually opening the document.

 NOTE Excel spreadsheet files, Access database files, and PowerPoint presentation files also have a Properties sheet where you can enter detailed information about each file.

There are three different types of file properties:

- *Automatic* properties are those that Word handles for you. For example, the size of the file and the date it was created are both automatic properties.

- *Preset* properties are those for which you can enter specific text information— for example, the title, subject, comments, and keyword information.

 NOTE Word's AutoSummarize feature, a tool for generating executive summaries or abstracts of documents, automatically fills in the properties for keywords and comments. To disable this feature, choose Tools ➢ AutoSummarize, and then clear the Update Document Statistics check box.

- *Custom* properties are those you select from a built-in set of named properties, or those you create yourself. Custom properties can be linked to specific items in a file. For example, you can link a bookmark in a Word document to a custom property, and then search for all Word files that contain a property with that bookmark.

 NOTE To display the Document Name Properties dialog box when you save each file for the first time, choose Tools ➢ Options ➢ Save. Check the Prompt For Document Properties box and choose OK.

To display and add to the preset document properties:

1. Choose File ➢ Properties, and then, if necessary, click the Summary tab to display the page shown in Figure 12.6.

2. Enter any of the following information in the corresponding text box:

   • The Title text allows you to search for the file based on the text entered. The title can be different from the filename.

   • The Subject text should contain a short description of the main topic of the document. The file's subject allows you to group it with files about the same subject, so you can search for all files about a particular topic.

   • Type the name of the document author in the Author text box. The username for the computer on which it was created is entered automatically.

   • The Manager text is used to group files with the same project manager. Users can search for all the files that have the same manager when looking at a particular project.

   • The Company text box contains the name of the company that was entered when Office 2000 was installed on that computer. Type the name of the company for which the document was created so users can search for all documents relating to that company.

   • If projects are grouped into classes or categories, type the class name in the Category text box. Users can use the information provided to search for all files in that category.

   • Type the keywords to use when searching for this file in the Keywords text box.

   • Type any notes about the file in the Comments text box so users can search for the file based on its comments.

   • Type the base address for all hyperlinks in the document in the Hyperlink Base text box. The address can be an Internet URL, such as `http://www.microsoft.com`; a path on your hard drive, such as `C:\My Documents\Personal`; or a path to a server, such as `\\Server\Shared\Newsletter Projects`. To use the hyperlink base address, you must type the name of the file, not browse for it, in the Type The File Or Web Page Name in the Insert Hyperlinks dialog box.

3. Check the Save Preview Picture box to display a preview of the first page of the document (if it is a template) in the New dialog box.

4. Choose OK in the *Document Name* Properties dialog box.

FIGURE 12.6

Display or edit the properties of the active document on the Summary page in the Document Name Properties dialog box.

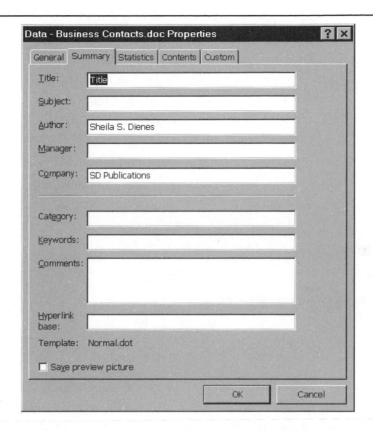

 NOTE When you check the Save Preview Picture box, it increases the size of the file. This option is not useful for a regular document file because you can preview it from within the Open dialog box before you open it.

To view the properties of an unopened document:

1. Click the Open button on the Standard toolbar to display the Open dialog box, and then highlight the name of the file.

2. Choose Tools ➤ Properties to display the *Document Name* Properties dialog box, and then click the Summary tab, if necessary.

 NOTE You can also click the Properties button in the Windows Explorer window to display the properties of the highlighted file.

PART

II

Creating Dazzling
Documents in Word

To preview the document:

1. Click the Open button on the Standard toolbar to display the Open dialog box, and then highlight the name of the file.

2. Click the Views drop-down list button to display its menu, and then choose Preview.

To search for all the files with a specified property, follow these steps:

1. Display the Open dialog box, and then choose Tools ➤ Find to display the Find dialog box.

2. Select the property that contains the information in the Property drop-down list.

3. Type the text for that property in the Value text box.

4. Choose Find Now to display the name of every file that contains the specified text as the value for the selected property.

Protecting Documents

Although you may not think there is much in your documents that anybody else would want, the sad truth is that your documents could become victims of corporate espionage or of unscrupulous colleagues out to pass your work off as their own. Add to that the risk that some well-meaning but misguided individual might revise one of your documents without your consent, and it's clear that it never hurts to be too careful.

Word 2000 provides the following options to protect your documents:

- You can require a password to open the document.

- You can require a password to modify the document. Users without the password can open a read-only copy of the document, which means that they cannot save any changes made to it.

- You can suggest, but not require, that users open the document as read-only so that, if they make changes, they must save it using a different name.

- You can prevent changes being made to a document you route for review, except for comments or tracked changes.

WARNING Word gives you a stern warning that password-protected documents cannot be opened if you forget the password. Take this warning seriously. If you forget the password for a document, it's gone for good.

Passwords, which are case-sensitive, must be at least eight characters but no more than 15 characters in length, and can consist of letters, numbers, spaces, and symbols. A combination of upper- and lowercase letters with numbers, spaces, and symbols is best—bl%Ack ?9 is an example of a difficult password to break. When you choose a password option, the password will not be visible on the screen as you type it. Instead, Word will ask you to reenter the password for verification.

 TIP Use one of several unique passwords for all of your documents. That way, if you forget the password for a document, you can try one of the other ones you are used to using to gain access to the file.

To apply document protection when you save a document for the first time, follow these steps:

1. Click the Save button on the Standard toolbar to display the Save As dialog box.

2. Choose Tools ➤ General Options to display the Save page, shown in Figure 12.7.

3. Choose any of the following options in the File Sharing Options For *Document* area:

   • Type a password in the Password To Open text box to allow those who know the password to open the document. Without the correct password, they will not be able to open the document.

   • Type a password in the Password To Modify text box to allow those who know the password to open the document and edit it. Users who don't know the password can open the file as a read-only document, and they can save any changes made to the document to a file with a different name.

   • Check the Read-Only Recommended box to have Word ask the user whether or not to open the document as a read-only document. You do not need to specify a password when you recommend that a document be opened as read-only.

4. Choose OK on the Save page. If you specified a password in step 3, the Confirm Password dialog box appears.

5. Type the password again in the Reenter Password To Open (or Modify) text box, and then choose OK.

6. Choose Save in the Save As dialog box.

PART

II

Creating Dazzling
Documents in Word

FIGURE 12.7

Display the Save page when you want to provide password protection or recommend read-only status to a document.

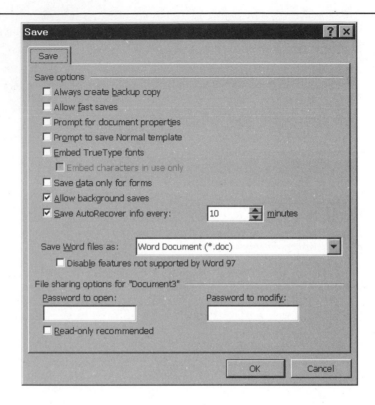

 NOTE To password-protect a file you've already saved, choose Tools ➤ Options and click the Save tab. Alternatively, choose File ➤ Save As and follow steps 2 through 4 above.

When you require a Password To Open, users will be prompted to input the password. Users who don't know the correct password for a file that requires a password to modify it can choose Read Only in the Password dialog box to open the document as read-only. Changes must be saved to a file with a different name.

To change or delete a password, open the document and reenter or delete the password on the Save page.

Protecting a Document You're Routing for Review

If you're sending a document to several people for review, you probably want to make sure that no one, whether by accident or intention, hides their changes by turning off the Track Changes option, or by accepting or rejecting changes. Or, you might want to make sure that the reviewers can insert comments, but not insert or delete any of the document's text. If the document is a form, you probably want to protect the form by making certain that only the data for the form's fields can be entered, but that users cannot alter the structure or labels in the form.

Follow these steps to protect your document against such revisions:

1. Open the document that is to be sent for review.

2. Check to see if the document contains more than one version. If it does, save the current version to a file with a different filename to prevent reviewers from seeing any previous versions of the document.

3. Choose Tools ➤ Protect Document to display the Protect Document dialog box shown in Figure 12.8.

4. Choose one of the following options:

   Tracked Changes: Tracks all changes made by reviewers and prevents reviewers from either turning off the Track Changes feature or from accepting or rejecting any changes. Reviewers can insert comments in the document.

   Comments: Prevents reviewers from making any changes to the document text. They can insert comments, however.

   Forms: Prevents reviewers making any changes to a document except in form fields or unprotected document sections.

5. If you chose Forms in step 4, choose Section, check the box before each section in the document you want to protect, and then choose OK. The sections are listed in the Protected Sections list box.

6. Type a password in the Password (Optional) text box, and then choose OK to allow reviewers who know the password to turn off the Track Changes feature, accept or reject changes, edit regular document text, or edit the structure or labels in a form. Retype the password in the Confirm Password dialog box, and then choose OK.

7. Save the document.

PART

II

Creating Dazzling
Documents in Word

FIGURE 12.8

The Protect Document dialog box contains options that allow you to protect your document or form from being changed by reviewers.

WARNING If you don't require a password, anyone can unprotect the document by just choosing Tools ≻ Unprotect Document.

When a password is required, users must enter the password before they can unprotect the document.

Routing Documents

Being connected to your colleagues—by a local or wide-area network or through electronic mail—makes sharing and exchanging documents a snap. Word 2000 even includes a routing slip, which specifies how to send an outbound document to reviewers. The routing slip can dispatch a document in either of the following ways:

- Use a routing slip to send a copy of the document to all reviewers simultaneously.

- Use a routing slip to send the same document to each reviewer, one at a time, in the order you specify, so subsequent reviewers can see the changes proposed by earlier reviewers. You can keep track of the location of the document when it is routed this way.

The routing slip can be saved with your document. A routed document is sent as an attachment to an e-mail message.

To attach a routing slip to a document, follow these steps:

1. Choose File ≻ Send To ≻ Routing Recipient to display the Routing Slip dialog box shown in Figure 12.9.

2. Click the Address button to display your Address Book. Highlight the name of a reviewer, and then choose To to place the name in the Message Recipients list box. Choose the name of each reviewer in this way, and then choose OK to return to the Routing Slip dialog box. Each name you selected appears in the To list box.

3. Type a subject for the e-mail message in the Subject text box.

4. Type the e-mail message to send with the attached document in the Message Text box.

5. Choose one of the following options to specify how the document is to be routed to the reviewers:

   One After Another: Sends the document to each reviewer, in the order in which they are listed in the To list box at the top of the Routing Slip dialog box. Click the ↑ or ↓ Move button to change the order of the highlighted name.

All At Once: Simultaneously sends a copy of the document to each person listed in the To list box.

6. Check either of the following check boxes as necessary:

Return When Done: Automatically sends the routed document back to you when the last reviewer closes it.

Track Status Automatically: Sends you an e-mail message when the document is sent to the next reviewer in the list when the document is routed using the One After Another option.

7. Select (none), Tracked Changes, Comments, or Forms as the method of protection for the document in the Protect For drop-down list.

8. Choose one of the following options to send the routing slip with the attached document:

Add Slip: Adds the routing slip to the document and closes the Routing Slip dialog box without sending the document. Choose this option when you want to edit the document before sending it.

Route: Adds the routing slip to the document and displays your Connection dialog box so you can send it and the attached document.

PART

II

Creating Dazzling Documents in Word

FIGURE 12.9

Use the options in the Routing Slip dialog box to send a document as an e-mail attachment to reviewers.

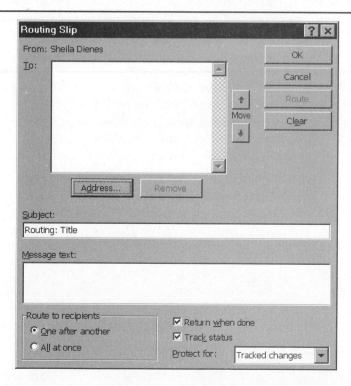

If you are routing the document to One After Another, choose File ➢ Send To ➢ Next Routing Recipient to open the Send dialog box, and then choose either of the following options:

Route Document To "*Reviewer Name*":   Sends the document to the next person on the list when you choose OK.

Send A Copy Of Document Without Using The Routing Slip: Opens Outlook Express to a new message with the document already attached. Select the name of the reviewer in the Address Book, type any accompanying e-mail message in the text area, and then choose Send to place the message in your Outbox. Choose Send And Receive to actually send the message.

Alternatively, choose File ➢ Send To ➢ Other Routing Recipient to open the Routing Slip dialog box again so that you can choose someone from the list or add someone new. As each reviewer finishes reviewing a document that is sent One After Another, he or she must select this option to send the document to the next reviewer in the list.

What's Next

In Part II, you've learned a great deal about using Word's features for all your documents, both printed and online. Part III moves on to using PowerPoint to create presentations. You'll see how easy it is to create a basic presentation (possibly incorporating text from a Word document), and then go on to more advanced topics such as formatting the slides and text in a presentation. You'll learn how to insert objects on a slide, how to create transitions for special effect, and how to animate your presentation. Finally, you'll learn how to use your workgroup to review your presentation online, prepare handouts and notes, and customize shows for different audiences.

PART III

And Now, Presenting PowerPoint!

LEARN TO:

- **Create basic presentations**

- **Format slides and text**

- **Add objects, transitions, and slide animation**

- **Prepare notes, handouts, and overhead transparencies**

- **Automate and narrate your presentation**

- **Present to a remote audience**

CHAPTER 13

Creating a Basic PowerPoint Presentation

FEATURING:

Steps to a quality presentation

Using the AutoContent Wizard

Entering and editing text

Using design templates or blank presentations

Voices in the room fall to a hush as you make your way to the podium. Several speakers have been before the board already, not one of them with an idea as good as the one you are about to present. You know what they say—it's all in the delivery. This is where you make it or break it. Gathering your notes and your wits, you take a deep breath and begin...

When you make your next presentation—whether it's to demonstrate a product, outline a project, or sell an idea—PowerPoint offers a way to take the focus off you and put it where it belongs—on what you have to say!

Use PowerPoint to create electronic slide shows that can enliven even the most apathetic crowd. If you don't want to give your presentation electronically, you can create vivid overhead transparencies and valuable audience handouts that will rival the most polished presentations. You can create presentations that run automatically, like those seen at kiosks at trade shows. With PowerPoint 2000's enhanced Web features, you can create Web-ready presentations for display on the Internet.

Whether you are creating slides for a departmental presentation or displaying information on the company Web site, PowerPoint allows you to quickly grab the attention of your audience and deliver your message in a most memorable way!

Steps to a Quality Presentation

Every PowerPoint presentation consists of a series of *slides*: text or objects displayed on a graphic background, as shown in Figure 13.1. You create your presentation by adding text and objects to slides.

FIGURE 13.1

A PowerPoint slide

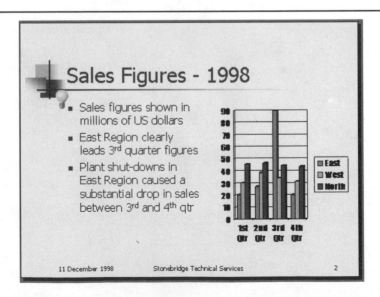

For every presentation you create in PowerPoint, you'll go through these steps:

1. Create the presentation, entering and editing text, and rearranging slides.

2. Apply a presentation design. Modify the design if necessary.

3. Format individual slides if you wish.

4. Add objects to the presentation.

5. Apply and modify transitions, animation effects, and links for electronic presentations.

6. Create audience materials and speaker notes.

7. Rehearse and add slide timings.

8. Present the presentation.

When you launch PowerPoint, the PowerPoint dialog box opens:

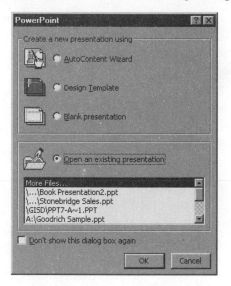

You can create a new presentation using one of the three listed options, or open an existing presentation. If you prefer to start PowerPoint without viewing this dialog box, you can disable it. To help you become familiar with PowerPoint, you'll create your first presentation using the AutoContent Wizard. The other creation methods are discussed later in this chapter.

PART

III

And Now, Presenting PowerPoint!

Creating a Presentation Using the AutoContent Wizard

The AutoContent Wizard is helpful for beginning users of PowerPoint because it generates an outline and applies a considerable amount of slide formatting automatically. It can also help the more advanced user who is not quite sure how to structure their presentation. As its name implies, it is designed to suggest content.

The AutoContent Wizard works like any of the other wizards in Office. You are taken through a series of steps with additional questions that help you design your presentation. In each step, click Next to advance or Back to return to a previous step. When you finish, the wizard leaves you in Normal view showing your first slide, the suggested outline, and a place to add speaker's notes if desired.

1. If you have just launched PowerPoint, choose AutoContent Wizard from the PowerPoint dialog box, and click OK to start the wizard. If PowerPoint is already running from an earlier presentation, or if you closed the PowerPoint dialog box, choose File ➤ New to open the New Presentation dialog box. On the General tab, choose the AutoContent Wizard. The first step explains the wizard. Click Next.

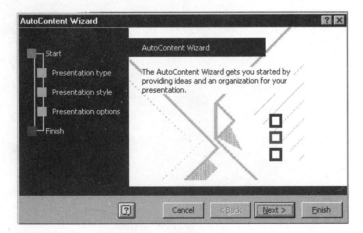

2. In the second step, choose the PowerPoint presentation type that most closely matches your topic. You can scroll through all the presentation types or narrow down your choices by selecting another category from the button list. Click Next when finished with this step.

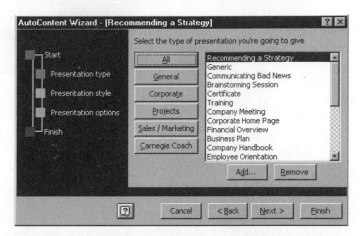

3. Next, select a style for your presentation. Will this presentation be displayed on the Internet? Will you be using black-and-white overheads? The choice you make here will not prohibit you from switching to another style later. Click Next.

 NOTE If you are creating an online presentation, refer to Chapter 43 for more on Power-Point's dynamic Web publishing features.

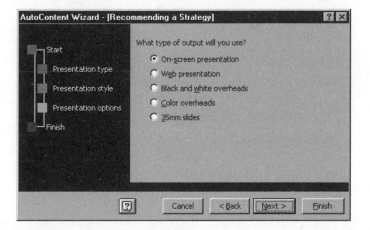

4. In the fourth step of the wizard, enter the title of your presentation. It will appear on the first slide. If there is additional information you would like to

include on every slide, such as a company name or the current date, activate those features here. Click Next.

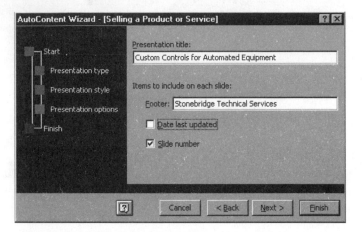

5. The Finish screen of the Wizard lets you know you have completed the process. Click Finish to have PowerPoint create and open this presentation.

Viewing Slides

One of the keys to working comfortably and efficiently in PowerPoint is understanding its different views. The term *view* refers to how you look at and work on your presentation. The PowerPoint 2000 window offers five different views: Normal view, Outline view, Slide view, Slide Sorter view, and Slide Show view.

Tri-Pane View   Three of the five views in PowerPoint are Tri-Pane windows. In other words, you can see three different aspects of your presentation within one window. The sections of the Tri-Pane window are different sizes so they emphasize different elements of the presentation. In Outline view, for example, the text of the outline occupies the largest pane.

In Figure 13.2, the AutoContent Wizard has just closed and the presentation has been opened in Normal view. The Outline (with text suggested by the AutoContent Wizard) is displayed on the left, your first slide is shown on the right, and a smaller pane at the bottom of the window allows you to add speaker's notes.

Five view buttons appear at the left end of the horizontal scroll bar; the Normal view button is pressed in, and the status bar displays the active part of the screen (that is, the pane where you last clicked). The status bar also shows which design template is applied to the displayed slide. The Drawing toolbar is on by default. You can hide it by choosing View ➤ Toolbars from the menu.

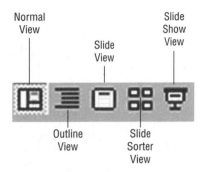

FIGURE 13.2

Normal view

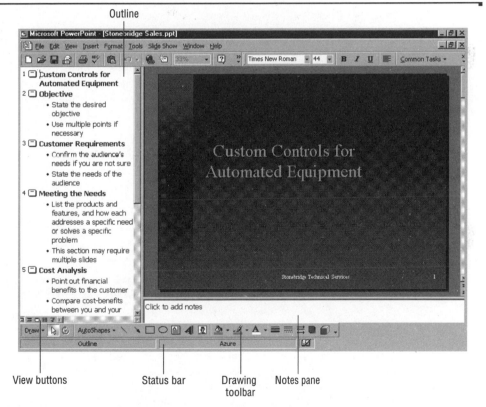

PART

III

And Now, Presenting
PowerPoint!

Each view provides a different way to look at and modify your presentation. Change views by clicking another of the view buttons at the bottom-left of the PowerPoint window.

In Outline view, presentation text is displayed in the main part of the Tri-Pane window. A miniature version of the selected slide is shown to the right of the outline. Below the slide miniature is an area for adding notes if you choose to use them. Your audience never sees these notes. They are for you to use while giving your presentation or as reminders while you are working on your presentation.

Slide view lets you work on one slide at a time. The main part of the Tri-Pane window displays the selected slide, while the left side of the window shows numbered slide icons with the selected slide shaded gray. The Notes pane is at the bottom of the main slide view window. If you don't see the Notes pane, point to the window divider directly above the five view buttons. Click and drag upward to open the Notes pane.

There are several different ways to move between slides in Slide view. You can click on the slide icon to the left to select a different slide to display, or you can use the vertical scroll bar on the right to move forward and backward through your slides. Notice that as you drag the vertical scroll bar, the slide number and slide title are displayed. If you wish to advance to the next or previous slide, you can use the buttons located at the bottom of the vertical scroll bar. You can also use the PgUp and PgDn keys to move one slide forward or one slide back.

 Slide Sorter view allows you to see many slides at once. The number of slides shown depends on the zoom setting. PowerPoint defaults to 75% zoom, which allows you to see approximately eight slides with display resolution settings of 800 × 600 pixels. If you wish to see more or fewer slides, adjust the zoom higher or lower, accordingly.

 The final button in this group is the Slide Show view. Click this button to see how a slide will look in full-screen mode. Click the mouse button or press Enter to move from one slide to the next; if a slide has multiple lines of text, you might have to click once for each line. After the last slide, PowerPoint will return to the previous view. Press the Esc key if you want to leave the slide show before the last slide.

When you switch from one view to another, the current slide remains current, regardless of view. If you are on the fifth slide in Slide view and switch to Outline view, the fifth slide will be selected. Clicking the Slide Show button begins the Slide Show with the fifth slide.

Which View Should You Use?

As you work in PowerPoint, you will discover that certain views lend themselves to certain types of formatting and editing. Similarly, you will find that there are certain types of editing that are possible *only* in a certain view.

In Outline view, the focus is on text, not objects or entire slides. Slide view lets you see one slide at a time; the focus is on text and objects, and how those items appear on each slide. In Slide Sorter view, the focus is on entire slides, their order, and how they appear during the presentation. Slide Show view lets you get a better idea of how your presentation will look when you eventually show it.

Continued

CONTINUED

In general, choose Outline view or Slide view to edit or insert text on slides. Use Slide view to insert objects and for animation (see Chapter 15 for information on slide animation). Choose Slide Sorter view to change the order of slides or to apply slide transitions (see Chapter 15 for more information on slide transitions). Slide Show view is best used to preview your presentation before showing it, or for full-screen preview of overheads. Normal view works well for those who find themselves frequently switching between Slide view and Outline view. Normal view lets you edit text either on the outline or on the slide, and the entire slide is displayed large enough to easily place objects and apply animation.

Working in Outline View

In the early stages of your presentation's development, you'll probably want to work in Outline view, which provides you with the most editing flexibility and allows you to see the text from multiple slides at one time. Figure 13.3 shows PowerPoint in Outline view.

The Standard and Formatting toolbars are available for editing functions. You work with text much the same as you would in Word.

FIGURE 13.3

Outline view

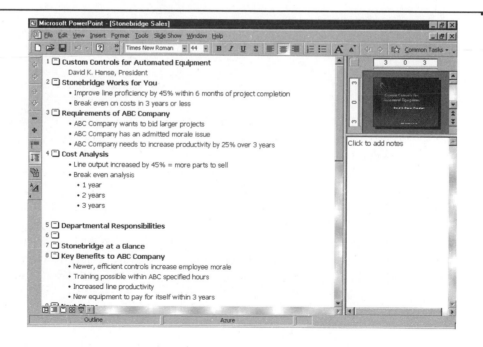

PART

III

And Now, Presenting PowerPoint!

NOTE When you begin your first presentation after installing PowerPoint, the toolbars may only be partially displayed. Drag a toolbar to a new location or click the drop-down arrow at the end of the toolbar to see more buttons.

Entering and Editing Text   You should replace the contents of the slides created by the AutoContent Wizard before making substantial formatting changes. Select the line of text you want to change by clicking on the bullet or slide icon in front of that line. Overtype with new text.

 Each level in the outline has a different size or shape of bullet. In PowerPoint 2000, font size appears the same at each level. PowerPoint automatically adjusts font size depending on the number of items contained on a slide, and the available space in the text box. You can enable or disable this feature by choosing Tools ➤ Options from the menu. On the Edit tab, click Autofit Text To Text Placeholder.

In a PowerPoint outline, there are five levels below the slide title:

Slide Title

■ Level 1

◆Level 2

◆Level 3

• Level 4

–Level 5

As you type in Outline view, press Enter at the end of each line of text. The next line will be on the same level as the previous line. If you are at the end of a bulleted point when you press Enter, the next line will start with a bullet at the same level as the previous one. If you position the insertion point at the end of a slide's title and press Enter, you will insert a new slide.

 Press the Tab key or click the Demote button to move to a lower level. By default, each level below the title is automatically bulleted. If you press Tab or click Demote again, you'll be at the next lower level. Text entered at any level other than the title level is a point or a subpoint.

 To move back a level, either hold Shift and press Tab or click the Promote button. Outline view in PowerPoint works the same as Outline view in Word. When you press return, you get a new line at the same level. To switch levels, you have to Promote or Demote.

You can also add new slides to follow the active slide in Outline view by clicking the New Slide button on the Formatting toolbar. The New Slide dialog box will open, and you will be prompted to select an AutoLayout. See "Selecting Slide Layouts" in the next section of this chapter.

Selecting Text, Lines, and Slides   Many of the methods used to select text in Word and Excel work here as well. Double-click a word to select and overtype it. To select a block of text, click at the beginning and Shift+click at the end. Most of the time, however, you will want to change an entire line. In that case, to select the line you want to change, place your mouse over the bullet or icon in front of the text and type the new text. You can also triple-click anywhere in the point to select and overtype it.

If you select a first-level point that has second-level points underneath it, the second-level points will also be selected. Click and drag to select only the main point. The sub-points will not be selected. Similarly, selecting the title using any method other than dragging selects the entire slide.

TIP   You can expand and collapse sections of the outline by right-clicking on a slide title and choosing Collapse from the Shortcut menu. To collapse multiple slides, select them and then right-click somewhere in the selection. To expand a collapsed section, right-click on it.

Checking Spelling   PowerPoint includes two spelling features. AutoSpell automatically underlines misspelled words that you enter. Right-click on an underlined word to see suggested correct spellings. Click the Spelling button on the Standard toolbar to check the spelling for an entire presentation. (For more information on spelling, see Chapter 2 and Chapter 5).

Using Find and Replace   Use PowerPoint's Find feature to locate a text string in your presentation. You can replace existing text strings with new text by using Find and Replace. Choose Edit ➤ Find from the menu bar to open the Find dialog box:

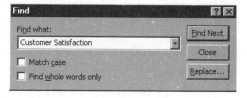

In the Find What text field, enter the text string that you want to find, and then set the Find options. Turn on the Match Case option to only find those text strings in the presentation that exactly match the string you enter. If you enter **Review** and turn on Match Case, Find will locate *Review* but not *review* or *REVIEW*. To find *Review* but not *Reviews*, turn on Find Whole Words Only.

If you use Find in Normal, Slide, or Outline view, clicking Find Next will move to and select the next text string that matches the Find what string. In Slide Sorter view, there isn't a Find Next button; instead, the button is Find All. Clicking Find All selects all the slides that contain the Find What string.

You can replace each occurrence of one text string with another. For example, you've created a presentation for the ABC Company; ABC has just come through a merger and been renamed DEF Company. You can find every occurrence of *ABC Company* and change it to *DEF Company*. Choose Edit ➤ Replace, or if the Find dialog box is already open, click the Replace button in the Find dialog box. Enter the string you want to find in Find What and the string you want to replace it with in Replace With.

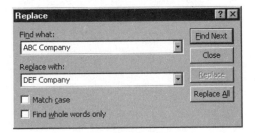

To replace all the occurrences, click Replace All. Or, you can work through the replacements one at a time. To find the next occurrence, click Find Next. Click Replace to make the replacement and Find Next to move to the next possible replacement. When you've replaced all occurrences of the text string, a message box appears to let you know that PowerPoint has searched the entire presentation and there aren't any more occurrences of the text string. A similar dialog box opens to let you know if the text string you entered in Find What doesn't appear in the presentation.

WARNING Be careful when using the Replace All button. You may make changes you do not want that damage other parts of the presentation. If you are not sure, walk through the presentation using Find Next, then select Replace to change that occurrence.

Inserting, Deleting, and Moving Points and Slides As you move your mouse over a bullet or slide icon, the pointer shape changes to a four-headed arrow, the tool for moving text and objects. To move a point (and all the subpoints underneath it), click and drag the bullet preceding that point. If you click a slide's icon, the entire slide—title and any body text—will be selected. Click and drag a slide icon to move the entire slide.

As you drag the selection toward its new location, the four-headed arrow is replaced by a two-headed arrow, and a horizontal line appears in the outline. If you drag-and-drop the horizontal line, the selected point(s) or slide will move to the new location. Figure 13.4 shows the horizontal line you see when moving a point or slide in Outline view.

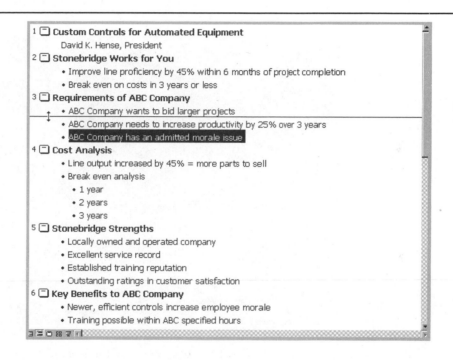

 NOTE You can also use the traditional cut/paste and copy/paste methods to move and copy sections of an outline.

When you use drag-and-drop to move text, be sure to move the mouse vertically. Horizontal dragging causes the selected line of text to change levels. If you drag a bulleted point horizontally to the right, a vertical line appears in the outline. Drag-and-drop the horizontal line to the right to demote the text, or to the left to promote the text.

If you drag an entire slide horizontally, PowerPoint 2000 will interpret it as an attempt to delete the slide. A dialog box will appear, prompting you to confirm deletion of the slide.

Delete slides, points, or subpoints as you would in a Word document. Select the text and press the Delete key, or right-click on selected text and choose Cut from the Shortcut menu.

Working in Slide View

It's easy to put too much on one slide in Outline view, so that some lines of text run off the bottom of the slide. If you prefer, you can edit and format slides in Slide view. Although you can only work with one slide at a time, Slide view gives you a better feel for how the slide will actually look when complete.

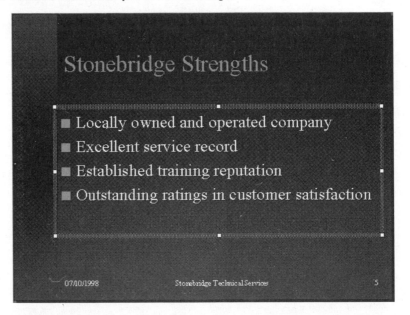

Most slides include two text boxes, one for the title and one for the body text. When you click in the title or body, a frame appears around the text box, as shown above. You can point to the frame and drag the text box to another location on the slide.

To add text to a slide, place your insertion point at the desired location in the text box. Promote or demote points and subpoints just as you would in Outline view, selecting the text first and either using the Promote or Demote buttons or pressing Tab or Shift+Tab. To format the text in the box, select the text by clicking or dragging as you would in Outline view; then change formats using the Formatting toolbar or Format menu.

Using the Slide Sorter

In Slide Sorter view, shown in Figure 13.5, you work with entire slides. You can't rearrange the text on a slide, but you can move or copy entire slides.

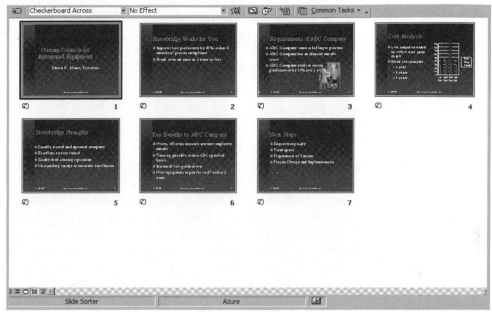

FIGURE 13.5

Slide Sorter view

Although moving slides is fairly easy in Outline view, you won't get the visual impact you see when arranging slides in Slide Sorter view. Drag-and-drop moving allows you to quickly and evenly distribute slides with graphic objects among those that are text-only, for an overall balanced presentation. You may want to return to Outline view to confirm that the text flows logically from slide to slide.

 TIP Double-click any slide in Slide Sorter view to return to the previous view. The double-click will not return you to Slide Show view, however.

To drag-and-drop slides, switch to Slide Sorter view and follow these steps:

1. Click a slide once to select it, or select multiple slides by holding Shift while selecting. A selected slide has a dark border around it, like Slide 1 in Figure 13.5.

2. To move a selected slide, drag the slide toward its new location. A gray vertical line will appear. Drag-and-drop to move the line and the selected slide to the new location.

3. To copy a slide, hold the Ctrl key while dragging; release Ctrl after dropping the slide in place.

4. To delete slides in the Slide Sorter, select the slide(s) and then press Delete.

PART

III

And Now, Presenting
PowerPoint!

TIP In Slide Sorter view, you can't always read the text on a slide. To see just the title, hold Alt and click on the slide. When you release the mouse button, the slide miniature returns to normal.

Adding Notes

The Speaker's Notes button lets you keep separate notes about slides in a presentation. You can use the Notes area of the Tri-Pane window for speaker notes during a presentation, but you can also use notes to keep track of other information about particular slides as you're creating a presentation. For example, there may be data that needs to be verified, or alternative information you've considered adding to the slide.

PowerPoint lets you add notes to slides in any view. Look for the pane that says "Click to add notes," as shown in Figure 13.6. If you click anywhere in the Notes area, those instructions will disappear, replaced by an insertion point for text entry. Slide Sorter view does not have a Notes pane. Instead, select the slide for which you wish to record notes, then click the Speaker Notes button on the Slide Sorter toolbar.

FIGURE 13.6

The Notes area is at the bottom of the window in Slide view.

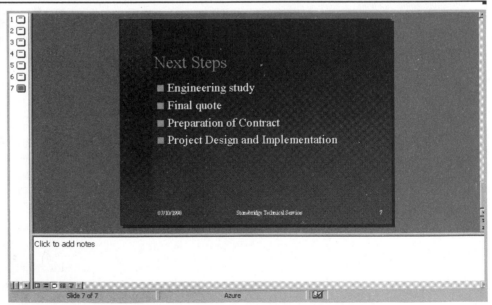

NOTE Remember, your audience never sees the text you have entered in the Notes pane unless you intentionally print your notes and hand them out.

To add notes from Slide Show view, right-click on any slide and choose Speaker Notes from the Shortcut menu.

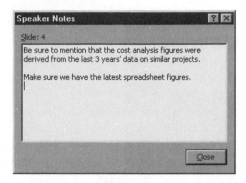

Enter text in the dialog box. When finished, click the Close button to return to Slide Show view. The text you entered will be displayed in the regular Notes pane in all other views except Slide Sorter.

 TIP In Slide view, the Notes pane may not be visible unless you drag the window adjustment tool up from the bottom of the screen, starting just above the Status Bar and View buttons. The Notes pane disappears from Slide view when you switch to another view and return.

Other Ways to Create Presentations

The benefit of the AutoContent Wizard is that it helps you to develop your content. It is also helpful to beginning users, because it automatically formats slides and applies transitions. (Slide transitions are more fully discussed in Chapter 15.) If you have already decided what should be in your presentation, and/or you are comfortable with formatting and slide transitions, you don't need to use the wizard. There are other ways you can create a presentation:

- Use a design template, which gives you a "look" without burdening you with text to alter or delete.

- Borrow the design from an existing presentation, which is useful if the presentations in your department should share a common design.

- "From scratch": enter your text first, and then apply a design.

- Import and modify an existing Word outline.

You can always apply another design template or presentation design to an existing presentation.

PART

III

And Now, Presenting
PowerPoint!

Using Blank Presentations or Design Templates

If you like to start "from scratch," choose Blank Presentation when you launch Power-Point, or choose File ➤ New from the menu bar to open the New Presentation dialog box. The General tab includes the AutoContent Wizard and Blank Presentation options for getting started. Choose Blank Presentation from the General tab, as shown in Figure 13.7.

You can also use the design elements from any existing presentation or template in a new presentation. To create a presentation using a design saved as a template, either choose Template in the dialog box that opens when you launch PowerPoint or choose File ➤ New from the menu. The Design Templates tab of the New Presentation Dialog Box displays templates. Select one of the templates to see a sample of its title slide in the Preview area, as shown in Figure 13.8. Double-click on a design template or click OK to choose the selected template.

You can change the design template of a presentation at any time by choosing Format ➤ Apply Design Template from the menu or by selecting Apply Design Template from the Common Tasks drop-down list.

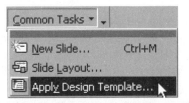

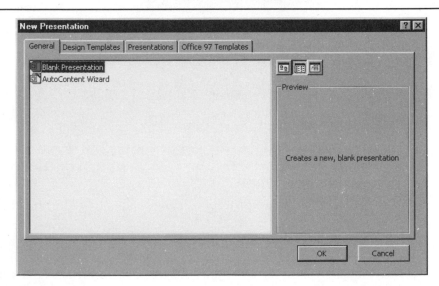

FIGURE 13.7

The General tab of the New Presentation dialog box

FIGURE 13.8

The Design Templates
tab of the New
Presentation dialog box

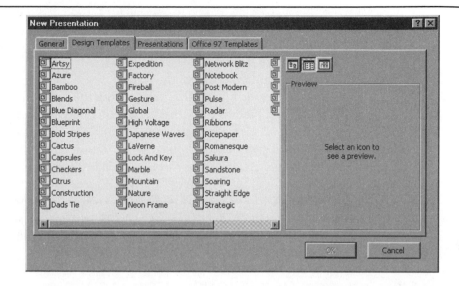

Selecting Slide Layouts

If you begin a presentation with a design template or choose to create a blank presentation, the New Slide dialog box opens, as shown in Figure 13.9. The New Slide dialog box also opens when you click the New Slide button on the Formatting toolbar, as mentioned earlier in this chapter.

FIGURE 13.9

The New Slide
dialog box

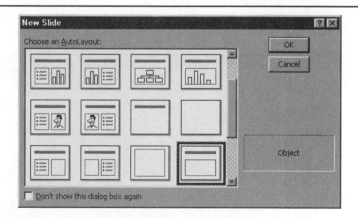

PART

III

And Now, Presenting
PowerPoint!

In the New Slide dialog box, you select an AutoLayout for each new slide. When you click the thumbnail for the layout, a description appears at the right of the dialog box. No choice that you make in this dialog box is carved in stone: you can always change a slide's layout. Notice that there is a scroll bar in this dialog box; there are other layouts you might want to look at.

Select the Title Slide layout for the first slide in the presentation. After you've selected the slide layout, PowerPoint puts you into Normal view. Click the Title text box (directly on the slide) and enter your title. Click the Subtitle text box and enter additional information you want to appear on the title slide. (If you prefer, you can enter all of the text for this slide on the Outline portion of the Normal view window.)

Choose Insert ➤ New Slide from the menu or click the New Slide Button to choose another AutoLayout for your next slide. You can also insert a new slide from the Common Tasks drop-down list on the Formatting toolbar. When you have finished entering text in a text box, click outside of the text box to turn off the selection. Depending on the slide layout you choose, there may be several text boxes for body text.

 WARNING If you add text to a slide using the Text Tool button on the Drawing toolbar, the text will not show up in your outline because you're adding a text box object, not slide text. Make sure you either enter text in your outline or select an AutoLayout that contains a text box.

Continue adding slides one by one to build your presentation. The New Slide dialog box allows you to easily vary the layout of your slides, providing a variety of slide styles for your audience. To change the layout of an existing slide, select the slide and choose Slide Layout from the Common Tasks menu. The Slide Layout dialog box will open.

Table Slides

 For times when you need to display information in multiple columns and rows, consider choosing a table slide from the New Slide dialog box. The enhanced tables featured in PowerPoint 2000 incorporate most of the powerful table tools from Word.

General Timeline

Item	Responsibility	Projected Completion
Engineering Study	Stonebridge	December 1998
Final Quote	Stonebridge/ABC	January 1999
Contract	Stonebridge	February 1999
Implementation	Stonebridge/ABC	February 2000

Now you can quickly and easily create and format tables. You can choose the number of columns and rows, insert and delete text, apply borders, apply shading, change fonts and alignment, resize columns and rows, and modify your table in a myriad of other ways.

1. In Slide view, choose New Slide from the Common Tasks drop-down list.

2. Select the AutoLayout that includes a table.

3. Activate the title text box and enter a slide title.

4. Double-click the icon to start a new table. The Insert Table dialog box will open.

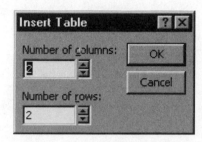

5. Use the spin boxes to indicate the number of columns and rows for your table, or select and overtype the default numbers.

6. Click OK. PowerPoint will display the empty grid and the floating Tables And Borders toolbar. The default tool is the pencil, which is used to draw new rows or columns and to split cells. You can drag the pencil vertically, horizontally, or diagonally.

7. Click the pencil tool to "put it away." Your mouse pointer will become an I-beam for selecting cells and typing text.

8. Use the other options on the Tables And Borders toolbar to apply formatting changes to borders, shading, and alignment.

NOTE There are numerous options for formatting and aligning tables. For a detailed description of Word's table features and more information on working with tables, see Chapter 6.

Multi-Object Slides

Choosing an AutoLayout from the New Slide dialog box will generally give you a good idea of how your next slide will look. Perhaps you are picturing a graphic next to a bulleted list, or a bulleted list with a graphic above it. The New Slide dialog box offers many

PART

III

And Now, Presenting
PowerPoint!

options for including several objects on one slide. Scroll down the list of choices in the dialog box to see options for multiple objects with text placement beside, below, or above objects.

Some layouts have placeholders for clip art. When you double-click the icon in the placeholder, it opens the Clip Gallery. Inserted clips are sized to fit the frame of the placeholder. Other layouts have placeholders for generic objects. Double-clicking those icons opens the Insert Object dialog box, offering you access to objects from other applications.

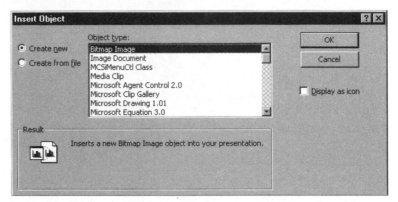

There are even layouts with placeholders for charts and media clips. Although placeholders aren't necessary—charts, clip art, media clips, and other objects can be placed on any slide—the placeholders provide shortcuts to the objects you include most often. They save time by eliminating a great deal of resizing, since objects are placed in a presized frame. They also provide for balanced layouts, giving you professional-looking slides.

MASTERING THE OPPORTUNITIES

Creating an Organizational Chart

You can create professional-looking organizational charts right on your slides. In the New Slide dialog box, choose the Slide layout that includes an organizational chart. Click in the title text box and type a title for the slide. Then double-click the Org Chart icon to launch Microsoft Organizational Chart. You may be prompted to install the program if this is the first time you have used it. The Org Chart program runs inside its own window within PowerPoint.

When the Org Chart window opens, you are automatically given four boxes: one manager and three subordinates. You are also given the option of including a title for your Org Chart. Select text and overtype it with the pertinent information. Delete boxes you don't want by clicking on them and pressing Delete.

Continued

Before you add a box, decide which level is appropriate for the person whose name will appear in the box. Click that level on the toolbar (manager, subordinate, assistant, etc.), then click in the box to which you wish to attach this person. A new box will appear with instructional text to select and overtype.

Choose a particular level or all levels for editing by clicking Edit ≻ Select from the menu bar. Change the color, shadow, and border options on selected boxes using the Boxes menu. Change the thickness and/or color of connecting lines using the Lines menu. Options for different chart styles and text formatting are also available from the menu.

When you are finished, click the Close button on the Microsoft Organizational Chart program window. You will be prompted to update the object in your presentation before proceeding. Click Yes. You will return to the PowerPoint view you were in when you double-clicked the Org Chart icon. If you wish to edit the Org Chart at any time, simply double-click the chart to re-launch the program.

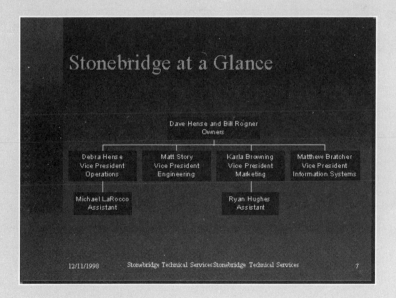

Using Existing Presentations

There may be times when you want to apply the design elements from a previously created presentation to your current project. Perhaps your company has a standard template for all sales presentations. PowerPoint allows you to duplicate the design from any existing presentation in a new presentation.

1. Begin by choosing any design template or a blank presentation.

2. Click Apply Design Template from the Common Tasks drop-down list.

3. When the Apply Design dialog box opens (see Figure 13.10), set the Look In control to the folder that contains the presentation with the formatting you wish to duplicate.

4. Change the Files of Type drop-down box at the bottom of the dialog box to All PowerPoint Files.

5. Select the presentation that has the design you want to use.

6. Click Apply.

Use the same method to apply any of the design templates in the Presentations folder to an existing presentation.

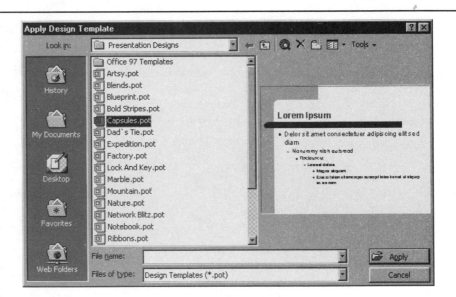

FIGURE 13.10

The Apply Design Template dialog box

Using Slides from an Existing Presentation

Applying a design uses a presentation's background, fonts, and formatting without any of the content. You can also use the Slide Finder to take entire slides from an existing presentation and add them to another presentation. To open the Slide Finder, choose Insert ➤ Slides From Files. Click the Browse button and select the file that contains the slides you want to add to your presentation; then click the Display button to add thumbnails of the slides to the Slide Finder, shown in Figure 13.11.

FIGURE 13.11

The Slide Finder

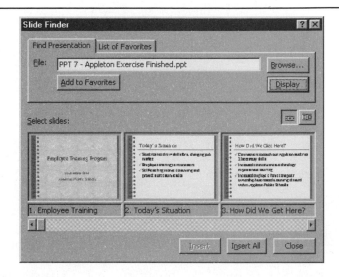

The slides appear with each slide's number and title below the slide. Use the horizontal scroll bar to move through the slides in order. To work more quickly, click the Show Titles button in the dialog box to display a list of slide titles with a single preview pane.

Click the Show Slides button to return to the thumbnails view. Select and then insert the slide or slides you want (hold Shift or Ctrl to select multiple slides). The inserted slides will appear in your presentation following the slide that was selected when you opened the Slide Finder.

As soon as you insert a slide, the text and any objects (like a picture or chart) on the slide are imported. The slide's design is *not* imported into the current presentation. Instead, each slide is reformatted upon being imported so it matches the design of the presentation you are currently working on.

Using Word Outlines

You can import a Word outline to create a PowerPoint presentation. (For more information on Word outlines, see Chapter 8.) The outline will be inserted into the active presentation so if you have just started, you can use the outline as the total presentation. You may also use an outline as additional content in a partially completed presentation. If you choose to insert an outline into an existing presentation, each first-level heading will become a new slide.

1. Choose Insert ➤ Slides From Outline on the menu.

2. Change the Look In field so it points to the folder containing the Word outline.

PART

III

And Now, Presenting
PowerPoint!

3. Select the Word file you want to insert.

4. Click Insert. New slides are inserted to follow the slide that was selected when you began the process.

 WARNING When you insert a Word outline, the complete document appears as part of your presentation. If you only want part of the outline, delete the extra slides after importing. If you have a rather lengthy outline from which you only need a few slides, consider copying those sections to a new Word document and importing from there.

What's Next

Once you have completed the outline, chosen a basic layout for slides, and applied a design template, you are ready to think about ways to customize your presentation. In Chapter 14, you will learn how to modify the colors and background of the design template to suit your own style and needs. Formatting issues such as text alignment and line spacing will be discussed. You will also learn to use PowerPoint's style checking features.

CHAPTER **14**

Formatting Slides and Text

FEATURING:

Changing the color scheme

Modifying the slide master

Customizing the background

Formatting and checking text

lthough PowerPoint offers many eye-catching design templates from which to choose, it won't be long before you feel the need to modify a template to suit your own style. It's easy to choose one of PowerPoint's design templates to establish the primary background for your presentation and then change the background or colors to meet your specific needs.

Consider the purpose of your presentation when changing colors or backgrounds. For overheads, the lighter the better. Dark backgrounds work well for on-screen presentations, but if you need to show a presentation with room lights on, choose a light background and dark text.

Changing the Color Scheme

Choosing Format ➤ Slide Color Scheme opens the Color Scheme dialog box, shown in Figure 14.1. The dialog box has tabs for Standard and Custom color schemes. The standard color schemes include the current color scheme, at least one alternate scheme, and one black-and-white choice. The number of standard schemes you see depends on the design template. Some have more than others. You can choose to apply a scheme to the current slide or to all of the slides in the presentation. To see how a slide will look, click the Preview button. (You'll have to move the dialog box out of the way to see the impact on the slide.) When you're satisfied, click Apply to change the selected slide or slides or Apply To All To change every slide in the presentation.

 NOTE You can't change the color scheme in a blank presentation; you must have already applied a design.

If you don't like any of the standard schemes, you can create your own. Select the scheme that's closest to what you want and click the Custom tab on the Color Scheme dialog box, shown in Figure 14.2. Select the color you want to change and click the Change Color button to open the Colors dialog box. Choose a color from the array of colors presented or, if you want to mix your own, click the Custom tab to open the Color Picker. If you wish, you can save the color scheme for future use with the current design by clicking the Add As Standard Scheme button on the Custom tab (see Figure 14.2). Added schemes are displayed on the Standard tab of the dialog box.

FIGURE 14.1

The Color Scheme dialog box

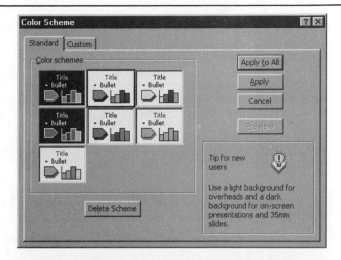

FIGURE 14.2

Custom color schemes

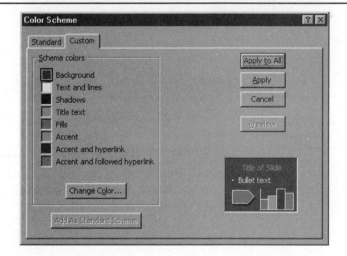

Modifying the Slide Master

Every design includes a *slide master* that identifies the position of the text and graphic objects, the style of the fonts, the footer elements, and the background for all slides (see Figure 14.3). There are one or two slide masters for each presentation; some designs include separate slide and title slide masters. Older templates from earlier versions of PowerPoint are more likely to have only one master.

All changes that you make to the master will be reflected in each slide that is based on the master. For example, if you want a graphic object (a logo perhaps) to appear on every slide, you could attach it to the master rather than inserting it on each slide. To change the title font for all slides or the vertical boxes shown on the left side of the slide in Figure 14.3, change it on the master.

FIGURE 14.3

The slide master

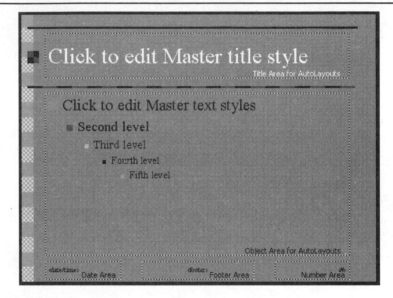

1. To open the slide master, either choose View ➢ Master ➢ Slide Master or hold the Shift key and click the Slide View button.

2. On the master, click any text box to edit its contents. Use the buttons on the Formatting toolbar to format text.

3. Choose Format ➢ Font to change text color, size, or style.

4. To change bullet characters, select the level of bullet you wish to change and choose Format ➢ Bullets And Numbering from the menu.

 NOTE For more information about modifying bullets, see Chapters 4 and 15.

While you're working with the slide master, you can select and move or delete placeholders, including graphic objects and text boxes. You can also insert logos or other graphics you want to appear on every slide by choosing Insert ➢ Picture from the menu.

Adding Slide Footers

When you use the AutoContent Wizard to start a presentation, you are offered the option of including the system date, slide number, and other text in a slide footer.

You can add, delete, or modify information in the footer area of all slides by using the slide master. Simply open the slide master and click on the footer area you wish to edit. Type in the new information.

 NOTE If you had already chosen to use text, dates, and/or slide numbering in the Auto-Content Wizard, those areas still show generic text in the slide master. Selecting one of the footer text boxes and typing in new information will overwrite the choices you previously made in the AutoContent Wizard.

For users who prefer to edit inside a dialog box, choose View ➤ Header Footer from the menu in any of the four editing views or from the slide master. The Header And Footer dialog box (shown in Figure 14.4) allows you to edit, add, or delete footer text on slides. Turn on the items you want to display, activate Don't Show On Title Slide, if desired, and click Apply to place a footer on the current slide only or Apply To All. If you opened the dialog box from the slide master, you can only choose Apply To All.

FIGURE 14.4

The Header And Footer dialog box

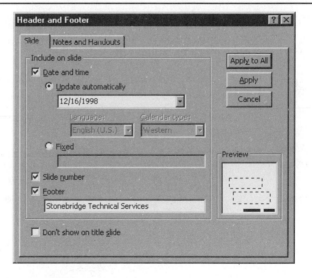

Customizing the Background

When you choose to apply a design template, the template includes, among other things, the color scheme and background color. Often, the background is more than just a solid color. It may have a shaded effect, a pattern, or a texture. There may be a picture or graphic object that is part of the background. All these characteristics—shading, patterns, textures and objects—form the background of the slide. Any text or additional objects that you place on the slide are positioned on top of the background.

To change the background, choose Format ➤ Background. The Background dialog box will be displayed. You can also open the Background dialog box by right-clicking on any slide (away from text boxes and objects) and choosing Background from the shortcut menu.

You can choose to Omit Background Graphics on an individual slide by activating that option in the Background dialog box and choosing Apply. (This means that master background graphics won't be applied to the selected slide, but all other slides will retain background graphics.) Figure 14.5 shows the same slide with and without background objects. By omitting background objects, your slide can retain the same basic appearance as the other slides, but background objects won't detract from other graphics, like charts, that you might place on the slide. If you Omit Background Graphics, you also omit the footer.

You can omit background graphics from all slides by activating that option in the Background dialog box and clicking Apply To All. It is probably a good idea to do this if your presentation contains charts, tables, or other graphics on most slides.

To make changes in the background fill, click the unlabeled drop-down arrow in the Background Fill area of the dialog box. You'll see a drop-down list of the slide background colors.

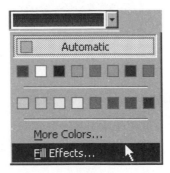

FIGURE 14.5

The top slide contains background objects. The bottom slide has its background objects omitted from the master.

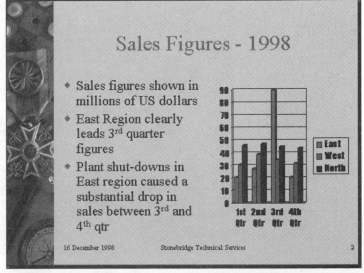

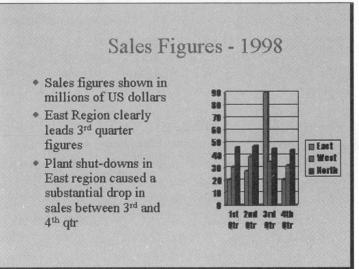

Choosing Automatic fills the background with the default fill color. Selecting a color from the eight color-scheme colors or choosing from More Colors (which opens the Color Picker) changes the background fill color. Choosing Fill Effects opens the Fill Effects dialog box to the Gradient tab, as shown in Figure 14.6.

FIGURE 14.6

*The Gradient tab of the
Fill Effects dialog box*

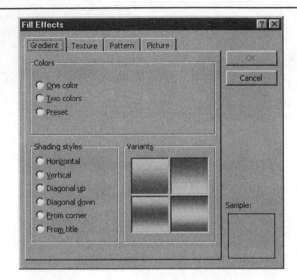

In this dialog box, you can select from four different types of fills: Gradients, Textures, Patterns, or Pictures. Gradients are variegated color mixes. Textures are photo-like fills; patterns are computer-generated patterns like diagonal lines or vertical stripes. On the Pictures page, you use the Browse button to select a picture to apply to a background. PowerPoint supports many different graphic formats, from Windows metafiles to JPEGs. Whether you choose a picture or texture, pattern or gradient, it's a good idea to Preview the fill before applying it.

To change the gradient of a slide background:

1. Choose Format ➢ Background from any of the four editing views, or right-click on a slide (outside of any text boxes or objects) and choose Background from the shortcut menu.

2. Open the fill drop-down list and choose Fill Effects.

3. Make sure the Gradient page of the dialog box is active. Select one of the gradient options: One Color, Two Colors, or Preset. The preset gradient schemes use two or more colors to create effects such as Early Sunset, Ocean, and Chrome.

4. If you have chosen the two-color option, select the two colors you wish to use to create a custom gradient.

5. Select a shading style to determine the direction of the gradient (Horizontal, Diagonal Up, From Title, etc.).

6. Click OK.

7. Preview the new gradient, and then click Apply or Apply To All.

To change the pattern of a slide background:

1. Choose Format ➤ Background from any of the four editing views or right-click on a slide (outside of any text boxes or objects). Choose Background from the shortcut menu.

2. Open the Fill drop-down list and choose Fill Effects.

3. Make sure the Pattern page of the dialog box is active (see Figure 14.7). Select a contrasting foreground and background color. The foreground color shows a pattern on top of the background color.

4. Click on one of the pattern styles displayed in the dialog box and click OK.

5. Preview the new pattern, and then click Apply or Apply To All.

FIGURE 14.7

The Pattern tab of the Fill Effects dialog box

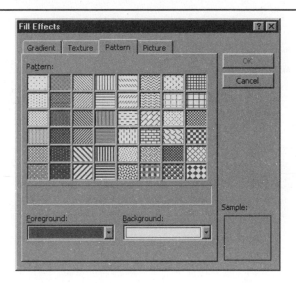

Formatting and Checking Text

When you format text on individual slides, the formatting takes precedence over formatting from the slide master. Even if you apply a new design, formatting applied to individual slides won't change, so you should make sure you are pleased with the overall design before formatting individual slides. You can apply standard text enhancements from other Windows applications to your PowerPoint slides. Select the text to be formatted; then change font typeface, size, and attributes using the Formatting toolbar or the Formatting menu.

Formatting always appears in Slide view. In Outline view and Normal view, you can decide whether or not to display formatting. The Show Formatting button on the Outlining toolbar toggles between displaying and hiding text formatting. In Slide Sorter view, the Show Formatting button toggles between displaying the slide thumbnail and slide titles.

Two buttons that do not appear in most other Office applications are the Increase Font and Decrease Font buttons. Each click changes the font size in standard increments that increase as font size increases. Fonts 10 points and smaller change in 1-point increments; larger fonts change in greater increments.

Add a shadow to selected text by clicking the Shadow button; change the color of the text by clicking the Font Color button on the Drawing toolbar. When you click the down arrow for Font Color, the colors from the current scheme are displayed.

NOTE Click View ➤ Toolbars to turn the Drawing toolbar on or off. You can also right-click any other toolbar (between buttons) and turn toolbars off and on from the shortcut menu.

TIP PowerPoint designers spend a considerable amount of time putting together templates with colors, fonts, and other attributes that "work." If you don't have a natural gift for aesthetics, ask a colleague to review any customized formatting you have applied.

Aligning Text

Selected text can be left-, center-, or right-aligned, or justified. Left, Center, and Right alignment are options on the Formatting toolbar. To justify text, choose Format ➤ Alignment ➤ Justify from the menu bar. The paragraph containing the Insertion Point will be justified. If you wish to justify multiple paragraphs, select them before choosing the menu commands.

A Word about Fonts

Most fonts fall into one of five categories: Serif, Sans Serif, Script, Decorative or Symbol.

Serif fonts like Times New Roman are easily recognizable from the serifs attached to the ends and tips of letters. For example, the uppercase "N" shown below has feet, and the lowercase "t" has a curvy bottom. Serif fonts are best for body text in paragraphs because they are easy to read.

Sans Serif fonts, like Arial, do not have fancy ends and tips on letters. They are rather plain and work well for headings.

Script fonts such as Lucida Handwriting or Brush Script are designed to look like cursive handwriting. It is best to stay away from script fonts at the office, as they project a more personal, rather than corporate, style.

Decorative fonts like Old English or Desdemona add impact to documents like flyers and banners. You'll most likely see a decorative font used on formal documents like wedding invitations. If you are the person in charge of creating and posting flyers for the annual company picnic, consider using a decorative font to draw people's attention to the posted document.

Symbol fonts are for inserting special characters like the © copyright symbol or for choosing bullet characters. You have probably seen the trademark symbol ™ used in business publications and the Greek letter Sigma Σ. Other symbols work well for bullet characters.

> This is Times New Roman, a Serif font
> This is Arial, a Sans Serif font
> *This is Brush Script MT, a Script font*
> THIS IS DESDEMONA, A DECORATIVE FONT
> Wingdings is a symbol font. Here are some Wingdings: ♎ ⚹ ☐ ♏ ◆ ⌂

Replacing Fonts

Use the Replace Font dialog box to substitute one font for another throughout a presentation. You might choose to replace fonts to change the look of a presentation, but there is sometimes a more pressing reason. If you open a presentation on a computer that doesn't have the presentation's fonts installed, another font is automatically substituted—unless the fonts were embedded in the presentation. (See Chapter 16 for pointers on saving presentations for use on another computer.) This substitute font may not be good-looking; and occasionally, it isn't even readable. Rather than changing various levels of the master, you can have PowerPoint change each occurrence of the font.

1. In Slide view or Normal view, select a text box that includes the font you want to replace.

2. Choose Format ➤ Replace Font to open the Replace Font dialog box.

3. Select a replacement font.

4. Click OK.

To replace fonts for *all* text boxes on *all* slides, switch to Slide Sorter view, select all slides (Ctrl+A is a quick way to select all slides), and follow Steps 2–4 above.

Adjusting Line Spacing

In PowerPoint, you can add or subtract space between lines and before or after paragraphs, much as you add leading in desktop publishing. Rather than entering extra blank lines between points or sub-points, adjust the line spacing.

In Slide view or Normal view, select the text you want to space. (This process works in Outline view as well, but it's difficult to see your results clearly because the slide is displayed so much smaller than in the other two views.) Choose Format ➤ Line Spacing to open the Line Spacing dialog box. Then set the lines or points (1 point = 1/72 inch) to be added as Line Spacing (between each line, even within a point or subpoint), Before Paragraph, or After Paragraph, and click OK.

Adjusting Tabs and Indents

The distance your insertion point moves when you press the Tab key is preset at one-half inch. You can see the default tab stops on the ruler most clearly in Slide view and Normal view. Choose View ➤ Ruler to turn your ruler on, if necessary. To change the default tab settings for your presentation:

1. Switch to Slide view, and display the ruler (View ➤ Ruler).

2. Select the text for which you want to change tabs.

3. On the ruler, drag the first default tab stop to its new position. All other tab stops will adjust so that the distance between each tab stop is the same.

If you click in a text box with multiple levels of main points and subpoints, you will see indent markers appear on the ruler. Each level of points has its own set of three indent markers. If you only have first-level bullets, you will only see three markers. If you have first- and second-level bullets, you will see six, and so on. You can use these indent markers to move text and bullets to the left or right or you can indent just the text, moving it farther from the bullet that precedes it.

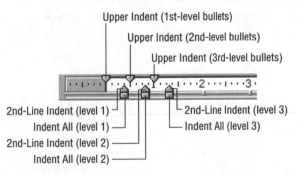

The upper marker sets the indent for the first line of the paragraph. Adjust the marker instead of pressing the Tab key if you want to give the appearance of a tabbed first line. Just drag the upper indent marker to the right; the other lines in that paragraph (and all paragraphs at that bullet level) will wrap to the left margin of the text box.

When you drag the triangular part of the lower indent marker, it adjusts all lines in the paragraph below the first line. If the first and subsequent lines of the paragraph are at the same setting (alignment), dragging this marker moves the entire paragraph farther or closer to the bullet character. (The rectangular part also moves when you drag the triangular part of the lower indent.)

Dragging the rectangular part of the lower marker allows you to move the entire paragraph while maintaining the relationship between the first line indent and the rest of the lines.

To change indent settings for the current slide:

1. In Slide view, select the text for which you want to set indents.

2. If the ruler isn't displayed, turn it on (View ➢ Ruler).

3. Drag the upper indent marker to change the indent for the first line of a paragraph.

4. Drag the lower indent marker to set the indent for other lines in a paragraph.

5. To change the indent for an entire paragraph, drag the rectangular box beneath the lower indent marker to move both upper and lower markers while maintaining the relationship between the upper and lower indent.

6. To change the distance from a hanging paragraph to the bullet that precedes it, drag the triangular portion of the bottom indent marker.

Style Checker

 PowerPoint 2000 automatically checks your presentation for consistency and style. When there are problems with punctuation and/or visual clarity, they are marked with a light bulb. You can choose to fix or ignore these errors, and there are options for changing the elements PowerPoint checks for.

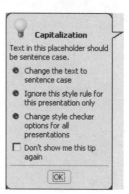

1. Open the presentation you want to check for style and consistency.

2. Locate slides that are flagged for errors.

3. Click the light bulb to see a list of options.

4. Click the option you want.

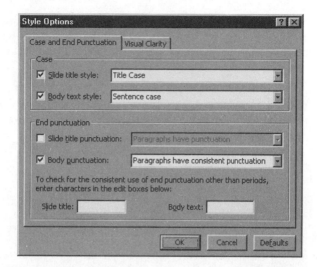

To change the elements that PowerPoint checks for, click Change Style Checker Options For All Presentations in the list. On the Case And End Punctuation tab of the dialog box, you can enable or disable case and end punctuation options so that your presentation is consistent. If you want all slides, including the title slide, to be in sentence case, enable those options. It is a good idea to check for consistent end punctuation on paragraphs. When you choose to use end punctuation, PowerPoint checks for periods by default. If you're using commas or some other end punctuation, type it in the edit boxes so the style checker can look for it.

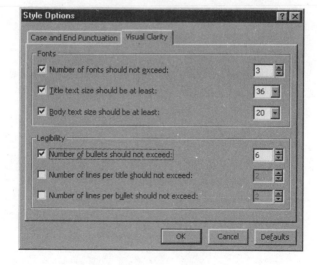

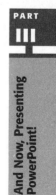

Click the Visual Clarity tab of the dialog box to enable or disable font and legibility checking. Use the spin boxes to set options for the number of fonts per presentation, font sizes, number of bullets, and number of lines of text.

 NOTE The style checker is not available if you have turned off the Office Assistant. However, you can still edit style checker options by choosing Tools ➢ Options ➢ Spelling And Style ➢ Style Options.

What's Next

By now, your presentation looks pretty good! You've customized the formatting just the way you want it. You've checked for consistency with the help of the Style Checker. In Chapter 15, you will learn how to add objects to slides. You'll enhance the appearance of your slides in Slide Show view by adding transitions and animation. And finally, you'll learn how to incorporate backup material through hiding and linking slides.

CHAPTER 15

Objects, Transitions, and Animation

FEATURING:

Adding objects

Creating graphical bullets

Modifying and adding transitions

Adding animation

Creating and animating charts

Hiding slides

Adding links to other slides

Once you are comfortable with the text that conveys the intended message of your presentation, you will want to think about ways to add visual impact to that message. Why not include your company logo on the introductory slide? Consider displaying those month-end sales figures in a Word table. Emphasize a particularly important point with a graphical bullet. This is your opportunity to add the design elements that can make a good presentation a great one.

Adding Objects

PowerPoint treats each item placed on a slide as an object. Even if you're typing text in Outline view, each slide has at least two text boxes, one for the title and one for the bulleted text; each text box is considered an object. Objects like clip art, WordArt, and charts add impact to your slides.

Inserting Objects

To add objects to slides, you will probably want to use Slide view or Normal view. If the object will appear on every slide (like a company logo or copyright information), add it to the slide master. If you want to insert an object, you may find it easiest to begin with a slide layout that includes the object, whether the object is text, clip art, a table, a chart, a sound or video clip, or any other object. (AutoLayouts and the New Slide dialog box are covered in Chapter 13.) Once you've selected the correct slide layout, just double-click on the object and you'll be taken to the appropriate application to either insert or create the indicated object.

Of course, you can also insert objects on slides that are not preformatted with placeholders. You will have to complete the extra steps of manually resizing and placing objects so text flows around them.

Inserting Clip Art

If you want to use clip art with your presentation, you may proceed a couple of different ways. You could choose Insert ➤ Picture ➤ ClipArt to open the Microsoft Clip Gallery (also called the Insert ClipArt dialog box). (See Chapter 7 to learn more about the Clip Gallery.) Or you might choose to insert a new slide and select a slide layout with a clip art placeholder (see Figure 15.1). Double-click the placeholder on the new slide to open the Insert ClipArt dialog box, shown in Figure 15.2.

FIGURE 15.1

Slide layout with a clip art placeholder

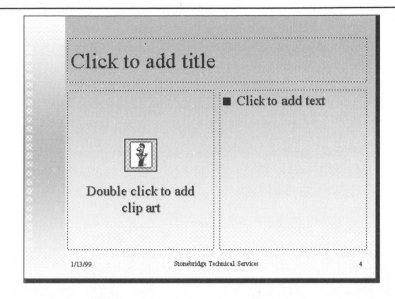

FIGURE 15.2

The Microsoft Clip Gallery offers hundreds of clip art images you can add to presentations.

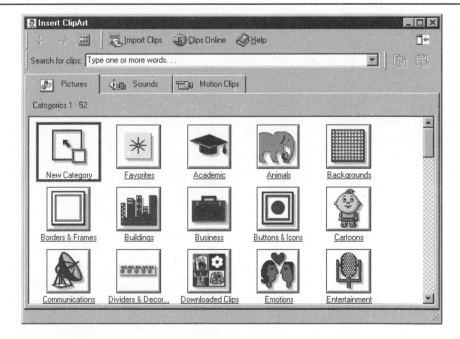

The Clip Gallery is arranged in categories. Click one of the icons displayed in the gallery to choose a category. Once a category choice is made, locate the thumbnail for the clip you want to insert.

PART

III

And Now, Presenting PowerPoint!

Not all clips in a category are displayed at once. If you wish to see additional clips, click Keep Looking at the bottom of the scroll list. Shift+Backspace will also display more clips when the Clip Gallery is open. Continue to choose Keep Looking to locate the exact piece you are looking for.

Once you are several layers deep in the Clip Gallery, you can use the Back and Forward buttons at the top of the dialog box to navigate between current and previous screens.

Select the picture; then click Insert. Click once on the object to select it and open a shortcut toolbar with choices to Insert the clip, Preview it, Add the clip to a category, or Find similar clips.

Choosing the Preview option enlarges the thumbnail so you can see more detail. Close the preview and choose Insert Clip if you decide you like it. You may decide to put this clip in another category. Choosing the third option on the shortcut toolbar allows you to reference the clip in an additional category you select from a list.

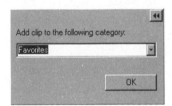

The Find option allows you to search for clips similar to the one you've selected. Click the Artistic Style button to see clips with the same general artistic style. If you've selected a black-and-white clip, for instance, this option will display other black-and-white clips. Click the Color & Shape button to see clips of the same shape and/or color. To see clips that are similarly categorized, click one of the keywords displayed below the buttons.

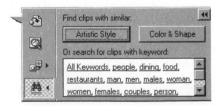

Your search history is kept on a drop-down list at the top of the Insert ClipArt dialog box. If you wish to duplicate a past search, simply choose the keyword from the list and press Enter to perform that search again.

 When you choose Add To Category or Search For Similar Clips, the pane that opens stays in view unless you click the Hide Pane button at the top-right corner of the dialog box.

Once you insert a clip and close the dialog box, you are returned to the view you were in when you opened it. Select the new object with a single click and you can drag it to another location on the slide or use its handles for resizing.

Recoloring a ClipArt Object When you select a ClipArt object, the Picture toolbar automatically opens:

 General use of the Picture toolbar is discussed in Chapter 36, which covers converting, linking, and embedding objects between Office applications, but one toolbar button is available only in PowerPoint: the Recolor Picture button. Clicking the button opens the Recolor Picture dialog box, shown in Figure 15.3.

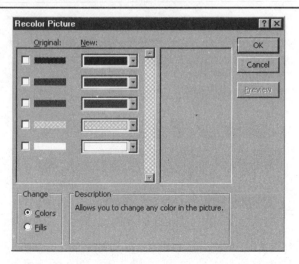

In the Change area, choose either Colors, which changes the colors of lines as well as fills, or Fills, which doesn't affect lines. To change a color, check the box in front of the color you want to change, then select a new color from the corresponding New drop-down list. The sample will change as you recolor different colors and fills.

Sound and Video

PowerPoint includes sounds and videos you can play during your slide shows. Some sounds, like the typewriter or laser sound, are included on the Animation Effects toolbar. Other sounds, music, and videos, are in the Microsoft Clip Gallery. To insert a sound or video file:

1. In Slide view, move to the slide you want to add an object to.

2. Choose Insert ➤ Movies and Sounds ➤ Sound From Gallery or Video From Gallery.

3. In the Clip Gallery, select the sound or video you want to add. Click the Play button to preview the selected sound or video.

4. Click Insert to insert the object and place a sound icon or video object on the slide. If you are inserting a sound file, PowerPoint will prompt you to choose whether it plays automatically or on mouse click.

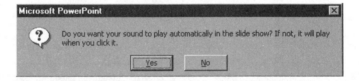

5. To play a sound or video that doesn't play automatically, double-click on the icon or object in Slide Show view.

 TIP To insert a sound or video that isn't in the Clip Gallery, choose the From File menu choice. Locate, select, and open the file.

Inserting Tables from Word

If you've already created a table in Word that you want to use in a presentation, you can copy it in Word and paste it onto a slide. A table any bigger than three columns by four rows will be too large to show up clearly on a slide, so keep it simple. If you want to create a Word table in the current presentation, choose Insert ➢ Picture ➢ Microsoft Word Table, or choose a Table AutoLayout from the New Slide dialog box and double-click the Table icon on the slide. You will be asked how many columns and rows you want:

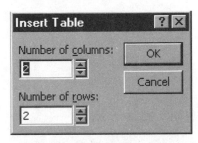

After you select the appropriate number of rows and columns and click OK, the Tables And Borders toolbar from Word appears. You will work with this toolbar to create the embedded table. (See Chapter 13 for more about table slides. For a thorough review of Word's table features, see Chapter 6.)

You can resize the table using the handles or reposition the table by dragging it to a new location. If you need to edit the table, double-click the table object, or manually turn the Tables And Borders toolbar back on.

Creating Graphical Bullets

Microsoft Office has always offered users the option of choosing bullet characters from the many font sets installed with Windows and Office. But now, you also have the capability to create a bullet character from any picture file, giving you endless possibilities for emphasizing points on slides.

Before you make a change to bullet characters, decide whether you want to make the change on all slides, or just the selected slide. If you wish to make the change for all slides, be sure you are working from the slide master. (See Chapter 14 for more information on working with master slides.)

1. Select the text for which you wish to change the bullet character. If you are working on the slide master, click in the appropriate level.

2. Choose Format ➢ Bullets And Numbering. The Bullets And Numbering dialog box will open as shown in Figure 15.4.

PART

III

And Now, Presenting PowerPoint!

FIGURE 15.4

Use the Bullets And Numbering dialog box to choose or customize bullet characters.

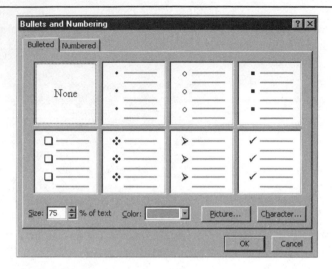

3. You can select one of the seven bullet types displayed here, or you can change the size and/or color of your bullet character. If you want to see more bullet choices, choose either Character or Picture.

4. Choosing Character takes you to the Bullet dialog box shown in Figure 15.5. Change the Bullets From selection to see another sheet of character choices. Click on a character to see a larger sample, as shown in the figure. Click on the character you wish to use and click OK.

FIGURE 15.5

Previewing a bullet character in the Bullet dialog box

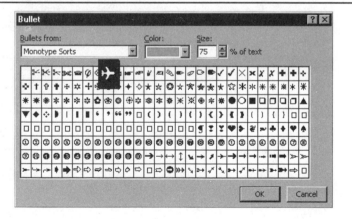

5. Choosing Picture takes you to the bullet character portion of the Clip Gallery, shown in Figure 15.6. (If you haven't installed the Clip Gallery, choosing Picture takes you to the Insert Picture dialog box.) Choose one of the displayed bullets, click for More Clips, or choose a picture from a file.

FIGURE 15.6

The Picture Bullet dialog box lets you choose a picture from the Clip Gallery to use as a bullet character.

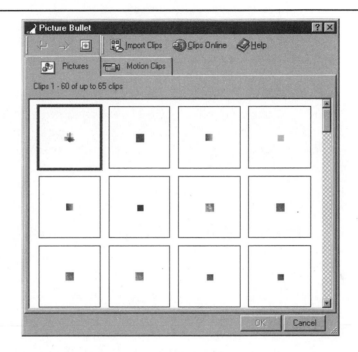

6. To select a bullet character from a picture file, click the Import Clips button near the top of the dialog box. Choose the drive and folder that contains the file you wish to use, select it, and click Import.

7. The first time you import a picture to use as a bullet, it appears on a page by itself. However, the next time you wish to use the same picture bullet, it will appear as a choice among others in the Clip Gallery.

Modifying and Adding Transitions

An electronic presentation, or *slide show*, is a presentation displayed on a computer screen or projected with an LCD projector. Since slides are "changed" by the computer

PART

III

And Now, Presenting
PowerPoint!

rather than by hand, you can add computerized special effects to a slide show that aren't possible when you use regular overheads for a presentation. A *transition* is a special effect added to the slide's initial appearance on screen. The slide can appear from the right, dissolve in gradually, or fade through the background of the previous slide. Some of the design templates also include animated features: for example, one of the background objects may streak into place.

Individual slides can include *animation*—different steps used to construct the slide, one placeholder at a time. For example, the slide can appear with a title only, and bulleted points can be added one by one.

If you started your presentation with the AutoContent Wizard or certain templates, you may find your slides already have transitions and/or animation assigned. You add or modify transitions in Slide Sorter view using the tools on the Slide Sorter toolbar, shown below. While you can add preset text animation in the Slide Sorter, you can't animate other objects, so you'll generally want to work with animation in Slide view.

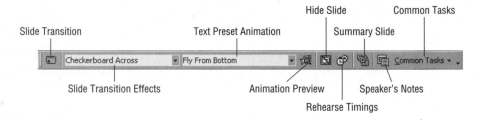

If a presentation doesn't have transitions, each slide simply appears in place of the previous slide—very "plain vanilla." Most of the PowerPoint 2000 design templates include transitions so there is more pizzazz. To change or add transitions, select the slide(s), and then choose a transition from the Slide Transition Effects drop-down list.

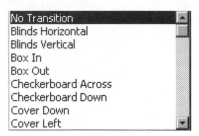

TIP To select a slide in Slide Sorter view, click on it. To select multiple noncontiguous slides, click on the first slide, hold down the Ctrl key, and click on the other slide(s) you want to select. To select all slides, press Ctrl+A.

Many of the transitions listed differ only in direction; for example, Cover Up, Cover Down, and Cover Up-Left. When you select a new transition from the list, PowerPoint provides a preview of the transition using the selected slide. (Look fast—it doesn't take long.)

 A *transition icon* appears below the lower-left corner of a slide with an assigned transition. Clicking this icon shows the transition again in the slide miniature. It might take some time to familiarize yourself with the various types of transitions. If you use PowerPoint regularly, you will become accustomed to them rather quickly.

Setting Transition Speed and Sound

The default speed for transitions is Medium. However, you may want to provide some variety to your audience by adding a fast or slow transition every so often. You can change the speed for transitions, choose a different transition, or add sound effects to accompany a transition in the Slide Transition dialog box.

Make sure the slides you want to affect are selected; then click the Slide Transition button on the Slide Sorter toolbar to open the dialog box, shown in Figure 15.7.

FIGURE 15.7

The Slide Transition dialog box

From the Effect drop-down list, select a transition, then choose one of the Speed options. Advance is used to enter timings for automatic slide advances (see "Setting Slide Timings" in Chapter 16). There is also a drop-down list of Sounds you can add to a transition. If you assign a sound, you can choose to have the sound loop until another sound is assigned. The last choice on the list, Other Sounds, opens a dialog box so that you can select a sound file. PowerPoint uses wave sounds, files with a .WAV extension. You'll find some wave files in the Media folder in the Windows folder, but you can purchase CDs of wave files at many computer stores. Free sound bytes are also available from the Internet (see the "Mastering the Opportunities" box below).

When you've finished setting options, choose Apply or Apply To All. Effects, including sound, can be previewed by clicking the transition icon in the Slide Sorter.

WARNING The Slide Transition dialog box only offers options to Apply or Apply To All. If you want to select every other slide to apply a transition, be sure you do it prior to opening the dialog box.

MASTERING THE OPPORTUNITIES

Using Sound Files from the Internet

If you work in a company or industry that frequently uses PowerPoint presentations, you may hear those canned sound bytes so many times they become ho-hum. Make your presentation stand out with different sounds—for free!

Use any Internet search engine to locate sites with the text string "WAV files." Select a site and browse the files until you find just the right sound. Right-click on the file and choose the Download or Save As option. Select a Save location and click OK. Once the sound file is saved to a folder you can access, assign it by choosing Other Sound from the drop-down list in the Transition dialog box.

Naturally, you will have to use discretion in selecting sound bytes for a professional presentation. Although *you* might want to communicate bad news using the Tragic Soap Opera Organ from Joe's Original Wave Files (http://www.sky.net/~jdeshon/joewav .html), your boss may not find it amusing! Further, many companies have strict policies regarding Internet usage and downloading of files. Be sure you are working within your company's policy before using Internet sounds.

Adding Animation

Transition effects are used *between* slides; animation effects occur *within* a slide. Each title, bulleted point, or other object on a slide can be added to the slide separately. This allows you to discuss individual points or add illustrations in a particular order during the presentation. PowerPoint provides a group of preset animation settings you can apply in Slide Sorter view. Select the slide or slides, and then choose a type of animation from the Text Preset Animation drop-down menu:

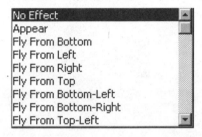

 The selected animation will be applied to all text (other than the title) in the slide. Preview the animation in Slide Show view or click the icon beneath the slide to see the animation on the miniature in Slide Sorter view. You can also preview animation in the Custom Animation dialog box (see "Adding Custom Animation" below).

When you animate body text, moving to Slide Show view will open the slide with the title and any background objects and graphics. Click anywhere and the first bulleted point will animate. Click again for each point.

Another group of animation effects is available from the context menu. Right-click on a selected slide in the Slide Sorter, and choose one of the Preset Animations that include sound:

Adding Custom Animation

Using Custom Animation tools can make your presentation stand out from all the others. Sound and motion can be combined in unique ways to generate a memorable electronic presentation. Use the custom animation tools to add sound and motion to individual graphic elements on a slide.

To open the Animation Effects toolbar, switch to Normal, Slide, or Outline view and click the Animation Effects button on the Formatting toolbar. To move quickly to your previous view (before using the Slide Sorter), double-click on the slide you wish to animate.

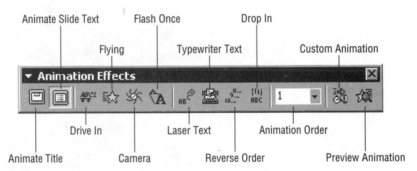

To have the slide title drop in from the top, click the Animate Title button. If you have already assigned animation effects to the slide, the Animate Slide Text button will be depressed as shown in the labeled picture above. Click the button to assign other animation.

The other Animation Effects buttons are used for specific graphic elements, including text boxes and objects. Click on the slide itself to select the object you want to animate, and then click one of the eight effects buttons on the Animation Effects toolbar. After you click one of these buttons, the object will be added to the slide's animation list. When the object is selected, its animation order number appears in the Animation Order drop-down list. Preview the animation using the last button on the toolbar.

Click the Custom Animation button to open the Custom Animation dialog box, shown in Figure 15.8. Click the Preview button to preview the current animations in order. On the Effects page of the dialog box, select one of the slide elements; assign animation and, if you wish, a sound. The After Animation drop-down allows you to change the color of animated text as the next animation occurs. You can use this in multiple-point slides with rather dramatic effect; for example, you can have each point animate as white text, then change to gray when the next point enters, drawing the viewer's attention immediately to the new point and away from the previous point.

FIGURE 15.8

The Effects tab of the
Custom Animation
dialog box

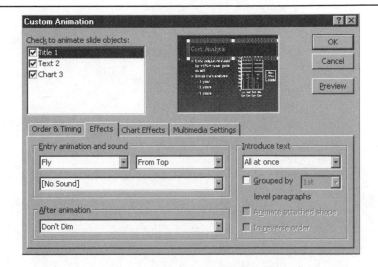

 WARNING Be sure to select an After Animation color that does not cause your text to become invisible. Gray works well unless the background color of your template is gray. This is particularly important when audience members choose to take notes during your presentation.

In the Introduce Text drop-down list (on the Effects tab of the Custom Animation dialog box), you can choose to bring in text for each bulleted point by paragraph, by word, or by letter. If you choose a Fly Effect and introduce text By Word, each word flies in separately, one right after the other.

Be sure to choose whether to introduce text by specific levels or all at once. If all your bulleted points are on the first level, introducing text by that level will cause them to appear with separate mouse clicks. However, if you have second- and third-level bullets and choose to introduce text by the first level, the second- and third-level bullets will appear with the first-level bullet they fall under.

Switch to the Order & Timing tab of the dialog box to modify the Animation Order using the Move Up and Move Down arrows. If you wish to automate animation so that it proceeds without mouse clicks, choose the option to start animation Automatically and set the number of seconds that should pass between the end of the previous animation and the beginning of the selected animation.

PART

III

And Now, Presenting
PowerPoint!

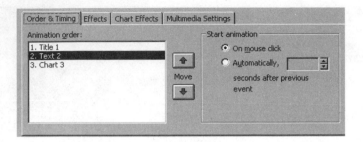

Chart Effects are disabled unless the selected object is a chart. You can introduce an entire chart at one time, or have chart elements appear separately. (See "Creating and Animating Charts" below.)

The Multimedia Settings are enabled when a sound or video object is selected. If you choose to assign the media an Animation Order, you don't have to click on the object to play it. You can choose to hide the object until it plays and you can assign a sound to hear as the video plays. Click More Options to have the video loop or rewind automatically.

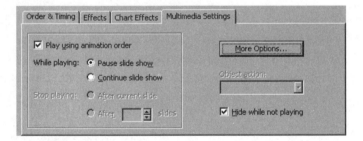

Tips for Transitions and Animation

When you give a slide show, you want the audience to remember your presentation's *content*—not just the flashy effects. Use one or two similar transitions throughout the presentation. For example, alternating left and right or top and down transitions of the same type provides variety without irritating your audience. When a presentation has transitions, slides without transitions stand out, so No Transition effectively becomes another type of transition. Sound can be attention grabbing, but new sound on every slide is too much.

The same tips apply to animation. Choose a small group of animation effects. Text that flies in from the right feels normal because the side we read first enters first. To add emphasis, then, have text enter from the left, top, or bottom. In general, you will want to develop an overall theme and keep it consistent throughout your slides.

Creating and Animating Charts

In Office 2000, there are two programs that create charts: Excel and Microsoft Graph. If you already have a chart in Excel, you can easily copy it and embed or link it to your slide. However, if you don't have access to Excel, Microsoft Graph will let you create charts quickly and easily in PowerPoint.

Creating Charts

To launch Microsoft Graph, click the Insert Chart button on the Standard toolbar or choose Insert ➢ Chart from PowerPoint's menu bar. If a slide already contains a chart, double-clicking that object also launches Microsoft Graph for editing.

In Figure 15.9, you can see that Graph contains two windows: a datasheet that includes sample data, and a chart. Replace the labels (text) in the top row and left column with your labels and the values in the remaining cells with your numbers, and you have a basic bar chart. To delete a column or row you don't need, click on its header and press Delete. Close the datasheet at any point to place the chart in your document.

FIGURE 15.9

Inserting a Microsoft Graph chart object

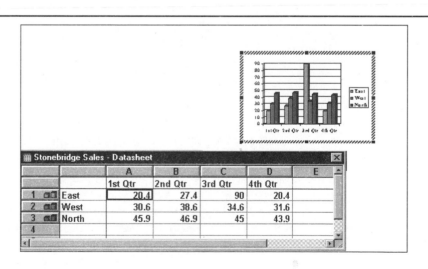

		A	B	C	D	E
		1st Qtr	2nd Qtr	3rd Qtr	4th Qtr	
1	East	20.4	27.4	90	20.4	
2	West	30.6	38.6	34.6	31.6	
3	North	45.9	46.9	45	43.9	
4						

You can resize and reposition the chart object as you would any other object. You must select the chart to resize it; a selected chart object has hollow handles. Double-clicking the chart opens the chart object so you can edit the individual objects inside it; when you can edit the chart, the object handles are solid, and you cannot move the chart object. To select the entire object again for moving or sizing, click outside of the chart to close it, then click once on the chart object.

Using Existing Data

If you already have data, don't reenter it—you can import or copy data into Microsoft Graph. Graph can convert data from Excel, text files, SYLK files, Lotus 1-2-3, and CSV (comma-separated) files that can be exported from most spreadsheet and database programs.

 To import data from an existing file, start Graph just as you would if you were creating a chart from scratch, choose Edit ➢ Import File on the Graph menu, or click the Import File button to open the Import File dialog box. Once you select a file in this typical Windows file window, the Import Data Options dialog box opens so you can select which part of the workbook or worksheet to use. Turn on Overwrite Existing Cells to replace the current data in the Graph datasheet. Turn this option off, and the imported data will be appended at the end of the current data in the datasheet.

Copying or Linking Existing Data   Use Copy and Paste or Paste Special to use existing data from Word or Excel to create a chart. Select and copy the data in its source application. In Graph, select the first cell where you want the data to appear. Choose the upper-left cell to overwrite the existing data, or select the left cell in an empty row to append the data. Paste the data, or choose Edit ➢ Paste Link from the Graph menu to link the chart to the table or worksheet. (With linking, changes you make to the data in the source application will be automatically reflected in the Graph chart.)

If you often work in Excel, you probably create most of your charts there. However, you can choose to create charts from within PowerPoint using Microsoft Graph and have access to most of Excel's formatting features as well.

Formatting a Chart

Graph has its own buttons that append themselves to the Standard toolbar once a chart is created. You have all the features you'll need to create a great-looking representation of your numerical data. Table 15.1 describes the buttons on the Graph toolbar.

TABLE 15.1: MICROSOFT GRAPH TOOLBAR BUTTONS		
Button	**Name**	**Use**
	By Rows	Displays data series by row. First row of the table provides x-axis labels.
	By Columns	Displays data series by column. First column of the table provides x-axis labels.
	Data Table	Toggles between showing and hiding the data table with the chart.
	Chart Type	Allows you to change to another chart type such as 3-D Pie or Area.
	Category Axis Guidelines	Toggles to show or hide major vertical guidelines on chart.
	Value Axis Guidelines	Toggles to show or hide major horizontal guidelines on chart.
	Legend	Toggles to show or hide legend.
	Drawing	Turns Drawing toolbar off or on.
	Fill Color	Fills the background of the selected chart area.

 You can hide the datasheet display using the View Datasheet button on the Graph toolbar. Turning the datasheet off won't prevent you from displaying it with the chart on your slide; you can still use the Data Table button referred to in Table 15.1. However, to edit numbers on the datasheet, you must display it.

With the chart selected, right-click and choose Chart Options to open the Chart Options dialog box. Use the dialog box options to add titles, display minor as well as major gridlines, show and position a legend, display data labels, and include the datasheet as part of the chart object.

 To format an individual chart object (for example, the columns, all the data in a row or column, the chart background, or the legend), select the object in the chart, or choose it from the Chart Objects drop-down list on the toolbar. Then double-click the selected object, right-click and choose Format [Object Name], or click the Format Object button on the toolbar to open the relevant dialog box. For example, the Format Data Series dialog box is shown in Figure 15.10.

FIGURE 15.10

The Format Data Series dialog box appears when you've selected a data series for formatting. Format dialog boxes for other objects offer similar options.

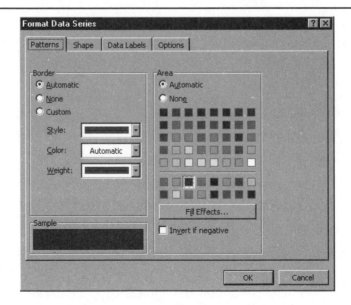

WARNING When you select an entire data series for formatting and then double-click an item in the chart to open the formatting dialog box, the formatting is *only* applied to whichever point in the data series you double-clicked on. If you want to apply formatting to the entire data series, select it using any of the methods described above, and then open the Format dialog box using the toolbar button, rather than double-clicking on the chart object.

Several options are available to you when you choose to format individual chart objects:

1. Use the Pattern tab of the dialog box to change borders and shading of the selected chart objects.

2. Use the Shape tab (when formatting a data series) for changing the shape of bars in your graph.

3. You can display values or percents on point in a series using the Data Labels tab.

4. Increase the depth of the chart and the space between each category of columns under Options.

5. When you've made all your choices, click OK.

Animating Charts

Chart animation allows you to provide dramatic illustrations of numeric data in your presentation. During your slide show, you can introduce an entire chart at one time, or have chart elements appear by category, by data series, or individually. Adding the data separately lets you apply emphasis where needed, and it allows your audience to digest one piece of information before you give them another.

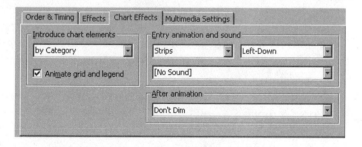

Open the Animation Settings dialog box to the Chart tab. In the Introduce Chart Elements drop-down list, select how you want your chart to appear. Choose By Series to have all bars from a category appear at once. (For example, you might have all four quarters of the West Coast data appear, then the East Coast, etc.). By Category brings in each group of bars separately (all first quarter, then all second quarter, and so on). By Element In A Series and By Element In A Category work essentially the same as By Element and By Category, respectively. The only difference is that only one bar appears at a time, rather than several bars at once.

Choose an effect from the drop-down list. You may find that if you choose to introduce data any way other than all at once, you can't use the particular effect you want. For instance, you can't have chart elements spiral in by category, but you can have them strip down. Turn on Animate Grid And Legend if you want to apply the effect to those chart elements as well. Assign a sound and an After Animation option if you wish.

NOTE Presentations with many different animation settings and transition effects require a fair amount of practice to show well. For a perfectly polished presentation, practice on your own until you have memorized which slides animate automatically and which advance on mouse click. Always keep in mind that your goal is to enhance the content of your presentation, not overpower it. If it's difficult to memorize your animations during practice, you're probably using too many.

Hiding Slides

Many presentations contain "emergency slides" that are only displayed if certain questions or topics arise during the presentation. Creating and then hiding, a slide gives you some leeway: If the question isn't asked, you don't have to show the slide. If, on the other hand, a member of the audience asks how you plan to raise the $10 million, you can whip out the hidden slide.

In Slide Sorter view, select the slide you want to hide, then click the Hide Slide button on the toolbar. A null symbol appears over the slide's number.

To display the hidden slide during the presentation, if you have access to the computer's keyboard, type **H** on the slide preceding the hidden slide.

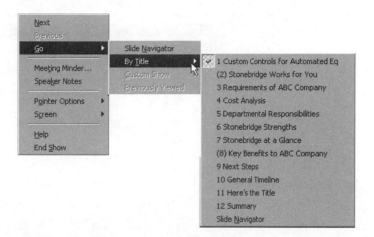

If you are across the room from the computer, using a remote pointing device, you can right-click on the slide before the hidden slide, choose Go ➤ By Title, and select the title of the hidden slide from the shortcut menu. However, the shortcut menu is very intrusive. Further, anyone who uses PowerPoint will know that the slide titles displayed in parentheses on the shortcut are hidden slides. That sort of defeats the purpose of hiding them. Hyperlinks provide a slicker way to show hidden slides.

Adding Links to Other Slides

Hyperlinks, like those used to navigate a Web site, can also be used in PowerPoint presentations. Clicking a hyperlink moves the user from the current slide to another slide, another presentation, or a site on the Internet.

To create a hyperlink, switch to Slide view and select the text that will be used as a hyperlink. Normally, this text will tell the user where they're going to end up: *Click Here to Exit the Presentation*, for example, or *Click to View More Options*. You don't want to have *Click Here for Hidden Slide*, so select some existing text that forms a logical jump-off point. With the text selected, right-click and choose Action Settings from the shortcut menu or choose Slide Show ➤ Action Settings from the menu bar to open the dialog box shown in Figure 15.11.

FIGURE 15.11

*Create hyperlinks in
the Action Settings
dialog box.*

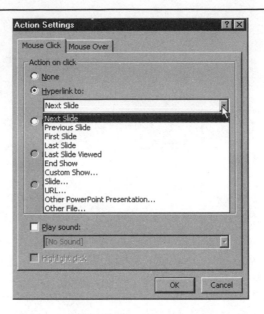

There are two ways to activate a hyperlink: clicking on it or moving the mouse over it. Both pages of this dialog box are identical—choose a page based on which mouse action you want to trigger the hyperlink. Click the Hyperlink To option and select the slide you want to link to. Choosing Next Slide shows the next slide, even if it's hidden. To choose a specific slide, choose Slide from the list to open the Hyperlink To Slide dialog box.

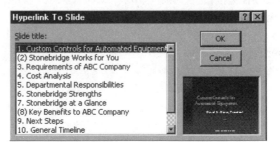

Choose a slide from the list, then click OK. Click OK in the Action Settings dialog box to create the hyperlink. (The Use Relative Path For Link option is used with Internet URLs and files; for a link to another slide, it doesn't matter whether or not this option is enabled.)

When text is turned into a hypertext link, its formatting is changed. The text will be underlined, and a contrasting font color applied. You won't be able to change the color or remove the underlining on the slide. If you want to camouflage hyperlinks, change their colors to match surrounding text by using the Custom tab of the Slide Color Scheme dialog box.

 WARNING Don't change the hyperlink color scheme to match surrounding text if you are displaying your presentation for users to click through themselves. They won't know it's a hyperlink if it doesn't stand out. (And even if you're presenting something you have created, it's possible you might forget the hyperlink without a visual cue.)

What's Next

Now you can create a full-featured presentation sure to grab and keep the attention of any audience. In the next chapter, you will learn how to adapt to different presentation environments. We'll look at the use of regular overheads, 35mm slides, and audience handouts. You will also learn about setting up remote presentations for times when you can't be in the same room as your audience.

CHAPTER **16**

Taking Your Show on the Road

Once you have created, polished and practiced your presentation, it's time to think about delivery. How will your audience see the presentation—in an auditorium, in a small conference room, over the company intranet? What are the differences between presenting on the road and presenting down the hallway? You will want to address setup issues thoroughly so that technical problems don't prevent you from showing a presentation you've worked hours creating. It's equally important to head off glitches that might occur during your presentation—hyperlinks that no longer work, linked files that aren't available, or animations that don't play as expected. No matter how convincingly you recover, technical problems will eventually detract from your message. Fortunately, there are steps you can take to ensure that your presentation runs smoothly.

Getting Feedback on Your Presentation from Your Workgroup

You probably wouldn't deliver new sales materials to a client without first having a colleague proofread them for you. Nor should you give a presentation that hasn't been scrutinized by someone else whose opinion you trust. The spelling checker catches most mistakes, but it can't do anything about a misspelled company name you've told it to ignore. Grammatical errors stemming from improper word usage (*too* instead of *to*, for example) leave the audience with a bad impression.

Few of us write a perfect first draft. Most presentations can benefit from others' input. Have a colleague check your presentation for spelling and grammar errors the Office tools can't catch. Get a second opinion about the appropriateness of your transitions and animations. Have someone outside your field of expertise check the presentation for clarity.

Fortunately, the people who proof your presentation don't have to be in the next office. They could be anywhere in the world! PowerPoint presentations can be attached to e-mail messages where others' comments can be added, or you can opt for online collaboration where you actually build your presentation with the help of another person at another location. Either way, getting suggestions from a second or third person is a great way to polish your presentation.

Incorporating Feedback

PowerPoint lets reviewers annotate slides with comments that you display or hide, allowing you to keep the comments with the presentation as you're working on it. Figure 16.1 shows a slide with a comment added in the default location.

To add a comment when you're the reviewer, in Slide view, choose Insert ➤ Comment from the menu bar. The Reviewing toolbar will appear, and a comment text box will open. Your name appears at the top of the comment. Begin typing, and the comment appears in the yellow text box on the slide.

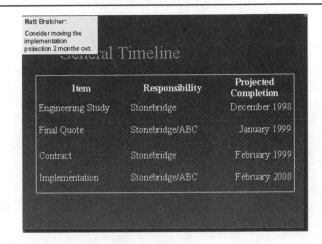

FIGURE 16.1

A slide with a reviewer's comment

To insert another comment, click the Insert Comment button on the Reviewing toolbar. You can have multiple comments for each slide. The Show/Hide Comments button displays or hides all comments in the presentation. When you hide comments, they will not appear in any view until you click the Show/Hide Comments button again.

If you show comments and leave them positioned on your slide, they will appear in Slide Show view (you probably don't want this to happen). You may choose to delete each comment as it is addressed. Simply click at the edge of the comment to activate the frame and press Delete, or click the Delete Comments button on the reviewing toolbar. Another solution is to drag comments into the gray background area of Slide view. That way, you can see them when you need them, but they won't show up during the slide show. Use the comment's handles to move or resize the comment as you would with any other text box.

E-mail your presentation to a colleague for review using your regular mail program or send it from within PowerPoint by choosing File ➤ Send To from the menu. You will have the option of sending the entire presentation as an attachment or sending the slide text as the body of your message.

Collaborating Online

You can get online help from live people without leaving your desk using Power-Point's online collaboration feature. For many organizations implementing Office 2000, the tools for online collaboration will be among the software suite's most valuable new networking features. Chapter 37 covers online collaboration in detail. This section simply shows how to use the tools from PowerPoint.

To access online collaboration, choose Tools ➢ Online Collaboration ➢ Web Discussions. The first time you access this feature, you will be asked to specify a discussion server in the dialog box shown in Figure 16.2. The network administrator in your office can provide you with a discussion server. Type its full name in the first field and a user-friendly description in the second field. Once you're online, others can see your presentation and offer feedback using the Web discussion tools, more fully discussed in Chapter 37.

FIGURE 16.2

*Specifying a discussion
server*

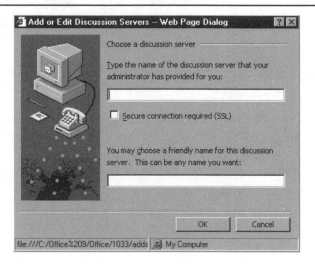

 TIP For general online help with tips and troubleshooting from Microsoft, choose Help ➢ Office On The Web.

MASTERING THE OPPORTUNITIES

Developing a Presentation as a Team

If you are creating a presentation jointly with one or more people in your workgroup, you may wish to keep it in a shared network folder. That way, each collaborator can access and edit the same file rather than having multiple unfinished drafts floating around the office.

Start by working together to develop an outline. Then decide on a template (customized, if you wish). Talk about the type of transitions and animations to be used. Decide whether each person should animate his own slides or if one person should do it after all slides have been created. Discuss which slides will have supporting graphics.

Once you have made those decisions, you can delegate parts of the outline to each team member for preparation of slides. Team members can work independently during the slide preparation stage, saving their work as they go along. When all slides are complete, you may wish to pull everyone together for a "polishing" meeting so each person has input as to the final draft. If more than one team member will speak during the actual presentation, it is important to do at least one "dress rehearsal" to ensure that the material flows smoothly between presenters.

If you don't have a network for sharing files, you can still collaborate on a presentation. Have each participant complete her slides in a separate presentation. Transfer them to one PC via floppy disk and use Slide Finder to incorporate all slides into one presentation. (See Chapter 13 for more about Slide Finder.)

Preparing Handouts and Notes

Handouts are pictures of the slides or the outline from a presentation that you give to participants. You can choose to arrange handouts so they have two, three, four, six, or nine slides to a page. Or you may choose to create a handout from your outline.

The Handout Master

You use the handout master to view the handout layouts. Choose View ➤ Master ➤ Handout Master or press Shift and click the Outline View button to open the master, shown in Figure 16.3.

PART

III

Taking Your Show on the Road

The dotted lines show where slides will appear in the layout selected in the Handout Master toolbar. The handout master contains areas for the footer, header, and page number. By default, the footer area displays the title of your presentation (not to be confused with the presentation's file name). If you have chosen to number slides or display the date and time in the presentation, the handout master will default to display these fields also.

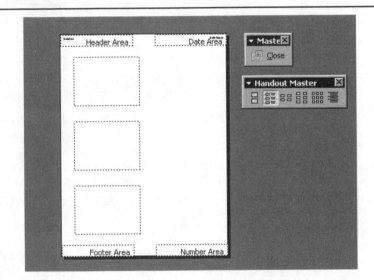

You can click in any of the areas to edit the contents. It's easiest to edit the master if you change the Zoom ratio to 75% or 100% so you can see the text. Or you can open the Header And Footer dialog box (View ➤ Header And Footer) and change any settings there. The header, footer, page, and date information you enter in the dialog box will replace the appropriate placeholders in the handout master when you print handouts.

Format the color scheme or background of your handouts by choosing Format ➤ Handout Color Scheme or Format ➤ Handout Background from the menu. The dialog boxes you see here should look familiar if you have customized slide backgrounds. Use these dialog boxes just as if you were formatting a slide (as explained in Chapter 14).

Printing in PowerPoint

Clicking the Print button on the Standard toolbar prints the entire presentation in the default setting—usually Slide view. If the slides have a background, this can take some time, even on a laser printer. In PowerPoint, it's always best to choose File ➤ Print to open the Print dialog box (shown in Figure 16.4) so you can select whether to print slides, handouts, notes, or an outline.

FIGURE 16.4

The Print dialog box

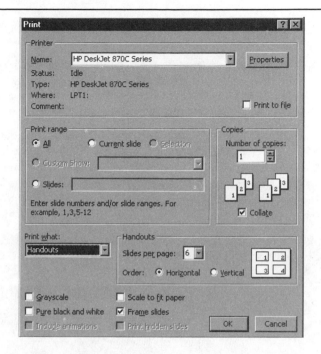

The default print setting is to print All Slides. If you just to want print some slides, enter their numbers in the Slides text box. Choose what you want to print (slides, handouts, an outline) in the Print What drop-down list. If you are printing a color presentation on a noncolor printer, click the Pure Black And White check box to speed up the printing process. Click the Grayscale check box to print black-and-white on a color printer.

 TIP You can change the default print settings by choosing Tools ➤ Options and selecting the Print tab of the Options dialog box.

Click the Frame Slides check box to print a simple box around each slide; this is a good idea if the slides themselves don't include a border. If there are hidden slides in your presentation, the default is to print them. You can disable that option by clearing its check box.

In the Print dialog box, you can also choose how many slides per handout page to print. If you have previously used the handout master to choose the number of slides per page, you can override that choice here.

PART

III

Taking Your Show on
the Road

MASTERING THE OPPORTUNITIES

Printing Report Covers from PowerPoint Slides

If your presentation setting is rather formal and you have to hand out a packet of materials, why not make the title slide of your presentation into a report cover?

If you are using a dark background for your presentation, it is a good idea to format the title slide temporarily with a light background. In Slide view, navigate to your first slide. Choose Format ➤ Slide Color Scheme and select a standard scheme that displays a light-colored or white background. If you only have access to a black-and-white printer, choose the black-and-white scheme. (See Chapter 14 for more on customizing color schemes.) Click Apply.

Select File ➤ Page Setup from the menu to open the Page Setup dialog box shown below. Change the orientation from landscape to portrait. Click OK.

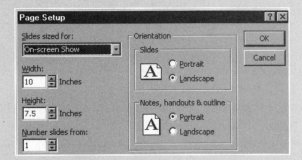

Make sure there is high-quality bond paper in your default printer tray. You might even choose to load card stock. Now print as many copies of the report cover as you need by choosing File ➤ Print from the menu. Be sure to click Current Slide in the Print dialog box, and use the spin box to select the number of report covers you need.

When you are finished printing, you will need to return your slides to their original landscape orientation, and the title slide should have its original color scheme restored. If you have just finished printing, click Undo twice. Or you can manually return your slides to their original formats by using the Page Setup dialog box and Slide Color Scheme dialog box referred to above.

Creating Handouts in Word

You can use the power of Office integration to create handouts and reports for a Power-Point presentation in Word. The Write-Up tool transfers the text and/or slides from the current presentation to a Word document, which you can then edit, format, and print. Choose File ➤ Send To ➤ Microsoft Word to open the Write-Up dialog box, shown in Figure 16.5.

FIGURE 16.5

When you create handouts from slides, the Write-Up dialog box lets you choose how the text you'll add in Word will appear in relation to your slides.

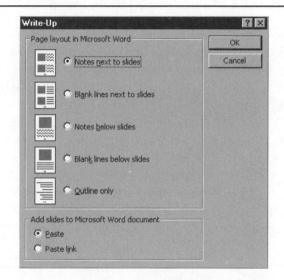

Select how you want the presentation to appear: in one of the four different handout-style layouts, or as an outline. Choose whether you want to paste a copy from your presentation or link the Word document to the presentation. If you choose Paste Link, changes to the presentation will be updated in the Word document; however, you'll lose some of the editing flexibility in Word.

When you have selected Page Layout and Paste options, click OK. PowerPoint will launch Word and export your outline or slides. Edit and print the document as you would a Word document. If you sent slides (instead of an outline), don't worry if it takes a few minutes. Each slide is exported as a graphic object, which takes some time.

PART

III

Taking Your Show on the Road

TIP If you're only transferring an outline, click the Black And White View button on the Standard toolbar before opening the Write Up dialog box for easier formatting in Word.

Preparing 35mm Slides and Overhead Transparencies

If you have a desktop slide printer, you can print your presentation as 35mm slides for use in a traditional slide projector. Even if you don't, you can still convert the Power-Point slides to 35mm. Genigraphics and other service bureaus can take your presentation (or selected slides from it) and convert it to 35mm. If you intend to do this, you need to install the Genigraphics Wizard from the Office CD. If the wizard is installed, you can choose File ➤ Send To ➤ Genigraphics and the wizard will walk you through packaging the slides.

To print black-and-white or color transparencies for an overhead projector, simply insert transparency film in your printer, and then print the slides (without animations) using the Print dialog box.

 TIP Transparencies look best with clear (white) backgrounds, black text, and occasional splashes of color. Avoid dark backgrounds or graphic-heavy templates more appropriate to on-screen presentations.

Setting Slide Timings

Once you have added transitions and animation, you are ready to run through your slides in preparation for the actual presentation. Rehearsal is vital—you'd rather discover problems in private than have them projected to a large audience.

Automated vs. Manual Advance

There are two ways to advance an electronic presentation. If the presentation is designed to run "on its own"—for example, in a booth at a trade show, you'll want to advance slides automatically. If your finished presentation will be used to illustrate a verbal presentation, or posted on an intranet, you will usually prefer to advance slides manually. If you use manual advance, then your presentation is essentially completed. You'll need to rehearse the presentation a few times, making sure that you know how many times to click on each slide to display all the animations.

Setting Automatic Timings

If you want to use automatic advance, a bit more work is required. There are two ways to set slide timings: through rehearsal, or manually in the Slide Transition dialog box. (You can only enter animation timings by rehearsal.) It's easiest to create timings through rehearsal and then alter individual advances manually. Before setting timings, run through the entire slide show two or three times. Try not to advance slides and animations too quickly for your audience, who will be seeing the slides for the first time. Make sure that your audience will have time to read the title, read each point, and see how a graphic illustrates the points. It helps to read the contents of each slide out loud, slowly, while rehearsing and setting the timings.

1. Click the Rehearse Timings button on the Slide Sorter toolbar. The first slide will appear, and the Rehearsal dialog box will open.

2. The dialog box has two timers. The timer on the right shows the total time for the presentation. The left timer is the elapsed time for the current slide. Click anywhere on the slide for your next animation or your next slide. The timers automatically record the number of seconds that pass between clicks.

3. The Rehearsal dialog box also has three buttons: Next, Pause, and Repeat. Clicking the Next button moves to the next slide or animation, but you can do this by clicking anywhere on the slide.

4. If you are interrupted in the middle of rehearsal, click the Pause button, and then Pause again to resume.

5. If you make a mistake while rehearsing a slide, click Repeat to set new timings for the current slide. If you don't catch a mistake before a slide has been advanced, you can either finish rehearsing and then edit the slide time manually, or close the dialog box and begin again.

6. When you complete the entire rehearsal for a presentation, you'll be prompted to save the timings. Choosing Yes assigns the timings to the slide transitions

and animations. In Slide Sorter view, the timing will appear below the slide. Choosing No brings you back to Slide Sorter view, with no timings assigned.

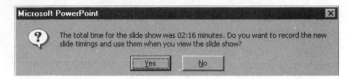

7. To edit an individual transition time, select the slide and click the Transition Effects button on the Slide Sorter toolbar. The rehearsed time, which you can edit, will be displayed in the dialog box.

Customizing Shows for Different Audiences

Sometimes you'll need to create multiple versions of the same slide show to present to different audiences. For instance, you might have an East Coast and a West Coast version of the same sales presentation. Both versions use identical slides 1–12, but slides 13–25 are different depending on where the client is located. The versions may differ only slightly, but until now you had to save each as a separate file. In Office 2000 you can create a presentation within a presentation using PowerPoint's new Custom Shows feature. Essentially, you group slides together under a certain name and then display or skip them depending on which version of the show you need for the current audience.

To begin customizing, choose Slide Show ➢ Custom Shows from the menu. The Custom Shows dialog box opens.

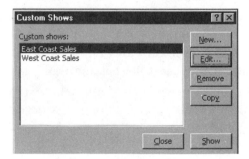

Click New to open the Define Custom Show dialog box.

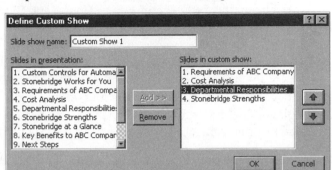

Name your show, overwriting the default of Custom Show 1. Select the slides you wish to include in this version of the show and click Add to move them to the list on the right. If you change your mind and want to remove a slide from the included list, simply select it and click the Remove button.

Use the arrows to change the order of the selected slide. Click OK to finish defining your custom show and return to the Custom Shows dialog box. Your newly defined show will be displayed there. Define another custom show using the New button, or edit the selected show by clicking Edit. If you no longer wish to keep a custom show, you can remove it here as well.

During the presentation, you can right-click, choose Go ➢ Custom Show on the short-cut menu, and then click the show you want. However, the shortcut menu is rather intru-sive. You may prefer to set up the presentation so it displays the custom version when you start the slide show. (See the next section, "Setting Up the Slide Show.")

 TIP You can also skip to a custom show by creating a hyperlink to that show. Choose Slide Show ➢ Action Settings or Insert ➢ Hyperlink from the menu. For more information, see "Adding Links to Other Slides" in Chapter 15.

Setting Up the Slide Show

You've designed a good presentation, had it reviewed by a colleague, and practiced clicking through the slides. Before you present the slide show, choose Slide Show ➢ Set Up Show or hold Shift and click the Slide Show button to open the Set Up Show dialog box, shown in Figure 16.6. In the Show Type area, select a presentation method and choose whether or not to use narration. (See "Recording Narration" later in this

PART

III

Taking Your Show on the Road

chapter.) In the Advance Slides area, choose Manually or Slide Timings. To show the presentation continuously, choose Using Timings and click the Loop Continuously Until 'Esc' check box. In the Slides area, you can choose to show the entire presentation, certain slide numbers, or a custom presentation.

During the presentation, you can use the mouse pointer to draw on the slides to emphasize a point (see "Drawing on Slides" below). You have a choice of colors for the pen. Choose a color that will contrast with both the background and text colors used in the slides. The Projector Wizard is helpful if you are setting up an LCD panel for an on-screen presentation. Click OK once you've made your choices.

FIGURE 16.6

The Set Up Show dialog box

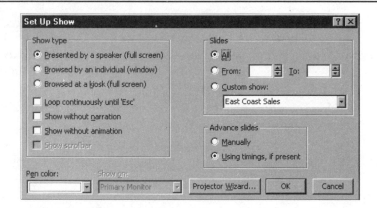

The slide show settings are saved with the presentation. Clicking the Slide Show button runs the slide show with the settings you previously chose in the Set Up Show dialog box.

When you click on the final slide in a slide show, you return to the PowerPoint window. To end on a blank slide, choose Tools ➤ Options to open the Options dialog box. Click the View tab, then click on End With Black Slide.

To start the slide show, click the Slide Show View button. When the show begins, a shortcut menu button appears in the lower-left or lower-right corner of the slide. Clicking the button opens a shortcut menu.

The shortcut menu gives you additional options for navigating through your presentation. Most often, you'll manually click as you present or use the slide timings you've previously set up. With the menu you can choose Previous or Next (PgUp and PgDn on the keyboard) to move to the previous or next slide. To move to a specific slide, choose Go ➢ Slide Navigator to open the Slide Navigator. Select a slide to move to, and click OK.

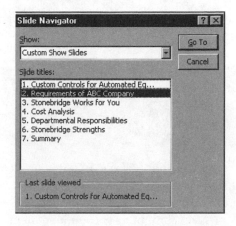

Recording Narration

There are times when you may need voice narration for your presentation. Perhaps a key team member can't attend but wants to view the slides at another time. Perhaps you want to keep a voice record of the meeting. Shows that run at a kiosk or on a Web site may also be good candidates for narration. You can record narration before you run the slide show, or you can record it during the presentation and include comments from meeting participants. When recording narration, you need a computer with a sound card and microphone. To show a presentation with narration, the computer needs only a sound card.

 WARNING Voice narration takes precedence over all other sounds. If you have included transition and/or animation sounds but choose to show slides using narration, only the narration will play.

PART

III

Taking Your Show on the Road

Choose Slide Show ➤ Record Narration from the menu. This opens the Record Narration dialog box shown in Figure 16.7.

FIGURE 16.7

*The Record Narration
dialog box*

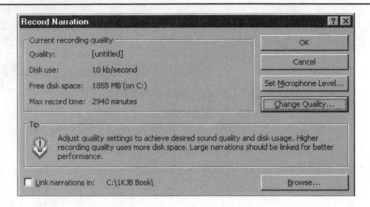

Choose Set Microphone Level to test your microphone and set up an appropriate volume for the narration. You can change the quality of your sound here as well, but be aware that higher-quality sound output takes up much more disk space and may run too slowly on computers with limited memory. To insert narration as a linked sound file, activate that check box. Click OK to begin recording narration. You will be prompted to choose whether you want to start on the current slide or the first slide.

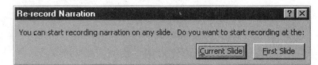

During recording you can right-click and pause if necessary. Right-click and choose Resume to begin recording where you left off. When you have finished recording, Power-Point saves the narration with each slide and asks whether you want to save the new timings as well. It is probably a good idea to save these new timings since they coincide with the narrations and any previously recorded timings may not. Slides with narrations display a speaker icon in the bottom-right corner.

You can delete unwanted narrations from a slide by selecting the speaker icon and pressing the Delete key.

There are times when voice narration is not appropriate. Noisy convention halls make it difficult to hear and understand narration at a kiosk. Participants in a meeting might be hearing-impaired, making voice narration unsuitable. And it's likely your Web presentation will sometimes be viewed on computers without sound cards. You can opt to show your presentation without previously recorded narration in the Set Up Show dialog box under the Slide Show menu.

Broadcasting Presentations

With Microsoft NetShow, you can show a presentation over a TCP/IP network or the Internet. Members of the audience view the presentation on their computers. You can schedule the meeting in advance either by phoning participants or by using Microsoft Outlook (see Chapter 20). You also have the option of starting a meeting at any time from within the presentation you want to share. During the presentation, you can choose to take complete control while audience members watch, or you can turn on Online Collaboration, allowing participants to make changes to the presentation. Chapter 46 discusses online presentations in detail, and Chapter 37 discusses the Online Collaboration option.

Drawing on Slides

During the slide show, you can use the Pen tool to draw on a slide, underlining or circling an object or text to make a point. Press Ctrl+P, or choose Pen from the shortcut menu, and the mouse pointer becomes a pen. Drag to draw on the current slide. Right-click and choose Arrow, or press Ctrl+A to turn the pen off. The drawing isn't saved, so no damage is done to the slide.

You can change the color of the pen tool before you begin a presentation by choosing Slide Show ➢ Set Up Show from the menu. Select a color from the drop-down list. Although it's somewhat intrusive, you can also change pen colors during your presentation. In Slide Show view, right-click and choose Pointer Options ➢ Pen Color from the shortcut menu. Click once on the color you want.

PART

III

Taking Your Show on
the Road

Generating Meeting Notes

During the presentation, you can enter minutes or action items in the Meeting Minder. Right-click in Slide Show view and choose Meeting Minder. Click the Minutes tab to enter meeting minutes.

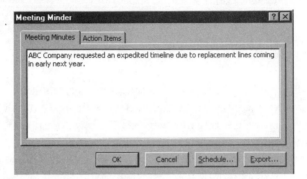

In the Action Items page, enter the "to do" list generated during the meeting, including due dates and the person responsible for the item. If the date or responsible person changes, or if the item is eliminated in later discussion, select the item from the list and edit or delete it. Click the Schedule button to launch Microsoft Outlook and enter this item on your calendar or To Do list.

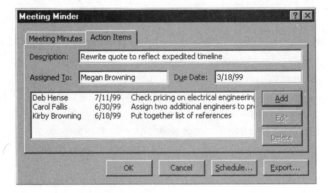

When the conference is finished, click the Export button to export the minutes to Word and the Action Items to Word and/or Outlook.

Viewing on Two Screens

If you're running Microsoft Windows 98 or Windows NT version 5, you can get the benefits of online broadcasting even if you're doing a live presentation to a group. PowerPoint's View On Two Screens option allows you to set up a show with one computer (say, your laptop) as the presenter and the other (a computer with a large monitor) as the audience. You get to see your slides and notes while the audience only sees the slides.

First, connect the two computers using a direct-connect serial cable. Then, on each computer, choose Slide Show ➤ Set Up Show to open the dialog box shown in Figure 16.6 earlier in this chapter. Click the drop-down list and select the monitor you wish to use to show the presentation.

Saving a Presentation for Use on Another Computer

Office includes a PowerPoint Viewer that you can copy in order to display a presentation on a computer that doesn't include PowerPoint. To bundle your presentation and the viewer in one easy, compressed package, choose File ➤ Pack And Go to launch the Pack And Go Wizard. As you proceed through the wizard, you'll be asked to select a presentation, a destination drive, linking and embedding options, and whether the file should include the PowerPoint Viewer. If your presentation includes linked objects or fonts that may not appear on the computer used to display the presentation, choose to include linked files and to embed fonts.

 WARNING When you embed fonts and include linked files, even compressed files can become very large, requiring five, ten or even more standard floppy disks. "Packing" time for these large files is considerable. You will probably want to use a Zip disk or other high-capacity medium to transport the presentation file between computers. If your e-mail system supports transmission of large amounts of data, consider sending the presentation that way.

When it's time to unpack the presentation, take the following steps:

1. Insert the disk created by Pack And Go if you used portable media, and then open Windows Explorer.

2. In Windows Explorer, select the drive and/or folder where the disk is located, and then double-click the Pngsetup.exe file.

PART

III

Taking Your Show on the Road

3. Enter a destination for the unpacked presentation and viewer.

4. To start the slide show, double-click the PowerPoint Viewer (`Ppview32.exe`); then click the presentation. If you did not include the viewer you can start the slide show immediately after you unpack it. Or you can launch PowerPoint and open the unpacked file.

What's Next

Now that you've delivered that stunning presentation, you will need to organize the business contacts you've made and follow up on their requests. The tool to use is Outlook 2000. With six applications available from one window, Outlook allows you to efficiently manage your calendar, e-mail, to-do list, business contacts, journal entries, and desktop notes. Set reminders for yourself so you don't drop the ball. Create categories for viewing your data in ways that make sense to you. Print portions of data to take on the road, or synchronize your PC with a hand-held unit. Use Outlook 2000 to stay on top of all those details that make the difference between doing business and doing business well.

PART IV

Getting Organized with Outlook

LEARN TO:

- **Work in the Outlook modules**

- **Create appointments and calendar events**

- **Create, assign, and manage tasks**

- **Send, receive, and manage e-mail messages**

- **Enter, edit, and manage contact information**

- **Record contact activities**

CHAPTER **17**

Understanding Outlook Basics

FEATURING:

Finding your way around Outlook

Using Outlook Today

Working in the Outlook modules

Printing in Outlook

O utlook can help you organize the mountains of information that inundate your working life. The first few times you launch Outlook, it's valuable to spend some time finding your way around. There is much to see and do here—as long as you know where to look and how to make it work for you. Outlook is six distinct applications all rolled up into one: Contacts, Inbox (e-mail), Tasks, Calendar, Journal, and Notes. You can use all six applications, called Outlook modules, or only one, depending on your individual needs and circumstances. The great part is that once you've learned how to use one module effectively, you know most of what you need to use each of them. If you are unsure of which Outlook modules you want to use, start working with the module that you have the greatest need for. Once you are comfortable with one of the modules, it will be much easier to move into the next one. Before long you'll throw away your paper-based planner and start wondering how you ever lived without Outlook.

 TIP When you launch Outlook 2000, be careful not to select Outlook Express, a more limited e-mail application that is included with Internet Explorer.

Outlook Uses and Outlook Users

Outlook 2000 is a flexible tool that can be used in any business environment and has many applications for managing personal information. You can use Outlook effectively on a stand-alone computer with no outside access or as part of a large corporate network with hundreds of computers and multiple sites around the globe. Regardless of your environment, you'll find tools that you can use to organize your information.

Outlook 2000 is referred to as a *desktop information manager (DIM)* but it's really that and more. You can use Outlook 2000 to organize all the information on your desktop, including a significant amount of information that you probably kept only in paper form up to now and some information that you may never have organized at all.

With Outlook 2000, you can:

- Record the names, addresses, and other information related to personal and business contacts.

- Keep your to-do list and organize it by priority, by due date, or in endless other ways.

- Manage your appointments and track birthdays, holidays, and other special events.

- Send electronic mail through the Internet or your corporate network.
- Keep notes about telephone conversations and meetings and, if desired, relate them to individual contacts.
- Schedule a meeting with other people in your workgroup or even across the Internet.
- Organize all of your personal information and files through one central interface.

And this is just the beginning. There is only one way to truly appreciate the power of Outlook 2000—you have to start using it. Once you do, you'll experience an increase in personal productivity and actually start to believe that you'll one day be able to control the incredible amount of information that crosses your desk. Maybe it will even improve your outlook!

Outlook as a Personal Information Manager

Outlook 2000 includes six modules:

Contacts replaces your manual address book. In Contacts, you keep personal and business contact information, names, addresses, e-mail addresses, and other information related to individuals. You can send contacts through Internet e-mail to other Outlook users.

Tasks is your online to-do list. You can list your tasks, assign due dates, prioritize items, and even include shortcuts to Microsoft Office documents that are related to the task. You can also delegate tasks through Internet e-mail to other people who are running Outlook.

Calendar records your appointments, meetings, and other date-specific information, such as birthdays, holidays, vacations, and anniversaries in a date book. You can easily assign times in your calendar to work on items in your Task list.

Inbox is your source for sending and receiving electronic mail from home, the office, or on the road. If you have Internet access, you can participate in Usenet (NNTP) newsgroups and create private discussion groups.

Journal lets you record what you've done. It can be used as a personal diary, a record of conversations and interactions with a client or customer, a time tracker to analyze how you spend your time, and a place to organize documents and communications related to a specific individual or project.

Notes is an electronic notepad to keep track of all those little pieces of paper scattered all over your desk.

Designed to Fit Your Environment

Outlook 2000 comes with three basic configurations depending on your particular environment.

No E-Mail: This is the configuration for stand-alone computers that do not have access to an Internet server on a network.

Internet Only: This option provides e-mail capability for users who have an e-mail service through an Internet service provider or other SMTP/POP3 or IMAP4 mail server. Users can use the Internet vCalendar protocol for sending meeting requests, iCalendar for sharing free/busy calendar information, and vCard for sharing Contact (business card) information.

Corporate/Workgroup: This is the richest of the three configurations, offering full support for e-mail, group scheduling, voting buttons, and message recall using Microsoft Exchange Server or other network mail server.

When you install Outlook for the first time, you are given a choice of which configuration best fits your situation. If you already have Outlook on your computer, the Office 2000 installation program uses your existing configuration.

 TIP If your e-mail services change (for example, if your company installs Microsoft Exchange Server), you can change Outlook configurations by choosing Tools ≻ Options to open the Options dialog box. On the page labeled Mail Services or Mail Delivery (depending on your current configuration), click the Reconfigure Mail Support button. If you change from Internet Only or No E-Mail, you'll need to configure your additional mail services immediately. If you move from Corporate/Workgroup, support for corporate mail services like Microsoft Exchange will be removed.

Outlook on a Small Network

If you work in a small-business setting where you have anywhere from two to twenty computers, you're probably running a peer-to-peer network or small LAN (local area network) using a mail client such as Microsoft Mail or Lotus cc Mail. In this situation, you should install the Corporate/Workgroup configuration. In addition to the personal information management tools listed in the previous section, in this configuration you can:

- Share contacts with others on the network.

- Assign tasks to other users and accept or decline task requests.

- Use group-scheduling features, such as those shown in Figure 17.1, to send and receive meeting requests and let others have access to your personal schedule.

- Store messages in multiple server folders (also available to IMAP4 users); apply Inbox rules, shown in Figure 17.2 (this option is available to SMTP/POP3 users); share public folders; or exchange e-mail without dialing up an Internet service provider.

FIGURE 17.1

Group scheduling features drastically reduce the amount of time spent scheduling meetings.

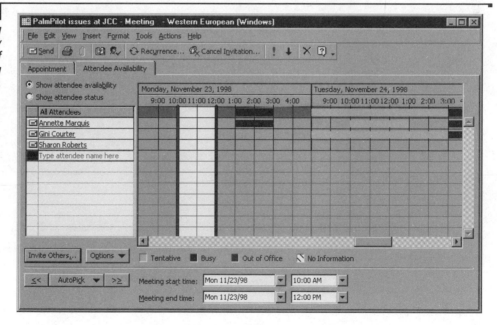

FIGURE 17.2

You can apply Inbox rules to e-mail with the Rules Wizard.

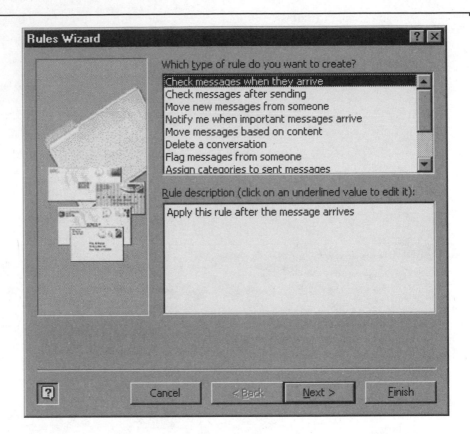

NOTE Users of MS Mail and other LAN mail servers cannot participate in NNTP news-groups or create private discussion groups.

With the advancement of Internet technology, users can also share data with others outside of the traditional networked environment. The biggest advantage of running a network is the ability to exchange e-mail and use other Outlook features collaboratively without connecting to the Internet. This reduces the cost of external phone lines and speeds access for users inside the company.

Outlook in a Corporate Setting

To experience all the incredible functionality of Outlook 2000, you must be running Outlook as a Microsoft Exchange Server client. You don't have to be a large corporation to use Exchange Server. Many small companies are seeing the benefits of running Exchange Server. It's an ideal system for companies organized around a virtual office. By setting up an Exchange Server, you can enable staff to dial in to the server from their homes or hotel rooms and have access to e-mail, to documents stored in public folders, and to shared calendars.

Whether you're in a corporation of thousands or one of five people working from your homes, Outlook 2000 running under Microsoft Exchange Server has this additional functionality:

Calendar lets you see when other users are free or busy; opens other's calendars with appropriate permissions; works with Microsoft Schedule+ for group scheduling; and lets you delegate access to schedule appointments on your calendar.

Inbox stores e-mail on the server in public folders; uses server-based rules to filter your mail; supports voting, message flags, and message recall; allows deferred delivery of e-mail; receives receipts when mail has been delivered or read; gives access to the Exchange Server Global Address List; allows users to access mail remotely; and uses client/server replication of messages.

Workgroup Functionality creates private discussion groups (available also to Internet users) and works with collaboration, workflow, and project tracking applications such as Microsoft Project, Microsoft Team Manager, and Microsoft Office products.

Outlook was clearly designed with the workgroup in mind. Its primary objective is to make collaboration in a workgroup setting efficient, friendly, and productive.

When Outlook is installed on a desktop, it creates a default *user profile,* a group of settings that define how you receive e-mail, where your personal information is stored, and what information services, such as Microsoft Exchange Server, are available to you. User profiles can be set up to be mobile, which means that in an office environment you could log on to any computer and have access to your personal information. You can find more information on profiles in *Mastering Outlook 2000* (Sybex, 1999).

Exploring the Application Window

The Outlook application window, labeled in Figure 17.3, has many elements that are familiar to Microsoft Office and Windows users. The application window itself has a title bar that identifies the name of the application and the module that is currently active. On the far right side of the title bar are standard Minimize, Maximize/Restore, and Close buttons that you can use to control the application window. Underneath the title bar are two toolbars, one that contains menu options and one with buttons to access most commonly used features.

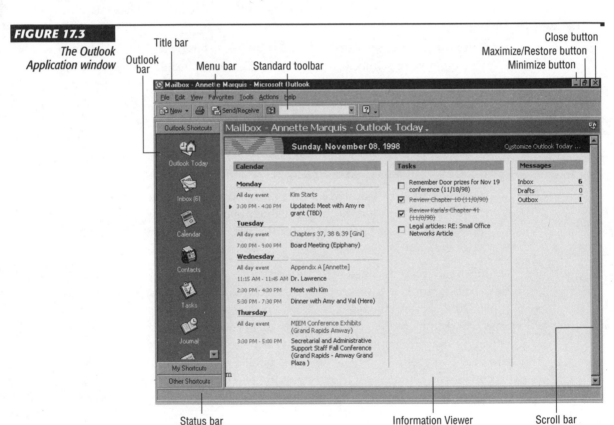

FIGURE 17.3

The Outlook Application window

The bar of icons on the left side of the application window is called the Outlook Bar. These icons let you move between the Outlook modules and easily access other folders. Outlook data is displayed in the larger window to the right of the Outlook Bar called the Information Viewer. You can use the scroll bars on the Information Viewer to see data that does not appear in the display. The status bar displays messages and information: for example, the number of items in an active module.

 NOTE Every record in Outlook—a contact, a task, an appointment, an e-mail message, a journal entry, or a note—is referred to as an *item*. Items are stored in folders designated by the module in which the item was created. You can create new folders and then move and copy Outlook items between folders to organize your data. See Chapter 21 for more about organizing items in folders.

Toolbars

The toolbar menu options and buttons are dynamic, which means that they change depending upon which module is active at the current time. For example, if you are in Contacts, the Actions menu has options related to creating a new contact, sending a message to a contact, calling a contact, and so on. If you are in Calendar, the options on the Action menu relate to creating new appointments, new events, and new recurring appointments.

If you have difficulty finding a menu option that you know you saw somewhere before, switch to the module in which you would most likely use that option, and you'll probably find it on one of the menus there. For more options, you can turn on the Advanced toolbar by choosing View ➤ Toolbars and clicking Advanced.

 If these aren't enough options to suit you, you can create your own custom toolbars and customize any of the available Outlook toolbars. (In Chapter 38, you can learn how to create and customize toolbars in any Office application.)

 The first button on the Standard toolbar is the New button. This button is the easiest way to create any new item—a new task, a new contact, or a new appointment, for example. Just remember that what it creates depends on the currently active module. When you point to the New button, a ScreenTip tells you what the button is currently set to do.

Regardless of which module you are in, you can choose to create any new item by clicking the New button's down-arrow. This opens up the New menu, shown in Figure 17.4, and gives you all the new item choices available in Outlook.

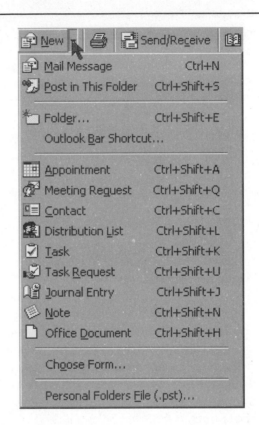

The Outlook Bar

The Outlook Bar on the left side of the application window (see Figure 17.3) gives you easy access to the Outlook modules and to other folders on your computer. Click any of the icon shortcuts to activate that module. Use the scroll bar button on the bottom of the Outlook Bar to see other icons on the Outlook Bar. Shortcuts on the Outlook Bar are organized into groups. Click one of the group buttons, such as My Shortcuts, at the bottom or top of the Outlook Bar to display the shortcuts available in that group.

To change the size of the icons on the Outlook Bar so that more can be displayed, right-click anywhere on the bar except directly on a button and choose Small Icons from the pop-up menu that appears.

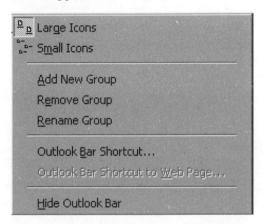

If you decide that the Outlook Bar takes up too much room on your screen, click Outlook Bar on the View menu to turn the Outlook Bar off. Click View ➢ Outlook Bar again to make it visible again.

The Information Viewer

The Information Viewer is where it all happens—where Outlook displays all of your data. The Information Viewer displays multiple items or records at once. This is where you see all of your unread e-mail, a catalog of your contacts, or a list of your tasks. The best part about the Information Viewer is that it displays your data the way you want to see it. You can sort your data, group it together, and find records that meet specific criteria.

Outlook Today

When you start Outlook for the first time, you will probably start in Outlook Today (See Figure 17.3). Using an interface like a Web browser, Outlook Today provides you with the day-at-a-glance view of your world by listing your appointments, e-mail that has yet to be handled, and tasks that are due to be completed. In an ideal world, you would spend your day completing these responsibilities and then start fresh tomorrow with a brand new list. Recognizing that few of us live in that ideal world, Outlook

Today by default displays appointments for the next five days and includes tasks that are overdue as well as those that are due today. However, if you'd rather focus only on today or see more than five days of appointments, you can change some of the basic options that control Outlook Today.

> **NOTE** If Outlook Today does not appear automatically when you launch Outlook, you can launch it yourself by clicking the Outlook Today icon on the Outlook Bar.

To change the options, click the Customize Outlook Today button in the upper-right corner of the Outlook Today window.

The Customize form, shown in Figure 17.5, opens so you can change the following:

Startup: If you like Outlook Today's view of your world, click the check box to have Outlook Today appear every time you launch Outlook.

Messages: You can choose to display messages from your Inbox, Drafts, or Outbox folder.

Calendar: Display between 1 and 7 days of your calendar by choosing the number from the drop-down list.

FIGURE 17.5

The Outlook Today Options form

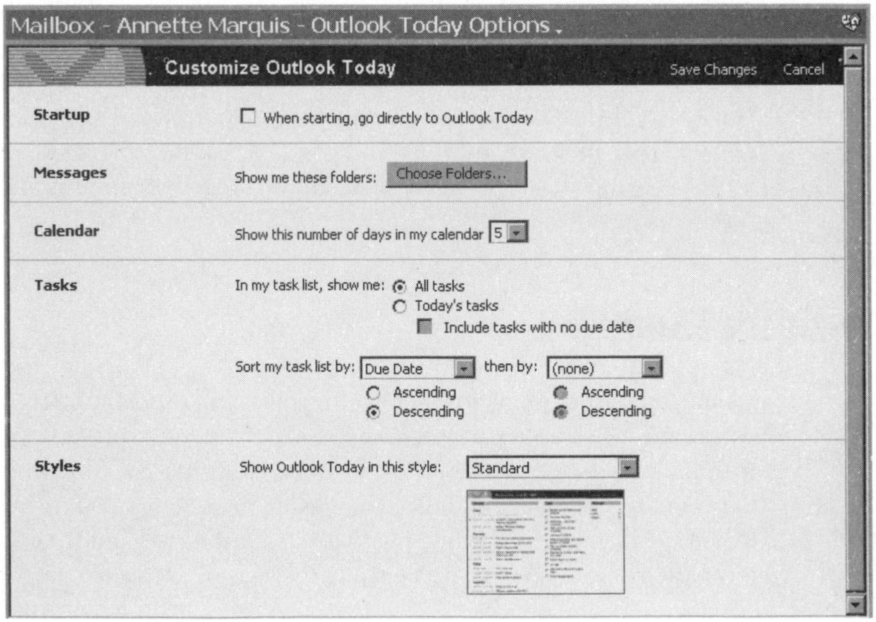

Mailbox - Annette Marquis - Outlook Today Options

Customize Outlook Today — Save Changes   Cancel

Startup ☐ When starting, go directly to Outlook Today

Messages Show me these folders: [Choose Folders...]

Calendar Show this number of days in my calendar [5 ▾]

Tasks In my task list, show me: ⊙ All tasks
⊙ Today's tasks
☐ Include tasks with no due date

Sort my task list by: [Due Date ▾]   then by: [(none) ▾]
○ Ascending   ○ Ascending
⊙ Descending   ⊙ Descending

Styles Show Outlook Today in this style: [Standard ▾]

Tasks: Select All Tasks or Today's Tasks, which shows only those incomplete tasks that are due today. You can also indicate how you'd like the tasks sorted.

Styles: Choose between different presentations of Outlook Today.

When you have finished setting your preferences, click Save Changes to return to Outlook Today.

Working in the Outlook Modules

Each Outlook module has some unique features. However, some operations, such as how you enter and edit text, are common to all six modules. In this section, we will explore the common features of the Outlook modules.

There are two ways to work with Outlook data: in the Information Viewer or on Outlook forms. As mentioned earlier in the chapter, the Information Viewer shows you multiple Outlook items or records. You can enter data directly in the Information Viewer or you can double-click a particular record to open that item in a form. By contrast, a form displays an individual Outlook record: all the information about a particular contact, the entire contents of an e-mail message, or the details of a scheduled appointment. The Information Viewer lets you look at your data as a group—all the people from the same company or all of your unread e-mail—while forms let you focus on one record and see all its data.

Viewing Data in the Information Viewer

One of Outlook's greatest strengths is its ability to display your data in a wide variety of ways. Because the Information Viewer lets you look at multiple records at one time, how you view your data here is paramount. Before you can enter or edit data in the Information Viewer, it's necessary to understand what you are seeing as you move between the Outlook modules.

Types of Views

A view is a defined set of fields, sort order, grouping, filters, and formats all contained in one of the five types of layouts available in Outlook. Each of the Outlook modules has a default view, but you can switch to or create different views. There are five types of views:

Card view: The default in Contacts, this view type displays contact data in an address book fashion, similar to the card file sitting on your desk. You can use buttons on the left side of the screen to navigate quickly between records.

Table View: The default in Tasks and commonly used in all modules, this view type is organized in rows and columns, as shown in Figure 17.6.

Timeline View: The default view type in Journal. Data is displayed along a time-line. The emphasis is on when things occurred—for example, when a journal entry was made or an e-mail message received.

Day/Week/Month View: The default view type in Calendar, shown in Figure 17.7, this closely resembles a day planner. Data for a day, week, or month is displayed. By default, a list of tasks is also displayed in table format.

Icon View: The default in Notes, this view type displays records as icons similar to the familiar icon view from My Computer in Windows.

FIGURE 17.6

Table view is the default view in Tasks.

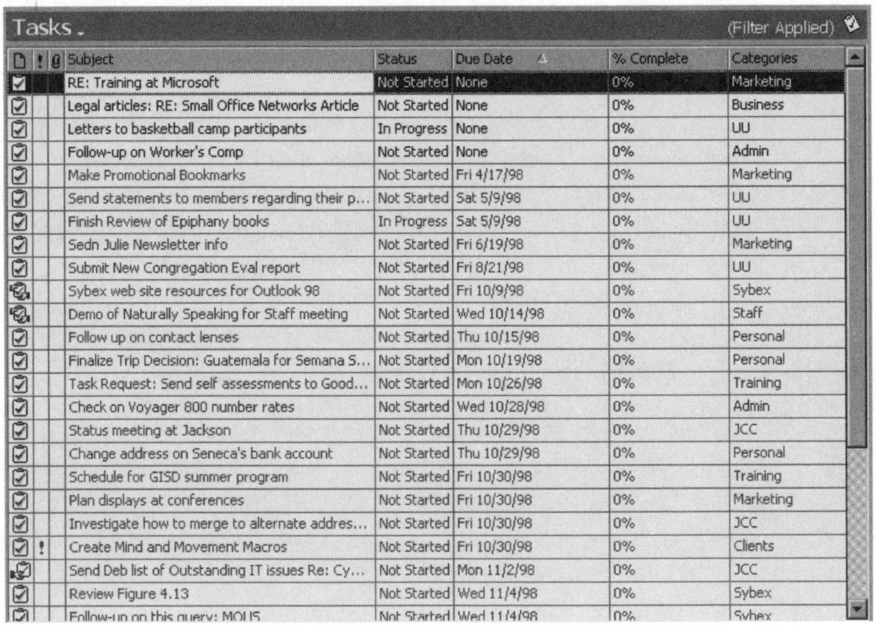

	!	0	Subject	Status	Due Date △	% Complete	Categories
			RE: Training at Microsoft	Not Started	None	0%	Marketing
			Legal articles: RE: Small Office Networks Article	Not Started	None	0%	Business
			Letters to basketball camp participants	In Progress	None	0%	UU
			Follow-up on Worker's Comp	Not Started	None	0%	Admin
			Make Promotional Bookmarks	Not Started	Fri 4/17/98	0%	Marketing
			Send statements to members regarding their p...	Not Started	Sat 5/9/98	0%	UU
			Finish Review of Epiphany books	In Progress	Sat 5/9/98	0%	UU
			Sedn Julie Newsletter info	Not Started	Fri 6/19/98	0%	Marketing
			Submit New Congregation Eval report	Not Started	Fri 8/21/98	0%	UU
			Sybex web site resources for Outlook 98	Not Started	Fri 10/9/98	0%	Sybex
			Demo of Naturally Speaking for Staff meeting	Not Started	Wed 10/14/98	0%	Staff
			Follow up on contact lenses	Not Started	Thu 10/15/98	0%	Personal
			Finalize Trip Decision: Guatemala for Semana S...	Not Started	Mon 10/19/98	0%	Personal
			Task Request: Send self assessments to Good...	Not Started	Mon 10/26/98	0%	Training
			Check on Voyager 800 number rates	Not Started	Wed 10/28/98	0%	Admin
			Status meeting at Jackson	Not Started	Thu 10/29/98	0%	JCC
			Change address on Seneca's bank account	Not Started	Thu 10/29/98	0%	Personal
			Schedule for GISD summer program	Not Started	Fri 10/30/98	0%	Training
			Plan displays at conferences	Not Started	Fri 10/30/98	0%	Marketing
			Investigate how to merge to alternate addres...	Not Started	Fri 10/30/98	0%	JCC
	!		Create Mind and Movement Macros	Not Started	Fri 10/30/98	0%	Clients
			Send Deb list of Outstanding IT issues Re: Cy...	Not Started	Mon 11/2/98	0%	JCC
			Review Figure 4.13	Not Started	Wed 11/4/98	0%	Sybex
			Follow-up on this query: MOUS	Not Started	Wed 11/4/98	0%	Sybex

Tasks (Filter Applied)

Regardless of what view you are in, items are initially sorted alphabetically or chronologically. In some views, data is also grouped according to common values or entries in a field. For example, to see all your contacts within a single company, you could group by company and then optionally sort the contacts within each company by last name. Grouped views usually are indicated with the word "by" in their name—for example, the By Company (see Figure 17.8) or By Category views in Contacts.

FIGURE 17.7

The Day/Week/Month view of Calendar resembles a day planner.

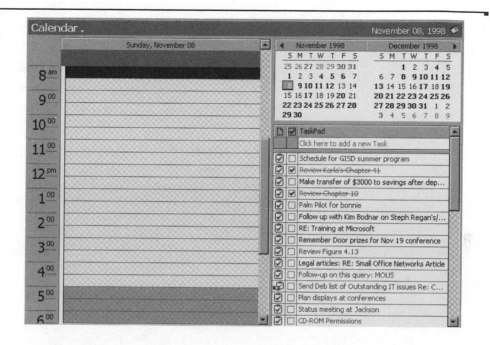

FIGURE 17.8

Contact data grouped in the By Company view

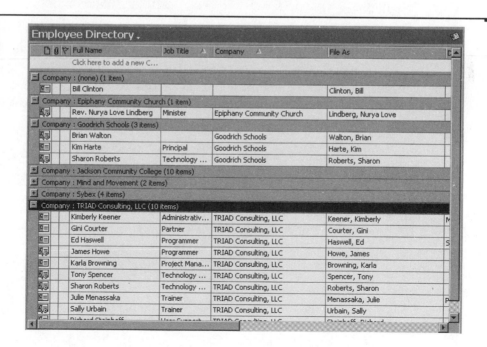

Changing Your View

Whether you want to switch to one of the predefined views, alter an existing view, or create your own from scratch, Outlook makes it easy to display your data in whatever view best suits you. To switch to another view, click on the View menu, choose Current View, and select from the list of available views. It's helpful to explore each of the views available in each module to see which one is closest to the view you want. Figure 17.9 shows the views available in Tasks.

FIGURE 17.9

Predefined views available in Tasks

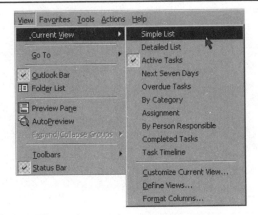

Rearranging a Table View   Table views are the easiest type to change. To rearrange the order of the columns in a table view, click on a column label in the header row, hold your mouse button down, and drag the column label to its new location. When you see two red arrows appear where you want the column to be, as shown here, release the mouse button.

To delete a column, drag the column off the header row and drop it when you see a large black X like the one in this example:

To sort the data in a different order, click the label of the column on which you want to sort. An upward or downward arrow will appear in the label. An up-arrow, shown below, indicates that the data is sorted on that column in ascending order; a down-arrow indicates descending order. Click the label again to change the sort direction.

Ascending sort

Entering Data in the Information Viewer

In many views, you can enter data directly into the Information Viewer. For example, to add a task in Task List view, click at the top of the list where it says *Click here to add a new task*. Type the task into the text box and press Enter to add the task to the list.

Most views allow you to edit data directly in the Information Viewer. To edit an item, click once in the field you want to edit. If an insertion point appears, you can edit the data. If it does not, you must edit the data in the item's form.

Using Forms to Enter Data

Creating a new record in any of the modules is as simple as clicking the New button on the Standard toolbar. Either switch to the module you want to use before clicking the New button or click the button's drop-down list to select the desired item. (See "Toolbars" earlier in this chapter for more information about the New button.) The default form for a module contains fields available in that module. To open the form for an existing record, double-click the item in the Information Viewer or right-click on the item and choose Open.

Navigating a Form

When you open a form, such as the Contacts form shown in Figure 17.10, the focus is automatically on the first field in the form. Each form has its own special toolbars with options available only in that module. Use the Tab key to move to the next field and Shift+Tab to move to a previous field. You can also click in any field to activate it. If a form has multiple pages, click the tab at the top of the form to move between the pages.

FIGURE 17.10

The Contacts form

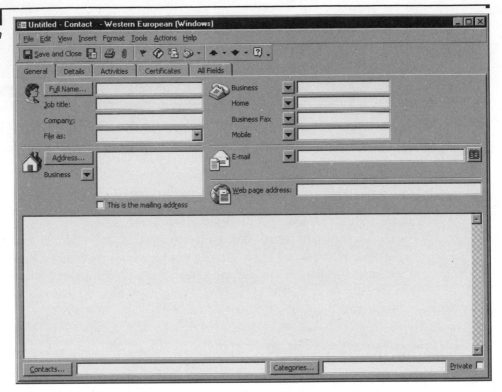

To move from record to record without closing the form and opening the next one, click the Previous Item or Next Item button; this moves you directly to the next record. Outlook will prompt you to save any changes that you made to the current record before moving on.

The drop-down arrows on each of these buttons let you move quickly to the first and last records in the module. Click the arrow attached to the Previous Item button and choose First Item in Folder; click the arrow on the Next Item button and choose Last Item in Folder.

Entering Text and Numbers

When you enter text into a form, you can use many of the same options you are used to in Word and other Windows-based word processors. You can:

- Select text by dragging over it with the mouse pointer.
- Double-click to select a word and triple-click to select a line of text.

- Select all the text in a field by clicking Edit ➤ Select All.

- Click the Edit menu to access Cut, Copy, and Paste options or use the shortcut keys: Ctrl+X to cut, Ctrl+C to copy, and Ctrl+V to paste.

- Choose Edit ➤ Undo and Redo to revert back to a previous state. You can click Undo multiple times to reverse several actions.

- Use Spelling to spell check your document (Tools ➤ Spelling).

Using AutoDate   One of the exciting features of Outlook is the natural-language feature called AutoDate, which lets you enter text in English and converts it into data Outlook can store or understand. For example, suppose you know you want to schedule a meeting for three weeks from today but you aren't sure of the date. Rather than scrolling through the calendar to find the date, you can just type **3 weeks from today** into the Date field and AutoDate will convert the text to the actual date. It can also convert holidays, but only those with fixed dates. Unfortunately, it cannot convert movable holidays such as Hanukkah or Easter, even if you add the appropriate year.

The following table shows examples of some of the common descriptions you may want to use. Experiment and you may find more that are particularly useful or at least entertaining.

TABLE 17.1: EXAMPLES OF OUTLOOK'S AUTODATE FEATURE

Dates and Times	Holidays
first of Jan	Boxing Day
noon	Cinco de Mayo
next Fri	Christmas
yesterday, tomorrow, today	Halloween
one month from today	Independence Day
next month	St. Patrick's Day
a week from now	Valentine's Day
a month ago	Veterans Day

 TIP   Outlook allows you to add national and religious holidays to your calendar, including Christian, Jewish, and Islamic holidays. Choose Tools ➤ Options ➤ Calendar Options ➤ Add Holidays.

Saving Data in a Form

Outlook gives you several ways to save data in a form. If you are interrupted while entering data, it's a good idea to choose File ➢ Save to make sure you don't lose your work. You won't be prompted for a file name because items are saved within the Outlook file. If you want to use the item in some other Windows application, such as a Word document, use File ➢ Save As to save the item as an RTF (Rich Text Format) file on your hard drive or network location.

NOTE Outlook supports several other file types in addition to RTF. You can choose to save an item as a text file (.txt), an Outlook template (.oft), or a message format (.msg). Contacts can also be saved as vCard files (.vcf) and Calendar items in vCalendar format (.vcs).

Once you have completed entering data in a form, click the Save And Close button on the Standard toolbar or click the Windows Close button and choose Yes to save the item when prompted.

Printing in Outlook

Printing in Outlook is essentially a what-you-see-is-what-you-get feature, which means that whatever is on your screen is pretty close to what will print. If you want to print a list of contacts, display that list in the Information Viewer. If you want to print the contents of an individual e-mail message, open the message before you print.

Clicking the Print button on the Standard toolbar will print whatever is in the Information Viewer.

Special Printing Options

Outlook has a number of advanced page setup features that allow you to print pages that will fit right into your favorite paper-based planner such as Day-Timer, Day-Runner, or Franklin. You can print attractive schedules and directories, such as the calendar shown in Figure 17.11, from the choices available. To access these options, change the view to one that most closely matches what you want to print. For example, to print a list of tasks, switch to one of the Task List views (View ➢ Current View).

FIGURE 17.11

*A monthly calendar
using special printing
options*

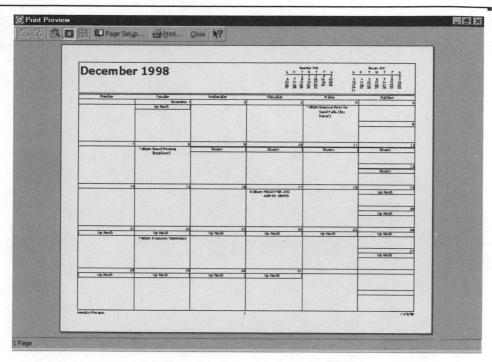

When you are ready to print, choose File ➤ Page Setup to choose your printing preferences. Then, choose the style of layout you want from the menu. The menu choices presented depend on the module and the current view. If the choice you want is not available, switch to a different type of view. There are two print styles that are available in every module:

Table: Data is presented in a traditional format of columns and rows, as seen in Figure 17.12.

Memo: The selected record will print as shown in Figure 17.13. This is the style that will print when you have one item open in a form.

After you choose a style, you can then choose other page setup options such as formatting options, paper type and size, margins, page orientation, and headers and footers. Figure 17.14 shows a typical Page Setup dialog box—this one is for the Daily style of Calendar.

FIGURE 17.12

An example of the
Table style

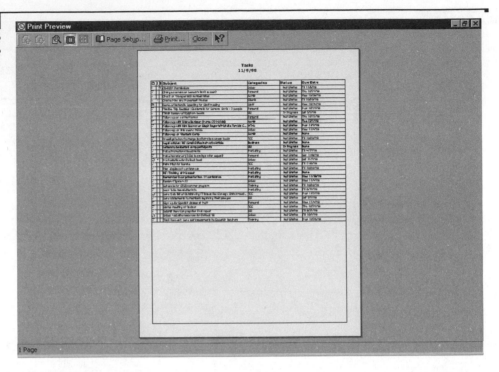

FIGURE 17.12

An example of the
Table style

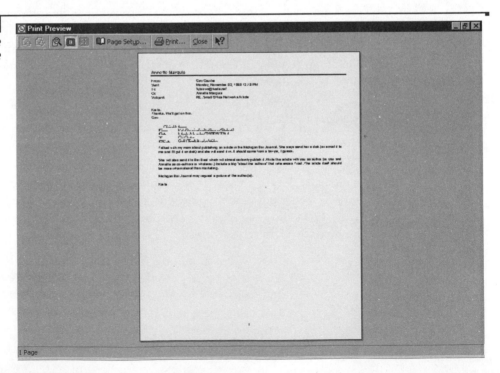

FIGURE 17.13

An example of the
Memo style

FIGURE 17.14

The Page Setup dialog box for Calendar

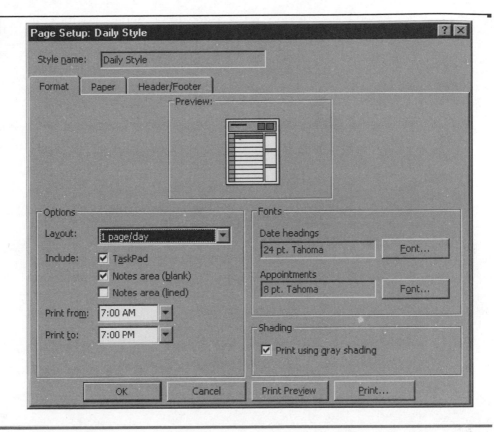

TIP The Calendar has several unique styles such as Daily, Weekly, Monthly, and Tri-fold styles. To find out more about printing calendars see Chapter 20.

Using Print Preview

Previewing your document before you print saves time and paper. You can get to Print Preview directly from the File menu or from any of the Page Setup dialog boxes. It's helpful to preview the document while you are making Page Setup choices so that you can see the results of your selections. The Print Preview toolbar is shown in Figure 17.15.

FIGURE 17.15

The Print Preview toolbar

When you are satisfied with the document's setup, click the Print button in Print Preview or return to Page Setup and print from there.

What's Next

Get out your address book or card file and get ready to organize contact information for your customers, colleagues, or friends. In the next chapter, you'll work in three of the Outlook modules: Contacts, Journal, and Notes.

CHAPTER **18**<u></u>

Tracking Contacts with Outlook 2000

FEATURING:

Creating contacts

Viewing your contacts

Finding contacts

Printing contacts

Tracking activities related to contacts

Automatically recording Journal events

Using the Notes module

ou probably have an existing address and phone list in a contact management system such as a DayRunner, Franklin Planner, or Rolodex. When you start using Outlook, entering data from your current system as Outlook contacts is the best place to begin. In Outlook, a *contact* is an individual or organization you need to maintain information about. The information can be basic—a name and phone number—or include anniversary and birthday information, nicknames, and digital IDs. As Outlook has evolved, it is growing into a solid contact management system. The other Outlook modules are designed to work in conjunction with Contacts, so the more time you spend developing accurate and useful contact information, the easier it is to use Outlook to schedule meetings, send e-mail and faxes, and document activities related to your contacts.

While Outlook is robust enough to help you easily manage business and professional contacts, don't forget to take time to add personal contacts like friends and family members so all your important names, e-mail addresses, phone numbers, and addresses are in one place.

Creating Contacts

An Outlook Contact form holds all the information you have about a contact. A blank form can be opened in several ways. If you're going to be entering a number of contacts, click the Contacts icon in the Outlook shortcut bar to open the Contacts module.

You can also choose File ➢ New ➢ Contact from the menu bar, click the New Contact button on the toolbar, or press Ctrl+Shift and the letter C. All of these methods open a Contact form, shown in Figure 18.1.

If you're working in another module (for example, the Outlook Calendar) you don't need to switch to the Contacts module to open a Contact form. You can choose File ➢ New ➢ Contact from the menu bar in any module, or click the New Item button's drop-down arrow and select Contact from the menu.

FIGURE 18.1

Use Outlook Contact forms to collect and manage information about business and personal contacts.

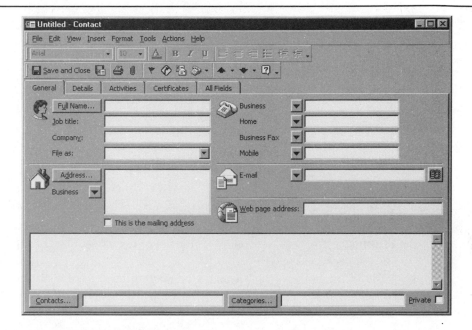

Entering General Information

The Contact form has page tabs labeled General, Details, Activities, Certifications, and All Fields. The form opens with the General page displayed, as shown in Figure 18.1. (To move to another page, simply click the tab for the page.) You'll enter the kinds of information stored in an address or telephone book in the text boxes on the General page.

Entering Names, Job Titles, and Companies

Begin by entering the contact's name in the first text box, next to the Full Name button. If you just want to enter the contact's first and last names, that's fine, but you can also include their title, middle name (or initial), and suffix. For example, **Mary Smith**, **Dr. Mary Smith**, **Richard M. Smith III**, and **Mr. Richard M. Smith** are all acceptable ways of entering names.

When you've finished typing the contact's name, press Enter or Tab to move to the next field. Outlook will parse (separate) the name into parts to store it. If Outlook can't determine how to separate the name, or if you enter an incomplete name, the Check Full Name dialog box, shown in Figure 18.2, opens so you can verify that Outlook is storing the name correctly.

FIGURE 18.2

The Check Full Name dialog box appears when you need to verify how a name should be stored in Outlook.

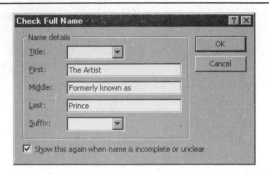

To instruct Outlook not to check incomplete or unclear names, clear the check box in the Check Full Name dialog box before clicking OK. To turn checking back on, open a Contact form, click the Full Name button to open the dialog box, turn the option back on, and click OK.

Enter the contact's job title and company in the respective text boxes. In the File As field, either select an entry from the drop-down list or type a new entry to indicate how the contact should be filed.

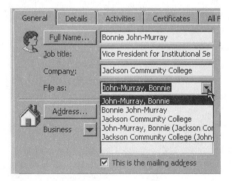

If you choose to file contacts with the first name first, you can still sort them by last name, so it's really a matter of personal preference. If you'll usually look up the company rather than the individual, it's a good idea to file contacts by company name.

You aren't limited to the choices on the File As drop-down list. Select the text in the File As text box, and then enter the File As text you'd like to use. This allows you to enter formal names for contacts but store them in a way that makes them easy to retrieve; you can enter **Dr. William Jones III** as the contact name, but file your friend as **Bill Jones** so you can find him quickly.

Entering Contact Addresses

Outlook allows you to store three addresses—Business, Home, and Other—for your contact and to designate one of the three as the primary address. To choose the type of address you want to enter, click the drop-down arrow in the address section and select the address type from the list.

The address type will be displayed to the left of the arrow. Click in the Address text box and type the address as you would write it on an envelope. Type the street address on the first or first and second lines, pressing Enter to move down a line. Type the city, state or province, country, and zip code or postal code on the last line. If you don't enter a country, Outlook uses the Windows default country.

NOTE The Windows default country is set in the Windows Control Panel under Regional Settings.

When you press Tab to move to the next field, Outlook will check the address just as it did the contact name. If the address is unclear or incomplete, the Check Address dialog box opens, as shown in Figure 18.3. Make sure the information for each field is correct, and then click OK to close the dialog box.

FIGURE 18.3

The Check Address dialog box opens to allow you to verify an incomplete or unclear address.

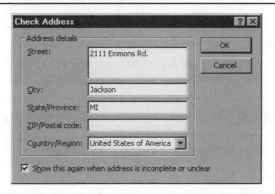

In Outlook, the primary address for a contact is called the *mailing address*. The mailing address is the address displayed in most views, and it's the address used when you merge a Word main document with your Outlook contacts. By default, the *first* address you enter for a contact is set as the mailing address. To use another address as the mailing address, make sure that address is displayed in the Address text box and click the This Is The Mailing Address check box.

Entering Contact Telephone Numbers

This is truly the age of connectivity. While three mail addresses are sufficient for nearly everyone you know, it isn't unusual to have five, six, or more telephone numbers that you use to contact one person: home phones, work phones, home and work fax numbers, mobile phones, ISDN numbers, and pager numbers. With Outlook, you can enter up to 19 different telephone numbers for a contact and display four numbers on the Contact form, as shown in Figure 18.4.

FIGURE 18.4

The Contact form displays four of the 19 numbers you can enter for a contact.

When you create a new contact, the four default phone number descriptions displayed are Business, Home, Business Fax, and Mobile. When you enter one of these telephone numbers, you don't need to enter parentheses around the area code, hyphens, or spaces—just enter the digits in the telephone number:

When you move out of the text box, Outlook will automatically format the digits, adding parentheses, spaces, and hyphens. If you enter a seven-digit telephone number, Outlook assumes the phone number is local, and adds your area code to the number.

NOTE If you include letters in your telephone numbers (like 1-800-CALLME), you won't be able to use Outlook's automated dialing program to call this contact.

To enter another type of telephone number, click the drop-down arrow for any of the four text boxes to open the menu of telephone number descriptions.

Assistant
Business
Business 2
Business Fax
Callback
Car
Company
✓ Home
Home 2
Home Fax
ISDN
Mobile
Other
Other Fax
Pager
Primary
Radio
Telex
TTY/TDD

The telephone number descriptions with check marks are those you've already entered. Choose the description of the telephone number you wish to enter from the menu; then enter the number in the text box. When you've finished entering telephone numbers for the contact, the numbers that are displayed in the four text boxes may not be the numbers you use most frequently. That's not a problem—just open the menu next to each text box and select the descriptions for the numbers you want to display from the menu.

Entering E-Mail Addresses

To enter an e-mail address, enter the entire address, including the username and the domain name. When you move out of the text box, Outlook analyzes the address you entered to ensure that it resembles a valid e-mail address looking for a username, the @ symbol, and a domain name. If Outlook doesn't find what it's looking for, it opens the Check Names dialog box, shown in Figure 18.5.

PART

IV

Getting Organized
with Outlook

FIGURE 18.5

Outlook uses the Check Names dialog box to clarify an incomplete or erroneous e-mail address.

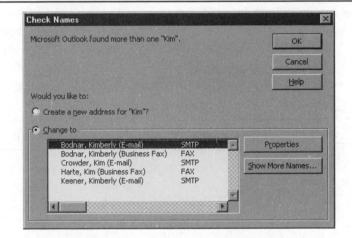

Because you can't use an existing Outlook Address Book entry for the e-mail address, click Cancel to close this dialog box and enter the e-mail address again, making sure you've included the @ symbol and the "dot" domain separator.

Assigning a Web URL to a Contact

When you enter a World Wide Web URL in the Web Page Address text box, enter the resource name (for example, www.disney.com) and when you leave the text box, Outlook will automatically add http:// to the beginning of the URL. However, if you're entering an address for another type of protocol like Gopher, Telnet, or FTP, you must enter the entire URL, including the protocol and the resource.

TIP When you're preparing for a visit, telephone call, or Internet meeting with a contact, you probably have a number of information sources you check. You'll look at your Calendar to see when you met last, check your Task list to ensure that all the tasks related to the contact are complete, and search online for recent news about the contact's organization. The contact's Web site is one of the places you'll want to search. Web sites often contain news about an organization, including recently announced products, promotions, legal actions, press releases, and other information of interest. By adding a *hyperlink* pointing to the site to the General page of the Contact form, you can access the contact's Web site with one quick click of the mouse.

Relating Contacts

 Outlook 2000 is designed to help you create relationships between the people you interact with and the things you do. Throughout the Outlook modules, a Contacts field has been added to forms make organizing your data even easier. This feature is valuable anytime you want to show connections between people—for example, tracking all the members of a family or relating a client to the person who referred them. To relate a contact to another contact, click the Contacts button at the bottom of the General Contacts page. Select the contact you want to relate to this contact and click OK or click Apply if you want to assign multiple contacts.

When you close the Select Contacts dialog box, a link to the related contact's form will appear in the Contacts text box. Double-click the link to open the contact's form. A link to the original contact will also appear in the related contact's Contacts text box.

Using Categories

A *category* is a key word or term that you assign to an item. Categories give you a way to group, filter, and locate contacts, tasks, and other Outlook items. Every type of Outlook item can be grouped by category. Outlook comes with 20 built-in categories, and you can delete categories or add other categories that reflect your work.

With categories, you can consistently organize items in all modules; this can serve as a way to relate items. If all the contacts, Journal entries, tasks and appointments related to Project XYZ are assigned to the Project XYZ category, you can use Advanced Find (see the "Mastering the Opportunities" box on the next page) to locate and display them. You can group and filter Outlook items based on categories within a module. Thoughtful use of categories is a key to effective Outlook organization.

To assign a category to a contact, either type a category description in the Categories text box or click the Categories button on the General page to open the Categories dialog box, shown in Figure 18.6.

FIGURE 18.6

Assign, add, and delete Outlook categories in the Categories dialog box.

You can add as many categories as you wish to a contact. Click the check box in front of each category that you wish to assign. Some categories, like Holiday and Time & Expenses, don't apply to contacts but can be used in Calendar or Tasks. As you click the check boxes, the categories you select are listed in alphabetical order in the Items Belong to These Categories box at the top of the dialog box. When you close the dialog box, the categories are listed in the Categories text box on the General page.

MASTERING THE OPPORTUNITIES

Using Advanced Find to Locate All Items Related to a Category

Managing and organizing all the activities, contacts, and documentation related to project can be a daunting task. You can simplify this process considerably through the use of categories. When you start a new project, create an Outlook category for it. As you add tasks, calendar items, contacts, and Journal entries, relate each of them to the project category. When you want to locate a particular item or pull together all the material

Continued ▐▶

MASTERING THE OPPORTUNITIES CONTINUED

(except e-mail) related to a project, use Advanced Find to list them all for you. Follow these steps to use Advanced Find:

1. Choose Tools ➣ Advanced Find to open the Advanced Find dialog box, shown below.

2. Change the Look For field at the top of the dialog box to Any Type of Outlook Item.

3. Click the More Choices tab and the Categories button to open up a list of your categories.

4. Select the project's category from the list.

5. Click Find Now to generate a list of all items related to the project, as illustrated.

6. Double-click any item in the list to open that item.

7. If you would like to save the search parameters to run again, click File ➣ Save Search. Enter a file location and name for the saved search (*.oss).

8. When you want to run the search again in the future, open Advanced Find, choose File ➣ Open Search and locate the search you saved. Any new items assigned to the project category will show up in the list.

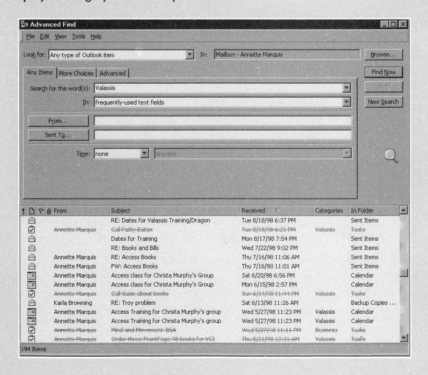

Adding and Deleting Categories

There are several approaches to changing and adding categories: you can add them one at a time as you need to use them, or you can do a bit of planning and add them all at once in the Master Category List.

You'll find that planning pays off. After you've looked at each of the Outlook modules, but before you create too many contacts, open the Categories dialog box and determine if the categories listed will meet your needs. Delete the categories you don't want to use, and add the categories you require to the Master Category List.

To access the Master Category List from any Outlook form, click the form's Categories button to open the Categories dialog box. Then click the Master Category List button at the bottom of the Categories dialog box. You'll see the Master Category List dialog box, shown in Figure 18.7.

Using the Master Category List dialog box is one way to create a customized list of Outlook categories.

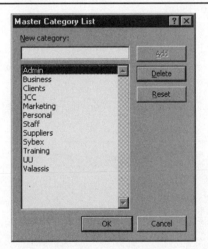

To remove a category from the list, select the category and click the Delete button. To add a category, type the category name in the New Category text box, then click the Add button. If you click the Reset button, Outlook returns the Master Category list to the 20 default categories shown in Figure 18.6.

Deleting a category from the Master Category List does not remove the category from Outlook items already assigned to it, but you won't be able to use that category with other Outlook items.

WARNING While Outlook allows you to assign multiple categories to items, many Outlook-compatible personal data assistants (PDAs) are more limited. There may also be a limit on the number of overall categories you may use. If you intend to synchronize your Outlook contacts with a PDA, see the owner's manuals for both the PDA and the synchronization software before assigning multiple categories or adding new categories to the list.

Assigning Multiple Items to Categories

After you have created a number of Outlook items, you can select multiple items and assign them to categories. These steps will guide you through the process:

1. Open the module, such as Contacts, where you want to assign categories.

2. Click Organize on the Standard toolbar and click Using Categories on the page that opens.

3. Select the items you want to assign to a category by clicking on the first item, holding Ctrl, and clicking the remaining items.

4. Select the Category from the Add [*Item*] Selected Below To drop-down list as shown in Figure 18.8.

5. Repeat steps 3 and 4 to assign additional categories.

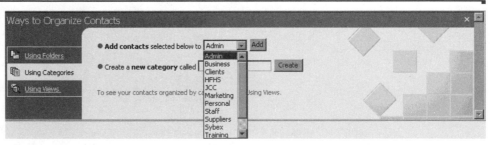

 MASTERING TROUBLESHOOTING

Deleted Categories Still Show Up When You Group by Categories

When you group your contacts by category, every category that's used in a contact shows up, even after you delete the category from the Master Category List. If you don't want to see contacts grouped under categories you've deleted from the list, you'll need to open each contact and delete the category from the contact. Advance planning in creating your categories can minimize a lot of rework.

Making a Contact Private

If you're using Outlook on a network, other users may have been given permission to share your Contacts folder, or you may place contacts in a public folder. In the bottom-right corner of the General page, there's a check box marked Private. By enabling the Private setting, you prevent other users from seeing this contact, even if they have access to your Contacts folder.

Adding Details

On the Details page of the Contact form, shown in Figure 18.9, you'll record less frequently used information about your contacts. Remember that you can sort and filter your contacts on these fields, so try to use standard entries. If, for example, you want to be able to find all the vice presidents in your Contacts folder, make sure you enter **Vice President** the same way for each contact.

FIGURE 18.9

Use the Details page to record other additional information about a contact.

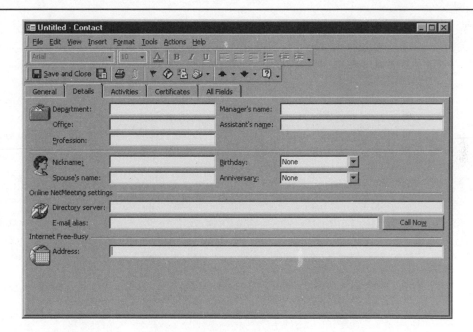

The Birthday and Anniversary fields have a drop-down arrow that opens a calendar. You can type dates in these fields using the *mm/dd/yy* format (3/5/57 for March 8, 1957), or you can select a date from the calendar. The Outlook calendar control is pretty nifty. Click the arrow, and the calendar opens, displaying the current month.

To choose the current date, click the Today button. To enter a different date in the current month, just click the date. Click the arrows in the calendar's header to scroll to the prior month or the next month. If you need to enter a date from 1945, you're probably better off just typing it.

Entering NetMeeting Addresses

Microsoft NetMeeting is Internet-based collaboration software included with Outlook. With NetMeeting, you can work with one or more contacts "face to face" over the Internet, using video and audio, as you would in a video conference call. Some hardware is required to support NetMeeting's high-end video and audio functions. But even if you don't use these, NetMeeting has a lot to offer. You can use NetMeeting to send files directly to a meeting attendee; have open chat sessions for brainstorming ideas about projects; diagram ideas on a whiteboard; and work with other attendees in real time in shared applications.

NetMeetings are held on an *Internet Locator Server (ILS)*; each meeting participant must log on to the server, which maintains a list of users so that other participants can find out who is available for a meeting. On the Details page, you can enter two NetMeeting settings. Enter the ILS used for meetings with the contact in the Directory Server text box, and the contact's E-Mail Alias (usually their e-mail address).

TIP To use NetMeeting outside of Outlook and to set up NetMeeting for the first time, launch NetMeeting from the Programs menu. A wizard walks you through the steps of configuring NetMeeting and provides you with a list of servers you can access.

Accessing Your Contact's Schedule on the Internet

The Internet Free-Busy setting in Details refers to the times that a user is available (for meetings, including NetMeetings) or unavailable according to their Outlook calendar. With Outlook 2000, you can publish your free-busy times in two ways: with the Corporate/Workgroup configuration of Outlook running Exchange Server on your local area network, and over the Internet, using the iCalendar standard. With Exchange Server, the only people who can see your free-busy times are colleagues who can log on to your network. By publishing your free-busy times on an Internet Server, you make the schedule of free time available to people outside your network.

Before users can access your free-busy schedule, you need to tell them where the file that contains the schedule is located. The file can be stored on a server, FTP site, or Web page. If a contact has given you the URL for their free-busy schedule, enter it in the Internet Free-Busy text box on the Details page.

Tracking Activities

After you've entered a contact, Outlook can track all your activities related to that contact, including e-mail messages, tasks, and Journal entries. Outlook no longer requires you to create a Journal entry to track every item related to a contact. Outlook 2000 automatically links to a contact any e-mail to or from the contact. You can manually link tasks and other Outlook items or files.

To view the activities related to a contact, click the Activities tab on the Contact form. Outlook automatically goes out and searches all your Outlook folders and lists all related items, as shown in Figure 18.10.

FIGURE 18.10

The Activities tab displays a list of all Outlook items and files related to a contact.

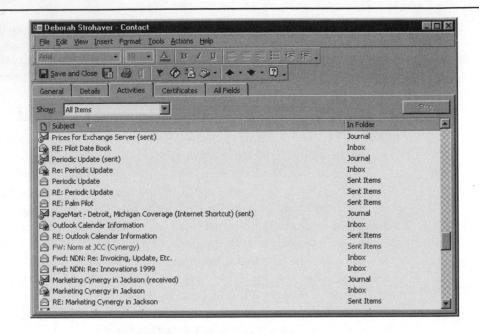

To relate additional items, such as tasks, to a contact, follow these steps:

1. Choose Actions ➤ Link and click Items.

2. Select the item or items you want to relate (hold down Ctrl to select multiple items).

3. Click OK to close the list or Apply to switch to a different folder and select additional items.

If you would like to relate files, such as Word documents, to a contact, Outlook will create a Journal entry for each file:

1. Choose Actions ➤ Link and click File.

2. Select the file you want to relate—you can only link one file to a contact at a time—and click Insert to open a Journal Entry form, as shown in Figure 18.11.

3. Click Save and Close to link the file. (You'll learn more about Journal entries later in this chapter.)

FIGURE 18.11

When you link a file to a contact, Outlook automatically creates a Journal entry.

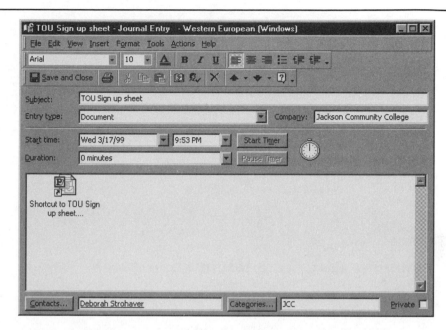

After you manually link items and files to a contact, they should immediately show up in the Activities list. Double-click any item on the Activities list to open it.

MASTERING TROUBLESHOOTING

Searching Public Folders for Activities

Outlook's Activities feature appears at first blush to be limited to personal folders. It is possible, however, to search public folders for related e-mail and other activities; it just requires a little more effort. Outlook cannot search public and private folders at the same time. You can search all local folders and their subfolders at once, but each individual public folder must be searched separately. To set up a public folder to be searched for activities, follow these steps:

1. Click Contacts.

2. Choose File ➢ Folder and click Properties For Contacts and the Activities tab.

3. Click the New button and select the public folder you want to search. If it is a subfolder, expand the main folder by clicking the plus symbol in front of the folder.

Continued

MASTERING TROUBLESHOOTING CONTINUED

4. In the Name box at the top of the View Title And Folders dialog box, enter a name for the Public Folder. (If you name it *Public–[Folder Name]*, it will make it easier to select the public folders from the list you want to search later.)

5. Click OK to close the dialog box and OK again to close the Properties.

When you click the Activities tab on an open contact form, Outlook automatically searches the default folder set (typically your personal folders). To search a public folder, select the folder from the Show drop-down list at the top of the page.

You can only search one public folder at a time, and each new search clears the previous list of items. That means that if you have items stored in public folders, there is no way to see all of the activities related to a contact in one list.

Viewing Certificate Information

The fourth page of the Contact form, Certificates, is a place to store digital IDs for a contact. A *digital ID,* or *certificate*, is used to verify the identity of the person who sent an e-mail message. Digital IDs have two parts: a *private key*, stored on the owner's computer, and a *public key* that others use to send messages to the owner and verify the authenticity of messages from the owner. You can view the properties of the ID, and choose which ID should be used as the default for sending encrypted messages to this contact.

Viewing All Fields

In the Contact form's All Fields page, you can display groups of fields in a table format. The default display is User Defined Fields In This Item. Unless someone has customized your Outlook forms and added fields, there won't be any fields displayed—but don't assume that this page is totally useless. Choose Phone Number Fields from the Select From drop-down list, and you'll see all the phone numbers associated with the contact, as shown in Figure 18.12. If you print the form now, you'll get the contact's name and a list of their phone numbers.

FIGURE 18.12

The All Fields page displays contact information for a group of fields.

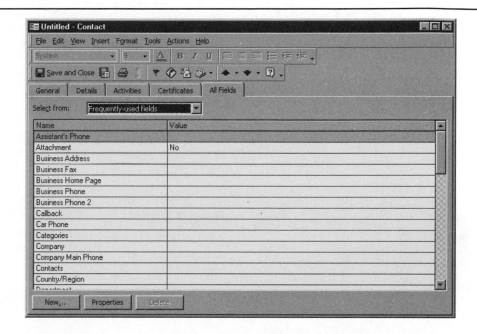

Change to any other category of fields to see only the information related to that category. You'll also find some fields in the All Contact Fields category that are not available on the Contact form's pages, such as Children, Hobbies, and Personal Home Page.

Saving a Contact

When you've finished entering information in the Contact form, click the Save And Close button, or choose File ➤ Save And Close to save this contact's information and close the form.

If you're going to enter another contact immediately, it's faster to click the Save And New button or choose File ➤ Save And New to save the current contact and open a blank form.

TIP To add another contact from the same company, choose New Contact From Same Company on the Contact form's Action menu. Outlook opens a new Contact form, retaining the company name and address, business phone number, and business fax number.

Deleting a Contact

To delete a contact, select the contact or open the Contact form and:

- choose Edit ➤ Delete from the menu, or
- right-click and choose Delete from the shortcut menu, or
- press Ctrl+D

You will not be prompted to confirm the deletion. However, if you immediately notice that you've deleted a contact erroneously, you can choose Undo Delete from the Edit menu to restore the contact.

Putting Contact Information to Work

Entering all your contacts is an important step to working efficiently with Outlook. But after they are all there, it's helpful to know how to organize your contacts, find the contact you are looking for, and communicate with your contacts.

Using Predefined Views

The Contacts module has seven predefined views: Address Cards, Detailed Address Cards, Phone List, By Category, By Company, By Location, and By Follow Up Flag. To switch to another view, click Organize on the toolbar, choose Using Views, and select the view you want to apply.

 NOTE Views do not affect your data in any way—they only change the way you see your data.

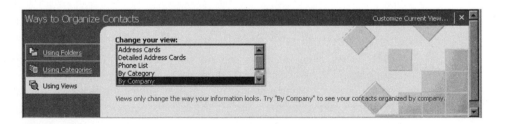

You can create your own views, adding fields, deleting fields, and setting up custom grouping. For information on creating views, see Chapter 21.

Sorting Contacts

Sorting is easy in any list view. To sort by a field in ascending order, click the heading at the top of the field. An up-arrow is displayed in the field heading to remind you that it is sorted in ascending order.

Click the heading again, and you sort the list in descending order. When the list is sorted in descending order, the heading arrow for the Sort By column points down.

 NOTE   You cannot sort by Categories in any view.

Locating a Contact

The easiest way to search through a long list of contacts is to enter a first or last name in the Find A Contact text box on the Standard toolbar. If Outlook only finds one name that matches your entry, it will open the Contact form for that person. If it finds more than one possible match, Outlook will display a list of possibilities that you can then choose from.

 When you don't remember the contact's first or last name, you can search for other information about the contact by clicking the Find button on the Standard toolbar to open the Find pane at the top of the list.

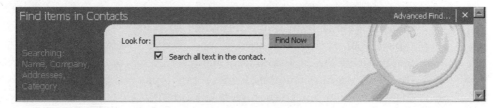

If you're looking for a contact, enter all or part of their name, company name, or address in the Look For text box. To search through all the fields (including Comments), leave the Search All Text In The Contact check box enabled. Disabling the check box limits the search to the fields displayed at the left and speeds up the search.

Click the Find Now button to find all the contacts that include the text you entered. Figure 18.13 shows the results obtained when searching for **Smith**. When you find the contact you're looking for, just double-click it to open the Contact form.

Find Now

FIGURE 18.13

Use Find to locate a contact based on their name, address, or text anywhere in the entry.

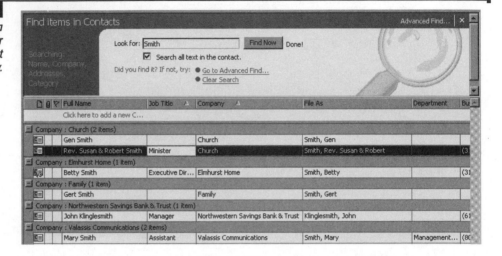

If you can't find the contact you're looking for in the Find pane, or if you're looking for text in specific fields or based on criteria other than text, consider using Advanced Find. You can either click the Advanced Find button at the top of the Find pane or run a basic search and then choose Go To Advanced Find if necessary:

On the Contact page of the Advanced Find dialog box, you can select the type of item, location, and fields to be searched. Open the In drop-down list and select the type of field you want to search. Choose Frequently Used Text Fields for the broadest search. Using the Time options, you can search for contacts that were created or modified within a particular time frame. For example, you can find contacts you created today or modified in the last week. In Figure 18.14, we're using Advanced Find to locate contacts modified in the last seven days with Oak in the company name.

FIGURE 18.14

Advanced Find lets you
search for contacts
based on when they
were created or
modified.

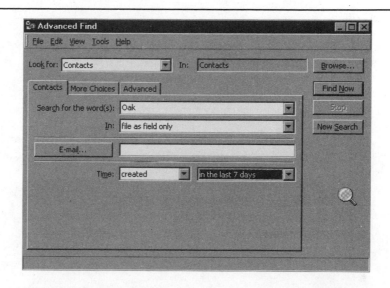

Flip to the More Choices page, and you can find contacts by categories. On the
Advanced page of the Advanced Find dialog box, shown in Figure 18.15, you can
enter multiple, specific search criteria based on the values in fields. To enter a search
criterion, click the Field button to open a menu of Outlook field types. Choose a type
(for example, All Contact Fields), and then select the field from the menu.

From the Condition text box, choose the appropriate operator. The operators in the
list depend on the type of data that will be in the field you selected. For example, with
text fields, you'll choose between Contains, Is, Doesn't Contain, Is Empty, and Is Not
Empty. In the Value text box, enter the value you want to find (or not find). You don't
have to enter a Value for Is Empty and Is Not Empty fields. When you're finished
building the criterion, click the Add To List button to add it to the Find Items list.
When you've entered all the advanced criteria you need to conduct your search, click
Find Now to find the contacts that match all the criteria you entered.

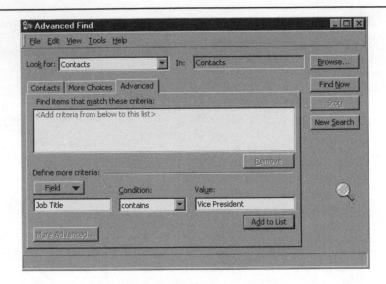

FIGURE 18.15

Use the Advanced page to find contacts based on one or more specific fields.

You can enter search criteria on more than one page and find, for example, contacts created in the last seven days in the Business category. If you're finished with one search and want to search for other contacts, click the New Search button to clear the criteria you entered from all three pages of the dialog box.

When you're finished with Advanced Find, choose File ➤ Close or click the Close button on the dialog box title bar to close Advanced Find and return to Contacts. To close the Find pane, click the Close button at the top of the pane, or switch to another view.

Printing Contacts

If you've ever been asked to create an employee directory for your organization, you know the potential pitfalls. Someone (probably you) has to enter data, choose a layout for the directory, format all the data, add headings. By the time you send the directory to your printer, you've invested a lot of time in design issues. Outlook 2000 includes a number of printing options that will help you quickly and easily create directories, phone lists, and other print resources that formerly took hours or days to create.

When you choose File ➤ Page Setup from the Outlook menu bar, you are presented with a list of styles to choose from, as shown in Figure 18.16. The available styles depend on the current view; so before you print, select the view that most closely resembles the printed output you want. For a simple employee telephone list, choose one of the Table views. For complete names and addresses, choose a Card view. Table 18.2 identifies the Contact views and their corresponding print styles.

TABLE 18.2: PAGE SETUP STYLES		
Style	**Type of View**	**Default Printed Output**
Table	Table	The view as it appears on the screen
Memo	Table	Data for the selected contact(s), with your name at the top of each entry
Phone Directory	Table	A two-column listing of names and phone numbers, with a heading for each letter of the alphabet (very slick)
Card	Card	A two-column listing of names and contact information
Small Booklet	Card	A multiple-section listing of names and contact information prepared for two-sided printing
Medium Booklet	Card	A two-column listing of names and contact information prepared for two-sided printing

FIGURE 18.16

Use the Page Setup
dialog box to set print-
ing options for the
style you selected

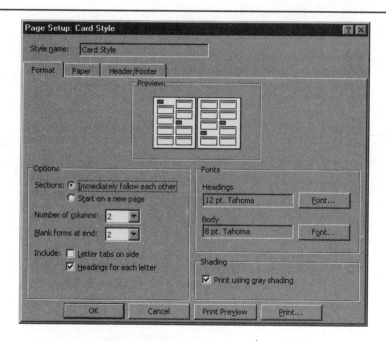

The dialog box has three pages: Format, Paper, and Header/Footer. In the Format page, choose the format options you would like to apply to the style:

Sections: To have each letter of the alphabet begin on a new page, choose Start on a New Page.

Number of columns: As you increase the number of columns, Outlook decreases the font size.

Blank forms at end: This option allows users to add new entries in the correct section.

Letter tabs on side: This check box will generate an index, like the index used in Address Card view, with the section's letters highlighted.

Headings for each letter: This feature gives you a highlighted letter at the beginning of each alphabetic section.

Fonts: These lists offer you choices of fonts for the letter headings and body.

Shading: This check box enables or disables gray shading in the letter tabs, letter headings, and contact names.

After you make a change, you can click the Print Preview button to see how the change affects your printed output. In Figure 18.17, we're previewing a booklet with letter tabs on the side and headings for each letter. Click anywhere in the preview to zoom in on the detail; click again to zoom out. To close Print Preview and return to the Page Setup dialog box, choose Page Setup. If you click Close, you close both Print Preview *and* Page Setup.

On the Paper page of the Page Setup dialog box, choose the settings that describe the dimensions of the paper you're going to use.

On the Header/Footer page, you can create a header and footer that contain text and document information. Headers and footers appear on each page of the finished product. If you're creating a 1/4-page booklet, a header will appear four times on the printed sheet, so it will be at the top of each page after it is folded.

The header and footer each have a left-aligned, a centered, and a right-aligned section. To include text in the header or footer, just click in the section and begin typing. Use the five buttons on the toolbar below the header and footer sections to include the page number, total number of pages, date printed, time printed, and username in the header or footer:

When you've finished setting print options, click the Print button to open the Print dialog box, shown in Figure 18.18. Select a printer from the Name list, the range of pages to print, and the number of copies. Click the OK button to send the job to the printer.

FIGURE 18.17

Use Print Preview to
see how your format
change affects the
printed document.

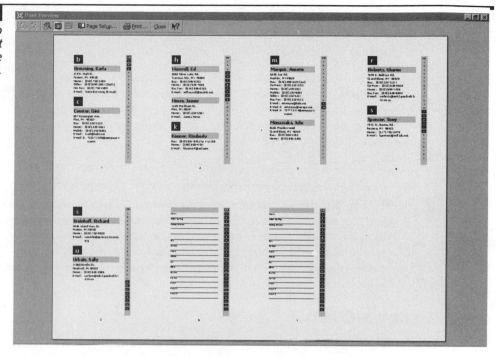

FIGURE 18.18

Change settings in the
Print dialog box to
specify the number of
copies, range, and
number of pages.

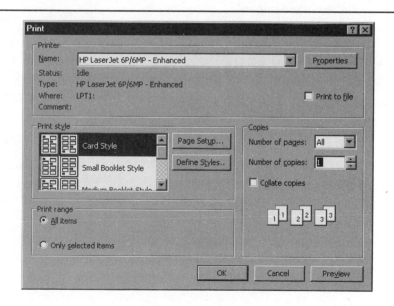

Printing a Booklet

If you want to print a booklet with two-sided pages and you have a one-sided printer, choose Odd in the Number of Pages drop-down list and print all the odd-numbered pages first. Turn the sheets over and reinsert them into the printer. Choose Even to print the rest of the pages. Outlook will order the pages so they can be folded into a booklet when they're all printed.

 NOTE The printing process is the same in all the Outlook modules. Begin by selecting a view that supports the output you want. Preview the output in Print Preview. Change views, if necessary, and then adjust the Page Setup options to further define the final output. Finally, send the job to the printer, and think about how easy this was.

Dialing a Contact

Newer multimedia computers support a full range of *telephony* accessories, including headsets and built-in or monitor-mounted microphones. You don't need a lot of fancy hardware to use Outlook's telephony features. As long as you have a telephone connected to the line your modem uses, you can place telephone calls from Outlook. You don't need a fast modem to make telephone calls—your voice is simply routed from one port in the modem to the other. Outlook's telephone dialing program is called *AutoDialer*. You must be in the Contacts folder to use AutoDialer.

 You can begin by selecting the contact you want to call. Then click the AutoDialer drop-down arrow to open the menu of all the telephone numbers for the contact. Choose a number from the list, and the New Call dialog box opens.

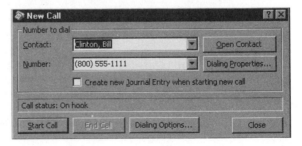

The contact's name appears in the Contact text box, and the phone number you select is in the Number text box. You can click the arrow in the Number box to see other numbers.

If you know your contact's telephone number, or have it in your telephone's speed dial listing, you could have dialed the number by now. AutoDialer is popular because of the check box that appears under the number. One simple click and Outlook will open a Journal entry for the contact while you place the call.

Click the Start Call button to have Outlook dial the number. If the Create New Journal Entry check box is enabled, a new Journal Entry form opens automatically. The New Call dialog box is still open (and remains open during the call). The Call Status reads *Connected*, and the End Call button is enabled.

When you've completed your call, click the End Call button to close the connection (you may have to move the Journal Entry form out of the way to see the New Call dialog box). Outlook automatically pauses the timer in the Journal item, and it enters the total time for the call in the Duration control. If you'd like to make some notes about the call, enter them in the open Notes area in the Journal item. You should also change the subject to describe the contents of the telephone call and assign a category if you wish. When you've finished entering information in the Journal form, click the Save And Close button to close the Journal entry.

Creating a Letter to a Contact

To write a letter to a contact (the traditional, snail-mail variety), select the contact and chooses Actions ➢ New Letter To Contact. This starts the Microsoft Word Letter Wizard. Information available in the Contact form is filled in for you. When you complete the additional information in the Letter Wizard, Outlook passes control over to Word so you can write your letter. Complete the letter as you would any Word document. Close or minimize Word to return to Outlook.

Mail Merging with Word Documents

For the past several versions of Office, you could connect to Outlook Contacts as a data source in a Word mail merge. In Outlook 2000, you can actually initiate a Word mail merge from within Outlook. To access the mail merge features in Outlook, switch to the Contacts module. Once you are in Contacts, follow these steps to initiate a mail merge:

1. Create a Contacts view, including the fields you want to merge and any filters you want to apply to the data (choose View ➢ Current View ➢ Customize Current View).

2. If you don't want to merge all of the visible contacts, select the contacts you want using Ctrl + Click.

3. Choose Tools ➤ Mail Merge to open the new Outlook Mail Merge Contacts dialog box.

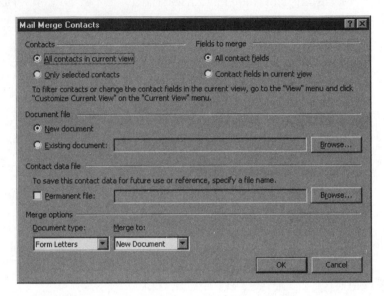

4. Check whether you want to merge all the records or the selected records.

5. Check if you want to merge all contact fields or only the fields in the view you selected—with over a hundred contact fields, it is generally better to choose the fields you want, as described in Step 1, to make the list more usable.

6. Identify if you want to create a new Word main document or if you have an existing Word document you want to use as the main document.

7. To save a copy of the contacts you include in the merge, check Permanent File and enter a file name.

8. Choose the document type and indicate whether you want to merge to a new document, a printer, an e-mail, or a fax.

9. Click OK to launch Word and open the main document. You can now add merge fields and finish the merge directly in Word.

 NOTE For more about Word's mail merge feature, refer to Chapter 9.

Recording Activities in the Journal

Outlook's Journal module is to activities what Contacts is to people. You can use the Journal to make notes about telephone conversations, record your impressions after a meeting, organize e-mail communications to and from a contact, and track how long you spent developing an Excel spreadsheet. The Journal is the place in Outlook where you can keep a running history of your daily activities. Using the Journal, you can automatically record e-mail messages to a contact or manually record information during a phone call or after a meeting with the contact.

Manually Recording an Event in the Journal

To access the Journal, click the Journal icon on the Outlook bar. The Journal will open in its default Timeline view, showing how you've spent your time and what events have occurred on a particular day. Figure 18.19 shows three phone calls that occurred over a two-day period.

FIGURE 18.19

The Journal's
Timeline view

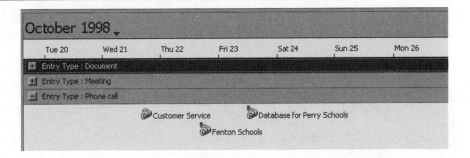

To expand a particular Entry Type so you can see all of the entries underneath it, click the Plus button to the left of the label Entry Type. To collapse a group that is already expanded, click the Minus button.

NOTE The first time you click the Journal icon on the Outlook bar you may be surprised to find that there are already entries in the Journal. This is because the Journal is working behind the scenes, automatically recording work that you're doing in other Office applications. For a better understanding of these entries, and to learn how to change the automatic settings, see "Automatically Recording Journal Events" later in this chapter.

There are only three types of Journal entries visible in Figure 18.19: documents, meetings, and phone calls. In all, there are approximately twenty types of Journal entries that you can make. To create a new Journal entry, click the New button on the Standard toolbar and choose Journal Entry from the list. The Journal Entry form shown in Figure 18.20 will open. The default entry type is Phone Call. Just click the down arrow in the Entry Type field to see the other choices, such as Conversation and Microsoft Excel.

FIGURE 18.20

A Journal Entry form

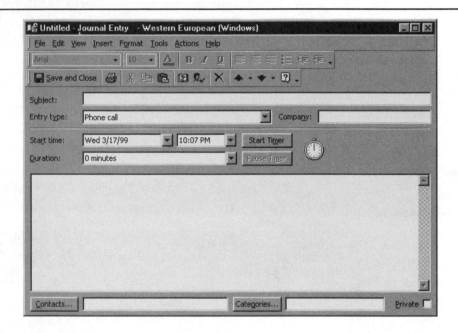

Creating a Journal entry is quite simple:

1. Enter a Subject for the Journal entry and choose the Entry Type from the drop-down list.

2. To associate a Journal entry with an existing contact, click the Address Book button and choose a contact from the Select Names dialog box.

3. Enter a Company name, if desired.

4. Enter a date and time in the Start Time field or, if you're making a phone call, click the Start Timer button to have Journal automatically time your conversation.

5. Record the length of the communication from the Duration drop-down list or type in an entry of your own. If you clicked the Start Timer button, click the Pause Timer button when you've finished your phone call to have Outlook automatically record the call's duration.

6. Type your notes about the communication in the open text box area.

7. Assign the Journal entry to a Category by clicking the Categories button.

8. To exclude anyone who has access to your Outlook folders from reading this entry, click the Private check box.

9. Click the Save And Close button to record your Journal entry.

Automatically Recording Journal Events

Working behind the scenes, Outlook can help you keep track of your communications and monitor how much time you spend on your projects. Any action associated with a contact such as sending or receiving e-mail, a meeting response, or a task request can automatically appear in the Journal. Additionally, Outlook can record what other Office documents you work on and for how long.

To set up Outlook to automatically record items:

1. Choose Tools ➤ Options from the menu and click Journal Options to open the Journal Options dialog box, shown in Figure 18.21.

2. Select the items you would like to automatically record from the list of choices, including e-mail messages, meeting requests, and so on.

3. Mark the contacts for whom you want to record items automatically.

4. Select the types of files you would like to record automatically from the list, which includes all of the Office applications and other compatible programs.

5. Choose whether you want double-clicking a Journal entry to open the entry itself (the default) or the item it refers to.

6. Click OK to save the Journal Options dialog box and click OK again to close the Options dialog box.

FIGURE 18.21

The Journal Options dialog box

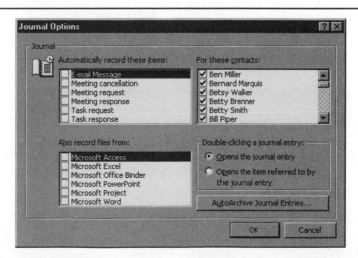

Unless you've chosen to open the referenced item directly, when you double-click a Journal entry, the Journal form opens containing an icon for the referenced item, as shown in Figure 18.22.

FIGURE 18.22

A Journal entry with a shortcut to an e-mail message

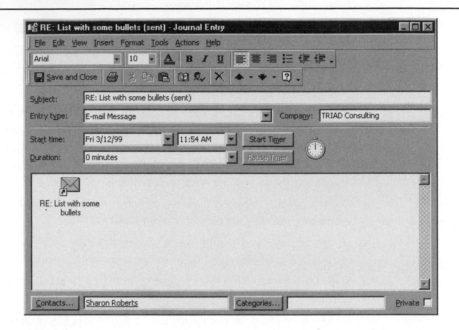

 NOTE When you set the Journal to automatically record documents that you work on in any of the Office applications, Outlook records the author of the document as the contact it associates with the Journal entry, using the Author field on the Summary page of the document's properties. (To get to the Summary page, open the document in the application, choose File ➢ Properties, and click the Summary tab.)

Inserting Items and Files into Journal Entries

You can insert documents and Outlook items (or shortcuts to them; see the accompanying box for a discussion of this choice) directly into Journal entries. For example, if you had a phone conversation about a proposal you were writing for a client, you could insert a shortcut to the Word document directly into the Journal entry. In the

future when you wanted to review what you talked about, you could directly reference the proposal. Follow these steps to insert an item or file into a Journal entry:

1. Open the Journal entry and click in the Notes area of the Journal form.

2. Choose Insert ➤ Object from the menu bar. The Insert Object dialog box opens.

3. Click Create From File and click Browse to locate the file.

4. Locate the file you want to insert and select it.

5. Click Display As Icon to insert an icon representing the document or clear this
   check box to insert the entire text into the Journal entry.

6. Click Link to insert the file as an object that is linked back to the original document. Changes you make in the original are reflected in the linked document.

7. Click OK to insert the file. In the notes area of the Journal entry, you'll see either
   the contents of the file, an object containing the file contents (if you chose
   Link), or an icon representing the document (if you chose Display As Icon).

8. Double-click the icon or link to open the document.

 NOTE Display As Icon does not create a shortcut to the document but inserts an actual
copy of the document into the Journal entry.

Inserting an Outlook item into a Journal entry is a simple as drag and drop. Locate
the item you want to insert and right-drag (drag with the right mouse button) it to
the Journal icon on the Outlook bar. When you release the item, you are offered a
choice to copy the item into a Journal entry as a shortcut, copy the item into a Journal entry as an attachment, or move the item into a Journal entry as an attachment.

 TIP You can drag files directly from the Windows Desktop or My Computer to the Journal icon on the Outlook bar to create Journal entries.

Which Insert File Option Should I Choose?

There are significant differences between inserting a file as Text Only, Attachment, or Shortcut; and you should make a careful choice each time you insert a file into an Outlook item. The default choice is *Attachment*. Be aware that when you insert an attachment, you are making a copy of the original document. When you double-click the icon in the Outlook item to open the document, you are opening and perhaps modifying the copy. The original document remains unchanged. Use this option if you want to send a file to someone who can open a Word attachment to an e-mail message.

The *Shortcut* option creates a pointer to the document on your local or network drive. Use this option if you are inserting the document for your own reference and do not plan to e-mail the item to anyone outside your network. When you double-click the icon to open this document, you are modifying the original document in its original location.

The *Text Only* option is useful if you plan to send this item to someone who cannot open a Word attachment to an e-mail message. The actual text of the document (sans formatting) is inserted into the Notes areas of the item. If the document is formatted (font formatting, headers/footers, etc.), you may get a lot of unreadable characters but somewhere in the midst of all of it you should find your text. Saving the file as Rich Text Format (.rtf) or Text (.txt) before your insert it will eliminate the garbage characters.

Your network may also have policies about version control and storage capacity. You may need to maintain a "paper trail" by keeping each stage of modification as a separate document; or you may need to minimize duplication of storage by keeping only a single copy of each document.

Making Notes

Even after you are using Outlook to its fullest, you will still run across those odd pieces of information that have nowhere to go or that you want to keep at your fingertips: your flight information, the type of battery your cell phone uses, or information about your car insurance. They aren't related to a contact and they aren't an event, so what do you do with them? Outlook includes an easy way to organize all those notes that don't belong anywhere else. Choose Note from the New Item button (or hold Ctrl+Shift and press N) to open a Note window. Enter your text in the Note window that opens.

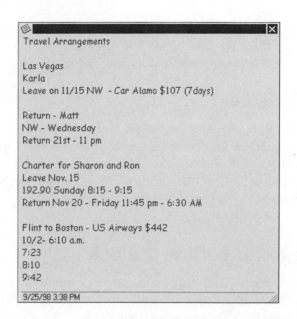

 TIP When you are entering a note, enter a title for the note and then press Enter before entering the contents of the note. Otherwise, the entire text of the note will be visible in the Notes Information Viewer.

Each note is automatically time- and date-stamped. Closing the window automatically saves the note. To view a note, click the notes icon on the Outlook Bar to go to the Notes window. Double-click a note to open it. Click the note icon to access options for deleting, saving, and printing notes.

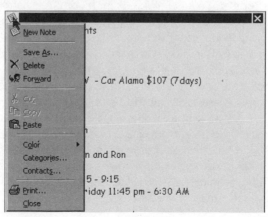

If a note gains importance and needs to become a task, a Journal entry, or an e-mail message, just drag the Note icon onto the appropriate icon on the Outlook bar or into the appropriate folder in the folder list.

Notes Views

Even though notes are small, you still have options for viewing them in different ways. Choose Small Icons, Large Icons, or List from the Notes Standard toolbar to change how the icons are displayed in the Information Viewer.

Choose View ➤ Current View to switch to a number of predefined views; for example, Notes List view shows you a list of your notes and gives an AutoPreview of their contents.

Using Notes outside Outlook

You can take a note with you to any application or even let it sit open on the Windows Desktop ready and waiting for you. To place a note on the Windows Desktop, restore the Outlook window (click the Restore button on the Outlook title bar) and drag the note to the Desktop.

Outlook does not have to be open for you to edit the note, makes additions to it, or delete the contents. However, if you close the note you'll have to reopen Outlook to view the note again.

MASTERING THE OPPORTUNITIES

Making Notes Mobile

If you carry a 3Com PalmPilot, Palm III, or other handheld computing device, chances are it synchronizes with Outlook's Notes module. It may have a different name for the folder; the Palm III, for example, calls it MemoPad—look at your handheld device to see if there is a similar folder. Once you discover it, it opens a world of possibilities for having information at your fingertips. For example, copy your travel itinerary into an Outlook note and you never have to worry about finding your travel agent's printout again. This is especially valuable in the age of electronic tickets where you don't even have a ticket to look at. If there is a document you want to take with you, copy and paste Word documents or Excel spreadsheets directly into a note. It's a good idea to check your handheld's documentation to see if there is a maximum file size, and you'll want to double-check the document on your handheld after you synchronize to make sure it made it there safely. Once you get in the habit of using notes, you'll find them an invaluable tool for the mobile professional.

What's Next

Now that you have people to communicate with in Contacts, Chapter 19 will introduce you to the power of Outlook's e-mail features. Outlook offers robust features for the Internet Only user and provides users on a Microsoft Exchange network with incredible workgroup features such as voting and message recall.

PART

IV

Getting Organized
with Outlook

CHAPTER 19

Using Outlook as a Communications Tool

FEATURING:

Creating and addressing e-mail messages

Attaching items and files to messages

Designing and using custom signatures

Setting message handling options

Using e-mail as a voting tool

Receiving and replying to mail

Outlook was designed first and foremost as an e-mail communication tool. In Outlook 2000, Microsoft has added new mail features like flagging and automatic message decryption, enhancing what was already an outstanding product. With Outlook, you can work collaboratively, using e-mail messages to distribute documents or vote on important issues in your company.

Outlook Configurations and E-Mail

There are three ways to send and receive mail, depending on how Outlook 2000 is configured on your PC:

- If Outlook was installed for Corporate/Workgroup use and you are connected to your organization's network, mail from within your organization is delivered directly to your Inbox. Internet mail may also be delivered directly, depending on your organization's connection to the Internet; if it is not, you use a separate dial-up connection to send and receive Internet mail.

- If you have the Corporate/Workgroup setup and are not connected to your company's network (for example, when you are working away from the office with your laptop computer), mail is only delivered on demand when you connect to your organization's server with a dial-up connection.

- If you chose the Internet Only mail option when Outlook was installed, you always need to tell Outlook to send and receive mail, either by changing the Mail Delivery options to automatically connect to your Internet Service Provider at specified intervals, or by telling Outlook to connect to your ISP when you wish to send and receive mail.

In this chapter, we'll focus on the first and third options. For more information on sending and receiving e-mail while working offline, refer to our *Mastering Outlook 2000* (Sybex, 1999). Mail settings are determined by your Outlook configuration; we'll point out the differences between the two configurations throughout this chapter.

 TIP   There is a fourth installation option, besides those just listed: No E-Mail. If Mail Message is not a choice on the File ➢ New menu, e-mail has not been installed. You must install it before you can send messages in Outlook. Choose Tools ➢ Options ➢ Mail Services, and then click the Reconfigure Mail Support button to change your e-mail configuration to Internet Only or Corporate/Workgroup.

Creating and Addressing E-Mail

 To create a message, choose File ➤ New ➤ Mail Message from the menu bar, or open the menu on the New Item button and choose Mail Message to open a message form, shown in Figure 19.1.

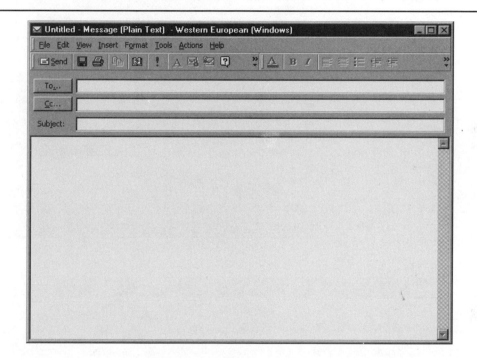

There are three View menu options that allow you to display text boxes in a message form: From, Message Header, and Bcc Field. The default view, Message Header, includes the Subject and Cc fields. Click any of the options to turn it on or off.

Entering E-Mail Addresses

There are three ways to enter e-mail addresses: from your address books, by typing the address manually, or by searching for the person's e-mail address with a directory service. Enter the recipient's name or e-mail addresses in the To text box, or click the To button to open the Select Names dialog box, shown in Figure 19.2. When you open the Select Names dialog box, the choices are based on the type of communication you're creating: To and Cc (courtesy copy) for letters; To, Cc and Bcc (blind courtesy copy) for e-mail messages and faxes. To and Cc recipients are listed in the header of the message, while recipients of blind courtesy copies are not. Therefore, recipients of the original message and courtesy copies won't know that the message was also sent to the Bcc recipients.

FIGURE 19.2

Select message recipients using the To, Cc, and Bcc buttons in the Select Names dialog box.

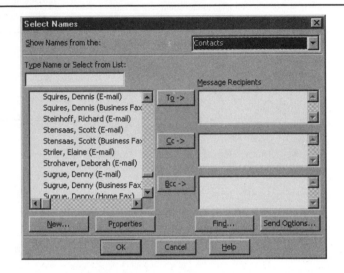

About Address Books

An address book is a list of names you can select addresses from. You may have only one address book (with the Internet Only configuration), three address books (with the Corporate/Workgroup configuration), or some other number of address books, depending on the services installed to handle mail messaging on your computer. The major address books are:

Global Address Book: An address book for members of your organization stored on a server; also called a *post office address list*. This address book can contain global distribution lists.

Outlook Address Book: The Outlook Address Book automatically contains the entries in your Contacts folder in the Corporate/Workgroup configuration. It only includes contacts that have an e-mail address or fax number listed.

Continued ▯▶

> **CONTINUED**
>
> **Contacts:** In the Internet Only configuration, this is your personal address book; it includes all your contacts, whether or not they have an e-mail address or fax number.
>
> If you have installed other mail services, such as CompuServe, you may have additional address books.

 NOTE Personal Address Books have been eliminated in Outlook 2000. Personal distribution lists can now be stored within Contacts folders. See "Creating and Using Distribution Lists (Groups)" in this chapter for more information.

In the Internet Only configuration, you select recipients from the Contacts folder. With the Corporate/Workgroup configuration, you will have more than one address book, so begin by choosing an address book from the drop-down list in the dialog box:

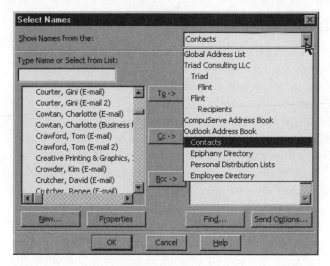

Either scroll to the person's name or begin entering the name in the Find text box and Outlook will find the name in the list. With the contact's name selected in the left pane, click the To, Cc, or Bcc button to add the name to the list of recipients. (Or right-click the name and select To, Cc, or Bcc from the shortcut menu.) You can hold Shift or Ctrl and click to select a contiguous list of names or multiple names before clicking the To, Cc, or Bcc buttons. After you've added all the recipients, click OK to close the Select Names dialog box and return to the message form.

Entering Addresses Manually

You can type an entire e-mail address, or enough of the contact's name for Outlook to find the recipient. When you enter text in the To, Cc, or Bcc text boxes, Outlook automatically checks the text against the names in the address books. If Outlook determines that the text is a valid e-mail address, it underlines it. If you have a display name entered in Contacts for this person, it may substitute the display name for the e-mail address.

If you enter a name that does not exactly match a name in an address book, Outlook marks it with a wavy red underline (just as Word marks a spelling error). Right-click the name and select the recipient from the shortcut menu. Select the person you want to send the message to from the menu. If you don't identify the recipient before sending the message, Outlook will open a dialog box so that you can select a name. The next time you enter **Susan** as a recipient name, Outlook will automatically select the name you chose from the menu this time. However, the name will have a green, dashed underline so that you know there are other Susans in the address book.

Using Directory Services

A *directory service* is an address book maintained in an LDAP directory. *LDAP* (Lightweight Directory Access Protocol), developed at the University of Michigan, is an emerging Internet/intranet standard, used in many networking programs, that defines a common format for electronic directories. The directory could be on a local network server running Microsoft Exchange or on a public directory service you access via the Internet, such as Four11 or Bigfoot. You use directory services when you know a person's name, but don't have their e-mail address.

Public directory services are automatically enabled in the Internet Only configuration. In the Workplace/Corporate configuration, LDAP directories are created or enabled by your network administrator. If clicking the Find button doesn't open a Find People dialog box, you don't have direct access to directory services. However, if you have an Internet connection, click Start ➤ Find ➤ On The Internet. Internet Explorer takes you to a search engine that allows you to search for individual e-mail addresses.

Adding Addresses on the Fly

You can quickly create a contact from any e-mail address you enter in a message. Right-click the address in the To, Cc, or Bcc text box, and choose Add To Contacts from the shortcut menu. Outlook will open a blank Contact form with the e-mail address in both the Name and E-mail text boxes. Correct the name, enter any additional information you wish, and then click Save And Close to close the form and return to your e-mail message.

Creating and Using Distribution Lists (Groups)

When you work with a team or are a member of a committee or task force, you'll often address e-mail to the same group of people: the other members of your team. *Distribution lists* streamline this process. With a distribution list, you create a named list in your Contacts folder, and then add all the members of your team or committee to the group. When you address your next e-mail message, you can send it to the distribution list (and all its members) rather than adding each of the members as individual recipients.

In the Internet Only configuration, you create *groups* rather than distribution lists. Groups and distribution lists work the same way, but you create them in a slightly different fashion.

Creating a Group (Internet Only Users)   If you're an Internet Only user, creating a group is easy. Just follow these steps:

1. Select Tools ➢ Address Book from the Outlook menu to open the Address Book dialog box.

2. Click the New Group button on the Address Book toolbar and select New Group.

3. In the Group Name box, type the name for the group.

4. Click the Select Members button to add names from the address book.

5. Select a name in the list and click the Select button to add the address to the group. Hold Ctrl to select multiple names before clicking the Select button.

6. To add people to the distribution list that aren't in your Address Book, click the New Contact button and create a new contact.

7. Click OK to close the Select Group Members dialog box. Click OK again to close the Group Properties dialog box.

  Creating a Distribution List (Corporate/Workgroup Users)   In the Corporate/ Workgroup configuration, you create distribution lists in your Contacts folder. Choose Tools ➢Address Book to open the Address Book window, and click the New button to open the New Entry dialog box.

Choose Personal Distribution List. You can store personal distribution lists in any Contacts folder—you may want to create a subfolder in your main Contacts folder to store distribution lists (see Chapter 21 for more about creating folders). Choose where you would like to store this list and click OK to open the New Personal Distribution List form. Enter a name for the list, and then click the Select Members button to open the Select Members dialog box, shown in Figure 19.3.

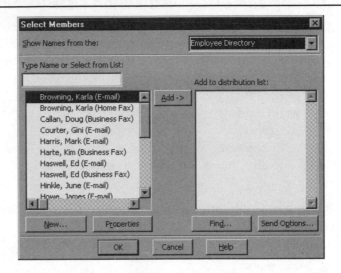

Choose the address book that contains the first member you wish to add. Double-click an address to add the address to the distribution list. To add a member who isn't in an address book, click the New button to open the New Entry dialog box again. Select an address type, in this case, New Contact; then choose whether you want to add the member to Contacts or just use it in this list. Complete the Contact form that opens. When you save and close the contact, select the newly created contact from the list.

When you've selected all the members of the distribution list, click OK to close the Select Members dialog box. Click Save And Close to close the Distribution List form.

NOTE If you click the Add New button from the Distribution List form, you can enter a display name and e-mail address and check whether you want to add this person to Contacts. If you do not add the information to Contacts, this person's address will be accessible only in the distribution list.

Figure 19.4 shows the contents of a Contacts subfolder called Personal Distribution Lists. If you store your lists in the Contacts main folder, the personal distribution lists will be intermingled with contacts—look for the special group icon to tell them apart.

FIGURE 19.4

Creating a Personal Distribution Lists subfolder makes all your lists available in one place.

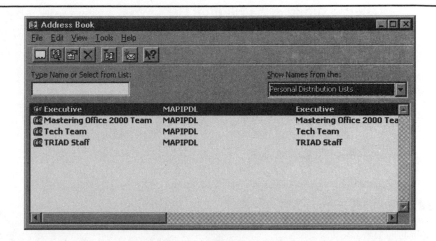

Addressing Mail to a Group or Distribution List   To send mail to all members of a group or distribution list, type the group name in the To, Cc, or Bcc text box on the message form, or click one of the three buttons to open the Select Names dialog box. Group names are bold in the Select Names dialog box and address books, and they are preceded by the group icon. Select the group name and click the To, Cc, or Bcc button to add the group's members as message recipients. If you need to check the member-ship of a group, right-click the group name in the message's address boxes or in the Select Names dialog box and choose Properties to open the group's properties sheet.

Adding or Removing a Name from a Group or Distribution List   The member-ship of a team or committee can change as members leave the team and new mem-bers are elected. You add and remove names from a group in the Address Book by following these steps:

1. Choose Tools ➢ Address Book from the menu, and select the address book that contains the group.

2. Double-click the name of the group you want to change or right-click a group name and choose Properties to open the group's Properties dialog box.

3. If you have Internet Only mail, click the Select Members button to add new group members. In a Workgroup or Corporate setting, Use the Select Members button to add names to the group.

4. To remove a member from a group, select the name you want to delete and click the Remove button in the Group Properties dialog box. In a Workgroup or Cor-porate setting, click the Remove button to delete members from the list.

5. When you've finished adding and removing members, click OK to close the Select Names dialog box, and click OK again to close the group Properties dialog box.

Delete a Group or Distribution List   When a team's work is complete or a committee is disbanded, you probably won't need the group or distribution list any more. To remove a group list, open the Address Book (Tools ➤ Address Book) and select the group you want to remove.

In the Internet Only configuration, click the Delete button to remove the group. The entries for the individuals included in the group list will not be deleted. With Corporate/Workgroup settings, right-click the name of the distribution list and choose Delete from the shortcut menu. When you delete the distribution list, any addresses that existed *only* in the list are also deleted.

Formatting Messages

Outlook supports four message formats. The mail editor you select determines the tools you can use to format the text, paragraphs, and background of your mail message.

Plain text is the default format, created with a plain text editor. With plain text, text appears in the computer's default e-mail font, usually Courier, and you can't apply formatting. With *Microsoft Outlook Rich Text* you can format fonts, align paragraphs, and use bulleted lists in your message. When you use an HTML editor, your message is created in *Hypertext Markup Language (HTML)*, the language used to develop pages on the World Wide Web. The HTML format supports an incredibly wide range of formatting, including backgrounds, horizontal lines, numbered and bulleted lists, and any other formatting you expect to see on a Web page. The fourth format, Microsoft Word, uses Word 2000 as your e-mail editor and lets you apply any formatting changes that are valid in Word.

To select a different editor, open the Format menu and choose from the list. Depending on the editor you selected, various tools are available on the Format menu and Formatting toolbar in the message form as shown in Table 19.1.

TABLE 19.1: OUTLOOK EDITORS

Text Editor	Formatting
Plain Text	No formatting
Microsoft Outlook Rich Text	Text formatting, bullets, alignment
HTML Text	Text formatting, numbering, bullets, alignment, horizontal lines, backgrounds, HTML styles, Web pages

NOTE You cannot change from Rich Text to HTML. You have to change back to Plain Text first. Any formatting you've already applied will be lost when you make this switch, so it's best to pick your editor and stick with it.

In the HTML editor, you have traditional Font and Paragraph options at your disposal, just as in Rich Text, but it doesn't stop there. You can also place horizontal lines, pictures, animated graphics, and multimedia files in the message and apply a picture or color as a background, as shown in Figure 19.5.

FIGURE 19.5

HTML messages can include text formatting and graphic lines.

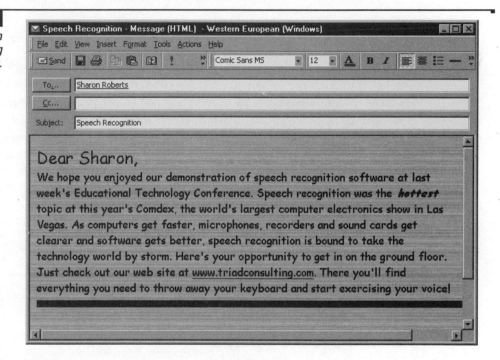

On the Insert menu, you'll find these options:

Horizontal Lines can be an effective way to divide a message into parts. To add a horizontal line to an HTML message, place the insertion point where you want to insert the line in the message body.

Picture allows you to insert a picture into the body of the message.

Hyperlink can be chosen to convert a Web address such as www.sybex.com to a hyperlink that your reader can just click to go to.

On the Format menu, you'll find the following choices:

Style includes bulleted and numbered lists and six levels of headings. To apply a style, select the paragraph(s) you want to format and then choose Format ➤ Style to open a menu of paragraph styles.

Background can include color and pictures. To choose a background color, choose Format ➤ Background ➤ Color from the message form's menu and select a color from the palette. To use a picture as a background, choose Format ➤ Background ➤ Picture to open the Background Picture dialog box. The dialog box list includes pictures suitable for use as backgrounds. Select from the list, or click the Browse button and select a picture from your local drive or a network drive.

Formatting Word Messages

The last format choice for e-mail messages is Microsoft Word. When you create a message, a Word session will be opened, so you can use most of the formatting and text-editing features available in Word: AutoCorrect, bulleted and numbered lists, drawing tools such as WordArt and AutoShapes, a spelling checker, and so on. When you install Outlook, you can choose Word 2000 as your default e-mail editor. As you'll see next, however, you can also switch editors for new messages at any point, so don't worry if you didn't make this choice during installation.

 TIP When you reply to a message, Outlook automatically uses the original message's format for the reply.

Setting Mail Format Options

There are three types of mail format options: the default editor, which determines the Message Format; Stationery and Fonts; and customized Signatures you can add to your messages.

Setting a Format for New Messages

With all these choices, how do you choose a format for e-mail messages? That depends on a number of factors, including the e-mail editor and other software you and your recipients have on their PCs. There are four steps to selecting an editor:

1. Choose Tools ➤ Options from the Outlook menu to open the Options dialog box.

2. Click the Mail Format tab.

3. Choose the text editor you wish to use in the Send In This Message Format text box (see Figure 19.6).

4. Click OK to close the dialog box.

FIGURE 19.6

Choose an e-mail editor and set message format options in the Options dialog box.

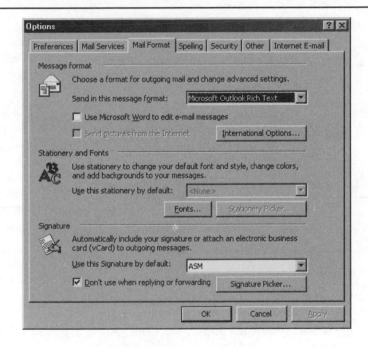

Table 19.2 summarizes the advantages and disadvantages of each format.

TABLE 19.2: COMPARING MESSAGE FORMATS

Format	Advantages	Disadvantages
Plain Text	Messages can be read with any e-mail editor; supports MIME encoding.	Lack of formatting makes it harder to add emphasis or get the reader's attention.
Outlook Rich Text	Allows font and paragraph formatting, supported by Microsoft Exchange and many PC mail editors.	No cross-platform support, so Unix and Macintosh users get plain text versions of messages.
HTML	Language is cross-platform; many users will eventually be able to read HTML messages. Support for encoding, graphics, formatting, and custom stationery.	Many e-mail editors don't support HTML messages, so some of your recipients will receive plain—or worse, garbled—text.
Word	Lots of formatting options and support for templates. Word users see the message exactly as it appears on your screen. If a recipient doesn't have Word but their mail editor supports Rich Text Format, most of the Word formatting is preserved.	You must have Word 97 or later to use this feature. Some of the best formatting features (like tables) are converted to plain text if the recipient doesn't have Word installed on their computer. Custom signatures must be created in Word templates; does not support digital signatures.

When you choose an editor, you're choosing the potential formatting for new messages. For example, if you create and send an HTML message to a recipient whose e-mail system doesn't support HTML messages, they see the text of your message in plain text. Formatting and graphics are reduced to text strings that look like a lot of garbled text. On the other hand, if your recipient is using a mail editor that supports HTML messages, they get to see your message in all its glory. The potential is there, provided the recipient's mail editor can support the format you choose.

PART
IV

Getting Organized
with Outlook

 MASTERING TROUBLESHOOTING

Encoding Messages

If you use a plain text or HTML editor, you can also choose an encoding format for messages that are sent over the Internet. (When you attach a Word document to a message, you're attaching more than just text. Applications add their own information to files. This information can't be translated by text editors, only by the application, in this case Microsoft Word.) Encoding translates your message and its attachments into a binary code that your recipient's mail program must then decode. Many mail programs decode messages automatically; if a recipient's mail system does not, there are programs like WinZip that decode encoded messages. Outlook supports two of the three primary encoding programs: UUencode and MIME. The third program, BinHex, was created for the Macintosh environment and is not supported by Outlook.

UUencode (which originally meant Unix-to-Unix encode) was designed to allow users of different word processors and operating systems to send information back and forth.

MIME (Multipurpose Internet Mail Extensions) was created by the Internet Engineering Task Force (IETF), and is the "official" standard for encoding Internet messages. UUencode works well for text, but MIME was designed to support a wide range of file types: video, e-mail, audio, and graphics. Most mail programs automatically handle MIME encoding and decoding; other mailers, particularly freeware or shareware mailers, automatically handle UUencode.

Whether you use UUencode or MIME, your recipient must have the appropriate decoding software to decode and read the message. If you are sending audio and video attachments, use MIME, and choose base64 (an encoding protocol for nontext content) in the Encode Using drop-down list. For more information and help using MIME, visit http://www.hunnysoft.com/mime/. To encode your plain text or HTML messages, click the Internet E-Mail tab of the Options dialog box. Choose UUencode or MIME. If you choose MIME, you can also have your message encoded using base64.

Choosing Stationery

If you use an HTML editor, you can personalize your e-mail messages by choosing HTML stationery, a scheme that includes a font and a background color or picture. To select stationery, you must select HTML as your mail editor in the Options dialog box. Then choose a Stationery pattern from the Use This Stationery By Default drop-down list. To see what the various Stationery patterns look like, click the Stationery Picker button on the Mail Format page of the dialog box to open the Stationery Picker dialog box. Each Stationery choice includes fonts and a background picture or color.

 TIP Can't find stationery to meet your needs? Just click the Get More Stationery button, and Outlook will launch your browser and visit the Microsoft Web site, where you can download more stationery patterns for free.

Designing Custom Signatures

A *custom signature* is text you add to the end of a message to provide any information you want all of the recipients of your e-mail to know, such as your contact data, confidentiality information, or advertisements for your products.

With Outlook 2000, you can create multiple custom signatures and select the signature you wish to use with each message you send. This lets you create a formal signature for business messages and a friendlier signature for messages to friends and family.

To create a custom signature or choose a default signature for all messages, choose Tools ➤ Options from the Outlook menu to open the Options dialog box. On the Mail Format tab, click the Signature Picker button to open the Signature Picker dialog box. Click New and enter the information requested in the dialog box shown in Figure 19.7.

FIGURE 19.7

Create one or more custom signatures in the Create New Signature dialog box.

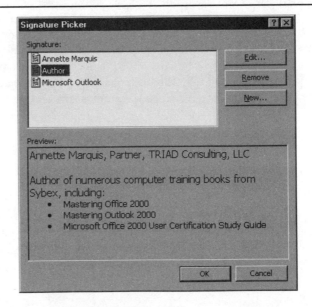

TIP If you use Word as your e-mail editor, the Signature Picker is disabled. To create a signature, include your custom signature in a template in Word; then select the template from the File ➢ New dialog box in Word. Look for information on creating Word templates in Chapter 8.

Clicking the Advanced Edit button on the second page of the Create New Signature dialog box opens Word (or WordPad) so you can enter and format text in a larger window. To delete the Signature Text and begin from scratch, click the Clear button. The vCard options allow you to include your contact information (as a "virtual card") in the signature. For information on vCards, see our *Mastering Outlook 2000* (Sybex, 1999).

When you've finished entering and formatting the text for your custom signature, click OK to close the Edit Signature dialog box and return to the Signature Picker. Close the Signature Picker to return to the Options dialog box. The signature you just created is automatically set as the default, appearing in the text area of every new message. You can choose another default signature (or None) from the drop-down list.

Selecting a Custom Signature

 To choose a custom signature for a message, place the insertion point where you want to insert the signature. Choose Insert „ Signature or click the Signature button and select a signature from the menu; if the custom signature you want to use isn't displayed on the menu, choose More to open the Signature dialog box. Select a signature, and then click OK to add the signature to the message.

Attaching Items and Files to Messages

You can *attach* a file or an Outlook item to an e-mail message. It doesn't matter which e-mail editor you use; you can attach items and files to messages in any format. Files and items can be inserted in a message as attachments, as shortcuts, or as text:

Attachment: The file or item retains its original formatting and is included in its entirety in the message. Use attachments when the recipient needs to work with a copy of the file or item in its original format. For example, you could send a colleague an Excel worksheet that they could open in Excel. Note that the attachment is a copy, so changes your colleague makes will not be reflected in the original file.

Shortcut: Inserts an icon in the message pointing to the file. Insert a file or item as a shortcut when you and the recipient both have access to the file. For example, if the Excel worksheet is stored on your departmental server, you could send a shortcut so that your colleague could find the file and both of you could work with the original file.

Text Only: Inserts the text of the file in the body of the message. Use this to send information from a Contact form to a friend who doesn't use Outlook.

NOTE When you send Outlook items with categories like Ideas or Hot Contact as attachments, the categories you used are automatically added to the recipients' categories. Unless you and your recipient use exactly the same categories, you should consider deleting the categories from the attached item before sending the message.

To attach a file to a message, choose Insert ➤ File from the message menu or click the Insert File button on the message toolbar to open the Insert File dialog box. Select the file and choose Text Only, Attachment, or Shortcut from the Insert button's drop-down list. Click OK to insert the file.

If you insert the file as an attachment or shortcut, an icon representing the file or file location appears in the message. Text (or something similar) appears for a file inserted as Text Only. In Figure 19.8, a Word file has been inserted as a shortcut, a graphics (.bmp) file as an attachment, and a Readme file as text only. When the recipient clicks on the files, the Word file will open in Word; the bitmap will be opened in the recipient's default graphics editor; and the Readme file is already open in the message. If your recipient doesn't have the program needed to open a file, they can't view it.

FIGURE 19.8

Mail message with an attachment, a shortcut, and text inserted from a file.

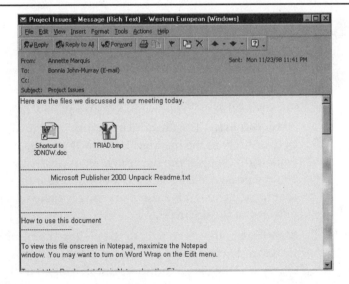

MASTERING TROUBLESHOOTING

Troubleshooting File Attachments

Only a few file types can be successfully inserted as Text Only. Files created in plain text editors like Notepad and Rich Text editors such as WordPad insert well; these programs create files with extensions like .txt, .bat, and .rtf. Other files contain formatting that can't be translated as text. For example, Microsoft Word files begin and end with embedded codes that specify the document's properties. If you insert a Word file as Text Only in a plain text or RTF message, it will begin and end with symbols—hundreds or thousands of symbols.

If your intended recipient doesn't have the application to open an attachment, you can send the text of the document in the message without attaching it. For a Word document, for example, open the document in Word, select the text, and copy it to the Clipboard. Open the message in Outlook, position the insertion point, and paste the text into the message. You can also use the new Office feature that allows you to send documents directly from an application (File ➢ Send To ➢ Mail Recipient).

To attach an Outlook item to a message, place the insertion point in the body of the message and choose Insert ➢ Item from the message menu to open the Insert Item dialog box, shown in Figure 19.9. Select the folder that contains the item you want to attach, then choose the item in the Items pane. You can use Ctrl or Shift and click to select multiple items.

If your recipient uses Outlook, send the item as an attachment. For recipients who use other e-mail editors, insert the item as Text Only. Outlook will add the text from the selected item to the message.

 TIP If you send an Outlook item as a shortcut, the recipient must have permission to access the folder that contains the item. By default, other users do not have permission to view items in your personal folders, so you'll generally want to send items as Attachments or Text Only. For more information on folders and permissions, see Chapter 21.

FIGURE 19.9

*Use the Insert Item
dialog box to select
Outlook items to
attach to an e-mail
message.*

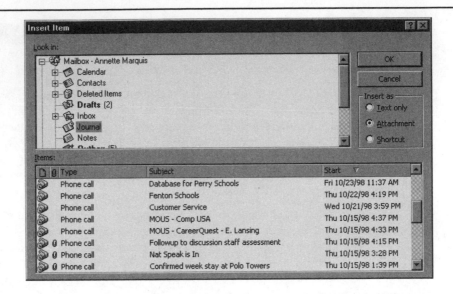

Sending Your Message

You've selected an e-mail editor, addressed your message, added and formatted text, and inserted attachments and custom signatures; now you're ready to send your message to the recipients. But first, take a moment and examine Outlook's message-handling options to make sure your message is delivered and received with the same care you took while creating it.

Setting Message Options

Unlike the Message Format options, Message options are set for the individual message you're creating now, not for all new messages.

Click the Options button in the message form's toolbar to open the Message Options dialog box. The Corporate/Workgroup Message Options dialog box is shown in Figure 19.10; the Internet Only version of the dialog box does not include Voting and Tracking options. Table 19.3 explains each of the message handling options.

FIGURE 19.10

*Message options are
set for a specific
message.*

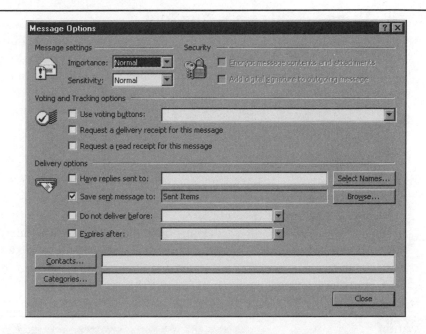

TABLE 19.3: MESSAGE HANDLING OPTIONS

Option	Description
Importance	Puts a flag on the message to alert the recipient about its importance. Click to select Normal, Low, or High.
Sensitivity	Puts a flag on the message to alert the recipient about how sensitive the message is. Click to select Normal, Personal, Private, or Confidential.
Use Voting Buttons	Enables use of e-mail as a voting tool (see "Using E-Mail as a Voting Tool" below).
Tracking options	Notify you when the message has been received and/or read (depending on the capability of the recipient's mail service or Internet Service Provider).
Have Replies Sent To	Allows you to designate an individual to collect replies to your message.
Save Sent Message To	Indicates which folder you want the sent message stored in.
Do Not Deliver Before	Keeps the message from being delivered before the date you specify.
Expires After	Marks the message as unavailable after the date you specify.
Contacts	Relates this message to a contact.
Category	Assigns a category to this message.

Using E-Mail as a Voting Tool

Gathering opinions, reaching agreement, and settling on a course of action are all part of working as a team. The Corporate/Worksgroup configuration of Outlook has built-in a tool to help generate and then gather responses from groups of e-mail recipients. It will even tabulate the results for you, showing you a log of everyone's vote. To activate voting, click the Options tab of an open e-mail message. Click the Use Voting Buttons and Have Replies Sent To check boxes.

You can add your own text to the voting buttons that appear, and you can add additional buttons—put a semicolon between the options or you'll get one big button. If you want to have someone else collect the results, enter their address in the Have Replies Sent To text box. When you've set up the options, click Send to distribute the ballots to the voting list.

Recipients respond by clicking one of the voting buttons below the menu bar, as shown in Figure 19.11. Their responses are sent to the Inbox like any other message, but a tracking form is added to the original message in the Sent Items folder so you can view the results, as seen in Figure 19.12.

FIGURE 19.11

Recipients click one of the voting buttons on the message to cast their ballots.

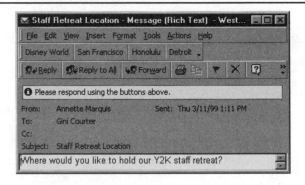

FIGURE 19.12

The Tracking page of a message with voting options lets you determine the status of the vote.

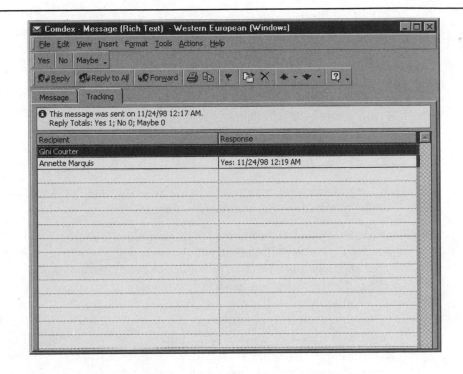

Sending Mail Messages

You're ready to send your message to its recipients. Click the Send button on the message toolbar. You may be wondering how long the message will hang around in the Outbox. The answer: it depends. There are three possible scenarios:

- In a Corporate/Workgroup installation where you are connected to a network, options are usually set to send messages immediately and your outgoing message will spend very little time in the Outbox.

- In an Internet Only or Corporate/Workgroup installation, you can establish automated Internet mail delivery at specified intervals (Options ≻ Internet E-Mail). Outlook connects to the Internet every *N* minutes or hours, and delivers and receives messages.

- On the other hand, you may be using Outlook with the Internet Only configuration without automated mail delivery (the default for Internet Only) or working offline in a Corporate/Workgroup configuration. In that case, mail waits in your Outbox until you instruct Outlook to send and deliver messages.

To move the message out of the Outbox and into the Internet or local mail server:

- Choose Tools ➤ Send from the Outlook menu to send, but not receive, messages from your mail server.

- Choose Tools ➤ Send And Receive ➤ All Accounts (or a specific account) to both send and receive messages.

- Choose Tools ➤ Send And Receive and then point to a specific account to send a receive messages from only one mail service.

If you access your mail server with a dial-up connection, a dialog box opens while Outlook is connecting to your server. This dialog box remains open while messages are being sent and received. Once Outlook has established a dial-up connection, you can move the dialog box to a less central location or switch to another application and continue working.

Internet Only users have the option to keep the dialog box open or close it down—and there's a good reason to close it. In the Internet Only configuration, message handling happens in the background, so you can create contacts, add items to your calendar, or even view newly received messages while Outlook continues to send and deliver mail. If you don't want to see this dialog box again, enable the Always Hide This Dialog check box.

You'll still be able to keep track of Outlook's progress, even with the dialog box hidden. Check the right side of the status bar to see reports as Outlook sends and receives your messages. If you need to cancel message receipt or delivery, click the arrow at the right end of the status bar and choose Cancel Mail Delivery from the menu. To redisplay the Details dialog box, choose Details from the menu. After the message has been sent, Outlook moves it from the Outbox to the Sent Items folder or another folder you specified in the message options.

Reviewing Mail Messages

As long as Outlook is running, you can tell you have received mail by the envelope icon that appears on the Windows task bar. Double-click the envelope to activate Outlook and review your messages. In the table view of the messages, unread messages are boldface, so they are easy to spot.

PART

IV

Getting Organized
with Outlook

Select a message, and the beginning of the message appears in the preview pane below the messages. If the preview pane is not open, choose View ➤ Preview Pane from the Outlook menu to display it. You can adjust the size of the preview pane by adjusting the bar at the top of the pane up or down with the mouse pointer.

TIP You cannot preview messages that have been encrypted for security by the sender.

The previews usually let you see enough of a message to gauge its urgency. The first four columns of the default Inbox view show the message's Importance, Message Icon, Flag Status, and Attachment information. If the sender set the importance of the message, it is displayed in the first column; high importance is marked with a red exclamation point, low importance with a blue arrow. Table 19.4 below shows the icons used in the Inbox.

TABLE 19.4: INBOX MESSAGE ICONS

Icon	Message
!	High Importance
✉	Unread
✉	Digitally signed message
✉	Read
✉	Forwarded
✉	Replied to
▽	Flagged for follow-up
▽	Flagged; follow-up completed
📎	Includes an attachment
📧	Meeting Request
📧	Task Request

Opening Mail Messages

To open a message, double-click the closed envelope icon in front of the message—the same icon that announced the message's arrival in the taskbar tray. Outlook opens the message in a separate window. An information bar above the message header indicates if the message was flagged or has importance or sensitivity settings other than Normal. In Figure 19.13, the message header indicates that this message has high importance.

FIGURE 19.13

The message header contains important information about the message.

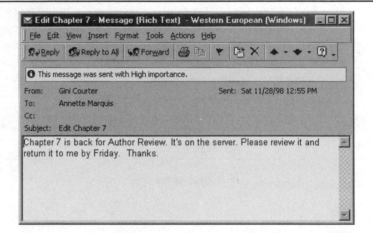

To close a message, click the Close button in the message's title bar, choose File ➤ Close from the message's menu, or press Alt+F4.

 TIP To open multiple messages, each in its own window, hold Ctrl and click to select each message in the list; then right-click and choose Open Selected Items.

MASTERING THE OPPORTUNITIES

Mastering Message Security

When you need to send or receive secure data over the Internet, a digitally signed message can give you confidence that the message has not been altered. To send or receive a digitally signed message, you must receive a digital ID or certificate from a certified security authority, such as VeriSign, Inc. Your Microsoft Exchange Server administrator may also be able to issue a digital ID. You can use your digital ID to verify your signature and to encrypt your message so only the intended recipient (who must also have a valid digital ID) can read it.

A secured message has a Certificate button just above the message box. To view the signature or encryption used with the message, click the Certificate button to open the Digital Signature dialog box. Outlook validates certificates by ensuring that:

- The contents of the message didn't change after the message was signed.
- The certificate is not revoked or expired.
- The e-mail address on the certificate matches the address on the message.
- The check mark in front of each item indicates that it is valid.

By default, Outlook notifies you before you open a message with an invalid certificate. You can check the Digital Signature dialog box to find the item that is not valid; it will be marked with a red *X* rather than a check mark.

If the certificate has expired, you can e-mail a message to the sender and let them know. Otherwise, it may be that the certificate is not from a certifying organization that Outlook already recognizes. If you know the certificate is acceptable, click the Edit Trust button in the Certificate or Digital Signature dialog box and choose Explicitly Trust This Certificate to accept this certificate in the future.

Opening Messages with Attachments

An icon in the message, as shown in Figure 19.14, represents a message attachment. To open the attachment, double-click the icon.

FIGURE 19.14

Icons in the message represent attachments.

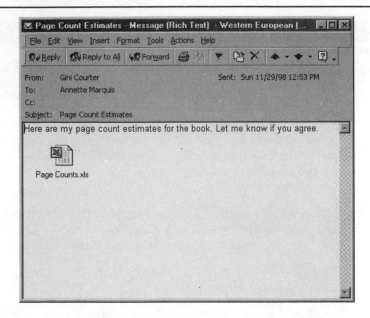

The first time you double-click an attachment from certain applications, an Opening Mail Attachment dialog box warns you that this type of file may include a virus. This is just a standard precaution and does not indicate that there is anything unusual about this particular file. Choose whether you want to open the file or save it to disk, and click OK. If the file isn't from a trusted source and you'd rather not open it, click Cancel.

With some file types, you can disable the Always Ask Before Opening This Type Of File check box, and Outlook will quit prompting you about the particular file type. You can't turn off checking on some file types, like Zip files, without turning off checking for all file types.

After you select Open or Save and click OK, Windows searches for the application needed to open the attachment, launches the application, and opens the file. If you don't have the required application, or if the file extension isn't properly registered in the Windows registry, you're notified that the file can't be opened, and told what action you could take to open the file.

MASTERING TROUBLESHOOTING

Troubleshooting Attachments and Encoded Messages

Attachments

If you receive a file created with an application that you do not have on your computer, you may be able to associate the file with another application. For example, you may not have Adobe Illustrator but you know that Corel Draw will open Illustrator files. You can associate files with the Illustrator extension to Corel Draw using Windows Explorer (View ➢ Folder Options ➢ File Types).

If you are uncertain whether you have a suitable application, look at the icon used to display the attachment. When the familiar Windows icon is displayed, there is no application associated with the file on your computer.

If you're not sure what program an attachment was created in, ask the sender before you follow the dialog box instructions. If the file can't be opened directly in any application, associating the file won't solve the problem. You may need to contact the sender and request that the file be converted to a format you can open.

Encoded Messages

Messages sent over the Internet are often encoded to preserve formatting and maintain the integrity of attachments. As discussed earlier, the most common encoding schemes are UUencode, the Unix-to-Unix encoding format, and MIME, the Multipurpose Internet Mail Extensions format.

Outlook automatically decodes messages encoded in both of these formats. The only way you will know that the message was encoded is by looking at the text at the beginning of the message. If you receive a message encoded with a scheme other than UUencode or MIME, the text of the message will appear to be garbled.

The sender may have chosen to encode the message. You can let them know that it isn't working, and that they can encode messages in MIME or UUencode and Outlook will decode them for you.

Often, however, the sender's mail program automatically encoded the message, so the sender doesn't know that the message was encoded. They may be able to change a mail format or delivery option and switch to UUencode or MIME, but they may not have the option. If you regularly receive encoded mail from users with other formats (like Mac users who use BinHex), consider a separate decoding program. There are several good shareware programs, such as XferPro (http://sabasoft.com), which allow you to decode messages encoded in a variety of encoding schemes.

Replying to Mail

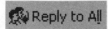

After you read a message, you can reply to the sender or to everyone who received the message (including courtesy copies of the message). Select or open the message you wish to reply to; then click the Reply button to address a reply only to the sender, or the Reply To All button to send a reply to all the other recipients of the message you received. Outlook opens a message form and enters the recipients' addresses in the To text box. You can add other recipients using the To, Cc, and Bcc buttons on the message form.

Keep in mind that when you reply to a message, Outlook uses the same format as the original message to ensure that the recipient can read the reply.

Forwarding Messages

Forwarding a message sends the entire message (and any text you add) to another recipient. To forward an open message, click the Forward button or choose Actions ➢ Forward from the message menu. If the message is not open, right-click it in the view list and choose Forward from the shortcut menu. To indicate how the original text and text you add should appear in the forwarded message, follow these steps:

1. Choose Tools ➢ Options on the Outlook menu to open the Options dialog box.

2. On the Preferences page, click the E-Mail Options button to open the E-Mail Options dialog box.

3. Choose a format from the When Forwarding a Message drop-down list:

    • Attach Original Message
    • Include Original Message Text (the default)
    • Include and Indent Original Message Text
    • Prefix Each Line of the Original Message.

4. To add comments to replies and forwarded messages, enable the Mark My Comments With check box and enter your name or other text in the text box.

5. Click OK to close the E-mail Options dialog box.

6. Click OK to close the Options dialog box.

Flagging Messages for Further Action

You can't always reply to, forward, or even fully read and review a message when you receive it. Flagging messages ensures a message doesn't get lost and helps you stay organized. When you flag a message, you note the type of action that's required. You can even set a reminder so you don't forget to follow-up on the message.

To flag an open message, choose Actions ➤ Flag For Follow-Up from the message menu, or click the Flag For Follow-Up button on the message toolbar. If the message is not open, right-click it in the Inbox and choose Flag For Follow-Up from the shortcut menu. Choose a flag description from the list of choices or enter your own description in the Flag To text box.

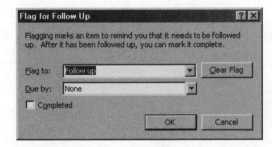

Choose a date to be reminded about the message by opening the Due By calendar control. When you're finished entering flag information, click OK to close the dialog box.

TIP   You can flag messages that you're sending or forwarding as well as those you receive.

When you've completed follow-up with the message, you can either clear the flag or mark the action complete. To clear the flag, open the Flag For Follow-Up dialog box, click the Clear Flag button, and click OK. To mark a flag as complete, open the Flag For Follow-Up dialog box and enable the Completed check box, then click OK to close the dialog box.

Organizing E-Mail Messages

One of the most persistent challenges facing the networked business is presented by the proliferation of electronic mail. Learning how to organize your mail will make you more efficient and help you maintain your sanity in the process.

Outlook makes it easy to organize and manage your Inbox, and all the tools you need are in one place—the Organize page. Click the Organize button on the toolbar to open the Organize page at the top of the Inbox, shown in Figure 19.15. Using the page, you create folders for message management, create rules to color-code your message, change Inbox views, or open the Rules Wizard and automate management of the messages you receive.

FIGURE 19.15

With the Organize page, all your message management tools are right at your fingertips.

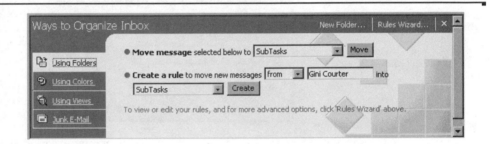

The Organize page has four tabs: Using Folders, Using Views, Using Colors, and Junk E-Mail. (Information about views, and more details about folders, can be found in Chapter 21.)

Creating Rules to Automatically Move Messages

No matter which tab you're using in the Organizer, you create rules by example. Here's how it works with Using Folders: If you want all messages from Karla Browning to be automatically placed in a specific mail folder, select a message from Karla in the Inbox or any other mail folder. Then choose From or Sent To in the Create A Rule drop-down list (shown in Figure 19.15) to indicate which type of messages should be moved. If you don't have a message from your recipient in any of your mail folders, enter the person's name in the text box. Use the Into drop-down list to select the folder where you want the messages to/from this person moved; then click the Create button to create the new rule. You'll know it worked because it will say Done next to the Create button.

The rule is applied to all new messages you send or receive.

Using Colors to Organize Messages

Message information (sender, subject, and so on) is displayed in the Windows text color by default; this is the color you get when you choose the Automatic color in any Windows application. The Using Colors tab, shown in Figure 19.16, lets you apply any of sixteen colors to message descriptions based on who sent the message, who it was sent to, and whether you are the only recipient.

Getting Organized with Outlook

FIGURE 19.16

Automatically apply colors to easily distinguish messages from each other

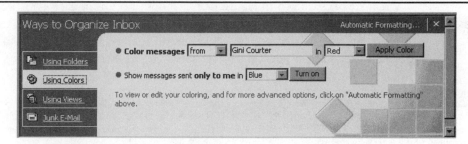

To set the color based on the sender or recipient:

1. Choose a message from the sender or addressed to the recipient in the list view.

2. In the Color Messages drop-down lists, choose From or Sent To and a color you wish to apply.

3. Click the Apply Color button to create the color rule.

4. To distinguish messages sent only to you from those sent to multiple recipients, choose a color in the Show Messages Sent Only To Me In drop-down list, and click the Turn On button to apply this rule.

You can create a new Automatic Formatting rule in the Organizer by clicking the Automatic Formatting button in the Ways to Organize Inbox pane. Click the Add button to create a rule that Outlook will temporarily name "Untitled." Type a descriptive name for the rule, click the Font button and choose a font, and then click the Condition button to open the Filter dialog box. In the three pages of the dialog box, set the filter conditions, and then click OK to create the condition.

Using Junk Mail and Adult Content Rules

Businesses have used direct mailing (via snail mail) to market to individuals and companies for years. What marketing companies call direct mailing, others call "junk mail." Junk mail delivered to your electronic mailbox can be just as annoying as it is on paper. Outlook 2000 can automatically color or even move junk mail messages (right to your Deleted Items folder if you prefer) so you don't waste your time with them.

Although you may or may not consider them junk mail, adult content messages can also be automatically formatted for easy identification or moved to a separate folder to read at a later time.

To format junk e-mail or adult content messages, click the Junk E-Mail tab in the Organize page, shown in Figure 19.17. Choose a color for each type of message (you can apply the same color to both), then click the Turn On buttons. If you'd prefer the messages were deleted or placed in a specific folder, Choose Move from the drop-down list and then select the folder to which you would like the messages moved.

FIGURE 19.17

Automatically format or move your junk and adult-content e-mail using Outlook rules.

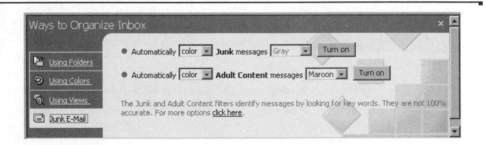

 MASTERING THE OPPORTUNITIES

Filtering Junk Mail and Adult Content Mail

Outlook 2000 recognizes junk mail and adult content mail by filtering message content. Outlook filters messages, searching for phrases commonly used in direct marketing messages and adult content messages. For junk mail, phrases include: "cards accepted," "extra income," "money-back guarantee," and "100% satisfied." With adult content mail, Outlook searches for phrases like "over 18," "adults only," "adult web," and "xxx" in the Subject.

Continued ▌▶

MASTERING THE OPPORTUNITIES CONTINUED

It's worth knowing how Outlook and other programs with content filters determine which messages may be junk mail or have adult content. If you include phrases like "we're brainstorming ways to generate extra income" or "there must be over 18 ways to complete this analysis" in a piece of regular business correspondence, don't be surprised if your recipient never reads the message. To see all the phrases Outlook uses to filter mail, open the file `filters.txt` in the folder where Outlook was installed.

There are other programs you can use to check incoming messages based on sender address that are compatible with Outlook. For more information, visit the Microsoft Web site (www.microsoft.com).

What's Next

Now that you've mastered Contacts and Inbox, you're ready to put Outlook 2000 to work managing your time and responsibilities. In Chapter 20, you'll learn how to create and track tasks and even delegate those tasks to others. You'll also learn how to keep your calendar, schedule appointments with other people, set reminders, and plan multiple-day events.

CHAPTER **20**

Managing Your Time and Tasks

FEATURING:

Creating tasks

Setting up recurring tasks

Assigning a task to someone else

Completing a task

Viewing and navigating the Calendar

Scheduling appointments

Configuring the Calendar

Printing the Calendar

Using the Calendar in a workgroup

I f you're a list keeper, you'll find that Outlook takes the To Do list to a new dimension by adding the ability to track progress, assign tasks to other people (our personal favorite), set reminders for tasks, schedule time to complete tasks, and evaluate the progress you are making. Even if making lists is not your favorite pastime, it's hard to ignore the power of Outlook's Tasks module. When you combine tasks with the flexibility and organization of Outlook's Calendar, it won't be long before you're keeping up with the most organized person you know.

Creating a Task

Creating a task can be as simple as typing the name of the task and the due date, or you can choose to enter more detailed information about the task, taking full advantage of the power that Outlook has to offer.

To enter a task, click the Tasks icon on the Outlook bar. The default view in Tasks is the Simple List view, shown in Figure 20.1. This view has four columns:

Icon: The icon in this column changes if a task is assigned to someone else or assigned by someone else.

Complete: A simple check box indicating if the task has been completed.

Subject: A descriptive name for the task.

Due Date: The date you expect or need to complete the task.

You can enter a task directly into the Information Viewer by clicking in the Click Here To Add A New Task text box. The row turns blue and the box that is active for editing is white. Type the subject in the Subject field. Press Tab to move to the Due Date field (Shift+Tab will move you back to Subject); the text box will turn white. Because Outlook recognizes natural language dates using its AutoDate feature, just about anything you type into the field that remotely resembles a date will be converted into a standard date format (Wed 8/19/99). You could type **8-19-99**, or **aug19**, or **three weeks from now**, or **a week from today**, or **tomorrow**, or **one month from next thu**. All are legitimate dates in Outlook (of course they wouldn't all return the same date).

If your objective is just to get the task recorded and then come back to it later to add additional information, you can click anywhere in the Task list to move the task into the list. (Where the task appears in the list depends on how the list is currently sorted.) You can now enter another task. This is the quickest and easiest way to enter tasks.

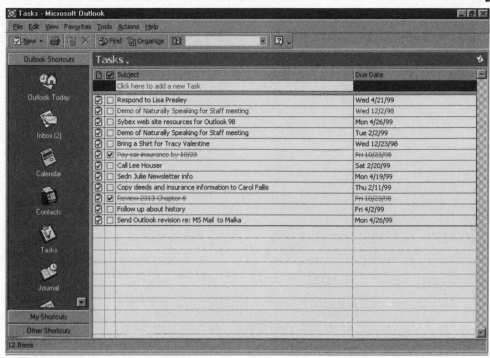

FIGURE 20.1

*The Simple List view
of Tasks*

Entering Details about a Task

To take advantage of the powerful features built into Outlook, you need to add additional information about the task. The most direct way to do this is to use a Task form. You can open the form on any existing task by double-clicking the task in the Information Viewer. To open a blank Task form, click the New button on the Standard toolbar (as long as Tasks is the active module in the Information Viewer) or click the New button's down arrow and choose Task from the list.

The Task form, shown in Figure 20.2, has two pages: Task and Details. The Task page focuses on a description of the task. (See "Completing a Task" later in this chapter for more information about the Details page.) Enter the Subject and press Tab to move to the Due Date field, where you can choose or enter a date. If the task is not scheduled to start right away, enter a Start Date to indicate when it should be started.

FIGURE 20.2

The Task form

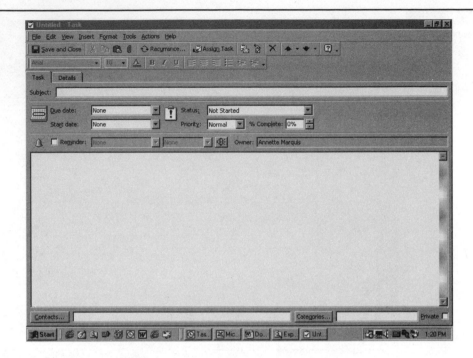

Setting Reminders

Click the Reminder check box to activate a reminder that will be displayed at a specified date and time.

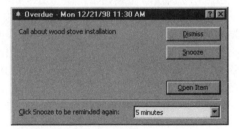

The Time drop-down list has a choice for every half-hour around the clock, so be careful to select the correct A.M. or P.M. time. There's nothing like setting a reminder for twelve hours after something was supposed to be done! You can also type an entry in this box if you need a reminder at the quarter hour.

Reminders come with a sound by default. You have the option of disabling the sound or changing the sound file it plays. Click the speaker icon to access the Reminder Sound options. Clear the Play This Sound check box if you'd prefer your reminders to appear on your screen silently. If you would like to hear a sound but prefer a different sound file, click the Browse button to locate the file you would like to use. Double-click the file name and it will appear in the Reminder Sound text box.

TIP If you change the sound file within a task, it will only be in effect for that specific reminder. To change the default sound file for reminders, close the task and go to Tools ➢ Options. Click the Other tab, choose Advanced Options ➢ Reminder Options, and enter a new .wav file name. If you would like to record your own reminder message or sound that plays when it is time to do a task, you can do so using the Windows Sound Recorder.

Updating Task Status

When you enter a task, Outlook assumes you haven't started working on it yet. To help you manage your tasks and assess the status of projects, you have four other Status options in addition to Not Started available to you. Click the Status drop-down arrow on the Task page of the Task form to open the list of choices:

In Progress: If a task is in progress, you might also want to indicate the percentage that is complete in the % Complete text box. Use the spin box to change the percentage, or type in the actual percentage directly in the box.

Completed: In addition to marking a task complete, there are some additional fields on the Details page that you might also want to complete. See "Completing a Task" later in this chapter.

Waiting On Someone Else: It's helpful to set a reminder to yourself to call this person if you don't hear from them in a reasonable amount of time.

Deferred: You may want to change the start and end dates so this task doesn't show up on your list of active tasks.

Setting Priorities

By setting a priority level for a task, you can be sure that your most important tasks receive most of your attention. The default priority is Normal. You have additional options of High and Low. High Priority items are designated by a red exclamation point in the Information Viewer. A blue drop-down arrow designates Low Priority items.

Owning a Task

The *task owner* is the person who creates the task or to whom it is currently assigned. If the task is all yours, the Owner field shows "Me" or reflects whatever profile name you are currently using.

Assigning Categories to Manage a Project

Categories are user-defined values that help to organize your data throughout Outlook. Chapter 18 shows how to create new categories and delete undesired categories. Although you have the same list of categories available, categories serve a slightly different purpose in Tasks than they do in Contacts or the other Outlook modules.

Categories play a vital role in tracking tasks related to a single project. When you create a task, the more specific you can be the easier it is to complete the task. For example, if the task you enter is **Complete database for Goodrich**, you will have a difficult time demonstrating progress toward your goal. When is the database complete—after the application is functioning or after the product is installed? Maybe it's not complete until the staff is trained and they are using the product successfully.

It would be a lot more helpful to break down the various steps of the project into its logical components. Categories could then pull all these individual tasks together into one project. Just click the Categories button and assign each task to the same category from the Categories dialog box. When you return to the Information Viewer, you can sort by category, group all the tasks in the same category together, or even filter out just those tasks related to a single category (see Chapter 21 for more about creating custom views). Figure 20.3 is an example of a Task list grouped by category.

FIGURE 20.3

A task list grouped by Category

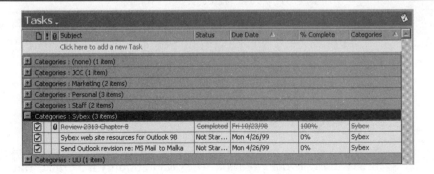

Getting Organized
with Outlook

Making a Task Private

If your Outlook files are shared on a network, there may be times when you don't
want others to see information about a task. Click the Private check box in the lower-
right corner of the Task form to keep the task in your personal Outlook folders. The
task will not synchronize with the server, so other users with permission to see your
folders will not be able to view it.

Setting Up Recurring Tasks

A *recurring task* is one that you must complete on a regular basis—a monthly report, a
weekly agenda, or a quarterly tax submission, for example. In Outlook you can enter
the task once and then set a pattern for it to recur on your Task list. Outlook doesn't
care if you've completed this month's report; when the time comes for next month's,
it will add another copy of the task with a new due date to your list.

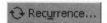

To set up a recurring task, enter the task as you would any other. When you have
the data entered for the first occurrence of the task, click the Recurrence button on
the Standard toolbar within the Task form. This opens the Task Recurrence dialog
box, shown in Figure 20.4.

FIGURE 20.4

*The Task Recurrence
dialog box*

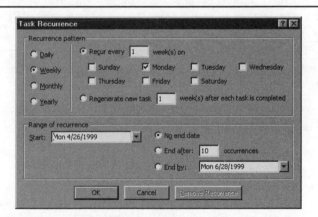

Here you can set the Recurrence Pattern and the Range of Recurrence. To set the
Recurrence Pattern, indicate whether the task needs to be accomplished Daily, Weekly,
Monthly, or Yearly. If the task needs to be completed every three days, choose Daily; if
it's every two months, choose Monthly—choose the option that most closely defines

the pattern you need to set. Each of the four options gives you different choices for defining the actual pattern.

Daily: Choose between Every *N* Days and Every Weekday.

Weekly: Indicate how often the task should occur: every week (1), every other week (2), every third week (3), and so on. This is the best option if the task needs to be completed every 6 weeks or every 8 weeks, because some months have more than four weeks. Then mark which day of the week the task needs to be accomplished.

Monthly: You can specify which date of each *N* month(s) or indicate the first, second, third, fourth, or last day of every *N* month(s). For example, you might specify the last Friday of every 1 month(s), the third Thursday of every second month, or the first weekday of the month.

Yearly: Indicate a specific date in a specific month or mark the first, second, third, fourth, or last day of a specific month (for example, the first Friday in May).

For each pattern, you are then asked to indicate how many days/weeks/months/years you want Outlook to wait after a task is marked as complete before it generates a new task.

Sometimes you have to be creative to figure out how often a task really occurs. For example, if a task occurs twice a year on February 28 and August 31, do you use Monthly or Yearly? Because these dates are six months apart use Monthly by setting the Start Date to one of the two dates and choosing the last day of every six months as the Recurrence Pattern.

However, if a task is not so evenly spaced, May 31 and August 31 for example, you probably will have to enter two tasks every year—one for the May date and one for the August date.

Defining the Range of Recurrence

The Range Of Recurrence option refers to when the first task in the series is due and how long the task will recur. You can indicate a specific number of occurrences or a specific ending date, or you can tell Outlook that there is no ending date.

Once you have set the range, click OK to return to the Task form. Click Save And Close to save the task and return to the Information Viewer.

Editing Task Recurrence

To make changes to the recurrence pattern or range that you set, open the task and click the Recurrence Pattern button. Make your changes and then save and close the task again.

PART

IV

Getting Organized
with Outlook

If you want to skip the next occurrence of a task but not interfere with the recurrence pattern, open the task and choose Skip Occurrence from the Actions menu. The due date will automatically change to the next date the task is due.

To delete the recurrence pattern without deleting the task, open the task and click the Recurrence button. In the Task Recurrence dialog box, click Remove Recurrence. Close the dialog box, and save and close the task. The task will still be on your list but for a single occurrence only.

Assigning a Task to a Contact

If you work as a member of a team or have people reporting to you, there are times when you may want to create a task for someone else to do. As long as the other person is running Outlook and you both have access to e-mail, you can assign tasks to each other. When you assign a task to someone else, that person becomes its owner.

To assign a task to someone else, create the task as you normally would, define task recurrence if appropriate, and then click the Assign Task button on the Standard toolbar of the Task form. This opens a message form with the task included, as shown in Figure 20.5.

FIGURE 20.5

*Assigning a task to
someone else*

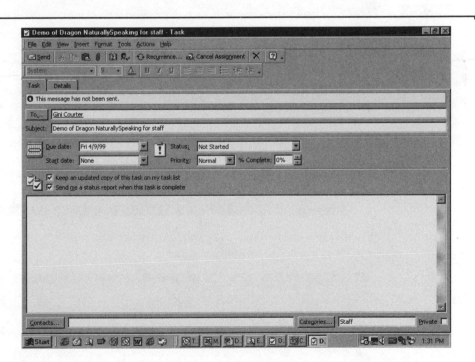

WARNING When sending a task to another person through Internet e-mail, make sure the properties for that person's e-mail address in Contacts include Always Send To This Recipient In Microsoft Outlook Rich-Text Format. This way, the recipient will be able to copy and paste the task directly into their Task list. Enter the person's e-mail address or click the To button and choose the name from your address lists.

You have two options related to this assignment:

Keep An Updated Copy Of This Task On My Task List: Even though you have assigned the task to someone else, you may still want to follow its progress. Every time the new owner revises the task in any way, you receive a message indicating that the task was updated, and the task is revised in your Task list. This option is not available if the task is recurring.

Send Me A Status Report When This Task Is Complete: When the new owner marks the task as complete, you receive a message automatically informing you that the task is complete, and the task is marked as complete on your Task list.

 NOTE Although you can assign a task to anyone who runs Outlook, if the person is not on your network, you will not receive automatic updates when that person updates or completes the task.

If you would like to send a message along with the task assignment, enter the text in the message box. Click Send to transfer the message to your Outbox.

Receiving a Task Assignment

When someone sends you a task, you receive an e-mail message labeled Task Request:

When you open the task, you can choose to accept or decline it by clicking the appropriate button on the message form:

If you click Accept, the task is automatically added to your Task list and you become its owner. If you click Decline, the person who sent you the task retains ownership. Either way, the person who originated the task is sent a message indicating your response. When you click Send, you are given the option of editing the response before sending it or sending it without editing. If you want to explain why you're declining a request from your boss, click Edit The Response Now and enter your explanation in the message.

Even after you accept a task, you can change your mind and decline the task. Just open the task and choose Decline Task from the Actions menu.

Passing the Task Along

If you receive a task from someone, it's possible for you to accept the task assignment and then turn around and assign the task to someone else (commonly referred to as passing the buck). When you accept the task, you become the owner of the task and changes and updates you make are returned to the task's originator. When you re-assign a task to someone else, that person becomes the owner and future updates are returned to you. In order to keep the task's originator up to date, you will have to generate updated status reports when an update is returned to you from the new owner.

To reassign a task:

1. Open the e-mail message that contains the original task request and click Accept. This sends a Task Update to the originator indicating you have accepted the task. You are now the owner of the task.

2. Open the task in your Task list and click the Assign button. Make sure the Keep An Updated Copy Of The Task On My Task List and Send Me A Status Report When The Task Is Complete options are both checked so you won't lose track of the task.

3. Enter the e-mail address of the person you want to assign the task to and click Send to send the Task Request to them. They are now the temporary owner of the task. When they accept the task, they become the task's owner.

4. When you receive a task update from the new owner, click Actions ➢ Send Status Report from the Standard toolbar of the open task. Type in (or copy and paste) your status report. Enter the e-mail address of the task's originator and click Send to send an update to them.

By following this process, you keep the task's originator informed and you have someone else doing the work—not a bad deal, if you can get it!

Viewing Tasks

One of the key ways to stay on top of what you have to do is to review your tasks from different perspectives. The default view for Tasks in the Information Viewer is the Simple List (shown in Figure 20.1 earlier). This view shows the Subject and Due Date of both active and completed tasks. It's quite simple to switch to another view that shows only active tasks or organizes the tasks in some other meaningful way. To change to another view, click View ➤ Current View. This opens the list of available views displayed in Figure 20.6.

FIGURE 20.6

Available views in Tasks

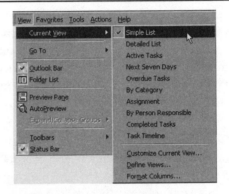

The Detailed List and the Active List are essentially the same view, except the Detailed List includes completed tasks while the Active List includes only those tasks yet to be completed. Figure 20.7 shows the Detailed List view.

FIGURE 20.7

The Detailed List view

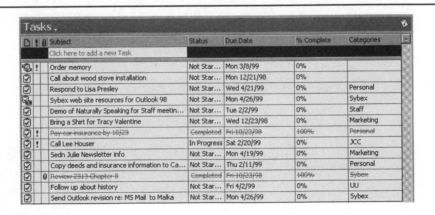

The Next Seven Days view displays the same fields as the Detailed List and Active List views, but it filters the view to show only those tasks whose Due Date is within the next seven calendar days.

When a task passes its Due Date, Outlook displays the task in red to distinguish it from current tasks. You can then choose Overdue Tasks from the Current View menu to see only those tasks that require immediate attention.

You can also examine your tasks by Category, by Assignment, and by Person Responsible. These views are especially helpful in managing the work on a particular project or managing the workloads of personnel because they group tasks together that have something in common (see Figure 20.3 earlier in this chapter for an example of tasks grouped by Category).

Finally, the Task Timeline view is designed to let you examine your tasks based on due dates. This view, shown in Figure 20.8, can be used to plan your activities for particular days based on the tasks you have to accomplish.

FIGURE 20.8

The Task Timeline view

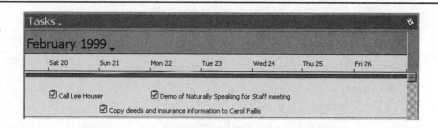

In Chapter 21, you'll learn how to design custom views to meet your particular needs. Refer back to Chapter 17 if you don't know how to sort based on any of the visible fields, change column width, rearrange the fields, and remove fields from any of the table views.

Creating Tasks from Other Outlook Items

One of Outlook's most powerful features is its integration—all of the modules work together to make your life easier. How many times have you received an e-mail message asking you to do something? Unless you print the message and put it in the stack of papers on your desk and hope you run across it before it needs to get done, you may find yourself forgetting it was even asked of you. Outlook changes all that. The next time you receive an e-mail message with a request, just drag the message to the Task icon on the Outlook bar.

Outlook will automatically open a Task form for you with the information already in it, including the contents of the e-mail message, as shown in Figure 20.9.

All you have to do is add in Due Dates, assign the task to a category, and add any other details you want. Then you'll be sure to not forget to do what is asked of you.

FIGURE 20.9

A Task form opens automatically from an e-mail message.

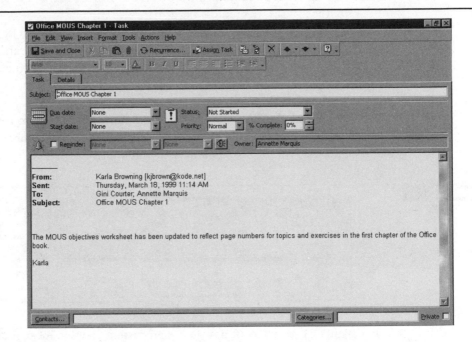

TIP You can drag any Outlook item to any Outlook icon on the Outlook bar (such as Journal, Calendar, or Note) to embed the item in a new Outlook item.

Completing a Task

When you have finally finished a task, there is nothing more satisfying than checking it off your list. Outlook has incorporated a check box into the Information Viewer for most of the standard views. To mark a task as complete, just click the check box:

The task is crossed out on the list. If the view you are using does not include completed items, the item is actually removed from the list altogether. If you mistakenly mark a task complete, just switch to Simple List view and clear the check box.

You can record further information about a completed task using the Details tab of the Task form, shown in Figure 20.10.

FIGURE 20.10

*Tracking additional
information about a
completed task*

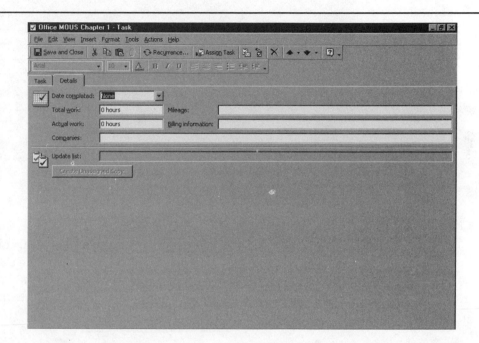

Here you can record the date the task was completed, the planned number of hours (Outlook will translate to days), the actual number of hours, the number of miles traveled on the job, and other information you may want to track. If you have to submit an expense or billing statement at the end of the month, this is a great way to track the information you need.

Scheduling Your Time in Calendar

When you first enter the Calendar by clicking the Calendar icon on the Outlook bar or choosing View ➢ Go ➢ Calendar from the menu, you are shown the Day, Week, Month view, seen in Figure 20.11.

FIGURE 20.11

The Calendar's Day, Week, Month view

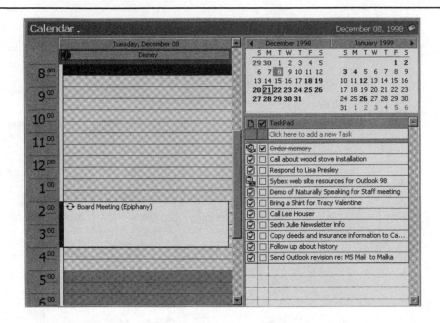

This view is actually a combination of a daily calendar, a monthly calendar, called the Date Navigator, and a list of active tasks on the TaskPad. Within this view, you can easily switch from Day view to Work Week view, Week view, or Month view using buttons on the Standard toolbar.

The first button, Day, is the default view. The next button, Work Week, displays a work week of five days. If your work week is made up of different days, you can customize the week, using the Calendar options. (See "Configuring the Calendar" later in this chapter.) The Week button shows all seven days of the week in the typical week-at-a-glance format. The Month button displays a month at a time, alternating gray and white backgrounds to differentiate the months. Personal preference dictates which view you use most frequently. Choose the view that gives you the best sense of where you have to be and what you have to do.

Using the Date Navigator

The Date Navigator not only shows you the monthly calendar but also lets you select days to view in the calendar itself:

Click any date in the Date Navigator and that date becomes visible in the Information Viewer. Click the left and right arrows next to the month headings to select a different month. To select an entire week, move your pointer to the left side of the Date Navigator. The pointer changes position and points toward the Date Navigator. Click your mouse to select the week. To select multiple weeks, hold your mouse button down and drag, as shown here:

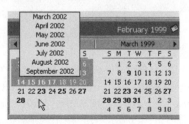

It's also easy to compare nonconsecutive days. Click one day and hold the Ctrl key down on the keyboard before selecting the next day.

To move quickly to a different month, click on the month name and select another month from the list. If the month you want is not immediately visible among the months displayed, pretend there is a scroll bar and drag outside the list:

Moving the mouse pointer farther away from the list will increase the speed of the scroll. To slow down the scroll rate, move the mouse pointer closer to the list. To move to a previous month, position the mouse pointer above the list.

Any time you want to move quickly back to the current date, click the Go to Today button on the Standard toolbar.

TIP If you prefer to display only one month in the Date Navigator, move your mouse pointer to the left side of the Navigator. The pointer will change to a resize arrow; drag the border of the Date Navigator to the right until only one month is visible.

Scheduling Appointments

Scheduling an appointment is as easy as clicking in the appointment slot in the Day view and typing in the information. Once you have typed in the entry, point to the lower border of the appointment slot and, with the two-headed arrow pointer, drag to identify the end time of the appointment. Drop the blue line just above the desired end time as shown in Figure 20.12.

FIGURE 20.12

Dragging to identify the appointment's end time

To change the start time of the appointment, drag the blue line above the appointment slot. If you want to maintain the length of the appointment but alter the start and end times, point to the blue line on the left side of the appointment and, with the four-headed arrow, drag the entire appointment to a new time. Once you begin dragging, the four-headed arrow will change shape to a pointer with a move box.

To change the appointment to a different day, switch to the desired month in the Date Navigator and drag the appointment with the four-headed arrow to the new date.

Entering an Appointment in the Appointment Form

When you want to enter more details about an appointment, double-click the appointment in the Information Viewer to open the Appointment form shown in Figure 20.13. In addition to the Subject and Start and End times, the Appointment form allows you to enter a location, to set a reminder, and to enter other notes about the appointment.

FIGURE 20.13

*The Calendar's
Appointment form*

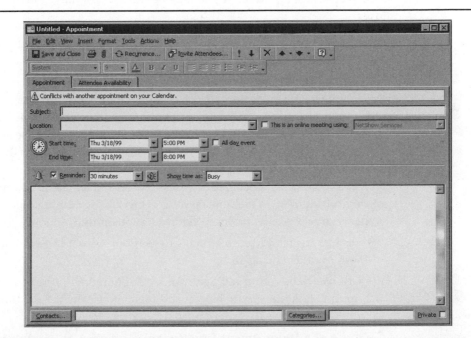

Appointment or Event?

Outlook 2000's Calendar feature distinguishes between appointments and events. An appointment has a start and end time and may last for less than one day or may span multiple days. An event, on the other hand, encompasses an entire day or perhaps several days but does not have a specific start and end time. For example, a vacation is designated as an event. To change an appointment to an event, click the All Day Event check box to the right of the Start Time on an Appointment form. The Start and End Time fields are removed from the form, and the Show Time As field is set to Free. Events appear as a banner in the Day view of the Calendar. See "Scheduling Events" later in this chapter for more information about events.

Click the This Is An Online Meeting check box if the meeting will occur over the Internet (for more information about online meetings, see Chapter 15).

To set the start and end times in an Appointment form, click the down-arrow to the right of the Start Time and End Time fields. The first arrow opens a calendar from which you can select the date for the appointment. Use the left and right arrows next to the month name to select from a different month.

The arrow to the right of the second field opens a list of times. Be careful to select the correct A.M. or P.M. time, or you may be expecting to have lunch some day at midnight.

Setting a Reminder

One of the biggest advantages of using an electronic calendar is that it can automatically remind you when it's time to go to your appointments. The default reminder is set for 15 minutes prior to a scheduled appointment, but you can select any time from 0 minutes to up to two days from the drop-down list, or you can type any reminder time in the text box. To turn off the reminder, click the check box to the left of the Reminder field.

When a reminder is scheduled, it will appear as a small dialog box in whatever application is running at the time (as long as Outlook is running in the background).

When you receive a reminder, you have several options:

- Dismiss the reminder, in which case Outlook assumes you are on your way and won't bother you again.

- Choose to be reminded again in a designated amount of time. To use this option, click the Snooze button and then choose the desired time interval from the Click Snooze To Be Reminded Again drop-down list.

- Open the Appointment form so you can review the appointment or make changes to it.

When the Reminder dialog box opens, clicking anywhere outside the dialog box will move it to the Windows Taskbar. You can then open it at any time to respond to the reminder.

By default, an appointment reminder is accompanied by the Windows "ding." You can change the sound, as described in the "Creating a Task" section of this chapter. When you have set the Sound Reminder options, click OK to return to the Appointment form.

Scheduling Recurring Appointments

You probably have appointments that occur on regular basis—for example, a weekly staff meeting, a daily project review meeting, or a monthly district sales meeting. With Outlook's calendar, you can set up a meeting once and it will automatically recur in your calendar. Recurring appointments can be set up in the same way as recurring tasks described earlier in this chapter. The only difference is that you have to enter a start and end time and duration as shown in Figure 20.14.

FIGURE 20.14

Enter a start and end time and duration to set up a recurring appointment.

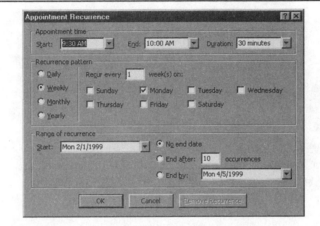

Scheduling Events

Recall that an event is an appointment that has no start or end time, such as a holiday, anniversary, or any other day that you want to note. To schedule an event, open an Appointment form, enter the subject and date information, and then click the All Day Event check box. This removes the Start Time and End Time fields from the Appointment Form. You can set a reminder for an event and set a Recurrence Pattern just as you would for any other appointment.

Outlook assumes that an event does not occupy your time and therefore shows your time as Free. You may want to change this, however. For example, if the event you are entering is your vacation, you could set the Show Time As field to Out Of The Office.

Because there are no times associated with an event, events are displayed differently than regular appointments in the Information Viewer. In the Day view, an event appears at the top of the day's schedule. In the Week and Month views, events are displayed in bordered boxes, such as those shown in Figure 20.13, earlier in this chapter.

Scheduling a Multiple-Day Event

Multiple-day events are scheduled activities that have no set start and end times and span across several days. To enter such an event, open the Appointment form and set the start and end time dates to coincide with the actual dates of the event.

MASTERING THE OPPORTUNITIES

Scheduling Time to Complete a Task

To help you manage your time more effectively, Outlook displays the TaskPad as part of the default Calendar view. This allows you to schedule time to work on individual tasks.

To schedule time to work on a task, display the day and select the time in the Information Viewer. Drag the task from the TaskPad to the designated time. Outlook will create an appointment based on the task and will open an Appointment form with the contents of the task already included in it. Set the other options just as you would for any other appointment.

When you complete the task, mark it complete on your Task list just as you would any other task. You'll be surprised at how much easier it is the check off items on your Task list when you schedule time in your daily calendar to complete them.

Configuring the Calendar

Because people work very different schedules these days, Outlook has included a number of options that let you define the days you work, the hours that you want to display in your calendar, and on which day your work week starts. To change the Calendar options, click Tools on the menu bar and choose Options. Click the Calendar Options button to open the dialog box shown in Figure 20.15.

FIGURE 20.15

Calendar Options let you customize the Calendar to fit your needs.

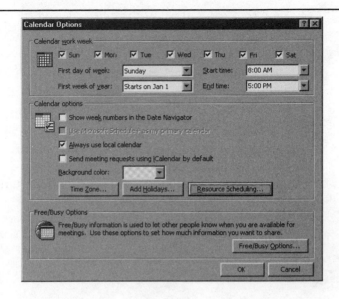

Set the Calendar options as follows:

1. Calendar Work Week:

   • Check the boxes for the days of the week to designate the days that make up your workweek. Set the start and end times of your typical day using the Start Time and End Time fields.

   • To keep your calendar in line with your staff schedules, you may want to indicate that your calendar starts on the first four-day week or first full week of the year rather than January 1. Make this selection from the First Week Of Year drop-down list.

2. Calendar Options:

   • Click the Show Week Numbers In The Date Navigator check box if you need to know what week you are in for planning purposes.

   • Check Always Use Local Calendar if you are on an Exchange Server network and want to make sure you are seeing your most accurate calendar.

   • Send Meeting Requests Using iCalendar By Default lets you use an Internet calendar rather than the standard Outlook meeting request function.

   • Background Color lets you designate a different color for your calendar's background in Day and Work Week views.

3. Time Zone lets you adjust the time zone you are in and set a second time zone to view simultaneously—an invaluable option if you schedule meetings in one time zone that you plan to attend in another.

4. Add Holidays adds a variety of religious and national holidays to your calendar.

5. Resource Scheduling lets you set options if you are responsible for scheduling resources such as meeting rooms, AV equipment, and the like.

6. Free/Busy Options allows you to control how far in advance your free/busy information is available for others on your Exchange server to see and how frequently it updates information with the server. If you want to share your free/busy information with others over the Internet, you can enter the URL where your information is available. See "Checking Others' Schedules First" later in this chapter for more about free/busy information.

Printing the Calendar

Before you can print your calendar, you need to decide what style you want to use. By default, the view that is visible on your screen is the view that will print. For example, if you are in Day view, you'll print all your appointments for that day.

If you are more particular about your calendar's layout, choose File ➤ Page Setup to have a world of options available to you. Before a dialog box even opens, you are presented with a list of choices.

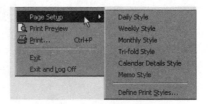

Choose the primary layout that you want for your calendar. The Page Setup options you see depend on the style you choose. Figure 20.16 shows the options for the Weekly view.

PART

IV

Getting Organized
with Outlook

FIGURE 20.16

*Page Setup options for
the Weekly view*

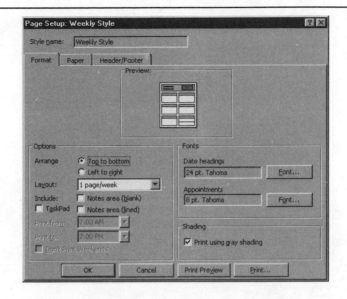

The first page of the Page Setup dialog box is the Format options. Here you can indicate what sections you would like to appear on the page. You can even include an area for those handwritten notes. At any point in the Page Setup process you can click the Print Preview button to see how your printed document will appear. If you are satisfied, click the Print button—if it needs more work, click Page Setup and you're brought right back here.

The second page of the Page Setup dialog box, shown in Figure 20.17, is the Paper page. This page is especially critical if you don't plan to print your calendar on standard 8.5" × 11" paper. You can set the paper type, size, dimensions, orientation, and margins and you can identify what tray of the printer the paper will be in.

TIP   If you are using a planner from the big three—Day-Timer, Day Runner, or Franklin—take special note of the Page Size list. Your planner is probably listed so you'll be able to select an exact match.

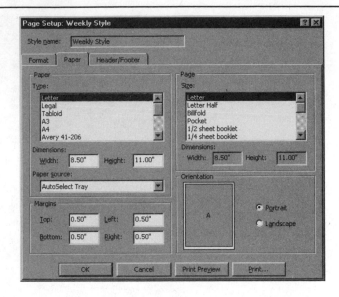

Headers and Footers

The Header/Footer page of the Page Setup dialog box, shown in Figure 20.18, closely resembles Excel's dialog box for defining headers and footers. If you're familiar with Excel, this will be a snap.

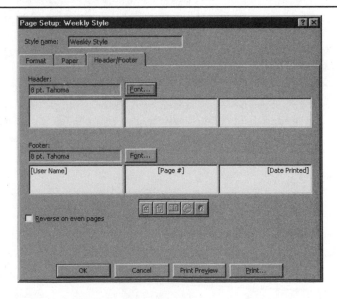

A header appears on the top of every page of your document, in this case, the calendar. A footer appears on the bottom of every page. Typically, you'll find the title and subtitle in the header. By default, Outlook includes the User Name (that's generally you), the Page Number, and the Date Printed in the footer. However, you can put any information anywhere you want it.

The header and footer sections are each divided into three subsections: left, center, and right. Click in any of the six text boxes to enter text in that section. Outlook provides you with placeholders for five variable fields that you can insert in either the header or the footer:

Page Number: Inserts the actual page number of the document.

Total Pages: Can be combined with the *page number* placeholder to create expressions like "Page 1 of 4" (Page [Page #] of [Total Pages]).

Date Printed: Displays the date the Calendar was printed, regardless of the date period shown in the Calendar.

Time Printed: Displays the actual time the Calendar was printed.

User Name: Displays the name of the user currently logged in to Outlook.

To insert a placeholder, click in the section of the header or footer where you want the placeholder to appear, and then click the placeholder button.

 TIP If you're printing a calendar in booklet form, you may want to reverse the header and footer on opposite pages. For example, if the date printed appears on the right side on odd pages, it would appear on the left on even pages. This gives your document a more professionally printed appearance.

When you have finished setting up the Page Setup options, click the Print button to print your calendar.

Creating Your Own Calendar Style

To save time and use a consistent format for your calendar from week to week, you can define a Page Setup style to use every time you print your calendar. Follow the steps below to define your own print style that will appear in the Page Setup menu list:

1. Click File ➢ Page Setup ➢ Define Print Styles.

2. Choose to edit an existing style or to create a new style by copying an existing style.

3. If you choose to copy an existing style, enter a name for the new style in the Style Name text box at the top of the Page Setup dialog box.

4. Create your custom style using the Page Setup options.

5. Click OK to save your changes.

6. Select your newly created style from the Page Setup menu.

To delete a custom style, choose Define Print Styles, select the style you want to delete, and click Delete.

 TIP If you are editing an existing style, the original style will no longer be available. However, you can reset the original style by choosing Define Print Styles from the Page Setup menu, selecting the style and clicking the Reset button.

Using the Calendar in a Workgroup

If you've ever worked in an office that holds lots of meetings, then you know firsthand the inordinate amount of time that is spent scheduling and rescheduling meetings. Some office studies have found that nearly 30 percent of secretarial time is spent scheduling meetings for managers and administrators. Group scheduling tools are one of the fastest-growing software markets today. Companies all over the globe are recognizing the need to simplify the process of scheduling meetings. Outlook is ready to address this challenge, as the Calendar module offers extensive tools for workgroup scheduling.

Planning a Meeting with Others

There are several ways in Outlook 2000 to invite others to attend a meeting. The simplest way is to click the drop-down arrow on the New button and choose Meeting Request from the list of choices. This opens the e-mail message form, shown in Figure 20.19. There are some differences between this and the standard message form.

FIGURE 20.19

*A meeting request
message form*

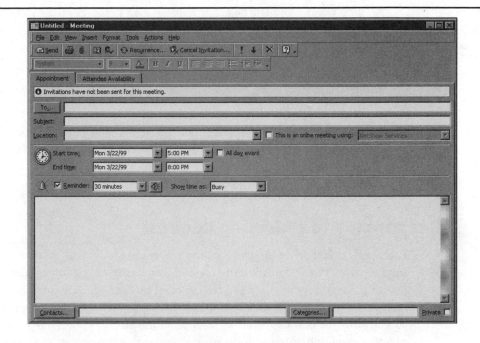

First, notice the message informing you that invitations for this meeting have not
yet been sent. Of course, you already knew that, but you can always find the status of
an invitation here even after you send it. Second, in addition to the To and Subject
fields, there is a Location field for you to identify where the meeting will take place.
The other fields on the Meeting Request form are similar to a typical Appointment form.

To create a meeting request, follow these steps:

1. Click the drop-down arrow on the New button and choose Meeting Request.

2. Click the To button to open the Select Attendees And Resources dialog box.

3. Double-click the names of those people whose attendance at the meeting is
   required.

4. If a person's attendance is optional, click their name and click the Optional button.

5. If you have meeting rooms and other resources set up with their own mailboxes,
   select the resource you want to assign to the meeting and click the Resources
   button.

6. If someone you want to invite to a meeting is not in your Address book, click
   the New Contact button and enter information about the contact in the Properties dialog box. Click OK to add this person to your Address book.

7. Click OK to close the Select Attendees And Resources dialog box and return to the Meeting Request form.

8. Enter the Subject and Location, and click the check box if this is an online meeting.

9. Fill in the Start Time, End Time, Reminder, and Show Time As fields just as you would for any other appointment.

10. If the meeting is going to be regularly scheduled, you can click the Recurrence button and set up the Recurrence pattern (see "Scheduling Recurring Appointments" earlier in the chapter).

11. Click the Send button to send out the meeting requests.

Responding to a Meeting Request

Each person you invited to the meeting will receive an e-mail message labeled Meeting Request. When they open the message, they will see the information about the meeting. Once they've decided whether they can attend, they can click one of the Accept, Decline, or Tentative buttons at the top of the Meeting Request form.

Clicking one of these three buttons generates an e-mail message back to you, the meeting request originator, indicating whether this person can attend. If the person accepted the meeting request, it's automatically placed on their calendar. In addition, all of the responses are automatically tabulated, so there is no need to keep a manual count. It really couldn't be easier. All you have to do is open the appointment in your calendar. Click the Attendee Availability tab to see a list of attendees and their responses to date, as shown in Figure 20.20.

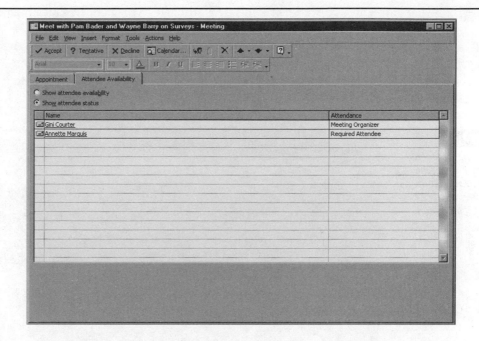

FIGURE 20.20

The Attendee
Availability tab of the
Appointment form
after a meeting
request has been
sent out

If, after seeing who has accepted your invitation, you decide to invite other people
to this meeting, click the Invite Others button on the Meeting Planner tab. You'll
then be able to generate new e-mail meeting requests.

That's all there is it is to it. Never again will you have to make 25 phone calls to
get four people to attend a meeting. Now you'll actually have time to get some real
work done.

Checking Others' Schedules First

Even the steps outlined above for requesting a meeting could backfire if you find
that the majority of the people you need at your meeting can't attend at the time
you requested. It might be easier to check individual schedules first and schedule
the meeting at a time when all of your key people can attend. A lot of people get
nervous when you talk about making their schedules available for others to see.
Outlook has found the best of both worlds. It allows you to look at the individual's
free/busy information; you can see when an individual is free, busy, out of the office,
or tentatively scheduled. You cannot, however, see what they are doing or how they
are spending their time (unless they have given you permission to do so). This seems
to relieve most people's anxiety about Big Brother looking over their shoulder and
still allows for the greatest success in scheduling meetings with the first request.

To check to see when someone is available to meet, open a Meeting Request form and click the Attendee Availability tab. The Attendee Availability page, shown in Figure 20.21, lists all attendees in the left column. When you first open this page, Outlook automatically goes out to the network to gather the most current free/busy information. The grid on the right side of the page shows each individual's free/busy status.

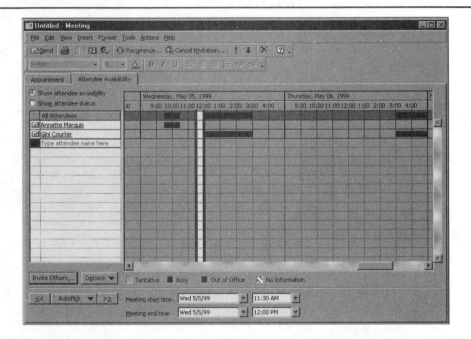

An individual's free time is not marked in the grid. If they are out of the office, a maroon bar extends across the time that they will be gone. If they are busy, you'll see a blue bar, and if they are tentatively scheduled you'll see a light blue bar.

The white vertical bar represents the duration of the meeting. The green border on the left indicates the start time and the brown border represents the ending time of the meeting.

The key to working with the Attendee Availability grid is to start by manually setting your preferred meeting time in the Meeting Start Time and Meeting End Time text boxes. Even if the desired attendees are not available at this time, this sets a beginning date and the duration of the meeting. Click the AutoPick button to locate the first time when all attendees are available. Notice that the Meeting Start Time and Meeting End Time text boxes change to correspond to the time indicated by the grid. As soon as you find an agreeable time, click the Make Meeting button at the bottom of the form. This will generate the attendees' e-mail message. Now you can be pretty confident that the attendees will accept the meeting request.

If you decide to invite others to the meeting, click the Invite Others button. Click the Options button to access the following three options:

- To show only work hours in the calendar, choose Show Only Working Hours.
- To see more dates in it at once, choose Show Zoomed Out.
- To force Outlook to update the free/busy information on the server, choose Update Free/Busy.

MASTERING THE OPPORTUNITIES

Scheduling Meeting Rooms and Equipment

In an office setting you may also often need to schedule meeting rooms and AV equipment. It's not unusual to spend hours setting up a meeting only to discover that there's no room available in which to hold it. Outlook 2000 provides a way for you to schedule meeting resources at the same time you schedule people to attend a meeting. First, the Microsoft Exchange network administrator needs to set up mailboxes for each room and each piece of equipment. These can be kept in a separate address book that is made available to all users on the network. The people or person responsible for maintaining the schedule of resources needs to have access to each of these mailboxes.

When you schedule a meeting, you can then select the meeting room and other resources from the Address list in the Select Attendees and Resources dialog box. Now when you check for attendee availability, the availability of the room and required resources will also be considered.

So, you may ask, who's supposed to handle all the e-mail generated by meeting requests? As long as the user has appropriate permissions to book the resource and the resource is available at the requested time, Outlook 2000 will directly book the appointment onto the resource's calendar instead of sending the resource a meeting request. If you are responsible for scheduling resources, you can also set options for a resource that will help you out. To do this, you first have to log in to Outlook as that particular resource. For example, if you want to set the options for Meeting Room A, you would log into Outlook under the user name Meeting Room A. Then go to Tools ➤ Options ➤ Calendar Options and click the Resource Scheduling button. Here you're given three options regarding a resource's mailbox:

Automatically Accept Meeting Requests And Process Cancellations: This option gives anyone the freedom to schedule any room or other resource as long as it's available.

Continued

MASTERING THE OPPORTUNITIES CONTINUED

Automatically Decline Conflicting Meeting Requests: With this option turned on, no one can schedule a resource if it's already tied up.

Automatically Decline Recurring Meeting Requests: You may have a policy that recurring meetings must be scheduled in person with the meeting coordinator. This option restricts users from booking a room or other resource for a regular meeting time every week or every month.

After you have set these options, scheduling for meeting rooms and other resources can happen behind the scenes with very little personal maintenance.

If you are planning a large meeting, you may want to invite the resource to the meeting before you invite any human beings. If the resource is available for your preferred time, you can then invite others to the meeting. If it's not available, you don't have to reschedule everybody else's time.

Canceling a Meeting

Suppose you need to cancel a meeting that you arranged. Don't despair, you still don't have to make a slew of phone calls. Open the meeting in your calendar and click the Cancel Invitations button on the Meeting form toolbar. This will generate an e-mail message to all attendees indicating that the meeting has been canceled. You'll be given an opportunity to explain why you are canceling the meeting. You can then follow it up with another invitation to the meeting at the new date and time. What used to take hours is now handled in just a few minutes. Everybody's notified, everyone's calendar is updated, and no one had to be interrupted from their work to make it happen.

What's Next

The more you work with Outlook, the more reasons you'll find for integrating the Outlook components. You may also find that it is easier to keep track of all your files in Outlook, not just your Outlook items. In Chapter 21, you'll see how to use Outlook to manage data and files, customize the Outlook environment, and you'll learn more about using Outlook in a Microsoft Exchange Server environment.

CHAPTER 21

Working Behind the Scenes in Outlook 2000

FEATURING:

Managing data and files in Outlook

Moving and copying items

Archiving and backing up your Outlook data

Customizing Outlook to work the way you do

Using Outlook on a Microsoft Exchange Server

Nowhere does Outlook do a better job of living up to its reputation as a desktop information manager than in its folder and file management features. You never have to launch Explorer or My Computer again. All of your file management needs can be accommodated from within Outlook. And when you want to exchange data with others over the Internet or a network, Outlook is ready to serve. Collaboration has never been easier.

Managing Data and Files in Outlook

Whether you've realized it or not, all of the Outlook modules are organized as folders, with all of the properties of other folders on your hard drive or network. Anything you already know about file management in the Windows Explorer applies to working with folders and items in Outlook. You can move files, copy them, rename them, create subfolders under them, and view them in different ways. The easiest way to grasp the Outlook folder structure is to choose Folder List from the View menu. This opens a third pane in the Outlook window that clearly shows the folders and subfolders that make up the Outlook modules (see Figure 21.1). Click any folder to see its contents.

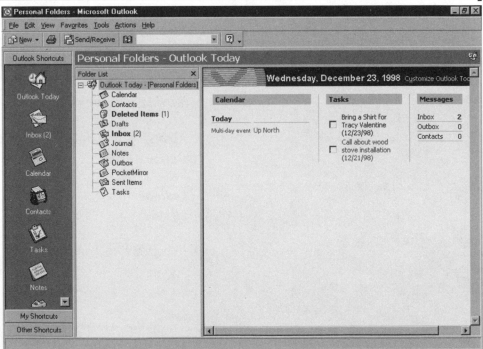

FIGURE 21.1

The Folder List view of Outlook

To create a new folder to organize Outlook items, follow these steps:

1. Choose File ➤ New ➤ Folder to open the Create New Folder dialog box shown in Figure 21.2.

2. Enter a name for the new folder.

3. Select the type of Outlook item you plan to keep in the folder.

4. Choose where you'd like to place the folder.

5. Click OK.

FIGURE 21.2

In the Create New Folder dialog box, create an Outlook subfolder to organize your items.

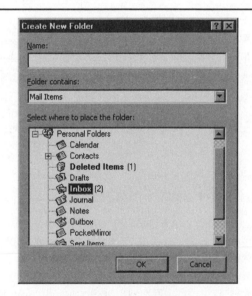

Moving and Copying Items into Outlook Folders

To move existing Outlook items into a subfolder, open the folder that contains the items and drag the items to the new folder in the folder list. To copy the items, hold down the Shift key while you drag. To select several noncontiguous items to move or copy, hold down the Ctrl key before selecting. To select contiguous items, select the first item and hold down the Shift key before selecting the last item in the list.

MASTERING TROUBLESHOOTING

Making a Contacts Subfolder an E-Mail Address Book

If you create a Contacts folder, you have to make it available as an Outlook address book in order to access the e-mail and fax addresses from the Select Name dialog box when you are creating messages. Follow these steps to make a folder available as an Outlook address book:

1. Right-click the new Contacts subfolder and choose Properties from the shortcut menu.

2. Click the Outlook Address Book tab of the Properties dialog box (discussed further in "Properties and Other Options" later in this chapter).

3. Click the Show This Folder As An Outlook Address Book check box.

4. Enter a different name for the address book if desired. This does not change the folder name—only the name of the address book.

5. Click OK to save the changes and close the Properties dialog box.

Deleting Items and Folders

To delete an item or a folder, select what you want to delete and click the Delete button from the Outlook menu. Deleted items (not folders) go into the Deleted Items folder, visible in the folder list. The Deleted Items folder is similar to the Recycle Bin in that items you delete go there before being gone forever. There are some important differences, however, between the Recycle Bin and the Deleted Items folder.

First of all, files remain in the Recycle Bin until you empty it or restore the files to their original location. By contrast, items can be removed from the Deleted Items folder in four ways:

- By emptying the folder. To do this, right-click the folder and choose Empty Deleted Items Folder.

- Automatically upon exiting Outlook. To set this option, choose Tools ➤ Options and click the Other tab. Click the Empty The Deleted Items Folder Upon Exiting check box.

- By archiving the folder. Archiving cleans out items that are older than the time period you specify. See "Archiving Items" later in this chapter.

- By moving the items to another folder.

The Recycle Bin and the Deleted Items folder also differ in that files erroneously deleted from the Recycle Bin may be recoverable using file recovery software, such as Norton Utilities or the Windows Undelete utility. Because Outlook items are stored in folders known as MAPI data stores, or containers—essentially, records in a database— rather than independent files, items deleted from the Deleted Items folder cannot be recovered.

Sharing Outlook Data with Another Outlook Item

Once you start working with multiple Outlook modules, you can be even more efficient by tying existing items together. For example, to create a task related to a scheduled meeting, drag the appointment into the Task folder. Outlook will open a new Task form and insert all the text from the appointment into the task. If you receive an e-mail about an appointment or want to schedule time to complete a task, dragging the Outlook item into the new activity is all you have to do to make sure you have the information when you need it.

 MASTERING THE OPPORTUNITIES

Maintaining Information Away from the Office

If you carry a personal digital assistant (PDA), such as a 3Com PalmPilot, and do not synchronize your e-mail, you can still carry the contents of e-mail messages with you on the road. Just drag the message into the notes folder. All of the contents will be placed in the note and the next time you synchronize, it will be transferred to your PDA. Copying and pasting the contents of a Word or Excel document into a note is another way to have the information you need without carrying a backbreaking briefcase everywhere you go. You'll learn more about synchronizing later in this chapter.

Archiving Items

The more you use Outlook, the more Outlook items you create. Pretty soon, your collection of Outlook items can become pretty unmanageable. Organizing Outlook items into subfolders is one way to keep things under control, but that won't solve the performance problems you may begin to experience when your folders become unwieldy. Deleting unneeded items can be helpful in maintaining manageable folders, but more than likely the day will come when you'll need something you deleted and have no way to retrieve it. So what's the answer? Archiving old Outlook e-mail, appointments, tasks, and Journal entries keeps Outlook fit and trim and still gives you access to your old data if you need it.

Outlook's archiving feature requires a few setup steps the first time you use it. After that, archiving will initiate automatically based on the time period you set. To set up archiving, follow these steps:

1. Turn the feature on. Go to Tools ➤ Options ➤ Other and click the AutoArchive button. Set the options shown in Figure 21.3.

2. Set the properties of each folder you want to archive. Right-click each folder (and subfolder) you want to archive and choose Properties. Click the AutoArchive tab and set the individual folder AutoArchive settings shown in Figure 21.4.

3. Activate archiving. Choose File ➤ Archive to open the Archive dialog box.

4. Indicate whether you want to use the AutoArchive settings you set in step 2 or override them this time only. If you do not choose to archive all folders according their AutoArchive settings, designate the folders you want to archive at this time and how old the items should be.

5. If desired, change the file name of the archive file.

6. Click OK to begin archiving.

While Outlook is archiving in the background, you'll see a message in the status bar, and Archive Folders temporarily appears above Personal Folders in your file list.

FIGURE 21.3

You can set the AutoArchive options to archive old Outlook items automatically.

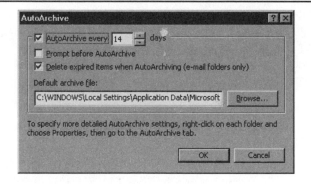

FIGURE 21.4

You can adjust each folder's AutoArchive properties to reflect how you'd like to archive the items in that folder.

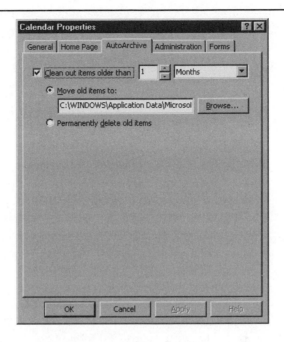

From this point on, AutoArchiving will commence the first time you launch Outlook after the interval you set in the AutoArchive options.

TIP If you would rather be prompted each time before AutoArchiving begins, be sure to set the Prompt Before AutoArchive option under Tools ➢ Options ➢ Other ➢ AutoArchive.

Retrieving Archived Items

When you need an archived item, all you need to know is where you stored the archive folders. Choose File ➢ Open and select Personal Folders File. Find the file named `archive.pst`.

TIP If you don't remember where you filed `archive.pst`, try the default file location: `c:\Windows\Local Settings\Application Data\Microsoft\Outlook\archive.pst`. If it's not there, you are on your own—use Windows Find to track it down.

When you locate the file, click OK and Outlook displays Archive Folders in the file list. Click the plus symbol to expand the list, locate the item you need and drag it into your active folder, and then print it or commit it to memory. When you have found the information you need, right-click Archive Folders in the folder list and choose Close "Archive Folders."

Backing Up Outlook Data

Growing to depend on Outlook as your personal information manager can be deadly if you don't regularly back up your Outlook folders. A hard-disk problem or a network snafu could wipe out all of your information. Backup is not as automatic as archiving, but it's just about as easy. The trick is remembering to do it—why not create a recurring Outlook task that reminds you to back up regularly?

To back up your folders, follow these steps:

1. Choose File ➤ Import And Export to launch the Import And Export Wizard.

2. Select Export To A File and click Next.

3. Choose Personal Folders File and click Next.

4. Select Personal Folders from the list and click Include Subfolders. You can also choose to back up a particular folder here (you can only choose one folder and its subfolders) and to filter the items based on criteria you set. Click Next when you've specified what you want to back up.

5. Choose a location and a file name for the backup (`C:\Windows\Local Settings\Application Data\Microsoft\Outlook\backup.pst` is the default name and location). Choose one of these options: Replace Duplicates With Items Exported, Allow Duplicates To Be Created, or Do Not Export Duplicate Items.

6. Click Finish to start the backup.

If you have a lot of e-mail and other items, expect the backup to take more than a few minutes. It's better to let the backup run without interference, so you probably want to set it up to run at the end of the day or as you are going to lunch.

Managing Windows Files and Folders

You can conduct all of your file management activities within Outlook; it's not just a tool for managing and organizing Outlook items. To access files and folders on your computer or network, click the Other Shortcuts button on the Outlook bar. Click the My Computer, My Documents, and Favorites icons to see all of the files you would expect to see using My Computer or Explorer in Windows. If you turn on the Folder

List (View ➤ Folder List), you get a split window just like you find in Explorer, with folders in the left pane and folder contents in the right pane. Move, copy, rename, and create folders and delete files using the same methods as you would in Windows.

The key advantages to managing files in Outlook are that you can customize the way you see your files and you can print your file list. Figure 21.5 shows a file list grouped by author. You may choose to group files by file type or view a folder in Timeline view to see what files were created or modified during a specific period (for more about Outlook views, see "Creating Custom Views" later in this chapter). When you need a hard copy of your file list, set up the view the way you want it and click the Print button on the toolbar. Try doing that in Explorer!

FIGURE 21.5

This file list grouped by author is just one of the ways you can view your documents in Outlook.

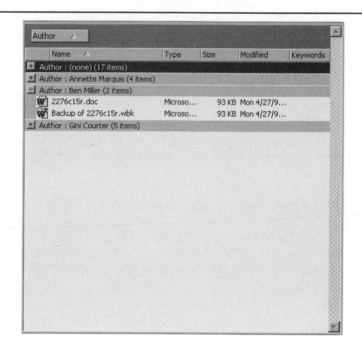

Customizing the Outlook Environment

There are many ways to customize Outlook to make it do things according to your working style. In fact, there are so many options scattered throughout Outlook that it is difficult to keep track of them all. Options or settings are found in three primary locations:

- On the Tools menu under Options
- On the Tools menu under Services (in a Corporate/Workgroup installation of Outlook) or Accounts (in an Internet Only installation)
- On the Properties page of a folder

Additional options are sprinkled around Outlook. For example, options related to toolbars are found on the Customize Toolbars dialog box (View ➤ Toolbars ➤ Customize), and options related to the Outlook Today home page are found by clicking the Customize Outlook Today button on the top of the page. Although Microsoft has made an attempt at streamlining, don't expect to find every option you need in one place—you probably won't. When you already know the option you are looking for but aren't sure where to find it, your best bet is to ask the Office Assistant. It does a pretty good job of pointing you in the right direction.

 NOTE Outlook's toolbars and menu bars are consistent with those in other Office 2000 applications. For information about customizing toolbars and menu bars, refer to Chapter 38.

Setting Options in the Options Dialog Box

The majority of Outlook options are available under Tools ➤ Options, but even navigating through there can give the most knowledgeable user a headache. The focus of this overview section is simply to help you know what options are available and where to find them. For a thorough discussion of Outlook options, refer to our *Mastering Outlook 2000* (also published by Sybex in 1999).

Preferences

The first page of options is the Preferences page for each of the Outlook modules: E-Mail, Calendar, Tasks, Contacts, Journal, and Notes.

E-Mail Options   In the E-Mail area you'll find Message Handling options, including Advanced Options related to saving messages, what happens when a message arrives, and default sensitivity and importance options. You'll also find options for tracking whether a message has been delivered and read, as well as options for replies and forwarded messages.

Calendar Options   In the Calendar area you'll find these options:

Calendar Work Week options include settings for the days you want to appear in your calendar and start and end times to each day.

General Calendar options include displaying week numbers, setting color, and sending meeting requests by default using iCalendar.

Time Zone lets you designate the current time zone and set up a second time zone to show in your calendar.

Add Holidays inserts religious and national holidays into your calendar.

Resource Scheduling is for use when you are responsible for maintaining schedules for rooms and other resources for meetings.

Free/Busy options let you determine how far in advance your calendar information should be available for others to use to schedule meetings and if you want that information posted to the Web.

Task Options   In the Task area you'll find these options:

Reminder Time changes the default time you are reminded to complete a task.

Color options change the colors to distinguish overdue tasks and completed tasks.

 NOTE   To find more options related to Tasks, see the discussion of the Other page later in this chapter.

Contact Options   In this area, the Name and Filing options determine how Full Name and File As names are displayed.

Journal Options   Here, the Automatically Record options let you set what type of items you would like to automatically record for which contacts. You can also set Outlook to automatically record files you work on in other Office and Office family applications.

Note Options   The Appearance options give you choices of note color, size, and font.

Mail Services/Mail Delivery

The second tab in the Options dialog box is Mail Services in the Corporate/Workgroup configuration or Mail Delivery in the Internet Only configuration. The Corporate/Workgroup settings are limited here to the following:

Startup Settings determine whether to prompt you for a profile on startup or use a default profile.

Mail options give you the option to identify which mail services Outlook checks when you tell it to check for new mail.

Reconfigure Mail Support lets you switch between Internet Only, Corporate/Workgroup, and No E-Mail Service options. This option was previously only available through Outlook setup and is much more conveniently located here.

In the Internet Only configuration, you can create and update new accounts, set up when Outlook sends and receives your messages, and determine how Outlook establishes and maintains connections to your mail services.

To add or remove mail services, you must go to Tools ➢ Services (Corporate/Workgroup) or click the Accounts button on the Mail Delivery tab (Internet Only). You can also edit existing mail services under Tools ➢ Services or Tools ➢ Accounts by opening the properties related to the mail service you want to edit. You'll learn more about Services/Account options later in the chapter.

Mail Format

Options under the Mail Format tab include message format settings, stationery and fonts, and signature.

Message Format options let you choose which format you want to use for your messages: HTML, plain text or Microsoft Outlook Rich Text. Plain text is the most generic and can be read by all of your e-mail recipients. You can also choose to edit your e-mail message using Word—this option requires additional memory resources that may drag down your system.

Stationery and Font options allow you to change the default fonts and stationery used for writing and replying to messages. Stationery options are only available if you choose HTML as your message format. Make sure the person you are sending to can read HTML messages.

Signature sets up an automatic signature that is included in all of your outgoing correspondence. Click Signature Picker to create a new signature.

Spelling

The Spelling tab offers settings related to automatic spell-checking and spelling dictionaries. When the Always Check Spelling Before Sending option is checked, you can be sure that every e-mail message is corrected before sending it out.

Security

E-mail and Web security is a major concern for businesses interacting over the Internet. Companies without adequate security controls in place are opening the door to corporate spying, sabotage, and other nasty stuff. Outlook 2000 has a number of features built in that help you secure your correspondence by validating who sent the e-mail and encrypting the contents so unauthorized people cannot view them.

On the Security page of Options you can secure and encrypt your e-mail, avoid downloading harmful content from the Web, and designate a digital ID for use in electronic transactions.

 NOTE Briefly, a digital ID is a unique code that can be assigned to companies or individuals (for a fee) by trusted third parties such as VeriSign, Inc. based on information supplied. The purpose is to guarantee that parties in Web transactions are indeed who they claim to be. You can learn more about digital IDs at http://www.webreference.com/ ecommerce/mm/column1/index.html.

Other

The Other page of the Options dialog box contains an assortment of options that have no apparent relationship to each other. If you're looking for a setting and you can't find it, you might just find it here. The Other page is where you assign Outlook's start-up folder, set appearance options such as the font for the Date Navigator, and choose specific options related to Tasks. The Other options are as follows:

General options include a setting to empty the Deleted Items folder on exiting and an Advanced Options button.

Advanced options include general settings such as providing a warning before permanently deleting items, turning on auto-selection, and providing feedback with sounds. You will also find additional options here related to Tasks, Notes, and Calendar to go with those on the Preferences page. If you are customizing Outlook and designing custom forms, come here to manage custom forms, install add-ins, and add COM components.

AutoArchive options create the default settings for managing your archiving preferences. (See earlier in this chapter for more information about archiving.)

Preview Pane settings control what happens when you read mail in Outlook's Preview pane.

Delegates

Delegates are people you designate to be able to send mail on your behalf. To give other users access to your mail without being able to send mail for you, right-click on the mail folder you want them to be able to open and change their permissions to that folder.

Internet E-Mail/Fax

The last page of the Options dialog box offers settings regarding Internet e-mail or fax, depending on which configuration of Outlook you have installed. Corporate/ Workgroup users have an Internet E-Mail tab, and Internet Only users who have a fax service installed have a Fax tab. In either case, you can set options regarding online connections and formatting.

NOTE Most of the options related to Internet e-mail and fax can be found on the Properties pages of the specific e-mail service or account. Open Tools ➤ Services or Tools ➤ Accounts to access these settings.

Managing Information Services or Accounts

To set up new information services such as a new Internet mail service, click Tools ➤ Service (Corporate/Workgroup) or Tools ➤ Accounts (Internet Only). Click the Add button and enter the information about this service. To set up an e-mail service or account, you need to know your account name and password and the names of the incoming and outgoing mail servers at your Internet Service Provider. Contact your ISP if you do not know this information.

TIP If you are using Dial-Up Networking (DUN) to access a new service, it's helpful if you create the DUN connection before setting up the information service.

To create a new Personal Folders file (*.pst) or connect to an existing one in the Corporate/Workgroup configuration, click Add and choose Personal Folders from the list of choice. Use the same steps to create a new personal address book (*.pab).

To edit an existing service, select the service and choose Properties. If you are on a network, do not edit Microsoft Exchange Service or other mail services without talking with your system administrator or help desk.

Properties and Other Options

Every Windows folder has properties, or attributes, related to it: how large it is, when it was created, and how many subfolders it has, for example. All of the Outlook modules and any subfolders you create also have properties that can affect the functioning of the folder. To access a folder's properties, like those shown in Figure 21.6, right-click the folder in the folder list or on the Outlook bar and choose Properties.

FIGURE 21.6

Every folder has properties that define it.

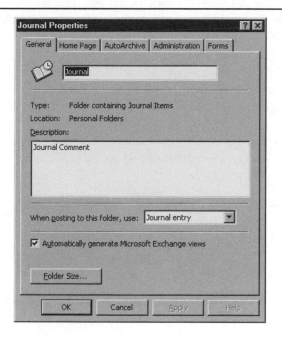

Use folder properties in Outlook to change the AutoArchive settings (discussed earlier in the chapter) for a folder, designate a home page to open when you open this folder (like the Outlook Today page), or assign a customized form to a folder. Every Outlook module has some settings that are unique to that folder type, and not all settings apply to all folders. Additional options may also be available if you are on a Microsoft Exchange Server network, so you'll want to explore the Properties dialog box of each folder in Outlook to see what options are available to you.

WARNING Changing the setting of an option may have unpredictable results if you don't know what the option is supposed to do. If you are unsure of an option's purpose, leave the default setting.

Customizing the Outlook Bar

The Outlook Bar is a navigational feature introduced in the original version of Outlook that has since become a standard tool available in a variety of other applications. FrontPage 2000, for example, uses a similar bar to navigate between views. The Outlook Bar has a lot of flexibility that some users love and others choose to ignore. It's up to you to decide what role the Outlook Bar will play for you.

The Outlook Bar offers groups of shortcuts. The default groups—Outlook Shortcuts, My Shortcuts, and Other Shortcuts—can be renamed or deleted completely if you choose. You can also add additional groups for your own shortcuts. To rename or delete a group, click to open the group and right-click the Outlook Bar (to add a new group, just right-click). Choose Add New Group, Rename Group, or Delete Group from the list of options.

To add a shortcut to the Outlook Bar, drag the folder from the Folder list to the Outlook Bar. Drop the folder when the black horizontal line appears where you want the folder to appear:

 A new feature of Outlook 2000 is that you can now create Outlook Bar shortcuts to documents. To add a document shortcut, follow these steps:

1. Click the Other Shortcuts button on the Outlook Bar and open My Computer.

2. Locate the document you want to create a shortcut to.

3. Drag the document to the Outlook Bar.

 TIP To turn off the Outlook Bar completely, choose View ➤ Outlook Bar or right-click the bar and choose Hide Outlook Bar.

Creating Custom Views

As you've seen while working in the various Outlook modules, views define how you see your Outlook data. There are five types of views available in Outlook:

Table view: The default view in Tasks, this shows data in columns and rows.

Timeline view: Used in Journal to see when activities occurred, this displays data across a timeline.

Card view: This displays Contact data in an address-card format.

Day/Week/Month view: Used with Calendar, this shows a Date Navigator and Day, Work Week, Week and Month buttons to display data.

Icon view: The default view in Notes, this displays a small or large icon for each Outlook item.

Views improve efficiency by making the data you need visible when you need it. Switching between views gives you a different perspective on your data and helps you capitalize on the powerful grouping features. Views also provide you with a valuable reporting tool. By creating custom views that are sorted, grouped, and filtered to extract the data you need, you can create time logs, calendars, project reports, schedules, company directories, correspondence logs and a whole host of other management reports. When you use views effectively, raw data is translated into priceless information.

If you would like to create a new view, you have three options:

• Modify an existing view.

• Copy an existing view and modify the copy, leaving the original unchanged.

• Create a new view from scratch.

To modify an existing view, follow these steps:

1. Switch to the view you want to modify.
2. Click View ➢ Current View ➢ Customize Current View to open the dialog box shown in Figure 21.7.
3. Click the Fields button to add or remove fields from the view.
4. Change the grouping of the data by clicking the Group By button.
5. Click the Sort button to set the fields you want to sort by.
6. Define criteria for records to display by clicking the Filter button.
7. Change display settings and fonts under the Other Settings button.

8. Click the Automatic Formatting button to apply special formatting rules to items, such as applying bold to unread items in the Inbox.

9. Click OK to apply the customized view.

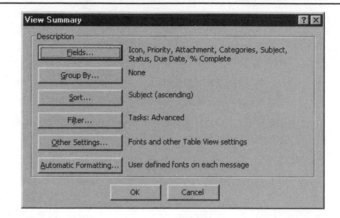

Making a copy of an existing view or creating a new view from scratch is essentially the same as modifying an existing view, but there are a couple of extra steps involved. To copy an existing view or create a new view, follow these steps:

1. Switch to the module for which you want the new view.

2. Click View ➤ Current View ➤ Define Views to open the dialog box shown in Figure 21.8.

3. To copy an existing view for modification, select the view from the list, click Copy, and enter a name for the new view.

To create an entirely new view, click New, enter a name for the view, and select the type of view.

With either option, if you are on an Exchange Server network, indicate if you want this view visible to everyone in this folder, visible only to you in this folder, or available in all Contacts folders.

4. Click OK and follow steps 3–8 in the procedure for modifying an existing view.

5. Click Apply View to make the new view the current view for this folder or OK to add the view to the list of available views but not apply it.

FIGURE 21.8

*In the Define Views
dialog box you can
create a new view,
make a copy of an
existing view, or mod-
ify an existing view.*

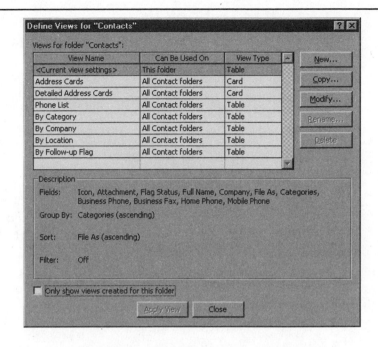

 TIP If you modify one of the default views and later decide to return it to its original
state, choose View ➤ Define Views, select the view, and click Reset.

To delete a custom view, switch to the module that contains the view you want to
delete. Choose View ➤ Current View ➤ Define Views, select the view you want to
delete, and click the Delete button.

Outlook 2000 and Microsoft Exchange Server

You can create shared Outlook mail folders on any network. However, to share schedules, tasks lists, or contact lists, these items must be on a network with a Microsoft
Exchange Server, and you must have the necessary network permissions for the public
folder you wish to create the shared item in.

 If you aren't on an Exchange Server network, you can synchronize offline folders in
Outlook 2000, but you will not be able to share Outlook folders.

Creating Shared Outlook Items

Shared folders are used to share schedules, contact information, and other kinds of Outlook items. The easiest way to create shared items is to copy an existing folder to a public folder. For example, you can copy your Contacts folder as a public Contacts folder, and then delete the contacts that don't need to be shared. Or you can simply create a new folder in All Public Folders.

Setting Permissions for Others

Outlook's default Calendar settings allow other users to find out when you are busy or available but not to see details about appointments. You might want to allow certain people—for example, an assistant—to see more details or add new appointments to your Calendar. Before they can do so, you need to change the default permissions for the folder.

Roles are bundled groups of folder permissions; to change a user's permissions for your folder, you assign that user to a role for the folder. The roles for folders, from most to least restrictive, are the following:

None: No access to the contents of a folder

Contributor: Allowed to create new items

Reviewer: Allowed to read existing items

Author: Allowed to create new items, edit or delete items they have created, and read existing items

Publishing Author: Same as Author but includes access to subfolders

Editor: Same as Author but can edit or delete all items

Publishing Editor: Same as Editor but includes access to subfolders

Owner: All permissions, including the right to change folder permissions

Add or remove permissions for other users in the folder's Properties dialog box, shown in Figure 21.9. To change permissions on a folder, follow these steps:

1. Open the folder.
2. Choose File ➢ Folder ➢ Properties For *Folder Name*.
3. Click the Permissions tab.
4. Click the Add button to open the Add Users dialog box.
5. Select the person that you want to allow access to your folder, and click OK.
6. Select the person's Name in the upper pane.

7. Choose the appropriate role in the Roles drop-down list.

8. Click OK.

FIGURE 21.9

*Set permissions for
other users in the
folder's Properties
dialog box.*

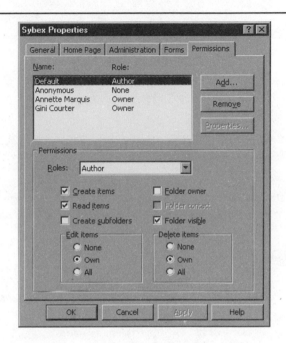

Finding Public Folders

If you work in a large company, the number of public folders on the Exchange
Server may make it difficult to find the information you are looking for. With Outlook 2000's new Find Public Folders option, shown in Figure 21.10, you can quickly
locate and open any public folder you need. To access this feature, follow these steps:

1. Select Tools ➢ Find Public Folder.

2. Click Browse to open up a Select Folders list if you want to narrow your search.

3. Enter the text you are searching for in the Contains Text box.

4. Indicate where you would like to look for that text: in the Name or Description,
the Internet Newsgroup Name, the Folder Path, the Folder Name or the Folder
Description.

5. Specify a Folders Created Since date if you want to search within a certain date
range.

6. Click Find Now to conduct the search.

FIGURE 21.10

Use the Find Public Folders option to locate a public folder.

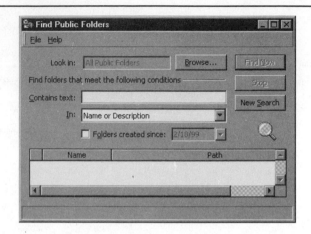

Outlook returns the name of the folder and the path where the folder is located. Just double-click the folder to open it in a separate window.

Working Away from the Office

Outlook has three methods for handling work while you're out of the office: *Remote Mail, offline folders,* and *personal folder synchronization*. With Remote Mail, you can download and read the messages that have been delivered in your absence, but you can't send messages. Offline folders, a second set of folders kept on your remote computer, allow you to send *and* receive mail, tasks, and other items. Personal folder synchronization is a new add-in for Outlook 2000 that lets you synchronize your Outlook folders without Microsoft Exchange Server.

 TIP To use Remote Mail and offline folders, you must have your home or laptop computer configured to use DUN. To use offline folders, you must have dial-up access to a Microsoft Exchange Server. See your system administrator for dial-up permissions and information on configuring DUN.

Managing Remote Mail

Remote Mail allows you to download selected messages from your computer at work. Before you can use Remote Mail, you must do the following:

1. Install Outlook on your remote computer.

2. Establish a Personal Folders file (.pst) on your work computer so messages can be delivered to your computer rather than the server. Choose Tools ➢ Services to see if Personal Folders is listed. If not, click Add.

3. Establish a dial-up connection from your remote computer and choose Tools ➢ Synchronize ➢ Download Address Book to copy the Address Book.

4. Set options for your Personal Folder in the Services dialog box.

5. Have Outlook direct new mail to your Personal Folders (Tools ➢ Services ➢ Delivery).

To connect to Remote Mail, click the Inbox and choose Tools ➢ Remote Mail ➢ Connect from the menu bar. After the connection is established, you can download messages or just the message headers. If you download the headers, you'll be automatically disconnected after the download is complete.

Browse through the headers and mark headers for messages you'd like to see by clicking the Mark To Retrieve or Mark To Retrieve A Copy buttons on the Remote Mail toolbar. You can click the Delete button to delete messages; however, when you delete messages remotely, they're actually deleted, not just moved to the Deleted Items folder, so use this feature cautiously. After you've marked all messages, reconnect to download or delete marked messages.

 TIP It's a good idea to make sure you've set up Remote Mail correctly and practiced using it before you grab your laptop and leave for the Bahamas.

Working Offline

Offline folders allow you to use a folder remotely, work with all the items in the folder, and then synchronize (update) both the offline folder and the folder on your work computer so the two are identical. Before you can work offline, you must:

1. Install and configure Dial-Up Networking.

2. Establish an Offline File Folder on your remote computer. If you indicated that you travel with the computer during Outlook Setup, it already exists. To check, open the Inbox, and choose Tools ➢ Services. If Offline File Folder isn't listed, add it.

3. Download the Address Book (see the previous section, "Managing Remote Mail").

4. Add any public folders you want to use offline to Public Folders Favorites.

5. Choose the folders you want to make available offline. Select the folder in the Folder List, choose File ≻ Folder ≻ Properties For ≻ Synchronization, and enable the When Offline Or Online check box. Click OK.

6. Synchronize the offline folders (see "Synchronizing Folders Offline" later in this chapter).

7. Set Outlook to work offline.

You might also choose to create offline folders on your work computer so that you can work when you're not connected to your network server. On a network computer, you don't need to set up Dial-Up Networking.

Setting Outlook to Work Offline   You can tell Outlook either to always work offline or to prompt you each time you start Outlook. If, for example, you have a laptop and use a docking station at work, you should choose to be prompted. However, if you only use your laptop for offline work, set Outlook to always start offline. To set Outlook to work offline:

1. Select the Inbox and choose Tools ≻ Services.

2. Choose Microsoft Exchange Server from the list, and click Properties.

3. On the General page, enable either the Work Offline And Use Dial-Up Networking or the Choose The Connection Type When Starting check box.

4. Click OK.

5. Exit and restart Outlook.

Synchronizing Folders Offline   *Synchronizing* your folders compares the contents of the offline and regular folders and adjusts items in both so that they are identical. For example, synchronization moves messages you've received at work to an offline folder and sends messages from your offline Outbox folder. If you delete a Contact item in your Offline folder, synchronizing will delete the item in your regular folder. Follow these steps to synchronize folders:

1. Choose Tools ≻ Synchronize.

2. To synchronize the current folder, select This Folder.

3. Choose All Folders to synchronize all offline folders and their corresponding folders on your workstation or server.

 TIP   To set the number you want to use for dialing into the Exchange Server, choose Tools ≻ Dial Up Connection and choose the connection you want to use. You can use this menu to change your Dial-Up Location and add or modify Location Settings.

Personal Folder Synchronization

Not everyone who needs to synchronize personal folders between two computers runs Exchange Server, yet until now that was the only option if you wanted to keep your Outlook folders in sync. Microsoft offers an Outlook 2000 add-in called Personal Folder Synchronization that will change all that. Even if you are not on a network, Personal Folder Synchronization will let you create a synchronized backup of your personal folders to a floppy disk or zip disk. On your second computer, you'll just open the synchronization file to update all of your data.

 NOTE Check the Microsoft Web site at www.Microsoft.com for information about obtaining the Personal Folder Synchronization add-in.

To use Personal Folder Synchronization, follow these steps:

1. Insert a floppy disk or zip disk in your drive or identify a network location for the file.

2. Choose Tools ➤ Synchronize Other Computer ➤ Save File.

3. Click New to identify your computer and the destination computer.

4. Enter a name for the computer you are using right now and a name for the destination computer.

5. Select the folders you want to keep synchronized and click OK.

6. Identify where you want the file saved and click OK. Synchronization will begin. It will prompt you to insert additional disks if necessary.

7. If you want to verify the contents of the synchronization file, click Details on the message that appears telling you the synchronization information was successfully saved. You'll see the detailed information in the lower pane of the window, as shown in Figure 21.11.

8. When you reach the destination computer, choose Tools ➤ Synchronize Other Computer ➤ Open File.

9. Locate the synchronization file and indicate how you would like it to handle conflicts that arise, as shown in Figure 21.12. Click the Details button to check the date this file was created and other file details.

10. Click OK to complete the synchronization.

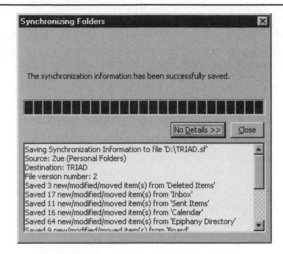

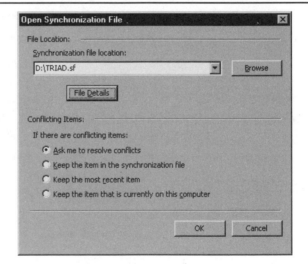

Depending on the size of your personal folder files, Personal Folder Synchronization may take some time the first time you run it, but after that it's pretty snappy because it just updates any changes.

What's Next

The next part of the book covers Microsoft Excel, which continues to be the market leader in spreadsheet applications because it is far superior to its competitors. In fact, Excel was the driving force for many companies to choose Office as its standard long before the Office suite held market dominance. Excel 2000 capitalizes on its success by expanding its database and query tools, improving its data analysis and pivot table tools, and adding support for OLAP cubes. In the following chapters, you'll learn about Excel's powerful calculation, analysis, charting, and database tools.

PART V

Number Crunching with Excel

LEARN TO:

- *Enter and format text and numbers*

- *Create charts*

- *Work with formulas and functions*

- *Manage data with Excel*

- *Link workbooks and use 3-D cell references*

- *Use Excel's proofing tools*

- *Use Excel in a workgroup*

CHAPTER 22

Creating and Printing Excel Worksheets

FEATURING:

Entering data in Excel

Working with numbers

*Changing worksheet layout and
other formatting*

Printing and previewing

Using functions and references

Working with ranges

*Using charts to express
information graphically*

This chapter provides a hands-on tour of the basic operations and concepts involved in creating and using Excel worksheets. If you're completely new to Microsoft Office 2000, you might want to review Chapters 1 and 2 before you return here to begin work in Excel. On the other hand, if you're already familiar with earlier versions of Excel, you'll probably want to skim through the introductory material here and look for the NEW marker in the margin to find out about the latest improvements. To illustrate Excel's features, we use sample data and practice worksheets; you may want to create these for yourself to try out the techniques before "going live" with your real data.

Entering and Editing Cell Entries

Welcome to Excel 2000, the number cruncher! If you've used prior versions of Excel, you'll find many new features that are welcome additions to Excel. If you're moving to Excel from another spreadsheet program, you're in for a real treat. Simply put, Excel 2000 is the best spreadsheet program ever designed—a powerful program with plenty of features to help you harness that power in your workplace.

The Excel Application Window

The Excel application window (see Figure 22.1) includes the standard title bar and command bars. Below the command bars is a strip that contains the *name box* and the *formula bar*.

The Excel status bar displays information about current selections, commands, or operations. The right end of the status bar displays NUM if the keyboard's Num Lock is on.

Excel 2000 uses personal toolbars, so the command bars may appear side by side or one above the other. You can drag-and-drop command bars to rearrange them if you wish. You can also click the toolbar and drag it to the left to elongate its display and make more buttons visible.

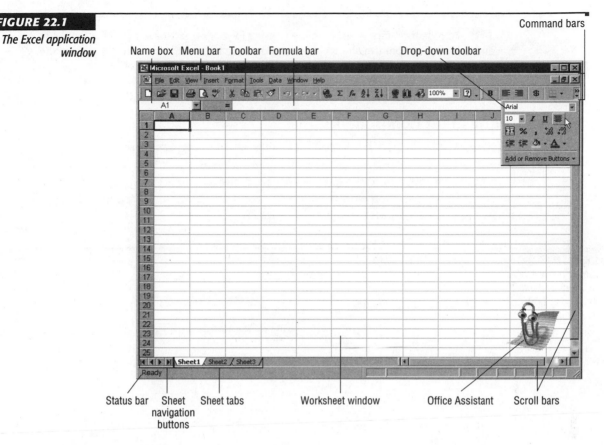

FIGURE 22.1

The Excel application window

Name box   Menu bar   Toolbar   Formula bar   Drop-down toolbar

Command bars

Status bar   Sheet navigation buttons   Sheet tabs   Worksheet window   Office Assistant   Scroll bars

Workbooks and Worksheets

When you launch Excel, the Excel application window opens with a new Excel *workbook*. A workbook is a multipage Excel document. Each page in the workbook is called a *worksheet*, and the active worksheet is displayed in the document window. At the left end of the horizontal scroll bar are *sheet tabs* and *navigation buttons*. Use the sheet tabs to move to another worksheet and the navigation buttons to scroll through the sheet tabs.

TIP To hide the Office Assistant while working in your spreadsheet, right-click the figure and select Hide from the shortcut menu. You can reactivate the assistant by clicking the Help button or pressing the F1 key.

Worksheet Components

Each worksheet is divided into columns, rows, and cells, separated by *gridlines*, as shown in the Payroll worksheet in Figure 22.2. *Columns* are vertical divisions. The first column is column A, and the letter A appears in the *column heading*. The horizontal *rows* are numbered. Each worksheet has 256 columns (A through IV) and 65,536 rows—plenty of room to enter all your numbers!

FIGURE 22.2

A worksheet consists of cells organized into rows and columns.

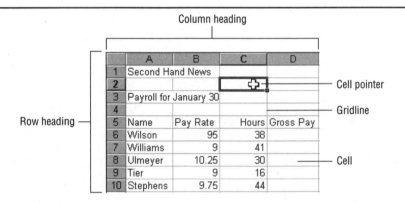

A *cell* is the intersection of a row and a column. Each cell has a unique *address* composed of the cell's column and row. For example, the cell in the upper-left corner of the worksheet (with the text *Second Hand News* in Figure 22.2) is cell A1. Even though some of the text appears to run over into cell B1 in the next column, it is really entered in cell A1. The *active cell*, C2 in Figure 22.2, has a box around it called the *cell pointer*, and the headings in the active cell's column (C) and row (2) are highlighted. When you enter data, it is always placed in the active cell.

 TIP Right-click any cell or selected cells to display a shortcut menu of frequently used commands. You can, for example, change the cell's format, or cut, copy, or paste its contents.

Moving the Cell Pointer

To move the pointer one cell to the left, right, up, or down, use the keyboard arrow keys. Other frequently used keyboard commands are shown in Table 22.1.

TABLE 22.1: KEYSTROKES TO MOVE THE CELL POINTER	
Key(s)	**Moves**
PgDn	Down one screen
PgUp	Up one screen
Home	To column A in the current row
Ctrl+Home	To cell A1

 TIP To activate a cell with the mouse, simply click in the cell.

Scrolling In the Worksheet

If you want to see other areas of the worksheet, use the scroll bars. To scroll up or down one row, click the arrow at either end of the vertical scroll bar. Use the arrows on the horizontal scroll bar to scroll one column to the left or right. To move up, down, left, or right one window, click the empty space above, below, or to the left or right of the scroll bar's scroll box:

Click here to scroll.

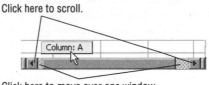

Click here to move over one window.

Drag the scroll box to scroll more than a couple of rows or columns. As you drag, a *ScrollTip* appears showing the location you are scrolling over. Note that scrolling doesn't change the active cell—scrolling lets you view other parts of the worksheet, but the active cell is wherever you left the cell pointer.

Power Scrolling To scroll long distances, hold the Shift key while dragging the scroll box, and Excel will scroll farther for each movement of the mouse. To use Excel efficiently, you should become comfortable moving the cell pointer using both the keyboard and the mouse. It's easier to use the keyboard when you are entering data and the mouse when you need to scroll a long way or already have your hand on the mouse for another task.

 TIP Use the navigation buttons in the lower-left corner of the Excel screen to scroll quickly through worksheets when you have so many sheets in your workbook that not all of the sheet tabs can be displayed. Right-click one of the tab scrolling buttons to display a shortcut menu of available worksheets.

Entering Text and Numbers

Three types of data can be entered in cells in a worksheet:

Numbers are values you may want to use in calculations, including dates. Dates are often used in calculations to determine, for example, how many days to charge for an overdue video or how many months of interest you have earned on a deposit.

Formulas are calculations.

Text is any entry that isn't a number or a formula.

 NOTE You can also insert data in worksheets, including maps, images, Web links, and more, but the process differs slightly from entering data directly in a cell.

 To enter data in a cell, first activate the cell, and then begin typing the data. As soon as you begin entering characters from the keyboard, an insertion point appears in the cell, the text you are entering appears in the cell and the formula bar, and the formula bar buttons are activated.

Correcting Data Entry Mistakes

If you make a mistake while entering data, click the Cancel Formula button (the red X) to discard the entry you were making and turn off the formula bar buttons. You can also cancel an entry by pressing the Esc key on the keyboard.

Using the Efficient Enter Key

Clicking the Enter button (the green check mark) finishes the entry and turns off the formula bar buttons. Pressing the Enter key on the keyboard does the same thing but also moves the cell pointer down one cell. So if you are entering columns of data, the Enter key is more efficient than the Enter button. Moving to another cell always finishes an entry as if you clicked the Enter button before you moved the cell pointer.

 NOTE Some Excel features are disabled while you are entering data in a cell, so you should always make sure you finish an entry by entering or canceling it before moving on to other tasks.

There is another way to finish an entry: simply move to another cell by clicking on the cell or using the arrow keys. Before Excel switches the focus to the new cell, it finishes the entry in the current cell.

Saving Time with AutoComplete

Excel has an *AutoComplete* feature, which keeps track of text entered in a column and can complete other entries in the same column. For example, if you have already typed **Jones** in cell A1 and then enter the letters **Jo** in A2, Excel will automatically fill in **nes** to make **Jones**. If **Jones** is the correct text, simply finish the entry by pressing Enter, moving to another cell, or clicking the Enter button. If the AutoComplete entry is not correct, just continue entering the correct text to overwrite the AutoComplete entry.

 NOTE AutoComplete is turned on by default. To turn it on or off select Tools ➤ Options, choose the Edit tab, and check or clear the Enable AutoComplete For Cell Values check box.

AutoComplete resets each time you leave a blank cell in a column. AutoComplete may seem annoying at first, but it's worth getting used to, particularly when you're entering columns of data with a lot of repetition: repeated department names, cities, states, or other such information. If your data doesn't have many repeats, simply ignore AutoComplete and enter your data.

 TIP If you type the same word or long number many times in your worksheet, consider adding it to Office's AutoCorrect list (Tools ➤ AutoCorrect). In the AutoCorrect dialog box, type in a few characters signifying the word or number, and then type out the full entry. Excel will automatically substitute the full entry when you enter the abbreviation. See Chapter 2 for a general introduction to AutoCorrect and Chapter 5 for its uses in Word.

PART

V

Number Crunching with Excel

Revising Text and Numbers

There are two ways to change an entry in a cell:

Type Over: If you activate the cell and type the new entry, the old entry will be replaced. This is the easiest way to change a number (for example, *15* to *17*) or to replace text with a short word.

Edit Portion: If the original entry is long and requires only minor adjustment, you might prefer to edit it. Click the cell and edit the entry in the formula bar, or double-click the cell to open it for editing and edit directly in the cell. When you are finished, press Enter or click the Enter button to complete the entry—you can't simply move to a new cell.

NOTE If you cannot edit in the cell by double-clicking on it, your Edit Directly In Cell option may be turned off. Select Tools ≻ Options and select the Edit tab in the Options dialog box to restore this option.

Deleting Cell Contents

To delete the contents of a cell completely, activate the cell and then either press the Delete key on the keyboard or right-click and choose Clear Contents from the shortcut menu. (Don't choose Delete—that deletes the cell, not just the entry in the cell.)

TIP If you've used other spreadsheet programs, you may be in the habit of deleting cell contents by pressing the spacebar to overwrite the contents. In Excel, cells with contents you can't see (like a space) have a way of messing things up later on, so you should get used to using the Delete key instead.

Selecting Multiple Cells

In Excel, at least one cell is always selected: the active cell. A group of cells is called a *range*. To select a range, move to the first cell in the range (check to be sure the mouse pointer is the large cross used for selecting), hold down the mouse button, and drag to the last cell you want to select before releasing the mouse button.

To select all the cells in a column or row, click the column heading or row heading. To select multiple columns or rows, select one heading and drag to select the others. When you point to row or column headers to select them, be sure that your mouse pointer looks like the fat selection cross as you do this, not a thinner black cross. To select the entire worksheet, click the Select All button, the gray rectangle at the upper-left corner of the worksheet above the row headings.

If the cells, columns, or rows you want to select are noncontiguous (not next to each other), select one of the ranges you want to select, and then hold down the Ctrl key while selecting the others.

Working with Numbers

You use a *formula* every time you want to perform a calculation in Excel, so you'll appreciate some of the new formula features built into Excel 2000. Formulas are what make a spreadsheet a spreadsheet—the driving force behind the magic of Excel. You don't have to be a math major to use formulas, because Excel does the math correctly every time. Even if your checkbook never balances, you can use Excel's formulas and your data to calculate totals, averages, and other results accurately, quickly, and easily.

Excel uses standard computer operator symbols for mathematical and logical operators, as shown in Table 22.2.

TABLE 22.2: MATHEMATICAL AND LOGICAL OPERATORS

Operation	Symbol
Addition	+
Subtraction	–
Multiplication	*
Division	/
Exponentiation (to the power of)	^
Precedence (do this operation first)	enclose in ( )
Equal to	=
Not equal to	<>
Greater than	>
Less than	<

Creating Formulas

There are a number of ways to create formulas, some more efficient than others. We'll begin with simple formulas that have one math operation. For example, the Second Hand News Payroll worksheet (see Figure 22.2) needs a formula to multiply Wilson's pay rate times the hours worked in order to calculate gross pay. There are two ways to create this formula: using point-and-click, or typing the formula using cell addresses.

Point-and-Click Formulas

Point-and-click is the highly reliable method that Excel is known for. The following steps will get you started with this intuitive approach:

1. Activate the cell where you want the result to appear.

2. Type an equal sign (=). Your formula elements will begin appearing in the formula bar as you type or select them.

3. Click the first cell you want to include in the formula.

4. Type an operator.

5. Click the next cell in the formula.

6. Repeat steps 4 and 5 until the entire formula is entered.

7. Finish the entry by pressing Enter or clicking the Enter button on the formula bar. (Don't just move to another cell—Excel will include it in the formula!)

Traditional Typing Technique

The traditional spreadsheet approach is to type the formula using the cell addresses of each cell you want to include in the formula. This is the most error-prone and therefore the least desirable way to create a formula. It's much too easy to glance at the wrong column or row, even when you're only working with a few numbers. If you need to reference widely disparate cells, consider naming the cells (see the "Naming Ranges" section in Chapter 23) and then referring to the names.

MASTERING THE OPPORTUNITIES

Using Natural Language Formulas

There is another technique for entering formulas, called *natural language formulas.* Support for natural language formulas was introduced in Excel 97 but didn't receive the rave reviews that Microsoft had anticipated. In Excel 2000, support for natural language formulas is available but is disabled by default. To turn on natural language formulas, choose Tools ≻ Options to open the Options dialog box. On the Calculation page, enable the Accept Labels In Formulas check box.

You'll notice in Figure 22.2 that Column B is labeled Pay Rate and Column C is labeled Hours. You can use the column labels to enter your formula. You can move to cell D6, type **=pay rate * hours**, complete the entry, and Excel will know exactly what you mean.

The natural language approach assumes that you know a couple of subtle things about worksheet design. You should always make sure that every row and column label is unique. There shouldn't be two columns or rows labeled Totals, or Excel will simply grab the nearest one, not necessarily the correct one. The entire label should fit into one cell. If the column label is Hours Worked, don't put Hours in one cell and Worked in the cell underneath. If you do, you can't refer to Hours Worked in a natural language formula (or anywhere else in Excel). For long labels, enter the label and then use the text-wrapping option discussed in "Aligning Text" later in this chapter.

Using the Formula Palette

Whatever formula construction method you use, you can use the *Formula Palette* to view the progress of your formula as it's being constructed. To activate the Formula Palette, click the = button in the formula bar (don't press the = key on the keyboard). As you enter the formula, the Formula Palette will show the results of the formula:

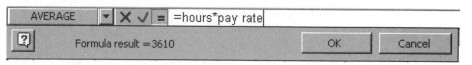

NOTE When you activate the Formula Palette, the cell drop-down list (or name box) next to the formula buttons in the Formula bar changes. It lists some of Excel's built-in functions. Click a listed function to display the function in the Formula Palette, where you can enter variables. Functions are discussed in detail in Chapter 23.

Click OK (or press Enter) to finish the formula entry, or Cancel if the results aren't what you expected. With simple formulas, the Formula Palette isn't very helpful, and it takes time to load and open the Office Assistant. As you use more complex formulas and functions, you will often want to begin a formula by opening the Formula Palette so you can get additional assistance or see the intermediate results of a formula.

 WARNING Formulas are dynamic, so the results automatically change each time the numbers in the underlying cells are revised. Typed-in numbers don't change unless they are edited. This is the reason for the first of two Very Important Excel Rules: *Never* do math "in your head" and type in the answer in a cell where you or other users would reasonably expect to have a formula calculate the answer. Before typing in any cell that may contain a formula, select the cell and check the Formula Bar. You will see the formula there and can avoid typing over it.

Complex Formulas

Complex formulas involve more than one operation. For example, you might have separate columns for hours worked in the first week of the pay period and hours worked in the second. You'll want to add the hours together before multiplying by the pay rate: = Hours Week 1 + Hours Week 2 * pay rate. When you have more than one operation in a formula, you'll need to know about the *order of operations*, a short set of rules about how formulas are calculated:

1. Formulas are calculated from left to right: 15/3+2 is 7, never 3.

2. Multiplication and division are always done before any addition or subtraction. Excel will make two left-to-right passes through the formula in the preceding paragraph and do the multiplication on the first pass. Then, it will come back through and add the hours worked in the first week to the gross pay for the second week. Calculating the gross pay this way would not make your employees happy, so parentheses are needed to change the order of operations.

3. Any operation in parentheses is calculated first. If you want the hours for the two weeks added together first, just throw a set of parentheses ( ) around the addition

part of the formula. Notice that you never need to include parentheses if you're only doing one operation, only when you need to tell Excel how to order two or more operations.

 TIP To add parentheses to an existing formula, select the cell containing the formula and click in the Formula Bar. Type parentheses around the expressions in the formula, but not around the initial = sign. Turn on the Formula Palette while you are adding parentheses to check whether you still have a valid formula.

Filling Formulas

In the Payroll example, the formula for each employee's gross pay is the same: hours * pay rate. Since you've already created one working formula, all you need to do is *fill* it to the other cells.

 There is a square box in the lower-right corner of the cell pointer called the *fill handle*. As you move the mouse toward the cell pointer, the mouse pointer changes shape to a black cross (as shown at left) to let you know that you can use the mouse for a fill operation.

 There are several shapes the mouse pointer assumes as you move it around the worksheet. When the mouse pointer is a large cross, you can use it to activate or select cells.

 If you move the mouse toward the border of the active cell, the mouse pointer will change to an arrow. When the pointer is an arrow, you can use it to move the cell (you'll learn more about moving cells in the "Adjusting Worksheet Layout" section in this chapter). You'll want to look at the mouse pointer frequently while working in Excel. A mouse movement of 1/32 inch is the difference between selecting, moving, and filling.

Filling is a form of copying. Begin by activating the cell that has the formula you want to copy. Move the mouse pointer toward the fill handle until the mouse pointer changes to the fill pointer shape.

 Press the mouse button and drag the fill handle down to select the cells you want to copy the formula to. Release the mouse button, and the formula will be filled to the other cells.

Now that you have read about the process, try it out by following these steps:

1. Select the cell that contains the formula you want to copy to other cells.

2. Drag the fill handle to select the cells where you want the formula copied.

3. Release the fill handle to fill the formula.

TIP A common mistake that novice Excel users make is to include the wrong cells in the initial selection. At this point in your fill career, if all the selected cells don't include formulas, you've selected incorrectly.

Using AutoFill Features

Excel supplies time-saving methods for filling cells with data without actually entering all the numbers, dates, or formulas. For example, if the value in cell B5 is the number 7, you can copy the 7 to the cells immediately below, above, right, or left of B5 as you would copy a formula. Just select B5, grab the fill handle, and drag to the cells you want to copy to. If you want to increment the value by one (7, 8, 9, 10), hold Ctrl while you drag. Excel automatically increments when you fill dates.

 TIP You can quickly use a simple fill feature by selecting the cell containing the value you want to use and an adjacent cell or range of cells you want to fill. Then choose Edit ➢ Fill ➢ *Down, Right, Up,* or *Left*. Excel swiftly copies the source cell contents into all of the destination cells. The shortcut keystroke to fill down is Ctrl+D; Ctrl+R fills to the right. When you fill using the menu or shortcut keys, dates are not automatically incremented.

Excel can fill your destination cells with a value from your source cell and increase this value in each successive cell in the series, based on a step value that you specify. For instance, if one cell contains the number 10, or the date 02/14/99, you can tell Excel to use these values to fill other cells and automatically add 2 to each successive cell value, or seven days to each succeeding cell date.

Excel will even fill your cells based on a series of values in successive cells. Let's say you select three cells, with successive values of 3, 6, and 9, plus three more blank cells after them. Excel can recognize the series and automatically fill the three selected blank cells with 12, 15, and 18 (the next values in the series where $n = n + 3$).

 TIP You can quickly fill a linear series by selecting two cells in the series and then dragging the fill handle. For example, if you select two cells with the values 5 and 10 and then drag the fill handle, Excel will fill with the values 15, 20, 25, and so on.

Here are the steps for using the AutoFill feature.

1. Select the starting fill value based on one of three approaches:

   One cell: Select a single cell if you are going to fill cells based on the contents of one cell, which will increase according to a step value that you specify.

   Series of cells: Choose a set of adjoining cells containing a series of values that you want to continue in other blank cells.

   Formula cell: Choose a cell containing a formula if you want to fill other cells with the formula.

2. Select the rest of the cells in the fill series. The destination cells must be adjacent to the target cell.

3. Choose Edit ➢ Fill ➢ Series to display the Series dialog box, shown in Figure 22.3. Excel automatically selects either Rows or Columns in the Series In area, depending on what range of cells you have selected.

4. Select the series category in the Type area. Your choices are:

   Linear: Choose this for series that increase linearly. For example, adding a number to each successive cell value is linear.

   Growth: Select this for series that increase geometrically or exponentially. For instance, multiplying each successive cell value by the preceding cell value is a growth increase in value.

   Date: Use this for dates to be incremented. Also select the date interval Excel should use in the Date Unit area. Your choices are Day, Weekday, Month, and Year.

   AutoFill: Use this for formulas or other series types. Determines what series type to use based on the cells selected. This option is the same as filling by dragging the fill handle.

5. For Linear or Growth series types, check the Trend box or fill in a Step Value and/or Stop Value, based on the following:

   Trend: Check this box if you selected a range of cells with progressive values. Excel will determine what the trend is and fill the blank cells accordingly.

PART

V

Number Crunching
with Excel

WARNING If you choose Growth and enable the Trend option, Excel calculates the trend and then adjusts the source cell values to smooth the trend, so the values you originally selected may also be changed.

Step Value: Enter the value you want Excel to use in incrementing the Linear or Growth series of values.

Stop Value: Optionally record the maximum (or minimum) value you want Excel to reach in the series.

6. Click OK to fill the cells, or click Cancel to dismiss the dialog box.

FIGURE 22.3

The Series dialog box

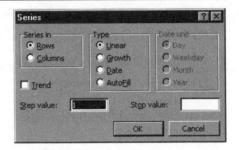

To quickly fill or copy numbers, formulas, series, and even formats, select the source cells and then drag using the *right* mouse button. Release the mouse button and choose the type of copy or fill operation you want from the shortcut menu.

Totaling Columns and Rows

 Excel has a one-step method for creating row and column totals using the *AutoSum* button on the Standard toolbar. Begin by selecting the cells that contain the numbers you want to total; you can include the empty cell that should contain the total in the selection. Then click the AutoSum button. Excel will add a formula to the empty cell (whether or not you selected it) and calculate the total.

 NOTE   If you do not select an empty cell to contain the total for the selection, Excel will place the total in the first blank cell in the row or column containing the selected range.

If you would like a blank row before the totals, simply select two extra cells. Excel always places the total in the last empty cell selected. If you want to create totals for multiple rows or columns and a grand total, select all the numbers before clicking AutoSum, as illustrated in Figure 22.4. In this example, Excel will create formulas in row 9 and column E for each selected row and column. In cell B9, the formula will be =sum(B5:B8), telling Excel to sum (total) the values in the range of cells B5 through B8.

FIGURE 22.4

Using AutoSum to total rows and columns

	A	B	C	D	E
1	Vacation Meisters Ticket Sales				
2	First Quarter				
3					
4	Destination	January	February	March	
5	Detroit	17	21	36	
6	Miami	119	101	89	
7	Phoenix	75	77	61	
8	Reno	93	87	90	
9					

PART

V

Number Crunching with Excel

Revising Formulas

There are two reasons you might want to revise a formula:

- You entered an incorrect formula.
- You've added new data and need to change the formula to reflect the new entries.

You can move to the cell that contains the formula and create a new formula, overwriting the original formula. Or you can edit the existing formula.

When you double-click a cell with a formula to open it for editing, Excel paints each cell address or range address in the formula a different color and places a border of the same color, called a Range Finder, around the cell or range. This makes it easy to see whether a formula refers to the correct cells.

Changing the Formula Reference   If you want to change the formula reference to another cell, you can use the keyboard or the Range Finder, as explained in the following steps.

To use the keyboard:

1. Select the cell reference to change in the formula.

2. Then, use one of these methods:

- Click the cell you want to replace it with.
- Type the replacement cell's address.

If the formula you're revising uses row labels instead of cell addresses, select the column or row label and type the correct label to replace the original entry.

To use the Range Finder:

1. Grab the border of the Range Finder and move it to the correct cell. (You're moving the Range Finder, so the mouse pointer should be an arrow.) If you need to include additional or fewer cells in a range, drag the selection handle at the lower-right corner of the Range Finder to extend or decrease the selection; the pointer will change to a fill pointer.

2. When you are finished editing the formula, press Enter or click the Enter button.

 WARNING If the cell reference you want to change is a range, the reference will include the first cell in the range, a colon, and the last cell in the range, like this: B10:B15. To revise this reference in a formula, select the entire reference, move into the worksheet, and drag to select the cells for the new formula, or move and then extend the Range Finder.

Unions and Intersections   Unions and intersections are two special types of ranges. A *union* is all the cells in two separate ranges. If you want, for example, to add a group of numbers in C2 through C8 and those in C20 through C28, the ranges would be (C2:C8,C20:C28). By using a comma to separate the two ranges, you're indicating that you want all cells from both ranges.

An *intersection* is just what it sounds like: a place where two ranges come together or overlap. For an intersection, use a blank space instead of a comma: The intersection (C2:C10 A10:J10) refers to just one cell, C10, where the two ranges overlap. Intersections are almost always used in natural language formulas, mentioned earlier in this chapter.

Formatting Numbers

Excel lets you present numbers in a variety of formats. *Formatting* is used to identify numbers as currency or percents and to make numbers easier to read by aligning decimal points in a column. You can format selected cells with three tools:

- the Formatting toolbar
- the Format Cells dialog box
- the shortcut menu

When you format a number, you change its appearance, not its numeric value. The default format for numbers, General, doesn't display zeros that have no effect on the value of the number. For example, if you enter 10.50, 10.5 has the same numeric value, so Excel doesn't display the extra or *trailing* zero.

Using the Formatting Toolbar

To format cells with the toolbar, select the cells and then click a button to apply one of the formats shown in Table 22.3. Click any cell to turn off the selection.

TABLE 22.3: NUMERIC FORMATTING FROM THE FORMATTING TOOLBAR

Button	Style	Effect
$	Currency	Displays and lines up dollar signs, comma separators, and decimal points: 75.3 as $75.30. Excel uses the currency symbol (for example, the $) selected in Regional Settings in the Windows control panel.
%	Percent	Displays number as a percentage: .45 as 45%.
,	Comma	Same as Currency, but without dollar signs: 12345.6 as 12,345.60.
+.0 .00	Increase Decimal	Displays one more place after the decimal: .45 as .450.
.00 +.0	Decrease Decimal	Displays one less place after the decimal: .450 as .45. If decreasing the number of digits eliminates a nonzero digit, the displayed number will be rounded. For example, if you format 9.75 with no digits following the decimal, Excel will display 10.

Formatting affects only the display of a cell, not the cell's contents. To view the contents of a cell, click the cell and look at the formula bar. The number entered in the cell appears in the formula bar exactly as entered regardless of the format that has been applied to the cell.

Using the Format Cells Dialog Box

Excel has more numeric formats, which you can select from the Format Cells dialog box. Select the cells you want to format. Then open the dialog box in any of three ways: either choose Format ➢ Cells from the menu bar, click Ctrl+1, or right-click to open the shortcut menu and choose Format Cells.

The Format Cells dialog box has separate pages for Number, Alignment, Font, Border, Patterns, and Protection. Figure 22.5 shows the Number page, which includes a list of format categories (see Table 22.4) and controls for the number of decimal places, thousands separator, and treatment of negative numbers. Choose a category, and then fill in the other options.

FIGURE 22.5

*The Format Cells
dialog box*

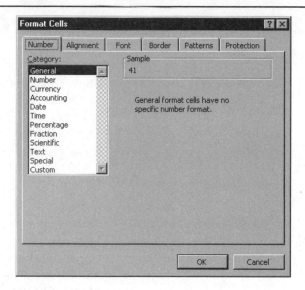

TABLE 22.4: NUMERIC FORMATTING IN THE FORMAT CELLS DIALOG BOX

Category	Description
General	The default format.
Number	Like General, but you can set decimal places, use a thousands separator, and include negative numbers.
Currency	Numbers are preceded with a dollar sign immediately before the first digit. Zero values are displayed.
Accounting	Dollar signs and decimal points line up. Zero values are shown as dashes.
Percentage	The same as the Percent toolbar button.
Scientific	Numbers are displayed in scientific notation: for example, 1.01E+03.

TIP   If you point to the button on the Formatting toolbar with the dollar symbol, the ScreenTip indicates it is the Currency Style button. However, when you apply this button's format, Excel applies the Accounting format, with dashes for zeros and the dollar signs lined up. Go figure!

The Format Cells dialog box includes six more specialized formatting categories:

Date formats: These are used for displaying dates in a variety of ways, even mixing text and numbers.

Time formats: This category includes options for mixed date and time displays, 24-hour clock times, and stopwatch results.

Fraction formats: The Fraction category allows you to choose from formats based on either the number of digits to display in the divisor (1, 2, or 3) or the fractional unit (halves, quarters, tenths, etc.).

 WARNING   Unlike the other formatting categories, Special and Text *change the underlying value of the number*. If you format a number with Special or Text, you will no longer be able to use the number in mathematical operations—unless you first reformat the cells with some other format.

Special formats: This category converts numbers to text and includes formats for kinds of numbers that aren't really mathematical values: Zip Code, Zip Code + 4, Phone Number, and Social Security Number. You wouldn't want to add or multiply any of these numbers—they are informational labels just like a last name.

Text formats: This option changes a number to text without adding other formatting. It is useful for numeric labels that may include leading zeros, such as employee ID numbers. All the regular numeric formats strip off leading zeros. Format the cell for text *before* entering the number.

 TIP   If you only have a few numbers that need to be treated as text, you can enter them manually. Simply type an apostrophe (') before the number, and Excel will treat the number as text.

Custom formats: This allows you to select from or make an addition to a list of formats for numbers, dates, and times (see Chapter 25).

Adjusting Worksheet Layout

As you add more data to your worksheet, it becomes increasingly important to understand how to modify its layout for optimum viewing of the cells you need to see. Reusing data within the same worksheet becomes a lot easier when you know how to insert, delete, move, copy, and drag not only cells and cell ranges, but even entire worksheets.

Adjusting Column Width and Row Height

By default, Excel columns are slightly more than eight characters wide. If the data in a worksheet is wider or much narrower than the column, you'll want to adjust the *column width* so it is wide enough to contain the data, but not so wide that data seems lost. You can adjust column width either manually, by dragging the column border, or by double-clicking to AutoFit the column width to the existing data. You can also select several columns and either adjust them manually to a uniform width or AutoFit each one to its contents. Here are the general steps:

1. Select the column(s) you want to adjust.

2. Position the mouse pointer at the right edge of one of the selected columns' headings. The pointer will change shape to a double-headed arrow.

3. Double-click to have Excel adjust the widths of the selected columns to fit their contents. Or, to adjust the columns manually to the same width, drag the right border of a column's heading to make the column wider or narrower.

 TIP You can change the default column width value by selecting Format ➤ Column ➤ Standard Width and typing a new value in the Standard Width dialog box.

 WARNING The second Very Important Excel Rule: *Never* leave blank columns in a worksheet as "spacers." Blank columns create problems with charts, sorting, and many other advanced features. Instead, adjust column widths to provide adequate space for and between entries.

Changing Row Height

You can adjust row height the same way you adjust column width. If you move the pointer to the lower edge of a row heading, the pointer will change to an adjustment tool. Double-click to adjust the row height to fit the font size; drag to manually increase or decrease size.

 TIP To copy a column width from one column to another, click a cell in the column with the desired width, and select Edit ➤ Copy or type Ctrl+C. Then select the destination column. Select Edit ➤ Paste Special and click the Column Widths option button in the Paste area of the Paste Special dialog box.

Inserting and Deleting Rows and Columns

To insert a column between (for example) the current columns A and B, begin by selecting column B. Right-click and select Insert from the shortcut menu or choose Insert ➤ Columns from the menu bar to insert a column. To insert multiple columns simultaneously, select more than one column before inserting. For example, you can insert three columns by first selecting B, C, and D. You can insert rows in the same fashion. When you insert or delete rows and columns, Excel automatically moves the surrounding rows and columns to fill the gap.

Deleting rows and columns is much like inserting. Begin by selecting one or more rows or columns. To clear the contents but leave the emptied row in place, press the Delete key on your keyboard. To delete the contents *and* remove the row or column, choose Edit ➤ Delete from the menu bar. When you delete a row or column, all information is deleted, including cells that may not be in the part of the worksheet you can see.

 TIP To quickly insert or delete a single row or column, select the row or column heading by right-clicking and selecting Insert or Delete from the shortcut menu.

Inserting and Deleting Cells

Sometimes you'll need to add or delete cells in part of a worksheet without inserting or deleting entire rows or columns. For example, Figure 22.6 shows a section of a

PART

V

Number Crunching with Excel

worksheet for a network switchover project. Columns A–D show information about specific tasks in the project, and column E lists software components needed for the project as a whole. Suppose we need to add more tasks for March 10. Adding entire new rows there would introduce blanks in column E, and we'd have to tediously move text back into place. Instead, we should insert new cells in columns A–D only.

FIGURE 22.6

To add new tasks for an existing date in this worksheet, we need to insert cells rather than entire rows.

	A	B	C	D	E
1	Cyclops Software Division				
2	Windows NT Network Conversion Project				
3					
4	Date	Task	Days	Resource	Project Components
5	10-Mar	Install NT Server 1	1.0	Ken	Windows NT Server
6	10-Mar	Install NT Server 2	1.0	Jody	Windows NT Client - 25
7	11-Mar	Switch sales printers	0.5	Ken	Innoculan Server
8	11-Mar	Switch service printers	0.5	Ken	Carbon Copy
9	12-Mar	Backup CS Sales files	0.3	Jody	
10	12-Mar	Backup CS Service files	0.5	Jody	

Follow these steps to insert cells:

1. Select the range where new cells should be inserted, right-click, and choose Insert. When you insert or delete cells, Excel needs more instruction to know how to move the surrounding cells, so the Insert or Delete dialog box opens:

2. If you choose Shift Cells Down, the cells in the selection and all cells below them in the same columns are shifted. If you choose Shift Cells Right, cells in the same row(s) are moved to the right. Notice that you can also use this dialog box to insert rows or columns.

3. Click OK to apply the selected action.

Moving and Copying Cell Contents

Basic moving and copying techniques in Office 2000 were discussed in Chapter 2; however, there are a few differences you'll notice when copying and moving cells and cell ranges in Excel:

- If you paste cells on top of existing data, the existing data will be overwritten, so make sure that there are enough blank cells to accommodate the selection you want to paste. For example, if you want to move the contents of column E to the right of column A without overwriting column B, begin by inserting a blank column between A and B.

 NOTE If you do accidentally paste from a larger to a smaller range of cells, Excel warns you before completing the operation, giving you a chance to confirm the order or perform an alternate task.

- *Cut-and-paste* and *copy-and-paste* now operate the same in Excel as in other Office applications. Thanks to the Office Clipboard, you can copy now, do a few other things, and then paste later. Enhanced in Office 2000, the Clipboard now saves the contents of up to 12 copy operations from any Office application.
- When you cut a cell in Excel, it is copied to the Clipboard but is not removed from the worksheet until you paste it in its new location by pressing Enter or clicking the Paste button.
- When you get ready to paste, just click the first cell, row, or column where you want pasted cells, rows, or columns to appear. If you select more than one cell to paste into, the selected range must be exactly the same size as the range you want to paste or an error will occur.
- When you copy a selection, you can paste it more than once. When you press Enter at the end of a paste operation, Excel empties the Clipboard, so use the Paste button to paste all but the last copy. Press Enter to place the final pasted copy.

The basic steps for using cut, copy, and paste are quite simple:

1. If there is data below or to the right of the paste area, begin by inserting enough blank cells, rows, or columns for the data you want to move or copy.
2. Select the data you want to move or copy. To move, click the Cut button, choose Edit ➤ Cut, press Ctrl+X, or select Cut from the shortcut menu. To copy, click

the Copy button, choose Edit ➤ Copy, press Ctrl+C, or select Copy from the shortcut menu.

3. Select the first cell, row, or column where you want to place the moved or copied data.

4. Press Enter to move or copy the data to its new location.

Data Transfers between Worksheets

To move or copy data from one worksheet to another, cut or copy the selection and then click the sheet tab for the sheet that you want to paste into. Click in the appropriate cell and press Enter to paste.

Data Transfers between Workbooks

To move or copy data from one workbook to another, make sure both workbooks are open. Select and cut or copy the data, choose Window from the menu bar, and pick the destination workbook from the list of open workbooks. Click in the destination cell and press Enter.

TIP To paste previously copied contents from the Office Clipboard, select View ➤ Toolbars ➤ Clipboard. The Clipboard appears, showing all of its copied contents. Copied material from different applications is denoted with the appropriate icon. Point to any pages with an Excel icon. A ScreenTip showing the content of that Clipboard page will appear. When you find the correct page, click it and its contents will be pasted into the spreadsheet.

Using Drag-and-Drop

When you're moving or copying cells between worksheets or workbooks, it's easiest to cut or copy and paste. Another method, called *drag-and-drop,* works well when you can see the cells to be copied and their destination on one screen. Following are the steps to use this approach.

1. Select the cells and move the mouse so that it points to any part of the cell pointer except the fill handle (the mouse pointer will change to an arrow).

2. Hold down the right mouse button and drag the cells to their new location.

3. Release the mouse button. A shortcut menu opens so you can select whether you want to move or copy the cells.

4. Choose the desired option from the menu.

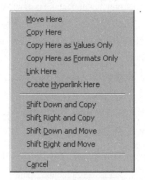

You can also move cells by dragging with the left mouse button. To copy with the left mouse button, hold the Ctrl key down, drag and drop the selected cells, and then release the Ctrl key.

Aligning Text

By default, Excel left-aligns text and right-aligns numbers. You can use the buttons on the Formatting toolbar to override the defaults and align text and numbers at the left, center, or right within cells:

Left		
	Center	
		Right

The default settings reflect some standard rules for aligning text and numbers:

- Columns of text should be left-aligned because we're used to reading left-aligned text.
- Columns of numbers should be kept in the default (right) alignment and formatted so that the decimal points align.
- Column labels should appear over the contents of the column. If the column is filled with numbers, the heading should be right-aligned or centered. Labels for text columns should be left-aligned or centered.

Excel has a fourth alignment called Merge and Center, which *merges* selected cells into one cell and centers the contents of the top-left selected cell across the new merged cell. Worksheet titles are often merged and centered.

PART
V

Number Crunching
with Excel

To merge and center a title, select the cell containing the title and the cells in the same row for all the used columns in the worksheet, and then click the Merge And Center button. Excel only centers the text in the top-left cell of the selection, so if your worksheet's title is in more than one row, you'll need to merge and center each title row separately.

There are more alignment options that aren't accessible from the toolbar but are set in the Alignment page of the Format Cells dialog box (choose Format ➤ Format Cells or right-click and choose Format Cells from the shortcut menu). Some of the more interesting alignments, including text rotation, are illustrated in Figure 22.7. The Alignment page of the Format Cells dialog box is shown in Figure 22.8.

FIGURE 22.7

Text alignments

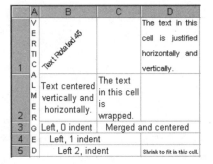

FIGURE 22.8

The Alignment page of the Format Cells dialog box

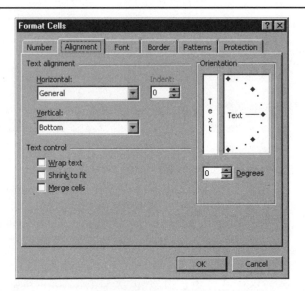

Rotating Text

Use the rotation tools to orient text vertically or to rotate text to a specific orientation.

These steps will guide you through the process:

1. Select the cell containing the words to be rotated, and then select Format ➤ Cells and click the Alignment tab in the Format Cells dialog box. Choose one of the following options:

   • To orient text vertically, click the box with the vertical word Text in it.

   • To rotate text to another orientation, either use the Degrees spin box or drag the Text indicator in the rotation tool.

2. Click Ok to apply the rotation.

Rotating text lets you create a splashy column or row label. Vertically orient and merge text (see Figure 22.7) to label a group of row labels.

Merge, Shrink to Fit, and Wrap Text

If you want a vertical title to cross several rows (such as the label *Vertical Merged* in column A of Figure 22.7), use these steps:

1. Select the title and several additional cells below the title.

2. Select Format Cells and check one or all of the following options in the Format Cells dialog box:

   • Click the Merge Cells check box to merge the cells.

   • Shrink to Fit reduces the size of the type within selected cells so the contents fit.

   • Wrap Text wraps the contents of a cell if it would exceed the cell's boundaries.

3. Click OK to apply these changes.

Both Shrink to Fit and Wrap Text use the current column widths. If you narrow or widen a column after you shrink or wrap a label, you'll need to reshrink or rewrap.

Borders and Color

Effective use of fonts, discussed in Chapter 2, can help make worksheets easier to understand. Borders and color provide further ways to highlight information in a worksheet. A *border* is a line drawn around a cell or group of cells. *Fill color* is used to highlight the background of part of a worksheet; *font color* is applied to text.

Even if you don't have access to a color printer, you might still want to use color in worksheets that you or other users use frequently. Color distinguishes between similar-looking worksheets; for example, the Sales Department's budget could have a blue title, and Production's title could be burgundy.

The Border, Fill Color, and Font Color buttons are found on the Formatting tool-bar. All three buttons are combination buttons that include a menu opened by click-ing the drop-down arrow attached to the button:

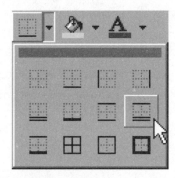

Borders can completely surround a group of cells, surround each cell individually, provide an underline, or double-underline the selected range. Selecting a border from the menu assigns it to the button and applies it to the selected cells.

After you have assigned a border to the button, the next time you click the Border button, the same border style will be applied to your currently active cell or range of cells.

 TIP The only way to change the color of the border is to select Format ➤ Cells and click the Border tab. Choose a border color from the Color drop-down list.

The Fill Color and Font Color buttons also have attached menus and are used the same way.

Use these steps to add colors or borders to your work:

1. To apply a Font Color or Fill Color, select the cells to be formatted. Click the color button's drop-down arrow and select a color from the menu.

2. To add a border, select the cells to be formatted. Click the Border button's drop-down arrow and select a border from the menu.

Opening Border, Color, and Font Menus

If you have a lot of borders, colors, or font colors to apply, you can open any or all of the menus as separate toolbars that float on your worksheet:

1. Open the menu and point to the dark gray bar at the top of the menu. The bar will turn the same color as your program title bar.

2. Drag the menu into the worksheet and release the mouse button.

3. When finished with the menu, close it with its Close button.

Previewing and Printing

Print Preview, Page Setup, Page Break Preview, and Print are interrelated. Print Preview, Print, and Page Setup function much as they do in the other Office 2000 applications. (See Chapter 2 for more information on these features.) *Page Break Preview* displays the current page breaks and allows you to adjust them.

Adjusting Margins in Print Preview

The Print Preview Margins button displays the current margin settings. Point to any of the margin lines, and the pointer will change to an adjustment tool, as shown in Figure 22.9. Press the mouse button, and the status bar will indicate the name and current setting for the margin. Drag a margin to adjust it.

FIGURE 22.9

*Adjusting margins in
Print Preview*

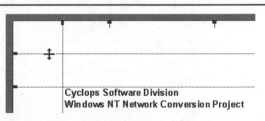

Cyclops Software Division
Windows NT Network Conversion Project

Excel's default margins are 0.75" on each side and 1" on the top and bottom, with a 0.5" header and footer margin. Headers and footers print in 0.5" of space between the header/footer margin and the regular margin. The top and bottom margins define the limits of the printed worksheet, and the header and footer margins define the areas where the header and footer will print. If you use headers and footers, the top and bottom margins need to be inside the header and footer margins, or part of the worksheet will print on top of the header and footer.

Changing Page Setup

To change page setup, choose File ➤ Page Setup from the menu bar to open the Page Setup dialog box. (If you're already in Print Preview, click the Setup button; from Page Break Preview, right-click and choose Page Setup from the shortcut menu.) The Page Setup dialog box splits page layout into four tabbed pages that contain Page, Header/ Footer, Margins, and Sheet settings.

Page Settings

Use the Page options of the Page Setup dialog box, shown in Figure 22.10, to set orientation, scaling, paper size, and print quality:

1. Open the Page Setup dialog box by choosing File ➤ Page Setup or by clicking the Setup button in the Print Preview window. Click the Page tab.

2. Change settings for Orientation, Scaling, Paper Size, Print Quality, or First Page Number.

3. Click OK to apply the settings.

FIGURE 22.10

Page settings in Page Setup dialog box

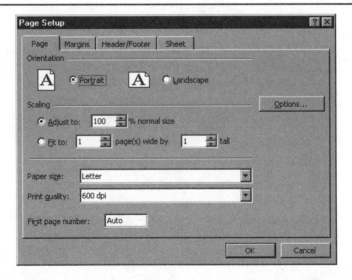

Orientation is the direction of print in relation to the paper it is printed on. Portrait, the default setting, places the short edge of the paper at the top and bottom. If your worksheet is wider than it is long, consider using Landscape orientation.

Scaling is used to reduce or enlarge the print. If you simply need to make the print larger, use the Adjust To control and choose a size greater than 100%. The Fit To control instructs Excel to reduce a worksheet that exceeds a specific number of pages so it will fit.

Paper Size lets you choose a paper size other than the default (for example, legal paper).

Print Quality is measured in dpi: dots per inch. Higher dpi means clearer print quality, but slower printing.

First Page Number is used to start printing from a page number other than 1.

 TIP The Options button appears on every page of the Page Setup dialog box. The button opens the Windows property sheet (or the manufacturer's property sheet) for the printer that's currently selected.

Headers and Footers

A header appears at the top of each page of a document. Footers are printed at the bottom of the page. The default setting is no header or footer. If you want a header or footer, choose or create it in the Header/Footer page in the Page Setup dialog box, shown in Figure 22.11.

FIGURE 22.11

*Setting up a page
header and footer*

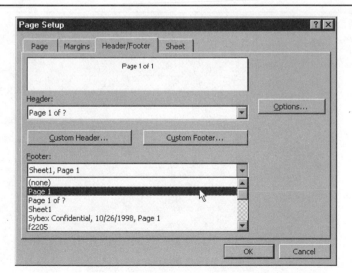

The currently selected header and footer are displayed in the two preview panes. To choose a different predesigned header, click the Header drop-down list. Choose a footer the same way, using the Footer drop-down control. When you select a different header (or footer), the preview pane will reflect the change.

 TIP To create a new header or footer, click the Custom Header or Custom Footer button.

Add or change headers and footers by the following these steps:

1. Choose File ➤ Page Setup from the menu bar, or click the Setup button in Print Preview.

2. In the Page Setup dialog box, select the Header/Footer tab.

3. Click the Header drop-down list and select a header, or click Custom Header to create a header. Click the Footer drop-down list and select a footer, or click Custom Footer to create a footer.

4. Press Enter (or click OK) to return to the Page Setup dialog box.

Setting Margins in the Page Setup Dialog Box

The preview in the Margins page of the Page Setup dialog box (see Figure 22.12) displays the margins as dotted lines. You can change the margins here using the spin arrows for each margin.

FIGURE 22.12

The Margins page of the Page Setup dialog box

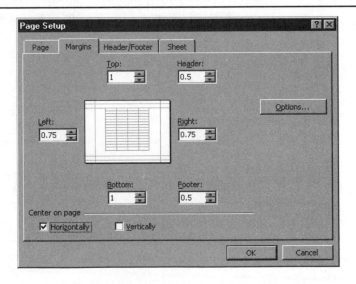

Use the Center On Page controls to center the printed worksheet horizontally between the side margins or vertically between the top and bottom margins. As you change settings on the Margins page, the Preview will change to reflect the new margin settings.

Here are the steps for using the Margins tab to adjust page setup factors:

1. In the Page Setup dialog box, select the Margins tab.

2. Using the spin arrows, set the top, bottom, left, and right margins.

3. If you are using a header or footer, use the Header and Footer spin boxes to set the distance for the header and footer margins.

4. Use the Center On Page check boxes to center the printed worksheet.

5. Click the OK button to apply the changes.

Changing Sheet Settings

The Sheet page (see Figure 22.13) contains settings that relate to the features that will appear in the printed copy, including the print area, repeating rows and columns, and gridlines.

FIGURE 22.13

Sheet settings

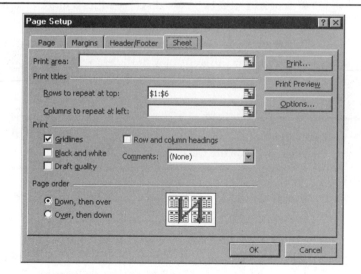

NOTE The Print Area, Rows To Repeat, and Columns To Repeat controls are only enabled when you open the Page Setup dialog box from the menu (File ➤ Page Setup or View ➤ Header and Footer). If you go to Page Setup from Print Preview or the Print dialog box, you won't be able to change these three settings.

Print Area: By default, Excel prints from the home cell (A1) to the last occupied cell in a worksheet. To specify a different range, type the range in the Print Area control, or select the area with the mouse. If the Print Area includes noncontiguous cells, each contiguous range will print on a separate page.

 TIP The easiest way to set the Print Area is from the menu bar. Select the cells to be printed and choose File ➤ Print Area ➤ Set Print Area from the menu bar. When you want to print the entire worksheet again, choose File ➤ Print Area ➤ Clear Print Area.

Print Titles: Prints column and row labels on each page of the printout. Specify these rows or columns in the Rows To Repeat At Top and Columns To Repeat At Left text boxes. (Excel requires a *range* with a colon for these entries, even if it's only one row or column.)

Print or Hide Gridlines: Determines whether gridlines will be printed but does not affect their display in the worksheet. Turning off the print gridlines gives your worksheet a cleaner appearance and can make it easier to read.

 TIP To turn off screen gridlines, choose Tools ➤ Options and clear the check mark in the Gridlines option on the View page of the Options dialog box.

Draft Quality: Prints the worksheet without gridlines or graphics.

Black and White: If you used colors in the worksheet but won't be printing on a color printer, click this control to speed up the print process.

Row and Column Headings: The row numbers and column letters will be included in the printout. This is a useful feature when you are editing or trying to locate an error in a worksheet.

Page Order: Establishes the order in which multipage worksheets are printed.

If you find it difficult to select cells with the Page Setup dialog box in the way, click the Collapse Dialog button to minimize the dialog box while you select cells. This button is located on the Sheet tab in the Page Setup dialog box to the right of the Print Area, Rows To Repeat At Top, and Columns To Repeat At Left text boxes.

Click the Expand Dialog button to return to the Print Setup dialog box. This button is located to the right of the same text boxes mentioned above, when they appear as solo floating text boxes. Take these steps to change sheet settings:

1. Choose File ➤ Page Setup to open the Page Setup dialog box. Click the Sheet page tab.

2. Specify ranges for a Print Area and rows and columns to be repeated as titles on each printed page by entering them from the keyboard or by using the mouse.

3. Enter option settings in the Print and Page Order sections.

4. Click OK.

 TIP You can set Page Setup options for multiple worksheets by grouping (selecting) the worksheets before opening the Page Setup dialog box. Remember to ungroup the worksheets after you've changed the Page Setup. Worksheet grouping is covered in Chapter 23.

Setting Print Options

Excel supplies some flexibility for manipulating page breaks and print areas in order to accomplish the often-difficult task of printing unwieldy spreadsheets on standard-size paper. The Page Break Preview feature is a good tool for managing the printable areas of a spreadsheet, while the Print dialog box delivers complete control over which pages will print.

Page Break Preview

Page Break Preview is a view of the worksheet window that shows you what will be printed and the order in which the pages will be printed. To turn on Page Break Preview, click the Page Break Preview button in Print Preview, or choose View ➤ Page Break Preview from the menu bar. In Page Break Preview, areas that will be printed are white; cells that won't be printed are gray. Each printed page is numbered. You can quickly change the range to be printed by dragging the edge of the page break with your mouse to include or exclude cells.

To view and adjust page breaks, follow these steps:

1. From the Print Preview window, click the Page Break Preview button; or choose View ➤ Page Break Preview from the worksheet window.

2. Using the mouse, drag the page break to extend or limit the range of cells to be printed.

3. Choose View ➤ Normal View to close Page Break Preview.

Inserting Manual Page Breaks   If a worksheet prints on multiple pages, you can adjust the breaks by dragging the page break. To add a manual page break, select the first column or row you want to appear in the page after the break. Right-click and choose Insert Page Break from the shortcut menu:

> Insert Page Break
>
> Reset All Page Breaks
>
> Set Print Area
>
> Reset Print Area
>
> Page Setup...

Removing Manual Page Breaks   To remove a manual page break, right-click in the row below the horizontal page break or in the column to the right of the vertical page break, and choose Remove Page Break from the shortcut menu. To remove all manual page breaks, right-click any cell and choose Reset All Page Breaks from the shortcut menu. In Page Break Preview, you can also remove a page break by dragging it outside the print area. To return to Normal view, choose View ➤ Normal View from the menu bar. Note that you can also go directly from the worksheet to Page Break Preview from the View menu.

Changing Print Settings

If you click the Print button on the Standard toolbar, Excel prints one copy of the selected worksheet(s) using the default print settings, including any settings you have changed in the Print Setup dialog box. To adjust print settings, choose File ➤ Print to open the Print dialog box, shown in Figure 22.14.

FIGURE 22.14

The Print dialog box

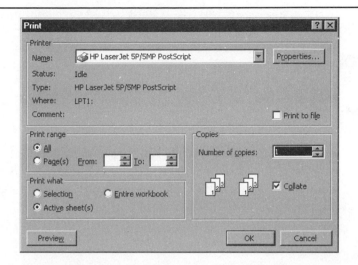

Use the Print Range controls to print some, but not all, of the pages of a multiple-page print job. You cannot specify noncontiguous pages in Excel, so if you want to print pages 1–4 and 6–8, you either have to print twice or choose the cells on those pages and specify them as your print area.

In the Print What control, specify which part of the worksheet or workbook you want to print. The Selection option provides another way to override the default print area: select the cells you want to print, and then print the selection. Choose Workbook to print all used worksheets in the active workbook. To print some but not all worksheets in a workbook, select the sheets before opening the Print dialog box, and then choose Active Sheets.

Checking Worksheet Spelling

Misspelled words automatically cast doubt on the accuracy of an entire worksheet. Excel includes two tools to help you correct spelling errors. *AutoCorrect* automatically fixes common typos and *Spelling* checks all the text in a worksheet to ensure that it is error-free. If you are not in the home cell when you begin the spelling check, Excel will check from the cell pointer to the end of the worksheet, and then ask if it should return to the top of the worksheet and finish checking. When Spelling is complete, Excel will notify you that it has finished checking the entire sheet.

Spelling is a shared feature of all the Office 2000 products, so words you add to the dictionary or to AutoCorrect are added to the common custom dictionary you use with Word, PowerPoint, and Access. For more information on AutoCorrect and Spelling, see Chapter 2.

What's Next

In the next chapter, you'll learn how to add more complexity to your worksheets, yet at the same time simplify your work with them. Excel's functions are used in formulas that involve more complex calculations. Names simplify your work by letting you use aliases to refer to cells and groups of cells.

CHAPTER 23

Managing Data with Worksheets, References, and Functions

Excel provides numerous tools to help you manage complex projects with finesse. Excel's flexible worksheet options allow you to easily manipulate multiple worksheets related to the same project. The functions and references included with Excel supply ready-made solutions for computing all types of standard and not-so-typical values. Ranges can also be very helpful in keeping track of large quantities of numerical data.

Naming a Worksheet

If you've moved to Excel from another spreadsheet program, you may not have realized what a powerful organizational tool an Excel workbook is. Some spreadsheet programs save each worksheet independently as a separate file, requiring you to open five or six files when you work on a large project. With Excel, you can cluster worksheets for similar projects in a single workbook, which lets you open the entire project in one step.

You can move through the various worksheets (Sheet1, Sheet2, and so on) associated with the project as easily as you flip pages in this book. To change a worksheet's name to something more descriptive, double-click the sheet tab, type a new name of up to 32 characters, and press Enter.

 TIP If you do not see any sheet tabs at the bottom of your Excel application window, they may have been turned off. To turn them on, select Tools ➢ Options and click the View tab. Check the Sheet Tabs box in the Window Options area.

Selecting Worksheets

To select one worksheet, click its sheet tab. To select more than one worksheet, hold the Ctrl key while selecting each worksheet or click the first, hold Shift, and click the last worksheet you wish to select. To select all worksheets in a workbook, right-click any tab and choose Select All Sheets from the shortcut menu.

Using Grouped Worksheets

When more than one worksheet is selected, the worksheets are *grouped*. Data entered into one sheet is entered into all sheets in the group, making it easy to enter the same title in cell A1 of five sheets in the same workbook.

WARNING When using grouped worksheets, you need to remember to ungroup worksheets immediately when you are finished entering, moving, or copying common data. Otherwise, entries you make on one worksheet will be made on all worksheets, overwriting the existing entries on the other sheets in the group.

Ungrouping Worksheets

To ungroup worksheets, right-click any grouped worksheet and choose Ungroup Sheets from the shortcut menu, or click any worksheet in the workbook that is not included in the group.

 TIP To ungroup one or more sheets from the group while maintaining the rest of the sheets as grouped, Shift+click the tabs of the sheets to be ungrouped.

 MASTERING THE OPPORTUNITIES

Creating Identical Worksheets

It's not unusual to need a number of worksheets with common formatting and data entry. For example, if you work with quarterly budgets, you might want to create a workbook with sheets that contain the same column headings, row headings, and formulas. With Excel, there are two ways to do this: by grouping the sheets and then entering the data and formulas common to all four sheets, or by creating one sheet and then copying it three times. Generally, it's easier to create and copy the worksheets, as you'll see in the next section.

Grouping is most useful when the sheets already exist and you need to enter the same information in the same cell on each sheet. Rather than enter a number in cell B16 on all four sheets, group them and enter the value once. Remember to ungroup sheets as soon as you are finished entering data that should appear on all grouped sheets.

PART

V

Number Crunching
with Excel

Copying and Moving Worksheets

You can copy or move one or more selected worksheets within and between workbooks. To move worksheets within the same workbook, drag the sheet's tab to the new location (marked by a small triangle just above the tab) and drop it:

To copy a worksheet in the same workbook, hold the Ctrl key while dragging. The copy will have the same name as the original sheet, followed by the copy number:

You can copy or move a worksheet to a new or existing workbook:

1. To move or copy a worksheet to an existing workbook, open the workbook first. (You can switch between open workbooks by using the Window menu.)

2. Select the worksheet you want to copy, and then either choose Edit ➤ Move Or Copy Sheet from the menu bar or right-click the sheet tab and choose Move Or Copy from the shortcut menu to open the Move or Copy dialog box, shown in Figure 23.1.

FIGURE 23.1

The Move Or Copy dialog box

3. In the To Book drop-down list, select the name of the open workbook where you want to move or copy the sheet, or choose New Book.

4. To copy the worksheet, turn on the Create A Copy option at the bottom of the dialog box before clicking OK. You can use this dialog box to move and copy

worksheets within the same workbook if you prefer the dialog box to the drag-and-drop method.

Inserting and Deleting Worksheets

To insert a new worksheet, choose Insert ➤ Worksheet from the menu bar. You can also right-click a sheet tab and choose Insert from the shortcut menu.

If you want a regular blank worksheet, it's faster to use the menu bar. When you insert a sheet from the shortcut menu, the Insert dialog box (which is similar to the New dialog box) opens and prompts you to select the type of file to open: a worksheet, chart, macro, dialog box, or one of the many templates available.

 TIP If you select an uninstalled template in the Insert dialog box, you'll be prompted to insert your Microsoft Office 2000 CD so the template can be installed.

To delete one or more selected sheets, choose Edit ➤ Delete Sheet from the menu bar, or right-click the sheet(s) and choose Delete from the shortcut menu. When you delete a worksheet, a dialog box will open, asking you to confirm the deletion, which cannot be undone.

 TIP Excel 2000 includes three worksheets in every new workbook. If you frequently find yourself adding sheets to workbooks, increase the default number of sheets in a new book. Select Tools ➤ Options from the menu bar, and change the Sheets In New Workbook setting on the General page of the Options dialog box.

Naming Ranges

You can apply a *name* to refer to a cell or a range of cells, rather than using cell addresses as references. Names provide multiple benefits:

- Names are more descriptive and easier to remember than cell addresses.
- When a cell moves, the name moves with it.
- You can use a name in place of a cell or range address in a formula or function argument, just like a row or column label.

- When you copy a formula that uses a name, the effect is the same as using an absolute cell reference.

The rules for using range names include the following requirements:

- Names can be up to 255 characters long and can include letters, numbers, underscores, or periods.
- The name must begin with either a letter or the underscore character.
- You cannot use spaces, commas, exclamation points, or other special characters.
- Names cannot be valid cell addresses: F1998 cannot be used as a name.
- Names are not case-sensitive: INTEREST RATE and Interest Rate are the same name.
- The traditional practice is to exclude spaces and to mix uppercase and lowercase letters, beginning each word within the name with an uppercase letter: InterestRate.
- A name can't be repeated within a workbook, so you can't use the same name on two different sheets in the same workbook.

There are three ways to name a range:

- Use the Name box in the formula bar.
- Use the Define Name dialog box.
- Create a name from a row or column of text.

All three methods are explained in the next sections.

Naming a Range Using the Name Box

Using the Name box at the left end of the formula bar is the easiest way to name ranges:

1. Select the range to be named; it can include noncontiguous cells.
2. Click in the Name box.
3. Type a valid name for the range and press Enter.

Using the Define Name Dialog Box

You can name ranges and change or delete existing range names using the Define Name dialog box, shown in Figure 23.2. The dialog box displays a list of the names already defined for the workbook. Here are the steps for defining, changing, and deleting range names:

1. To define a name, select the range of cells you want to name.
2. Choose Insert ➢ Name ➢ Define from the menu bar.

3. In the Names In Workbook text box, type a valid range name and click Add.

4. To change a name, select the name from the Names In Workbook list. Select the name in the Names In Workbook text box; overtype the old name with the new name and click Add.

5. To delete a name, select the name from the Names In Workbook list and click the Delete button.

6. When you are finished, click OK.

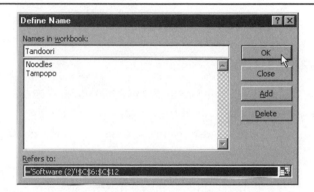

FIGURE 23.2

In the Define Name dialog box, you can define, delete, or edit a range name.

MASTERING THE OPPORTUNITIES

Creating External and 3-D References

After you click Define in step 2, you can click in the Refers To text box and select cells in any open workbook. For example, you may have one budget workbook that includes sales totals for the third quarter. Rather than re-create these figures in your annual sales workbook, you can create names (Total3rdSales, Total3rdExpenses) that refer to them.

When you create a name in one workbook that refers to cells in another workbook, it's called an *external reference.* There is a potential downside—if the other workbook is deleted, moved, or renamed, Excel won't be able to find the named range.

A *3-D reference* refers to the same cell in more than one worksheet in a book. For example, suppose that in a budget workbook the total sales figure is always in cell D87. You can create a name that refers to all the monthly worksheets in the workbook. Click in the Refers To text box, select all three worksheets, and then select cell D87 on any of the selected sheets. As you'll see in Chapter 27, 3-D range names are particularly useful in formulas.

Creating Names from a Row or Column

You can define a group of labels in a row or a column at one time using the Create Names dialog box, shown in Figure 23.3.

1. Select the range to be named. Include the cells you want to use as names as either the top or bottom row, or the first or last column selected.

2. Choose Insert ➤ Name ➤ Create from the menu bar to open the Create Name dialog box.

3. In the Create Names In area, select the row (Top or Bottom) and/or column (Left or Right) that contains the labels you want to use to name the selected range.

4. Click OK to apply the names and close the dialog box.

 TIP Excel automatically allows you to use labels in the row immediately above and the column to the left of your data in formulas if you've enabled labels in formulas (Tools ➤ Options ➤ Calculation).

How Excel Creates Range Names From Text

Excel edits text as needed to make valid names. Excel uses these standards to generate names from labels or other text:

- If the label for a column or row contains spaces, Excel will replace the space with an underscore: Interest_Rate.

- If the cell contents begin with a number, like 8-Mar or 4 bags, Excel will add an underscore to the beginning of the name: _8-Mar or _4_bags.

- Excel will not create a name from a cell that contains *only* a number (like 1998, 78, or 1254.50). Excel will let you go through the motions, but it won't create the names.

Using Names as References

Once you've defined a range, you can enter it anywhere a regular cell reference is valid. For example, you can type in the name of a range as an argument for a function: =SUM(Totals). Names also serve a valuable navigation function, particularly in large workbooks and worksheets. To select and display a named range anywhere in the workbook, click the down arrow in the Name box and select the name from the list.

Both names and column and row labels can be used to refer to specific cells at the intersection of a row and a column. In the Vacation Meisters Ticket Sales worksheet shown in Figure 23.4, Detroit (the row label) refers to row 6 and Total (the column label) refers to column E. The formula =Detroit Total will return the value (74) at the intersection of row 6 and column E.

FIGURE 23.4

The formula in this worksheet uses row and column labels to return the value at the intersection of row 6 (Detroit) and column E (Total).

	A	B	C	D	E	F	G
1	Vacation Meisters Ticket Sales						
2	First Quarter						
3							
4	Destination	January	February	March	Total	Average	% TOTAL
5							
6	Detroit	17	21	36	74	25	9%
7	Miami	119	101	89	309	10	143%
8	Phoenix	75	77	61	213	71	288%
9	Reno	93	87	90	270	90	87%
10							
11	Total for Month	304	286	276	866		
12	Average for Month	76	72	69	217	=Detroit Total	
13	Minimun for Month	17	21	36	74		
14	Maximum for Month	119	101	90	309		
15							

Using Functions and References

In Chapter 22 you used the SUM function (by clicking the AutoSum button) to total numbers. Excel includes hundreds of other functions that you can use to calculate results used in statistics, finance, engineering, math, and other fields.

Functions are structured programs that calculate a specific result: a total, an average, the amount of a monthly loan payment, or the geometric mean of a group of numbers. Each function has a specific order or *syntax* that must be used for the function to work properly.

Functions are formulas, so all functions begin with the equal sign (=). After that is the *function name*, followed by one or more *arguments* separated by commas and enclosed in parentheses:

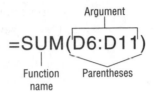

Excel's functions are grouped into 10 categories, as indicated in Table 23.1.

TABLE 23.1: EXCEL FUNCTIONS	
Category	**Examples**
Financial	Calculates interest rates, loan payments, depreciation amounts, etc.
Date & Time	Returns the current hour, day of week or year, time, or date.
Math & Trig	Calculates absolute values, cosines, logarithms, etc.
Statistical	Includes common functions used for totals, averages, and high and low numbers in a range; advanced functions for t-tests, Chi tests, deviation.
Lookup & Reference	Searches for and returns values from a range; creates hyperlinks to network or Internet documents.
Database	Calculates values in an Excel database table.
Text	Converts text to upper or lower case, trims characters from the right or left end of a text string, concatenates text strings.
Logical	Evaluates an expression and returns a value of TRUE or FALSE, used to trigger other actions or formatting.
Information	Returns information from Excel or Windows about the current status of a cell, object, or the environment.
Engineering	Included with Office, but must be installed separately from the Analysis Toolpack.

You don't have to learn all the functions—but you should know the common functions thoroughly and know enough about other functions so that you can find them as you need them. SUM is the only individual function included on the Standard toolbar. You can access all the functions (including SUM) using the Formula Palette.

Entering Functions

Before entering a function, make sure the cell where you want the results to be displayed is activated. Click the = in the formula bar to open the Formula Palette. The Name box (to the left of the formula bar) will change to a Function box, displaying the name of the last function that was used (SUM), as shown in Figure 23.5.

FIGURE 23.5

*The Formula Palette
and Function box*

	File Edit View Insert Format Tools Data Window Help				
IF	X ✓ = =				
Formula result =			OK	Cancel	
5					
6	Detroit	17	21	36	74	25
7	Miami	119	101	89	309	10
8	Phoenix	75	77	61	213	71
9	Reno	93	87	90	270	90
10						
11	Total for Month	304	286	276	866	
12	Average for Month	76	72	69	217	74
13	Minimun for Month	17	21	36	74	
14	Maximum for Month	119	101	90	309	
15						
16						
17			=			

Click the Function box drop-down arrow to open the list of recently used functions:

If the function you want is on the list, select it, and Excel will move the function to the formula bar and the Formula Palette. The Formula Palette will expand to include a description of the function and one or more text boxes for the function's arguments, as shown in Figure 23.6. For common functions that use a single range of cells as an argument, Excel will "guess" which numbers you might want to sum or average and place the range in the argument text box. Required arguments are bold, like Number 1 in Figure 23.6. These text boxes must be filled in to successfully use the function.

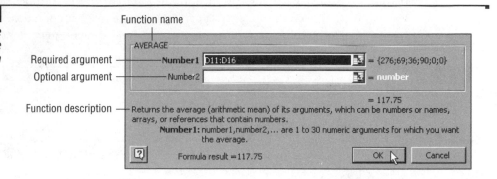

In Figure 23.6, you can't tell whether the range in the Number 1 text box is correct, because the Formula Palette covers the cells. Click the Collapse Dialog button to shrink the Formula Palette.

Confirm that the correct cells are selected, or use the mouse to select the correct cells, before expanding the palette with the Expand Dialog button. After you have selected all the required arguments, click OK to finish the entry and close the Formula Palette.

As with any formula, the results of the function are displayed in the active cell. The function itself is displayed in the formula bar when the cell is active.

If the function you want is not listed in the Function box, choose More Functions at the bottom of the list to open the Paste Function dialog box, shown in Figure 23.7.

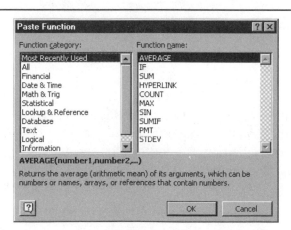

If you know you want a rarely used function, you can open this dialog box directly by clicking the More Buttons drop-down button on the Standard toolbar and then clicking the Paste Function button:

Select a function category from the left pane of the dialog box, and then scroll the right pane and select a function. If you need more information, clicking the Office Assistant button opens the Assistant, which will offer help on the selected function. Click the OK button to choose the selected function and return to the Formula Palette.

These steps summarize how to use Excel functions:

1. Activate the cell where you want the result of the function to appear.

2. Click the = button on the formula bar.

3. Choose a function from the Function box drop-down list; or, if the function does not appear on the list, choose More Functions to open the Paste Function dialog box. Choose a category in the left pane and a function from the right pane. Click OK to return to the Formula Palette.

4. In the Formula Palette, select the Number 1 text box. Click the Collapse Dialog button if necessary, and then select the cells you want to include in the argument. Click the Expand Dialog button to return to the Formula Palette.

5. Click the OK button to complete the entry.

Relative and Absolute Cell References

When you copy a formula from one cell to another, Excel automatically adjusts each cell reference in the formula. If, for example, the formula in cell J15 is =H15+I15 and you copy the formula to J16, it is automatically adjusted to =H16+I16. The references to H15 and I15 are *relative cell references*, so they were changed during the copy operation to keep the same relationship relative to the new cell, J16. Most of the time, this is exactly what you want Excel to do. However, there are exceptions.

For example, in the Vacation Meisters worksheet shown in Figure 23.8, we would like to know the percentage of tickets sold for each destination city. We calculate a city's percentage by dividing the city's total into the grand total for all cities. In Figure 23.8, a formula was entered to divide the total Detroit tickets (74) into the grand total (866). The formula for Detroit is fine—but it's obviously wrong when used with the other cities.

FIGURE 23.8

Calculating percentages

	A	B	C	D	E	F	G
1	Vacation Meisters Ticket Sales						
2	First Quarter						
3							
4	Destination	January	February	March	Total	Average	% TOTAL
5							
6	Detroit	17	21	36	74	25	9%
7	Miami	119	101	89	309	10	143%
8	Phoenix	75	77	61	213	71	288%
9	Reno	93	87	90	270	90	87%
10							
11	Total for Month	304	286	276	866		
12	Average for Month	76	72	69	217		
13	Minimum for Month	17	21	36	74		
14	Maximum for Month	119	101	90	309		

So what happened? The formula in G6 was =E6/E11. When it was AutoFilled from G6 to G7, Excel changed each cell reference, just as it did when AutoFilling the totals in Column E. You can see which cells were referenced in each formula by double-clicking on a formula.

The formula in G7 was changed to =E7/E12, and the change from E11 to E12 created the problem. Rather than dividing Miami's total into the total for all destinations, it divided it into the average in cell E12. The formulas for Phoenix and Reno have a similar problem.

When you fill this formula, you want E6 to change to E7 *relative* to the formula's new location, but you don't want E11 to change at all. The reference to E11 should be *absolute*—not changeable.

Absolute Cell References

You can instruct Excel not to change the reference to E11 by making it an *absolute cell reference*. Absolute cell references are preceded with dollar signs: $E$11. The dollar signs "lock in" the cell reference so Excel doesn't change it if you fill or copy the formula to another cell.

The dollar sign in front of the E instructs Excel not to change the column; the dollar sign in front of the 11 locks in the row. So as you fill the formula to the other cities, E6 will change to E7, E8, and E9, but E11 will always be E11.

You create the absolute cell reference in the original formula. If you never intend to fill or copy the formula, you don't need to use absolute references, and they won't fix a formula that doesn't work correctly to begin with. (The original formula for Detroit in G6 worked just fine.) If you are typing the formula, just precede the column and row addresses with a $. You can also create the absolute cell reference using the F4 key, as you will see in the steps below.

 TIP Another way to handle this situation is by naming cell E11 and using the name in the formula. Names are always absolute.

Use these steps in creating an absolute cell reference:

1. Place the cell pointer where you want the results of the formula to appear.
2. Begin entering the formula. After you indicate the address of the cell that contains the absolute value, press the F4 key once to add $ to the row and column of the cell reference.
3. When the formula is complete, press Enter or click the green check mark.
4. Fill the formula to the appropriate cells.

Mixed Cell References

You can also create a *mixed reference*, making part of a cell address absolute and part relative, by locking in either the column or the row. Use mixed references when you want to copy a formula down *and* across and to have a reference change relatively in one direction but not in the other.

For example, E$5 will remain E$5 when copied down because the row reference is absolute, but it can change to F$5, G$5, and so on when copied across because the column reference is relative.

 TIP The Absolute key (F4) is a four-way toggle. The first time you press it, it locks both the column and row: $E$11. Press again, and only the row is locked: E$11. The third time you press, the column is locked: $E11. Press a fourth time, and both row and column are relative: E11.

PART

V

Number Crunching
with Excel

Using Excel's Financial Functions

Excel has more than fifty built-in financial functions, and you don't have to be an accountant to find ways to use them. You'll find functions for a variety of essential operations, including:

- Five ways to calculate depreciation on assets or inventory
- Tools to manage the profits you invest
- Functions that help you determine the cost of borrowing against your business line of credit

The financial functions use a variety of arguments, but these are the most common:

Fv: Future value; what a loan or investment will be worth at a future time when all payments have been made

Nper: Number of periods; the number of months, years, days, or other periods for an investment or loan

Pmt: Payment; the amount you periodically receive from an investment or are paid on a loan

Pv: Present value; the initial value of an investment or loan

Rate: The interest rate on a loan; the discount or interest rate on an investment

The amount of a periodic payment, present value, interest rate, and the total number of payments have a fixed relationship to each other. If you know any three of these, you can use one of the Excel financial functions to calculate the fourth:

NPER calculates the number of periods.

PMT calculates the payment amount.

PV returns the present value for the amount loaned or invested.

RATE returns the interest rate.

With these four functions, you can determine how much interest you paid on a loan or how much income you would receive from an annuity. The worksheet in Figure 23.9 uses the PMT function to calculate a monthly payment for various present values at an interest rate entered by the user.

When you work with the financial functions, you need to make sure that all the arguments in a function are based on the same period: a day, month, or year. For example, in Figure 23.9 the payments are monthly, but the number of periods and user-entered interest rate are based on years.

FIGURE 23.9

*A worksheet for calcu-
lating loan payments*

1	LOAN PAYMENT CALCULATOR						
2							
3	Enter an Interest Rate Here:		12%				
4			Amount Borrowed				
5	Loan Life (Years)	$5,000.00	$10,000.00	$15,000.00	$20,000.00	$25,000.00	
6							M
7	1	$444.24	$888.49	$1,332.73	$1,776.98	$2,221.22	O
8	2	$235.37	$470.73	$706.10	$941.47	$1,176.84	N
9	3	$166.07	$332.14	$498.21	$664.29	$830.36	T
10	4	$131.67	$263.34	$395.01	$526.68	$658.35	H
11	5	$111.22	$222.44	$333.67	$444.89	$556.11	L
12	6	$97.75	$195.50	$293.25	$391.00	$488.75	Y
13	7	$88.26	$176.53	$264.79	$353.05	$441.32	
14	8	$81.26	$162.53	$243.79	$325.06	$406.32	P
15	9	$75.92	$151.84	$227.76	$303.68	$379.61	M
16	10	$71.74	$143.47	$215.21	$286.94	$358.68	T

In the PMT function arguments, then, Nper has to be multiplied by 12 and Rate divided by 12 so that all the arguments are based on a period of one month, as shown in Figure 23.10.

FIGURE 23.10

*The Formula Palette
showing PMT argu-
ments for the Loan
Payment Calculator
worksheet*

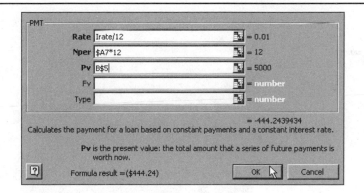

The Depreciation Functions

Businesses must select a depreciation method as assets are placed in service, and the method can't be changed later (unless you want to file additional paperwork). The worksheet in Figure 23.11 uses several of the depreciation functions to model methods a business could use to depreciate assets.

FIGURE 23.11

A worksheet for comparing different asset depreciation methods; Excel has a built-in function for each method.

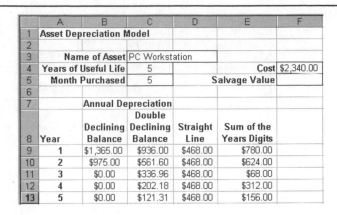

The depreciation functions use other arguments:

Life: The years of useful life of the asset (similar to Nper)

Salvage: How much the asset will be worth when it's past its useful life

Months: The number of months the asset was in service the first year

The arguments for the Declining Balance function are shown in Figure 23.12.

FIGURE 23.12

Arguments for the Declining Balance (DB) function

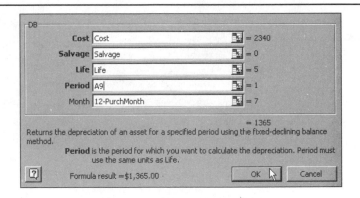

Working with Statistical Tables

Excel includes a fistful of complex statistical functions. However, you're most likely to use the everyday statistics functions like AVERAGE, MIN, MAX, and these:

- COUNT, which returns the number of numbers in a selected range
- MEDIAN, another kind of average, which is used to calculate the value in the middle of a range
- MODE, which returns the value that occurs most frequently.

If you don't have a statistics background, don't worry. All three of these functions are useful and easy to understand.

Using COUNT, MEDIAN, and MODE

The COUNT function tells you how many numbers there are in a selected range. If you've got a small worksheet, it's a breeze to glance down column C and say "Looks like four numbers to me." It's a bit harder with larger worksheets, and the problem is compounded when some cells in a column are blank. COUNT is used to calculate the number of survey responses in Figure 23.13.

 TIP If you want to count the number of entries including text entries in a range, use the COUNTA function rather than COUNT.

AVERAGE returns a value called the arithmetic mean—the total of all the values in a range divided by the number of values in the range. When we talk about averages—bowling scores, test grades, speed on several typing tests—it's the arithmetic mean we're referring to.

However, there are two other types of averages: MEDIAN and MODE. MEDIAN tells you which value is the middle value in a range, and MODE tells you which value occurs most frequently, as shown in Figure 23.13.

The marketing department's survey question is "What is the most you are willing to pay for this product?" The AVERAGE answer is $47, but is it fair to say "The average person is willing to pay $47 for our product?" No—only one person is willing to pay that much: the person who'll pay up to $150. If the marketing department uses the average, they'll price the product so high most customers won't buy it.

FIGURE 23.13

Functions that return averages

Question 14: How much would you be willing to pay for this product?	
Survey Number	**Response**
109871	30
109874	30
109880	40
109881	150
109889	40
109899	30
110001	40
110051	30
110060	33
Number of Responses	9
Mean Average	47.00
Median	33
Mode	30

That's where MEDIAN and MODE come in. The response in the middle (the MEDIAN) is $33. There are as many people willing to pay less than $33 as people willing to pay more than $33, so this might be a good price.

You can routinely use MEDIAN to test the AVERAGE. If MEDIAN and AVERAGE values are close to each other, then there aren't too many bizarre values (like the $150 answer) in the range. MODE tells us that there are more people are willing to pay $30 than any other price—more useful information for the marketing department to know.

Enter arguments for the financial and statistical functions as you would any other function.

What's Next

Pie charts, line charts, bar charts, and column charts present numerical information in ways that are attractive and easy to comprehend. In the next chapter, you'll find out how to make the most of Excel 2000's charting tools.

CHAPTER <u>24</u>

Creating Easy-to-Understand Charts

C harts are graphical representations of numeric data. Charts make it easier for users to compare and understand numbers, so charts have become a popular way to present numerical data. Every chart tells a story. Stories can be simple: "See how our sales have increased" or complex: "This is how our overhead costs relate to the price of our product." Whether simple or complex, the story should be readily understandable. If you can't immediately understand what a chart means, then it isn't a good chart.

Charts are constructed with *data points,* which are the individual numbers in a worksheet, and *data series,* which are the groups of related data points within a column or row. For example, Figure 24.1 shows the Vacation Meisters Ticket Sales worksheet we've used to create the chart illustrations in this chapter. Each of the numbers is a data point. There are many possible sets of data series in this worksheet: one set includes four data series—one for each city's row. Another set includes a data series for each month's column. Each column or row of numbers is a series.

FIGURE 24.1

Each number in this worksheet is a data point, and each row or column can be considered a data series.

	A	B	C	D	E
1	Vacation Meisters Ticket Sales				
2	First Quarter				
3					
4	Destination	January	February	March	Total
5					
6	Detroit	17	21	36	74
7	Miami	119	101	89	309
8	Phoenix	75	77	61	213
9	Reno	93	87	90	270

Understanding Chart Types

Excel comes with a wide variety of charts capable of graphically representing most standard types of data analysis, and even some more exotic numeric interpolations. The type of data you are using and presenting determines the type of chart you will plot the data on. This chapter discusses some of the most frequently used chart types. Excel has charts in the following categories:

Pie charts: These work best for displaying how much each part contributes to a total value. Pie charts can be exploded for greater visual clarity, or turned into doughnut charts, which can represent more than just one set of data.

Line and area charts: These show data points connected with lines, indicating upward or downward trends in value. Area charts show the area below a line filled in. Both types can be combined with column charts to show more data.

Column and bar charts: These compare values across categories, with results presented vertically in column charts and horizontally in bar charts. The composition of the column or bar can be stacked in more than one color to represent the contribution of each portion of a category's data to the total for that category.

Specialty charts: Excel includes a number of charts suitable for presenting scientific, statistical, and financial data. Scatter charts are used to present experimental results. Surface and contour charts are good for presenting 3-D and 2-D changes in data. Radar charts show data values in relation to a single metric. Stock charts present values for between three and five series of data, including open, high, low, close, and volume trading information.

Pie Charts

Use *pie charts* to show the relationships between pieces of an entity. The implication is that the pie includes *all* of something. In the example shown in Figure 24.2, the pie shows all the tickets sold in the first quarter. The pie chart isn't appropriate for illustrating *some* of anything, so if there's not an obvious "all" in the data you're charting, don't use a pie.

FIGURE 24.2

*A pie chart from the
Tickets worksheet*

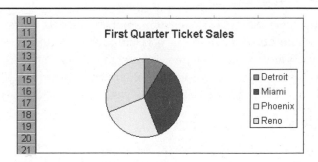

A pie chart can only include one data series. If you select more than one data series, Excel uses the first series and ignores all others. No error message appears, so you won't necessarily know that the chart doesn't show the data you intended to include, unless you examine the chart carefully.

TIP Pie charts almost always show relationships at a fixed point in time—the end of the year, or a specific month, day, or week. It is possible to create a pie chart with more than one time frame; however, this kind of information would be better represented in a series chart.

When you create a pie chart, Excel totals the data points in the series and then divides the value of each data point into the series total to determine how large each data point's pie slice should be. Don't include a total from the worksheet as a data point; this doubles the total Excel calculates, resulting in a pie chart with one large slice (50 percent of the pie), as shown in Figure 24.3.

FIGURE 24.3

Including the total value as a data point generates this incorrect pie chart.

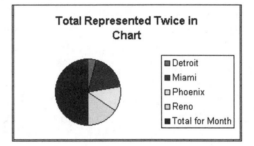

Series Charts

In a *series chart*, you can chart more than one data series. This lets you compare the data points in the series, such as January vs. February, or Reno vs. Phoenix. Series charts are open-ended; there is no requirement that the data shown is all the data for a month or year. There are several types of series charts. You can give the same set of data a very different look by simply changing the chart type.

Line and Area Charts

The series chart shown in Figure 24.4 is a *line chart* showing the relationship between ticket sales and each city during the first quarter. Each data series is a city. Line charts are available in a 2-D version (as shown) or in a 3-D version that is sometimes called a *ribbon chart*. An *area chart* is a line chart with the area below the line filled. Line charts and area charts are typically used to show one or more variables (such as sales, income, or price) changing over time.

FIGURE 24.4

A line chart typically includes these elements.

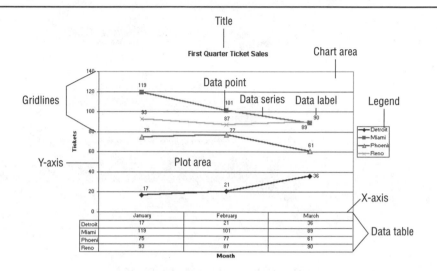

Column and Bar Charts

Figure 24.5 shows the same information presented as a *bar chart*. The bars give added substance to the chart. In the line chart (Figure 24.4), what the reader notices is the trend up or down in each line and the gaps between the lines. The bar chart makes all ticket sales seem more substantial, but it also makes the difference between destinations even clearer—like why doesn't anyone spend a winter vacation in Detroit.

Line and area charts share a common layout. The horizontal line is called the *x-axis*, and the vertical line is the *y-axis* (the same x- and y-axes you may have learned about in algebra or geometry class when plotting data points). In a bar chart, however, the axes are turned 90 degrees so that the x-axis is on the left side.

Excel can also combine columns with line or area charts and embellish line or column charts with 3-D effects. You can make the columns and lines on your charts into tubes, pyramids, cones, or cylinders; or transform regular bars into floating 3-D bars. Plotting data on two axes is also possible with column charts.

PART

V

Number Crunching
with Excel

FIGURE 24.5

A bar chart

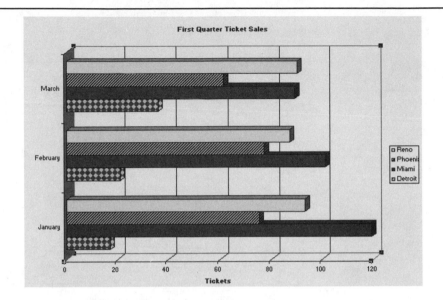

Bar and Column Chart Variations

Column charts are the same as bar charts, but with the x-axis at the bottom. There are three-dimensional varieties of bar and column charts, which add depth to the regular chart. Cylinders, cones, and pyramids are variations of a column chart.

Excel also offers another style of bar and column chart—the *stacked chart*. A stacked 3-D column chart, using the same data as Figures 24.4 and 24.5, is shown in Figure 24.6. In a stacked chart, parallel data points in each data series are stacked on top or to the right of each other. Stacking adds another dimension to the chart, since it allows the user to compare sales between as well as within time periods—like providing a column chart and a pie chart for each time period.

The 3-D charts have three axes. In a 3-D column chart, the x-axis is on the bottom. The vertical axis is the *z-axis*; the y-axis goes from front to back, providing the "third dimension" of depth in the chart. Don't worry about memorizing which axis is which in each chart type; there are ways to know which is which when you're creating or editing the chart.

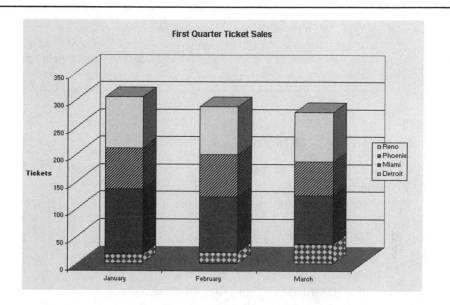

FIGURE 24.6

A stacked 3-D column chart

 TIP As you'll see when working with the Chart Wizard in the next section, the x-axis is often called the *category* axis, and the y-axis is usually called the *value* axis. In a 3-D chart, the y-axis becomes the *series* axis, and values are plotted on the *z-axis*.

Creating a Chart

The easiest way to create a chart is by using the Chart Wizard. Begin the charting process by selecting the data to be used in the chart. With the exception of the chart's title, everything that appears in the chart should be selected somewhere in the worksheet.

Make sure that the ranges you select are symmetrical: if you select four labels in rows 9–12 of column A, select data points from the other columns in rows 9–12. If you select labels in columns A–D of row 5, then the data series you select should also be in columns A–D.

TIP If you include blank rows or extra empty columns in your selection, you'll have empty spaces in your chart. Remember that you can hold the Ctrl key to select noncontiguous ranges of data. If you select some cells you don't want to include, press Esc and start again.

Using the Chart Wizard

When you have your text and numbers selected, click the Chart Wizard button on the Standard toolbar. The Chart Wizard and the Office Assistant both open. You can close the Assistant; the Chart Wizard includes a button to reopen the Assistant if you want help.

In the first step of the Chart Wizard, choose a chart type in the Chart Type list box (see Figure 24.7). If the type of chart you want isn't listed, check out the chart types on the Custom tab.

If your Office Assistant is turned off and you want more information about a particular chart type, select that type, click the Chart Wizard's Office Assistant button, and choose Help With This Feature. The Assistant will offer to provide a sample of the selected chart. Microsoft Excel Help will then slowly be displayed, showing detailed explanations of all the charts and their respective elements. If your Assistant is on, you will automatically see the prompt asking if you want help with this feature. Select Yes to see Excel Help. If you just want a quick preview of what the chart looks like, use the technique described next.

After choosing a chart type in the left pane on the Standard Types tab, choose a subtype in the right pane. To see a rough sample of the type and subtype using your data, use the Press And Hold To View Sample button in the Chart Wizard. When you've selected a type and a subtype, click Next to continue.

In the second step, shown in Figure 24.8, you have an opportunity to make sure the range you selected is correct on the Data Range tab. If it isn't, use the Collapse Dialog button and reselect the proper range before continuing. Choose Rows or Columns in the Series In option group. The preview will change to reflect the range and series arrangement you specify. Click Next, or click the Series tab to make additional changes.

FIGURE 24.7

Chart Wizard, Step 1–
choosing a chart type

FIGURE 24.8

Chart Wizard, Step 2–
verifying the range in
the Data Range tab

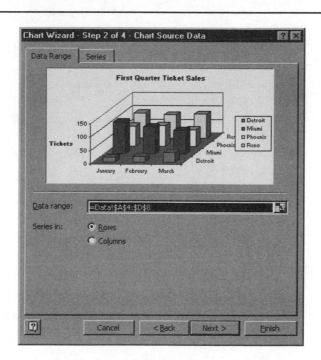

Use the Series tab in Step 2 of the Chart Wizard (Figure 24.9) to check selected ranges and values for the series used in the chart. Click any of the items listed in the Series list box to see which cells or cell ranges in the spreadsheet correspond to the selected series item. Use the Collapse Dialog button next to either the Name or Values text boxes to modify these chart elements. You can also specify or change the cells used for x-axis labels in the Category (X) Axis Labels text box.

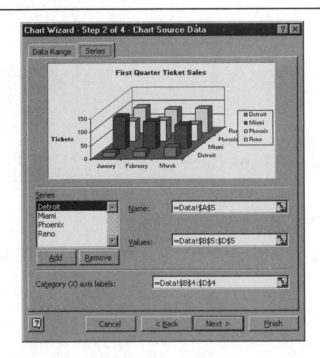

In the third step, use the tabs (shown in Figure 24.10) to change options for various aspects of the chart:

Titles: Enter titles for the chart and axes.

Axes: Display or hide axes.

Gridlines: Display gridlines and display or hide the third dimension of a 3-D chart.

Legend: Display and place a legend.

Data Labels: Display text or values as data labels.

Data Table: Show the selected range from the worksheet as part of the chart.

As you change options, the chart preview will reflect your changes. When you've finished setting options, click Next to continue.

FIGURE 24.10

*Chart Wizard, Step 3—
setting chart options*

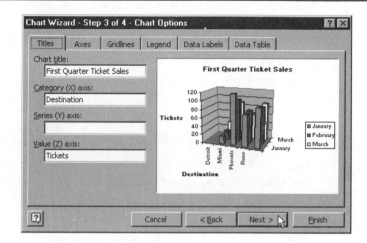

 TIP Every chart needs a title. The title provides information that is not already included in the graphical portion of the chart. The chart's picture, legend, and title taken together should answer any questions about the timing, location, or contents of the chart.

In the last step of the Chart Wizard (Figure 24.11), you can place the chart on the current worksheet or on a new, blank sheet in the same workbook. If the chart is placed on its own sheet, it will print as a full-size, single-page chart whenever it is printed. If you add it to the current worksheet as an object, it will print as part of the worksheet, but it can also be printed separately.

FIGURE 24.11

*Chart Wizard, Step 4—
placing the chart*

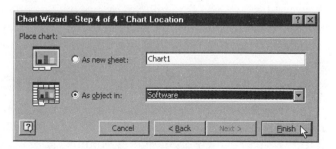

Don't spend a lot of time deciding whether to place the chart in this worksheet or its own worksheet. You can easily move it later. Enter a new sheet name (or choose As Object In and select the worksheet in which to place the chart) and click Finish to create and place the chart. The Office Assistant will open and offer further help with charts. The Excel Chart toolbar will also appear in its floating form.

Here's a quick summary of the steps for creating an Excel chart with the Chart Wizard:

1. Select the cells to be included in the chart.

2. Click the Chart Wizard button on the Standard toolbar.

3. In the first wizard step, select a chart type and subtype; then click Next.

4. In the second step, verify that you have selected the correct range, and choose to have the series represented by rows or by columns. Click Next.

5. In the third step, use the tabs to move to the various options for the chart. On the title tab, enter a chart title. Set other options as you wish, then click Next.

6. In the fourth step, either enter the name for a chart worksheet or leave the default setting to have the chart placed as an object in the current worksheet. Click Finish.

 TIP You can always move a chart object to its own worksheet or make a chart an object in another worksheet. Select the chart or chart object, right-click, and choose Location from the shortcut menu to open the Chart Location dialog box.

Editing and Formatting Charts

After you create and save your chart, you can use Excel's editing and formatting tools to modify it or improve its appearance. You will probably want to move and resize the chart to place it correctly in an existing report or presentation slide.

Excel also gives you the ability to change or update the data plotted in the chart by adding, deleting, or reordering data series. You can display error bars and additional data labels, or change the color and spacing of various chart elements.

Moving, Sizing, and Printing Chart Objects

If you have Excel place the chart as an object in the current worksheet, you might find that you'd like to move or resize the chart—especially if the chart is too small or if it covers part of the worksheet data. Fortunately, moving a chart in Excel is a snap!

When the chart is placed in the worksheet, it is selected: it has square *handles* on the corners and sides. If the chart isn't selected, clicking once on the chart selects it. To deselect the chart and return to the worksheet, click once on part of the worksheet that isn't covered by the chart. Once the chart is selected, you can move it by pointing to the chart and holding the mouse button down until the pointer changes to a four-headed arrow. Drag the chart to its new location. To change the chart's size, move the mouse pointer to one of the chart's handles. Press the mouse button and drag the handle to stretch or shrink the chart. Handles on the sides of the chart change the size in one direction (width or height). To increase width and height in proportion, use a corner handle.

 TIP You might want to turn on Page Break Preview when sizing and moving charts to make sure they remain within the boundaries of a page. Page Break Preview isn't an option while a chart is selected, so click anywhere in the worksheet to deselect the chart, and then choose View ➤ Page Break Preview.

Printing Charts as Objects or Worksheets

Even if you placed your chart as an object in the current worksheet, you can still print it separately. If the chart is selected when you print, it will print by itself on a full page. If the worksheet is selected, the worksheet prints, including the chart object.

- To print a worksheet, including a chart object, activate any worksheet cell before printing.
- To print a chart object as a full-page chart, select the chart before printing.

Adding a Data Series

Excel's charting tools allow you to modify charts quickly and easily. You can, for example, create a simple series chart like the chart shown in Figure 24.12, and then add another data series using drag-and-drop. (You can't add individual data points, just data series.) Here are the steps for adding a data series to a chart:

1. In the worksheet, select the data series to be added.
2. Drag the series and drop it in the chart.

Selecting a new series in the worksheet and dragging it into the chart area (top) automatically adds it to the chart (bottom).

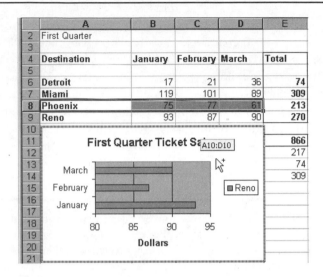

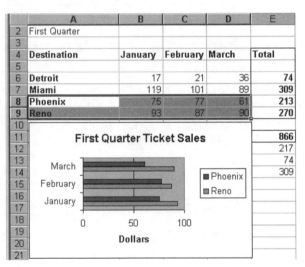

Deleting a Data Series

A chart is a collection of graphic objects. To access the objects, first select the chart. Then click the object you wish to select. The selected object (data point, data series, title, etc.) will have handles. When an object is selected, you can delete or format the object. Use these steps to delete a data series from a chart:

1. In the chart, select the data series or any data point in the series.

2. Press the Delete key on the keyboard.

WARNING If you select the entire chart, pressing the Delete key will delete the chart itself.

Formatting Charts

The *chart area* (see Figure 24.13) is a rectangular area within the chart window bounded by the chart border. Changing the size of the chart window changes the size of the chart area. All objects in a chart must be within the chart area.

FIGURE 24.13

The chart area

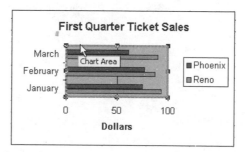

The *plot area* is bounded by the axes and contains the columns, lines, wedges, or other objects used to represent the data points. Objects within the plot area have fixed locations and cannot be moved or individually sized. For example, the x-axis labels must be located near the x-axis.

You can, however, resize all the objects in the plot area by increasing or decreasing the plot area itself. (There's an exception to this rule; see "Exploding Pies" later in this chapter.) Objects outside the plot area and axes can be sized or moved to other locations in the chart area. The title and legend can be placed above, below, or in the plot area.

Any object in a chart can be selected and then formatted or deleted, with the exception of individual data points. Data points can be formatted, but only data *series* can be added or deleted. To select a data point, first select the data series, and then click the data point once.

Using the Chart Toolbar

Common formatting options are available on the Chart toolbar (use View ➤ Toolbars ➤ Chart), as indicated in Table 24.1. Select the chart object you want to format from the Chart Objects drop-down list; then use the toolbar buttons to format the object or the entire chart.

TABLE 24.1: CHART TOOLBAR BUTTONS

Button	Button Name	Function
	Format Object	Opens the Format dialog box for the selected object.
	Chart Type	The drop-down arrow opens a menu of chart types; clicking the button applies the type indicated on the button face.
	Legend	Displays or hides the legend.
	Data Table	Displays or hides the data table.
	By Rows	Uses the selected worksheet rows as a data series.
	By Columns	Uses the selected worksheet columns as a data series.
	Angle Text Downward	Angles selected text downward.
	Angle Text Upward	Angles selected text upward.

Double-click any object to open the formatting dialog box for the object. For example, double-clicking any column in a data series opens the Format Data Series dialog box, shown in Figure 24.14.

PART

V

Number Crunching
with Excel

FIGURE 24.14

*The Format Data
Series dialog box*

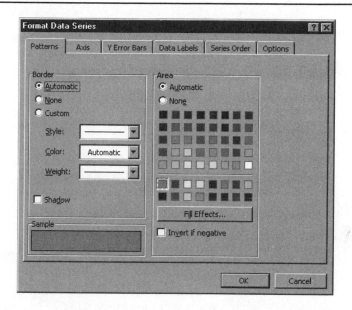

There are five or six tabs in this dialog box. Each contains a group of settings for the selected data series. Depending on the chart type, the dialog box may include a tab for Shape and may not include Axis or Y Error Bars tabs.

Patterns: Used to set the color and pattern for each series.

Axis: If the chart has more than one series, allows you to add a second vertical axis at the right end of the plot area scaled to the selected series.

Y Error Bars: Adds a graphic display of the standard error; used to approximate sampling error when the data in a chart is a statistical sample being applied to a larger population.

Data Labels: Adds a descriptive label or the numeric value for each data point in the series.

Series Order: Allows you to reorder the series in a chart; this is especially helpful with 3-D charts, where the selected range is charted in reverse order.

Options: Settings for the bar or column overlap, gap, and color variation.

For more information on a specific control within the Data Series dialog box, click the Help button and then click the control.

Similar options are available when you double-click a selected data point, the plot area, chart area, or other chart object.

TIP You can select any object or series: right-click, then select Format from the shortcut menu. Chart Type is always a shortcut menu option, giving you access to all the types and subtypes. If the entire chart is selected, Chart Options appears on the menu.

These steps summarize how to format chart objects:

1. Select the chart.

2. Double-click the object you want to format (or select the object, right-click, and choose Format) to open the appropriate dialog box.

3. Change formatting options; then click OK to apply the changes and close the dialog box.

Inserting and Formatting Titles

If you didn't give the chart a title while creating it, you can add one at any time. Select the chart, right-click, and open the Chart Options dialog box from the shortcut menu. You'll see the Titles page of the dialog box. You can edit or format existing titles (including placeholders) in a selected chart without having to use the Chart Options from the shortcut menu. To change the text in a title, click once to select the title, and then edit the selected text.

To wrap a title into multiple lines, place the insertion point where you want the second line to begin, hold the Ctrl key, and press Enter.

Double-click a title (or select the title, right-click, and choose Format Title from the shortcut menu) to open the Format Title dialog box. Use the controls in the Pattern, Font, and Alignment pages to format the title as you would format other text.

 TIP To change all the fonts used in a chart, double-click in the chart area and change fonts in the Format Chart Area dialog box. If you don't like the results, you can revert to the original style by using Edit ➤ Undo or Ctrl+Z.

Exploding Pies

If you want to emphasize specific data points in a pie chart, you can *explode* the pie chart by moving one or more pieces of the pie farther from the center (see Figure 24.15). Usually, you'll move one or two individual slices to emphasize specific data points in the chart. In Figure 24.15, the Detroit slice has been exploded.

Although you can select an exploded pie in the Chart Wizard, the wizard explodes either all slices of the pie or the first slice, depending on which explosion sample you choose. It's easier to create an unexploded pie of the type you wish, and then edit the chart to explode selected slices.

FIGURE 24.15

An exploded pie chart

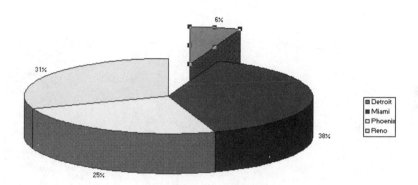

First Quarter Ticket Sales

If you want to explode all the slices in an existing chart, first select the chart and then select the pie in the plot area. Excel will put handles on the outside edge of each slice of the pie. Drag any slice away from the center to explode all the pie slices.

To explode a single slice, select the chart and then click the pie to select the data series. With the series selected, click to select the slice you want to explode. Drag the slice away from the center.

When you explode all slices in a pie, each slice gets smaller as you increase the space between the slices. If you explode slices individually, the other slices remain centered in the plot area, and the slices don't get smaller.

MASTERING THE OPPORTUNITIES

Changing 3-D Views

If you are working with one of Excel's 3-D chart types, you can change the perspective using the 3-D View tool in the Chart menu. This is helpful for tilting pies and exploded pies to a better viewing angle or for emphasizing one particular chart element that gets your point across.

Continued ▮▶

PART

V

Number Crunching
with Excel

MASTERING THE OPPORTUNITIES CONTINUED

For example, here's the pie from Figure 24.14 rotated and tilted so that the pulled-out slice is at the bottom in the foreground where it is more noticeable. The slice also stands out better, because its lighter color is next to the darker color of the adjacent slice. The chart legend has also been pulled closer to the exploded slide, so viewers can see immediately which data the emphasized slice represents.

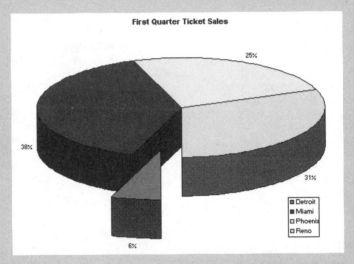

Optimizing the view of more complex 3-D charts is essential for conveying the data's message to viewers. Sometimes, important chart objects can be obscured by other, closer chart objects. Larger chart objects will dominate the chart's visual impact, possibly drawing attention away from smaller elements that could be important points in a presentation or report.

Use these steps to change a chart's 3-D view:

1. Select the chart and choose Chart ➢ 3-D View. The 3-D View dialog box appears, as shown here:

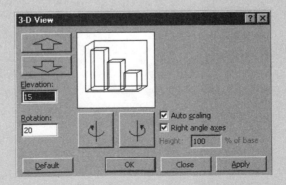

Continued ▐▶

> ### MASTERING THE OPPORTUNITIES CONTINUED
>
> **2.** Click the large arrows on the left to change the *elevation,* or degree of tilt of the chart. The wire-frame preview changes to show the effects of your setting, as does the number in the Elevation box.
>
> **3.** Click the clockwise or counterclockwise rotation buttons to change the chart's horizontal orientation. The Rotation settings and the preview will change to reflect your choices.
>
> **4.** Type in a different percentage in the Height text box to collapse or expand the chart's height (the z-axis) relative to its width (the x-axis). A higher percentage will make the chart taller or wider; a lower percentage will make it shorter or smaller.
>
> **5.** Click OK to make all the changes and close the box.
>
> If your chart gets distorted from the 3-D view changes, click the Default button and check the Auto Scaling box to restore it to its original settings and orientation.

What's Next

The techniques you have learned in this chapter give you superior ways to display data using all of Excel's charting features. Chapter 25 covers methods of ensuring a consistent look in your Excel files with custom formats, the AutoFormat tool, and spreadsheet styles. You'll also learn how to enforce consistent formats during data entry by using special codes for numbers, text, times, and dates (even Y2K dates).

CHAPTER **25**

Using Custom and Special Formats

Formatting—controlling the appearance of cell contents and the overall layout of worksheets—is a fundamental skill that any Excel user needs to master. Chapter 22 introduced the topic and showed how to apply formats from the toolbar and the Format Cells dialog box. This chapter looks briefly at applying the built-in AutoFormats and then moves on to styles, conditional formatting, and creating custom formats. You'll also learn about formatting issues related to the year 2000 (Y2K) and the emerging Euro currency.

Using AutoFormats

Excel includes a number of canned worksheet designs, including formal business, list, and 3-D formats. If you're in a hurry, the predesigned formats offer a quick way to apply a standard format to all or part of a worksheet.

Before you AutoFormat, select the cells to be formatted. This will usually include all the text and numbers in your worksheet, but you might want to apply an Auto-Format to titles or data only.

Choose Format ➤ AutoFormat from the menu bar to open the AutoFormat dialog box. Click the Options button to expand the dialog box to display the formatting elements you can apply, as shown in Figure 25.1.

For example, you might choose not to apply column widths if you've already adjusted column widths and don't want them changed. As you select formats from the Table Format list and turn the Formats To Apply options on and off, the worksheet in the Sample pane will change.

Follow these steps to AutoFormat a worksheet:

1. Select the portion of the worksheet you wish to AutoFormat.

2. Choose Format ➤ AutoFormat from the menu bar to open the AutoFormat dialog box.

3. Choose a format from the Table Format list.

4. Click the Options button to show Formats To Apply. Deselect any options you don't want to include.

5. Click OK to apply the selected formats as shown in the Sample pane.

FIGURE 25.1

The AutoFormat
dialog box

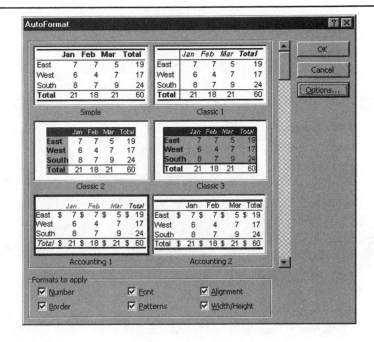

Working with Styles

AutoFormats are composed of *styles*: specifications about one or more formatting options. Most AutoFormats include several styles, such as these:

- Arial 14-point teal bold for the title
- Arial 12-point accounting format for the numbers
- Arial 12-point bold with a top border for totals

Creating Styles

While you can't create your own AutoFormats, you can create individual styles and apply them to ranges in a worksheet. There are two ways to create a style:

- From existing formatted entries
- By specifying formatting options as you create the style

If the formatting you want to save as a style already exists in the worksheet, select a range that includes the formatting; if not, select a cell that's close to what you want so you'll have less formatting to modify. Choose Format ➤ Style from the menu bar to open the Style dialog box shown in Figure 25.2.

FIGURE 25.2

The Style dialog box

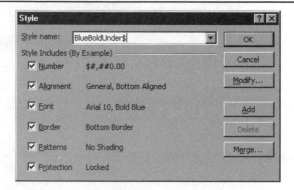

Don't begin by clicking options. First, enter a descriptive name for the new style, as shown in Figure 25.2. As soon as you begin entering the name, previously disabled options will be enabled. Use the check boxes to exclude format settings from the style, or click the Modify button to open the familiar Format Cells dialog box and set other formatting attributes before clicking OK. When you return to the Style dialog box, the style will include the options you selected in the Format Cells dialog box. Click the Add button to create the style.

These steps summarize how to create a style:

1. Select cells whose formatting is the same as, or similar to, the style you want to create.

2. Choose Format ➤ Style from the menu bar.

3. Enter a new name for the style.

4. Use the check boxes to disable formatting features that should not be included in the style.

5. Click the Modify button and change any format options you wish in the Format Cells dialog box. Click OK to close the dialog box.

6. Click the Add button to add the new style. Click Close to close the dialog box, or click OK to apply the style to the current selection and close the Style dialog box.

4. Select a conditional operator.

5. In the Condition text box enter a value, cell reference, or formula.

6. Click the Format button. Set up a format for this condition, and click OK.

7. If you have additional conditions or formats, click the Add button and repeat steps 3–5 for each condition.

8. Click OK to close the dialog box and apply conditional formatting.

FIGURE 25.3

This Loan Payment worksheet uses conditional formatting, highlighting payment amounts over $300.

Interest Rate 10%					
			Amount Borrowed		
Loan Life (Years)	**$5,000.00**	**$10,000.00**	**$15,000.00**	**$20,000.00**	**$25,000.00**
1	$444.24	$888.49	$1,332.73	$1,776.98	$2,221.22
2	$235.37	$470.73	$706.10	$941.47	$1,176.84
3	$166.07	$332.14	$498.21	$664.29	$830.36
4	$131.67	$263.34	$395.01	$526.68	$658.35
5	$111.22	$222.44	$333.67	$444.89	$556.11
6	$97.75	$195.50	$293.25	$391.00	$488.75
7	$88.26	$176.53	$264.79	$353.05	$441.32
8	$81.26	$162.53	$243.79	$325.06	$406.32
9	$75.92	$151.84	$227.76	$303.68	$379.61
10	$71.74	$143.47	$215.21	$286.94	$358.68

PART

V

Number Crunching with Excel

FIGURE 25.4

The Conditional Formatting dialog box

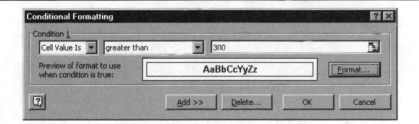

Setting the First Condition

From the first drop-down list, choose Cell Value Is to base the formatting on the value in the cell or Formula Is to base the formatting on a formula that returns a value of true or false. Don't let this confuse you; it doesn't matter whether the cell contains a typed-in value or a formula. If you want the format to be applied based on the number or text that appears in a cell, use Cell Value Is. You'll only use Formula Is with specialized functions like the Date and Logical functions.

In the second drop-down list, choose one of the conditional operators: Between, Not Between, Equal To, Not Equal To, Greater Than, Less Than, Greater Than Or Equal To, or Less Than Or Equal To.

In the text box, either type a constant (like **300** or **Florida**), select a cell in the worksheet, or enter a formula. (There's more about the second and third options under "Using Cell References in Conditions" later in the chapter.)

Now click the Format button to open an abbreviated version of the Format Cells dialog box. Some of the formats are disabled (like font type and size), so you know you can't use them for conditional formatting. You can, however, pile on borders, shading, and different colors to make cells jump off the page.

Choose the format options you want to apply when the condition is true, and then click OK to return to the Conditional Formatting dialog box. Click OK to close the dialog box, and the formats will be applied to the appropriate cells.

Adding Another Condition

What if you want more than one alternate format? For example, you might want to show sales increases over last month in blue and decreases in red. In this case, you need two conditions. Create the first condition in the Conditional Formatting dialog box, then click the Add button to add another condition, as shown in Figure 25.5.

FIGURE 25.5

The Conditional Formatting dialog box with a second condition

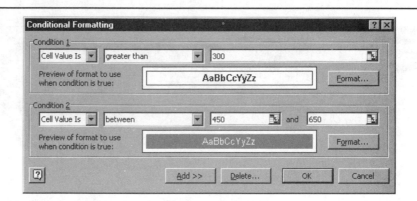

Using Cell References in Conditions

You can compare the value in a cell to the value in another cell in the worksheet. For example, you might select a cell that shows an average and apply a conditional format to all the numbers that are above that average.

In this case, each cell you conditionally format will refer to the cell that contains the average, so you'll use an absolute cell reference. Simply click on the cell with the average to place the absolute reference in the condition text box.

Using relative references in conditional formats isn't much trickier. In the section of the Tickets worksheet shown below, February sales that were greater than January sales are bold and shaded:

	A	B	C
1	Vacation Meisters Ticket Sales		
2	First Quarter		
3			
4	Destination	January	February
5			
6	Detroit	17	21
7	Miami	119	101
8	Phoenix	75	77
9	Reno	93	87

To decide what kind of reference to create, think about how you would create a formula for each cell in column C to compare it to the value in column B. The conditional format will be testing whether C6 > B6, C7 > B7, and so forth. Each cell in column C would need a formula that changed relative to column B, so to create this condition, make sure that you use relative cell references. In this example, select the cells, open the Conditional Formatting dialog box and choose Cell Value Is and Greater Than. Click in the Conditions text box, and then click cell B6. B6 is added as an absolute cell reference: $B$6. Use the F4 key to change the reference to a relative reference.

Extending Conditional Formatting

You don't have to apply conditional formatting to all the cells in a range at once. You can create one or more conditional formats for a single cell and tweak them until they're exactly what you want. Then select the entire range you want to format, including the formatted cell.

Choose Format ➢ Conditional Formatting, and the dialog box will open, displaying the format you created. Just click OK, and the format will be adjusted and applied to the other selected cells.

Using Formulas as Conditions

Now add one more flourish: you can compare a cell to a formula. For example, you only want to bold and shade a cell in column C if the value is at least 3 greater than the value in column B. If sales didn't go up by at least three tickets, it's not a substantial enough increase to warrant special formatting.

To achieve this, you will expand the definition of the condition greater than B6 to create the condition greater than B6+3. Use formulas like this to format the sales that went up more than 20 percent or individual items that represent more than 5 percent of the total budget.

Creating Custom Formats

Excel includes a huge number of formats, but you might need a particular format that isn't part of the package. You can create *custom formats* to handle specialized formatting needs.

A common use of custom formats is creating formats that include a text string: 10 mpg, $1.75/sq ft, or $3.00/dozen. If you simply enter 10 mpg in a cell, the entry is text, so you can't average the miles per gallon across a line of automobiles. With a custom format, the number 10 is a value; the mpg is a format like a dollar sign or percent sign. You create custom formats in the Format Cells dialog box. But before you open the dialog box, let's look at the codes you'll use to create custom formats.

Codes for Numbers

Each of the codes shown in Table 25.1 is a placeholder for a digit or a character. You string together a number of placeholders to create a format. If a number has more digits to the right of the decimal than there are placeholders, the number will be rounded so it fits in the number of placeholders. For example, if the format has two placeholders to the right of the decimal, 5.988 will be rounded to 5.99.

 TIP Excel differentiates between significant digits and insignificant digits. A significant digit is part of a number's "real value." In the value 3.70, the 3 and 7 are significant; the zero is an insignificant digit, because removing it doesn't change the real value of the number. Only zeros can be insignificant. Insignificant zeros after the decimal are called trailing zeros. Different placeholders display or hide insignificant zeros.

TABLE 25.1: NUMBER FORMAT CODES

Code	Use	Example
#	Displays significant digits.	###.## formats 3.50 as 3.5 and 3.977 as 3.98
0	Displays all digits; placeholders to the right of the decimal are filled with trailing zeros if required.	##0.00 formats 3.5 as 3.50 and 57.1 as 57.10

Continued ▶

TABLE 25.1: NUMBER FORMAT CODES (CONTINUED)

Code	Use	Example
?	Displays significant digits and aligns decimal or slash place-holders.	???.?? displays 3.50 as 3.5, 57.10 as 57.1, and 3.977 as 3.98, and aligns decimals
/	Displays a number as a fraction.	# ??/?? displays 7.5 as 7 1/2
,	Thousands separator, also used to format numbers as if they were divided by a thousand or a million.	##,### displays 99999 as 99,999 ##, displays 9,000 as 9 ##,, displays 9,000,000 as 9
( )	Parentheses, used to format negative numbers.	(##,###) formats −99999 as (99,999)
-	Hyphen, used to place a hyphen in a number.	000-000 formats 123456 as 123-456
" "	Used to indicate a text string.	### "miles per hour" formats 100 as 100 miles per hour
[colorname]	Applies one of eight reserved colors to a format	[BLUE] ###.## formats 3.5 as 3.5 with blue font color

There are several approaches to conditional formatting within a custom format. If you include two formats, separated by a semicolon, Excel uses the first format for positive numbers and the second for negative numbers. The format ##,###; [RED]##,### will format negative numbers in red.

 TIP   The reserved colors are [BLACK], [WHITE], [BLUE], [RED], [YELLOW], [GREEN], [CYAN], [MAGENTA]. To apply other colors, use conditional formatting rather than a custom format.

If you have three sections of format, the third format is used for zero. The format [BLUE]##; [RED]##; [WHITE]## will display blue positive numbers, red negative numbers, and white zeros. On a white background, this makes zeros disappear. A fourth section can be used for text that appears in the cell (see "Codes for Text" below).

PART

V

Number Crunching with Excel

You can enter a condition in brackets, followed by the two formats to be used based on whether the condition is true or false. A common use for a conditional custom format is formatting zip codes when some have nine digits and others have five.

The condition [>99999] will be true for nine-digit zip codes, so the format [>99999]00000-0000;00000 will format both nine-digit and five-digit zip codes correctly, including leading zeros.

MASTERING THE OPPORTUNITIES

Getting Ready for the Euro

Financial spreadsheet users and those of you working for multinational companies will probably soon be encountering the Euro, a new currency unit being adopted by many of the countries in the new European Union (EU). The EU began implementing the Euro for electronic transactions only on 1/1/1999. Euro coins and bills will be introduced in 1/1/2002, and the Euro will be standard currency in eleven EU countries by July 2002.

Microsoft has built Euro support into Office 2000 applications; however, Windows 95 and Windows NT 4.*x* do not automatically support the Euro. You must download a system upgrade from Microsoft's TechNet Web site (www.microsoft.com/technet) and install it in order to update these operating systems.

You must also update your printer fonts to obtain the special Euro character:

Fortunately, Windows 98 and Windows NT 5 both include fonts, drivers, and everything else you need to support the Euro. (Note that you can always use the three-letter code for the Euro (EUR) if you are having problems getting the symbol to display or print.)

Of course, displaying and printing the Euro is only the first step in using this new currency in spreadsheets. You must also convert old European currencies into this new currency. You may also need to convert the Euro values into whatever currency is of primary interest at your company. Check at the Microsoft Office Web site (www.microsoft.com/office) periodically to see whether they have posted a solution you can download for converting currencies based on the triangulation-of-values method. Microsoft will also be posting a list of third-party vendors offering products that address this conversion issue.

Codes for Dates and Times

Use the format codes shown in Tables 25.2 and 25.3 to create date and time formats. The m code is used for both months and minutes. Excel treats m as a month code unless it appears directly after a code for hours or before a code for seconds.

TABLE 25.2: DATE FORMAT CODES

Code	Use	Examples
m	Months as ##	m formats January as 1 and December as 12
mm	Months as 00	mm formats January as 01 and December as 12
mmm	Months as three-letter abbreviation	mmm formats January as Jan
mmmm	Month named spelled out	mmmm formats January as January
mmmmm	Month's first letter	mmmmm formats January as J and December as D
d	Days as ##	d formats 1 as 1 and 31 as 31
dd	Days as 00	dd formats 1 as 01 and 31 as 31
ddd	Days as weekday abbreviation	ddd formats 1/1/99 as Fri
dddd	Days as weekday	dddd formats 1/1/99 as Friday
yy	Years as 00	yy formats 1999 as 99
yyyy	Years as 0000	yyyy formats 1/1/99 as 1999

PART V

Number Crunching with Excel

TABLE 25.3: TIME FORMAT CODES

Code	Use	Examples
h, m, s	Hours, minutes and seconds as ##, international (24 hour) clock	h:m formats 3:13 p.m. as 3:13, but treats it as 3:13 a.m.
hh, mm, ss	Hours, minutes and seconds as 00, 24 hour clock	hh:mm formats 3:13 p.m. as 03:13, but treats it as 3:13 a.m.
AM/PM	12-hour clock, upper case	h:m AM/PM formats 3:13 as 3:13 AM
am/pm	12-hour clock, lower case	hh:mm am/pm formats 3:13 as 03:13 am
a/p	12-hour clock, short form	hh:mm a/p formats 3:13 as 3:13 a

If you don't include one of the versions of am/pm, Excel bases time on the 24-hour clock.

MASTERING THE OPPORTUNITIES

Year 2000 Date Settings

Like all the other Office 2000 components, Microsoft Excel has been equipped with a "factory setting" that automatically takes into account the year 2000 problem when saving and displaying dates—even if they have been entered with ambiguous two-digit years.

This new setting uses "29" as the cut-off date when determining whether a two-digit year should be saved as a year from the twentieth century or the twenty-first century. For example, if you enter **2/14/28**, Excel 2000 will convert that entry into 2/14/2028. If you enter **2/14/30**, Excel saves and displays that date as 2/14/1930. (Excel 97 and Office 97 use the same automatic cut-off date of "29" for saving and displaying dates.) If this cut-off date does not work in your business, don't worry; the date can be customized. Windows 98 and Windows NT 5 both include a way to modify the cutoff date in the Regional Settings properties dialog box found in the Windows Control Panel.

Windows 95 and Windows NT 4.*x* users can also customize their cut-off date with the Date Cutoff tools supplied in the Office 2000 Resource Kit. Excel 95 used a cut-off date of "19" instead of "29."

Excel 2000 also includes two new date formats using the four-digit year, which will minimize confusion in spreadsheets and give you more formatting flexibility. The two extra formats are M/D/YYYY and DD-MMM-YYYY.

To use these formats, select a cell or range of cells, choose Format ➢ Cells, and click the Number tab in the Format Cells dialog box. Choose Date as the formatting category, and scroll to the bottom of the Type list box, where you can choose one of the two new formats.

If you will be using spreadsheets from previous versions of Excel with your new Excel 2000 application, you might want to check out the Date Migration Wizard included in the Office 2000 Resource Kit. This wizard helps you audit workbooks and worksheets from earlier versions of Excel to look for date functions and correct date formatting problems. You can also download both the Date Migration Wizard and the Date Fix Wizard add-ins for Excel 97 from Microsoft's Web site at http://www.officeupdate.microsoft.com.

Codes for Text

If you want to include text along with a number in a cell, put quotes around the text string or precede the text with a backslash (\). If you want to include a format for text entered in a cell, make it the final section in your format.

The @ symbol stands for any text typed in the cell, so **[BLUE]@** will format text in the cell in blue. (If you just type the format **[BLUE]**, the text won't appear at all.)

If you don't include a text format, text entered in the cell is formatted according to the defaults or the formatting applied with the toolbar and Format Cells dialog box.

Spacing Codes

There are two reasons you'll use spacing codes: alignment and filling. In some formats, negative numbers are surrounded by parentheses. If you use parentheses in a custom format, you need to add a space to the end of the positive format that will line up with the right parenthesis in a negative value. (This keeps the decimal points lined up.) To create a one-character space in a format, include an underscore: ##,##0.00_.

You can fill any empty space in a cell by entering an asterisk (*) and then a fill character (such as a space) in the number format. For example, the accounting format begins with an underscore and a dollar sign, followed by an asterisk and a space before the digit placeholders: _$* #,##0.00. This ensures that the dollar sign is one space from the left edge of the cell, and that all the room between the dollar sign and digits is filled with spaces.

Using the Custom Format Codes

To create a custom format, select the cells to be formatted and open the Format Cells dialog box. On the Number page, choose Custom from the Format Type list. The Type list already includes formats. Scroll the list and choose a format similar to the custom format you want to create, then edit the format, adding or deleting placeholders.

You can also select the format in the Type text box and begin typing a format from scratch. As you enter a format, the Sample area will reflect your changes. Click OK to create the format.

To delete a custom format, select it from the Format Type list, then click the Delete button in the Format Cells dialog box.

Create a custom format by following these steps:

1. Select the cells to be formatted. Choose Format ➤ Cells from the menu bar or right-click and choose Format Cells from the shortcut menu.

PART

V

Number Crunching
with Excel

2. On the Number page of the Format dialog box, choose Custom from the category list.

3. Enter a format in the Type text box.

4. Click OK to apply the custom format.

What's Next

Chapter 26 looks at Excel as a data-management tool. You'll see what the essential elements of a database are, explore sorting and filtering, and learn how to bring data into Excel from other sources effortlessly. Further topics include creating forms for data entry and for searching, data-analysis tools like the PivotTable and PivotChart Wizard, and the Data Map tool.

CHAPTER 26

Managing Data
with Excel

You've worked with Excel's spreadsheet and charting features. In this chapter, you'll use Excel's database capabilities to create and manage lists. You will also discover other special Excel features, such as pivot tables and data mapping.

One of the first questions many Office users may have about working with databases is when it's OK use Excel and when it's really necessary to use Access. This chapter will help you evaluate that issue in terms of your own needs. If you anticipate database operations more complex than we describe here, you should probably plan to use Access, the subject of Part VI.

Basic Database Concepts

In its simplest form, a *database* is a list with a specific structure, defined by its *fields:* the categories of information it contains. A telephone directory, for example, is a printout of a computer database whose fields include last name, first name, middle initial, address, and telephone number.

An individual listing in the phone book is a *record* in the database, containing a single set of the fields: one phone user's last name, first name, middle initial, address, and telephone number. Each field must have a unique *field name:* LastName, last name, LASTNAME, and LastNameforListing are all possible field names for a field containing last names. In Excel, fields are columns, and each record is an individual row.

The Traverse Tree Sales worksheet (shown in Figure 26.1) is an Excel database. Each field is a separate column. Field names (*Month*, *County*, *Type*, *Quantity*, and *Bundles*) are used as column labels. Each individual row is a record.

Again, what we've just described is the very simplest type of database. A more elaborate database structure might consist of many such database *tables*, related by one or more common fields. (In the Traverse Tree Sales example, the tree Type might be a field used by a whole set of tables.) A *relational* database allows you to manage very large amounts of information efficiently and to pull together information from different tables in order to answer complex questions.

Microsoft Access is designed specifically to create databases, particularly relational databases, and it allows you to create and manage incredibly large numbers of records, limited only by the amount of space on your hard drive. Excel databases are limited to the number of rows in a worksheet: 65,536. Despite these and other limitations, Excel's list management features are powerful tools for creating small databases and manipulating smaller sets of records from larger databases.

FIGURE 26.1

*The Traverse Tree Sales
database*

TRAVERSE TREE SALES				
County Cooperative Tree Orders				
Month	County	Type	Quantity	Bundles
00-Apr-1999	Genessee	White Pine	37000	74
00-Apr-1999	Oakland	Blue Spruce	22500	45
00-Apr-1999	Oakland	White Pine	15500	31
00-Apr-1999	Oakland	Concolor Fir	13500	27
00-Apr-1999	Genessee	Blue Spruce	12500	25
00-Apr-1999	Oakland	Scotch Pine	11000	22
00-Apr-1999	Genessee	Frazier Fir	6500	13
00-May-1999	Lake	Blue Spruce	42500	85
00-May-1999	Lake	White Pine	32000	64
00-May-1999	Lake	Frazier Fir	14500	29
00-May-1999	Kalkaska	Blue Spruce	13500	27
00-May-1999	Lake	Concolor Fir	12000	24
00-May-1999	Kalkaska	Concolor Fir	10000	20
00-May-1999	Kalkaska	Frazier Fir	7500	15
00-Sep-1999	Lake	Blue Spruce	3100	62
00-Sep-1999	Lake	White Pine	26500	53

Creating a database is as simple as creating any other worksheet, but there are two additional rules for worksheets that you intend to use as databases:

Blank rows signal the end of a database. Don't leave a blank row between column headings and data records. DO leave a blank row after all records and before totals, averages, or other summary rows.

Field names at the tops of columns must each be in a single cell and unique within a worksheet. Be consistent: Label every column.

Any worksheet you've already created can be used as a database, but you might have to delete or add rows or edit column labels to meet these requirements.

Sorting a Database

Database software must allow you to do two distinct things: organize, or *sort*, the data in a specific order (for example, alphabetized by state), and separate, or *filter*, the data to find specific information (for example, all your customers who live in Oregon).

To sort the data in a database, first select any cell in the database; then choose Data ➢ Sort from the menu bar to have Excel select the records in the database and open the Sort dialog box, shown in Figure 26.2.

FIGURE 26.2

The Sort dialog box

Excel will select all cells above, below, to the right, and to the left of the cell you selected until it encounters a blank column and row. Excel will examine the top row of the database and either assign it as a record by including it in the selection, or deselect it, assuming it is a row of column headings. The last section of the Data Sort dialog box lets you correct an incorrect selection by specifying whether you have a header row.

 TIP If you didn't select a cell within the database before choosing Data ➤ Sort, Excel will warn you that there was no list to select. Click OK, select a cell in the database, and choose Data ➤ Sort again.

In a telephone book, records are sorted initially by last name. This is called a *primary sort*. What if there is a tie: for example, all the people whose last name is Smith? If you know that lots of your records will have the same entry in the primary sort field, you can do a *secondary sort* on another field, like the first name. And if you might have two David Smiths, you can use the middle initial for a *tertiary sort*. Note that the secondary and tertiary sorts occur only in case of a tie at a higher level of sorting.

You can sort up to three levels using the Data Sort dialog box. Records can be sorted in *ascending order* (A–Z or 1–100) or *descending order* (Z–A or 100–1). In the Sort By box, enter or select the field name you want to sort by. Choose a sort order. If some of the records may have the same value in the Sort By field, use the first Then By text box to select the field you want to sort by when there is a tie in the primary sort field. For databases with many similar records (like a long customer list), you might want to add a tertiary sort, using the second Then By box. When you have made all the sort selections, click OK to sort the database according to your specifications.

Here's a summary of the steps for sorting data using the menu bar:

1. Select any cell within the database.

2. From the menu bar, choose Data ➤ Sort.

3. Select the field you want to sort by from the Sort By drop-down list. Click the Options button to set any special sorting options for text dates or case sensitivity.

4. Use the Then By drop-down lists to select secondary and tertiary sort fields.

5. Click the OK button to sort the database.

Using the Toolbar Sort Buttons

You can also sort a database using the sort buttons on the Standard toolbar. Select a single cell within the column you want to sort by. Click the Ascending Sort or Descending Sort button to sort the database.

This is an easy way to sort, but it has one major drawback: Excel doesn't allow you to verify that the correct cells have been selected as the database. It's best to sort each database once using the Sort ➤ Data dialog box to ensure that the correct rows and columns have been selected before using the toolbar.

 WARNING When you sort a database, it is vital that all of its columns are selected. If some columns are not selected, the selected columns will be sorted but the unselected columns will not be, ruining the integrity of the data by mixing up the records. (This is why you never include empty columns in a worksheet.) Always check to be sure that all columns were included before sorting. Click Undo immediately if some columns were omitted in a sort.

Use these steps to sort using the toolbar buttons:

1. Select any cell within the database in the column you want to sort by.

2. Click the Ascending or Descending Sort button.

3. For secondary, tertiary, and other sorts, use the Ascending and Descending Sort buttons to work through the sorts in reverse order.

Once you know how Excel sorts, you can use the sort buttons to do secondary and tertiary sorts. When Excel sorts the records in a database, it only rearranges records when necessary. If a list is already sorted by city, sorting it by state will create a list sorted first by state, and then by city within each state, because the existing city sort will only be rearranged to put the states in order.

If you need to sort by more than the three fields allowed in the Sort dialog box, sort the least important field first and work backward through the sort fields to the primary sort field.

Filtering a Database

There are many times you'll want to work with a database *subset:* a group of records in the database. For example, you might want to print all sales records for one sales-person, all the orders from one client, or all the customers who haven't made a purchase this year. A *filter* is used to select records that meet a specific criterion and temporarily hide all the other records. You enter criteria to set the filter.

Using AutoFilter

To have Excel set up an AutoFilter, select any cell in the database and choose Data ➤ Filter ➤ AutoFilter. Excel reads every record in the database and creates a filter criteria list for each field. Click the drop-down arrow that appears next to each field name (see Figure 26.3) to access the field's criteria list.

Month	County	Type	Quantit	Bundle:
00-Apr-1999	Genessee	White Pine	37000	74
00-Apr-1999	Oakland	Blue Spruce	22500	45
00-Apr-1999	Oakland	White Pine	15500	31
00-Apr-1999	Oakland	Concolor Fir	13500	27

- The default criteria setting in each field is All, which means that the contents of the field are not being used to filter the records.

- Top 10 is used in numeric fields to display the top or bottom 10, 5, or any other number or percentage of values.

- Custom prompts you to create a custom filter (see *Creating a Custom Filter,* below) for choices that don't appear on the list.

When you apply a filter, all the records not included in the subset are hidden, as shown in Figure 26.4, where the records are being filtered on Lake County. The number of records found and the total number of records in the database are displayed in the status bar. Each record retains its original row number; the row numbers of filtered records appear in blue. The drop-down arrow for the filtered field turns blue to show that it is being actively used to filter the database.

FIGURE 26.4

Filtering a database

4	Month	County	Type	Quantit	Bundle:
12	00-May-1999	Lake	Blue Spruce	42500	85
13	00-May-1999	Lake	White Pine	32000	64
14	00-May-1999	Lake	Frazier Fir	14500	29
16	00-May-1999	Lake	Concolor Fir	. 12000	24
19	00-Sep-1999	Lake	Blue Spruce	3100	62
20	00-Sep-1999	Lake	White Pine	26500	53

You can filter on more than one field to select, for example, all the Scotch Pine sales in Oakland County. Set the criteria using each relevant field's drop-down list. Only records that meet all the criteria you selected will be included in the filtered subset.

To redisplay the entire database, change the filter criteria for all filtered fields back to All, or simply choose Data ➤ Filter ➤ Show All. You'll know at a glance that all filters are set to All because the drop-down arrows and the row headings will all be black again.

Applying and using the AutoFilter is easy when you follow these steps:

1. Select any cell in the database.

2. Choose Data ➤ Filter ➤ AutoFilter to turn on the filter.

3. Click on the drop-down arrow for the field you want to use to filter, and choose a filter from the criteria drop-down list.

4. To see all the records in the database, reset all filter criteria to All.

Using the Top 10 Filter

When you choose Top 10 as your filter criterion, the Top 10 AutoFilter dialog box opens:

In the first box, choose Top or Bottom, depending on whether you want to see the highest or lowest values in the database. In the spin box control, enter a number larger than 0. In the last control, choose Items or Percents. For example, to see the top 10 percent of the scores in a column of test scores, choose Top, enter **10**, and then choose Percents.

 NOTE The Top 10 filter only works with numbers (including dates and times).

Creating a Custom Filter

When you filter using the drop-down criteria, you are always looking for records that exactly equal specific criteria or fall in a Top 10 criterion. Custom filters give you access to other ways to set criteria:

- All records with fields that are NOT equal to a criterion
- Records that are greater than or less than a criterion
- Records that meet one condition OR another

To create a custom filter, choose Custom from the drop-down criteria list to open the Custom AutoFilter dialog box, shown in Figure 26.5.

FIGURE 26.5

The Custom AutoFilter dialog box

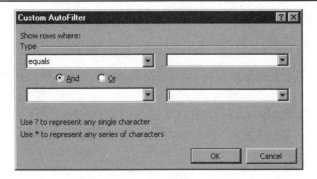

The first drop-down under Show Rows Where opens a list of operators. The list includes regular logical operators like Equals and Is Greater Than Or Equal To, but as you scroll the list you'll notice other operators that allow you to look for entries that do or do not begin with, end with, or contain a *string* you specify. A string is a pattern of text characters, such as a word or part of a word.

The right drop-down list shows the record entries in the field from the field criteria list. To find all records that are NOT in Lake County, choose Does Not Equal as the operator, and select Lake from the drop-down list. You can also enter text in the criteria controls.

 TIP Notice in the dialog box that you can use the wildcard characters * and ? to broaden the search string.

To find all orders for Oakland and Ottawa counties, you could

- Use the wildcard character and search for `equals O*`
- Use the Begins With type and search for `begins with O`

The AND and OR options are used when you want to filter by more than one criterion in a column. AND is used to establish the upper and lower ends of a range and is almost always used with numerical entries: `Quantity is greater than 100 AND Quantity is less than 201` leaves only the quantities between 101 and 200.

OR is used to filter by two different criteria: Lake County OR Oakland County. If you use AND when you mean OR, you'll often get a *null set:* no records. (There are no records in Lake County AND Oakland County—it's one or the other.) If you use OR when you mean AND, you'll get all the records. (Every record is either less than 201 or greater than 100.)

The following steps summarize how to create a custom filter:

1. If the AutoFilter is not turned on, turn it on (Data ➤ Filter ➤ AutoFilter). Choose Custom from the relevant column's drop-down list to open the Custom AutoFilter dialog box.

2. In the upper-left list box, set the operator for the first criterion.

3. Enter or select the first criterion from the upper-right drop-down list.

4. Set an operator, and enter or select the second criterion in the lower list boxes.

5. Set AND for a range; set OR to filter for more than one possible value.

6. Click OK to apply the custom filter.

The filter criteria drop-downs don't appear when you print a database, so there usually isn't a reason to turn the AutoFilter off until you are done working with a database. To turn the AutoFilter off, choose Data ➤ Filter ➤ AutoFilter again.

Working with Filtered Records

You can work with the filtered set of records in a number of ways. If you print the database while it is filtered, only the filtered records will print, so you can quickly generate reports based on any portion of the information in the Excel database.

Filtering is also useful when you need to create charts using part of the data in the database. Filter the records you want to chart, then select and chart the information as you would normally.

When you create a chart based on a filter, you need to print the chart before changing the filter criteria. Changing the criteria changes the chart. If you need to create a permanent chart, see the following section on creating a subset database.

Creating a Subset

There are times when you will want to work with or distribute a subset of the database. For example, you might have a database with 5,000 records—but only 700 of them pertain to your current project. It would be easier to work with a smaller database that included only the 700 records you need.

You can copy the filtered subset to the clipboard and paste it in a new location in any open workbook to create a new database containing only records from the filtered subset. Here are the steps for creating a new database from a filtered subset:

1. Filter the active database to create a filtered subset.

2. Select the filtered database, including the column labels and any other titles you wish to copy.

3. Click the Copy button or choose Edit ➤ Copy.

4. Select the first cell where you want the new database to appear.

5. Press Enter to paste the database.

Extracting a Subset

If you prefer, you can create a subset by *extracting* the subset's records from the database using Excel's Advanced Filter. The advanced filter requires you to establish a *criteria range* that includes the column labels from your database and one or more criteria that you enter directly below the labels.

The criteria range is the heart of advanced filtering. If the criteria range is incorrect, the extracted data will be wrong—so take your time with this. The column labels must be precisely the same as they are in the database, so begin by copying the column labels to another location in your workbook (a separate worksheet that you name *Criteria* is good).

Then, type the criteria you want to establish. For example, if you want to extract records where the Quantity is over 10,000, enter **>10000** in the cell just below the Quantity column label. If you have more than one criterion in a single column (for example, County = Genessee OR County = Oakland), use one cell for each criterion:

Month	County	Type	Quantity	Bundles
	Genessee			
	Oakland			

There are two ways to filter for two criteria in separate columns, based on whether you want to use AND or OR. Enter criteria on the same row for an AND condition:

Month	County	Type	Quantity	Bundles
	Genessee		>20000	

Or place criteria on separate rows for an OR condition:

Month	County	Type	Quantity	Bundles
	Genessee			
			>20000	

In this example, criteria are established to find quantities over 20,000 in Oakland County or over 10,000 in Lake County:

Month	County	Type	Quantity	Bundles
	Oakland		>20000	
	Lake		>10000	

You can't create this last criterion with an AutoFilter in one pass. You would need to find each county separately. A need to mix AND and OR conditions is one of the two reasons you might want to use an advanced filter.

 TIP You'll need to refer to the criteria range in the Advanced Filter dialog box, so you might want to name it.

When the criteria range is set, click anywhere in the database and open the Advanced Filter dialog box (Data ➤ Filter ➤ Advanced Filter) to see the second reason to use an advanced filter: You can instruct Excel to return only unique records, as shown in Figure 26.6.

PART

V

Number Crunching
with Excel

FIGURE 26.6

*The Advanced Filter
dialog box*

Excel will automatically select your entire database for the List Range text box. Use the Criteria Range text box to identify your criteria range, including the column labels.

Choose whether you want to filter the records in their current location (as Auto-Filter does) or extract the records by copying them to another location. If you choose another location, the Copy To text box will be enabled so that you can select the first cell of the range where the filtered records should be copied.

As with any copy operation, just select one cell—if you select a range, it must match exactly the range required by the extracted data. Be sure that there is room in the destination area for the incoming data.

You can enter a cell in any open workbook in the Copy To text box, so you can put the filtered subset of your database in a different workbook or a different worksheet than the original database.

If you want to eliminate duplicate records from the filtered list, turn on the Unique Records Only check box. Finally, click OK and Excel will filter in place or extract data as you have indicated.

 TIP Suppose you've got a database with 10,000 records, many of them duplicate records. Don't eliminate the duplicates manually. Set up a criteria range without criteria and use the Unique Records Only option to extract a list without duplicates.

When you use advanced filtering to filter in place, the filtered subset will have blue row numbers, just as it does with AutoFilter. To turn the filter off, choose Data ➤ Filter ➤ Show All.

Here's a summary of the steps for advanced filtering:

1. Copy the database column labels to another location.

2. Enter criteria in the cells directly under the column labels.

3. Select any cell in the database, and choose Data ➤ Filter ➤ Advanced Filter to open the Advanced Filter dialog box.

4. Check to ensure Excel has accurately identified the database range. If not, adjust it in the List text box.

5. Enter the criteria range in the Criteria list box.

6. Choose the Filter In Place or Copy To option.

7. If you are extracting (copying) the filtered list to another location, enter the upper-left cell of that location in the Copy To text box.

8. Enable or disable the Unique Records check box.

9. Click OK to create the filter.

Creating Subtotals

You can create subtotals based on any field in the database. A *subtotal* is not necessarily a sum: it can be an average, count, minimum, maximum, or other statistical calculation based on a group of records.

Before subtotaling, you need to sort the database on the field you wish to subtotal on. For example, if you want to subtotal each month's orders, first sort by month. Then, select a cell anywhere in the database and take the following steps:

1. Choose Data ➢ Subtotals to open the Subtotal dialog box, shown in Figure 26.7.

2. Select the numeric fields to be subtotaled when the value of the At Each Change In field changes.

3. Select a type of subtotal from the Use Function drop-down.

4. In the Add Subtotal To control, select each field you want to subtotal. You can subtotal more than one field at a time, but you have to use the same function: average three fields, sum three fields, etc.

FIGURE 26.7

The Subtotal dialog box

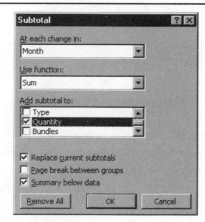

5. If necessary, change the settings for Replace Current Subtotals, Page Break Between Groups, and Summary Below Data.

   • Use Replace Current Subtotals if you have subtotaled earlier and want to replace the former set with new subtotals. If you want both sets of subtotals to appear (for example, sums and averages), deselect this option.

   • If you are going to print the worksheet with subtotals and want each sub-totaled set of records to print on a separate page, insert a Page Break Between Groups.

   • Summary Below Data places a summary (grand total, grand average) row at the bottom of the database.

6. When you have entered the information for subtotals, click the OK button to add subtotals, as shown in Figure 26.8.

PART

V

Number Crunching with Excel

To remove subtotals from a worksheet, open the Subtotal dialog box again (see Figure 26.7) and click the Remove All button.

FIGURE 26.8

The Traverse Tree Sales worksheet with subtotals

Month	County	Type	Quantit	Bundle
00-Apr-1999	Oakland	Blue Spruce	22500	45
00-Apr-1999	Oakland	White Pine	15500	31
00-Apr-1999	Oakland	Concolor Fir	13500	27
00-Apr-1999	Oakland	Scotch Pine	11000	22
	Oakland Total		62500	125
00-May-1999	Lake	Blue Spruce	42500	85
00-May-1999	Lake	White Pine	32000	64
00-May-1999	Lake	Frazier Fir	14500	29
00-May-1999	Lake	Concolor Fir	12000	24
00-Sep-1999	Lake	Blue Spruce	3100	62
00-Sep-1999	Lake	White Pine	26500	53
	Lake Total		130600	317

Saving Custom Views

If you find yourself manipulating your workbooks or worksheets frequently to display different portions on the screen together, you may want to save these views as custom views. Views allow you to preserve different ways of looking at a worksheet or workbook, so that you do not have to re-create these settings every time you want to revisit that workbook and see all of the same data at once.

You can save any of the following settings as a custom view:

- Column widths
- Window size or location on screen
- Frozen panes or split windows
- Hidden rows, hidden columns, or filter criteria
- Selected cells
- Print settings

Here are the steps for creating and saving a custom view:

1. Set up your spreadsheet or workbook full of spreadsheets the way you want the view to be saved. Apply filters, hide columns, split panes, freeze heading rows, and so on. Select View ➢ Custom Views.

2. In the Custom View dialog box (shown next), click the Add button.

3. Type a name for the new view in the Add View dialog box. It is best to include the name of the worksheet used in the view (or enough of the name so that you can readily recognize it in a list of multiple views).

4. Check boxes in the Include In View area to preserve Print Settings, or Hidden Rows, Columns And Filter Settings, or both.

5. Click OK. The new view will be added to the list of custom views for that workbook. These views are listed in the Custom Views dialog box.

To use the stored views, open the workbook you need, select View ➤ Custom Views, choose the correct view name in the Views list, and click the Show button. Your saved view will be applied to the correct worksheet in the workbook.

To eliminate an unneeded view, select its name in the Custom Views dialog box and click the Delete button. You cannot modify views, but you can open a view, make changes to it, and save it as a new view with the same name as the old view. Excel will ask you if you want to delete the old view and continue saving the new one. Click Yes, and the modified view will replace the old view.

Importing Data from Other Applications

Often, Excel users need to get data stored in files created in other programs into an Excel worksheet or workbook. It's easy to obtain data from files in other Microsoft

Office applications, but getting the stuff from non-Office programs can be more challenging. Fortunately, Excel readily opens files saved as plain text, and most programs can save files in this format.

 TIP When you open your file in Excel, some of its formatting and features may not translate well into the new environment, so be prepared to do some "data massaging" by replacing broken or missing formulas, reformatting columns, reapplying fonts, and so on.

Here are the steps to open a file from another application in Excel:

1. Select File ➢ Open. In the Files of Type list box, select the relevant source file type (for example, an earlier version of Excel) or simply display All Types. Locate and select the file, and click Open.

2. If your file opens, save it as an Excel file and begin working with it. If it does not open, or looks very garbled in Excel, open it in the original application and save it as a text file; then use the steps in the next section to get it into Excel.

 TIP In some instances, Excel may give you a "file not valid" error message, in which case you must return to the original application, save the file as a text file, and reopen it in Excel with the Text Import Wizard, described in the next section. In other cases, as with some word processing files, Excel will jump right into the Text Import Wizard.

Parsing Imported Data with the Text Import Wizard

When Excel can't open an imported file directly, you can use the Text Import Wizard to open the file and parse it into an Excel spreadsheet. *Parsing* is a process in which Excel examines a file, converts text items to relevant data types, and formats it into rows and columns. In order to be parsed, a text file must already resemble a spreadsheet or table, with each paragraph corresponding to a record or row, and with some character, usually a comma or tab, marking the column breaks.

Here's how to open a text file, parse its contents, and convert it into an Excel format with rows and columns using the Text Import Wizard:

1. Select File ➢ Open and select Text Files in the Files Of Type list box.

2. Navigate to your file using the folder structure in the Look In list box. Select your file and click Open. The first step of the Text Import Wizard appears, as shown in Figure 26.9.

PART

V

Number Crunching
with Excel

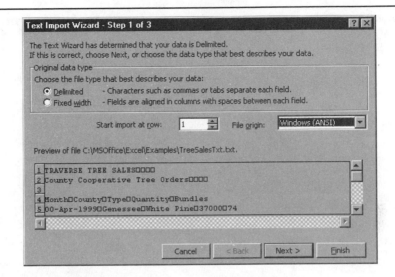

FIGURE 26.9

The Text Import
Wizard, step 1

3. The wizard attempts to determine what type of text file it is opening. If it has guessed correctly, click Next, if not, select the appropriate option in the Original Data Type area and click Next. Your choices are:

> **Delimited** Used for text files where words or data are separated by commas or tab markers.

> **Fixed Width** Used when the data or words in the text file are separated only by spaces.

4. Excel adds the column boundaries in Step 2 of the Text Import Wizard, as you can see in Figure 26.10. If the columns are not laid out properly, examine the Delimiters area. You can specify a different separator here, if your text file uses a comma instead of a tab to separate data, for example. Click Next.

5. The final step in the Text Import Wizard (Figure 26.11) lets you set the format for each of the newly defined columns. By default, all of the columns will be set to General format, unless you say otherwise. The format used in the column appears in the header. If you want all of the columns to have the same format, but something other than General, hold down the Shift key and click on each column until all are selected. Choose a format from the options in the Column Data Format area. Click Finish when the formats have been set.

TIP You can parse data that's already in Excel to, for example, separate a column of full names into first and last names. Select the data, and then choose Data ➤ Text To Columns.

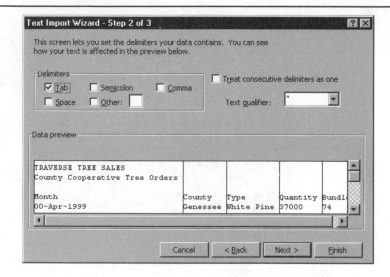

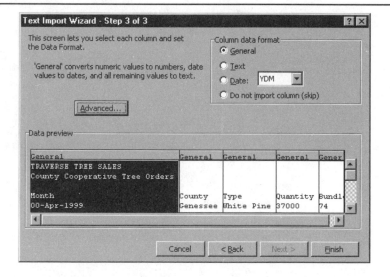

Excel displays your new spreadsheet. You can resize rows and columns as needed, and you can format row and column headers using tools on the Formatting toolbar.

Using Refreshable Text Importing

If you will be updating the original text file containing the data you plan to import, you can establish a link to this source file so that every time it is changed, those modifications will appear in the Excel file, too. This process, known as *refreshable text importing*, uses the Text Import Wizard, too, but accesses it through a different menu command.

To implement refreshable text, use these steps:

1. Open the Excel workbook and select the worksheet where you will be importing the data. Click in the cell where you want the insertion point, and select Data ≻ Get External Data ≻ Import Text File.

2. Find the text file containing the data using the Look In list box in the Import Text File dialog box. Select the file and click Import.

3. Follow steps 3 through 5 in the "Parsing Imported Data" procedure to use the Text Import Wizard to import the file as a refreshable file.

 NOTE Refresh the data by selecting Data ≻ Refresh Data, selecting the appropriate text file in the Import Text File dialog box, and clicking Import. If you only want to import a portion of the text file as refreshable text, you should construct a query using the Microsoft Query tool, discussed in Chapter 34.

Using Data Forms

Data forms provide an easy way to enter or search for data yourself, and they offer a bulletproof way to let a less-accomplished user enter data. Select any cell in a database and choose Data ≻ Form to open a data form. The first record in the database will be displayed in the data form. The data form for Traverse Tree Sales is shown in Figure 26.12.

Because data forms have a portrait orientation, they're particularly helpful when the columns in your database exceed the width of the screen. Using the form allows you to see all the database fields at once without scrolling horizontally.

In the form, use the vertical scroll bar or the Up and Down arrow keys to browse the records. Use the Tab key to move between fields in the form; pressing Enter moves to the next record.

You can change the contents of a field by editing the text box next to the field name. The contents of *calculated fields* are displayed without a text box, because you can't edit them. However, if you change a value that a calculated field is based on, Excel will recalculate the field. To discard changes made to a record, click the Restore button before moving to another record.

FIGURE 26.12

A data form for the Traverse Tree Sales database

Adding and Deleting Records

Clicking the New button or scrolling to the last record of the database opens the New Record form. Enter each field in the appropriate text box control. When you have entered information for the last field, press Enter or click the New button again if you want to keep entering new records. Press the ↑ (Up arrow) key or click the scroll bar to close the New dialog box.

To delete the record currently displayed in the data form, click the Delete button. A dialog box will appear, warning that the record will be permanently deleted. Pay attention to the warning—clicking Undo will not bring the record back. Click the OK button to delete the record's row from the database.

It isn't always more convenient to use the data form. Excel's AutoComplete feature doesn't work with the data form, so you have to type each entry fully.

Searching for Records

You can use the data form to search for individual records that meet specific criteria. This is like filtering, but you view the records one at a time. This is a good way to locate specific records that you need to delete.

The following steps outline how to search for records with the Data Form:

1. Open the data form if it is not already open.

2. Click the Criteria button to open the Criteria form:

3. Enter the search criteria for one or more fields in the text box controls. Excel joins two criteria with AND, so it will only find records that meet both criteria. You can't search for records that meet either criteria (OR). For advanced searching, use a filter. If you want to erase the search criteria, click the Criteria button again. Click the Clear button to delete the criteria, then click the Form button to return to the form.

4. Click Find Next to find the first record that meets the criteria. Use Find Next and Find Prev to view the records that meet the search criteria.

5. Click the scroll bar to view all records in the database.

Creating Pivot Tables and Pivot Charts

Pivot tables are a powerful tool for data analysis. A *pivot table* summarizes the columns of information in a database in relationship to each other. (The graphical equivalent of a pivot table, a *pivot chart* displays different views of data, depending on what you choose to put in it.) Our Traverse Tree Sales example is a small database, but it would still take time and effort to answer the following questions accurately:

• How many trees of each type were delivered each month?

• How many Blue Spruces were delivered each month?

- How many White Pines were delivered in 1999?
- What was the average number of each type of tree sold to Oakland County?

You could sort the list and then add subtotals to answer any one of these questions. Then, to answer any other question, you would have to sort and subtotal again. A single pivot table will allow you to answer all of the above questions, and more.

Using the PivotTable Wizard

Select any cell in a database, and choose Data ➤ PivotTable and PivotChart Report to launch the PivotTable and PivotChart Wizard (see Figure 26.13).

Step 1: Identifying the Data Source and the Type of Report

In step 1 of the wizard, you tell Excel what kind of data you have: data in a single Excel database, data from an external source like Microsoft Access, data that you want to consolidate from several worksheets or sources, or an existing PivotTable. You also specify whether you want just a pivot table or a pivot table with a pivot chart. Clicking Next moves you to the second step.

FIGURE 26.13

Step 1 of the PivotTable and PivotChart Wizard

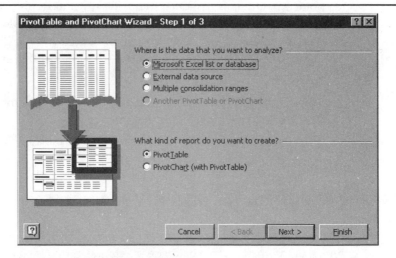

Step 2: Verifying the Data Range

In step 2 (Figure 26.14), verify the range of the database. A flashing line should appear around a suggested range of cells. Use the scroll bars to verify that the entire database—including the field names—is selected. If there is no range selected, or if the range is incorrect, select the correct range before clicking the Next button.

Step 3: Layout and Destination

In the third step (see Figure 26.15), you'll specify the destination, final layout, and any options. The default destination is a new worksheet. To place the pivot table in an existing worksheet, click Existing Worksheet. Then enter a cell address for the upper-left corner of the Pivot Table in the text box.

FIGURE 26.14

Step 2 of the PivotTable and PivotChart Wizard–identifying a data range

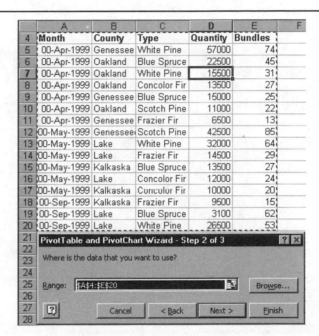

	A	B	C	D	E	F
4	Month	County	Type	Quantity	Bundles	
5	00-Apr-1999	Genessee	White Pine	57000	74	
6	00-Apr-1999	Oakland	Blue Spruce	22500	45	
7	00-Apr-1999	Oakland	White Pine	15500	31	
8	00-Apr-1999	Oakland	Concolor Fir	13500	27	
9	00-Apr-1999	Genessee	Blue Spruce	15000	25	
10	00-Apr-1999	Oakland	Scotch Pine	11000	22	
11	00-Apr-1999	Genessee	Frazier Fir	6500	13	
12	00-May-1999	Genessee	Scotch Pine	42500	85	
13	00-May-1999	Lake	White Pine	32000	64	
14	00-May-1999	Lake	Frazier Fir	14500	29	
15	00-May-1999	Kalkaska	Blue Spruce	13500	27	
16	00-May-1999	Lake	Concolor Fir	12000	24	
17	00-May-1999	Kalkaska	Concolor Fir	10000	20	
18	00-Sep-1999	Kalkaska	Frazier Fir	9500	15	
19	00-Sep-1999	Lake	Blue Spruce	3100	62	
20	00-Sep-1999	Lake	White Pine	26500	53	

PivotTable and PivotChart Wizard - Step 2 of 3

Where is the data that you want to use?

Range: $A$4:$E$20   Browse...

Cancel   < Back   Next >   Finish

FIGURE 26.15

Step 3 of the PivotTable and PivotChart Wizard–selecting a destination

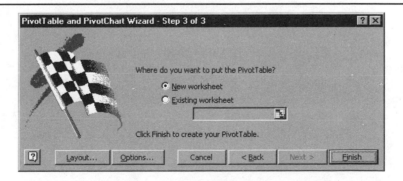

PivotTable and PivotChart Wizard - Step 3 of 3

Where do you want to put the PivotTable?

○ New worksheet
○ Existing worksheet

Click Finish to create your PivotTable.

Layout...   Options...   Cancel   < Back   Next >   Finish

Click the Layout button to display the Layout settings. A pivot table contains four areas: the Page number, the Column labels, the Row labels, and the Data. Each area has a corresponding layout area in the dialog box, shown in Figure 26.16. At the right side of the dialog box is a group of *field buttons*, one for each field name in the database. In this step you design the pivot table layout by dragging the field buttons into one of the four sections of the layout area. The Row, Column, and Data areas must have fields assigned to them; Page is an optional area.

FIGURE 26.16

Designing a table's Layout in the PivotTable Wizard

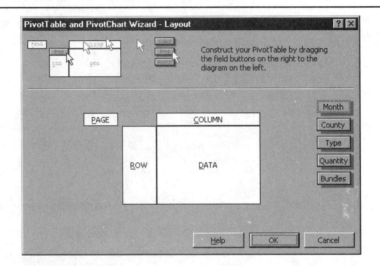

 TIP Place fields you want to compare in the Row and Column areas. For example, you might want to compare sales regions by month, or types of trees sold by county. The Row and Column areas are somewhat interchangeable; however, your pivot table is easier to use if it isn't too wide.

When the table is created, Excel will examine the fields you've chosen. Each unique entry becomes a row or column heading in the pivot table. If you have 5 unique entries in column A, but 10 in column C, using column A for Column and C for Row will create a pivot table report that fits on a screen. If you put column C in the Column, you will have 10 columns of data—too wide to view without scrolling.

If you need to create separate reports for values in one or more columns, drag those field buttons to the Page area. The Page area works like a filter in the completed pivot table.

Information in the Data area is mathematically summarized, so numeric fields are generally placed there. For Traverse Tree Sales, we could place either Quantity, Bundles, or both in the Data area.

As you drop a field button into the Data area, Excel will indicate the type of summary that will be done with the data. SUM is the default. To change the type of summary, drag the field button to the Data area, and then double-click on the field button to open the PivotTable Field dialog box. Choose the type of summary you want to use from the scroll list.

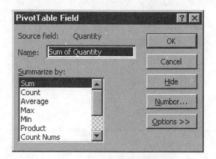

The default numeric format in a pivot table is General. You can click the Number button in this dialog box to format the numbers for this field, or you can wait and format the completed pivot table. Clicking the Option button extends the PivotTable Field dialog box so that you can perform custom calculations (see "Using Custom Calculations in Pivot Tables," later in this chapter). When you are finished laying out the pivot table, click the OK button to return to step 3 of the PivotTable Wizard.

To name the pivot table and specify other options, click the Options button to open the PivotTable Options dialog box, shown in Figure 26.17. You can name the pivot table just as you name any other range of cells. If you don't name it, Excel will give it a name like PivotTable1. For more information about any other option, click the dialog box Help button, and then click on the option. When you are finished setting options, click OK to return to the PivotTable Wizard and finish the process.

Click Finish to close the Wizard and create the pivot table report, as shown in Figure 26.18. The PivotTable toolbar will also open, so that you can change the completed table's layout and options.

PART

V

Number Crunching with Excel

FIGURE 26.17

The PivotTable Options dialog box

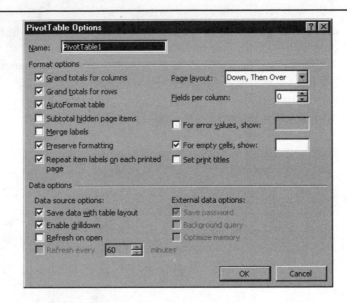

FIGURE 26.18

A completed PivotTable report

Sum of Quantity	Month			
County	00-Apr-1999	00-May-1999	00-Sep-1999	Grand Total
Genessee	56000			56000
Kalkaska		31000		31000
Lake		101000	29600	130600
Oakland	62500			62500
Grand Total	118500	132000	29600	280100

Using the PivotTable Toolbar

If the PivotTable toolbar does not appear, turn it on by choosing View ➤ Toolbars ➤ PivotTable:

Using Custom Calculations in Pivot Tables

Excel 2000 supports custom calculations in the Data fields of a pivot table. You create custom calculations in the third step of the PivotTable Wizard. In the wizard's Layout window (Figure 26.16), double-click the button for the field you want to calculate to open the PivotTable Field dialog box. Click the Options button to expand the dialog box; then choose one of the functions listed in Table 26.1 from the Show Data As drop-down list.

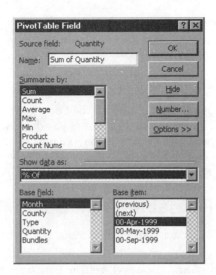

Many of the functions use a *Base field* and a *Base item*. Base fields and Base items are like filter criteria: the Base field is a column in your database, and the Base item is a value from that field.

TABLE 26.1: FREQUENTLY USED CUSTOM PIVOT TABLE FUNCTIONS

Function	Result/Use
Difference From	Shows the data in the data area as the difference from the value you specify for the Base field and item. Used to compare sales in dollars or units to a specific sales figure.
% Of	Displays the data in the data area as a percentage of the value you specify for the Base item. Used to show a percentage comparison between sales or revenues and a target figure, where sales that hit the target would be 100%.
% Difference From	Shows the difference between the data in the data area and the value you specify as the Base item, as a percentage of the base data. Used to show how much sales exceeded or fell short of a target; sales that hit the target would be 0%.
Running Total In	Displays the data in the data area as a running total. Used to show cumulative progress (by month, week, or other time period) toward a goal.
% of total	Displays each data item as a percentage of the grand total of all the data in the PivotTable. Used to show each entry's contribution to the grand total as a percentage.

PART

V

Number Crunching
with Excel

If your table is already completed and you want to change a summarization method, click the PivotTable Field button to open the dialog box.

TIP A chart that contains thousands of bars or columns for the rows in a database is meaningless. Instead, base your chart on a pivot table. Don't begin by selecting a cell that includes a field button, because as you drag away the button will move. Begin at the lower-right corner and end on the field button.

Creating Pivot Tables from External Data Sources

If you have external data created in an application other than Excel that you want to use in a pivot table or chart, you can obtain this data while using the PivotTable and PivotChart Wizard. However, getting data from the wizard involves using the add-on program Microsoft Query, which comes on your Office 2000 CD-ROM but is not installed during a regular setup operation. The wizard will also install Microsoft Query for you. (Chapter 34 discusses Microsoft Query.)

The following steps will initiate the process of getting external data through the PivotTable and PivotChart Wizard:

1. Select Data ➤ PivotTable and PivotChart Report and choose External Data Source in the first step of the three wizard steps.

2. In the Step 2 dialog box, click the Get Data button. If Microsoft Query is not installed on your system, you will be prompted to install it from the Office 2000 CD-ROM.

3. After Microsoft Query is installed, the Microsoft Query Choose Data Source dialog box appears. Refer to Chapter 34 for instructions on using this tool to pull data from other applications into Excel.

Changing Pivot Table Layout

You might need to summarize a database in a number of different ways. Rather than create a new pivot table, you can change the layout of an existing pivot table. The field buttons you placed in the Page, Column, and Row areas are in the pivot table. You can change the table by dragging a field button to another area, and Excel will update the pivot table. For example, if you want to view the data in Figure 26.18 by county and date, you can drag the County button to the Column area and Month to the Row area. The pivot table will change to reflect the new layout.

To remove a field from the pivot table, drag the field button out of the pivot table area. A large *X* will appear on the button. Release the mouse button to drop and delete the field. To add a field to the pivot table, select any cell in the table and choose Data ➤ PivotTable And PivotChart Report to reopen the Layout page of the wizard. Add, delete, or rearrange the field buttons, then click the Finish button to return to the pivot table.

Keeping the Pivot Table Updated

A pivot table is dynamically linked to the database used to create the table. If you edit values within the database, simply choose Data ➤ Refresh Data, or click the Refresh Data button, and Excel will update the pivot table to reflect the database changes.

However, if you add rows or columns to the database, you *cannot* simply refresh the data. You must return to the Pivot Table And PivotChart Wizard and identify the new range of records that should be included in the table. If you don't, the pivot table values won't include the added data.

To update the range being used by the pivot table, choose Data ➤ PivotTable and PivotTable Chart Report from the menu bar or click the PivotTable menu in the toolbar and choose Wizard. The PivotTable Wizard will open at Step 1. Click the Next button to go to Step 2 and reselect the database. Click the Finish button to close the wizard and return to the updated pivot table.

Creating Separate Pivot Tables

Rather than printing different departments' or counties' pivot tables on different pages, you might want to create a series of pivot tables—one for each department or county. You can do this quite simply. First, make sure that the field you want to create each table for (like County) is in the Page area of the table. Then take the following steps:

1. Arrange the pivot table layout so that the field that you want to use to separate the tables is in the Page area.

2. Click the Show Pages button or select any cell in the table, right-click, and choose Show Pages.

3. Choose the field you want to create separate pivot tables for, and click OK.

Excel will insert new worksheets and create a pivot table for each unique entry in the selected field.

Drilling Down in a Pivot Table

Even though the cells in the Data area contain summary information, you can *drill down* through a pivot table to view all the detail that underlies an individual summary figure. Double-click any nonzero value in the Data area, and Excel opens a new worksheet to display the records that were used to create that cell of the summary.

Figure 26.19 shows the results of drilling down in the cell for Oakland County in April 1999.

FIGURE 26.19

Drilling down to details

Month	County	Type	Quantity	Bundles
00-Apr-1999	Oakland	Scotch Pine	11000	22
00-Apr-1999	Oakland	Blue Spruce	22500	45
00-Apr-1999	Oakland	White Pine	15500	31
00-Apr-1999	Oakland	Concolor Fir	13500	27

Creating Pivot Charts

Pivot charts can be created at the same time you generate a pivot table or later on, after you have studied the pivot table. The default PivotChart type is a simple column chart, but you can change the chart to any of Excel's other chart types, except for the scatter, bubble, and stock charts.

You can rearrange the way the pivot table data fields are displayed on the chart, but the pivot chart will start out with the row fields in the table becoming the category fields (the horizontal, or x-axis) in the chart. Similarly, the column fields in the table become the series (the vertical, or y-axis) fields in the chart. Pivot charts also have page fields, which are optional. Refer to the earlier section, "Using the PivotTable Wizard," to decide what to drag onto the Category, Series, and Data areas of the chart.

Here are the steps for creating your pivot chart:

1. Open the workbook containing the worksheet you want to use for the chart and select the appropriate worksheet tab. Select Data ➤ PivotTable and Pivot-Chart Report.

2. In the first step of the wizard, select PivotChart (With PivotTable) and click Next.

3. In the second wizard step, make sure the correct data range is selected and click Next.

TIP If you have already created a pivot table with the selected data range, Excel will ask whether you want to create a chart based on the existing pivot table. If more than one pivot table exists for the data, Excel will prompt you to pick the one you want to use.

4. The third and final step in the wizard asks you where to put the pivot table, if you are creating one along with the chart. You can change the layout and other

options here, as described in "Using the PivotTable Wizard." Choose either New Worksheet or Existing Worksheet, and click Finish.

5. You will see the blank pivot chart and the PivotTable toolbar with fields from the pivot chart (shown in Figure 26.20). Drag fields from the toolbar onto the labeled chart areas to create the chart.

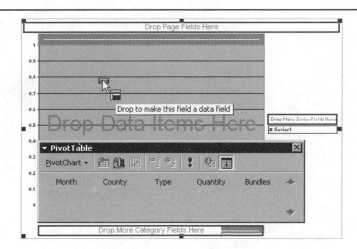

The fields you drag onto the chart become labels with list buttons. Click on these labels to change the data displayed. In the example shown below, clicking on the County label displays a list of counties and the All selection, which displays data for all the counties on the chart. You can select any of these data display options and click OK to redisplay the chart with your data choice.

 TIP Use the Chart menu to modify the pivot chart in the same way you would modify a regular Excel chart. See Chapter 24 for more information on the Chart menu commands.

Data Mapping in Excel

Use Excel's Data Map tool with geographic data: countries, states, or zip codes. With Data Map, you can create amazing, shaded maps to illustrate any figures that are tied to major geographic areas. The map in Figure 26.21 shows the population by state from the U.S. Census of 1990.

FIGURE 26.21
Population data map

State	Population
Alabama	4040587
Alaska	550043
Arizona	3665228
Arkansas	2350725
California	29760022
Colorado	3294394
Connecticut	3287116
Delaware	666168
District Of Columbia	606900
Florida	12937926
Georgia	6478216
Hawaii	1108229
Idaho	1006749
Illinois	11430602
Indiana	5544159
Iowa	2776755
Kansas	2477574
Kentucky	3685296
Louisiana	4219973
Maine	1227928
Maryland	4781468

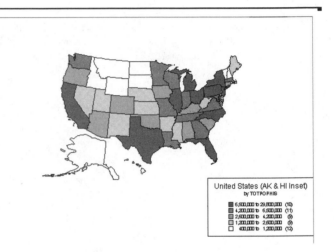

TIP Excel comes with extensive demographic information, including population figures by age range and gender for the world, U.S. states, Australian territories, and Canadian and Mexican provinces. All this information is contained in the `Pfiles\Common Files\Msshared\Datamap\Data\MAPSTATS.XLS` file.

You can create a data map from any worksheet that contains a column of geographic data: country, state, and province names, zip codes, or postal codes. If you use zip codes, first format them as text. Select the column of geographic data and the columns that contain the numerical data you want to map.

Click the Data Map button, and use the crosshairs pointer to drag a place for the data map in the worksheet; Excel will begin analyzing your data. If there's any ambiguity about your data, you will be prompted to select a map. Excel always asks which U.S. map you want if you use U.S. state information.

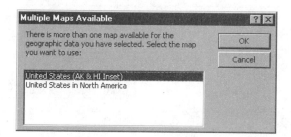

Select a map and click OK. Click within your worksheet. The data map will appear in your worksheet, the Microsoft Map Control panel will open, and the Microsoft Map command bars will replace the Excel menu bar and toolbar, as shown in Figure 26.22.

MASTERING TROUBLESHOOTING

Installing Data Map

Depending on how Office 2000 was installed on your system, you may have to add Data Map separately after the main installation process. If you have a file from a previous version of Office that contains a Data Map object, just click on the map and Office 2000 will automatically prompt you to install the Data Map add-on. You will need your Office 2000 CD-ROM to proceed, however.

If you are starting fresh and do not have old Data Map files to open, use the following procedure to install Data Map:

1. Insert the Office 2000 CD-ROM and select Start ➤ Settings ➤ Control Panel ➤ Add/Remove Programs. Choose Microsoft Office 2000 from the list on the Install/Uninstall page, and then click Add/Remove.

2. Expand the Microsoft Excel features list.

3. Click the Microsoft Map drop-down list and select Run From My Computer.

4. Continue to follow the prompts until the installation is complete.

After you run the setup program to add Data Map, you should see the Data Map globe button on your Standard Excel toolbar. If you do not, use the Tools ➤ Customize command to add the Data Map button to any toolbar, as explained in Chapter 38.

FIGURE 26.22

A data map and its Control panel

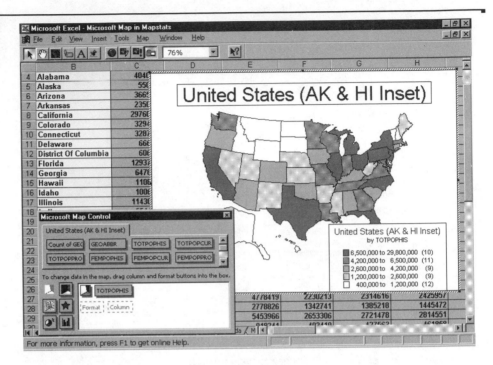

 You can display or hide the Map Control panel with the Show Map Control button on the toolbar. The Map Control panel is similar to the PivotTable layout page. If you begin by selecting multiple columns of data, you can see how each looks by dragging the column's button into the box in the control. To remove a data category, drag the column button out of the box, and drop it back in the category area.

On the left side of the control are format buttons. Drag a format button into the space next to a column to format it. When you remove a column, its format is automatically removed, and vice versa. Table 26.2 describes each format button.

TABLE 26.2: DATA MAP FORMATS		
Button	**Name**	**Description**
	Value Shading	Shows numeric data in different shades.
	Category Shading	Shows text data in different shades; used to show membership in a region or category.

Continued ▶

TABLE 26.2: DATA MAP FORMATS (CONTINUED)		
	Dot Density	Shows numerical data as dots; larger quantities are represented by more dots.
	Graduated Symbol	Shows numerical data as symbols; larger quantities are represented by larger symbols.
	Pie Chart	Places a small pie chart over each area of the map to represent local data.
	Column Chart	Places a small column chart over each area of the map to represent local data.

You can combine different formats to show multiple categories of information in the same data map. The data map in Figure 26.23 shows the total population with value shading and the population separated into age groups in the pie charts.

FIGURE 26.23

*A combination
data map*

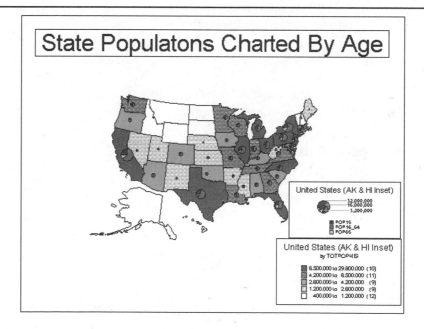

The data map, like a chart, is an object embedded in your worksheet. Use the handles to move and size it as you would any other object. Click anywhere in the worksheet to close the object and return to the worksheet.

Beefing Up the Data Map

To see a list of other features that are attached to the map, right-click on the data map and choose Features from the shortcut menu.

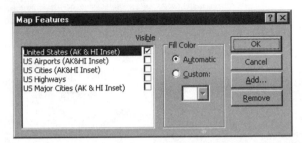

Use the check boxes to turn features on or off. If you want the feature to appear in a different color, select the feature, choose the Custom option, and select a color from the drop-down list. Don't expect realism here: oceans, for example, can be either blue or pink. When you're done setting features, click OK to apply them. If the feature you want to add doesn't appear on the list, right-click on the data map and choose Add Features from the menu to open the Add Features dialog box. After you've added a feature, it will appear, turned on, in the list in the Features dialog box. Adding Australia Highways to the map in Figure 26.23 doesn't change the map at all, since Australia isn't anywhere near this map. But if you add Canada Highways or Airports, they'll appear, in place, above the northern U.S. border.

Fun and Games with the Data Map

Once you're happy with the map's overall appearance, it's time to use some of the tools on the Data Map toolbar.

 The pointer, enabled by default, is used to select objects. You can move and size legend and text box objects in the data map.

 Use the Grabber to move the map around within the data map object window.

 When you click the Center Map button, the mouse pointer turns into a centering tool. Click the part of the map you want centered in the data map object to move the map.

 The Map Labels button offers a drill-down capability. Click the button, and the Map Labels dialog box opens.

In the first drop-down, select the feature you want to label. Then, choose whether you want the labels to display the names of the features on the map or the values from a column in the drop-down list. (The Values From list shows all the columns you initially selected, not just the ones included in the data map—so choose carefully.) Click OK to turn on map labels. The pointer will turn into crosshairs, and as you move the pointer into the center of a feature (like a state), the map label for that feature will appear. Click the Pointer tool to turn map labels off.

Use the Text tool to add a text box to the data map. You can add a text box at the side for explanatory material, or place a text box on top of the map to label a feature.

Click the Custom Pin Map button and a dialog box will open, prompting you for a new name for the pin map or for the name of an existing pin map. Use the Pin Map tool to show the location of regional offices, corporate headquarters, or reported cases of Legionnaires' Disease.

The Display Entire button centers the map in the middle of the data map object and expands or contracts it so the entire map is visible.

If you've recently used the Grabber, click the Redraw button to redraw the current view of the map and eliminate the distortion caused by the Grabber.

When the Map Refresh button is enabled, you know there's been a change in the data map's underlying data. Click the Refresh button to rebuild the map to reflect the changes. If you're changing a lot of data, you might prefer to have the map automatically refreshed. Choose Tools ➤ Options, and turn on automatic refresh in the Options dialog box.

The Zoom Percentage of Map menu zooms in (or out) to show you a more detailed view of the map. When you zoom, the center of the map remains in the same place, so the easiest way to zoom in on a feature is to use the Center Map tool first to center the feature. After the map is zoomed, use the Grabber to move to other areas of the map. Remember that when you click back in the worksheet, the map remains in the view you left it in. If you want it zoomed in, leave it that way. If you want the entire map, click the Display Entire button before moving back to the worksheet.

PART

V

Number Crunching with Excel

Printing Data Maps

Data maps print as objects in a worksheet; you can't print them separately. Of course, you can always move or copy a data map into a blank worksheet if you don't want it to print on its original worksheet.

What's Next

Now that you've mastered different ways of using and displaying Excel data, it's time to move on to some more advanced topics. Chapter 27 presents Excel's linking and proofing tools. It shows you how to share data between workbooks and manage multiple workbooks easily using 3-D cell references, linking commands, and file management techniques. This chapter also covers Excel's auditing features, which will assist you in finding and correcting data entry errors and logical errors in formulas.

CHAPTER 27

Linking and Proofing Tools

Excel provides a number of options for ensuring that the data you store and manage in workbooks remains up-to-date and accurate. Excel's linking features help you get the most out of your data by letting you use it in more than one worksheet while minimizing the amount of tedious reentry required to do so. Excel also has extensive auditing functions for detecting and correcting errors, repairing broken formulas, and untangling complicated spreadsheet calculations and cell references run amuck.

Linking Workbooks

A *link* is a reference to a cell or range in another workbook. Links are commonly used to avoid double-entering workbook information. For example, say you work in a company where departments are responsible for their own budgets. As the time to finalize the coming year's budget approaches, each manager is working furiously on his or her budget. The vice president for finance has a master budget that summarizes the department budgets.

It's not practical to put all the department worksheets and the master budget in one large workbook, because many people would need to use the workbook at the same. Instead, if the managers link the workbooks together, they won't have to fight with each other or with the vice president over whose turn it is to work with the budget. (Experience indicates that the vice president almost always wins.)

The vice president's workbook will include links to cells in the departmental budget workbooks. As the department managers change their numbers, the changes can be reflected in the vice president's master budget workbook.

Each link establishes a relationship between two workbooks. The vice president's workbook is called the *dependent workbook*, because each value there depends on a value in another workbook, which is called the *source workbook*.

There are two ways to create a link: by using an open workbook as a source or by referring to a workbook's disk or network location. The first method is much easier to use. It's the same as creating any other reference in a formula, but you need to switch to the source workbook before selecting the cell to reference in the formula.

Before creating the formula that includes a link, open the source workbook. Then, in the dependent workbook, begin entering the formula with an equal sign (=). At the point in the formula where you want to include a cell reference from the source workbook, choose Window on the menu bar and select the source workbook. Click on the cell that you want to reference, and it will be included, as shown in Figure 27.1.

FIGURE 27.1

Creating a link

VP Master Budget

	A	B	C	D	E	F
1	**Proposed Budget - 1999**					
2						
3						
4	**Employee Expense**	**Sales**	**Service**	**Acct**	**Totals**	
5	Salaries	='[Proposed Dept. Budget.xls]Sales'!$B$4				
6	Benefits					
7	**Total Employee Expense**					
8						
9						
10						
11						

Total Budget / Sheet2 / Sheet3 /

Notice that the cell reference includes the workbook and worksheet names as well as the cell address:

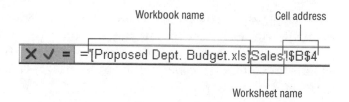

Workbook name   Cell address

✕ ✓ =   ='[Proposed Dept. Budget.xls]Sales'!$B$4

Worksheet name

You may prefer to arrange the source and dependent workbooks so that you can see the "result" cell and the cell to be referenced at the same time. With both workbooks open, choose Window ➤ Arrange to open the Arrange Windows dialog box:

Choose how you want the open workbooks arranged, and then use each workbook window's sizing tool to further size and arrange the windows.

TIP You can also arrange copies of a single workbook in order to work in different areas of the workbook in separate windows. Choose Window ➤ New Window and then open the Arrange Windows dialog box and arrange the windows.

If the workbook is not open, you must provide all the information that Excel needs to find the source workbook, including the full path. For example, if you want to refer to cell D4 in the Sales sheet of the Proposed Dept. Budget workbook, stored in the Sales Management folder on the C drive, the reference would be: `'C:\Sales Management\[Proposed Dept. Budget.xls]Sales'!D4`. There are many places to make a mistake when typing an entry like this. Try to create links with open source workbooks whenever possible.

Linking with Paste Link

If you simply want to include a cell from another workbook (as opposed to using it in a formula), create a link by copying and paste-linking.

Open both workbooks; then select and copy the cell(s) from the source workbook. Activate the destination workbook, and choose Edit ➤ Paste Special from the menu bar to open the Paste Special dialog box.

A normal paste simply pastes the formula(s) from the Clipboard. With Paste Special, you can paste values, formulas, formats, and other cell attributes, or perform a math operation during the paste:

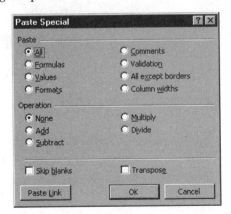

Click the Paste Link button, select a destination for the pasted selection, and press Enter to paste the link to the source workbook.

Updating Links

When you open the dependent workbook and the source workbook is not open, Excel will ask if you want to update the links. If both workbooks are open, changes in the source workbook are automatically updated in the dependent workbook.

If the source workbook can be opened by other users, however, they could be making changes to that workbook while you are working with the dependent workbook. In this case, the links will not be updated automatically; you have to instruct Excel to update the links.

With the dependent workbook open, choose Edit ➤ Links to open the Links dialog box (see Figure 27.2). From the Source File list, choose the source workbook that you want to update. Click the Update Now button to update the dependent workbook with information from the latest saved version of the source workbook.

FIGURE 27.2

*Use the Links dialog
box to update links
manually.*

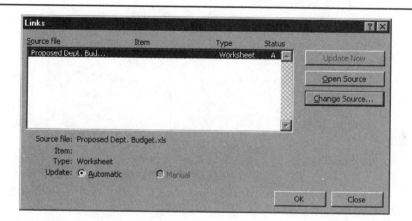

Creating 3-D Cell References

In Excel, you can reference ranges that occur in the same cell or group of cells on two or more worksheets. For example, Figure 27.3 shows the January, February, and March worksheets for reporting different types of media sold at various locations; all three worksheets have exactly the same layout. The FirstQuarter worksheet summarizes the figures from the three monthly worksheets. Because all the worksheets have exactly the same layout, you can total all worksheets at one time with a 3-D cell reference.

FIGURE 27.3

*Three monthly work-
sheets combined into a
summary quarterly
worksheet by using
3-D cell references*

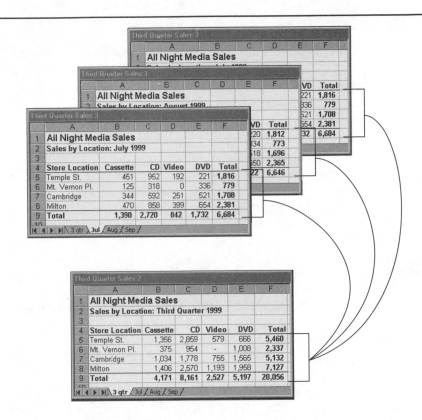

First make sure that the worksheets you want to reference are next to each other.
Then simply create the formula as you normally would, using AutoSum.

To insert a 3-D argument, hold Shift and select the worksheets that include the
cells you want to insert in the argument. (The sheet with the formula will also appear
to be included; just ignore it.) Then, select the cell(s) that you want to include and
finish creating the formula:

=SUM(Jan:Mar!B5)

 NOTE Formulas with 3-D references can be filled like other formulas.

Using Multiple Workbooks

If you plan to create and use many 3-D cell references, or 3-D references that span workbooks as well as worksheets, you should consider using 3-D range names. For example, if cell B10 in three worksheets is the value for April's Salaries, you could name all three cells SalaryApr. You can then use this range name in your 3-D reference.

Follow these steps to define a 3-D range name:

1. Choose Insert ➤ Name ➤ Define from the menu bar.

2. In the Names In Workbook text box, type the range name.

3. Delete any reference in the Refers To text box, and type **=**.

4. Click the tab for the first worksheet you want to reference, hold Shift, and select the tab for the last worksheet to be referenced.

5. Select the cell or range to be named.

6. Click Add to add the name, then OK to close the dialog box.

 TIP Don't forget to include all the information Excel needs to find the source workbook and worksheet, including the full name and path, such as **'C:\Sales Management\ [Proposed Dept. Budget.xls]Sales'!D4**.

Auditing Excel Worksheets

Excel's auditing tools will assist you in scanning worksheets and workbooks for errors, correcting any errors, and resolving data entry mistakes. You can apply the auditing tools to track down errors so you can fix them immediately.

However, you can also prevent errors from ever occurring by specifying values that will be permitted during data entry. If someone enters a value outside the permitted range, Excel gives them an error message (which you can also customize). If the invalid data still gets entered, you can check the worksheet or workbook later to highlight all invalid entries, and correct them yourself.

Checking for Errors

You know how to use Excel to create flashy worksheets and reports, complete with bar and pie charts. Excel makes numbers *look* believable—even when results are so incorrect that no one should believe them. Part of creating a worksheet is checking the completed worksheet for errors, before you or other people rely on the results for decision making.

There are two kinds of errors you can make when creating a worksheet. One is a data-entry error: typing the wrong number, misspelling a word or name, or forgetting to type both parentheses in a pair.

You can use Excel's Spelling tools to check for misspellings, and Excel will let you know when you miss a parenthesis, but there is no software tool that can check to be sure you enter all your numbers correctly. You can ensure that a number is in an acceptable range (see "Validating Entries" later in this section), but you also need to use your personal observation tools.

Resolving Logical Errors

The other kind of error is a logical error: adding rather than subtracting, or multiplying the wrong numbers. Some logical errors violate Excel's rules about how formulas are constructed and result in an error message in the cell or an interruption from the Office Assistant. Those errors are the easy ones to catch and correct.

But errors that don't violate Excel's internal logic are the really nasty ones, because there is nothing that jumps out and says "This is wrong!" You have to find these errors on your own.

Finding errors is easier when you have real knowledge about your data. For example, suppose you're creating a worksheet to calculate each salesperson's salary plus commission. When you've entered and filled all your formulas, you notice that each of the salespeople will be making over $20,000 this week. This should make you suspect an error, if the salespeople normally only earn weekly commissions of $2,000 because they are selling lower-priced consumer items. At this point, alarms should be going off in your head—it's time to check the logic of your formulas.

Excel doesn't "know" anything about your data, but you do. If you see results that don't seem reasonable, trust your own knowledge, and double-check the values and formulas in the worksheet. Investigate.

What if you don't have personal knowledge of the data in a worksheet? Before you print 100 copies of the worksheet and send them to division heads and corporate vice presidents, review the worksheet with someone who *is* conversant with the data.

Working with Error Codes

Excel has eight standard error codes that pop up in cells to let you know that a formula requires your attention. The first is the ###### error, which may be telling you that the data is too wide for the column. This is easy to fix (hardly an error, but you get the idea). The codes, listed in Table 27.1, give you information about what caused the error.

TABLE 27.1: ERROR CODES

Error Code/Error Name	Cause
#####	1. Data too wide for the cell, or 2. You subtracted one date from another, and the result is a negative number. Double-check your formula.
#DIV/0 Division by Zero	The number or cell reference you divided by is either zero or blank. If you see this in cells you just filled, you needed an absolute cell reference in the original formula.
#N/A Not Available	1. You omitted a required argument in a function, or 2. The cell that contains the argument is blank or doesn't have the kind of entry the function requires.
#NAME	1. You misspelled the name of a range or function, or 2. You referred to a name that doesn't exist, or 3. You used text in a formula or format without putting it in quotes, or 4. You left out the colon in a range (B3:D7).
#NULL	You referred to an intersection that doesn't exist, by using a space between two ranges in an argument.
#NUM	1. You used text or a blank cell in an argument that requires a number, or 2. You entered a formula that creates a number too large or too small for Excel to handle.
#REF Invalid Reference	You deleted some cells that this formula requires, so the formula can't find the cell that it refers to. You may have deleted some cells by pasting other cells over them.
#VALUE	1. You entered the wrong data type for a formula or argument, or the wrong type of data or the wrong argument for a matrix or array, or 2. You entered a range when the function or operator can only work with a single value, or 3. You pressed Enter instead of Ctrl+Shift+Enter after working with an array formula.

Resolving Circular Cell References

Circular cell references result in immediate messages from Excel. A circular cell reference occurs when a formula refers to the cell that it is in. For example, when the formula =SUM(J15:J20) is in cell J20, Excel tries to add J20 to itself over and over again. This is called *iteration*. Excel will iterate 100 times before giving up and showing an error message:

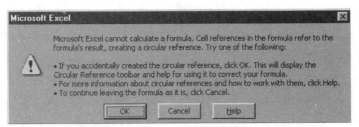

Click OK, and Help opens with information about circular references. Excel places a blue plus sign next to the formula that created the circular reference, and *Circular:* and the reference for the offending cell appears in the status bar.

When two or more formulas are involved, arrows will also appear on the worksheet. If this isn't the first circular reference you've created in this Excel session, you'll have to open the Circular Reference toolbar yourself (View ➤ Toolbars ➤ Circular Reference).

The drop-down list in the toolbar displays the current circular reference and other formulas with cells that could be the cause of the circular reference. The first two buttons on the toolbar are used to trace dependents and precedents.

  Dependents are cells with formulas that rely on the cell in the drop-down list; *precedents* are the cells that are referred to in this cell's formula. For diagnosing circular references, you'll want to trace precedents. Click the Trace Precedents button, and Excel will show you the precedent cells, as in Figure 27.4. The arrow shows that all the cells in the column, including cell E22, are included in the formula in E22, which reads +E5+E22.

 Click the Remove All Arrows button, and Excel will turn the arrows off. Then move to the circular reference cell and fix the formula so that it does not include a reference to itself.

PART

V

Number Crunching
with Excel

FIGURE 27.4

Tracing precedents

	A	B	C	D	E
4	Month	County	Type	Quantity	Bundles
5	Apr-99	Genesee	White Pine	57000	114
6	Apr-99	Oakland	Blue Spruce	22500	45
7	Apr-99	Oakland	White Pine	15500	31
8	Apr-99	Oakland	Concolor Fir	13500	27
9	Apr-99	Genesee	Blue Spruce	15000	30
10	Apr-99	Oakland	Scotch Pine	11000	22
11	Apr-99	Genesee	Frazier Fir	6500	13
12	May-99	Genesee	Scotch Pine	42500	85
13	May-99	Lake	White Pine	32000	64
14	May-99	Lake	Frazier Fir	14500	29
15	May-99	Kalkaska	Blue Spruce	13500	27
16	May-99	Lake	Concolor Fir	12000	24
17	May-99	Kalkaska	Concolor Fir	10000	20
18	Sep-99	Kalkaska	Frazier Fir	9500	19
19	Sep-99	Lake	Blue Spruce	3100	62
20	Sep-99	Lake	White Pine	26500	53
21	▼ Circular Reference			✕	
22	$E$22		▾ ⟨□ ⟨□ ℛ		0
23					

 TIP If there's a circular cell reference anywhere in an open workbook, the message *CIR-CULAR* appears on the status bar. Use the drop-down list in the Circular Reference toolbar to find the reference. Or you could try closing workbooks until the message goes away. This doesn't fix it, but it might make you feel better.

With an indirect circular reference, the problem is just as easy to find in Excel 2000. For example, suppose the formula in cell J24 is =SUM(J19:J22). Cell J19 refers to K24, which refers to J24. When the Circular Reference toolbar opens, it will already have traced the precedents from J24 to J19 to K24 and back to J24. You can clearly see the path tracing back to the circular reference. The Navigate Circular Reference control lets you move through the cells. Click the first cell in the control and examine its formula in the formula bar. If that formula is OK, select the next cell in the Navigate Circular Reference list to review it. Continue working through the cells shown in the list until you find the formula you need to correct.

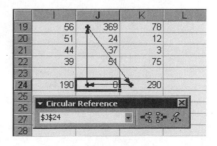

Minimizing Data Entry Errors

You're entering payroll. You're in a hurry. Instead of entering 10 hours for Jill Jones, you enter 100. When payday rolls around, Jill is a very happy person. You, on the other hand, are not. You could have checked your entries more closely, but if you barely have time to enter data, it's hard to make time to double-check it.

There's a helpful tool called *data validation*, which allows you to build business rules into each cell so that grossly incorrect entries result in error messages. Business rules are the policies and procedures, formal and informal, that govern how a business operates. Here are a few examples of business rules: no refunds after 30 days; no one ever works more than 80 hours in a week; and all employees must be at least 16 years of age.

Validation isn't a last-minute process—you have to establish the validation rules in advance. But validation, like using data forms, makes your worksheet more bullet-proof in the hands of novices, and it can make your own data entry work easier, too.

To create a validation rule, select the cell or range of cells that have the same business rule. Then choose Data ➢ Validation to open the Data Validation dialog box, shown in Figure 27.5. The dialog box has three pages: Settings, Input Message, and Error Alert.

The business rule you want to enforce goes on the first page. On the second page, you can enter a prompt that lets users know how to enter data in the cell. And on the third page, you can enter a message that a user will see when invalid data is entered.

Let's use the error in entering payroll hours mentioned above as an example. In the Settings page, select the type of value that's an acceptable entry for this cell from the Allow drop-down list. There are two possible numeric choices: whole number and decimal. When you select either, additional text box controls will open so you can enter values. In the Data drop-down list, choose the operator that you need.

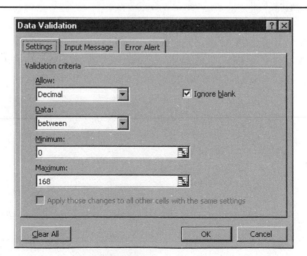

In Figure 27.5, we've used the Between operator because there is an upper and a lower limit that employees can work. Enter values for the Minimum and Maximum values. No one can work less than 0 hours. If there is no maximum established in the workplace, you could use 168. It's not possible to work more than 168 hours in a week—that's all there are. Notice that you can use the value in another cell as the minimum or maximum.

If the Ignore Blank check box is checked, then the user can leave the cell blank. Turn off the check mark if entries are required in all the selected cells.

The Input Message page lets you display a message (like a ScreenTip) to tell the user how to enter data in the cell. The message is displayed each time a user selects one of the cells in the range. This is great help if you have a number of different users working infrequently with this worksheet. However, if the same people use the worksheet over and over, input messages can become irritating.

If you want to enter an input message, do so. If you add a title, it will appear in bold above the message. You can't enter only a title. The message only appears if there is some text in the Input Message text box.

 TIP Input messages are great additions to worksheets you build for other people to use, even if you don't want to validate the data they enter in a cell. On the Settings page, leave the default Any Value setting; then enter your message on the Input Message page.

Use the Error Alert page to build an error dialog box like those used throughout Excel. Choose one of three styles—Stop, Warning, or Information—based on the severity of the error.

The Information style is a casual notice. A Warning is a bit more severe, and Stop uses the same icon that users see when a problem-ridden program is about to shut down, so it really catches people's attention. Include an error message and a title if you wish.

You don't have to include an error message. You might prefer to enter data, then have Excel show you all the data that isn't valid. Whether or not you show error messages is a matter of practicality.

If someone else is entering data in the worksheet, you should probably let them know when the data is incorrect so they can immediately find the correct data and enter it. Sometimes, the person entering data isn't in a position to correct it; in that case, you might want to dispense with the error message and handle the validation afterwards (see "Using the Auditing Toolbar" below).

Follow these steps to use the Data Validation tool to verify data and provide input messages:

1. Select the cells you want to validate.

2. Choose Data ➤ Validation to open the Data Validation dialog box.

3. If you want to set validation rules, on the Settings page set validation criteria for entries allowed, including the data type and minimum and/or maximum values.

4. If you want to include an input message, enter a message and optional title on the Input Message page. Make sure the Show Input Message check box is checked.

5. If you want to display a user message when invalid data is entered, choose a Style and enter an Error Message and optional Title on the Error Alert page. Make sure the Show Error Alert check box is checked.

6. Click OK.

7. Test the input message, validation, and error message by entering invalid data in one of the cells you selected.

To remove Data Validation or Input Messages, select the cells, open the dialog box, and click the Clear All button to clear all three pages of the dialog box.

Using the Auditing Toolbar

The Auditing toolbar includes the tracing tools from the Circular Reference toolbar, a tool to check the precedents for error codes, and a button to circle any entries that violate the validation rules you established.

The Auditing toolbar is one-stop shopping for error checking in your worksheet. Turn on the toolbar from the Tools menu (not the View menu) by choosing Tools ➤ Auditing ➤ Show Auditing Toolbar.

The first four buttons on the toolbar are used to trace precedents and dependents and to remove either the precedent or the dependent arrows.

The Remove All Arrows button is followed by a Trace Error button. The Trace Error button works like the Trace Precedents button, but you use it in a cell that contains one of the error codes listed in Table 27.1.

Use the New Comment button to insert a comment in the selected cell to help you keep track of your progress while auditing the worksheet. There are other reasons to insert comments that have nothing to do with auditing: to note the rationale behind a formula or the reason for changing data entries, or to flag data that needs later verification.

You can insert a comment in any cell by right-clicking and choosing Insert Comment from the shortcut menu. To delete a comment, select the commented cell, right-click, and choose Delete Comment.

The last two buttons on the Auditing toolbar are used to locate and circle invalid entries and to remove the circles. You use these buttons to check for data that violates the validation criteria established in the Data Validation dialog box, as shown in Figure 27.6.

FIGURE 27.6

Circling invalid data entries

Name	Pay Rate	Hours	Gross Pay
Wilson	$ 9.50	38	$ 361.00
Williams	$ 9.00	41	$ 369.00
Ulmeyer	$ 10.25	30	$ 307.50
Tier	$ 9.00	-3	$ (27.00)
Stephens	$ 9.75	44	$ 429.00

What's Next

In this chapter you saw that linking files can make it easier for members of a team to work independently on different phases of a project, using current, updated information. In the next chapter, you'll learn about workgroup tools, which provide other ways to share information with other users.

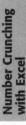

CHAPTER **28**

Using Excel's Workgroup Tools

Excel supplies powerful assistance for maintaining spreadsheet consistency throughout your workgroup or even your entire company. Use Excel templates to develop a corporate look for your worksheets and other shared files. If you share files among many different reviewers, Excel's revision features will help you keep track of changes and comments.

Using and Creating Templates

Templates are workbook models that you use to create other workbooks. Templates let you quickly construct workbooks that are identical in format, giving your work a standardized look. Excel includes some templates; you can create others for your personal use or for users in your workplace unfamiliar with the corporate look and how to format documents consistent with that look.

An Excel template can include text, numbers, formatting, formulas, and all the other features you already use. When you open a template, a copy is opened and the original template is not altered.

Working with Existing Templates

Excel includes predesigned templates that you can use or modify. To open a template, choose File ➤ New from the menu bar to open the New dialog box. (You can't simply click the New button on the Standard toolbar. The New button opens the default template: an empty workbook.)

Click the Spreadsheet Solutions tab to view the built-in Excel templates. Some templates are included in the Typical installation; others require a Custom installation, but they can always be added later. Click on any template icon to preview the template. To open a template, select it in the Spreadsheet Solutions window and click OK.

Entering Data

The Invoice template, shown in Figure 28.1, is a typical template. There are two worksheets in the template: Invoice and Customize Your Invoice (Invoice is displayed initially). Each template includes a special toolbar. As you use each template, its toolbar is added to the list in the Toolbars dialog box.

PART

V

Number Crunching
with Excel

FIGURE 28.1

The Invoice template is typical of Excel's built-in templates

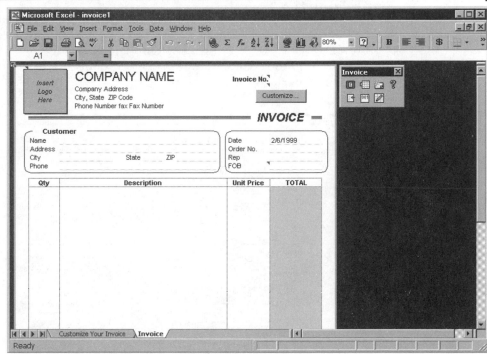

The Invoice toolbar initially appears as a palette in the worksheet window. You can move the toolbar if you wish. To view the entire worksheet template, click the Size to Screen button on the Invoice toolbar. Clicking the button again returns the worksheet to its original size.

Cells with a red triangle include *comments* to explain the information you should enter in the cell. To view a comment, move the mouse pointer over the cell. You can click the Hide Comments/Display Comments button on the Invoice toolbar to suppress or enable comment display.

Click the New Comment button to add your own comment to the template. (You can also quickly add a comment to any cell in a workbook by right-clicking and selecting Insert Comment from the shortcut menu.)

The canned templates include sample data that you can examine as a guide for entering your data. To view the sample data, click the Display Example/Remove Example button on the template's toolbar. To enter data in the template, turn off the example, activate the cell, and enter the information. Template cells with a light blue background contain formulas, so don't enter information in those cells.

Customizing the Template

The Invoice sheet includes placeholders for generic title information: the company name and a place for a logo or picture. To add your personal information, click the Customize button in the Invoice worksheet to move to the Customize Your Invoice worksheet, shown in Figure 28.2.

FIGURE 28.2

The Customize Your Invoice worksheet

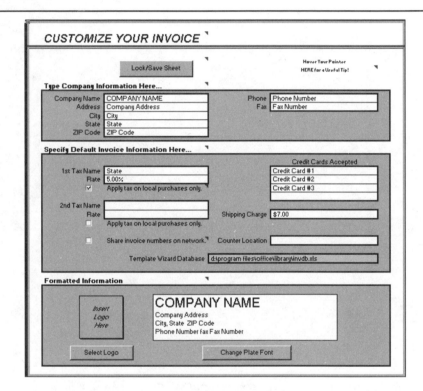

At the top of the worksheet is a Lock/Save Sheet button. *Locking* a template prevents users from accidentally changing the customized information in this workbook, but it does not alter the template. You can always choose to customize again and unlock the template if you want to change it.

Or you can save a copy of the template that includes the custom information you entered. It's more convenient to alter the template permanently by saving. To lock or save template changes, click the Lock/Save Sheet button. The dialog box shown next opens so that you can select either locking or locking and saving.

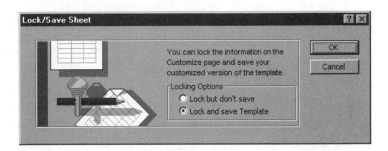

Here's a summary of the steps to customize your template:

1. Activate the Customize worksheet.

2. Enter your custom information as indicated in the worksheet.

3. Click the Lock/Save Sheet button.

4. Choose either Lock But Don't Save or Lock And Save Template; then click OK.

Creating Templates

You can create a template for workbooks that you use frequently. For example, you might use Excel to complete a weekly payroll and put all the payroll worksheets for one month into a separate workbook.

Rather than constructing a new workbook each month, you can create a monthly payroll template. At the beginning of each month you can create a new workbook from the template. Your template will differ from a regular workbook in four specific ways:

- You'll save the file as a template rather than a regular workbook.

- It will contain only the text, formulas, and formatting that remain the same each month.

- The template will include visual formatting clues and comments to assist users.

- It will be saved in the Office 2000 Templates folder.

You can create a template from scratch or base it on an existing workbook. If you're using an existing workbook, first make sure that all the formulas work, and that numbers and text are formatted appropriately.

Remove the text and numbers that will be entered each time the template is used. Don't remove formulas—although the results of the formula change, the formulas themselves remain the same. If you're creating a template from scratch, you still need to enter (and then remove) values to test the template's formulas before saving the template.

PART

V

Number Crunching
with Excel

Use borders and shading to let users know where they should—and shouldn't—enter text or other information. The Invoice template is a good model. Add comments (choose Insert Comment from the shortcut menu) to provide assistance where users might have questions about data entry.

Remove any extra worksheets from the workbook to improve its overall appearance. When you're finished formatting the worksheet, choose File ➢ Save As, and save the workbook as type Template.

TIP You can create a folder within the Templates folder to hold your personal templates. Other than the General tab, tabs in the New Workbook dialog box represent folders in the Templates folder.

When saving a template, be sure to follow these steps:

1. Click the Save button or choose File ➢ Save As.

2. In the Save As Type control, choose Template from the drop-down list. The Save In control will change to the default Templates folder.

3. Enter a name for the template in the File Name text box.

4. Click the Save button.

When you choose File ➢ New, the template will be included on the General page or the specific folder you saved it in. The template itself will not be altered when you or other users create new workbooks.

To modify a template, open the template from the Templates folder with File ➢ Open rather than File ➢ New. When you are finished editing, save and close the template.

As you gain experience with Excel, you can add other features to templates, like the buttons and toolbars used in the Invoice template. Use Excel's Help feature to find more information on template design and modification. Chapter 38 shows how to add custom buttons to toolbars and templates, and Chapter 39 shows how to record simple macros (which you can attach to buttons or menu options).

TIP The File menu includes a list of recently opened files that will include the template you just created. If you or another user open the template from the File menu, the template—not a copy of the template—will open. To clear the entries from the menu, first save and close the template; then choose Tools ➢ Options and click the General tab. Turn off the Recently Used Files check box, and then click OK to close the Options dialog box. Reopen the Options dialog box and turn the check box back on, and Excel will resume displaying recently used files with the next files you save.

Working with Workgroups

Excel's features for sharing workbooks and tracking changes make it easy for you to collaborate with others by sharing the same workbook file among multiple users. However, Excel minimizes the problems associated with multiple users by giving you control over how the changes made by all of the users are merged into a single, error-free file.

Sharing Workbooks

Excel is designed to allow multiple users to view and modify a single workbook simultaneously. If you want others to be able to use a workbook while you have it open, you need to share the workbook and ensure that it is stored on a shared drive that other users can access. Choose Tools ➢ Share Workbook from the menu bar to open the Share Workbook dialog box:

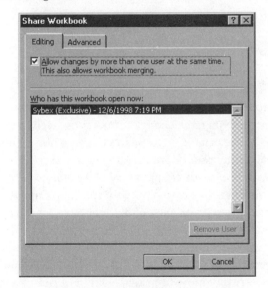

Before you make any changes in this dialog box, note that the current user has exclusive rights to this workbook. On the Editing page, click in the Allow Changes check box to make the file accessible to other users. Then activate the Advanced page to set options for tracking changes and resolving conflicts.

PART

V

Number Crunching
with Excel

Tracking and Updating Changes

You can only track changes in shared workbooks. If you choose to track changes in a *change history*, select the number of days each change should be kept. If you don't want to track changes, tell Excel not to keep a history.

Whether you track changes or not, you need to determine when changes are updated. The default is to updates changes only when the file is saved. This means that each time you (or another user) save, Excel will save your changes and update your workbook with changes made by other users.

Or you can choose to have your workbook updated Automatically every set number of minutes; if you then choose the Save My Changes option, your changes will be saved when the update occurs. (If you update changes Automatically, other users still won't see your changes until you save; however, they can also choose to see saved changes Automatically rather than waiting until they save.)

When two or more users make different changes in the same cell, it causes a conflict. Set the Conflicting Changes option to indicate how conflicts should be resolved. Excel can prompt you to resolve conflicts, or it can automatically accept the saved changes.

The Personal view contains your print and filter settings for the workbook. These settings do not affect other users' view of the workbook. Use the check boxes to include or exclude these settings when the workbook is saved.

Here's a quick summary of the steps to set up a shared workbook:

1. With the workbook open, choose Tools ➤ Share Workbook from the menu bar.

2. On the Editing page, enable Allow Changes By More Than One User.

3. On the Advanced page, set Track Changes, Update Changes, Conflicting Changes, and Personal View options.

4. Click OK to close the dialog box.

When you close the dialog box, Excel will save the workbook as a shared workbook; if you haven't previously saved it, the Save As dialog box will open.

Once you return to the Shared Workbooks dialog box, you'll notice that you no longer have the workbook open Exclusively, as other Excel users can now open it.

You can restrict who can open and use the data in a workbook by setting a password to open or save the workbook. Choose File ➤ Save As; then click the Tools button in the Save As dialog box and select General Options in the button drop-down list to open the Save Options dialog box.

Enter passwords that users (including you) must enter to open or modify the workbooks. Click OK to return to the Save As procedure. Make sure you keep track of the password; if you lose it, you lose the rights to open or modify the file.

Working in a Shared Workbook

When Tracking Changes is enabled, each change made is noted in a comment, and changed cells are flagged. For example, if you delete the value in a cell, a triangle appears in the upper-left corner of the cell. When you move the mouse pointer over the cell, a comment tells you who changed the cell, when they changed it, and what the former value in the cell was.

Excel assigns a different triangle color to each user who modifies the workbook, so you can visually inspect the workbook to find all the changes made by one user.

PART

V

Number Crunching
with Excel

When you save the workbook, you accept the changes, so the triangle and comment disappear.

> **Sybex, 12/6/1998 7:30 PM:**
> Changed cell D18 from '9500' to
> '7500'.

Some Excel features aren't available in shared workbooks. For instance, while a workbook is shared, you can't do any of the following:

- Delete worksheets
- Add or apply conditional formatting and data validation
- Insert or delete ranges of cells (you can still insert and delete individual cells, rows, and columns), charts, hyperlinks, or other objects (including those created with Draw)
- Group or outline data

However, you can use the features before you share a workbook, or you can temporarily unshare the workbook, make changes, and then turn sharing on again. See Excel's Online Help for the complete list of limitations of shared workbooks.

Resolving Conflicts

If changes you are saving conflict with changes saved by another user, you'll be prompted to resolve the conflict (unless you changed the Conflicting Changes setting in the Advanced page of the Share Workbook dialog box). In the Resolve Conflict dialog box, you can review each change individually and accept your change or others' changes, or accept/reject changes in bulk.

Viewing the Change History

You can examine all the changes that have been saved in a workbook since you turned on the change history. Choose Tools ➤ Track Changes ➤ Highlight Changes to open the Highlight Changes dialog box shown on the next page.

In the dialog box, select the time period for the changes you want to review, and specify the users whose changes you want to see. If you only want to see changes for a particular range or sheet, select the range you want to view. You can view the changes on screen or on a separate worksheet in the workbook.

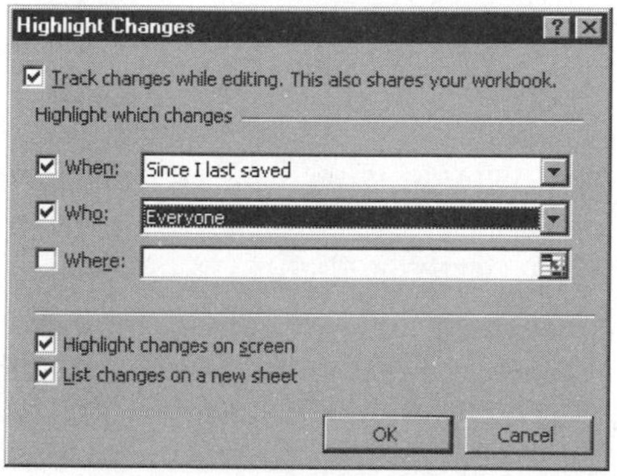

Highlight Changes ? X

☑ <u>T</u>rack changes while editing. This also shares your workbook.

Highlight which changes

☑ Whe<u>n</u>: Since I last saved ▼

☑ W<u>h</u>o: Everyone ▼

☐ Whe<u>r</u>e: ▢

☑ Highlight changes on <u>s</u>creen
☑ <u>L</u>ist changes on a new sheet

OK   Cancel

When you view the history on a separate worksheet, you can filter the changes to find changes made by different users or on specific dates, as shown in Figure 28.3. When you remove a workbook from shared use, the change history is turned off and reset. If you want to keep the changes, select the information on the History worksheet and copy it to another worksheet before unsharing the workbook.

FIGURE 28.3

Viewing the change history

Action Number ▼	Date ▼	Time ▼	Who ▼	Change ▼	Sheet ▼	Range ▼	New Value ▼	Old Value ▼	Action Type ▼	Losing Action ▼
1	12/6/1998	7:30 PM	Sybex	Cell Change	TreeSales	D18	9500	7500		
2	12/6/1998	7:42 PM	Sybex	Cell Change	TreeSales	A18	00-Sep-1999	00-May-1999		
3	12/6/1998	7:42 PM	Sybex	Cell Change	TreeSales	B12	Genesseee	Lake		
4	12/6/1998	7:42 PM	Sybex	Cell Change	TreeSales	C12	Scotch Pine	Blue Spruce		
5	12/6/1998	7:42 PM	Sybex	Cell Change	TreeSales	D5	57000	37000		
6	12/6/1998	7:42 PM	Sybex	Cell Change	TreeSales	D9	15000	12500		

Merging Workbook Changes

If you anticipate many conflicting changes in a shared workbook, or if you want users to be able to make changes independently, and then review all changes at once, make and distribute copies of the shared workbook.

To create the copies, use Save As and give each copy of the workbook a different name. Then you can merge the copies when users are done with their changes. You can only merge workbooks that have the same change history, so it's important that none of the users turns off sharing while using the workbook. Also, the history must be complete when you merge the workbooks.

If, for example, you set the number of days for the history at 30 days and users keep the workbooks for 32 days, you won't be able to merge the workbooks. Before you make copies of the shared workbook, make sure you set the history to allow enough time for changes and merging. If you're uncertain, set the history to 600 days or an equally ridiculous length of time.

These steps quickly review how to merge shared workbooks:

1. Open your copy of the shared workbook that you want to merge changes into.

2. Choose Tools ➤ Merge Workbooks. If you haven't saved your copy of the workbook, you'll be prompted to do so.

3. In the Select Files To Merge Into Current Workbook dialog box, choose the copy (or copies) of the shared workbook containing the changes you wish to merge. Click OK.

What's Next

This chapter concludes our exploration of Excel features, but some of the concepts you have examined here will come into play as you proceed to Part VI, which presents Access as a tool for nonprogrammers. Chapter 29 begins the discussion by showing how to plan a database; in doing so, it takes you beyond the simple database techniques used in Excel files and shows you the real power of Microsoft Access for managing large amounts of complex data.

PART VI

Access for the Nonprogrammer

LEARN TO:

- *Plan a custom database*
- *Create and customize data tables*
- *Set table relationships to join related data*
- *Insert subdatasheets to look up related data quickly*
- *Enter data in tables*
- *Import and link to data in other files*
- *Organize data by sorting and filtering*
- *Create and customize forms for data entry*
- *Create and customize reports for professional data presentation*
- *Build queries to extract precise data from tables*

CHAPTER 29

Planning a Database

FEATURING:

Creating a database with the Database Wizard

Understanding database objects

Designing your own database

Determining your database needs and purposes

Planning the database structure

Determining fields for your tables

Understanding table relationships

I n this chapter, you'll find an overview of planning and designing Access databases. For many computer users, databases represent a quantum leap in data-management capability beyond other business software, in which the most powerful and sophisticated features often require programming. That's also true of Access to some extent, but you can handle many of your company's database needs without writing a line of code. This part of the book, "Access for the Nonprogrammer," does not assume any familiarity with Access or database concepts, but it does assume that you're a knowledgeable Windows computer user; if you are new to Office 2000, you may want to review Part I for an introduction and then return here to work in Access 2000.

 MASTERING THE OPPORTUNITIES

About Access Project Files: Access Grows Up

Until now, it was common to hear complaints that while Access functioned well with a modest amount of data, it was too small to handle large volumes of data. In Access 2000, that limitation has disappeared. You can create a file called an Access *project*, which contains only forms, reports, macros, and modules; this part of a database is often called a *front end*. You can then link the project file to a large, SQL Server-type database, often called a *back-end data store*. To learn more about projects in Access, check out *Mastering Access 2000*, by Alan Simpson and Celeste Robinson (Sybex, 1999).

Creating a Database with the Database Wizard

If you need to create a database fast, whether to start storing data immediately or just to have a functional database to look at while you learn about database objects and structure, you can use one of the Database wizards to whip up a fully functional database with sample data. Several Database wizards are installed with Access; each wizard asks you some questions about your preferences, then uses your answers to create a new database. The Contact Management database is a useful sample database to create with these wizards.

If you haven't started Access before, follow these steps to get started:

1. Click Start ➢ Programs ➢ Microsoft Access. Access starts, and the Microsoft Access dialog box shown in Figure 29.1 appears in the Access window.

2. In the Microsoft Access dialog box, click the Access Database Wizards, Pages, And Projects option, and then click OK.

FIGURE 29.1

Starting Access

TIP You'll see the Microsoft Access dialog box only when you start Access; if you're already working in Access and want to create a new database with the wizard, click File ➢ New to open the New dialog box.

To create a database using the Database Wizard, follow these steps:

1. In the New dialog box, on the Databases tab, double-click the icon for the database you want to create.

2. You're asked what to name the new database and where to save it. In the File New Database dialog box (shown in Figure 29.2), type a file name in the File Name box. In the Save In box, navigate to the folder where you want to save the database. Then click Create.

FIGURE 29.2

The File New Database dialog box

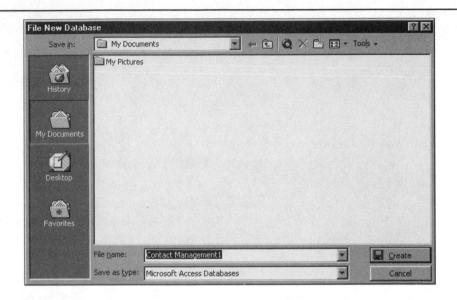

3. In the first wizard dialog box, the wizard tells you what kind of data this database is designed to store. Click Next.

TIP To create the database immediately by using all the wizard's default choices, click Finish in any Database Wizard dialog box.

4. In the second wizard dialog box (shown in Figure 29.3), select the specific fields you want to include in each table: in the list on the left, click a table; in the list on the right, mark or clear fields to include in that table. Then click Next.

5. In the third wizard dialog box, select a style for database screen displays (such as forms), and click Next. (Click each style name to preview it.)

6. In the fourth wizard dialog box, select a style for printed database reports, and click Next. (Click each style name to preview it.)

7. In the fifth wizard dialog box, type a title for your database (or accept the wizard's suggestion), and click Next.

8. In the sixth (and last) wizard dialog box, click Finish.

The wizard creates the database, and it appears on your screen as in Figure 29.4. What you see is the Main Switchboard, a form that simplifies your interaction with the database.

FIGURE 29.3

The second Database Wizard dialog box

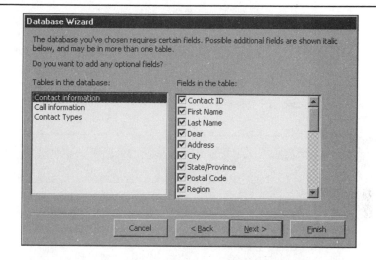

FIGURE 29.4

The new database created by the Database Wizard

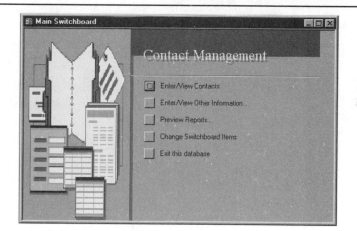

TIP If you just want to open an existing database to look at while you learn, but don't want to build one, you can open the Northwind Sample Database that's provided with Access 2000. Many of the figures in these chapters show the Northwind database. If you don't see it listed in the Microsoft Access dialog box when Access starts, you'll need to install it from the Office 2000 CD. After you've opened several databases, you may not see the Northwind database listed in the Microsoft Access dialog box; but if you click More Files, you can navigate to the Northwind database in the `C:\Program Files\Microsoft Office\Office\Samples` folder.

Understanding Database Objects

Access databases include seven types of objects: tables, forms, reports, pages, queries, macros, and Visual Basic modules. The object types are listed in the left pane of the database window (shown in Figure 29.5); to see a group of specific objects, such as forms, click the object name.

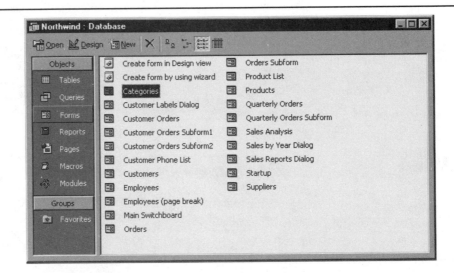

In this part of the book, you'll learn about Access tables, forms, reports, and queries. In Chapter 39, you'll be introduced to macros and the VBA programming language, and in Chapter 45 you'll learn about pages and other Web features.

Groups let you organize your database by putting shortcuts to related objects in one place. For example, you can create a group that contains a table, queries based on the table, and forms used to enter data in the table. When you need to make changes to the table, you can easily identify the other objects that might be affected. You create a group by right-clicking in the area under the Groups bar (see Figure 29.5) and choosing New Group from the shortcut menu. After you've named and created the group, you can drag objects from the other pages of the Database window to add shortcuts to the objects to the group. You can add an object to as many groups as you wish.

A database is a file in which you store all the data pertaining to a specific enterprise or business. Data for a single business might include product details, product categories, customer information, customers' orders, employee details, and shipping company details. All of this data is kept in a single Access file, the database, and is easily interrelated so you can find answers to questions such as 'How many orders were placed from customers in Arizona in November?' or 'Which employee handled the largest quantity of orders in the first half of 1998?'

Database structure is provided by *tables*, which are designed to store data easily, accurately, and without redundancy. Tables are composed of *fields*, or categories of information, and *records*, or individual line-item entries. A good example of a database is a telephone directory: fields in a telephone directory include last name, first name, address, and telephone number; and each name-address-telephone entry is a record.

Simple databases, sometimes called *flat-file* databases, only allow you to work with one list or table of information at a time (Microsoft Excel is an example of a flat-file database). Programs like Access, which is a *relational database*, let you separate your data into different tables and store each item of data (such as a customer address) only once. Then you relate the tables to each other so you can connect data such as a customer address and several customer orders. In a relational database, data storage is flexible, never duplicated, and takes up minimal hard drive space.

MASTERING THE OPPORTUNITIES

Do You Need the Complexity of a Relational Database?

Does your data need a relational database? If your data is simple and can be kept in a single table with no duplication (like a list of business contacts), it's easier to keep it in a flat-file database like Microsoft Excel. If your data requires lots of calculation and manipulation, those tasks are easier to perform in Excel. When you need to relate two types of data to each other (students and classes, sales managers and client accounts), you need to move to Access.

Whether you keep your data in Access or Excel, you can easily transfer it between the two programs. If your contacts are already in an Excel workbook, you can *import* the Excel file into Access as a table in a database. If you need data that's kept in another department and changes regularly, such as shipping charges, you can *link* to that table from your database and always have current data. And if you want to perform lots of calculations on data that's in an Access table, you can *analyze* it (by exporting a copy) in an Excel workbook.

Naming Conventions for Objects and Controls

Although Access will allow you to name objects any way you wish, we suggest that you follow the Leszynski/Reddick naming convention with your own objects so that databases you create can be easily understood by other people who work with Access. In the L/R convention, an object name begins with a tag that identifies the kind of object it is: tbl, frm, rpt, qry, mcr, or bas. There are no spaces or punctuation in object names, and the first letter of each word in the name is capitalized. (While Access allows spaces in object names, many other databases do not. Omitting spaces makes it easier to transfer data to other programs.) For example, a table of customer orders might be named tbl-Orders; a query showing customer order information might be called qryCustOrders. Access wizards don't use these naming conventions, but you can add these tags to new object names yourself whenever you create an object with a wizard.

 NOTE Leszynski/Reddick? Stan Leszynski and Greg Reddick are a couple of well-known database developers who came up with this logical naming convention in the early 1990s to provide a common language for developers so they could coordinate their efforts more easily.

Designing Your Own Database

Before you begin constructing your own database, you need to spend some time designing it. A bad design virtually ensures that you'll spend extra time reworking the database. Database developers often spend as much time designing a database as they do constructing it in Access. To design a database, you should follow these steps:

1. Determine the need or purpose of the database, and what sort of output you'll need to generate.

2. Decide what kinds of tables the database should include.

3. Specify the fields that each table should include, and determine which fields in each table contain unique values.

4. Decide how the tables are related to each other, then review and finalize the design.

5. Construct and relate the tables, and enter sample data for testing the database.

6. Create forms, reports, and queries to accomplish your data tasks.

The rest of this chapter is an overview of the design process. Details and procedures for creating database objects—tables, queries, forms, and reports—can be found in Chapters 30 through 33.

Determining Need or Purpose

Every database begins with a problem or need that creating a systematic data tracking system can solve. You might, for example, need to keep track of certain data about customers. Think about why you need the database: what will it allow you to do better than you do now? Send mailings to existing customers? Track orders? Study current customer trends to help identify potential new customers? You'll be able to answer all of these questions by creating the appropriate tables, queries, and reports.

If all of this data pertains to the same business, and one person is responsible for updating the data, it should all be kept in the same database; don't create a different database for each different purpose, because you'll create a lot more work for yourself in the long run. A situation in which you'd want to create separate databases within the same business might be in a large company, where several different departments are responsible for updating different aspects of company data. In that case, each department might have its own database, and your database designed for one department, would link to tables in other departments' databases. (Never keep two copies of the same data, because they're sure to be out of sync eventually.)

Deciding What Should Be Included

A customer database might include specific sets of data such as customer information, order details, salespeople who took customer orders, the results of customer surveys, or any combination of these. Determine each set of data to include; each separate data set will become a table in the database, and all the information in a specific data set will appear in only one table. It would be redundant, for example, to keep the first name, last name, and address of a customer in each of their orders. Customer data belongs in a Customers table, and Order data belongs in an Orders table. When the customer moves, you only have to change the address once in the Customers table, and it will always be current.

The tables you build are the backbone, or structure, of your database; all the other database objects you create use the data in these tables.

Deciding on a Structure for Your Database

To determine whether the structure accomplishes your objectives and is easy to work with, begin by entering a few records that are a representative sample of the data. Typically, you'll return to the structure and fine-tune it based on your analysis of how the database handled this test data. (See "Entering Data in a Table" in Chapter 30 to learn about data entry.)

Finally, you'll create forms for data entry, reports for output, and queries to gather information from more than one table. If the database will be used by others, you'll want to have someone who was not involved in the design test the forms and reports to make sure that other people find them easy to use.

Determining Table Fields

Once you've established the tables you'll be creating, determine what information about each entity should be included. Every data field must be part of a specific table, and every field should be atomic: that means you store data in its smallest logical components. Street address, city, state, and zip code should be stored separately, rather than in one big field, so that you can find all the customers in one state or zip code later on.

 TIP If you're converting your business records into a database for the first time, include tables and fields for all the data you have. Your decisions will be about how best to divide it up among tables and among fields within each table, but don't leave any of it out. Later, when you come up with new types of data you want to include, it will be easy to add new fields to the appropriate tables.

Identifying Unique Fields

In a relational database, tables are connected to each other through unique fields: fields with values that occur only once in a table. Social security numbers, for example, uniquely identify one living person. A field or combination of fields that uniquely identifies each record in a table is called a *primary key*. Other common primary key fields are the item number in a catalog, an employee ID, and a UPC for retail products. In some tables, it takes more than one field to create a primary key. For example, in a table that contains visits to a clinic, the primary key might be both the patient ID field and the visit date and time field, because neither field alone could uniquely identify a visit.

When you use the Table Wizard to create a table, you can let Access create a primary key for you; in that case, Access adds a field called "ID" that contains consecutive, nonrepeating numbers. Access assigns the numbers automatically, so each record in the table has a unique numeric identifier, but unlike an employee ID or UPC, the numbers themselves have no meaning outside the database. Whenever possible, you should identify a primary key within the data rather than having Access create an ID field.

Understanding Relationships

A *relationship* links two tables by specifying a common field that appears in both tables. There are three types of relationships: one-to-one, one-to-many, and many-to-many. If two tables are related in a *one-to-one relationship*, each record in Table A will have only one record in Table B. In the more common *one-to-many relationship*, one record in Table A can be related to many records in Table B. For example, in a Customer Orders database, for each one customer there can be many orders.

A *many-to-many relationship* means that a record in Table A can be related to many records in Table B, and a record in Table B can be simultaneously related to many records in Table A. For example, an order can include many products, and a product can be included in many orders. Relational databases don't allow you to create many-to-many relationships directly, but these relationships abound in real data. You build *junction tables* (or *linking tables*) to handle the many-to-many relationships in your database—a junction table exists in the middle of the many-to-many relationship, and splits it into a pair of one-to-many relationships.

The relationship between two tables allows you to select a single record in one table and see all the related records in a different table, called a *subdatasheet*. For example, in Figure 29.6, the Customers table is related to the Orders table; clicking the small plus symbol next to the Customer ID opens a subdatasheet that shows all the orders (in the Orders table) that the customer placed. The plus symbol becomes a minus symbol when the subdatasheet is opened; click the minus symbol to close the subdatasheet.

Subdatasheets are sometimes created automatically, such as when two tables are related through a Lookup field, or you can create them yourself. (You can learn more about subdatasheets in "Adding Subdatasheets to Look Up Related Records" in Chapter 30.)

A relationship also allows you to create multitable queries, which pull related data out of two or more tables, and reports that summarize data drawn from two or more tables. (To learn more about relationships, see "Working With Relationships" in Chapter 30.)

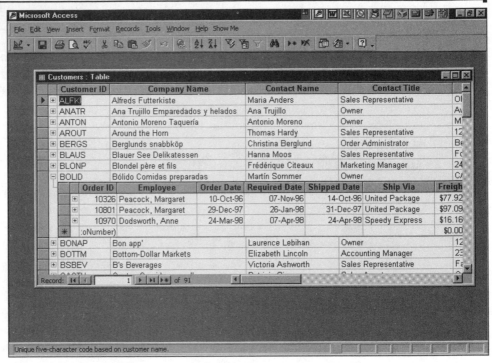

Understanding Primary and Foreign Keys

A relationship ties one table to another by including the primary key from one table in the related table. In the example above, including a Customer ID number in the Orders table clearly identifies which customer placed the order, so you can find a customer's name and address for any given order.

A table's primary key is the field or fields used to uniquely identify each record in the table. When you include the key field in another table and use it to relate the two tables, the field in the related table is called a *foreign key*.

TIP Customer telephone numbers are often used as a primary key because they're easy to remember; you can look up a customer's data quickly by simply asking for their phone number.

In the Orders table shown in Figure 29.7, the Order ID field is a primary key. When you include it in an Order Details table, it becomes a foreign key. To relate the two tables, you connect the primary key from the table on the "one" side of a relationship (the *primary table*) to the foreign key in the "many" table (the *related table*).

FIGURE 29.7

*Two related tables:
Orders and Order
Details*

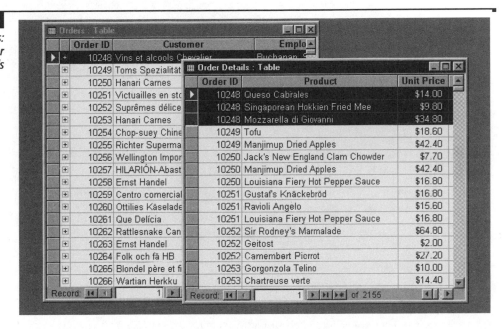

There are two ways to create relationships in Access 2000: you can create a Lookup field in a table or create the relationship directly in the Relationships window. In Chapter 30, you can learn about Lookup fields in "Creating Lookup Fields" and about creating relationships in "Working with Relationships."

Reviewing the Design and the Table Relationships

After you've planned the tables and relationships, and before you begin constructing tables and typing data, you need to reexamine the structure of the database: tables, fields, and relationships. When you're convinced that the design is well conceived, you can begin creating tables and setting relationships.

To design the database structure with minimum frustration and wasted time, get out a pencil and paper and draw the structure of your tables and relationships graphically. Access has a Relationships window where you can view the structure of your tables and relationships, and create, delete, and edit those relationships. You can look at the Relationships window in an existing database to get an idea of what database structure looks like; Figure 29.8 shows the Relationships window in the Northwind database.

PART

VI

Access for the
Nonprogrammer

FIGURE 29.8

*The Relationships
window*

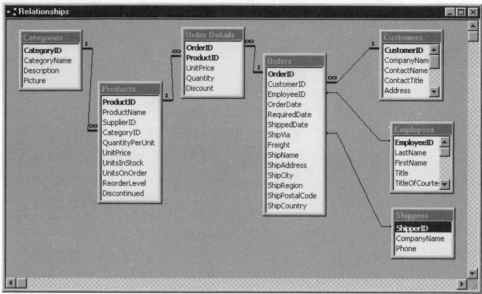

Each rectangle in the window represents a table and lists the fields in the table. The lines between the tables are called *join lines*; they represent the relationships between the tables, and each one connects a primary key to a foreign key. The Order Details table, although it contains some data not found in any other tables, also serves as a junction table between the Orders table and the Products table. The "1" and "infinity" symbols on the join lines indicate referential integrity; see "Setting Referential Integrity" in Chapter 30 to learn more about them.

 To open the Relationships window, click the Relationships button on the database toolbar. To close the window, click its close button. Whenever you make any changes in the Relationships window, even just moving a table a tiny bit, you'll be asked if you want to save the layout (you're only saving the picture in the window, not the relationships). If you want the window to open looking exactly as you left it when you closed it, click Yes.

What's Next

In this chapter, you learned what a relational database does and how to plan and design a relational database to fit your needs. In the next chapter, you'll learn how to create database tables, put data in them, and relate them to one another.

CHAPTER 30

Creating the Database Structure

n Chapter 29, you learned how to plan and design an Access database to meet specific needs. In this chapter, you'll continue the process as you learn about creating and modifying database tables and entering data into those tables. You'll also learn about working with relationships between database tables, particularly establishing and maintaining referential integrity.

Creating a New, Blank Database

To create a database, you can either start entirely from scratch or customize one of the predesigned databases that come with Access. When you create a database from scratch, you have complete control over the database objects, their properties, and their relationships. When you start Access, you immediately see the Microsoft Access dialog box (shown in Figure 30.1). To create a database from scratch, choose Blank Access Database and click OK.

FIGURE 30.1

Starting Access displays the Microsoft Access dialog box.

After you click OK, you're prompted to enter a filename and location for the database in the File New Database dialog box. A new database must be saved before you begin creating tables. Once you've entered a filename and clicked Create, a new, blank database opens, and you're ready to go to work.

Creating and Modifying Tables

Now that you have a new database, the first thing you have to do is get data into it. How you get data into the database is both a matter of personal preference and a question of where your data currently exists (on paper or in an electronic file).

If your data exists on paper, or doesn't exist yet, you'll create new, empty tables. To create a new table in an existing database, display the database tables by clicking Tables in the left pane of the database window. In the database window, three methods are listed (see Figure 30.2):

- Create Table In Design View
- Create Table By Using Wizard
- Create Table By Entering Data

FIGURE 30.2

Methods of creating tables in the database window

If your data exists in another electronic file, don't retype it. You can import it into your database or link to a table in an external file. (To learn more, see "Importing vs. Linking" in this chapter.)

Creating a Table in Datasheet View

You can create a new table in Datasheet view by double-clicking the Create Table By Entering Data icon in the Tables group in the database window. A new table like the one in Figure 30.3 appears. Decide what kind of data you want to store in this table; then follow these steps to set up the table quickly:

1. Double-click the Field1 column header and type the first field name (see Figure 30.3).

PART

VI

Access for the Nonprogrammer

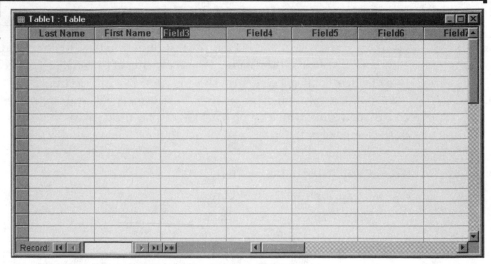

FIGURE 30.3

Creating fields in Datasheet view

2. Enter the rest of your field names the same way. Don't worry about the order, because you can drag-and-drop the columns to rearrange them later.

3. Enter a single record of data. It doesn't have to be real data (mock data is fine), but you must make an appropriate data entry in each field. Access guesses the probable data type for each field based on what you enter.

4. Switch to Design view by clicking the View button on the toolbar. You'll be asked to save the table. Type a table name and click OK. (Include the prefix **tbl** if you're following the L/R convention, discussed in Chapter 29.)

5. You'll be asked if you want to create a primary key. You don't have to—you can create it later. To skip the primary key, click No; to allow Access to create another field for a primary key, click Yes.

The table is saved and opened in Design view (shown in Figure 30.4), and all the extra columns in the unsaved table are deleted. You'll need to make changes to some of the data types and field properties, as discussed later in this chapter, in "Adding Fields in Design View."

Creating a Table in Design View

Design view is another way to create new tables from scratch. The biggest difference between the Design view and Datasheet view methods is that in the Datasheet method, Access tries to guess the field properties (and is sometimes wrong); in the Design view method, you set all the properties yourself. When you double-click Create Table In Design View, a table design window opens, as shown in Figure 30.5. In the upper pane of the design window, there's a row for each field. You'll give each field a name, data type, and optional description. Field names should be intuitive, as in CustomerFirstName.

PART

VI

Access for the
Nonprogrammer

FIGURE 30.4

A new table in Design view

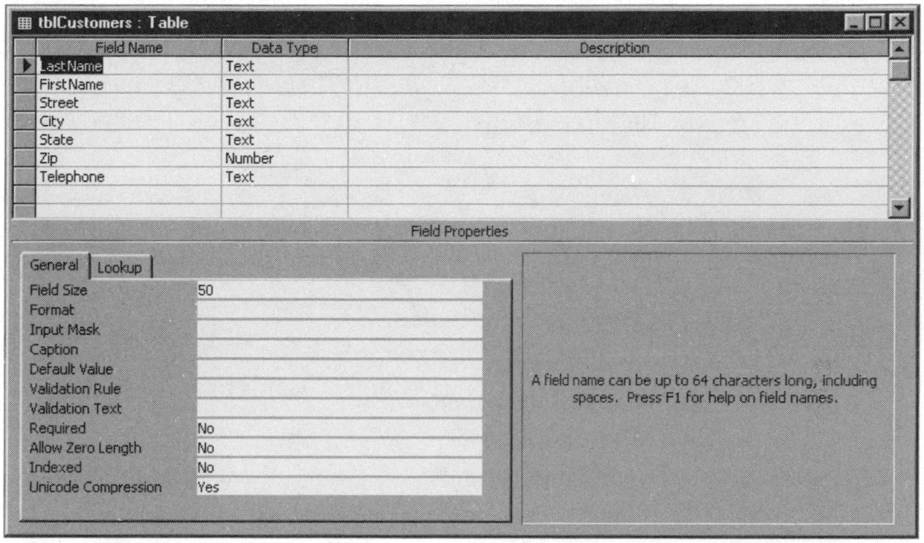

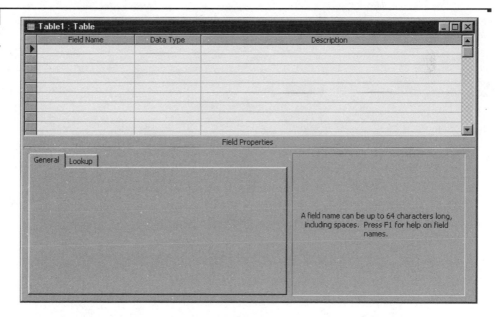

FIGURE 30.5

The Table design window

To create a table in Design view, follow these steps:

1. Begin by entering a Field Name.

2. The Data Type indicates the kind of data that can be entered in the field. Click the Data Type drop-down list to select a data type (see Figure 30.6). There are nine data types:

   Text: Used for words or for numbers that won't be used in calculations (such as phone numbers and Social Security numbers). It is the default setting because it is used most frequently.

   Memo: An open field that is used for comments.

   Number: Numbers, or integers, that are negative or positive values (not numbers that have no numeric value, such as Social Security numbers).

   Date/Time: Various formats for dates, times, and combinations of the two.

   Currency: Numbers in dollars or in dollars and cents.

   AutoNumber: A numeric field automatically entered by Access, used in a primary key field when none of the fields (or combination of fields) in a table is unique.

   Yes/No: A logical field that can have only one of two values: Yes or No.

   OLE Object: An object, such as a photograph, that was created in another application.

   Hyperlink: Used to store hyperlinks (URL and UNC addresses).

   Lookup Wizard: Not really a data type, this is used to create a Lookup field, which lets the database user select a value from a list, enhancing data accuracy by preventing typos (see "Creating Lookup Fields" later in this chapter).

3. Enter a description for the field, if the name is at all ambiguous. The Description entry appears in the status bar during data entry when the insertion point is in that field.

4. Press Enter to drop to the next blank row and enter the information for the next field. Continue until all fields are entered.

5. After you enter all the field names and data types, select a field or fields to designate as a primary key, then click the Primary Key button on the toolbar or right-click the row selector and choose Primary Key from the shortcut menu. (See "Selecting a Primary Key" later in this chapter.)

6. Save the table, and enter a unique table name when prompted.

7. To begin entering records, click the View button on the toolbar (see "Entering Data in a Table" later in this chapter); if you're not ready to enter data, close the table to return to the Database window.

...

MASTERING THE OPPORTUNITIES

Names with Spaces

Access 97 allowed spaces in object names, but spaces were discouraged because they presented a big problem if the database was upsized to a SQL Server or another database tool. In Access 2000, the spaces are no longer a problem when the data is migrated to a SQL Server because Access assigns a unique identifier to each name. So, if SQL Server is the database you'll upsize to, the decision to use spaces in your field names is up to you and your IS department.

If you need to change names to remove the spaces (for example, to migrate Access data to a database that does not accept spaces in object names), Access 2000's new Name AutoCorrect feature will change the names for you throughout the database. When you change the field name in one place, the name is changed wherever it occurs in the database. (Name AutoCorrect is turned on by default; you can turn it on/off by clicking Tools ➤ Options, selecting the General tab, and marking or clearing the check boxes under Name AutoCorrect.)

FIGURE 30.6

Data types

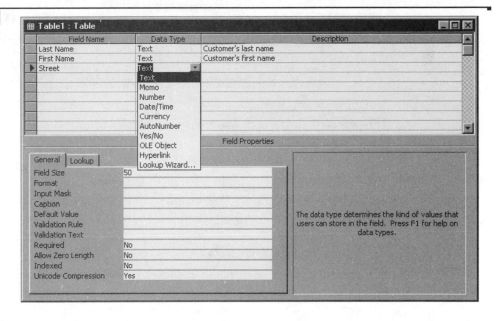

TIP   You can select a data type by typing its first letter; for example, if you know you want a Number data type, type **n** and press Enter.

Using the Table Wizard

The Table Wizard is fast, sets the correct data types and properties, and may remind you to include fields you might not have thought of when creating the table from scratch. To create a table using the Table Wizard, in the database window double-click Create Table By Using Wizard.

1. In the wizard's first dialog box (shown in Figure 30.7), click a category option, scroll through the list, and click a Sample Table. Double-click each Sample Field you want to include, or click the >> button to include all the fields. Then click Next.

FIGURE 30.7

Select a table and fields in the Table Wizard.

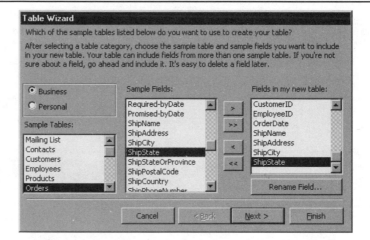

2. In the second wizard dialog box, type a name for your table and select a primary key option. Then click Next.

- If you choose not to let Access set a primary key for you, the next wizard dialog box will ask which field will be a unique identifier (for example, it could be a Part Number field in a Products table, or a Phone Number field in a Customers table). Set your options and click Next.

- If you did let Access set the primary key for you, the unique identifier field is the primary key. Click Next.

3. If there are already other tables in your database, the next wizard dialog box asks if you want Access to create relationships to those other tables for you. You can allow Access to create the relationships, or create them yourself later. To let Access create the relationships, click Relationships, set up the relationships in the Relationships dialog box (shown in Figure 30.8) by clicking options for the relationships you want, and click OK. When you're finished with this step, click Next. If this is the first table in your database, you won't be asked about relationships.

FIGURE 30.8

You'll see this dialog box if you let the wizard create relationships.

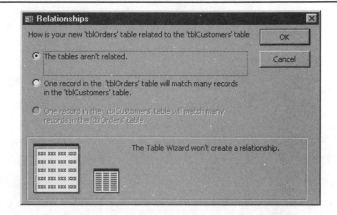

4. In the last wizard dialog box, choose an option to open the finished table in Design view (so you can tweak the design further) or in Datasheet view (so you can start entering data), or close the table and let the wizard create an AutoForm for data entry. If you open the finished table in Design view, you can begin modifying field properties next.

Modifying Fields in Design View

No matter how your table was created, you can add and modify fields in Design view.

Every field has properties that control how the field's contents are displayed, stored, controlled, or validated. Some properties are common to all fields, and some properties are only relevant to particular data types. In a table's Design view, the selected field's properties are shown at the bottom of the window. For example, Figure 30.9 shows the field properties for the Telephone field in a Customers table.

All data types except AutoNumber have the following general properties:

Format: Indicates how the field's contents will be displayed.

Caption: Provides the label that will be attached to the field on a form or report.

Default Value: Specifies values for new entries. Enter the most frequently entered value for the field.

Validation Rule: Indicates a range of acceptable entries.

Validation Text: Help message that appears in the status bar when the field is active.

Required: A Yes/No setting that indicates whether the field must have an entry.

PART

VI

Access for the Nonprogrammer

FIGURE 30.9

Telephone field properties

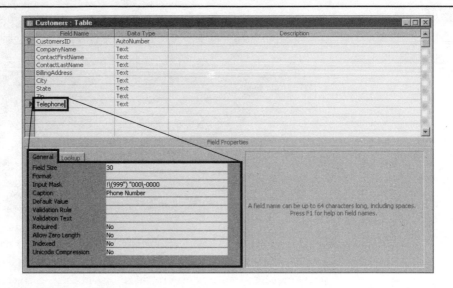

The following general properties apply primarily to text fields:

Field Size: Indicates the maximum number of characters allowed in the field. For example, you might set the size for a State field to 2.

Input Mask: Limits and formats the values that can be entered.

Allow Zero Length: A Yes/No setting that determines whether a text string with no length ("") is a valid entry.

Indexed: Instructs Access whether to create an index for the field. Indexing a field speeds up sorting, searching, and filtering the field's contents; however, too many indexes slow down record editing and entry. The primary key for a table is always indexed. You should index fields that will be frequently sorted for reports or forms.

Number and Currency fields have one additional general property: Decimal Places, which specifies the number of digits that will be displayed and stored after the decimal.

An Access database isn't limited to typed entries. The OLE Object (*OLE* stands for Object Linking and Embedding) data type allows you to store different types of objects in a database. You can store a variety of objects in an OLE Object field, including graphics, pictures (including pictures of bar codes), sounds, and Word documents. For example, a Products table could include pictures of products, the logo for commercial suppliers, or musical sound bites.

Selecting a Primary Key

In a customer database, a telephone number is often used as a primary key, since it's unusual for two customers to have the same telephone number. If a single field can't serve as a primary key, try combining two fields. For example, in the Order Details table shown in Figure 30.10, neither the OrderID nor the ProductID could be a primary key, since either could occur several times in the Order Details table. However, because each individual order lists each ordered product just once, every order-product combination will be unique. If no combination of fields is suitably unique, then you may need to add an AutoNumber field for a primary key. AutoNumber fields are, by definition, always unique.

FIGURE 30.10

The Order Details table has a two-field primary key.

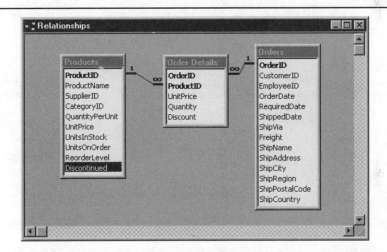

 To set the primary key, click the row selector (to the left of the Field Name column) to select the field or fields that will serve as the primary key. Right-click and choose Primary Key from the shortcut menu, or click the Primary Key button on the toolbar.

After your fields are set up, you can enter data in the table, but you can't enter data in Design view. Click the View button (on the left end of the toolbar) to switch to the table's Datasheet view. You'll be prompted to save the table. Choose Yes; if you choose No, you remain in Design view. Enter a name for the table in the Table Name dialog box (beginning with **tbl** if you're using the L/R naming convention). If you forgot to assign a primary key, a warning appears. Click Cancel, assign a primary key, and save again.

PART

VI

Access for the
Nonprogrammer

TIP When you change to a different view, the toolbars change to correspond to the view you are in, so don't be surprised if a toolbar looks different when you switch from Design to Datasheet view.

Entering Data in a Table

Datasheet view (see Figure 30.11) looks much like a spreadsheet, and skills that you've learned with Excel or other spreadsheets will serve you well here.

FIGURE 30.11

The Customers table in Datasheet view

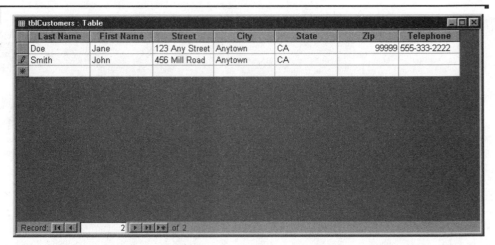

	Last Name	First Name	Street	City	State	Zip	Telephone
	Doe	Jane	123 Any Street	Anytown	CA	99999	555-333-2222
∅	Smith	John	456 Mill Road	Anytown	CA		
*							

Record: |◄ ◄ 2 ► ►| ►* of 2

Click in the first field and begin typing the entry; then press Tab to move to the next field. Continue entering field information and pressing Tab until you reach the end of the record; then press Tab again to start another record.

TIP Click in any field you want to enter data in; press Shift+Tab to move one field to the left. Press the arrow keys to move one cell at a time in the arrow direction. Press Ctrl+' (apostrophe) to copy the entry in the cell above. Press Crtl+Z to undo an entry immediately after you type it.

The table columns are all the same default width, so some of the field data, like addresses, won't fit in the column. Maximizing the window displays more of the data, and you can adjust the widths of individual columns. Move the mouse to the right edge of the column heading. The mouse pointer will change to a two-headed arrow. Drag to manually adjust the column, or double-click to resize the column to fit the existing data. When you close the table, you will be asked if you want to save the layout changes made when you adjusted the columns.

Move around in the datasheet using the arrow keys on the keyboard and pan the width of the table with the horizontal scroll bar at the bottom of the screen. The vertical scroll bar at the right screen edge moves up and down through the datasheet. (Scroll bars only appear when there is data that cannot be viewed within the current window.) The navigation buttons at the bottom of the screen are used to move to the first, previous, next, last, or new record.

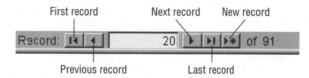

Modifying Data in a Table

To edit data, move the mouse over the field you want to edit. The mouse pointer changes to an I-beam, and when you click in the field, an insertion point appears. You can double-click the I-beam to select a single word, and then type over the word. To select and overtype the entire field, move the mouse to the left edge of the field.

The pointer will change to a selection tool. Click to select the field.

Deleting Records

To delete a record, click the record selector (the gray box to the left of the record's first field) to select the entire record, and then press the Delete key or click the Delete Record toolbar button. (You can drag the record selectors or Shift-click to select consecutive records.) Or, right-click the record selector and choose Delete Record from the shortcut menu. Deleting records can't be undone, so a message box appears, prompting you to confirm the deletion.

When you are finished entering or modifying table data, close the table. If you have changed the table layout, you'll be prompted to save the changes. You will not be prompted to save the data you entered; each record was saved as soon as you moved the insertion point to a different record.

NOTE The record you're entering data in has a small pencil icon in its record selector, indicating that the data in that record isn't saved. When you move to or click in a different record, the pencil icon disappears, indicating that the record has been saved.

PART

VI

Access for the
Nonprogrammer

Sorting Records

Records can be sorted in ascending (*A–Z*) or descending (*Z–A*) order. They can be sorted by any field or by more than one field. For example, you can sort records by last name and then by first name, or by zip code and then by last name within each zip code.

When you sort a table, Access will ask whether you want to save the changes to the table's design when you attempt to close the table. Choosing Yes will save the sort order so that when you open the table again, the records will still be sorted. While a table is sorted, added records are automatically sorted into position.

  To sort a table, switch to Datasheet view. Click anywhere in the column (the field) you want to sort by, and then click the Ascending Sort or Descending Sort button. To remove the sort order and return records to their original order, choose Records ➤ Remove Filter/Sort.

Multilevel Sorting   A *multilevel sort* sorts the records on the first field you specify, and then sorts records with the same value using another specified field. For example, you can sort all the customers by state, and then by zip code within each state.

To apply a multilevel sort, click Records ➤ Filter ➤ Advanced Filter/Sort. The Advanced Filter/Sort window (shown in Figure 30.12) appears.

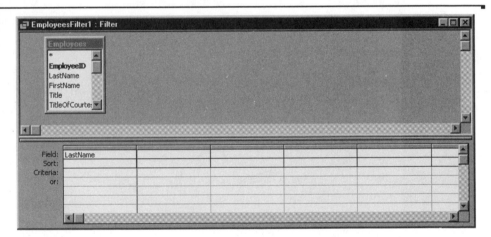

FIGURE 30.12

*The Advanced Filter/
Sort window*

1. In the field list in the upper pane, double-click the field name for the first field you want to sort by (in this Employees table, the LastName field). The field name appears in the left end of the grid in the lower pane. Then double-click the next field you want to sort by (in this example, FirstName).

2. Click in the Sort box for each field and select a sort order (in this case, Ascending) from the drop-down list.

 3. Click the Apply Filter button on the toolbar; the window disappears and the sort order is applied. To remove the sort, click Records ➤ Remove Filter/Sort.

Filtering Records

Applying a *filter* to an Access table temporarily hides records that don't meet your criteria. You can create a filter based on text or a value you have selected, use a blank form to type in the values you want to see, or enter complex filtering and sorting criteria in a way similar to writing a query.

 Filter by Selection/Filter Excluding Selection The easiest way to apply a filter in Access is with Filter by Selection. Click in the field you want to filter on, then click the Filter by Selection button. For example, to find all the customers in Mexico, click in a Country field entry that reads Mexico, then click the Filter by Selection button.

Only the records for Mexico will be visible; all others will be hidden (as shown in Figure 30.13). The navigation buttons at the bottom of the table show the number of filtered records only.

FIGURE 30.13

A filtered table

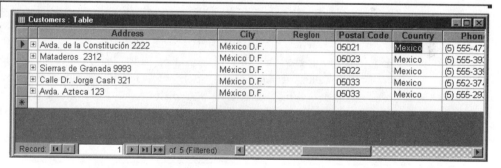

 To remove the filter, click the Remove Filter button. If you wish to reapply the filter, click the same button again, which has now become an Apply Filter button.

If you want the filter to match only part of a field, select the part of the data you want to see. For example, if you want to see all the companies in area code 317, select the string "317" in the telephone field. You can apply filters to filtered data to narrow the search even further.

If you would like to see all the records except those with a certain value—for example, all the customers that aren't in Mexico—locate a record with the value you want to exclude, right-click to open the shortcut menu, and choose Filter Excluding Selection.

PART

VI

Access for the Nonprogrammer

Filter By Form   The Filter By Form method works the same way as filtering by selection, except that you set up your criteria on a blank form or datasheet.

Click the Filter By Form button to open the Filter By Form window. All the table's field headings appear across the top. When you click in a field, a drop-down list containing all the values in the field appears. Select the value to use as a filter, and click the Apply Filter button. Using this method, you can apply multiple filters to display records that meet all the criteria you select, called an AND filter because it filters for records that each meet criterion A *and* criterion B *and* criterion C, etc.

You aren't limited to the values in the drop-down lists; you can use *comparison operators* (also called *logical operators*) such as less than (<), more than (>), and greater than or equal to (=>) in your criteria. For example, you can filter a Products table for records that show less than 10 Units In Stock and more than 10 Units On Order, as shown in Figure 30.14.

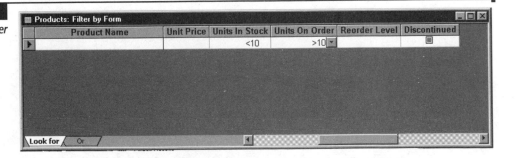

FIGURE 30.14

An AND filter

To see records that meet any of the specified criteria, but not necessarily all of them (an OR filter), click the Or tab at the bottom of the form before selecting the additional criterion. For example, you might want to see all customers in CA or AZ. After you set criteria on the Look For and Or sheets, click the Apply Filter button.

Adding Subdatasheets to Look Up Related Records

 Subdatasheets allow you to quickly look up the records in a related table, as shown in Figure 30.15. They make use of a one-to-many relationship by allowing you to open the "one" table and display the related records in the "many" table. Essentially, you are "drilling down" to more detailed information available in the related table, a type of analysis similar to that provided by pivot tables in Excel (as discussed in Chapter 26).

To display a subdatasheet, click the small plus symbol next to the record you want to see details for. To hide the subdatasheet, click the small minus symbol next to the record.

FIGURE 30.15

Looking up related records with a subdatasheet

	Order ID	Customer	Employee	Order Date	Required Date	Shipped Date
⊞	10248	Vins et alcools Chevalier	Buchanan, Steven	04-Jul-96	01-Aug-96	16-Jul-96
⊞	10249	Toms Spezialitäten	Suyama, Michael	05-Jul-96	16-Aug-96	10-Jul-96
⊞	10250	Hanari Carnes	Peacock, Margaret	08-Jul-96	05-Aug-96	12-Jul-96
⊞	10251	Victuailles en stock	Leverling, Janet	08-Jul-96	05-Aug-96	15-Jul-96
⊞	10252	Suprêmes délices	Peacock, Margaret	09-Jul-96	06-Aug-96	11-Jul-96
⊟	10253	Hanari Carnes	Leverling, Janet	10-Jul-96	24-Jul-96	16-Jul-96

	Product	Unit Price	Quantity	Discount
	Gorgonzola Telino	$10.00	20	0%
	Chartreuse verte	$14.40	42	0%
	Maxilaku	$16.00	40	0%
*		$0.00	1	0%

Record: 1 of 3

	Order ID	Customer	Employee	Order Date	Required Date	Shipped Date
⊞	10254	Chop-suey Chinese	Buchanan, Steven	11-Jul-96	08-Aug-96	23-Jul-96
⊞	10255	Richter Supermarkt	Fuller, Anne	12-Jul-96	09-Aug-96	15-Jul-96
⊞	10256	Wellington Importadora	Leverling, Janet	15-Jul-96	12-Aug-96	17-Jul-96
⊞	10257	HILARIÓN-Abastos	Peacock, Margaret	16-Jul-96	13-Aug-96	22-Jul-96
⊞	10258	Ernst Handel	Davolio, Nancy	17-Jul-96	14-Aug-96	23-Jul-96
⊞	10259	Centro comercial Moctezuma	Peacock, Margaret	18-Jul-96	15-Aug-96	25-Jul-96

Record: 1 of 830

PART **VI**

Access for the Nonprogrammer

Subdatasheets are created automatically when you create a Lookup field (which creates a one-to-many relationship), but you can insert them yourself if no lookup fields connect the two tables. To insert a subdatasheet:

1. Open the table that's on the "one" side of the relationship.
2. Click Insert ➤ Subdatasheet. The Insert Subdatasheet dialog box shown in Figure 30.16 appears.

FIGURE 30.16

*The Insert Subdatasheet
dialog box*

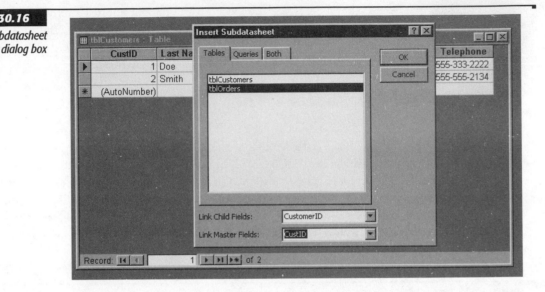

3. Click the name of the table on the "many" side of the relationship.

4. Drop the list in the Link Child Fields box and click the name of the foreign key field in the related table, then drop the list in the Link Master Fields box and click the name of the primary key field in the primary table.

5. Click OK. If there isn't a relationship already existing between the two tables, Access will ask if you want to create one. Click Yes.

To remove a subdatasheet, click Format ➤ Subdatasheet ➤ Remove.

Modifying Field Properties

Some fields need further modification to make your database really easy to use and ensure data accuracy. Here are some things you can do to tighten up your database:

- Create Lookup fields to look up complete and accurate entries.
- Set input masks to ensure complete entries and proper formatting.
- Require data entry in a field.
- Establish data validation rules to ensure data accuracy.
- Create an OLE field to store objects.
- Set a Hyperlink data type so a field can store hyperlinks.

Creating Lookup Fields

A Lookup field gets its entries from either another table or a fixed list of items. Lookup fields are handy for entering data such as an employee's name in an Orders table, product items in an order, existing customer names in an order, or shipping choices from a fixed list. They are created to represent the "one" side of a one-to-many relationship.

Lookup fields make data entry much faster, and they ensure data accuracy because the user can't inadvertently misspell the entry. It's important that all identical entries be spelled precisely the same way so that filters and sorts are complete and accurate.

To create a Lookup field, first decide whether you want to look up the entries in another table or in a fixed list. A fixed list is good if the data possibilities are few and seldom change, because you don't need to create another table to hold the entries. For example, if you need to enter a credit card type (such as VISA, MasterCard, American Express, or Discover) on an Orders form, your form works faster if you create a fixed list of these names for the Lookup field. If you need to look up product names for an Orders form, a table lookup is a better idea because the list will probably be fairly long and will change periodically. When you look up items in a table, you'll always get a current list of items.

To enter data in a Lookup field, the user clicks a drop-down arrow and chooses a value from a list (as shown in Figure 30.17) rather than typing the entry. If you choose to look up entries in another table, the table of looked-up entries (the *lookup table*) must exist before you can create the Lookup field that does the looking up.

FIGURE 30.17

Looking up an entry in a Lookup field

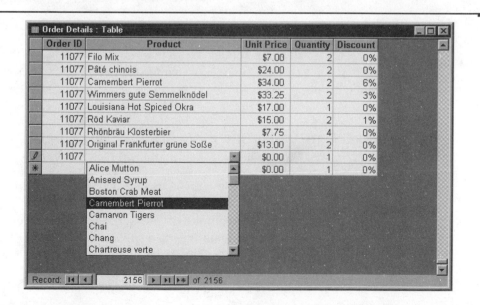

After you've created the lookup table, create the Lookup field by opening its table (again, the table on the "one" side of the relationship) in Design view.

1. Add the Field Name if it's a new field and choose Lookup Wizard as the data type; if you're changing an existing field, just switch to Lookup Wizard in the Data Type column.

2. In the first wizard dialog box (see Figure 30.18), choose whether the data in the lookup will come from a typed-in list or an existing table; then click Next.

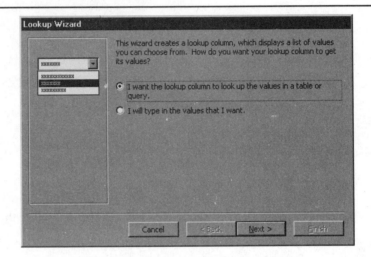

Looking Up Entries in a Fixed List   If you choose a fixed list, in the next wizard dialog box you'll choose a number of columns for the list and type in each item, as shown in Figure 30.19. (Press Tab at the end of each item to create the next entry.) Then, adjust the width of the column so that it is slightly wider than the longest entry, and click Next.

In the last wizard dialog box, enter a label for the lookup column; the label will become the new field name when you click Finish.

Looking Up Entries in a Table   If you choose to look up values in a table, you'll be prompted to select a table (or query) in the next wizard dialog box.

Then, you'll choose the columns that you want to include in your lookup. In Figure 30.20, adding the ProductName field will allow a user to select the product name from a list (the ProductID field, the primary key, will be included automatically). If you choose more than one field, all the fields will be visible in the final lookup list, but only the first field will be visible in the table datasheet after the user selects a value.

Double-click each field you want to add, and then click Next.

FIGURE 30.19

Entering a fixed lookup list

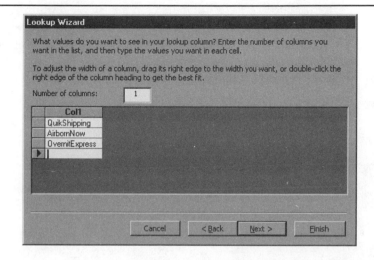

FIGURE 30.20

Choosing fields to look up values

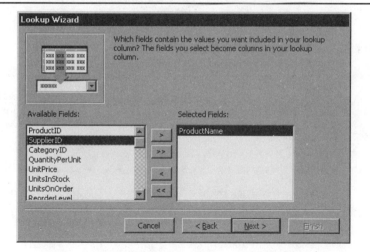

In the next wizard dialog box, set the width of the column by dragging the right border of the column label. Leave the Hide Key Column check box marked (this allows Access to use the primary key field to identify the looked-up record). Then click Next.

In the last dialog box of the Lookup Wizard, enter a label for the lookup, which becomes the new name for the field. Then click Finish. You'll be prompted to save the table so that Access can create the relationship between the table with the Lookup field and the table that provides the field's values.

PART

VI

Access for the Nonprogrammer

Verifying Lookup Relationships   To review the relationship Access created, open the Relationships window (close the table, then click Tools ➤ Relationships). There may be a number of relationships already defined, depending on how many lookups you've created in your database.

Click the Show All Relationships button to make sure all the relationships are displayed. The relationship between a Products table and a Categories table is shown in Figure 30.21. The CategoryID is the primary/foreign key field that relates the two tables.

FIGURE 30.21

The new lookup relationship

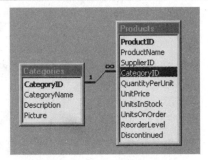

TIP   A Lookup field lets you enter data quickly, by typing the first letter or two of the entry; the matching entry in the list is filled in, and when you press Tab, it's completed.

Creating Input Masks

When a user enters data in a Telephone field, it would be helpful to have the punctuation (usually parentheses and hyphen) that's normally found in a telephone number entered automatically, without the user typing it. Formats for data entry, such as placeholders and punctuation, are called *input masks*.

To set an input mask, open the table in Design view and take the following steps:

1. Select the field; then click the Input Mask box in the lower pane.

2. Click the Build button (the button with three dots) that appears at the right end of the Input Mask box to start the Input Mask Wizard. (You will be required to save the table first.)

3. In the first wizard dialog box (shown in Figure 30.22), select the type of input mask you want to create; then click Next.

Select a mask.

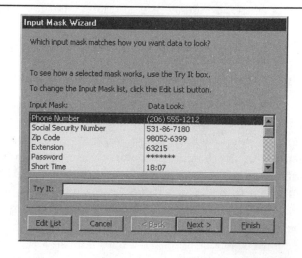

4. If you wish, you can edit the input mask (for example, a telephone number might be punctuated as 000-000-0000 or 000.000.0000). If you alter the punctuation, take care not to delete the **!** at the beginning (see Figure 30.23).

Accept or change the mask punctuation.

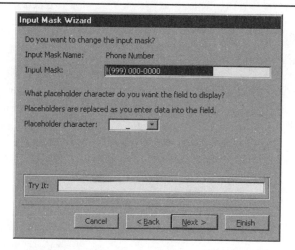

5. Then select the placeholder that will appear where the user should enter text, and click Next.

6. In the last step, click an option to choose whether you want the data stored with or without the input mask. Storing the data with the input mask in place

PART

VI

Access for the Nonprogrammer

makes the database file a bit larger, but preserves the special formatting so it appears in reports.

7. Click Finish to complete the input mask.

Setting the Required and Indexed Properties

When a field's Required property is set to Yes, a user must enter data in the field before saving the record. No means that data entry in the field is optional. These properties are important for primary key fields, but they can be set for any field in which you find them helpful for controlling your data accuracy and completeness. For example, in an Employee table, you might require entries for first and last names.

There are three possible values for a field's Indexed property: No, Yes (No Duplicates), and Yes (Duplicates OK). Choosing Yes speeds up searching, sorting, and filtering by creating an index for the field. Yes (No Duplicates) means that the value entered in the field must be unique (duplicate values won't be accepted).

For a single-field primary key, Access will set the Required property to Yes and the Indexed property to Yes (No Duplicates). With a multiple-field primary key, all fields are required, but duplicates are allowed within each field.

To set the properties, open the table in Design view and select the field in the upper pane. In the lower pane, in the Required box, select No or Yes; in the Indexed property, select No, Yes (Duplicates OK), or Yes (No Duplicates).

Validating Entries

Validation is a way to screen data being entered in a table or form to ensure greater data accuracy. Entering a value in a field's Default property is a passive way to validate data; if the user doesn't enter anything in the field, at least the default value is there. For more active validation, create a validation rule that all data entries must meet, and validation text to let the user know what constitutes a valid entry. In Access 2000, you can set validation for fields and records in tables and for controls in forms.

Field validation is set in a field's Validation Rule property. When you tab or click out of the field during data entry, Access checks to make sure the data you entered matches the rule. If not, the validation text is displayed.

Record validation is set in the property sheet for the table. When you move to a new record during data entry, Access checks to make sure the entire record is valid. Record validation is used to compare one field to another to check, for example, that an employee's HireDate occurred before the TerminationDate.

Many field properties set in a table are *inheritable*. That means that the validation rule set in a table passes through to any form control based on the field. So, normally you won't use control validation, which is set in a form control's property sheet and functions in the form but not in the underlying table. It's better to set validation once in the table than four times in four forms. However, in some cases you can only perform validation in a form. For example, you can create a form that displays information from an external linked table (see "Importing vs. Linking"). The linked table isn't part of your database, so you can't set validation at the table level, only in a form control.

To enter a validation rule for a field, open the table in Design view. Select the field in the upper pane, and click in the Validation Rule property box in the lower pane. If the rule is simple (for example, minimum pay rate is $10), enter it using logical operators such as **>=10** (shown in Figure 30.24). In the Validation Text property box, enter an error message that will appear on the Status bar when invalid data is entered.

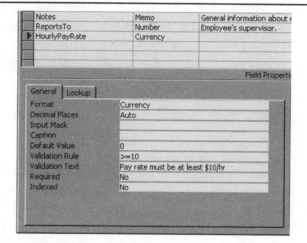

FIGURE 30.24

Defining a field's validation rule and text in the Design view lower pane

 TIP If you need more space in which to type validation text, right-click in the property box and choose Zoom to open the Zoom box. When you are done entering text, click OK to close the Zoom box.

To validate records, right-click anywhere in the Design view window and choose Properties from the shortcut menu to open the Table Properties window (shown in Figure 30.25).

You can use the Expression Builder, shown in Figure 30.26, to create complex field and record validation rules. To open the Expression Builder, click the Build button at the right end of the Validation Rule text box. With the Builder, you can access common functions and, for record validation, field names from the current table.

If you add validation rules for fields that contain data, you'll be asked whether you want Access to apply the rules to the existing data when you save the table. If you choose to apply the rules to existing data, Access will scan the existing data and tell you whether there are entries that violate the new rule. Access won't change the existing entries, or tell you which ones they are; it just tells you whether any violate the rule (you'll have to filter or sort the table and locate the existing errors yourself).

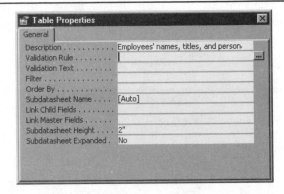

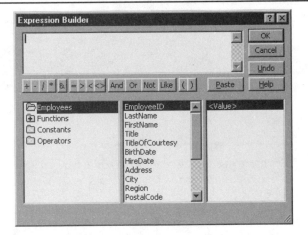

Adding Objects and Hyperlinks to Records

You can store objects such as pictures or sound files in records by creating a field with an OLE Object data type, and you can store hyperlinks to other files or Web sites in records by creating a field with a Hyperlink data type.

Adding Objects to Records   To add an OLE Object field to a table, open the table in Design view. Add the field and choose the OLE Object data type.

To enter an OLE object in a record, you can't just type in the object's file name—you have to insert the file. In the table's Datasheet view, right-click in the OLE field in the record and choose Insert Object to open the Insert Object dialog box. You can create a new object to place in the field by choosing Create New, but if the object already exists on a local or network hard drive, choose Create From File (shown in Figure 30.27).

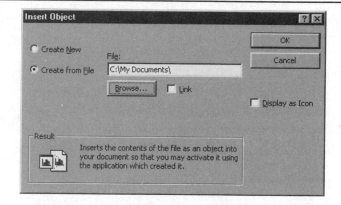

Click the Browse button and locate the OLE object file. If you want the object in the database to be updated if the file changes, choose Link. If you instead want a copy of the object in the database, leave the Link box blank, and the object will be *embedded* in the database (which means it won't be updated if the file changes). Click OK to insert the OLE object file in the record.

 TIP To learn about the advantages and disadvantages of linking and embedding, see Chapter 36.

Either the object or the object's type (such as a Word document, MIDI sequence, or bitmap) appears in the field. If only the type is displayed, double-click the entry to open the object in its native format. For example, a Word document will open in Word; a video clip will open the Windows Media Player and begin to play.

Adding Hyperlinks to Records   To add a Hyperlink field to a table, open the table in Design view. Add the field and choose the Hyperlink data type. To enter a hyperlink in a record, open the table in Datasheet view. Type the URL or UNC for the hyperlink (but don't type the http:// part). The hyperlink will turn blue and be underlined.

PART

VI

Access for the Nonprogrammer

When you click the hyperlink, your browser launches and goes to the site, or the file and program open. You cannot edit the link by clicking it, because that triggers the hyperlink. To edit or delete the hyperlink, right-click the hyperlink entry, then point to Hyperlinks on the shortcut menu and click the command you want. If the hyperlink was misspelled or the address changes, click Edit Hyperlink, and then change the URL text in the Type The File Or Web Page Name box in the resulting dialog box. To change the entry in the table to something more meaningful than the URL, change the entry in the Display Text box. To delete the hyperlink, click Remove Hyperlink.

Working with External Data

In Access 2000, you can add copies of tables from other applications to your database or work with tables that exist in a separate database or spreadsheet. Access 2000 can import (copy) or link (connect to) data from prior versions of Access, other databases like FoxPro and Paradox, spreadsheets like Excel and Lotus 1-2-3, and HTML tables from the Internet or an intranet. The ability to work with data from a variety of sources makes Access a powerful tool in today's workplace, where data can originate in a variety of applications. Before you retype data that already exists, it's worth your time to see if you can import it directly into Access or transfer it to a program that Access can use.

 Access considers any and all data files (files that consist of tables of data) usable, and can turn them into database files. If you click File ➢ Open to open an existing database, the Open dialog box shows a list of all data files (Excel spreadsheets, other database types, text files, etc.) in the folder. Opening a file such as Excel starts the Link Spreadsheet Wizard, which guides you through setting up a new database for the data file. The new database contains a single table, linked to the original file, so you can use the data in Access without duplicating any data on your hard drive. Creating an entire database for a single linked table isn't always the most efficient way to work with data, however, so read through the following sections on importing and linking tables into existing databases before you decide which method is most appropriate.

Importing vs. Linking

Importing data creates a copy of the data in a table in your database. Because a copy is created, the original data isn't affected, and further changes in the original data are not reflected in Access. With linked data, you are working with original data; when the source file changes, the changes are reflected in Access, and changes you make in Access are reflected in the source file.

Before you can import or link data, you need to decide which you want to do. For example, you're creating a new database and a colleague in another department offers you an Excel spreadsheet that lists all the cities, states, and zip codes for your region. Should you import or link? If you know that the data doesn't need to be updated in another program, you should import it. Cities, states, and zip codes rarely change, so updating isn't an issue with this table. And when you import data, you can change field properties and rearrange or delete fields if you need to, so importing is more flexible from your point of view. If, however, another user of your database also needs the data in its original form, or someone else keeps it updated, then you need to link to the data.

 TIP If you share an Access database with other users, you can put the data tables in one database and your forms and reports in another, then link the two databases together to allow multiple users to access the data tables. Access 2000 has a Database Splitter add-in to help you divide a database.

Importing Data

To import external data, choose File ➣ Get External Data ➣ Import to open the Import dialog box (shown in Figure 30.28). Click the Files Of Type drop-down arrow to select the type of file you want to import. Select the file and then click Import. Not all import file types are included in a Typical install. If the file type you want is not listed, you can install its import filter from your Office 2000 CD-ROM.

FIGURE 30.28

Importing a file

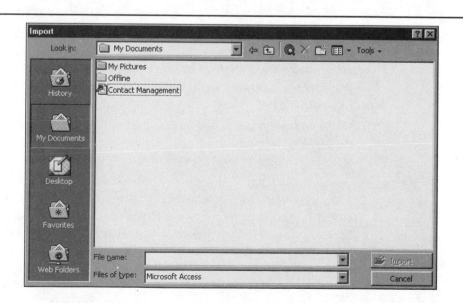

Importing Data from Spreadsheets and Other Databases

You can import data from Excel or Lotus 1-2-3. When you click the Import button, the Import Spreadsheet Wizard opens. You can import worksheets or named ranges from a spreadsheet (see Figure 30.29). If an Excel spreadsheet file contains more than one worksheet or named range, you can choose the one you want.

FIGURE 30.29

The Import Spreadsheet Wizard

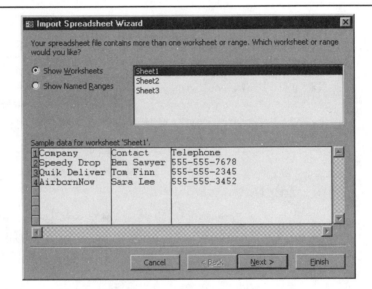

1. In the second wizard dialog box, indicate whether the spreadsheet's first row is data or column labels, then click Next.

2. In the third wizard dialog box, choose whether you want Access to create a new table with this data or place it in an existing table that you've already created. If you choose an existing table, the column labels in the spreadsheet and the field names in the table must be identical.

3. In the fourth wizard dialog box, shown in Figure 30.30, indicate whether the data in each column is indexed; you can omit any columns of data you don't want by skipping them.

4. In the fifth wizard dialog box, choose whether to have Access add an Auto-Number primary key, or select an existing column as the primary key, or indicate that there is no primary key field. (If the primary key will be more than one field, choose No Primary Key Field and set the primary key in the table's Design view after you've imported the data.)

5. In the last wizard dialog box, name the table and then click Finish. Access will import the data and add the table to your database.

After the table is imported, you may want to make some changes in Design view. For example, if the Social Security numbers were imported as numbers, you'd want to change the data type to Text and add an input mask to speed up data entry.

FIGURE 30.30

Choosing which columns to import

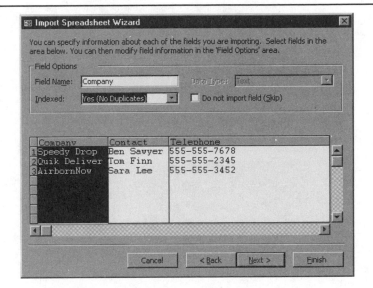

TIP Numbers that won't be calculated, such as zip codes and part numbers, should always have Text data types because if you leave them with Number data types, they'll lose any leading or trailing zeroes.

When you import from a database other than Access, the Import Database Wizard opens, and the steps are similar to the steps in the Import Spreadsheet Wizard.

Importing from Access

If you import from another Access database, you aren't limited to data. You can import forms, reports, macros, and even relationships. When you choose an Access database in the Import dialog box, the Import Objects dialog box opens. Click the Options button to extend the dialog box to show other available options, as shown in Figure 30.31.

PART

VI

Access for the
Nonprogrammer

Click the tabs in the dialog box to move from one type of object to another. On each object tab, click Select All to import all the objects or click each specific object you want to import. You can import tables with all their data, or import table structures only. When you've selected all the objects you want to import, click OK to add the objects to the current database.

FIGURE 30.31

Importing Access objects

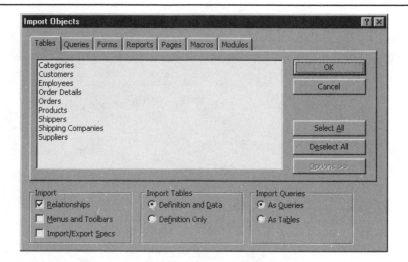

Linking to a Spreadsheet or Database

If the data you want to include from another source can change, you'll want to link rather than import the data. Examples of dynamic data include a list of current customers or products. Linking to a table or worksheet is even less complex than importing. You can't change the structure of the linked table or worksheet, so you don't get an opportunity to skip columns.

Follow these steps to link to an external data source:

1. Choose File ➢ Get External Data ➢ Link Tables.

2. Select the type of data source you want to link to in the Files Of Type list, select the file you want to link to, and click Link to open the Link Wizard.

3. If you're linking to a spreadsheet or other non-Access file, select the worksheet, named range, or table you wish to link to, and click Link. If you're linking to another Access table, select the table name and click OK.

If you're linking to another Access table, the table is linked and you're finished. If you're linking to a non-Access file, continue with step 4.

4. In the wizard, indicate whether the first row contains data or column labels, and click Next.

5. Enter the name you will use to refer to the external table or worksheet, and click Finish.

You can tell which tables in a database are actually links to other tables. Linked Access tables have a link arrow in front of the Access table icon; other linked file types have their own icons with the link arrow. In Figure 30.32, the Shipping Companies table is a linked Excel worksheet.

FIGURE 30.32

A linked external file

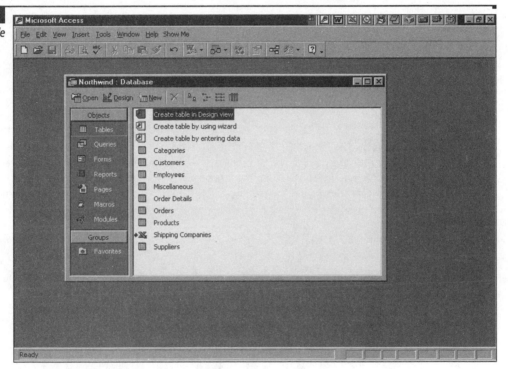

If you decide later that you don't want to be linked to the data, select and delete the link in the Table page of the Database window. The link will be deleted, but the original table won't be affected.

Working with Relationships

Working with table relationships begins with creating relationships in the Relationships window; then you can edit each relationship to set referential integrity if you need it, and set cascading updates and cascading deletes as part of the referential integrity if you want them.

PART

VI

Access for the
Nonprogrammer

Creating Relationships

If you create Lookup fields or subdatasheets, Access creates the required relationships for you, but some of the relationships in a database may not be used for lookups or subdatasheet lookups. For queries, reports, and forms based on multiple tables, you may need to establish relationships yourself. To create a relationship, the primary key field in the primary table must be included as a foreign key in the related table. To create a relationship:

1. Open the Relationships window by clicking the Relationships button on the toolbar. The Relationships button is on the Database toolbar and is available when the database window is active. To create a relationship, make sure that both the primary and related tables are visible. If not, right-click in the Relationships window and click Show Tables, then add the table(s) to the window.

NOTE The foreign key field in the related table must have the same data type and size as the primary key in the primary table—with one exception. If the primary key uses an AutoNumber data type, then the foreign key field must use the Number type with a size of Long Integer, which is the data type of the entries that AutoNumber fields create.

2. Select the primary key field in the primary table and drag-and-drop it onto the matching field in the related table.

3. In the Edit Relationships dialog box, check that the related field names are correct and click Create.

Setting Referential Integrity

Referential integrity ensures that records in a related table have related values in the primary table. Referential integrity prevents users from accidentally deleting or changing records in a primary table when records in a related table depend on them, making sure that there are no orphaned records in the related table, such as orders without customers or salaries without employees.

NOTE When referential integrity is applied, the join line in the Relationships window will have a "1" symbol and an "infinity" symbol. The symbols indicate a one-to-many relationship between the tables (Access figures out which is the "one" side and which is the "many" side).

For example, suppose a database includes two tables: Departments, with DepartmentID as the primary key, and Employees, which includes DepartmentID as a foreign key to show which department an employee is assigned to. When referential integrity is enforced in the relationship between two tables, three restrictions are applied:

- Access won't allow you to use a DepartmentID in the Employees table that doesn't already exist in the Departments table.
- Foreign key values (DepartmentIDs) that have been used in the related Departments table protect their matching records in the primary table, so a user can't delete a department in the Departments table that's currently used in the Employees table.
- The entries in the primary table are protected. A user can't change the DepartmentID OPS to Operations in the Departments table, because OPS is already referenced in the Employees table.

When you try to enter, delete, or change data that violates the referential integrity rules, Access displays a warning dialog box and ignores the change.

To change referential integrity in a relationship, open the Relationships window. Right-click the join line and click Edit Relationship. In the Edit Relationships dialog box (shown in Figure 30.33), mark the Enforce Referential Integrity check box to set it; clear the check box to undo it. Then click OK.

FIGURE 30.33

Setting referential integrity

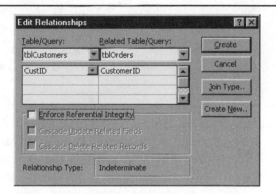

Cascading Updates and Deletes

You can override the second and third restrictions outlined above and still maintain referential integrity by enabling Cascade Update Related Fields and Cascade Delete Related Records.

When Cascade Update Related Fields is enabled, changing the value of a primary key in the primary table automatically updates that value in the foreign key of the related table's matching records. With Cascade Update enabled, you *can* change OPS to Operations; the change will be automatically reflected in any Employees record that included OPS.

When Cascade Delete Related Records is enabled, deleting a record in the primary table deletes any related records in the related table. Deleting the Operations record from the Departments table will delete the record for any employee of the Operations department in the Employees table.

Cascading Updates and Deletes make your database more efficient by ensuring that related records always match their primary records, but you can still edit or delete the related records without affecting their primary records. In other words, cascade operations only work in one direction, from primary to related records; changes to related records never travel backwards to the primary record.

Choosing When to Use Referential Integrity

You need to decide whether to use referential integrity, cascading updates, and cascading deletions on a relationship-by-relationship basis. To make this decision, ask four questions about each relationship:

- Do you want to limit the values in the related table to values that are already included in the primary table? For example, do you want to make sure that the only DepartmentIDs entered in the Employees table are those listed in the Departments table? If you do, then enable referential integrity. If, however, users should be allowed to enter departments that aren't already in the Departments table, then don't enable referential integrity.

- Does the primary key include an AutoNumber field? If so, then there's no reason to enable Cascade Update Related Fields, because users can't change the values in AutoNumber fields.

- Do you want users to be able to change the existing values in the primary key? If the department ID for OPS changes to MGMT, do you want to automatically update the employees who work in OPS to MGMT? It depends on the purpose of the table. If you need to keep a record to document that an OPS department once existed and had employees assigned to it, then don't allow the user to change the primary key value; leave Cascade Update Related Fields disabled. However, if you want to be able to immediately update all the OPS references, then allow cascade updates.

- Do you want to allow users to delete records from the primary table and all related records in the related table? If the OPS department is merged into another department, should deleting OPS from the Departments table also delete all the OPS department employee records? If not, don't enable Cascade Deletes.

A negative answer to the fourth question often takes you back to the first question. You have to choose between accurate supporting data, now and in the future, and the amount of dead data (from closed departments or customers who haven't ordered for years) you're willing to tolerate in lookup tables.

 TIP You can't set referential integrity if existing table data already violates the rules. For example, if you have entered employees in a department that isn't in the Departments table, you'll get an error. Add the department to the Departments table and try again. The error won't tell you where the problem occurred, just that there is one.

To set or change the Cascade settings, open the Relationships window. Right-click the join line and click Edit Relationship. In the Edit Relationships dialog box, mark or clear the Cascade check boxes, then click OK.

What's Next

In this chapter, you learned how to create and modify tables, add data into those tables, and build relationships between tables. In the next chapter, you'll learn how to create forms and use them to enter and edit data in tables.

CHAPTER **31**

Creating and Using Forms

FEATURING:

Creating AutoForms

Printing forms

Searching in forms

Creating forms for multiple tables

Modifying form design

Formatting and arranging form controls

Changing control properties

F orms provide a way for users to enter data without having to know how a table is designed, or getting lost in a sea of data and inadvertently editing an entry in the wrong row. Also, you don't have to include all of a table's fields in a form; you can leave out fields where users can't enter data, such as AutoNumber.

A single form can include data from multiple tables, providing one-stop data entry. You can create a customized layout so that a form looks just like its source document: a membership application, customer data form, or other document used to collect the data to be entered in the database. When an entry form closely resembles the source document, data-entry errors are less likely to occur. As with tables, there is more than one way to create a form. Access provides three form-creation methods: AutoForms, the Form Wizard, and Form Design view.

Using AutoForms

An *AutoForm* can have one of three layouts: datasheet, tabular, or columnar. Figure 31.1 shows a datasheet AutoForm for the Customers table. The datasheet AutoForm looks just like the table's Datasheet view, right down to the navigation buttons. You can move the columns and rows around, just as in the table.

FIGURE 31.1

A datasheet AutoForm

Custo	CompanyName	ContactName	ContactTitle	Address
ALFKI	Alfreds Futterkiste	Maria Anders	Sales Representative	Obere Str. 57
ANATI	Ana Trujillo Emparedados y helad	Ana Trujillo	Owner	Avda. de la Constitución
ANTO	Antonio Moreno Taquería	Antonio Moreno	Owner	Mataderos 2312
AROU	Around the Horn	Thomas Hardy	Sales Representative	120 Hanover Sq.
BERG	Berglunds snabbköp	Christina Berglund	Order Administrator	Berguvsvägen 8
BLAU	Blauer See Delikatessen	Hanna Moos	Sales Representative	Forsterstr. 57
BLON	Blondel père et fils	Frédérique Citeaux	Marketing Manager	24, place Kléber
BOLID	Bólido Comidas preparadas	Martín Sommer	Owner	C/ Araquil, 67
BONA	Bon app'	Laurence Lebihan	Owner	12, rue des Bouchers
BOTTI	Bottom-Dollar Markets	Elizabeth Lincoln	Accounting Manager	23 Tsawassen Blvd.
BSBE	B's Beverages	Victoria Ashworth	Sales Representative	Fauntleroy Circus
CACTI	Cactus Comidas para llevar	Patricio Simpson	Sales Agent	Cerrito 333
CENT	Centro comercial Moctezuma	Francisco Chang	Marketing Manager	Sierras de Granada 999
CHOP	Chop-suey Chinese	Yang Wang	Owner	Hauptstr. 29
COMM	Comércio Mineiro	Pedro Afonso	Sales Associate	Av. dos Lusíadas, 23
CONS	Consolidated Holdings	Elizabeth Brown	Sales Representative	Berkeley Gardens

Record: 1 of 91

A tabular AutoForm for the Customers table is shown in Figure 31.2. Like the data-sheet form, the tabular form presents multiple records, as though you were looking at the table. However, the form itself looks a bit more formal, and movement within the form is more limited. Using keystrokes, you can only move from field to field within each record, and from the last field in one record to the first field in the next record; you can't move up and down with the arrow keys.

FIGURE 31.2

A tabular AutoForm

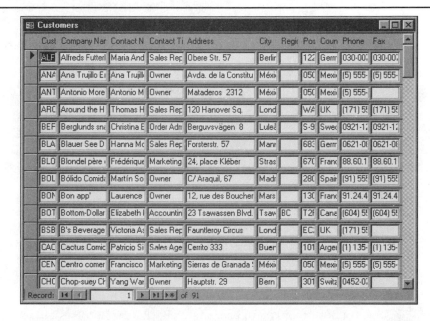

A columnar AutoForm, like the one shown in Figure 31.3, displays one record at a time. Click the navigation buttons to move between records or to enter a new record. If the primary purpose of a form is data entry or editing one record at a time, a columnar form is best. If you're designing a form to allow users to view several records at once, a datasheet or tabular form is a better choice.

FIGURE 31.3

A columnar AutoForm

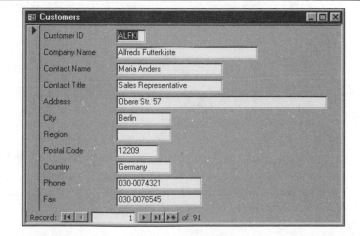

PART

VI

Access for the
Nonprogrammer

Creating AutoForms

To create an AutoForm, click the Forms button in the left pane of the Database window. With the Forms page displayed, click the New button at the top of the window to open the New Form dialog box. In the drop-down list at the bottom of the dialog box, select the table you want to base the form on. Choose the AutoForm type, and click OK.

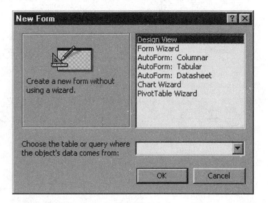

 You can also begin by selecting the table on the Tables page, clicking the New Object button on the toolbar, and then clicking AutoForm. If you click AutoForm, you get an instant columnar form; if you click Form, you get the New Form dialog box, where you can choose different types of AutoForms. When you close the form, you will be prompted to save it. Remember to use the **frm** tag to prefix the form's name if you're using the L/R naming convention (discussed in Chapter 29).

AutoForms are a good choice when you need a quick form that includes all the information from a single table. If you don't want to display all the fields, or if you need data from multiple tables, you'll want to use the Form Wizard or Design view instead. See "Creating Forms for Multiple Tables" to learn about the Form Wizard and "Modifying Form Design" to learn about Design view. First, however, we'll look at some basic operations you'll perform no matter how a form is created.

Entering and Editing in Forms

In the datasheet form, enter and edit information exactly as you would in the table's Datasheet view: select and edit a field by moving the mouse pointer to the left edge of the field and clicking. In tabular and columnar forms, drag to select all the text in a field before entering the correct data. To move to the next record in a form, tab out of the last *text box control* for the previous record. (A text box control is a box or area on a form that displays data from a table and allows data entry.) In all forms, you can use the navigation buttons to move between existing records and the Delete Record button on the toolbar to delete the selected record.

 NOTE Broadly, a *control* is any element of a software interface that a user can interact with: a text box, a button, and so on. You'll see the term often in this chapter, because in building Access forms, you are essentially creating an interface to your database.

Printing Forms

Access allows you to print forms just as you see them on the screen. However, there are a few things to be aware of before you print. If you click the Print toolbar button, you will print a form for every record in your database. If the form is a columnar form, that can amount to many printed pages. You should only use form printing when you need a copy of a single record in a hurry. (Reports give you many more options for printing multiple records.)

To print the current record, display the record you want to print. Choose File ➤ Print from the menu bar to open the Print dialog box, choose Selected Record(s) under Print Range, and click OK.

 MASTERING THE OPPORTUNITIES

Printing Forms for Manual Use

A good use for printed forms is a blank form that you can distribute to others, so they can fill it out and return it for data entry. To print a blank form, open the form and display a new record. Type a small character in one field (perhaps a period or space), so that Access thinks it's a record with data even though it looks like a blank form, and then print that record. (If the underlying table has other data-entry requirements, you'll have to meet those before you can print the record.)

Searching, Sorting, and Filtering in Forms

You can search for, sort, and filter data in forms just as easily as in a table, and the techniques are often quite similar.

Searching for Records

Access provides an easy way to find individual records; it will even allow you to look for a partial name if you are unsure about how the name is spelled.

To use the Find tool in Access, click in the field that contains the data you're searching for (for example, the Company Name field), and then click the Find button on the toolbar to open the Find And Replace dialog box.

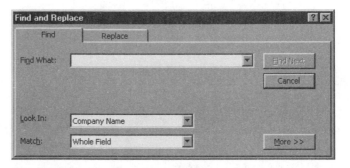

Access will search the field you clicked in. Type the search string you are looking for and click Find Next. Access will search the field and find the first occurrence of the text you entered (as shown in Figure 31.4). If the search string occurs more than once, you can click Find Next again to find the next occurrence. (You might need to move the dialog box out of the way to see the search results.)

FIGURE 31.4

Finding an entry

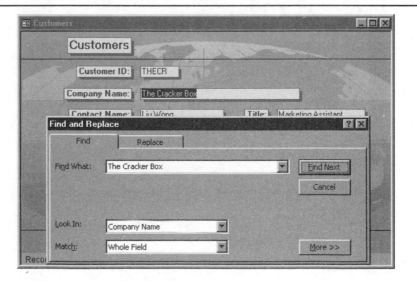

Access provides a number of options that can help when your search isn't quite so straightforward. Let's say you only remember that the person's name starts with *Has*. You can change the search parameters in a number of ways. You could look for all records starting with *Has* by choosing Start Of Field in the Match box. If all you know about the name is that it has a *ch*, you could choose to match Any Part Of Field.

You can choose to have Access search the single field or the entire table by selecting one or the other in the Look In box.

To further refine your searches, click the More button. You can specify that you want to match the case of the text string, and you can search up or down from your current position in the field instead of searching the whole field. (Searching up or down is only an issue if the database has many thousands of records, and searching in one direction would save time.)

Replacing Data

You can replace any text string by clicking the Replace tab in the Find And Replace dialog box. The Replace tab settings are identical to the Find tab settings (see Figure 31.5), except that when you find the text string, you can replace it with whatever you type in the Replace With box.

For example, if an employee's name changes, you can find and replace the name easily (and if the relationship between the Employees table and the Orders table was set up with Referential Integrity and Cascade Updates, the employee name will be changed wherever it occurs in the Orders table, too).

FIGURE 31.5

Replacing an entry

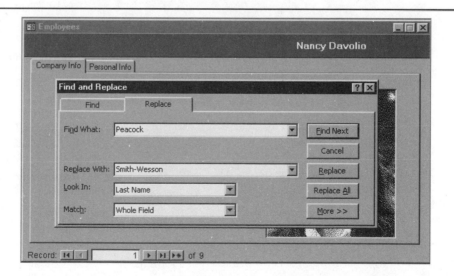

You can replace text strings one at a time by clicking the Find Next and Replace buttons, or you can replace all instances of the text string by clicking the Replace All button. Be careful using Replace All, because you could inadvertently replace lots of text strings that shouldn't have been replaced.

Using Wildcards

You can construct search criteria using wildcards, symbols that represent one or more characters. Table 31.1 lists wildcard characters you can use in Find.

	TABLE 31.1: WILDCARD SYMBOLS	
Wildcard	**Usage**	**Example**
*	Can be used at the beginning or the end of a string to match any number of characters.	Par* finds *Parker* and *Parson*. *son finds *Parson* and *Williamson*.
?	Matches any single alphabetic character.	w?ll finds *wall*, *well*, and *will*.
#	Matches any single numeric character.	4#5 finds *405*, *415*, *425*, etc.
[ ]	Matches any single character specified in the brackets.	w[ai]ll finds *wall* and *will*, but not *well*.
–	Identifies any one of a range of characters in ascending order.	[c-h]ill finds *dill*, *fill*, *gill*, and *hill*, but not *kill*, *mill*, etc.
!	Used within brackets to specify any character not in the brackets	w[!a]ll finds *well* and *will*, but not *wall*.

Sorting and Filtering Records in Forms

Records in forms are really records in tables, viewed through the window of a form. This means that while working with a form you have essentially the same sorting and filtering options discussed for tables in Chapter 30, and you use the same techniques. Here we'll look at the sorting and filtering features specific to forms.

When you sort a form and then close it, the sort order will be saved with the form automatically. The sort order saved in a form has no effect on the sort order in the underlying table; and changing the sort order in a table doesn't affect the sort order in forms.

Form filters are also saved with and limited to their forms; filters in a form don't affect the underlying table, and filters in a table don't affect forms based on the table.

The only difference between filtering a table and filtering a form is in what you see on the screen when you filter by form. In a table, the Filter By Form window resembles the table's datasheet layout; in a form, the same window resembles the form layout. To filter a form using the Filter By Form method, follow the procedures for filtering tables using Filter By Form (see Chapter 29).

Creating Forms for Multiple Tables

Forms based on multiple tables are often necessary in the real world, to make data entry quick and efficient. When you base a form on multiple tables, the result will be a form (a *subform*) nested within another form (the *main form*).

The Form Wizard can create forms that display data from related tables—the *related* part is important, because if you haven't already created a relationship between two tables, you can't relate them in a form (see "Creating Relationships" in Chapter 30, to learn more).

The easiest way to create a form that includes a subform is to use the Wizard. Select the Forms page in the Database window, and double-click Create Form By Using Wizard.

In the first step of the Form Wizard, shown in Figure 31.6, select one of the tables you want to use in the Tables/Queries drop-down list. Then, in the Available Fields list, double-click the fields to include from that table. Next, select the second table you want to use in the form, and double-click the fields to include from that table. When you have selected all the fields you need, click the Next button.

FIGURE 31.6

Selecting tables and fields in the Form Wizard

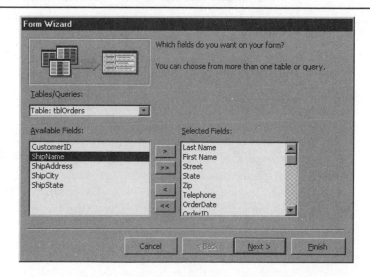

If you choose fields from unrelated tables, the Form Wizard will stop and display an error message that tells you to cancel the wizard, set the relationships, and then start the Form Wizard again. If the tables have a one-to-many relationship, you will be asked how you want to view your data—whether the form's primary focus should be the primary or the related table. In a typical Customers database, switching between By Customers (the "one" side) and By Orders (the "many" side) changes the sample in the wizard's right pane. Figure 31.7 shows the sample form when By Customers is selected; it's a main form with a subform that shows all the orders a specific customer has placed. The sample By Orders form is shown in Figure 31.8; it's not as useful.

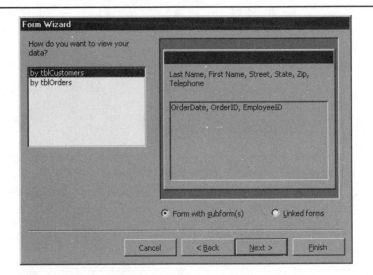

When the form is arranged by Customers, the order data appears in a sunken area of the preview. The main form will include a datasheet or tabular subform to display the customer's orders. The subform in the By Customers form (see Figure 31.7) will display the many order records—a visual representation of the one-to-many relationship between the Customers table and the Orders table.

If the main form is already fairly complex, you can choose to display the subform as a linked form, as shown in Figure 31.9. The main form will contain a button that opens the linked subform. Click the Linked Forms option to create linked forms.

When the primary focus of the form is the table on the many side of the relationship, there is only one related record to display, so the data from the related table is displayed on the main form. The By Orders layout (see Figure 31.8) doesn't include a subform. Each order was placed by one customer, so there is no need for a subform to display multiple customers for a single order.

After choosing a layout, the wizard will ask you to select form styles and enter form names to finish the subform/main form combination.

The same form
arranged by Orders
(the related table)

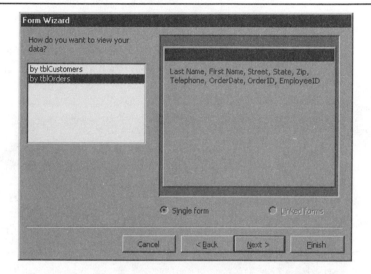

A linked subform

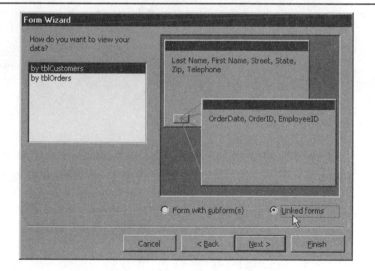

Modifying Form Design

The built-in Access forms have limited graphic appeal. To let you exercise some creativity, forms have a Design view, just as tables do, and Access includes many tools for modifying a form's design. First, open the form in Design view, as shown in Figure 31.10. (The form illustrated has a picture background. You can add and change the background pictures in your forms; see the section "Using a Background Picture" to learn how.)

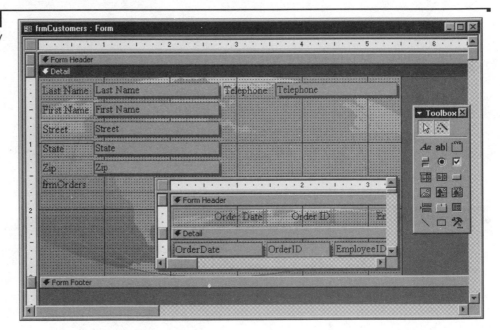

The Design window includes horizontal and vertical rulers and Form Design and Formatting toolbars. There's a toolbox that will help with adding objects to the form. If the toolbox doesn't appear when you open a form in Design view, click the Toolbox button on the Form Design toolbar.

In Design view, a form includes three sections and a number of different controls. The three sections are:

- a Form Header at the beginning of the first page of the form, usually used for titles

- a Form Footer at the end of the last page of the form, used for user tips or other miscellaneous information

- a Detail section, where each record's data is displayed

If the Form Header and Form Footer bars aren't visible, choose View ➤ Form Header/Footer from the menu bar to turn them on. The Detail section includes the form background, controls (Figure 31.11 shows controls commonly used in Access forms, and a label for each control. In tabular and datasheet forms, labels appear in the Form Header section, and controls appear below the labels in the Detail section. Any section can include various graphic objects like horizontal lines.

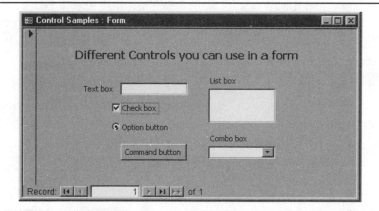

If you want to rearrange a form, it's easiest to begin by enlarging the form's area. Move the mouse pointer to the bottom of the Detail section, just above the Form Footer. When the pointer changes to a two-headed arrow, drag the Footer bar down to increase the height of the Detail area. To increase the Header section, drag the Detail bar down to make the Header area larger.

 TIP After you resize a form's Design view, the Form view window won't fit properly. To resize the Form view window after you finish working in Design view, switch to Form view and be sure the window is *not* maximized; then click Window ➤ Size To Fit Form.

Using a Background Picture

When you create a form using the Form Wizard, you can add a background picture by selecting it in the third wizard step (the "styles" step). If you create a form in Design view or by using an AutoForm, you'll get a form with a standard gray background, but you can add a picture to the background at any time. You can use one of the Access background pictures or a bitmap picture of your own (perhaps a company logo).

PART

VI

Access for the
Nonprogrammer

To add a picture to the background, open the form in Design view. Double-click the gray box in the upper-left corner of the form window, at the intersection of the vertical and horizontal rulers. The property sheet that appears should say Form in its title bar.

In the property sheet, click the Format tab. Scroll down and click in the Picture box. Click the Build button (the button with three dots) that appears on the right end of the Picture box. In the Insert Picture dialog box that appears, navigate to the graphics file you want to use. Select the file name and click OK. (For example, the background picture shown in Figure 31.10, named "globe," can be found in the `C:\Program Files\Microsoft Office\Office\Bitmaps\Styles` folder.)

Working with Objects in a Form

To select an object (a control or a graphic object), click it so that handles appear. If you select a text box, the corresponding label also appears to be selected. Actually, it is only partially selected; it will *move* with the text box, but if you change the *format* of the text box, the label format will not change. (To format the label, you must click the label.)

 NOTE Controls that display data, such as text boxes and check boxes, are *bound* to fields in the underlying table; labels, however, are just text on the form, and are *unbound*.

There are several ways to select multiple objects:

- Move the pointer to either ruler bar. The pointer changes to a bold arrow pointing toward the form. Press the mouse button, and a line drops directly through the form. When you release the button, all the objects the line passed through will be selected.

- Hold the mouse button down and drag the pointer to select a range of objects.

- If the objects you want to select aren't grouped together, you can select one object and hold the Shift key while selecting additional objects.

Delete selected objects by pressing the Delete key on the keyboard.

Moving and Sizing Objects in a Form

 To move an object, first select it; then move the pointer to an edge of the selected object, being sure not to point directly at any of the resizing handles. The pointer changes shape to a small hand. Hold the mouse button and drag the object to its new location. If you move an object beyond the form's grid, the form area will increase.

If you point directly at the handle in the upper-left corner of a text box or label, the hand changes to a finger pointing at the handle. If you drag using the pointing finger, only the object you are pointing at will move. If you point to a control and drag it, the label will remain in place; if you drag the label, the control won't move.

Adjust the size of controls as you would any graphic object: by dragging the resizing handles at the corners and sides of the object. Note, however, that changing the size of a text box control does not change the size of its underlying field. To change field size, you must go to the table's Design view and change the field size properties.

TIP If you have a hard-to-control mouse or want extra precision, select the control and use Shift+arrow keys to resize and Ctrl+arrow keys to move.

Formatting Labels and Controls

You can add and format labels in any section of a form. All labels can be edited and formatted with no effect on the data in the underlying table. Click once on a selected label, and you can edit the text in the label.

WARNING *Don't* change the field name in a control, because you'll break the link between the control and its underlying field; then data from the table won't appear in that control.

Adding a Title

The header section is used for a form title. Use the Toolbox Label tool to create a title or other text, to label the form itself, or to add extra information for a user. In the toolbox, click the Label tool; when you move the pointer back into the design area, it changes to a large letter *A* with crosshairs. Move the pointer into the header area, click where you want to place the label and type the label text. When you are done entering text, click elsewhere in the form to close the label control. Then you can select the control and use the Formatting toolbar to format the title.

Formatting Text

Much of the formatting for controls is the same as text formatting in other Office 2000 applications. Select one or more controls, and then choose formatting options from the Formatting toolbar or right-click and select options from the shortcut menu.

Font/Fore Color is the color used for text. Some colors, such as dark blue, make a very attractive form that is easy to read. Other colors, such as yellow, are very hard to read and should be used sparingly, unless you make the background dark and contrasting.

The Fill/Back Color is the color for the fill behind the text. The default for labels is transparent, which means the color from the form background appears as the label's background color. The default background color for text boxes is white.

To change the appearance of text, select the controls that contain the text you want to change (to save time, you can select and format several controls at once). Use the Font, Font Size, weight and style, alignment, and color buttons on the Formatting toolbar to format the selected controls.

Changing Borders

Every Access control and label has a border around it. Borders have three properties: color, line width, and special effect.

Although you can't delete the border, you can effectively disable all three properties by choosing Transparent as the border color. A transparent border has no visible width, color, or effect. This is effective for labels, but text boxes should have borders so that the form's user knows where to enter data.

You can change border width using the Line/Border Width button on the Formatting toolbar, selecting widths from a hairline thickness to a 6-point width. Typically, a 1- or 2-point border is appropriate for a text box control; but thicker borders can be used for titles and graphic design.

Border effects can also help differentiate types of controls and draw the user's attention to important controls. Figure 31.12 shows the six special effects you can access from the Special Effects button's drop-down list:

Flat: Appropriate for controls that are not used for data entry.

Sunken: The best choice for text boxes for editing or entering data.

Shadowed: A good choice for titles.

Raised: Another useful choice for data entry, titles, or to draw attention to a part of the screen.

Etched: A good choice for text boxes that cannot be changed.

Chiseled: Applies a single inverted line underneath the control.

When you apply the Sunken, Raised, Etched, or Chiseled effects, you turn off any other choices for border color and line width. Only Flat and Shadowed are affected by the border-color and line-width formatting options.

To apply borders and special effects, select the controls you want to change. Then use the Border Color, Border Width, and Special Effects buttons on the Formatting toolbar or the shortcut menu to format the borders for the selected controls.

FIGURE 31.12

Special effects

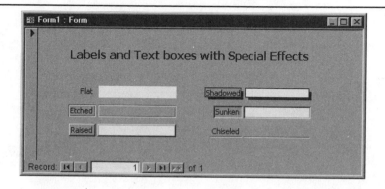

 Changing several controls one by one can be a time-consuming task. You can select and format several controls all at once, or you can use the Format Painter to paint all the formatting—color, borders, special effects, and alignment—from one control onto another. If you're going to apply the selected format to more than one other control, double-click the Format Painter button to lock it on (and click it again to turn it off).

Conditional Formatting

 Conditional formatting appears in a control when its value meets specific criteria that you set. For example, you can conditionally format a Unit Price text box to have a bright red text on a yellow background if the Unit Price in the displayed record is more than $100.

To create a conditional format, open the form in Design view. Click the control to select it, and click Format ➤ Conditional Formatting. In the Conditional Formatting dialog box (shown in Figure 31.13), under Condition 1, set a value range in which formatting will apply, and set the formatting with the formatting buttons. The example in Figure 31.13 shows a format for values more than $100; the conditional format is bold, bright text on a dark background. Click Add if you want to add more conditions to the same control (you can set up to three conditions on a control). Click OK when you're finished; click Delete to remove the conditional format.

Dividing Pages and Page Sections

A form that's cluttered with lots of loosely related fields will be hard to use. With Access you can separate your forms into individual pages and use graphic lines and rectangles to segment the form visually.

FIGURE 31.13

Setting a conditional format

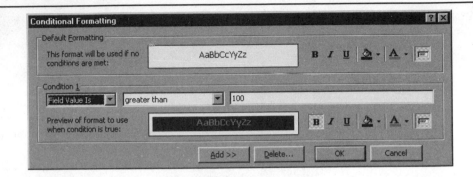

 A *page break* is a marker that separates pages in a form that's too large to be entirely displayed on screen. To insert a page break, click the Page Break button on the toolbox. When you move the pointer back into the design area, it changes to a crosshair with a piece of paper below it. Click the form where you want the page break to appear.

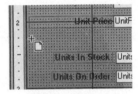

The page break will automatically position itself at the form's left margin. After you add a page break, resize the form so that only one page is visible at a time in Form view (switch to Form view and click Window ➢ Size To Fit Form).

To move from page to page in a multiple-page form, press the Page Up and Page Down keys (or click in the form's scrollbar).

To delete the page break, switch to Design view; select the page break mark and press the Delete key.

Relative Sizing and Alignment

A form's background has a grid of one-inch horizontal and vertical guide lines and points. If the grid points aren't visible, choose View ➢ Grid. When you move a control, it automatically lines up with the grid, both horizontally and vertically. If you try to place the edge of the control between two grid points, Access moves it to align with one grid point or the other. This is a feature called *Snap to Grid*. Sometimes you might want to place two or more controls so they aren't on a grid point—closer together than the grid allows or not as far apart as two grid points require. To do this, you must first turn off Snap to Grid by clicking Format ➢ Snap To Grid. The Snap to Grid feature is not one you will need to turn off very often, but working without Snap to Grid is essential for small refinements in your Access forms.

Aligning, Sizing, and Spacing Controls

You can manually adjust the size and position of every control on a form. However, Access automates size and positioning features so you can manipulate multiple controls at one time for perfect layout results.

Aligning Controls

Begin by selecting two or more controls, and then choose Format ➤ Align or choose Align from the shortcut menu bar to see the list of options:

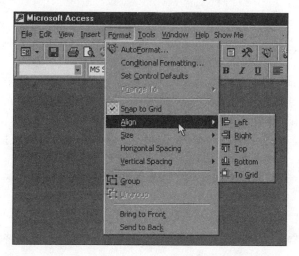

Align ➤ Left will align the left edges of all selected controls with the leftmost of them (Align ➤ Right works the same way, but to the right, as shown in Figure 31.14). Use Align ➤ Top or Align ➤ Bottom to adjust controls on the same horizontal line.

FIGURE 31.14

Control alignment

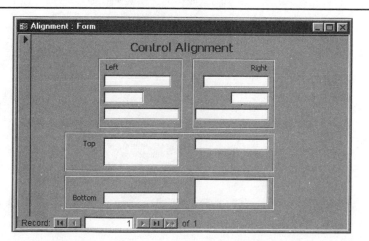

TIP Access has trouble differentiating between controls that are overlapped. Separate overlapping controls before attempting to align them to ensure that you only select the controls you want to align.

Sizing Controls

Choosing Format ➤ Size ➤ To Fit or double-clicking any sizing handle will instantly resize labels to fit their text. You can select two or more controls and use the other sizing options to resize all the selected controls to the same size; this is a good way to create identical command buttons. Tallest and Shortest refer to vertical height and Widest and Narrowest refer to horizontal width.

Spacing Controls

Spacing allows you to increase or decrease the relative position of selected controls by one grid point either horizontally or vertically. This is valuable if you need to spread out the controls or move them closer together for a neater visual layout. You can also use spacing to make sure controls are evenly spaced. Select the controls, and choose Format ➤ Vertical Spacing (or Horizontal Spacing) ➤ Make Equal (or Increase or Decrease).

Rearranging the Tab Order

A form's *tab order*—the sequence of controls you move through when pressing Tab—is assigned when the form is created. After you rearrange controls on a form, the tab order may be out of sequence. Users expect to be able to move through the form sequentially, so an inconsistent tab order almost guarantees data-entry errors. To change a form's tab order, choose View ➤ Tab Order, or right-click and choose Tab Order, to open the Tab Order dialog box.

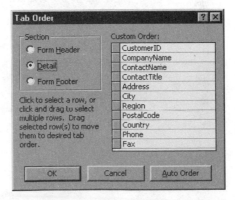

You can set the tab order for each of the three sections on the form, but you'll usually only care about the Detail section. Clicking Auto Order will generally rearrange the fields in the correct order, so it always makes sense to try this option first. If the Auto Order is not correct, you can set the order manually. Click the button to the left of a control name to select the control; then drag the control up or down into position in the tab order.

 TIP It's important to test how well your forms work each time you make any substantive change. Enter sample data and make sure everything operates as you expect it to.

Formatting Subforms

Making formatting changes to a form that has a subform is in most ways no different than formatting a single form. You can format it just as you would any form, using the toolbox and the Formatting toolbar. To size a subform, stretch the borders of the subform control in the main form, not in the subform itself. If the subform has a datasheet format, open the main/subform combination in Form view and resize the columns by dragging or double-clicking the column headers.

Adding Controls to Existing Forms

If you add a field to a table, existing forms won't include the field; or you may change your mind about the fields you omitted when you created the form.

 To add a field's text box control to the form, click the Field List button on the toolbar to open the Field list.

Drag the desired field from the Field List into the form, drop it in place, and then format the control. Because you created the control by dragging the field from the Field list, the control is bound to the table field.

TIP If the table field has a Yes/No data type, the default control will be a check box, not a text box, and a check mark will enter "Yes."

Formatting Datasheets

A form's Datasheet view looks like its underlying table, but only shows the fields you included in the form. Like a Form view, it's just a window into the table where the data is stored. All the formatting changes you can make to a table can also be made to a form's Datasheet view, including row height, column width, hiding, freezing, and conditional formatting.

To display a form in Datasheet view, open the form, click the arrow on the View button, and choose Datasheet view. All of the formatting options can be found on the Format menu.

Changing Properties of Forms and Controls

Every Access object—including tables and forms, controls such as text boxes and labels, and individual fields in a table—has properties. For example, the properties of a text box include its color, font, size, and control source: the table or query that supplies data to the text box. Field properties include size, input masks, and field type. Form properties include the size of the form, how the form can be viewed, and its record source: the table or query the records come from.

It's not essential to know every available property to work successfully in Access. However, whenever an object doesn't behave as you expect it to, it's a good idea to look for a property that might be affecting how the object acts. To view the properties for a control, double-click the control in Design view to open the property sheet (or right-click the control and click Properties).

 To open a form's property sheet, open the form in Design view and double-click the Form Select button at the intersection of the vertical and horizontal rulers in the Form window. A form has four categories of properties (the All tab lists all the properties found on the other four tabs):

Format: Shows properties related to formatting: what the form or control looks like, what buttons and bars are activated, what views are allowed.

Data: Shows where the data comes from: the record or control source and whether or not the data can be edited.

Event: Lists all the macros and programming code assigned to an object or control.

Other: Includes any other properties that relate to the object or control including, for example, a field's tab order.

The property sheet title bar includes the name of the selected object. If you want to look at properties for one of the form's other controls, don't close the property sheet, just click the control to switch the object described in the property sheet.

Changing the Property Settings on Multiple Fields

Often you'll want to change the property settings on multiple controls at the same time. If you select more than one control and open the property sheet, only those properties that affect all the selected controls will be displayed. For example, if you selected a label and a text box, there would be no Data or Event properties displayed; the text box has Data and Event properties, but the label does not.

It's helpful to understand a few properties when you are designing forms. If you don't know what a property does, you probably don't know what will happen if you change the setting. Unless you're feeling very adventurous, you should leave strange and unusual properties in their default settings.

Hiding Form Features

A number of elements are enabled by default on every form, including scroll bars, record selectors, and navigation buttons. All these elements can be turned off in the form's property sheet. For example, the scroll bars are only needed if parts of the form don't fit on the screen. Record selectors may or may not be necessary. Navigation buttons are generally not needed on a subform. All these features take up valuable screen space and can cause confusion during data entry. You can turn off features you don't need by opening the form's property sheet and changing the item's setting to No on the Format page. These changes, relatively easy to make, can make the form much easier to use.

What's Next

In this chapter you learned how to create forms for data entry and editing. You learned how to select a form type, how to combine forms into main/subform combinations for more efficient data entry, and how to format them to be both attractive and easy to use. In the next chapter, you'll learn how to create and customize Access reports, so your data is presented in a professional, easy-to-read format.

CHAPTER **32**

Creating Reports

A *report* is the printed output of the data in a database. Access gives you the freedom to report your data in a variety of ways. A report can show all or only some of the data related to a record, and it can be based on either a table or a query. The flexibility to customize reports and to organize the data in useful ways—in other words, to make it accessible—is really what gives Access its name.

A report is a static picture of current data. When you save a report, Access saves only its structure, so the data shown in a report is only as current as the records in the database when the report was created.

 TIP All reports except the most basic AutoReports have the date and time included in the page footer. Because a report is always created "fresh" whenever you open it, the date and time in the page footer reflect when you opened the report, not when you created or saved it.

Most reports are either columnar or tabular. A *columnar report*, like the report shown in Print Preview in Figure 32.1, shows each field on a separate line in a single column down the page. The columnar report is the printed version of a columnar form.

FIGURE 32.1

A columnar report places each record field on a separate line.

Products	
Product ID	1
Product Name	Chai
Supplier	
Category	
Quantity Per Unit	10 boxes x 20 bag
Unit Price	$18.00
Units In Stock	39
Units On Order	0
Reorder Level	10
Discontinued	☐
Product ID	2
Product Name	Chang
Supplier	
Category	
Quantity Per Unit	24 - 12 oz bottles

Page: 1

A *tabular report* (shown in Figure 32.2) is like a tabular form and for most data offers a better use of page space.

FIGURE 32.2

A tabular report shows records in table rows and fields in columns.

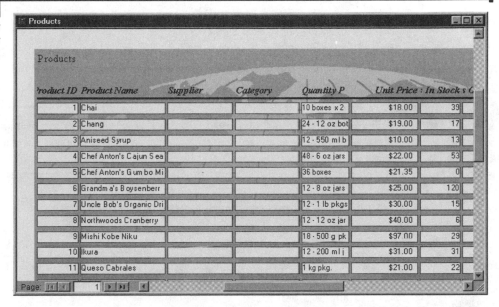

There are three ways to create reports:

- In Design view, where you can design a report completely from scratch
- With the Report Wizard, which lets you customize a report
- By choosing one of two AutoReports, which automatically include all of the fields in the table or query you select

In addition, there are two more wizards, each of which creates a specialized report:

- The Chart Wizard, which walks you through the steps to create a chart
- The Label Wizard, which creates mailing and other labels

Creating a report in Access is as simple as creating a data form; however, there are a few additional tricks you should have up your sleeve to format the report so it looks its best and displays precisely the information you want to see. Sometimes you merely need to show data in some kind of organized way: an individual data sheet or a listing of names and addresses. But it is through reports that you can bring together independent bits of data and summarize them into useful information that managers can use to make decisions, launch studies, and understand their businesses better.

Generating AutoReports

The simplest reports to produce are AutoReports. As with forms, there are columnar and tabular AutoReports, which provide a good place to start if the data you want is already contained in one table or query.

1. On the toolbar, click the New Object button, and then choose Report from the drop-down list to open the New Report dialog box.

NOTE If you choose AutoReport, you'll get a columnar AutoReport (with no date/time in the page footer and no layout graphics); choose Report if you want a choice between columnar and tabular.

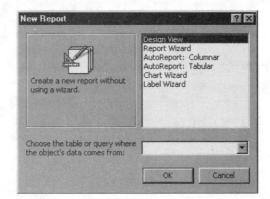

2. In the New Report dialog box, choose AutoReport: Columnar or AutoReport: Tabular. Then click the drop-down Tables/Queries list and choose the table or query that contains the data for your report.

TIP If you select the table name on the Tables page (or the query name on the Queries page) before clicking the New Object button, the table or query name will appear in the New Report dialog box.

3. Click OK to create the report and open it in Print Preview (a columnar Auto-Report is shown in Figure 32.3).

4. To print the report, click the Print button on the toolbar.

When you close the Print Preview window, you'll be prompted to save the report.

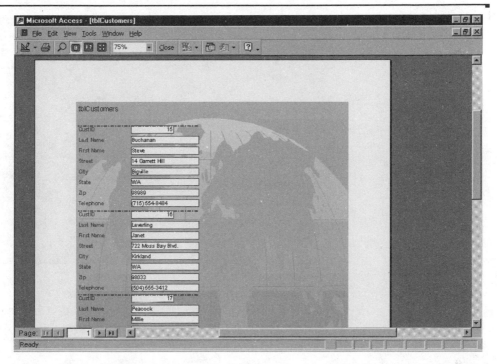

Although AutoReports are fast, they are not very attractive. To create a more professional report, use the Report Wizard.

Using the Report Wizard

The Report Wizard lets you choose the fields you want in the report—including fields from more than one table—and designate how the data should be grouped, sorted, and formatted. When you click Finish, Access will create the report and open it in Print Preview.

To start the Report Wizard, follow these steps:

1. Open the Reports page in the database window and click Create Report By Using Wizard.

2. In the wizard, choose the main table or query on which to base the report by clicking its name in the Tables/Queries drop-down list (shown in Figure 32.4).

FIGURE 32.4

The Report Wizard

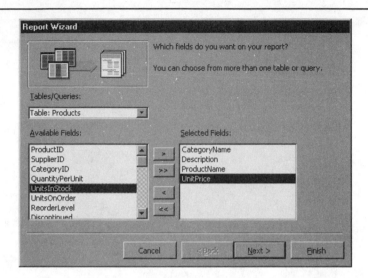

3. Double-click each field you want to include in the report (or click the >> button to include all the fields). If you want to include data from another table or query, select its name in the Tables/Queries list and double-click the fields you want to include. Then click Next.

4. If you're drawing data from more than one table or query, the next wizard step asks you to choose which table or query to use in organizing your data. Make your choice and click Next.

FIGURE 32.5

Organizing data from multiple tables

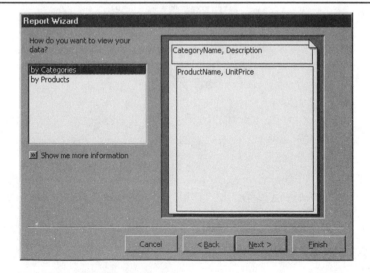

5. In the next wizard step, add any grouping levels you want that are different from the default. Until you become familiar with report results, you may want to use the default choices, as shown in Figure 32.6. Then click Next.

FIGURE 32.6

Setting the report grouping levels

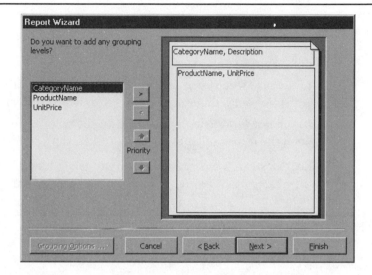

6. In the next wizard step, whether your data is drawn from one table/query or several, you can set sorting options for the report. Select the first field you want to sort by in the 1 box, and choose ascending or descending by clicking the sort button to the right of the box (shown in Figure 32.7). The default sort order is ascending. Set second, third, and fourth sort levels (if any) in the 2, 3, and 4 boxes. Then click Next.

FIGURE 32.7

Setting the sorting options

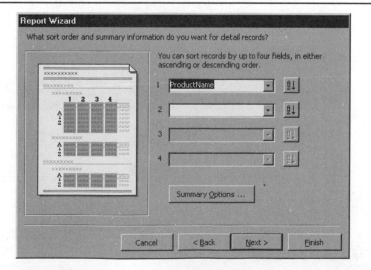

PART

VI

Access for the Nonprogrammer

NOTE If you want to summarize your data by group (for example, with totals or averages), click the Summary Options button shown in Figure 32.7, and choose a calculation for each field you want to summarize.

7. In the next wizard step, select a layout and orientation, and whether you'd like the field width adjusted to fit on one page. Click the different options to see layout previews, and then click Next.

8. In the next wizard step, select the style you'd like for the report. Click the different style names to see style previews. When you've made a choice, click Next.

9. In the last wizard step, type a title for the report, choose whether you'd like to open the report in Print Preview or Design view, and then click Finish.

Figure 32.8 shows a report drawn from two tables, Categories and Products. It's grouped by category and sorted within each category by product name.

FIGURE 32.8

A two-table, grouped report created with the Report Wizard

Products by Category

Category	Description	ProductName	UnitPrice
Beverages	Soft drinks, coffees, teas, beers, and ales		
		Chai	$18
		Chang	$19
		Chartreuse verte	$18
		Côte de Blaye	$264
		Guaraná Fantástica	$5
		Ipoh Coffee	$46
		Lakkalikööri	$18
		Laughing Lumberjack Lager	$14
		Outback Lager	$15
		Rhönbräu Klosterbier	$8
		Sasquatch Ale	$14
		Steeleye Stout	$18
Condiment	Sweet and savory sauces, relishes, spreads, and seasonings		
		Aniseed Syrup	$10
		Chef Anton's Cajun Seasoning	$22
		Chef Anton's Gumbo Mix	$21

Printing a Report

Printing a report is simple: Open the report in Print Preview and click the Print button on the toolbar. If a report is really long (for example, an invoice report that prints a page for each customer), you may want to print only a page or two. In that case, open the report in Print Preview and navigate to the page you want to print. Take note of the page number in the navigation area, and click File „ Print. In the Print dialog box, type the page number(s) in the Pages From and To boxes, and click OK.

 TIP If you want to print only one page, type its number in both the Pages From and To boxes.

MASTERING THE OPPORTUNITIES

Saving a Report as a Word Document

To save a report as a Word document (with most of its formatting included), either open the report in Print Preview or select the report name in the Reports group in the database window. Click Tools ≻ Office Links ≻ Publish It With MS Word. The report is saved automatically as a Rich Text Format (.rtf) file in your My Documents folder and can be opened and edited in most word processing programs.

Modifying a Report in Design View

Most of what you know about Access form design (Chapter 31) can be applied to report design. After you open the report in Design view, maximize the report so you have more room to work. Figure 32.9 shows the Design view of a grouped report named Products by Category. The report header includes the date the report was printed (the date appears once, beneath the report title), and the page footer includes page numbers.

FIGURE 32.9

A report in Design view

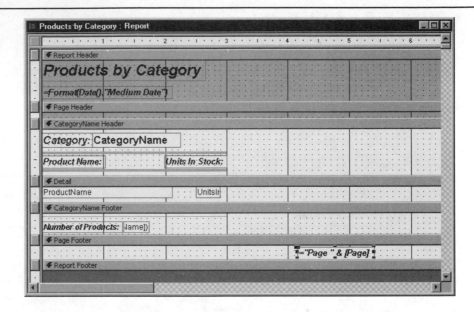

There are seven sections in a report:

Report Header: Appears at the top of the report (page 1) and includes the title and other report information.

Page Header: Appears at the top of every printed page of the report.

Group Header: Appears at the top of the identified group; there will be a separate group header for each grouping level.

Detail: Contains the data from the tables/queries.

Group Footer: Appears at the bottom of the identified group and contains summaries of group details.

Page Footer: Appears at the bottom of every page.

Report Footer: Appears on the last page of the report.

You can choose to incorporate any or all of these sections into your report. Use the mouse pointer to increase or decrease the size of the sections by dragging section bars up or down.

The Snap To Grid, alignment, and size features all work the same as they do in forms (see Chapter 31). All the colors, lines, borders, special effects, fonts, and other formatting features you can use with forms are also available in reports (but don't bother with the colors if you're going to print in black-and-white). You can edit any of the report's labels without worrying about affecting the contents of the report, but be careful not to edit the text boxes that contain data fields. If you do, the control will no longer be bound to a field, so it won't display data. To be certain that you're editing a label rather than a text box, look at the control's properties (right-click the control and choose Properties to display the control's property sheet).

TIP When a control is selected, its name appears in the Object box, at the left end of the Formatting toolbar. Labels are identified as labels, and bound text boxes are identified by their field names.

In a report's Design view, there are two preview choices on the View menu: Print Preview and Layout Preview. Print Preview produces the entire report just as it will look when printed, with all the pages.

Layout Preview shows only a single page with sample data. If you have a database with hundreds of records, it takes time to produce a preview of all the pages. By using sample data, Layout Preview quickly generates a preview so that you can check design features without a long wait.

Specifying Date and Page Number Codes

In Design view, the Page Footer contains two controls: the current date and the current page number out of the total number of pages. This information is important for general efficiency and office organization, because it assures you that the report you're reading is current and complete. Each of these controls can be customized if you would like to change their appearance.

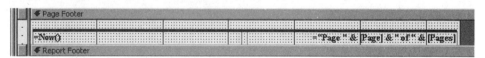

The date control, which displays the current date at the time the report is opened, contains the function =Now(). You can choose different date formats in the control's property sheet: On the Format tab, click the Format box drop-down arrow and select a date format: General Date, Long Date, Medium Date, or Short Date. If you want to add a date to a different part of the report or to a report that doesn't already have a date, choose Insert ➢ Date and Time from the menu bar to open the Date And Time dialog box.

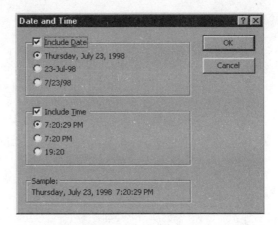

After you set your preferences and click OK, a text box control with the appropriate code will be inserted at the top of the active report section. Drag the control to wherever you want to position it in the report.

If your report is only one page, you might want to delete the page number altogether; select the control and press Delete. If you want to change the page number format, it's easier to delete the control and then reinsert a new page number control with the format you want. Choose Insert ➤ Page Numbers to open the Page Numbers dialog box:

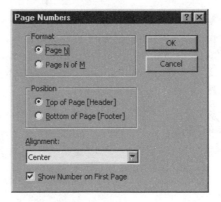

There are two formats: Page N (for example, Page 1) and Page N of M (Page 1 of 2). You can place the page number in the header or the footer and have it aligned on the left, center, or right of the page. For two-sided printing, choose either Inside or Outside alignment. You can also suppress the page number on the first page of a multiple-page report. When you click OK, a page number control appears in the position on the page that you selected in the Page Numbers dialog box.

Changing Sort Order and Grouping Levels

After you've used the wizard to create a report, you can open the report in Design view and change the sort order and grouping levels of the data. *Sorting* organizes items into alphabetical or numerical order, and *grouping* organizes them into categories of similar items. If you group items, you can sort the groups and sort the items within each group. Both grouping and sorting make it much easier for a reader to find and compare specific items in the report.

Click the Sorting and Grouping button on the Standard toolbar to open the Sorting and Grouping dialog box.

The first item, DepartmentID, is a group level for the report, as shown by the Sorting and Grouping icon to the left of the Field/Expression column. When you click on the DepartmentID field, you see a Yes under Group Header, indicating that there is a group header for the field. The grouped data is then sorted by LastName. If you were to click on the LastName row, you'd see that the Group Header property is set to No, indicating that the report doesn't include a header for last names.

- To rearrange the sorting or grouping order, select a row and then drag it into the desired order.

- To insert a new sort or group level, select the field from the Field/Expression drop-down list.

- To add a header or footer for the group level, set Group Header or Footer to Yes.

- To remove a group level, select the row and press the Delete key. You will see the following warning:

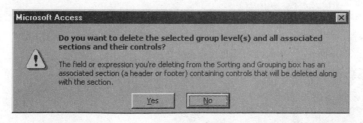

If you click OK, the group level, the group header, and the associated controls will be removed from the report. This does not affect the data displayed in the Detail section of the report, just the summary data for the group.

Adding and Deleting Report Controls

You can add and delete report controls in the same way that you add or delete form controls (see Chapter 31).

To add a field to a report, click the Field List button on the Standard toolbar to open the Field List dialog box, and drag the field name into the appropriate section of the report. (You might have to format and resize the label and the text box controls once you drop the field into place.)

NOTE A field with a Yes/No data type will appear as a check box in the report. You can change it to a toggle button or an option button by clicking Format ➢ Change To.

To delete a field's control from the report, select the control and press Delete.

You can calculate fields in a report by adding a calculated field to every record of a report, but it's easier to add a calculated field to the query underlying the report (see Chapter 33).

1. To access the query, open the Data tab of the report's Properties sheet.

2. Click the Build button on the Record Source box to open the query. (If the report is based on a table, you'll be notified that the report will now be based on a query. Click OK.)

3. Set up the calculation in the query using the Expression Builder, then close and save the query.

The calculated field will be available in the report's Field list.

Conditionally Formatting Controls

You can apply special formatting that depends on a field's value, called a *conditional format*. Conditional formats are helpful for drawing a reader's attention to particularly interesting values.

To create a conditional format, follow these steps:

1. Open the report in Design view.

2. Select the control and choose Format ➢ Conditional Formatting.

3. In the Conditional Formatting dialog box (shown in Figure 32.10), under Condition 1, set a value range at which formatting will apply, and set the formatting with the formatting buttons. The example in Figure 32.10 shows a format for values more than 50; the conditional format is bold type.

4. Click Add if you want to add more formatting options to the same control (for example, to add different formatting for values under 10).

Setting a Conditional Format

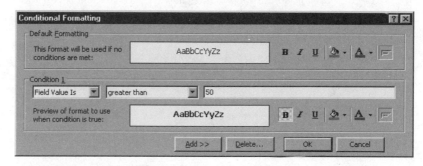

5. Click OK when you're finished.

To remove the conditional format, open the Conditional Formatting dialog box and click Delete. In the Delete Conditional Format dialog box, mark the check boxes for the specific conditional formats you want to delete, then click OK.

Saving a Report as a Snapshot

After you create a report, it's easy to show the data to others even if they don't have Access. You can save the report as a snapshot file that contains a high-quality picture of each page of the report. Other people can open the file, read the report, and print whichever pages they need.

Anyone who receives a snapshot file can read it by opening it in the Snapshot Viewer, a separate program they can download from the Microsoft Access Developer's Web site or install from the Office 2000 CD-ROM.

PART

VI

Access for the Nonprogrammer

MASTERING THE OPPORTUNITIES

Using Snapshots on the Web and in E-Mail

You can post a snapshot of a report on a Web page by creating a link to the file. Including a link to Microsoft's download page for the Snapshot Viewer is a way to ensure that your readers will be able to view the file, whatever their browser setup might be. They only need to download the viewer once, and Web users are accustomed to downloading add-ins to be able to view files of different types.

You can send report snapshots via e-mail, also. Your correspondents will need Snapshot Viewer to open and read the snapshot, so include a link to the download page on the Microsoft Web site for your readers' convenience.

Creating a Report Snapshot

To create a snapshot, take these steps:

1. In the database window, click the name of the report to select it.
2. Click File ➤ Export.
3. In the Export Report dialog box, select Snapshot Format in the Save As Type box (shown in Figure 32.11). Navigate to the folder where you want to save the file, enter an appropriate file name, and click Save.

FIGURE 32.11

Saving a Report Snapshot

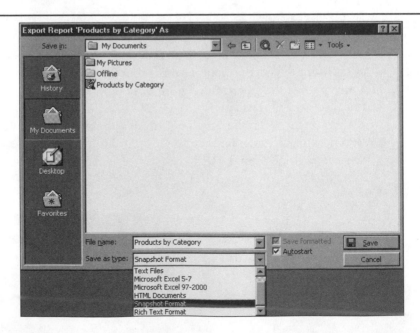

The snapshot is created and displayed in Snapshot Viewer (shown in Figure 32.12). If the Snapshot Viewer isn't already installed, Access will ask if you want to install it when you create your first snapshot.

FIGURE 32.12

A report snapshot in Snapshot Viewer

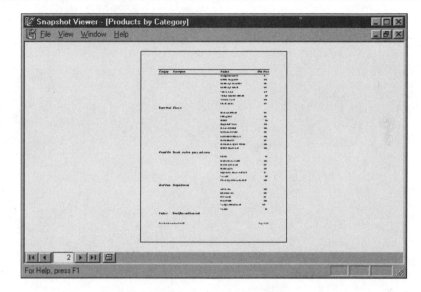

The snapshot file is saved separately from the database file, in the folder you selected in the Export Report dialog box. You can send it as an attachment in an e-mail message like any other file.

 TIP If you want to create an interactive HTML report that's linked to your data and that others can edit or add to, create a Data Access Page instead. It looks like an Access form but is an editable Web page that others can open, read, and edit in a browser. See Chapter 45 to learn about Data Access Pages.

What's Next

In the next chapter you'll learn about creating queries, which are like sophisticated filters. With queries, you can pluck out just the data you want, sort and organize the data, and base reports and forms on the queried data so they run faster.

PART

VI

Access for the Nonprogrammer

CHAPTER 33

Creating Queries

The advantage of a relational database is that data is stored without redundancy in separate tables. There's less data to store, and it's easier to keep data current because there's only one copy of it. But when you want to answer a question such as "How many orders did we get from Massachusetts last year?" you'll need to join data from separate but related tables to get the answer. Furthermore, you don't want all the data from each related table, just the specific data that answers your question (in this case, the state from a Customers table and numbers of orders from an Orders table).

A *query* displays records and fields from one or more tables based on criteria you specify. Queries are like filters, but much more flexible. When you create a query, you can choose which tables to draw data from, which fields you want from those tables, and which sets of records you want from those fields. You can also sort a query's resulting set of records any way you want without affecting the sort order in the underlying tables, and you can set up a query to perform mathematical operations on the data. You'll learn how to do these tasks and more in this chapter.

 TIP If you base forms and reports on queries that contain only the data you want to show, your forms and reports will be more efficient because Access won't have to look through all the data in each table when it generates the forms or reports.

Creating Simple Queries

There are different types of Access queries: select queries, parameter queries, crosstab queries, and action queries. Most of the queries used in databases are called *select* queries because they "select" records based on criteria you set; commonly these are referred to as *simple* queries.

 NOTE A query doesn't contain any data itself; rather, it consists of instructions about what data to select and which tables to select the data from. The instructions are in SQL (Structured Query Language), and you can see the SQL code for a query by opening the query and then choosing View ➢ SQL View.

Queries, like other database objects, can be created in a variety of ways. You can use one of the query wizards, or build your query in Design view, or type SQL statements if you're familiar with SQL. If your intention is to enter or report data in multiple tables, it's easiest to use the Form and Report Wizards to retrieve the data you want because the Wizard will create the query that the form or report uses. If, however, you need to work with a recordset independent of a form or report (for example, if you need to quickly see on screen a list of customers in Oregon and Washington who ordered more than $3000 last month), a query is faster.

Using the Query Wizard

To create a simple query, open the Queries page in the database window. Double-click Create Query By Using Wizard.

When the Simple Query Wizard (shown in Figure 33.1) starts, use the Tables/Queries drop-down list to choose the first table or query that contains the fields you want to include in the query, and double-click the fields you want to include in the query. Select any additional tables or queries and their fields you want to include. Click Next when all fields have been selected.

FIGURE 33.1

The Simple Query Wizard first asks you to select the tables or queries and fields to include.

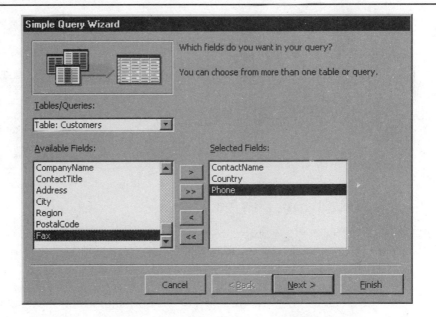

PART

VI

Access for the Nonprogrammer

If the fields you selected include a number field, you'll be asked to choose whether to create a summary or a detail query. To see each record, choose Detail. To see totals, averages, or other summaries of the data (instead of details), choose Summary and set the summation options you want. Then click Next.

Give the query a name, and click Finish to run (or "open") the query. Figure 33.2 shows the *result set* produced by a query that selects the ContactName, Country, and Phone fields in a Customers table.

 TIP The wizard won't use L/R naming conventions, so if you are using them, be sure to add the prefix **qry** to the query name.

FIGURE 33.2

A query's result set

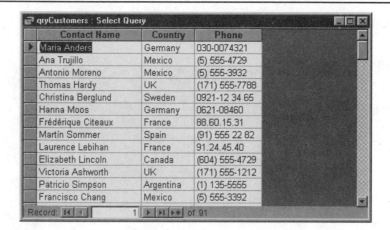

Understanding Design View

 Clicking the View button on the toolbar switches the query to Design view for modification (as shown in Figure 33.3). The query window is separated into two panes. The lower pane (called the *Query By Example grid* or *QBE grid*) uses one column for each field included in the query. It shows the field name, the table the field comes from, whether the query is sorted based on the field, whether the field is shown in the query results, and criteria that have been applied to the field to limit the query results.

PART

VI

Access for the
Nonprogrammer

FIGURE 33.3

A query in Design view

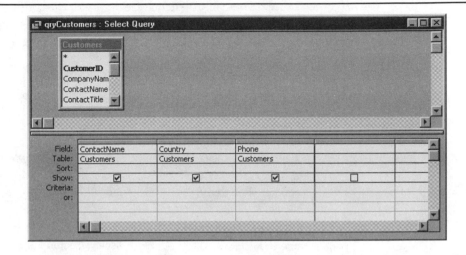

The upper pane (called the *table pane*) shows the tables included in the query and any relationships between the tables.

Changing Criteria

Criteria can further limit the records displayed in a query, so that you see only the records and fields you need to see and nothing else. For example, if you want to see the ContactName, Country, and Phone only for contacts in Germany, you can use criteria to limit the records to those with Germany in the Country field.

Criteria are entered in the Criteria cell for a field, in the query's design grid (shown in Figure 33.4). Don't type the quote marks; Access enters those for you.

FIGURE 33.4

Entering query criteria in the design grid

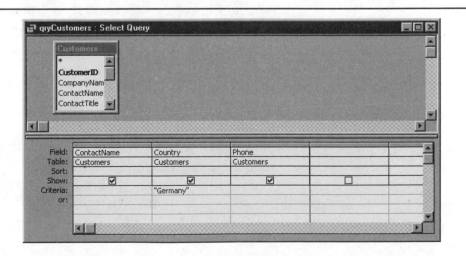

You can enter a specific field entry, such as **Germany** in the country field, to show records with that entry; you can also use criteria expressions and operators to further narrow the recordset selection. Table 33.1 lists some common criteria operators you can use in queries.

TABLE 33.1: QUERY CRITERIA OPERATORS

Operator	Purpose	Example
And	Selects records having one characteristic AND another characteristic in the field.	`Unit Price >20 AND <80` displays records with unit prices between $20 and $80.
Or	Selects records having one characteristic OR another characteristic in the field.	`Category Seafood OR Meat/Poultry` displays Seafood and Meat/Poultry records.
Not	Selects records that do NOT have the specified characteristic in the field.	`Category NOT Condiments` displays all records except those in the Condiments category.
Is Null	Selects records with no entry in the field.	`ZipCode Is Null` displays addresses with no zip code entered.
Is Not Null	Selects records that have an entry in the field.	`PhoneNumber Is Not Null` displays records with phone numbers entered.
=, <>, >, <	Selects records with a value that's equal to, not equal to, greater than, or less than a specified value.	`UnitPrice > 100` displays items with a unit price more than $100. You can enter an expression either with or without a space following one of these symbols.

Adding and Removing Fields

What makes a query more useful than a filter is that you can select not only the records you want to see, but also the fields within those records.

To add a field to a query, open the query in Design view. In the table pane, double-click the field you want to add to the query. It's added at the right end of the existing fields in the grid, but you can move it to a new position by clicking the gray bar at the top of the column to select it and then dragging the gray bar to move the column.

To delete a field from a query, click the gray bar at the top of the column to select it and press Delete.

If you need to include the field so you can sort or set criteria in it, but don't want to display it in the Datasheet result set, clear the check box in the Show cell. Keep in mind that the field not only isn't displayed, it isn't included in the result set.

 TIP Even though clearing the Show check box prevents the field's data from being displayed in the query's result set, you can still sort the result set by that field or limit the result set by setting criteria in that field. For example, if you combine a LastName field and a FirstName field into a single FullName field (see "Combining and Separating Field Entries," later in this chapter) you can still sort the result set by last name if you include and sort the LastName field and clear its Show box.

Understanding Table Joins

If you create a new query from related tables, Access will display the relationships as you place the tables in the upper pane. If you haven't already defined the relationships between the tables, you can create relationships in the upper pane the same way you do in the Relationships window when defining the database structure (see Chapter 30). However, these relationships are created only for the query—they aren't automatically placed in the Relationships window. A relationship between tables, as shown in Figure 33.5, is called a *join*. There are two types of joins, called *inner* joins and *outer* joins. Outer joins are further divided into right outer joins and left outer joins. Double-clicking the join line opens the Join Properties dialog box.

FIGURE 33.5

*The Join Properties
dialog box*

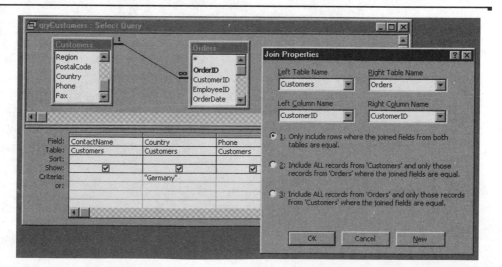

The first join type listed is an *inner join,* which is the default join in queries. In an inner join, the only records displayed in the query are those with identical values in the joined fields. In this example, if there are no orders for one of the customers, the customer won't be listed; similarly, an order with no customer will not be included in the result set.

The second join type is a *left outer join.* With a left outer join, all the records in the primary table in the relationship are displayed, even if they don't have matching entries in the related table.

A *right outer join* includes all the records from the related table (in this example, the Orders table), even if no matching records exist in the primary Customers table. The join symbol points from the table that will have all records listed to the table that will only have matching records displayed. All three joins use the same tables and relationships, but each returns a different query result set. To remove a join, select the join and press Delete.

 TIP You don't need to worry about remembering the terms "inner" and "outer" join, because the Join Properties dialog box tells you which option to click to get the results you want and never uses those terms.

Ambiguous Joins

If your database is simple and straightforward, you'll never see the error message "Query contains ambiguous outer joins"; but if you create a multiple-table query that's intricate or complex, you may well see this confusing message. Unfortunately, although Access tells you that your query contains ambiguous joins, that's all it tells you (and it doesn't tell you what they are or how to fix them).

Ambiguous joins are combinations of joins that don't tell Access exactly what you want; the specific problem depends on your database and the data you're attempting to join, and the solution is usually a result of changing join types. When you get this message, double-click a join line in the query. In the Join Properties dialog box, there are three options, numbered 1, 2, and 3.

Continued

CONTINUED

Join type 1 is the safest (it tells Access to show all records that have entries in *both* the joined fields). If all the joins in your query are type 1 (the default), this often solves the problem.

Join types 2 and 3 tell Access to show all the records in one table—either the left (type 2) or the right (type 3)—and only those records in the other table that have entries in the joined field. Sometimes this is exactly the information you need. If you apply either join type 2 or 3, the join line will be an arrow that points from the table where all records are shown to the table where only records with entries are shown. If you need to use join types 2 and 3, set them up so that all the arrows in the table pane point in the same direction (this is simplistic, but it works).

If you need to include two join types 2 or 3 and the result is an ambiguous outer join message, consider creating two queries. In the first query, include two of the tables with a type 2 or 3 join. Then, join this query to the remaining table to create your second query.

Sorting a Query

To sort a query, open it in Design view. In the Sort row of the column you want to sort by, choose Ascending or Descending.

You can sort by multiple fields, but the fields need to be in the proper order to achieve the sort you want. Access sorts fields from left to right in the query grid; so if you want to sort customers by last name and then by first name, for example, move the LastName field to the left of the FirstName field in the query grid, and set each to sort Ascending.

You can rearrange the columns in the query's Datasheet view to be in any order you like; the Datasheet view column positions are independent of the column positions in the Design view query grid.

Printing a Query

When you print a query result set, the results appear in Datasheet view. A query's datasheet view looks exactly like a table's Datasheet view, and if you need to see the query's result set on paper in a hurry, printing the query is faster than creating and printing a report.

To print a query, open the query to display the result set, then click the Print button on the toolbar.

PART

VI

Access for the
Nonprogrammer

Creating a Parameter Query

A *parameter query* displays a dialog box that prompts the user to enter *parameters*, or criteria, for selecting records. Parameter queries are useful when you frequently need to access a subset of a table or tables. For example, if you want to look up the names and phone numbers of customers in one state at a time, you can create a parameter query that asks you to enter the state abbreviation and then displays only the records from that state. It's the same as entering a specific state abbreviation in the Criteria row for the State field in the query grid, but it saves you having to create a separate query for each state.

To create a parameter query from an existing query, open the query in Design view. In the Criteria cell of the field you want to use as a parameter, enter a question or message (a *prompt*), enclosed in square brackets:

Field:	ContactName	Country	Phone	OrderDate	
Table:	Customers	Customers	Customers	Orders	
Sort:					
Show:	☑	☑	☑	☑	
Criteria:		[Which country?]			
or:					

The prompt appears in the Parameters dialog box to ask the user to enter criteria. Every time you run the query, either by opening it or by switching to Datasheet view, you'll see the Parameter dialog box before the query runs.

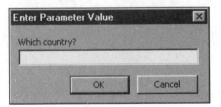

Type the parameters, the specific records you want to see, and click OK (or press Enter). Figure 33.6 shows the result set of a parameter query for customers in Germany.

To save the parameter query separately from the nonparameter (simple) query, save it under a new name. To change the parameter query back to a nonparameter query, delete the prompt from the Criteria cell in the query grid.

FIGURE 33.6

The result set of a
parameter query for
customers in Germany

Creating a Summary Query

A *summary query* is a query that returns summaries or totals rather than detailed
records. If the fields you select in the Simple Query Wizard include numeric fields,
you can create either a detail or summary query, but you can also turn any select
query into a summary query. First, open the query in Design view.

Σ On the toolbar, click the Totals button to open the Totals row of the query grid. All
fields in the grid are automatically set to Group By; fields you are not summarizing
will retain that setting.

For fields you want to summarize, click the drop-down arrow in the Totals cell
and choose a summary calculation. Table 33.2 lists the aggregate functions used in
queries.

TABLE 33.2: AGGREGATE QUERY FUNCTIONS

Function	Result	Used with Field Types
Avg	The average of the values in the field.	AutoNumber, Currency, Date/Time, Number
Count	The number of records that hold data in this field. The count includes zeros but not blanks.	All
First	The contents of the field in the first record in the result set.	All

Continued ▶

PART

VI

Access for the
Nonprogrammer

TABLE 33.2: AGGREGATE QUERY FUNCTIONS (CONTINUED)		
Function	**Result**	**Used with Field Types**
Last	The contents of the field in the last record in the result set.	All
Min	The lowest value in the field.	AutoNumber, Currency, Date/Time, Number, Text
Max	The highest value in the field.	AutoNumber, Currency, Date/Time, Number, Text
StDev	The standard deviation of the values in the field.	AutoNumber, Currency, Date/Time, Number
Sum	The total of the values in the field.	AutoNumber, Currency, Date/Time, Number
Var	The variance of the values in the field.	AutoNumber, Currency, Date/Time, Number

Figure 33.7 shows a summary query on the Customers table. Data is sorted by the Country field and then grouped by the Count function. The result set illustrated in Figure 33.8 shows the number of customers in each country.

FIGURE 33.7

*A summary query
ready to run*

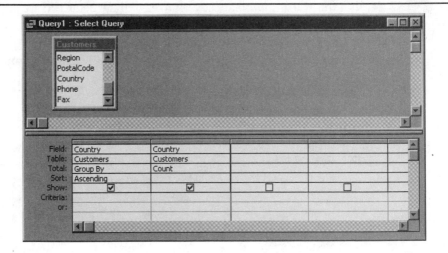

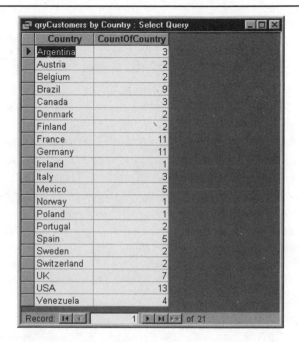

FIGURE 33.8

The summary query's result set

Adding Calculations to Queries

To perform a calculation in a query, you add a new column, called a *calculated field*, to the query. A calculated field can calculate the numbers in a table, so you don't have to enter the calculated values in a table yourself. For example, you can multiply one field by another, add two or more fields together, or use constant values (such as a tax rate) in calculations.

Common uses for calculated fields are to calculate Price × Quantity for a subtotal in an Orders query and the sales tax for an order (multiply the calculated subtotal field by the fixed tax rate). You can also use calculated fields with text functions to combine, for example, first name and last name to display full names in a single column.

PART

VI

Access for the Nonprogrammer

Combining and Separating Field Entries

Two tasks you might want to perform are combining multiple fields into a single field (for example, combining FirstName and LastName fields into a single FullName field), and separating a single field of full names into separate fields for first and last names. Combining (concatenating) is a simpler process than separating (parsing); combining can be done in a calculated field in a query, and separating can be done using Excel and the Text Import Wizard.

To combine two fields into one (for example, a FirstName and LastName field into a FullName field), open a query in Design view. Be sure the table with the fields is in the Table pane. In the Field cell of a blank column in the QBE grid, type a concatenation expression, such as **FullName:[FirstName]&" "&[LastName]**, and press Enter. In this example, FullName is the new field name, the existing field names are encased in square brackets, and the ampersands (&) join the first name to a space, followed by the last name.

To separate entries in a field, use Excel to parse the entries and the Text Import Wizard (see Chapter 26) to bring the table back into Access. Open Excel and Access in half-screen windows (so you can see them both). From the Tables group in the database window, drag the name of the table with the combined entries into the Excel window and drop it in a worksheet (the Access table is copied to the worksheet). Insert a new column on the right side of field you want to parse, and give it a field name in the same row as the other headers. Select all the cells in the field you want to parse, and click Data–Text To Columns. In the Convert Text To Columns Wizard, select Delimited, click Next, and then choose Space as the delimiter to separate the names.

After you parse the names, bring the Excel table back into Access to replace the version that has combined names. Use the Access Import Wizard to import the table (see the section "Importing Data from Spreadsheets and Other Databases" in Chapter 30). Import the table using the existing table name, and click Yes to overwrite the existing table.

Queries can also calculate with dates. For example, suppose an Employees table includes the year each employee was hired; the Human Resources department would like to quickly calculate the number of years each employee has worked here. To calculate the years of service, you would create a query based on the Employees table. In Design view, add another column to the table to contain the calculated field (in Datasheet view, the calculation will have its own column). Click in the Field cell of the column and enter the calculation, or click the Build button on the toolbar to open the Expression Builder.

The Expression Builder gives you more room to build calculation expressions, and it provides the correct spelling of field names (which is critical). Field names in calculations are always encased in square brackets. You can use field names, constant values, and built-in mathematical *functions*, or named equations, in expressions.

To produce the data the Human Resources department wants, you can use a combination of the Now() function, the Year() function, and a table field. The built-in Access function Now() returns the current date and time, and the function Year() returns the year from a date. By nesting the two functions, you can calculate the current year, Year(Now()), and the year hired, Year([HireDate]). Then, subtract the year hired from the calculated current year: Year(Now())-Year([HireDate]).

NOTE If dates are formatted with two-digit years, Access assumes that dates between 1/1/00 and 12/31/29 fall between the years 2000 and 2029; dates between 1/1/30 and 12/31/99 are assumed to fall between the years 1930 and 1999.

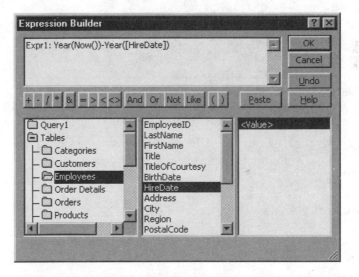

Click OK to close the Builder. Access will name the column Expr1, but you can select all the characters left of the colon (:) and enter a new name, like YrsSvc, in query Design view. You can base a form or report on a query, and you can have the calculations you need in the form or report done for you in the query.

PART

VI

Access for the
Nonprogrammer

Creating Crosstab Queries

Crosstab queries summarize information about two or more columns in a table or query. (If you want to create a crosstab query that involves more than one table, first use the Simple Query Wizard to create a select query that has all the fields you need, and then base your crosstab query on the select query rather than a table.) To continue our example, we can create a crosstab query to show the number of new hires by department each year based on the data in the calculated summary query created in the previous section, shown in Figure 33.9.

We can create a crosstab query from the results of the qryEmployeeYears query.

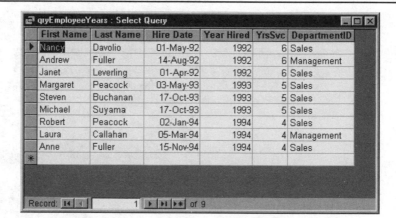

1. To create a crosstab query, click the New button on the Queries page in the database window, and then double-click Crosstab Query Wizard.

2. In the first step of the wizard, identify the table or query that contains the columns you want to summarize, and click Next.

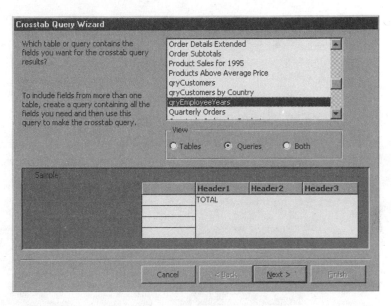

3. The second step of the wizard asks which fields contain the information you want to present as rows within the query. You can select up to three fields from the table to use as rows. As you select each field, Access adds it to the row headings. (Here, the Year Hired field is used for row headings and DepartmentID for column headings. We made this choice simply because there are more years than departments, so placing Year Hired on the left side means the completed query is more likely to fit on the width of the computer screen.) When you have selected the row headings, click Next.

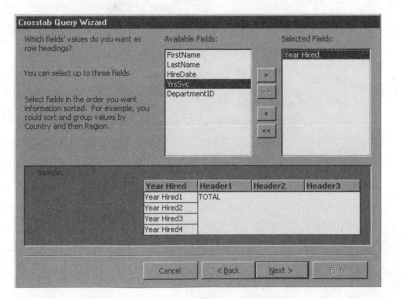

4. In the next wizard step, select the single field that you wish to use for column headings, and then click Next.

5. After you've selected a field for column headings, the following step has three choices:

- Which field do you want to calculate?
- How do you want to calculate your data?
- Do you want totals for each row?

The field you select determines the information that will be summarized in the crosstab query's result set, and the type of field you select determines the summary methods you can choose (see Table 33.1).

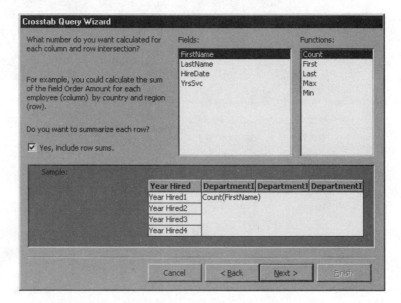

6. In the last step of the Crosstab Query Wizard, enter a name for the query. The finished results for this example are shown in Figure 33.10.

You'll find that crosstab queries are not as reusable as regular (simple or select) queries, because the column headings in a crosstab query come from the items in the field. If the items in the field change, the structure of the crosstab query is not updated, and data will be left out. For example, suppose you create a crosstab query of the current month's sales by state, using the State field to provide the column headings. If during the initial month you sold items only in CA, MI, and OH and the next month's data includes sales in NY, the NY data won't appear in the query results because the structure of the query (the column headings) doesn't automatically change. The solution to this problem is to anticipate it and make a new crosstab query.

FIGURE 33.10

A finished crosstab query

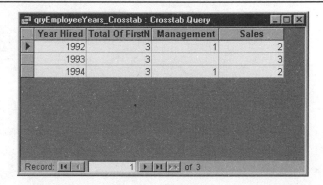

Year Hired	Total Of FirstN	Management	Sales
1992	3	1	2
1993	3		3
1994	3	1	2

Understanding Action Queries

Action queries are queries that take specific actions to change or copy large quantities of data all at once. You can use action queries to make a new table out of a query datasheet (a *make-table* query), add a set of additional records to a table (an *append* query), delete many records at once from a table (a *delete* query), or perform extensive data updates on a table (an *update* query).

Running a Make-Table Query

Sometimes you need to create a new table from a subset of data in an existing table. For example, suppose you have a large table of historical customer records that you want to keep intact, but you need a separate table of customers who placed orders within the last two years. You can query the historical-data table for the current customers, and then use a make-table query to create a new table from the current-customer query. Here are the steps:

1. First, create a query that contains the records you want to put in the new table. Have the query open in Design view.

2. Click the arrow next to the Query Type button on the toolbar, and select Make-Table Query from the drop-down list. The Make Table dialog box appears.

3. In the Table Name box, enter the name of the table you want to create. Click Current Database to put the new table in the currently open database, or click Another Database and type the name of a different database you want to put the new table in. Then click OK.

PART

VI

Access for the Nonprogrammer

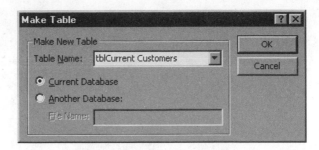

4. Use the querying techniques discussed throughout this chapter to select the data you want to include in the new table, and enter any criteria you need to get the records you want.

5. To preview the records in the new table before you create it, switch to Datasheet view. Make any changes you need in Design view so that the records and fields you want in the new table are shown in the query.

6. When the preview shows exactly the records you want, click Run on the toolbar to create the new table. In the warning message, click Yes and then close the query without saving it (unless you anticipate needing to make a new table with this query again).

Running an Append Query

If you need to add a group of records from one or more tables to the end of an existing table, run an append query instead of creating a new table. Here are the steps:

1. First, create a query that contains the table whose records you want to append to another table. The structure—that is, the field names and order—of the records you're appending should match the structure of the table you're appending them to.

2. In query Design view, click the arrow next to the Query Type button on the toolbar, and then click Append Query to display the Append dialog box, shown below.

3. In the Table Name drop-down list, select the name of the table you want to append the records to. Click Current Database if the table is in the currently open database, or click Another Database and type the name of a different database where the table is stored. Then click OK.

 NOTE You can also enter a path to a Microsoft FoxPro, Paradox, or dBASE database, or a connection string to a SQL database.

4. Use the query techniques discussed earlier to select the data you want to append to the table. If the primary key field you're appending has an AutoNumber data type, it may cause problems, so it's usually best not to include that field.

5. If the fields you're appending have the same name in both tables, Access automatically fills the matching name in the Append To row that appears in the query's QBE grid. If the fields in the two tables don't have the same name, use the Append To row to enter the names of the fields in the table you're appending to.

6. To preview the records before you append them, switch to Datasheet view. Make any changes you need in Design view so that the records and fields you want to append are shown in the query.

7. When the records are ready to append, click Run on the toolbar to add the records to the table. In the warning message, click Yes, and then close the query without saving it (unless you anticipate needing to run this append query again; if you do, save it with a clear identifying name).

Running a Delete Query

If you want to "clean out" a table (for example, to delete records older than two years), you can run a delete query.

 WARNING The results of a delete query are irreversible and can wipe out tremendous amounts of data, so use caution whenever you decide to use a delete query.

You can use a delete query to delete records from a single table in a single action. If you want to delete all related records from multiple tables in a one-to-many relationship, be sure that the table relationships are set up with referential integrity enforced and cascading deletes turned on, so that deleting the records from the "one" table will automatically delete related records in the "many" table. (See the section "Cascading Updates and Deletes" in Chapter 30 to learn more about referential integrity and cascading deletes.) Follow these steps to create and run a delete query:

1. First, create a query that contains the table whose records you want to delete. In query Design view, click the Query Type drop-down arrow on the toolbar, and then choose Delete Query.

2. Use the querying techniques discussed earlier to select the records you want to delete.

3. To preview the records before you delete them, switch to Datasheet view. Make any changes you need in Design view so that the records you want to delete are shown in the query.

4. When you're ready to permanently delete the records shown in the query, click Run on the toolbar. In the warning message, click Yes, and then close the query without saving it.

Running an Update Query

If you need to make large-scale changes to data in a table, you can run an update query. The advantage of an update query over find-and-replace operations is that you can query for the specific records that need updating before you make the changes (so you won't inadvertently change records that shouldn't be changed). An example is a change to the tax rate for a particular city in an Orders table; you don't want to change all the cities' tax rates, just the records for orders shipped to that specific city. Follow these steps to create and run an update query:

1. Create a query, selecting the tables or queries that include the records you want to update and the fields you need to set criteria for.

2. Open the query in Design view, and click Update Query from the Query Type button drop-down.

3. Use querying techniques to select the records you want to update.

4. In the Update To cell for the fields you want to update, type the expression or value you want to use to change the fields.

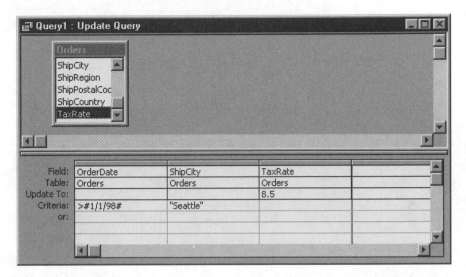

5. To preview the records before you update them, switch to Datasheet view (this list won't show the new values). Make any changes you need in Design view so that the records you want to update are shown in the query.

6. Click Run on the toolbar to complete the updates. In the warning message, click Yes, and then close the query without saving it (unless you anticipate needing to run this append query again; if you do, save it with a clear identifying name).

What's Next

The next two chapters build on the query skills you've learned in this chapter. Chapter 34 shows you how to use Microsoft Query to retrieve data from Access or any other ODBC-compliant database for use in Excel. In Chapter 35, you'll create OLAP queries that take crosstabs and pivot tables into completely new dimensions.

PART

VI

Access for the
Nonprogrammer

PART VII

Using the Office Data Analysis Tools

LEARN TO:

- *Create queries in Microsoft Query*

- *Manipulate query data in Query and Excel*

- *Create and connect to ODBC data sources*

- *Construct and use OLAP cubes*

CHAPTER **34**

Using Microsoft Query and ODBC

FEATURING:

Understanding ODBC

Selecting a data source

Setting up a new ODBC data source

Creating a query

Running queries

Just as you use the query features of Access to retrieve information from Office 2000 data sources, you use Microsoft Query within Excel to query data from a variety of sources. Using Query to retrieve data means you don't have to import or reenter the data in Excel, and this is what makes it a powerful Office tool. When you import data and manipulate it in Excel 2000, the data is frozen in time: If you're working with data you imported yesterday, the data set doesn't include changes made today. Query creates a path to the data, so that you can always retrieve the most current data.

 NOTE For general information about using queries in Access, see Chapter 33.

Excel is the Office 2000 application generally used with Query, so in this chapter we'll assume you're using Query within Excel. There are several good reasons to work with Query data in Excel, including the number of users who are already familiar with the application's tools. If you offer to create a Microsoft Query for a colleague, they'll probably express some degree of gratitude. When you offer to help them access the data they need in Excel, you'll generate some real excitement.

 TIP You can launch Query without Excel; you'll find the msqry32.exe program in the folder where the other Office 2000 applications are installed.

Understanding ODBC

Access 2000 is a great database, but large companies and institutions store the bulk of their information on mainframes or large minicomputers in heavy-duty databases, not in PC-based databases. Until recently, that wealth of organizational data was only accessible to mainframe users. If new reports or queries were required, it was time to call in the programmers.

Improved software and hardware for microcomputer access to mainframe data have radically changed the role of PCs in business, and Office 2000 continues the trend toward greater desktop access to hard-core corporate data with support for the

Using the Office Data Analysis Tools

latest version of ODBC (Open Database Connectivity). ODBC is an open API standard for database access. ODBC was not developed by Microsoft, but it is often thought of as a Microsoft standard because Windows was the first operating system to support ODBC. Access and SQL Server are both *ODBC-compliant*, as are many other database programs. Widespread use of the ODBC standard means that you can query data from a variety of sources on your PC, whether or not the data was created on a PC. For example, you may want to retrieve information from an Oracle database using Excel. To do this, you will use a combination of software:

- Microsoft Query to create a query
- Excel 2000 to open the query
- The ODBC Driver Manager, which is part of Windows
- A specific ODBC driver designed to allow Query to "talk to" the Oracle database
- The Oracle database

The combination of a database and the ODBC driver to connect to it is called a *data source*. Office 2000 automatically installs ODBC drivers for the following programs:

- dBASE
- Microsoft Access 2000
- Microsoft Excel
- Microsoft SQL Server
- Microsoft SQL Server OLAP Services
- Oracle
- Paradox
- Text database files (for example, comma-delimited files)

A driver for Microsoft FoxPro is available from the Microsoft Web site.

ODBC-compliant databases usually ship with their own ODBC drivers, and there are third-party drivers available. If you want to use Office 2000 to analyze information in a database that's not listed above, first check with the database manufacturer to find out how to get a 32-bit ODBC driver; often, you'll find that it was included with the software. You can also check the Microsoft Web site for ODBC drivers that were not included with Office 2000. The driver will have a setup program to assist with installation.

MASTERING THE OPPORTUNITIES

ODBC Drivers

Before you can set up a data source, you must have the appropriate driver. There are two types of ODBC drivers: 16-bit and 32-bit. If you're using Office 2000 you can use the 32-bit drivers. Use of the 16-bit drivers depends on your operating system. Windows NT Workstation supports both 16- and 32-bit drivers; only 32-bit drivers are supported under Windows 95 or 98. If you're running Windows 95/98 and working with vendors to acquire an ODBC driver, make sure you specify that you require a 32-bit driver.

The newest ODBC drivers have their own installation programs. Older drivers, which required setup through the Control Panel, are no longer supported in the version of ODBC that ships with Office 2000.

Selecting a Data Source

From an Excel worksheet, choose Data ➤ Get External Data ➤ New Database Query to launch Microsoft Query. Query will display the Choose Data Source dialog box, shown in Figure 34.1. The Databases page of the dialog box shows data sources that have already been created as well as available ODBC drivers you can use to connect to databases and create data sources. The Queries page has a list of queries you've previously created and saved. You'll find out about OLAP Cubes (the third page) in Chapter 35.

FIGURE 34.1

Select a data source so you can create a query.

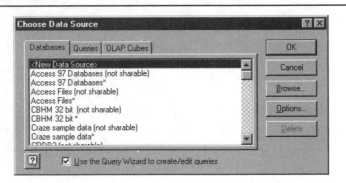

TIP There are default folders that Query searches for data sources and queries. To add other folders, click the Options button in the Choose Data Source dialog box.

Microsoft Query isn't the only program that creates ODBC data sources, so if you've created data sources to use with programs like Seagate Crystal Reports, Cognos Power-Play, or Cognos Impromptu, they'll be listed on the Databases page. If you've already created a data source for the database you want to query, simply select it from the list and click OK.

Setting Up a New Data Source

To create a new data source, choose New Data Source at the top of the list on the Databases page and click OK to open the Create New Data Source dialog box, shown in Figure 34.2. In the first text box, enter an easy-to-remember name for your data source; you can use the name of the database. In the second text box, choose the appropriate driver from the list of ODBC drivers, and then click the Connect button to launch the ODBC driver.

FIGURE 34.2

Enter a name for the data source and select a driver.

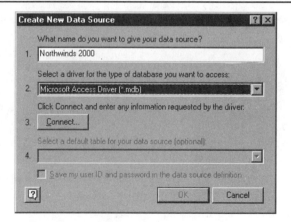

Setting Up Your Database

The ODBC Manager will display the Setup dialog box for the driver you selected. Figure 34.3 shows the ODBC Setup dialog box for Microsoft Access; if you choose a driver for a different type of database, the dialog box you see may request different information to complete the ODBC connection.

Setting up an Access ODBC data source

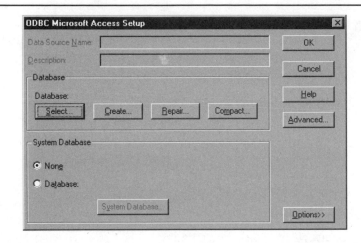

Click the Select button to choose an existing database in the Select Database dialog box. (You can click the New button to create a database, but we advise you to spend some time designing it first!) If the database is secured, use the second section of the dialog box to choose the system database that validates your login, and then click the Advanced button and enter your login name and password in the Set Advanced Options dialog box. If there is no security set for the database, leave the default System Database setting of None. (Contact your database administrator if you need more information about these choices.) Click OK to close the Select Database dialog box and return to the Create Data Source dialog box (see Figure 34.2).

Selecting a Default Table and Login

If you're going to create a number of queries based on the same table in the data source, you may want to set that table as the default table in the Create Data Source dialog box. If a default table is selected, it's the only table displayed in the Query Wizard, which can really speed up creating queries in a large database with many tables.

The check box at the bottom of the Create Data Source dialog box allows you to save your user ID and password as part of the data source so you won't have to re-enter them each time you connect to the data source.

Click OK to create the data source. You'll return to the Select Data Source dialog box, where you can choose the data source. Query includes a wizard that you'll use to create simple select queries as you would in Access. For more complex queries you'll use the Microsoft Query window. The Query Wizard is enabled by default. To turn it off, clear the check box at the bottom of the dialog box before you click OK to close the Select Data Source dialog box and open Microsoft Query.

PART

VII

Using the Office Data
Analysis Tools

 MASTERING THE OPPORTUNITIES

Limiting Access to Data Sources

When you set up your data source, you can restrict access to it so that you're the only user, or so that only people who have access to your computer can use the data source. Access restrictions depend on the type of data source you create: User DSN (data source name), System DSN, or File DSN. User data sources are specific to the current user and are available only on the machine where they're created. Create a User data source when you're the only person who needs to use the data source. System DSNs are local to the machine but are not user-specific, so they can be shared with other people who use your computer. File DSNs are available to all users whose computers have the ODBC driver used to create the data source, so you can share them with other people in your department or workgroup. Some ODBC drivers only let you set up one or two of the types of data sources. For maximum control when creating data sources, use the ODBC Data Sources (32-bit) application in the Windows Control Panel.

Creating Queries with the Query Wizard

The Query Wizard opens with a list of the *views* (database queries), tables, and columns (fields) in your data source. In Figure 34.4, the open data source is the Northwind sample database that is included with Office 2000. The left pane works like the Windows Explorer. Tables and views have a plus sign; click the plus sign to display the table's fields.

The right pane displays the columns included in your query. Select a view, table, or individual column, and use the pick buttons to move the selection to the right pane. If you need a reminder about the contents of a column, select the column in the left pane, and then click the Preview Now button in the dialog box to display data from the column.

You can select data from more than one table or view. When you have finished selecting columns, click the Next button. If you selected columns from more than one table, the Query Wizard will check to see if there are existing relationships between all the tables before proceeding. If any of the tables from which you included columns is not related to the others in the data source, you'll be dumped out of the Query Wizard and into Query so you can indicate the appropriate relationships. (If this happens, see the next section, "Defining Relationships in Query.")

FIGURE 34.4

Select fields or entire
tables to include in
your query.

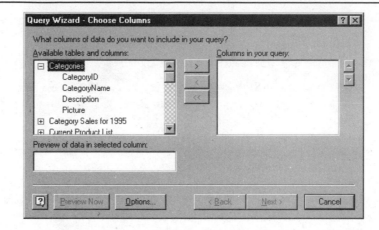

In the next step of the Query Wizard, use the drop-down lists and text boxes to specify filter criteria if you want to restrict the results based on values in specific columns. Use the And operator between criteria when all conditions must be met; use Or when any of the conditions should place a record in the query result set. For example, use Or to see Products in both the Meat/Poultry and Seafood categories, as shown in Figure 34.5. After the filters have been set, click Next.

FIGURE 34.5

Set one or more filter
criteria in the Query
Wizard.

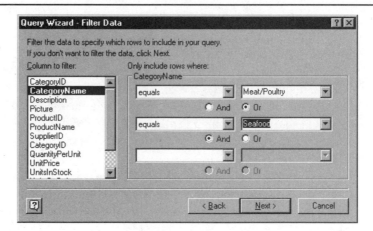

You can set up to three sort columns; then click Next. In the final step of the Query Wizard, shown in Figure 34.6, you can save the query by clicking the Save Query button. Then, choose one of three ways to work with your data. You can return the data to Excel, work with it in Query, or create an OLAP cube (see Chapter 35). If you choose to return the data to Excel, you can use all the Excel tools you're familiar with to work with the data. After choosing an option, click OK to close the Wizard and work with your result set. If you choose the first option, an Excel dialog box will open so you can specify the placement of the results.

FIGURE 34.6

Choose a destination for your result set in the final step of the Query Wizard.

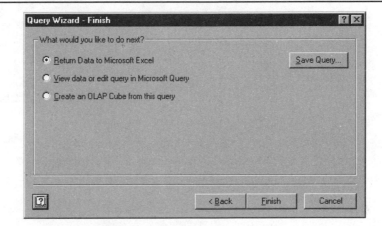

Defining Relationships in Query

Sometimes Query makes you clean up relationships simply because you didn't choose fields from enough tables. In Figure 34.7, we selected fields from Employees and Categories because we wanted to determine the total value of each employee's sales in each category. The problem is, there isn't a related field that appears in both the Employees and Categories tables. (In a well-built database, the fast way to figure this out is to see if the primary key of either table appears as a foreign key in the other table. For more information about keys, both primary and foreign, see "Determining Table Fields" and "Understanding Relationships" in Chapter 29.) Employees take Orders, which have Details about Products, and Products fall into Categories. We need related fields from the Orders, Order Details, and Products tables to create the query, so the Query Wizard closed.

FIGURE 34.7

Use the Query window
to create relationships
between tables.

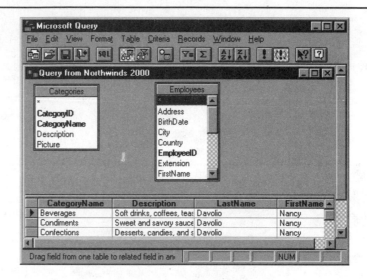

 We add other tables to the window just as we would in Access. Click the Add Tables button to open the Add Tables dialog box, select a table, and then click Add to add the table to the grid. Click Close when you're finished adding tables.

When the tables you selected are all related, you'll be able to follow the join lines from the first table to the last, as shown in Figure 34.8.

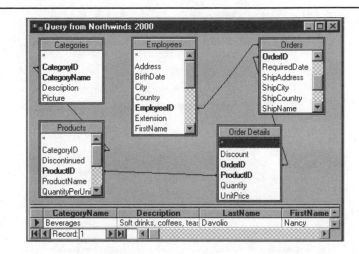

How does Query do this? It joins fields with the same name, which means that the joins it creates may not be the joins you need, particularly if the person who designed the database wasn't consistent when naming fields. To delete a join, select it and press Delete. To create a new join, drag the field from one table and drop it on the field that represents the same data in the other table.

To edit a join, select it and double-click to open the Joins dialog box shown in Figure 34.9. Choose the join that best describes the data you would like to see in your query results.

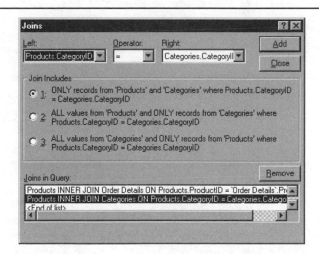

Working with Query Results in Excel

In Excel, you can use the query result set as you would any native Excel data. You can, for example, add formulas, create totals or averages, and chart the information. The real power of Query, however, is the ability to refresh the data any time you wish. When the query results open in Excel, the External Data toolbar also opens.

 If you want to change the query design, click the Edit Query button to launch Microsoft Query and reopen the Query Wizard so you can add or delete tables and columns, or change filters or sort order.

 TIP If you rearrange the columns or change the sort order or filter criteria in Excel, Query uses the new layout when it refreshes the data. See "Setting Excel Data Range Properties" later in this chapter for information on retaining or discarding layout changes.

 To view the latest data from the data source, click the Refresh Data button, and Query will rerun your query. The Refresh All button reruns all queries in the current workbook. If your queries are complex and take a long time to run, or if you have a number of queries, you'll appreciate being able to Cancel A Refresh or get Refresh Information at the click of a button.

MASTERING THE OPPORTUNITIES

Creating Parameter Queries

You can create a parameter query in Query just as you would in Access. In the final step of the Query Wizard, choose View Data Or Edit Query In Microsoft Query, and the Query window will open. If the Criteria grid is not displayed, choose View ➤ Criteria to display it. In the Criteria Field drop-down list, select the field for which you want to set a parameter. For example, to create a parameter query where users determine the state (Michigan, Nevada) used in the query, set the appropriate state field as the Criteria Field.

In the Criteria row just below the field, enter the user prompt in brackets: **[Enter a two-letter state abbreviation:]**. Query will immediately create the message box with the user prompt. You can simply cancel the message box, ot enter a value to see how your criteria work. Enter additional Or criteria in the remaining rows. To create an And criteria, set a Criteria Field and criteria in the next column.

Continued ▯▶

To return to Excel when you're finished, choose File ➣ Return Data To Microsoft Excel from the Query menu.

Creating a parameter query is particularly helpful when users need to change criteria frequently. In Excel, click the Query Parameters button on the External Data toolbar:

This opens the Parameters dialog box, where you can change the source for a parameter to a cell in the workbook (or a fixed value). This way, you can let users enter a value in (for example) cell A3, click the Refresh Data button, and see the query results for the new value they entered.

Setting Excel Data Range Properties

One of the disadvantages of working with Query data in Excel is that users can forget to refresh the data or to copy formulas in adjacent columns when more records are returned in the query results. Automated refresh settings are just one of the properties you can set for the range of data returned by Query.

Begin by clicking the Data Range Properties button on the External Data toolbar to open the External Data Range Properties dialog box shown in Figure 34.10. These properties don't affect the query that you saved (or didn't save) in Microsoft Query. They change how the query behaves in Excel:

Save Query Definition (on by default) saves the definition as part of the Excel worksheet so that it can be refreshed later without choosing Tools ➣ Get External Data and retrieving the saved query.

Save Password saves the password you entered to open the query data source.

Enable Background Refresh allows you to work on other tasks in Excel while data is being refreshed. If you disable this check box, you must wait for Query to refresh the data before continuing.

Refresh Every X Minutes ensures that the data range is refreshed at the interval you specify. Be careful with this, particularly when a query result set can grow or is accessed over a network with high peak volumes. You can become incredibly unpopular with colleagues who use this workbook if you refresh every 30 minutes and it takes 15 minutes for Query to refresh the data range.

Refresh Data On File Open launches Query and refreshes the data each time the workbook is opened rather than waiting for *X* minutes to refresh. This is a good option when data changes less frequently than users open the workbook. Many corporate data stores are refreshed once a day or once a week during off-peak hours, so a refresh when the file opens is probably adequate. With Refresh Data On File Open selected, you can choose to Remove External Data From Worksheet Before Saving. When the file is saved and closed, the external data is dumped, which saves drive space. The next time the workbook is opened, the query is run again and the data refreshed.

FIGURE 34.10

Use the External Data Range Properties dialog box to set refresh information for the query data.

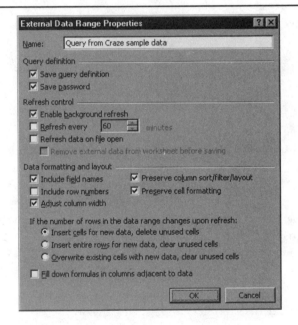

There are two distinct types of Data Formatting and Layout options. The first two options on the left pertain to the external data source; the options in the right column relate to Excel. You can Include Field Names (or omit them if you want to create different column labels) and Include Row Numbers from the external data source. When data is refreshed, Excel will automatically Adjust Column Widths to fit the data unless you turn this option off.

Preserve Column/Sort/Filter/Layout and Preserve Cell Formatting are both enabled by default. This means that if you rearrange columns in Excel and then apply a format to a column of query results, both the new arrangement and the format will be retained when the data is refreshed.

The last time you ran your query, it returned 10 rows of data; if it returns 13 rows next time, how should Excel deal with the extra rows? Use the option buttons to choose the method you want Excel to use (cell replacement, row replacement, or both) when the Number Of Rows Changes On Refresh. If you have other worksheet columns with formulas that rely on the external data range, enable the Fill Down Formulas In Columns Adjacent To Data check box to have Excel copy the formulas down to extra rows or remove formulas from rows that no longer have external data.

When you've adjusted the properties to meet the needs of the workbook's users, click OK to save the properties and close the dialog box.

What's Next

In Chapter 35, you'll extend your ODBC and query skills into another dimension with online analytical processing, a three-dimensional approach to data analysis.

CHAPTER 35

Using OLAP

OLAP *(Online Analytical Processing)* is a natural extension of traditional Excel pivot tables and Access crosstab queries. Both of these tools analyze data in two dimensions. For example, you can create a pivot table to analyze your company's sales by area, by date, or by product. If you create a pivot table to summarize dates by quarter and sales by region, you can drill down and view sales for a month or a particular day, or you can look at sales for the states within a region. However, until Office 2000, these two-dimensional tools had a limitation: you couldn't adequately analyze three or more dimensions (sales by region *and* date *and* product) simultaneously. OLAP is a three-dimensional data analysis tool for analyzing the multidimensional data that abounds in corporate databases. Support for OLAP is new in Excel 2000 PivotTables.

 NOTE OLAP uses PivotTable reports, Microsoft Query, and ODBC. This chapter assumes you're familiar with all of those concepts and the related Office operations, covered in Chapters 26 and 34.

Understanding OLAP Cubes

An *OLAP cube* is a special type of query with data organized in the categories you'd use for analysis so you can quickly generate new information or reports based on the data. You can create OLAP cubes from any ODBC data source with Query, or you can attach to an existing data cube created by one of your co-workers or an OLAP provider. If cubes are well designed, you won't need an abundance of them. One cube containing data on, for example, sales, can replace a plethora of queries created about specific aspects of sales information.

The cube is organized in *dimensions*, and a given dimension may have two or more *levels* of information, ranging from the more inclusive and general to the more specific and detailed. In a PivotTable or PivotChart report, a dimension is placed in a row, column, or page area. For example, a cube of data about sales might have these dimensions and corresponding levels:

    Sales dates: Years, quarters, months or weeks, days

    Geography: Country, state/province, city

    Product ordered: Product category, product

The lowest level of this cube, called a *measure*, would be the details about sales: the quantity of each product sold. The measures are placed in the data area of a pivot report. People who use your cube will analyze data by expanding and collapsing dimensions and swapping dimensions to see the changes in the measures.

If you serve as an information technology person in your company or department (formally or informally), you'll quickly realize that OLAP is a powerful feature. You can create cubes to help your users analyze data, even if they know nothing about joins or queries, rather than spending your time creating end-user reports. If you're an end user, you'll appreciate the power to robustly analyze and report on your data.

Opening an Existing OLAP Cube

There are three ways to access an OLAP cube. If the cube was already used in an Excel PivotTable or PivotChart, just open the Excel workbook. The workbook includes the information required to launch Microsoft Query and connect to the OLAP data source.

Using an Existing OLAP Query

If the OLAP cube was saved in Microsoft Query but not in Excel, choose Data ➢ Get External Data ➢ Run Saved Query from the Excel menu and select the OLAP query. Excel will launch Microsoft Query, run the query, and prompt you to choose a location for a pivot table.

Selecting an Existing OLAP Data Source

If there is no query based on the OLAP cube but a data source using the cube exists, select the data source as you would for any query based on an external data source. Open Excel and choose PivotTable Chart/PivotTable Report from the Data menu. In the first step of the wizard, choose External Data Source. In the second step, click Get Data to open the Choose Data Source dialog box. Click the OLAP Cubes tab and select an OLAP data source; then click OK to connect to the data source and return to the PivotTable Wizard.

Creating a New OLAP Data Source

If you need to create a new data source using a cube or OLAP server, begin by choosing an external data source as described in the previous section. On the OLAP Cubes tab, choose New Data Source and click OK to open the Create New Data Source dialog box, shown in Figure 35.1.

Create a new data source to connect to a cube or server.

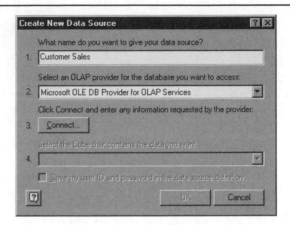

You'll connect to your OLAP data using the OLE DB Provider for OLAP Services, which is included with Office 2000. Click the Connect button to open the Multi-Dimensional Connection dialog box, shown in Figure 35.2.

If you're connecting to an OLAP server, enter the server resource name provided by your system administrator or database administrator in the text box. To connect to a cube, choose the OLAP Cube option, and then enter the Cube file name or browse and select it. Click Finish to connect to your server or cube and return to the Create New Data Source dialog box. Click OK to create the data source and add it to the list in the Choose Data Source dialog box. Click OK to return to the PivotTable Wizard.

 TIP There are two ways that OLAP data is delivered to a desktop: from a relational database using Microsoft Query and ODBC, or from an OLAP database. With an OLAP database, summary calculations are performed on the OLAP server and then sent over the network to Excel. OLAP database queries run much more quickly than those based on relational databases that require Excel to receive all the detail data and then perform summary calculations on your workstation. OLAP servers allow users to analyze data sets that have too many records for Excel to manage. On the other hand, OLAP cubes created with relational databases give you a way to look at complex data even if your company doesn't have an OLAP server. You can create the cube to filter the records returned from a database, allowing Excel to handle a larger number of records (without running out of system resources) than it would be able to if all fields were being retrieved by Excel.

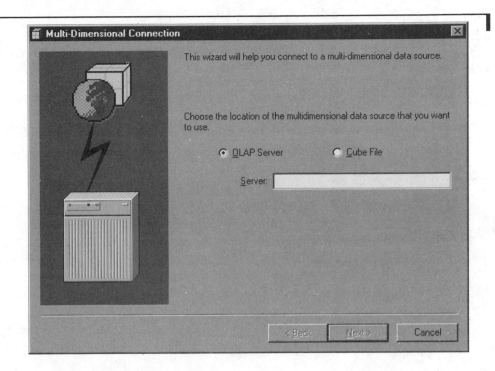

Creating a New OLAP Cube

If you can connect to an ODBC relational data source, you can create OLAP cubes by
setting up a data source, creating a query based on the data source, and saving the
query as an OLAP query. To try this from Excel, choose Data ➤ Get External Data ➤
New Database Query. If necessary, create and then select a Database data source as discussed in Chapter 34. In the illustrations that follow, we're creating a cube using the
Northwind database included with Access 2000.

In the Query Wizard, choose the tables and fields that you need for your cube.
Choose carefully: you can't edit a cube, so if you omit a field, you have to create a
new cube. Select tables and fields that represent the levels, dimensions, and measures
you'll want to analyze in the cube. In the last step of the Query Wizard, select Create
An OLAP Cube From This Query. If you think you may want to create a similar cube
later with slightly different fields, click the Save Query button. Click Finish to launch
the OLAP Cube Wizard.

TIP You'll select measures that you want to summarize when you create the cube. If you want to summarize a field twice, you need to add it to the query twice. For example, if you want to count *and* total the values in a field, you'll have to place the field in your query twice. You can't select a field more than once in the Query Wizard, but you can in Query itself. In the last step of the Query Wizard, choose View Data And Edit Query In Microsoft Query to return to Query, where you can drag additional fields into the query grid. After you've examined the query results, choose File ≻ Create OLAP Cube from the Query menu bar to launch the OLAP Query Wizard.

The OLAP Cube Wizard opens with an explanatory page. Click Next to move to the first step of the wizard, shown in Figure 35.3. In this step, you decide which of the fields you want to use as measures *(data fields)*. The fields you select here will end up in the data area of your PivotTable Report in Excel. The OLAP Cube Wizard examines your data, checks the fields that may be measures, and assigns a summarization method: COUNT for text and primary key fields, and SUM for other numeric fields. You need to select at least one data field and have at least one field that is not a data field when you're finished selecting. The fields that you don't check can be used in the next step as dimensions/levels. Of the fields selected by the wizard in Figure 35.3, we'll keep two: Orders and Quantities.

FIGURE 35.3

Select fields to be summarized in the OLAP Cube Wizard.

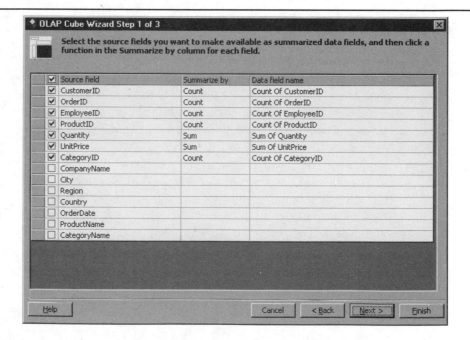

To change the summarization method for a field, click in the Summarize By column and select the function (Sum, Count, Min, Max) you want to use. Edit the Data Field Name to change the display name for a field. For example, in Figure 35.3 you might choose to change Count of Order ID to Number of Orders or even simply Orders. You can also change field display names later in Excel, but shortening the names now creates easier-to-use buttons in Excel's PivotTable toolbar. Click Next to move to the second step, selecting dimensions and levels.

The wizard does not select dimensions for you; instead, you begin with a blank screen. In your PivotTable Report, dimensions will be placed in the row, column, and page areas. Select the highest level in any dimension in the left pane, and drag and drop it on Drop Fields Here To Create A Dimension in the right pane to create a dimension, as shown in Figure 35.4. Add more dimensions the same way.

FIGURE 35.4

Select dimensions in the second step of the wizard.

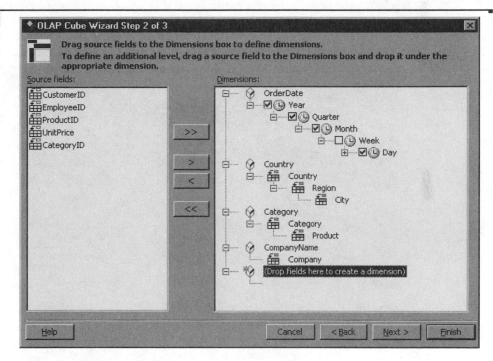

Date fields create their own levels—years, quarters, months, weeks, and days—that you can choose to include or omit. (You can't select both months and weeks to include, because weeks can cross months.) For other dimensions, you'll need to create your own levels. For example, to create a Products level within the Categories dimension, drop the Products field directly on Categories to create another level within Categories (see Figure 35.4). Similarly, you would drop Region on Country and City on Region to create a geographical dimension.

 TIP To edit a level or dimension name, right-click and choose Rename from the short-cut menu. You can also delete, cut, and paste dimensions. You cannot copy a dimension.

The third step of the wizard, shown in Figure 35.5, offers three ways to save your OLAP cube. The correct choice depends on several factors: the system resources available to the people who use the cube, the amount of data the cube will contain, and how frequently users change pivot reports. If a cube will see heavy-duty use, you may want to create three identical cubes, saved three different ways, and test the response of each to determine which choice is best.

FIGURE 35.5

Choose a save method for the cube.

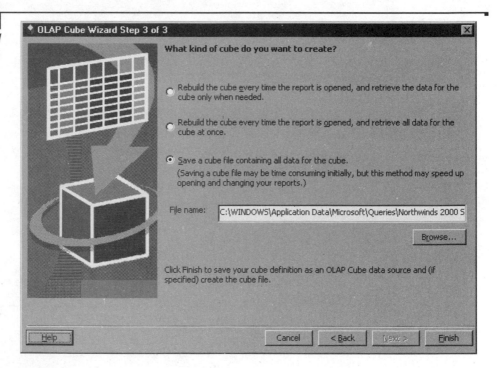

OLAP Cube Wizard Step 3 of 3

What kind of cube do you want to create?

○ Rebuild the cube every time the report is opened, and retrieve the data for the cube only when needed.

○ Rebuild the cube every time the report is opened, and retrieve all data for the cube at once.

◉ Save a cube file containing all data for the cube.
(Saving a cube file may be time consuming initially, but this method may speed up opening and changing your reports.)

File name: C:\WINDOWS\Application Data\Microsoft\Queries\Northwinds 2000 S

Browse...

Click Finish to save your cube definition as an OLAP Cube data source and (if specified) create the cube file.

Help   Cancel   < Back   Next >   Finish

The first option stores the information required to generate the cube in your OLAP Query (and PivotTable report in Excel). When you open the query, the cube is created and populated with the data immediately required. Additional data is retrieved on demand. The limited initial data means that this is a good choice when users frequently *look* at the PivotTable Report based on this cube but don't *change* the report very often.

The second option stores the cube information the same way, but when the cube is opened in Query or Excel, all data that might be required by the PivotTable is downloaded at once. This is a better choice when users often change the layout of the PivotTable, but it will, of course, take longer to load initially and it requires more memory than the first option.

The third option creates a separate cube file (with a .cub extension) that includes all the data for the cube. If you've got disk space and memory in quantity and need to rearrange your PivotTables a lot, this is a great choice. It takes longer to save this file the first time, but it will open more quickly than the first or second options because it doesn't have to re-create the cube. The cube file also functions as an offline cube; you can work with the cube even when you can't connect to the database it was created from, and refresh the data when you reconnect.

Select an option and click Finish. Immediately, Query opens a Save As dialog box to prompt you to save a *cube definition* (.oqy) file. This file is separate from the cube file or cube creation instructions you created in the wizard. You can't edit the cube, but the .oqy file is the next best thing. You can open the cube definition file in Query and launch the OLAP Cube Wizard again to create a new cube. The .oqy file is added to the Queries page of the Choose Data Source dialog box, so you can use it as you would any other query in Excel. Save the .oqy file, and Query will begin creating the OLAP cube. You'll be asked whether you want to return the cube to Excel and begin analyzing your data.

Working with a Cube in Excel

In Excel, the OLAP cube dimensions and measures appear on the PivotTable toolbar. It's worth noticing a field's ScreenTip; if the field is a summarized field, the tip includes the field name with the note "Drag button from here to the PivotTable data area." You can't place dimensions in the data area, or measures in the page, row, or columns areas of the table. Each dimension's field button includes all the levels you chose or added for the dimension, so dragging the OrderDate dimension into the PivotTable column area or the PivotChart x-axis brings along the years, quarters, and so on. They just aren't displayed yet.

Digging into Dimensions

There are three ways to see more data in a dimension: drilling down a dimension, using the Show Detail and Hide Detail buttons on the PivotTable toolbar, and selecting from a tree view of the dimension. Drill down by double-clicking the level in which you want to see more detail. In Figure 35.6, for example, you could double-click 1996 to see the four quarters; double-clicking one of the quarters would expand the months or weeks.

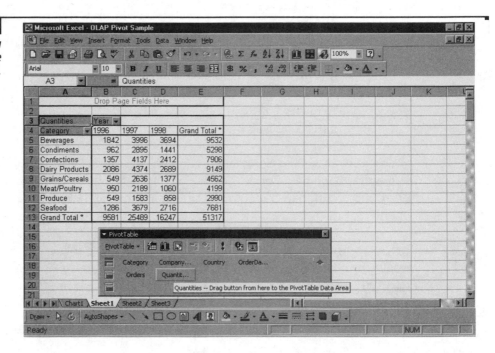

Instead of double-clicking each entry to expand a dimension, use the Show Detail and Hide Detail buttons. Select the row or column button and click the Show Detail button to expand every entry one level. Click again to expand the detail by two levels. You can show or hide a selected item as well as an entire row or column.

To expand, collapse, or filter a dimension, click the drop-down arrow on the dimension button to open a tree view of the dimension. A portion of the Categories dimension is shown here.

Use the plus and minus icons to expand and collapse the display, and use the check boxes to show or hide levels and items in a level. Click once on a checked box to add a double check mark, which displays the data in that level and the next level of detail.

If you save your Excel workbook, the next time you need to work with this cube you can simply open the workbook and Excel will connect to the cube file.

What's Next

In the next chapter, you'll learn how to use another type of server in Office 2000: an OLE server. Like OLAP, OLE breaks the boundaries of the individual applications and lets you select the tool that best fits the task you're working on.

PART VIII

Integration and Automation

LEARN TO:

- *Use OLE in the Office 2000 applications*

- *Collaborate using online documents*

- *Customize the Office environment*

- *Create and use macros in Office applications*

- *Create VB code in Office documents*

CHAPTER 36

Converting, Linking, and Embedding

FEATURING:

Converting files to Office formats

Linking and embedding objects

Inserting clips and pictures

I f you find yourself retyping information that already exists in another Office 2000 application, you're working way too hard. This chapter features a variety of methods to copy information from one application into another document by embedding, linking, or converting the existing data.

Object Linking and Embedding, or *OLE* (pronounced o-lay), is a protocol that allows applications to communicate with each other to create or update *objects:* data that can be embedded or linked in another application. Word documents, Excel worksheets and charts, Access tables, and PowerPoint slides are all examples of objects you can insert (embed or link) in other Office 2000 documents. For example, if you need to use an Excel chart in a Publisher or Word document or a PowerPoint presentation, don't re-create it—reuse it. You can also insert graphics, sounds, video, and virtually anything else you can select and copy to the Clipboard.

When you *convert* a selection, it is translated from its *native format* (the format used by the application it was created in) to a format that can be used directly by the application you place the selection into. Converting creates a copy, like a snapshot. After the selection is converted, you use the tools in the destination application to work with it. You can change the converted data without affecting the original.

Converting Data

The easiest way to convert (and embed or link) data in an Office application is to copy-and-paste. Open the *source application* that contains the text, picture, or other object you want to place in the *destination application.* Select the object and copy it to the Clipboard. In Figure 36.1, we've selected and copied data in an Excel workbook that we'll use in the examples that follow. You can close the source application if you wish; with some programs, you'll be asked if you want to retain the contents of the Clipboard. Choose Yes.

FIGURE 36.1

Data in Excel selected for copying to the Clipboard

	A	B	C	D	E	F
1			Unicorn Software Payroll			
2			Week Ending			
3						
4	Name	Hours	Rate	Gross Pay	Taxes	Net Pay
5	Azimi	32	$ 8.75	$ 280.00	$ 53.20	$ 226.80
6	Barzona	28	$ 9.00	$ 252.00	$ 47.88	$ 204.12
7	Buckley	32	$ 8.00	$ 256.00	$ 48.64	$ 207.36
8	Chiu	28	$ 10.00	$ 280.00	$ 53.20	$ 226.80
9	Collins	41	$ 10.00	$ 415.00	$ 78.85	$ 336.15
10	Jones	0	$ 9.50	$ -	$ -	$ -
11	Retzloff	42	$ 7.75	$ 333.25	$ 63.32	$ 289.93
12						
13	Totals	203		$ 1,816.25	$ 345.09	$1,471.16

Open the destination document and place the insertion point where you want to paste the selection. To convert the data, simply paste it into the document. In Figure 36.2, the data from Excel has been pasted into Word, which converted the Excel data into a Word table. You can use all the tools you normally use in Word tables to manipulate the converted table. Changes you make to the table, such as adding or deleting rows and columns, do not affect the original data in Excel.

FIGURE 36.2

Simply pasting the Excel data into Word converts it to a table.

As you can see from the information below, hours are not distributed evenly among employees. This causes both costs for unnecessary overtime and dissatisfaction among underutilized full time employees.

Name	Hours	Rate		Gross Pay		Taxes		Net Pay	
Azimi	32	$	8.75	$	280.00	$	53.20	$	226.80
Barzona	28	$	9.00	$	252.00	$	47.88	$	204.12
Buckley	32	$	8.00	$	256.00	$	48.64	$	207.36
Chiu	28	$	10.00	$	280.00	$	53.20	$	226.80
Collins	41	$	10.00	$	415.00	$	78.85	$	336.15
Jones	0	$	9.50	$	~	$	~	$	~
Retzloff	42	$	7.75	$	333.25	$	63.32	$	269.93

You don't have to convert the Excel data to a table. You can also paste it as a picture and use Word's drawing tools to position the graphic. To see further conversion choices, choose Edit ➤ Paste Special to open the Paste Special dialog box, shown in Figure 36.3.

FIGURE 36.3

Use the Paste Special dialog box to convert, embed, or link.

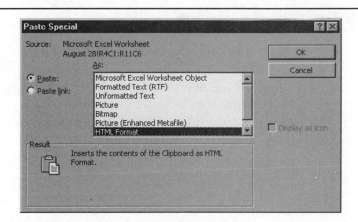

The source for the object (the name and range of worksheet cells) is displayed at the top of the dialog box. The list in the As box allows you to select how the information should be pasted:

Microsoft Excel Worksheet Object creates an object that can be linked or embedded (see the next section).

Formatted Text (RTF) is the default and converts the worksheet to a Word table.

Unformatted Text converts the selection to Word tabular columns.

Picture and **Bitmap** both convert the worksheet selection into a graphic that you can work with in Word using all the Word graphic tools. The Picture option creates a higher-quality graphic than Bitmap. You can place the graphic in a separate drawing layer by enabling the Float Over Text option.

Picture (Enhanced Metafile) converts the selection into a Windows Metafile graphic.

HTML Format converts the table to an HTML table.

Unformatted Unicode Text converts the entries in the cells to unformatted Unicode text columns.

Of the choices listed above, all but the first, Microsoft Excel Worksheet Object, convert the data. Choose a format and then click OK to convert the selection and paste it into your document.

Embedding and Linking

When you *embed* an object, a copy of the object that retains its native format is placed in the destination document. The Excel object is still "in" Excel, but it appears in the Word document. If you change the object pasted in Word, the original selection in Excel remains unchanged.

With a *link,* a relationship is established between the selection in the native application and the pasted entry in the destination document. When you open the Word document, Word reloads the Excel selection directly from the worksheet. When you begin to edit the object, Word launches Excel, and you make your changes there. This ensures that the original data and the linked copy are synchronized; changes to the original data are reflected in the linked object. Linking has two advantages: it saves disk space, but, more importantly, linking is *dynamic*. If the source for the object changes, the change is reflected in all linked objects.

Embedding an Object

To embed or link, you use the Paste Special dialog box. First, copy the object to the Clipboard. In the destination application, choose Edit ➤ Paste Special to open the Paste Special dialog box. Choose the description in the As list that includes the word *object* (for example, Microsoft Excel Worksheet Object) and click OK. Figure 36.4 shows the Excel object embedded in the Word document. You can tell it's an object because it has handles when selected. If you double-click the object to edit it, the native application (Excel) toolbars open right in the Word application window, as shown in Figure 36.4. From the computer's point of view, OLE is a complex operation. Give the destination document a moment to accept and place the new object.

FIGURE 36.4

Choosing Microsoft Excel Worksheet Object embeds the data.

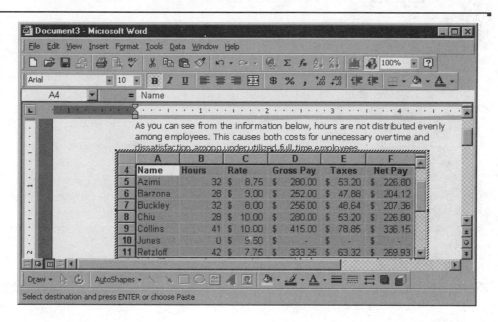

Creating a Link

To link the selection rather than embed it, enable the Paste Link check box in the Paste Special dialog box (Figure 36.3). You can link any of the converted or embedded file types listed. For example, if you copy an Excel worksheet range and choose to Paste Link it into a Word file as a Microsoft Excel Worksheet Object, you create a dynamic link to the range in the original worksheet. Any changes you make to the worksheet are reflected in the Word document.

If you would like to create a hyperlink to another document, choose Edit ➤ Paste As Hyperlink. The text in the pasted object is underlined and colored blue to indicate it is a hyperlink. When you click the hyperlink you are taken to the document in the native application.

 WARNING If a linked file is moved or renamed, an error message will appear when you open the destination document, and it will load without the object.

Working with Embedded and Linked Objects

To select a linked or embedded object, click it. Use the object's handles to size it, or press Delete to delete it. The real magic of OLE occurs when you double-click the object. After you click, wait a moment. If the object was embedded, the toolbars from the object's native application will open in the destination application. With a linked object, double-click and you'll be transported to the source document to edit the object.

 TIP Sometimes when you double-click an object, you will see a message that the source application cannot be opened (especially if the source application is already open). If the source application is installed on your computer, click OK to close the message box, and double-click again.

Automatic and Manual Updating

When you create a link with Paste Special, *automatic link updating* is enabled. The object is updated each time the destination document is opened and each time the source document changes. You can choose to update links manually rather than automatically, giving you control over when a file is updated. To change to *manual link updating,* select the linked object and then choose Edit ➤ Links to open the Links dialog box. As the Update Method, choose Manual. When you are ready to update links in the destination document, open the Links dialog box again and click the Update Now button, or right-click a selected object and choose Update Link from the shortcut menu.

WARNING If you use manual linking, you should adopt a consistent method for updating so you don't pass off last month's information as the latest data.

Embedding and Linking Files

If you want to embed or link an entire file instead of a selection, it is often easier to insert the object than to copy-and-paste. Choose Insert ➤ Object ➤ Create From File to open the Create From File page of the Object dialog box, shown in Figure 36.5.

FIGURE 36.5

Use the Create From File page of the Object dialog box to embed or link an entire file.

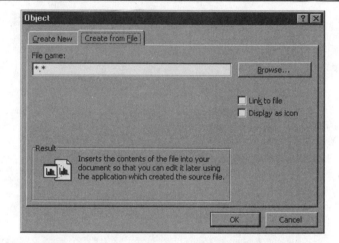

Select and open the file you want to embed or link, and set the other options as you did in the Paste Special dialog box. Click OK to insert the object in the destination document. Some files are inserted as icons whether or not you choose Display As Icon. Multimedia files, for example, place an icon in Word documents. Double-clicking the icon plays the file.

 NOTE To insert or import sound or video files, you must have Microsoft Media Player installed on your system. Media Player comes with Windows 95/98 and can be found on the Programs menu (Start ➤ Programs ➤ Accessories ➤ Multimedia ➤ Media Player).

Inserting and Converting Files in Word

If you're like many users, you use Word to pull together reports that include data from a variety of applications. Word is designed to let you convert files "on the fly" using the Insert command. To convert a file to Rich Text Format, choose Insert ➤ File from the menu to open the Insert File dialog box, shown in Figure 36.6. If you want to insert only part of a selected Excel workbook or Word document, click the Range button and then enter a range of cells or bookmark name before clicking the Insert button. This is a powerful tool. If you insert a 10-sheet Excel workbook, for example, all 10 sheets are converted, each in its own table.

FIGURE 36.6

When you insert a file, it is converted to the default format for the destination application.

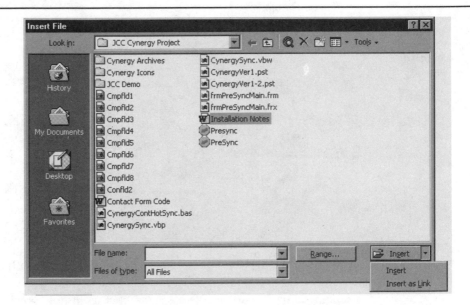

 To link the converted text back to the source document, click the arrow on the Insert button and choose Insert As Link. The linked data is placed as a field; when you click any part of the linked text, the gray field background appears. There's one major difference between inserting and pasting links in Word—the inserted link will be set for manual updating. You have two choices: change the updating method to automatic, or remember to occasionally right-click the linked object and choose Update Field from the shortcut menu.

Creating New Objects

You can use the Object dialog box to create a completely new object. For example, you may want to include an Excel chart in a Word document. You don't have to open Excel and create the chart; you can create an Excel object directly in Word.

 TIP Because new objects only exist in the destination document, they cannot be linked, only embedded.

You probably have other applications on your computer, such as Microsoft WordArt and Microsoft Graph, that also create objects. Choosing Insert ➤ Object from the menu bar opens the Object dialog box. The scroll list in the Create New page displays the objects that can be created using applications installed on your computer, as shown in Figure 36.7.

FIGURE 36.7

Insert objects using the Object dialog box.

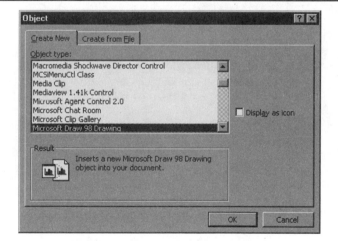

Select an Object Type and click OK to launch the application in which you will create the object. Create the object, and then close the application to return to the destination document. The Object Type list is amended as new applications are installed, but applications may remain on the list even if they have been removed from the computer. If you select an application that has been moved or removed, the destination application will provide an error message, warning you that it cannot find the application needed to create the object.

MASTERING THE OPPORTUNITIES

Working with OLE in Office 2000

OLE requires a source application that can create an OLE object (an *OLE server*) and a destination application that can accept OLE objects (an *OLE client*). Excel, Word, and PowerPoint are both servers and clients: they can create and accept OLE objects. Access and Outlook are OLE clients, but not OLE servers; they cannot create OLE objects. You can paste Access tables, fields, or records and Outlook items in Excel or Word but the result will be an Excel worksheet or a Word table, not an object. Selections pasted from Access and Outlook can't be linked. As OLE clients, Access and Outlook accept objects from other applications. You can link or embed part of a Word document or Excel worksheet in an Access form or report or an Outlook item. You can also choose Insert ➢ Object (or, in Access, click the OLE Object button on the Form Design toolbar) to embed a new object or embed or link an existing file in an Access form or Outlook item.

When you create an Access table from an Excel worksheet, you don't use copy-and-paste. Access uses importing to create a new table from an Excel worksheet or create a link to a worksheet. To add an Excel worksheet as a table in an existing database, open the database in Access 2000. Choose File ➢ Get External Data ➢ Import (or Link Tables). Select Microsoft Excel in the Files Of Type control. Select the Excel workbook from the file list, and then follow the steps of the Import Wizard to create a table from the file. From Excel, you can choose Data ➢Convert To Access to convert a worksheet to a table. To create a new database from an Excel workbook, simply launch Access and open the Excel workbook to begin importing the workbook.

In Outlook, use the Import and Export Wizard (File ➢ Import And Export) to swap data with Excel and Access.

Inserting Clips and Graphics

You can insert multimedia files in any Office application, but each application gives you menu or toolbar access to the types of media objects you'd be likely to place. For example, PowerPoint is the only program that has Movies and Sounds as a choice on the Insert menu, which makes perfect sense. In every application, you begin by selecting Insert from the menu. If the type of media you want to insert is listed on the Insert menu, select it. If not, choose Object and choose the media type from the list in the Insert Object dialog box.

Adding Clips to Documents

The Microsoft Clip Gallery, included with Office 2000, has a broad selection of media clips. You access the Clip Gallery from Publisher, Word, Excel, and PowerPoint by choosing Insert ➤ Picture ➤ Clip Art. Click the tab for the appropriate file type, and select the media file you wish to insert. A toolbar appears so you can insert the clip, preview it, add it to a category, or find similar clips, as shown in Figure 36.8.

Click the Insert button to add the clip to your document.

FIGURE 36.8

The Clip Gallery con-tains pictures, movies, and sounds.

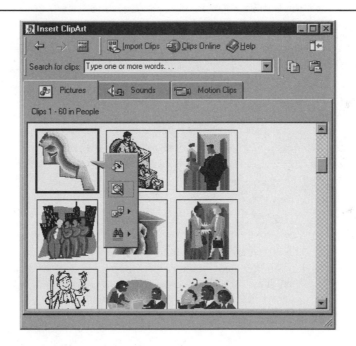

Even though the Insert menu choice says *Clip Art,* you can insert any of the files in the Gallery, including sound and video clips.

Improving Your Clip Collection

Microsoft adds new clips to their Web site every month. To download a new clip, click the Clips Online button in the Insert ClipArt dialog box (see Figure 36.8). You'll be connected to the Web site via the Internet so you can select and download new clips. The clips are automatically added to the Gallery.

PART

VIII

Integration and
Automation

Inserting Other Pictures

If the picture you want to insert isn't in the Clip Gallery, choose Insert ➢ Picture ➢ From File from the menu bar to open the Insert Picture dialog box. Locate and select the file. A preview appears in the right pane; if the file is large, it may take some time to load. Click Insert to insert the selected picture in your document.

You can add your frequently used picture files to the Clip Gallery for easy selection in Office 2000 applications. You can move or copy files to the gallery, or include a link to a file's location in the gallery. Click the Import Clips button in the Insert Clip Art dialog box (Insert ➢ Picture ➢ Clip Art) to open the Add Clip To Clip Art dialog box and add your files to the gallery.

Inserting Scanned Graphics

If a TWAIN-compliant scanner or digital camera is installed on your computer, you can scan images into Office 2000 using PhotoDraw, which is available from Microsoft. Choose Insert ➢ Picture ➢ From Scanner Or Camera, and the Photo Editor will launch. You'll be required to set some options; the specific options vary for different scanners and cameras. Make sure the document you want to scan is in the scanner (or that the image you wish to add is in the camera), and then click OK or Scan. After the image is loaded, you can alter it in PhotoDraw. (See PhotoDraw's online Help for more information.) When you close PhotoDraw, the image will be placed in your Office document.

 NOTE TWAIN (depending on whom you believe, either an acronym for Technology Without An Important Name or not an acronym at all) is a cross-platform standard interface that allows image files created with a scanner or digital camera to be inserted into compliant applications such as Microsoft Office. See http://www.twain.org to learn more about it.

Moving and Resizing Clips

To move a selected clip, drag it with the mouse. Drag the clip's handle to resize the clip; hold Shift while dragging to maintain the clip's proportions. You can resize a video clip as you can any other object by dragging a sizing handle. However, badly resized video is blurry and sometimes skips during playback. PowerPoint includes a resizing feature designed for video that sizes it at its best size for viewing. If you need to resize a video clip for an onscreen document in Word, Publisher, or Excel, consider placing the clip in PowerPoint, resizing it, and then cutting the clip and pasting it in the destination document.

To resize a video clip in PowerPoint, place the clip on a slide. In Slide view, select the clip and choose Format ➤ Picture to open the Format Picture dialog box. On the Size tab, enable the Best Scale For Slide Show check box, and then select the screen resolution commonly used by your viewers from the Resolution drop-down list. Click OK to resize the image and close the dialog box.

Modifying Pictures

After you've placed a picture from a file, a scanner, or the Clip Gallery, you can adjust the picture using the Picture toolbar. If the toolbar doesn't automatically appear, right-click and choose Show Picture Toolbar from the shortcut menu. For clip art, you may have to be a bit more aggressive: choose View ➤ Toolbars ➤ Picture from the menu, or right-click a toolbar and choose Picture from the shortcut menu. Table 36.1 describes the buttons on the Picture toolbar.

TABLE 36.1: PICTURE TOOLBAR BUTTONS

Button	Name	Use
	Insert Picture from File	Inserts another picture.
	Image Control	Lets you choose Automatic, Grayscale, Black & White, or Watermark format.
	More Contrast	Increases color intensity.
	Less Contrast	Decreases color intensity.
	More Brightness	Adds white to lighten the colors.
	Less Brightness	Adds black to darken the colors.
	Crop	Trims rectangular areas from the image.
	Line Style	Formats the border that surrounds the picture.
	Recolor Object	Lets you change individual colors in the object; only available in PowerPoint.
	Text Wrapping	Sets wrapping properties of surrounding text.

Continued ▶

PART

VIII

Integration and Automation

TABLE 36.1: PICTURE TOOLBAR BUTTONS (CONTINUED)		
Button	**Name**	**Use**
	Format Picture	One-stop shopping for picture properties.
	Set Transparent Color	Used like an eyedropper to make areas of the picture transparent. Used extensively for Web graphics.
	Reset Picture	Returns the picture to its original format.

The Crop, Recolor, and Set Transparent Object/Color buttons are used with areas of the picture. All other buttons affect the entire picture.

What's Next

Whether your computer is part of a large network or is a stand-alone computer with a modem connection to the Internet, Microsoft Office 2000 makes it easy to collaborate with others. In the next chapter, you'll learn how to share your work with others on the Internet using Web folders, discussion servers, and NetMeeting.

CHAPTER 37

Working Online with Office 2000

The Office 2000 programs allow you to work on a local network, intranet, or the Internet in a variety of ways: commenting on Office documents, collaborating in real time, and saving documents on Web servers. Much of this Web functionality is new or improved with this version of Office, so mastering these features quickly is a good way to be known as the online guru in your company or workgroup.

Understanding Web Servers

A *Web server* is a file server at a Web site that serves files to a *client* (a Web browser) in response to an HTTP request (HTTP, the Hypertext Transfer Protocol, is the technical standard or specification behind the Internet's World Wide Web and corporate intranets or Webs). When you save an Office document in a Web folder, view a page in a browser, or add a page to your organization's intranet, you're relying on a Web server.

A *Web discussion server* is Microsoft's term for a Web server that includes the *Office Server Extensions (OSE)*. You need access to a Web discussion server to start or participate in Web discussions based on Word, Excel, or PowerPoint documents. OSE, included with Office 2000, allow Web servers to support discussions. OSE can be installed on a Windows NT Server or on a workstation that already includes Web server software such as Microsoft's Internet Information Server or the Personal Web Server included with Office 2000. Information on system requirements for OSE is included on the Office 2000 CDs. *Web folders* are shortcuts to folders on Web servers where you have permission to read and/or write documents.

An *FTP server*, or *File Transfer Protocol server*, is a server that can send files in response to an FTP request. (The File Transfer Protocol is one of the Internet's oldest standards, first used long before the rise of the Web and still considered the most efficient way to exchange files.) When you download a file from an Internet Web site, you're using an FTP server. If you need to send a relatively small file to a group of users, you probably attach it to an Outlook e-mail message. However, Internet Service Providers (ISPs) typically limit the size of messages that e-mail users can receive as well as the amount of space they can use to store messages. If you have to deliver (or give users who aren't on your network access to) files in excess of 5MB over the Internet, you'll want to know how to save files on an FTP server.

Microsoft NetMeeting is included with Internet Explorer 5. To hold a NetMeeting, you access a *directory server*. Microsoft, Bigfoot, and other companies provide free access to directory servers. *NetShow servers* are used to broadcast PowerPoint 2000 presentations over an intranet or the Internet. See Chapter 46 for more information about presentation broadcasting.

Adding Web Folders to a Server

Add Web
Folder

Before you can save to a Web folder, you need to secure permission and get the information (such as the folder's URL) required to add the Web folder to your folder list. If you want to use Web folders on the Internet, talk to your ISP to see if their server supports Web folders. For a corporate intranet, speak with your system administrator.

To add one or more Web folders, open My Computer or Windows Explorer. Select Web Folders in the Folders pane. In the Files pane, double-click the Add New Web Folder icon to start the Add New Web Folder Wizard.

You can also start the wizard from any Open or Save As dialog box in Office by choosing Web Folders on the Places bar and then clicking the New Folder button. In the first step of the wizard, enter the URL for the Web folder you want to add as shown in Figure 37.1, or click the Browse button to launch your browser and search for the folder online.

FIGURE 37.1

*Enter or browse for
your folder's URL.*

PART

VIII

Integration and
Automation

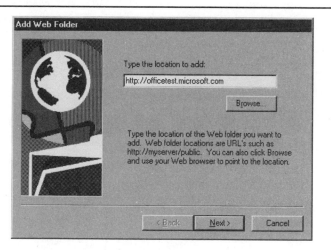

When you click Next, the wizard will attempt to verify your information. If you use a dial-up connection to the folder, the wizard will make the dial-up connection. You may be prompted to enter a login name and password to attach to the Web folder. In the next step, enter the name you'll use to refer to the Web folder, and click Finish to create the folder.

To save a file in your folder, click Web Folders in the Places bar of the Save As dialog box to display your list of Web folders. As a file is being saved or opened, Office 2000 displays a Transferring File progress meter. Treat the Web folder as you would other folders, subject to the restrictions placed on the folder by the provider. For example, you may be limited to 10MB of storage or two levels of subfolders in your Web folder. Copy, move, delete, and rename files and folders using the Windows Explorer. Save and open files or create folders in the Office 2000 Save As and Open dialog boxes.

 TIP If your Web folder is on a Web server running the Office Server Extensions, you can use your browser to look at the files in the Web folder.

Saving to an FTP Location

 If you've downloaded programs or add-ins from Microsoft or other software companies, you've used an FTP site. If you need to distribute large files to business partners, you may want to save them on an FTP server, so that your users can download the files when they need them. Before you can save a file to an FTP site, you have to add the site to your list of FTP Locations—and before you can do that, you'll need to talk to your system administrator and your ISP or Web server administrator to get permissions and settings that you'll need to add the site.

To add the FTP site to your list, open any Office 2000 Open or Save As dialog box. Open the Look In or Save In drop-down list, and you'll see Add/Modify FTP Locations at the bottom of the list:

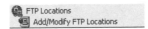

Choose the shortcut to open the Add/Modify FTP Location dialog box, shown in Figure 37.2. Type the URL for the FTP site, omitting the `ftp://` prefix. If you have a user name at the site, select the User option and enter the name. If you also enter your password here, you won't be prompted to type it each time you save files. (Your system administrator may not think it's OK to bypass this security feature, and we're not actually recommending it.) Click Add to add the FTP location to the list and begin adding another location. Click OK when you have finished. The FTP site will then appear at the bottom of the Look In and Save As lists in Open and Save As dialog boxes.

FIGURE 37.2

*Adding a new FTP
location*

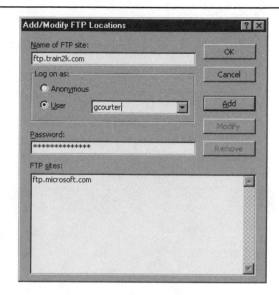

Using Web Discussions to Work on Documents

One of the most useful workgroup features in Office 2000 is a *Web discussion*, an online client/server feature that allows several users to collaborate on a document by inserting comments. Discussion comments are *threaded*, so you and your collaborators can ask questions, respond to comments, and get replies as you would using an e-mail client. Web discussions give you the opportunity to get lots of feedback on a Word document, Excel worksheet, or PowerPoint presentation on the way to creating your final document.

NOTE The Office Server Extensions (OSE) must be installed on your server if you want to use the Web Discussion and Subscription features. You can install OSE on a workstation that includes a Web server such as the Personal Web Server installed with FrontPage 2000.

Starting and Viewing Discussions

Before starting a discussion, you must save the Office 2000 document you wish to discuss. Place your insertion point in the part of the document you wish to discuss and choose Tools ➤ Online Collaboration ➤ Web Discussions from the menu. The first time you set up a Web discussion, the Add Or Edit Discussion Servers dialog box, shown in Figure 37.3, will open so you can specify a server.

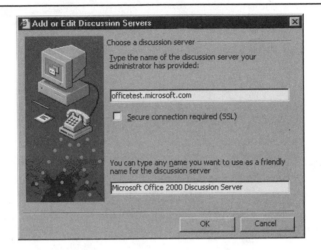

Enter the server name provided by your system administrator, enable SSL (Secure Sockets Layer) if required, type a friendly name you'll use to refer to the server, and click OK. The Office 2000 application will connect to the server and open the Discussion Options dialog box, shown here:

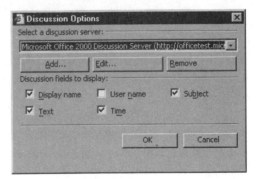

If you've set up more than one discussion server, select the server you wish to use. Enable or disable the types of information that should be displayed in the discussion, and then click OK to open the Enter Discussion Text dialog box, shown in Figure 37.4. Enter your discussion subject (like the subject of an e-mail message) and your text, and then click OK to post the comment.

FIGURE 37.4

*Enter your comment in
the Enter Discussion
Text dialog box.*

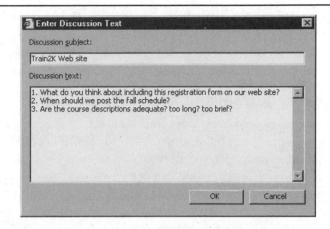

The posted comment appears in a discussion pane at the bottom of the document above the Discussion toolbar, as shown in Figure 37.5. The text header displays the options you enabled in the Discussion Options dialog box.

Use the Show/Hide Discussion Pane button to hide or redisplay the discussion pane.

FIGURE 37.5

*Discussions appear in
a separate pane.*

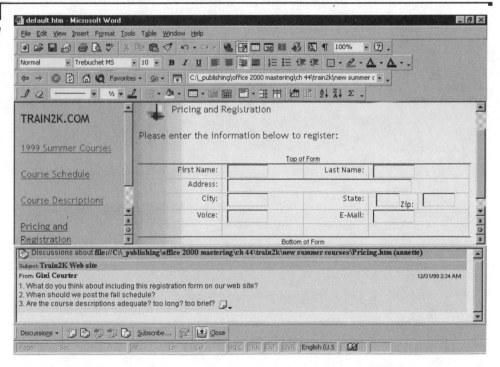

Editing, Deleting, and Replying to Comments

A comment icon is placed at the end of the text (see Figure 37.5). The author of a comment can edit or delete the comment by right-clicking on the icon to display the shortcut menu. Other users use the same icon to reply to a comment.

Discussions in and about Documents

There are two types of discussion comments: those *in* a document, and those *about* a document. By default, comments are placed in a document. The assumption is that discussion participants want to talk about document content.

 To start a new discussion in a document, click the Insert Discussion In This Document button. However, you may wish to start a discussion about the entire document—where it should be distributed, how many copies should be printed, who should have final editorial approval, and so on.

 Start a discussion *about* a document by clicking the Insert Discussion About The Document button.

  After other users have added comments, you can use the Previous and Next buttons to scroll through their comments in the discussion pane. To view a subset of the comments in a document, click the Discussions button and choose Filter Discussions to open the Filter Discussions dialog box. In the Filter Discussions dialog box, select a particular user or timeframe to display, and then click OK:

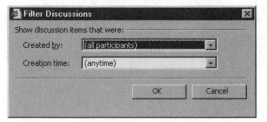

 To show all the discussions pertaining to a document, click the General Discussions button.

 When you're finished reviewing and making comments, you can close the Discussions toolbar to gain some space in your document window. To display the toolbar, choose Tools ➤ Online Collaboration ➤ Web Discussions again; you can't select the Discussions toolbar from the View menu or the command bar shortcut menu.

Subscribing to a Document

It's not unusual to send e-mail to colleagues asking them to examine a document. You can attach the document to the e-mail message or send a shortcut, but either way, it's your notification that prompts them to look. When you're working toward a deadline, it's easy to forget to send the e-mail. *Subscriptions* provide an alternative. When your colleagues subscribe to your Web document, they're notified when the document is edited, moved, or deleted. They can also subscribe to the entire Web folder that holds a project. Folder subscribers are notified when a folder is edited, moved, or deleted, or a new document is created in the Web folder. Subscriptions are designed to facilitate Web discussions; with subscriptions, you don't have to open the discussion document periodically just to see if there are changes or comments you need to respond to.

Subscribe...

To subscribe to a document or folder, open the document (or a document in the folder you want to subscribe to). Click the Subscribe button on the Discussions toolbar to open the Document Subscription dialog box, shown in Figure 37.6.

PART VIII

FIGURE 37.6

Setting up a subscription to a file

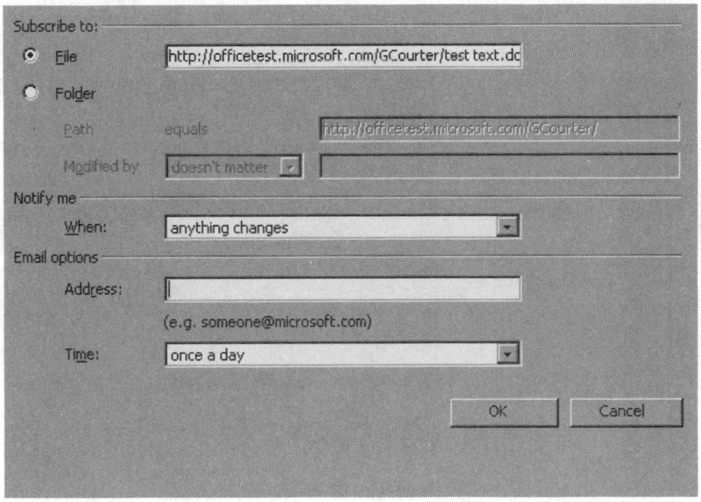

Integration and Automation

In th Subscribe To area, select either File or Folder. The folder that contains the current document is entered by default, but you can type the URL for another folder. Choose which type of event should trigger notification from the When drop-down list. For the Address, enter the e-mail address you want the notification sent to. In the Time list, choose to be notified of any changes immediately, daily, or weekly. Click OK to submit your subscription. In a few seconds, you'll be notified that your subscription has begun:

Many subscription notification messages include a link you can click to unsubscribe. Clicking the link launches your browser and opens a form so you can confirm deleting your subscription.

Setting Up an Online Meeting

Microsoft NetMeeting, included with Internet Explorer 4 and 5, is a toolkit for remote meetings. The tools include chat, a whiteboard for illustrating concepts, video, audio, file sharing, and online collaboration in Word, Excel, and PowerPoint documents. You need a camera and video card in order to send video, but no extra hardware is required to see video sent by other participants. You'll need a sound card and speakers to use any of the audio capabilities of NetMeeting, and a microphone to add your own voice to the discussion. But you can use NetMeeting even without video or audio. Many companies encourage the use of NetMeeting for group work when it isn't possible or convenient to gather at one location. For information about using NetMeeting, choose Help on the NetMeeting menu.

In Office 2000, you can invite participants to an online meeting using the Outlook Calendar. In the Meeting Request form, enable the This Is An Online Meeting check box before sending the meeting request, as shown in Figure 37.7.

Select a location for the meeting from the drop-down list of servers. There is no charge for using NetMeeting servers. If you want to collaborate on a document, enter the full path and filename or click the Browse button and select the document you'll use. The document's application must support the Office 2000 Online Collaboration features (so it's safest to use Word, Excel, or PowerPoint documents). Enable the AutoStart options to have Outlook automatically launch NetMeeting and log on to the server prior to the call. The amount of time prior to the call is your default Reminder interval for Outlook 2000. To change the interval, change the Reminder.

If you haven't used NetMeeting before, the NetMeeting Wizard opens so you can create a directory listing and test your sound card, speakers, and microphone. Work through the steps in the wizard so you're prepared for the meeting.

FIGURE 37.7

Inviting attendees to an online meeting

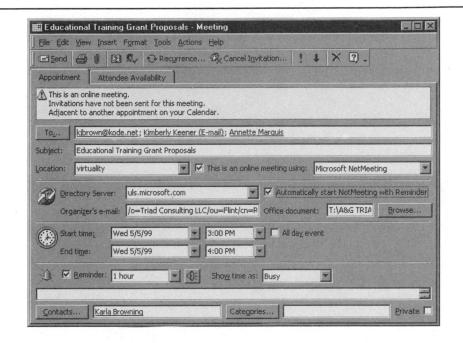

Starting Meetings Immediately

You don't have to schedule meetings in advance. If you're in the middle of a telephone conversation about a project, you can decide to move to a more visual conversation with just a few clicks.

You can start an immediate NetMeeting with an Outlook contact. Select the contact, and then choose Actions ➢ Call Using NetMeeting from the Outlook menu bar.

In Word, Excel, or PowerPoint, choose Tools ➢ Online Collaboration ➢ Meet Now to select a server and launch NetMeeting. Or click the NetMeeting button on the Windows taskbar to connect to a NetMeeting server. Your counterpart will need to log on to the same server and will then be able to select you from the list of users for a conversation.

What's Next

In the next chapter, you'll learn how to customize the Office 2000 user interface, including toolbars, menu bars, and other options to make routine tasks easier.

CHAPTER <u>38</u>

Customizing the Office Environment

FEATURING:

*Working with the Microsoft Office
Shortcut Bar*

Creating Taskbar shortcuts

Customizing application command bars

Customizing shortcut menus

Setting application options

As you work in Office 2000, you'll develop your own approach to routine Office tasks. While there may be a plethora of ways to get a job done, you'll generally use only one or two of those methods. Adding your frequently used programs to your favorite launch point, customizing command bars, and setting personalized application options will help you work more efficiently in all the Office 2000 applications.

Customizing the Office 2000 Shortcut Bar

When you install Office 2000, the Shortcut Bar is automatically added to the Windows Startup group. The Shortcut Bar is a collection of toolbars designed to provide quick access to commonly used functions: opening documents, creating tasks in Outlook, or launching your browser. The Office Shortcut Bar behaves the same way as application toolbars do. The default location for the Shortcut Bar is the right edge of your screen, but, like the Taskbar, it can be dragged to any edge of the screen; the Shortcut Bar illustrated below was placed at the top of the screen, so it's horizontal. If you drag the bar into the Desktop, the Shortcut Bar becomes a palette.

 NOTE The Shortcut Bar contains more than one toolbar. The toolbar shown here is the Office toolbar, but your Shortcut Bar may be displaying another toolbar, such as the Favorites toolbar. Click the Office button to display the Office toolbar.

 A small Office icon appears in the upper-left corner of the Shortcut Bar. Click the icon to open the menu shown here:

Choosing Restore restores the minimized Shortcut Bar to its prior location. Minimize minimizes the Shortcut Bar. As with the Windows Taskbar, AutoHide hides the Shortcut Bar, giving you more space on the Desktop. When you point to the edge of the screen where the bar is located, it is automatically displayed. If you AutoHide the Windows Taskbar, you can also AutoHide the Shortcut Bar, but you must place it on a different edge of the screen.

The Customize option lets you change the properties of the Shortcut Bar. If you want help with the Shortcut Bar, choose Contents and Index. About Microsoft Office displays your Office 2000 license number and gives you direct access to your computer's system information. Exit closes the Shortcut Bar; when you close the Shortcut Bar, a dialog box opens, asking whether you wish to display the bar the next time Windows is launched. To display the bar again without restarting Windows, choose the bar from the Startup menu (Start ➤ Programs ➤ Startup ➤ Office Shortcut Bar).

The default toolbar displayed in the Shortcut Bar is the Office toolbar. The Shortcut Bar creates another toolbar with the contents of the Favorites folder. It's configured to create other toolbars for the Programs menu, Accessories, and your Desktop. To create one of the preconfigured toolbars, right-click the Shortcut Bar's background to open the shortcut menu:

Choose the toolbar you want, and it will be created for you. A message box briefly appears, letting you know that the toolbar is being created. To display any other toolbar, click its icon in the Shortcut Bar.

If you have a lot of program groups (like Microsoft Office or Accessories) on your Programs menu, the Programs toolbar won't be very useful, as you'll have a toolbar linked to lots of program group folders. Clicking a program group button won't launch an application; instead, it will open the group folder in a window. Then, you have to select the application you wish to run and close the window. Fortunately, you can customize each of the Shortcut Bar's toolbars, removing the useless buttons and adding buttons for the programs and folders you use frequently. Right-click in the bar's background area and select Customize from the menu to open the Customize dialog box, shown in Figure 38.1. If you mistakenly right-click a button, you'll know it because the shortcut menu for individual buttons doesn't include Customize.

FIGURE 38.1

*Use the Customize
dialog box to change
Shortcut Bar properties.*

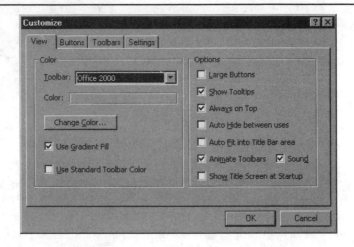

The Customize dialog box has four pages of settings: View, Buttons, Toolbars, and Settings. The View page, shown in Figure 38.1, includes options for the colors of individual toolbars on the left side and Shortcut Bar options on the right side. To change a toolbar's background color, first select the toolbar from the drop-down list. To use the Windows color scheme in your toolbars, enable the Use Standard Toolbar Color check box. To select other colors, click the Change Color button to open the Color dialog box. Select a color, or click the Custom Color button to mix a color using the Color Picker. Select the Use Gradient Fill and Smooth options if you wish.

 TIP If the toolbar you want to customize doesn't appear in the list, switch to the Toolbars page and turn it on.

The options on the right side of the View page apply to the entire Shortcut Bar:

Large Buttons: Makes the buttons easier to see, but the Shortcut Bar will take up more space on the Desktop.

Show Tooltips: Enabled by default, so when you point to a button the button's name is displayed.

Always On Top: Also on by default, this prevents application windows from encroaching on the Shortcut Bar.

AutoHide Between Uses: The same as the option available from the shortcut menu.

AutoFit Into Title Bar Area: Places the Shortcut Bar in the title bar of the active application. At most screen resolutions, this shrinks the buttons, making them hard to see.

Animate Toolbars: This sounds much more exciting than it is. When you click (for example) the Programs toolbar button, the Programs toolbar slides into the Shortcut Bar.

Sound: With this enabled, the switch to another toolbar is accompanied by a "whoosh" sound.

Show Title Screen At Startup: Displays the Office 2000 splash screen when the Shortcut Bar is loaded.

On the Buttons page (see Figure 38.2), you can remove buttons, add files or folders, and rearrange the toolbar buttons. To add a button to the Office toolbar, first select Office from the Toolbar list, and then click the check box in front of the application. Use the ↑ and ↓ buttons on the page to move a selected item up (or left when the Shortcut Bar is displayed horizontally) or down the list. Use the Add Space button to insert a space between the selected button and the next button on the list.

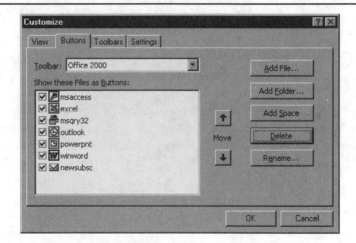

The Add File button lets you add other applications to a toolbar so all your frequently used programs are in one place.

On the Toolbars page (Figure 38.3), you can display, hide, and create toolbars. Use the check boxes to select the toolbars you want to display. To delete a toolbar permanently, click Remove; use the Rename button to change the name of the selected toolbar. Moving toolbars up or down changes the order of the toolbar button on the Shortcut Bar.

WARNING If you remove one of the toolbars that is included with the Shortcut Bar, you'll have to run the Office installation program to get it back.

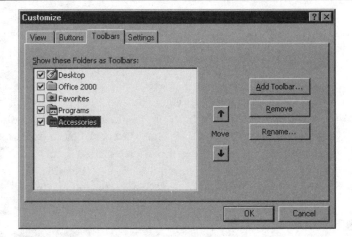

On the Toolbars page, you can add a blank toolbar and populate it with files and folders, or use the contents of a folder to create a new toolbar. (Office uses the second method to create the Desktop and Programs toolbars using the Desktop and Programs folders.) To create a new toolbar, click the Add Toolbar button to open the Add Toolbar dialog box. Enter the name for a blank toolbar, or select the Make Toolbar For This Folder option and click the Browse button to select the folder. A toolbar made from a folder will have the folder's name; you can use the Rename button to change the name after it's created.

The Settings page (Figure 38.4) isn't related only to the Shortcut Bar, but sets the default location for the templates used by all Office applications. To change the settings for the templates on your local drive, change the User Templates location. The default setting is provided by Office during installation; you should only modify it if you've actually moved the templates to another location. Workgroup Templates are generally stored on a network file server. You'll usually have to modify this setting so that Office can locate templates you share with your co-workers.

FIGURE 38.4

The Settings page of the Shortcut Bar dialog box is used to modify the location for templates.

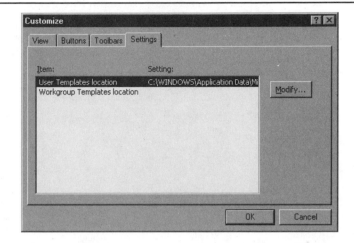

PART

VIII

Integration and Automation

Customizing Application Menus and Toolbars

Office 2000 is designed to create an environment that supports the way you use each application. When you initially launch an Office application, it displays by default a "Personal" toolbar, containing the most frequently used buttons from the Standard and Formatting toolbars, and a menu bar with similarly limited options. What makes these command bars "personal" is that as you use menu selections and toolbar buttons, they are added to the menu or toolbar. When an entire toolbar cannot be displayed, the buttons you have used most recently are displayed, and others are hidden. For many users, this is enough customization. And for some of us, spontaneously regenerating toolbars are a bit too much customization. If you want to control which menu options and toolbar buttons are visible, you can customize all of the menu bars, toolbars, and shortcut menus.

Changing Command Bar Options

To access options for command bars, right-click any Office 2000 toolbar or menu bar and choose Customize from the shortcut menu to open the Customize dialog box. Click the Options tab to view the options for menus and toolbars (see Figure 38.5).

FIGURE 38.5

You can change command bar options in the Customize dialog box.

Two options in this dialog box are specific to the application: Standard And Formatting Toolbars Share One Row, and Reset My Usage Data. All the other options affect all of Office 2000, regardless of which application you set them in:

Standard And Formatting Toolbars Share One Row: Enabled by default. Turn off the check box to stack the toolbars, resulting in more room to display buttons.

Menus Show Recently Used Commands First: With this option (enabled by default), each application shows you a personalized menu (short menu) with the commands you use frequently. Turn this off, and you'll see full menus in all applications.

Show Full Menus After A Short Delay: If you like personalized menus, you will generally want to leave this turned on, or you'll never get to see the items you don't select without customizing the menu to add items.

Reset My Usage Data: For menus to be personalized, there has to be a mechanism for tracking how often you use different menu options and toolbar buttons. Office tracks and saves your *usage data* when you close each application. This button resets the buttons displayed when a toolbar is not wide enough to display all the buttons and the menu commands shown in the personalized menu.

Large Icons: Intended for users with limited vision, these are truly large. Just turn them on for a moment, and you'll either love them or rush to return them to their normal size.

List Font Names In Their Fonts: This option affects only the Font drop-down list on the Formatting toolbar. It makes it easier to choose a font, but you take a slight performance hit, particularly if you have a large number of fonts installed on your computer.

ScreenTips: Formerly called ToolTips, these are enabled by default; remember that turning them off here turns them off throughout Office.

Menu Animations: Although interesting initially, these effects (Unfold, Slide, and Random) can get cloying rather quickly. Animation is disabled by default.

After you've changed the options, click OK to close the Customize dialog box and apply the options you chose.

 TIP To make command bars appear and behave as they did in Office 97, disable two check boxes: Standard And Formatting Toolbars Share One Row, and Menus Show Recently Used Commands First.

Customizing Command Bars

While the Customize dialog box is open, all displayed command bars are open for editing. Drag menu items or buttons to new locations to rearrange them, or drop them in the document window to delete them. To add a toolbar button or menu command, click the Commands page of the Customize dialog box. The Commands page from Word is shown in Figure 38.6. In the other Office applications, there is no Save In text box on the Commands page.

Drag commands from the Commands page to a toolbar or menu.

Commands are grouped into categories. Choose a category in the Categories pane, and then locate the command you want to add in the Commands pane. (Click the Description button to see a brief description of the selected command.) Drag the command onto a toolbar or the menu bar. To add a command to an existing menu, point to the menu, and then place the command in the appropriate place when the menu opens.

 NOTE Choosing the Macros category displays a list of macros that can be added to command bars. See Chapter 39 for more information about creating macros in Office 2000.

You can rearrange, delete, or display toolbar buttons and menu items without opening the Customize dialog box. Simply hold the Alt key while you drag the command.

 Each toolbar has its own set of *built-in buttons*. To quickly add or remove built-in buttons on a toolbar, click the More Buttons drop-down arrow, and choose Add or Remove Buttons from the menu. Buttons displayed on the menu have a check mark. Click the button name to add or remove the button from the toolbar.

 TIP The default settings for an application's built-in menu and toolbars are retained even after you customize the menu or toolbar. To return a command bar to its original settings, switch to the Toolbars page of the Customize dialog box, select the command bar, and then click Reset.

You aren't limited to the built-in toolbars. Creating a new toolbar gives you the opportunity to gather all the toolbar buttons you frequently use into one place. To create an entirely new toolbar, click the New button on the Toolbar page of the Customize dialog box. You'll be prompted for a new toolbar name, and the application will open the toolbar. Drag buttons onto the toolbar from the Commands list. To copy a button from an existing toolbar, hold Ctrl while dragging the button.

Adding or Modifying Shortcut Keys

Click the Keyboard button in the Customize dialog box to open the Customize Keyboard dialog box, shown in Figure 38.7. (This option is not available in Outlook.)

PART

VIII

Integration and
Automation

FIGURE 38.7

Change or add short-cut keystrokes in the Customize Keyboard dialog box.

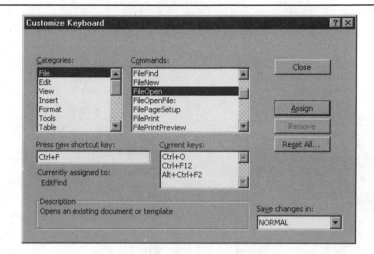

Choose the command you wish to add shortcut keys for. A description of the command appears in the Description section of the dialog box. Existing shortcut combinations for the command are displayed in the Current Keys list (in Figure 38.7 you can see the three preset combinations for File ➤ Open). If there's already a combination, you may just want to memorize it, or you can add another shortcut combination.

To add a shortcut combination for the selected command, click in the Press New Shortcut Key text box and execute the keystroke combination. If the combination is already assigned to another command, that information will appear just below the text box. In Figure 38.7, the keystroke combination entered is already used for the Find command on the Edit menu. Click Assign to assign the shortcut to the command, overwriting the current assignment, or select the information in the Press New Shortcut Key textbox and try again. When you have finished creating keyboard shortcuts, close the dialog box.

 WARNING Beware of using Alt-key combinations for keyboard shortcuts. Nearly all are used, but the keyboard customization routine doesn't seem to know it. For example, if you enter Alt+F as a shortcut, the Customize Keyboard dialog box will tell you that it's currently unassigned although it's the keyboard shortcut used to open the File menu in every Windows program, including the Office 2000 applications.

Customizing a Shortcut Menu

This is the first version of Office that allows you to customize the shortcut menus. You can't create or delete shortcut menus, but in some applications you can customize them as you would other command bars. On the Toolbars page of the Customize dialog box in Word, PowerPoint, or Access, enable the Shortcut Menus check box. A small toolbar with the three categories of shortcut menus opens:

Click a category to open its list of shortcut menus. Choose the menu you want to customize, as shown in Figure 38.8. With the menu open, add commands by dragging them from the Commands page of the Customize dialog box. Delete commands by dragging them from the menu. You can right-click shortcut menu items and change their options as you would command bar item options.

FIGURE 38.8

Even shortcut menus can be customized in Office 2000.

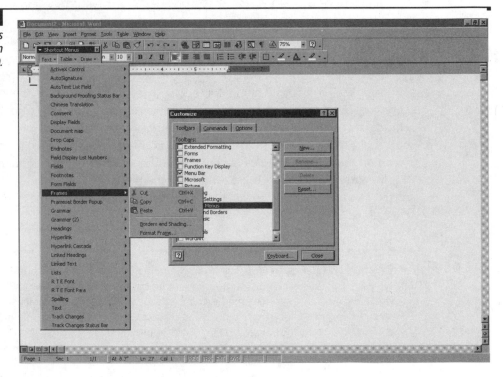

Changing Command Bar Item Options

While the Customize dialog box is open, you can change the properties of toolbar buttons and menu items. Right-click a button to display the shortcut menu:

Table 38.1 summarizes the customization options available for individual command bar items.

PART

VIII

TABLE 38.1: COMMAND BAR ITEM OPTIONS

Item	Use
Reset	Returns the item to its original image and style.
Delete	Removes the item from the command bar.
Name	Shows the name that will be displayed for the command. The ampersand (&) appears before the "hotkey" letter, which will be underlined.
Copy Button Image	Copies the image so it can be pasted onto another button.
Paste Button Image	Pastes an image from the Clipboard.
Reset Button Image	Restores the default image for the button.
Edit Button Image	Opens the Button Editor. Some button images cannot be edited or changed.
Change Button Image	Displays a palette of button images.
Default Style	Displays the command or button in its default style: buttons for toolbars, text for menu items.
Text Only (Always)	Displays text without an image, whether the command is displayed on a toolbar or menu.

Continued ▶

TABLE 38.1: COMMAND BAR ITEM OPTIONS (CONTINUED)

Item	Use
Text Only (Menu)	Displays text without an image on a menu, and the default image on toolbars.
Image and Text	Displays text and an image.
Begin a Group	Places group dividers on either side of a button, or above and below a menu command.
Assign Hyperlink	Creates a hyperlink to open a Web page or document, or insert a picture in the current document.

This is a good place to point out that you shouldn't change the built-in toolbars for Office 2000 if you share your computer with your colleagues. Removing menu commands or changing the image on the Copy button to the image for the Paste button is a swift and reliable way to decrease workplace harmony.

MASTERING THE OPPORTUNITIES

Creating Document-Specific Command Bars in Word

Creating and displaying toolbars for a specific document used to require Visual Basic code. With Word 2000, you can easily create customized menus, shortcuts, and toolbars for individual documents.

You can save a customized command bar or set of shortcut keys in the Normal template (NORMAL.DOT), any other active template, or a specific document. The Normal template is loaded each time Word is launched; so customizations saved in Normal become the new default command bars. When you save in another template, the command bars and shortcuts are loaded when the template is loaded. If you save changes in the current document, the customized items are only displayed when the document is opened. Use the Save In drop-down list on the Commands page of the Customize dialog box (see Figure 38.6) to choose where to save your customized command bars before clicking OK to close the dialog box. For keyboard shortcuts, use the Save In list in the Customize Keyboard dialog box.

The Assign Hyperlink command bar option opens up some creative opportunities for presentation of online Word documents. You can create a Supporting Documents toolbar that contains links to other documents and Web pages that your reader might be interested in. Save the customization in the document, and the Supporting Documents toolbar will be loaded each time the document is opened.

Setting Application Options

Each Office 2000 application has other user-customizable option settings. Outlook has the widest range of option settings because of the number of modules and the large number of options related to electronic mail. Publisher wins the award for the fewest options.

Options control overall application appearance and behavior. In Excel, for example, option settings determine whether you see sheet tabs, where the cell pointer goes when you press Enter, and how zero values are treated in series charts. In Outlook, Rich Text Format for messages is an option; a mail option determines whether the text of an original message is included in a reply. Word's scroll bars appear or disappear based on an option setting. If an Office program behaves differently than you think it should or remember it did, it's a good idea to check the option settings. To open the Options dialog box in any Office 2000 application, choose Tools ➤ Options from the menu bar. The Options dialog box for Excel is shown in Figure 38.9.

PART

VIII

Integration and
Automation

FIGURE 38.9

Option settings control application behavior.

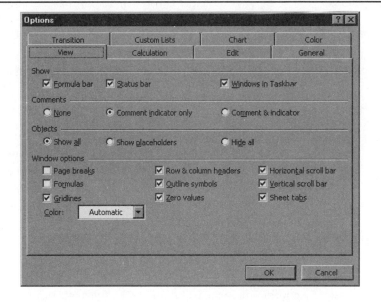

In every application, the settings on the General page include global settings that are required when the application launches such as the number of recently opened files to display on the File menu and the default file location. The View options display or hide features like scroll bars and the application status bar. Edit options determine how the application should respond to your actions (like selecting and dragging text or cells). Other options differ between applications. Table 38.2 lists the types of option settings available in each Office 2000 application.

TABLE 38.2: OFFICE 2000 OPTIONS

Application	Types of Options
Access	Advanced, Datasheet, Edit/Find, Forms/Report, General, Keyboard, Tables/Queries, View
Excel	Calculation, Chart, Color, Custom Lists, Edit, General, View
FrontPage	Configure Editor, General, Reports View, AutoThumbnail, Compatibility, Color Coding, Default Font, General, HTML Source, Spelling
Outlook	Delegates, Internet E-mail, Mail Format, Mail Services, Other, Preferences, Security, Spelling
PowerPoint	Edit, General, Print, Save, Spelling & Grammar, View
Publisher	General, Edit, User Assistance, Print
Word	Compatibility, Edit, File Locations, General, Print, Save, Spelling & Grammar, Track Changes, User Information, View

To change options, choose Tools ➤ Options to open the dialog box. If you have a question about a specific option, click the Office Assistant button for fast help on the option. After changing option settings, click OK to close the dialog box and apply the changes.

What's Next

Chapter 39 focuses on automating Office 2000 applications with macros and Visual Basic. By combining those techniques with the skills from this chapter, you'll be able to create customized documents and simple Office applications for yourself or your colleagues.

CHAPTER 39

Using Macros and Visual Basic in Office 2000

FEATURING:

Creating macros using the Macro Recorder

Creating macros in Access

Creating command bars in Access

Understanding Automation

Using the Visual Basic Editor

Using controls to create a user interface

Creating Access switchboards

Office 2000 is more than just the applications you install from CD or your network. In the previous three chapters, you've seen numerous tools for customizing Office 2000 applications and tailoring them to your business needs. This chapter looks at the most powerful Office customization tool of all—its *programmability*. In all the Office applications except Publisher, you can create your own software telling Office exactly how you want it to work. You'll use Visual Basic (VB) to program in Office 2000. There are essentially two ways to create VB programs. The simplest method, available in Word, Excel, and PowerPoint, is to record *macros*—VB programs that run within a host application (there's no such thing as a "stand-alone macro"). Or, if you're already familiar with Visual Basic, you can create Office macros by opening a VB module and typing code. You'll learn about Visual Basic and Visual Basic for Applications later in this chapter, but you don't have to know how to program in any version of VB to create macros in Office 2000. Most of the Office 2000 applications include recorders or macro windows to help you create code. We'll begin our work using these macro-creation tools.

Creating Macros in Word, Excel, and PowerPoint

In Word, Excel, and PowerPoint, you can use the Macro Recorder to create macros. You turn on the recorder, complete the steps you want to repeat, and then save the macro. The next time you need to complete the steps, you run the macro. Before recording a macro, you should practice the steps you want to record, because once you begin recording, all your actions are recorded, mistakes included. Take note of the conditions your macro will operate under and set up those conditions. Will you always use the macro in a specific document? If so, open the document. Will the macro be used to change or format selected text or numbers? Then have the text or numbers selected before you begin recording the macro, just as you will when you run the macro at a later time.

When you have practiced the steps and set up the same conditions the macro will run under, select Tools ➢ Macro ➢ Record New Macro to open the Record New Macro dialog box. The Excel Record New Macro dialog box is shown in Figure 39.1.

The suggested name is Macro1. (Microsoft didn't waste a lot of imagination here.) Enter a more descriptive name for the macro. Visual Basic names, including macro names, can be up to 255 characters long, and they can contain numbers, letters, and underscores but not spaces or other punctuation, and they must begin with a letter. You can enter uppercase and lowercase letters in a name; while Visual Basic will preserve your capitalization style, it is not case sensitive (that is, it won't recognize FixMyName and fixmyname as different names).

PART

VIII

Integration and
Automation

FIGURE 39.1

The Record Macro
dialog box in Excel

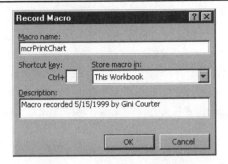

 TIP In both Word and Excel, any macro named AutoExec will run automatically when the application is opened.

If you're using a naming convention, you'll probably prefix the macro name with mcr for macro or bas for Visual Basic code. (Some companies only use the bas prefix, whether or not you create the macro with a macro recorder. Check the standards for your organization if you're not sure.) Enter a new description. If other users will have access to the macro, include your name and contact information (extension or e-mail address). Figure 39.2 shows the Record New Macro dialog box from Word.

FIGURE 39.2

The Record Macro
dialog box in Word

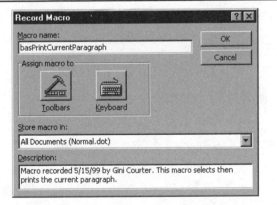

Storing a Macro

In the Store Macro In drop-down list, select the document you want the macro stored in. When you use the Macro Recorder in PowerPoint, you can store the macros you create in any open presentation. (Generally, you'll create macros in the presentation you intend to save them with.) In Word and Excel, a macro's storage location determines how you'll be able to access and run it later:

- If you select the current document (or another active document), the macro will only be available in that document. If you want the same macro somewhere else, you'll have to copy or re-create it. Macros that are stored in a document or workbook, including a template, are called local macros.

- Storing a Word macro in the default template (NORMAL.DOT) or an Excel macro in the Personal Macro Workbook creates a global macro, which is available to all documents created in the application.

From the description, you'd think that you should save every macro as a global macro, but all the global macros will be loaded each time you launch Excel or Word. They'll take up space in memory. And any macro names you use globally can't be reused in individual documents. Unless a macro is going to receive wide usage, it's best to store it in the current document.

In Excel, you can assign a shortcut keystroke combination to macros, and Word lets you assign a shortcut or place the macro on the toolbar. While you can assign macros to shortcut keys, you should use extreme caution when making assignments. Most of the Ctrl combinations and many of the Ctrl+Shift combinations are already in use. It's safer to assign frequently used macros to a command bar or a button. You don't have to make this decision when you record the macro; you can always add a macro to a command bar later (see "Customizing the User Interface" later in this chapter).

 MASTERING THE OPPORTUNITIES

Macro Storage and the User Interface

The decisions about where to store macros and where to place buttons or menu items that let users run the macros are related. Users should *always* be able to find the buttons for available macros. And they should *only* be able to see buttons if the macros are available. Clicking a button for a macro that the application can't find will result in an error message.

For example, let's say you're creating macros to automate an Excel workbook that will be distributed to your clients at a variety of locations. In this case, you should store the

Continued

Once you've set the options in the dialog box, click the OK button to begin macro recording. The message *Recording* is displayed at the left end of the status bar to show that you are recording a macro. The Stop Recording toolbar will open. The Macro Recorder records the actions you take, but not the delay between actions, so take your time. If you want the macro to enter text, enter the text now. Type carefully—if you make and correct a mistake, the mistake and correction will be included when you replay the macro until you edit the mistake (see "Working with the Visual Basic IDE"). To include menu commands in the macro, just make menu selections as you normally would.

When you are finished entering all the steps in the macro, click the Stop button on the Stop Recording toolbar. The toolbar will close automatically. You don't need to do anything special to save the macro now. Local macros are saved when you save the document. Excel saves global macros automatically, and Word will prompt you to save changes to NORMAL.DOT when you end your Word session.

TIP If you want to format text in a macro, choose the formatting options from a Format dialog box rather than clicking toolbar buttons to select font, font style, size, and alignment. If you use the buttons, the results when you run the macro would be unpredictable because the toolbar buttons are toggles. For example, if selected text is already italicized, clicking the Italics button will turn italics off.

PART

VIII

Integration and Automation

Cell References in Excel Macros

In Excel macros, all cell references are absolute by default. If you click in a cell during macro recording, the macro will select that exact cell each time you play it back. This wouldn't be terribly useful. For example, you might want to format cells, and then move to the cell below the selection. When you record the macro, the cell below the selection is J22. But each time you play the macro, you don't want Excel to select J22; you want to select the cell below the cells you just formatted.

To instruct Excel to use relative cell references, click the Use Relative References button on the macro toolbar. The macro will record references relative to the current cell until you click the button again to turn relative references off. Then you can record other actions using absolute references.

MASTERING THE OPPORTUNITIES

Updating Macros from Previous Versions

Older versions of Excel used a macro programming language called XLM. Visual Basic for Applications replaced XLM as the programming language beginning with Excel version 5. Excel 2000 supports both languages: if you have workbooks that contain XLM macros, Excel will let you play them. However, all new macros you create in Excel 2000 are recorded in VBA.

Word also had its own macro language, called Word Basic. When you open a Word document from a prior version that contains macros, Word automatically converts the macros. You will not be prompted. Some complex macros created in Word Basic will not run in Word 2000.

Running Macros from the Macros Dialog Box

It's always a good idea to save any documents you have open before you run a new macro. If you've made a mistake during recording, the playback results may not be what you expected.

TIP If there is an error, you can record the macro again using the same name. You may also have to click Undo a few times to back out of any problems the macro created.

To run a macro, choose Tools ➤ Macro ➤ Macros to open the Macro dialog box. The Word Macro dialog box is shown in Figure 39.3. (Writers spend a lot of time in Word, so we have an excessive number of macros.) Select the macro from the scroll list and click the Run button. The macro will execute. You can't enter text or choose menu options while the macro is executing. When the macro is done playing, the application will return control to you.

FIGURE 39.3

The Macro dialog box

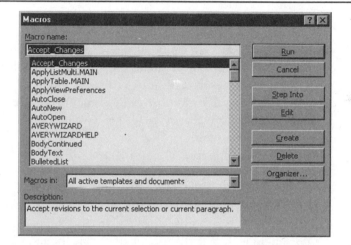

MASTERING TROUBLESHOOTING

Terminating a Macro during Execution

You can accidentally create a macro that won't be able to run to completion because it gets caught in a loop. Often this will happen when you make a logical error or a typing error while creating a macro in Visual Basic. If, for example, you write a macro that subtracts B9 from the value in cell B10 until B10 >=20, it will run forever, continually subtracting, if the initial value in B10 is already less than 20 (unless the value in B9 is negative).

When a macro won't stop on its own, you need to be able to terminate it. If you need to stop a macro during execution, press Ctrl+Break. A Visual Basic dialog box will open, offering you options to End program execution or Debug the macro in the Visual Basic Editor.

If Ctrl+Break doesn't stop macro execution, press Ctrl+Alt+Del once to open the Close Program dialog box. Select the application that contains the macro, and click the End Task button. When you reopen the application, you'll probably need to revert to the copy of the document that you saved before running the macro.

Deleting Macros

There are two ways to delete a macro. If you need to improve the way a recorded macro executes, you can record the macro again, using the same name. You will be asked if you want to overwrite the existing macro with the new one. If you no longer need a macro, you can choose Tools ➤ Macro, select the macro from the macro list, and click the Delete button to delete the macro from the template.

Opening a File That Contains Macros

If you can add code to an Office 2000 document, so can the people who write viruses. Viruses are self-replicating programs. When you open a document that contains a virus, the virus copies its code into the default template, effectively becoming a global virus. From that point forward, every document you save using that template will be infected, which means that every file you give to someone else on a disk or via the Internet will also contain the virus.

Office 2000 does not include virus detection software (although you should install some unless you never receive files from another computer by disk, network, or Internet connection). However, Word, PowerPoint, and Excel scan documents you open to see if the documents contain macros. The application notifies you if *any* macros exist in a workbook that you are trying to open. You can decide whether you want to open the document with macros enabled, or disable them:

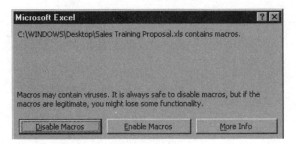

Disabling the macros gives you an opportunity to look at them in the Visual Basic Editor without endangering your computer. If you decide the macros are legitimate, just close the Visual Basic Editor and reopen the document. If you know that the workbook contains macros that you or a co-worker put there, choose Enable. If, on the other hand, you received the workbook unsolicited in an e-mail message from the Cosmic Hackers Union (or from a friend who just loves to pass along "cool" stuff from the Net), you should consider disabling the macros or not opening the file.

TIP The macro's code includes the macro's description (see Figures 39.1 and 39.2). This raises yet another good reason to always note your name and contact information when creating a macro: it gives other users less reason to delete the macro, and a way to reach you if they're still not sure.

Creating Macros in Access

Access doesn't include a Macro Recorder. Instead, you use the Macro window to create macros. In Access, choose Macro from the Objects list in the Database window and click the New button to open a new Macro window. The Macro window has two columns: Action and Comment. *Actions* are commands. Excel users often think of actions as the Access equivalent of functions. Like functions, actions have both required and optional arguments. Comments serve the same purpose as field descriptions in Table Design view; they allow you to document your design so that you or another developer can debug or change code when business rules change. In Figure 39.4, we've created a simple macro that exports a table to an Excel workbook and then displays a message confirming that the file has been exported. When the macro executes, the actions are executed in order.

PART

VIII

Integration and Automation

FIGURE 39.4

In Access, choose actions and their arguments to create macros.

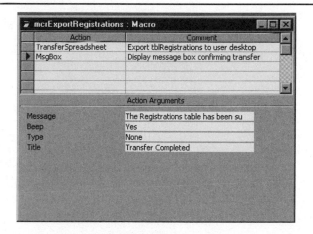

To create a macro, first select an action from the drop-down list. Controls for the action's arguments appear in the bottom pane. For the MsgBox action in Figure 39.4, there are very few arguments; all but the first and last arguments can be selected from drop-down lists. The TransferSpreadsheet action shown in Figure 39.5 has more arguments, including the full file path and name for the file the table will be exported to. If you want more information about an action's arguments, select the action and press F1 to get Help on the action.

Different arguments are required for the Transfer Spreadsheet (top) and Msg Box (bottom) actions.

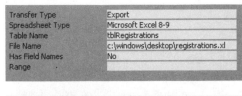

Transfer Type	Export
Spreadsheet Type	Microsoft Excel 8-9
Table Name	tblRegistrations
File Name	c:\windows\desktop\registrations.xl
Has Field Names	No
Range	

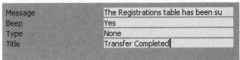

Message	The Registrations table has been su
Beep	Yes
Type	None
Title	Transfer Completed

When you've entered all the actions and typed documentation in the Comments column, click the Save button to save your macro. Click the Close button or choose File ➤ Close to close the Macro window.

 TIP Use the `mcr` prefix for macros in Access, and save the `bas` prefix for Visual Basic procedures. Macros run more slowly than Visual Basic, so if the responsiveness of your Access database begins to deteriorate because users have entered lots of records, you can speed up an application by converting all the macros to Visual Basic. If you always use these two prefixes to identify the type of code, it's easier to figure out where you're still using macros.

Running Access Macros

 You can run your Access macros from the Database window. Choose Macros in the Objects list, select the macro, and click the Run button. If you're writing macros for your own use, there's nothing wrong with this approach. But if the macros are part of a solution you're creating for other users, you'll probably want to avoid letting users into the Database window for any reason. You'll need another way for users to run macros. In Access (as in Word, Excel, and PowerPoint), you can add macros to toolbars and menus so that users can run a macro without opening the Database window or Macro window (see Chapter 38).

 TIP To set startup options, including hiding the Database window, choose Tools ➤ Startup from the menu.

Creating Macro Groups

If you have several related macros that you intend to run programmatically (for example, from a button) rather than from the Database window, you can store the macros together as a macro group. Macro groups put all your related macros in one place. But the big advantage of grouping macros is that you can automatically generate a toolbar, menu bar, or shortcut menu with one button for each macro.

The macro mcrExportRegistrations we created earlier (see Figure 39.4) was one of four different macros we need to export tables to Excel. We also need macros to export three other tables in our sample database: tblTrainees, tlkpCourses, and tblSections. We could create three additional macros, but it's just as easy to group them together in one macro. First, we'll rename our existing macro mcrXLExport (right-click and choose Rename from the shortcut menu). Then, we'll select the macro in the Database window and click the Design button to open the Macro window and make our changes.

In the Macro window, choose View ➤ Macro Names from the menu or click the Macro Names button to display the Macro Names column at the left side of the window. In the Macro Names column, enter a name for the code at the right. For example, we've named our existing code Registrations. We'll refer to the macro with the macro group name, followed by a period and the macro name: mcrXLExport.Registrations.

Now we're ready to create additional macros in the group. You can simply add another macro name on the first blank line, and then choose actions and arguments. We're creating three more macros that are nearly identical so we're going to copy and paste the Registrations macro and then change the table name, file name, message box text, and comment. The entire group is shown in Figure 39.6.

FIGURE 39.6

*Grouping similar
macros helps you
stay organized.*

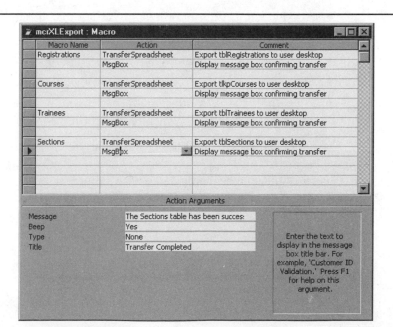

To create a command bar for a macro group, select the macro in the Database window and choose Tools ➤ Macro ➤ Create Menu From Macro or Create Toolbar From Macro. If you blink, you won't even notice the menu, docked with the other command bars. Here's the menu Access created for the macro group shown in Figure 39.6:

Automation in Office 2000

Most people understand the concept of creating a new application by developing an Access database, but when you talk about creating an application in Word, Excel, PowerPoint, or Outlook, even sophisticated users can get confused. We often think of the Office 2000 applications other than Access purely as end-user tools, not as programs that can serve as the basis for powerful desktop applications. And yet, Office 2000 is an ideal platform for custom application development for a number of reasons. The established user base is huge, so if you don't go out of your way to break the existing application, your users will know how to use much of the functionality of your customized application. You don't have to start from scratch. Each Office program is a powerful application, and you can build that power into your custom application. For example, you don't have to add a spelling utility or a charting routine to an application based on Excel. The depth and breadth of Office offers a variety of tools for development:

- Word for online forms or other applications that are largely text-based

- Excel for financial reporting and calculation applications

- PowerPoint for onscreen tutorials, sales presentations, and product overviews

- Outlook for contact and communication applications

- Access for financial management systems, student registration systems, and other types of data management and reporting

The major Office 2000 applications are *automation servers* (formerly called *OLE automation servers* or *OLE servers*). An automation server is an application that exposes its objects so they can be manipulated with a programming language. It's not as risqué as it sounds. In Excel this means you can use Visual Basic programming commands to, for example, change the appearance of any of the following:

- A workbook

- A worksheet in the workbook

- An object like a chart on the worksheet

- A data series in the chart object

Each of these items is an *object*. In object-oriented programming languages like C++, an object is an entity that has both data and instructions. In Visual Basic, an *object* is a distinct entity that you can refer to programmatically: a workbook, an application, a Desktop icon, and the Standard toolbar in Word are all objects. Except for the Desktop icon, each of these objects contains other objects: worksheets, toolbars, and toolbar buttons, for example.

 MASTERING THE OPPORTUNITIES

Understanding the Visual Basic Family and Office 2000

Visual Basic (VB) is a friendlier and vastly more powerful version of the easy-to-learn BASIC programming language that has been included with every version of DOS. VB isn't just an Office 2000 automation language; you can use VB to create programs without Office. VB is an interpreted rather than a compiled language, which makes it easier to learn. When you run Visual Basic code, the code is interpreted line by line, so you can receive instant feedback on code errors. This makes debugging—finding and fixing your errors—far easier. Visual Basic code can also be compiled, which makes it run faster. You can create code in the interpreter and then compile the debugged VB code.

Visual Basic is an event-driven language, which means that it responds to user *events* like clicking on a button or switching between worksheets. You write a VB program and attach it to an event. For example, if you write code that should run when the user clicks a particular button, you'll attach it to the button's Click event.

Visual Basic for Applications (VBA) is a streamlined subset of Visual Basic that works within a *host application* like an Office 2000 application. VBA's focus is extending the capabilities of the host application, so it doesn't include the tools needed to create applications outside of a host. Instead, it includes huge libraries describing all the objects you can program in each application.

The commands used in VB and VBA are identical. Some programmers, however, suggest that VBA is harder to use effectively, because it's not enough to just know the Visual Basic language. You also have to be a power user in every Office application you want to use as a basis of a custom application. If you're not a great Excel user, you'll probably never create a stunning application based on Excel.

Another subset of Visual Basic is called *VBScript*, a more simplified programming language for use on the Internet. VBScript was designed to compete with Netscape's JavaScript. VBScript is generally used in two places: HTML pages (Web pages) and Outlook 2000 forms. Unlike VBA, VBScript does not support all of the Visual Basic syntax. There are things you can do in VB that you cannot do in VBScript, including using financial and statistical functions and certain input/output operations. (You can also use VBA to automate Outlook 2000, so you have the best of both worlds.) VB and VBA code are interchangeable, but both types of code require fairly extensive rewrites for use in VBScript.

Working in the Visual Basic IDE

Office 2000 macros (with the exception of Access macros) are stored in Visual Basic *modules*. So the macros you've already created with the Macro Recorder are written in VB. To examine or edit a macro, choose Tools ➤ Macros to open the Macros dialog box, select the macro you want to examine, then click the Edit button to open the Visual Basic Integrated Development Environment (IDE), also referred to as the VB Editor (see Figure 39.7). To go directly to the VB Editor from an application, choose Tools ➤ Visual Basic Editor.

FIGURE 39.7

The Visual Basic IDE includes a Code window, the Project Explorer, and a Properties window.

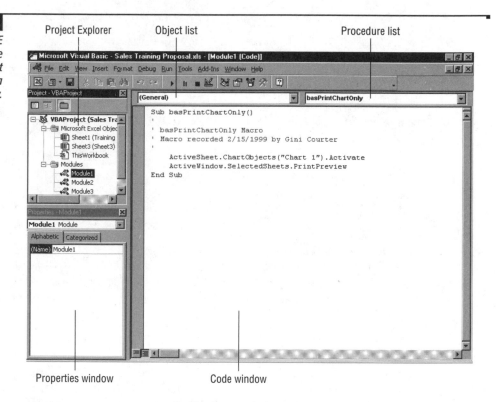

The Visual Basic IDE includes a number of tools. In Figure 39.7, the Project Explorer and Properties window are open to the left of the Code window. The Project Explorer shows all the open VBA projects. Every document can have one project associated with it; the project is stored with the document. The project in Figure 39.7 has two types of project components: *application objects* (worksheets and a workbook) followed by three *modules*. A module is a container for VB code. Each macro you create with the Macro Recorder is placed in a new module, so this workbook contains three macros created with the recorder. Projects can include three other types of project components: forms for user interaction, classes, and references to templates or other documents.

TIP If you have lots of macros, the Project Explorer will quickly fill up with modules. You can use cut-and-paste to move the macros to one module window, or use two or three modules to organize your macros by functionality, and then delete the empty modules. To delete a module, right-click it in the Project Explorer and choose Remove Module *N* from the shortcut menu.

The Properties window displays the properties for the object selected in the Project Explorer; it will be familiar if you've worked with Access objects, such as form controls in Chapter 31.

The Code window displays code from the active component in the Project Explorer. Double-click a module or select the module and click the View Code button in the Project Explorer to display the module's code in the window. If there are a number of macros in a module, select the macro name from the Procedure list at the top of the Code window.

Code lines that begin with an apostrophe (') are *remarks* that explain the code. In the Visual Basic Editor, remarks are color-coded green. The code itself is displayed in the default text color, black.

The code below (which also appears in Figure 39.7) is a simple Excel macro that selects and previews the first chart in the workbook, Chart 1. We created the macro by recording two actions with the Macro Recorder: selecting the chart, and clicking the Print Preview button on the Standard toolbar. The Macro Recorder generated this Visual Basic code:

```
Sub basPrintChartOnly()
'
' basPrintChartOnly Macro
' Macro recorded 2/15/1999 by Gini Courter
'
    ActiveSheet.ChartObjects("Chart 1").Activate
    ActiveWindow.SelectedSheets.PrintPreview
End Sub
```

You don't need to know much about programming to do some simple editing here. For example, you could have the macro print Chart 2 simply by changing the name of the chart object. When you finish editing, close the Visual Basic window to save

PART

VIII

Integration and Automation

your changes and return to the Office application. If you want to learn about Visual Basic, recording macros and studying the resulting code is a good way to begin.

Independent blocks of VB code are called *procedures*. There are three kinds of procedures in VBA: functions, subroutines, and property procedures. You already know what a *function* is from your work with Excel functions: code that returns a value as the result of one or more calculations, comparisons, or other operations. A *subroutine* is code like our macro that performs an operation, but doesn't return a value.

 NOTE Property procedures are beyond the scope of this book—but please don't confuse them with plain old properties, which you'll be working with a lot in this chapter.

The code begins with the word Sub (for *subroutine*) and ends with End Sub. Following Sub is the macro name we entered in the Record Macro dialog box and a set of parentheses. In a function, the parentheses show the names of the argument variables that are used or generated by the function. Most macros don't have input or output variables, so the parentheses are empty. The username, the date recorded, and other remarks are from the Description in the Record Macro dialog box.

Two lines of code follow. The first line activates Chart 1 on the active sheet:

```
ActiveSheet.ChartObjects("Chart 1").Activate
```

`ActiveSheet.ChartObjects("Chart 1")` identifies the object; `Activate` is a *method* of the object. Methods are actions for objects. Activate is a method common to many objects, because you can click on almost anything you see on screen.

The second line sends the selected sheets to Print Preview. Because the chart is selected, the preview only includes the chart—that's how Excel always behaves when you print or preview with a chart selected. The object is `ActiveWindow. SelectedSheets`, and `PrintPreview` is the method being used:

```
ActiveWindow.SelectedSheets.PrintPreview
```

When the VB interpreter hits the End Sub line, it's finished running the macro. It returns *focus* (control) to the host application, Excel, which is displaying Chart 1 in the Print Preview window. The user can choose to print the chart or close the Preview window.

Creating a Procedure in the VB IDE

The `basPrintChartOnly` macro is a *general procedure*. The code isn't tied to any particular button or control, and only runs on demand. General procedures are very useful. To launch this macro you can assign it to a toolbar button, a command button, the macro menu, a menu bar, or all of the above. We'll create our next general procedure in Microsoft Word.

In Word, switch to the VB IDE. Then insert a new module (Insert ➤ Module), or open an existing module. Choose Insert ➤ Procedure from the menu to open the Add Procedure dialog box, shown in Figure 39.8.

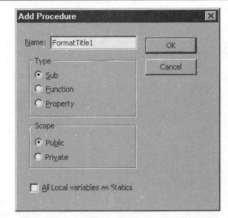

FIGURE 39.8

Use the Add Procedure dialog box to create new procedures.

Enter a name for the procedure in the text box. Choose the Type of procedure you're creating: Subroutine, Function, or Property. The Scope is a procedure's range: Private procedures can only be called by other procedures in the same module; Public procedures can be called by any procedure in the same application. Click OK to add the first and last lines of the procedure (called a *snippet*—no relation to Clippit) to the Code window.

This is a good time to begin documenting your procedure. Type an apostrophe, hit the space bar, and then enter at least your name and today's date. Feel free to add more descriptive information if you wish. Press Enter to move to the next line, type an apostrophe, and press Enter again to leave a blank line between your remarks and the code.

MASTERING TROUBLESHOOTING

Getting Help with VBA and Office 2000 Objects

When you enter code, you need to know which objects are available, and what properties and methods the object has. For a list of objects, use the VBA libraries, which are just a click away in the Object Browser. Click the Object Browser button (or choose View ➤ Object Browser) to open the browser, shown next.

Continued

MASTERING TROUBLESHOOTING CONTINUED

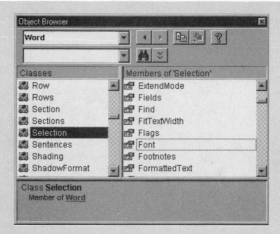

The library for the current application should already be selected, but you can choose other libraries from the Project/Library drop-down list. To search for an object, enter part or all of the object's name in the Search Text box and click the Search button. When you choose an object in the Classes pane, you'll see a list of properties and methods for the object in the right (Members) pane of the browser. If you want more information about the selected object, click the Help button in the Object Browser.

For a more global view of application objects, browse the object model, the map of all the objects in an application. The model shows each object and how it relates hierarchically to other objects in the application. To access the object model for an application, open the application, launch Help, and search for the word *object*.

The model uses different colors for objects and *collections*, which are groups of objects. For example, there is a collection of paragraphs in a document and a collection of documents in an application. Collections are important application features from a programming point of view. You can iterate through a collection if you want to count the number of paragraphs or save all open documents, but you also have the ability to affect one item in the collection. Select any object or collection in the model to get more information on the object, including samples of code using the object.

Our Word procedure will apply Tahoma 14 point Small Caps formatting to a selection. Every application has a Selection object that represents whatever is currently selected. Type the word Selection, followed by a period. Visual Basic's AutoList feature will automatically display choices that could complete the Selection statement, as shown next.

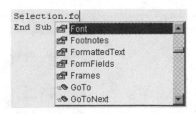

It's the font properties of the selection that need to be changed, so Font is a good choice. Hit the period again, and you'll see the AutoList with new choices appropriate to the Selection.Font object. Let's choose Name the first time through. Type an equal sign, followed by the name of the new font in quotation marks. The font name has to be enclosed in quotes because it's a string (text) variable. Your first line of procedural code should look like this:

```
Selection.Font.Name = "Tahoma"
```

The second line of code is pretty easy to predict now. We don't need to put the size in quotes because it's a value, not a string:

```
Selection.Font.Size = 14
```

The third line is a bit trickier. SmallCaps is a property, just like Name and Size, but it's a toggle: either on (True) or off (False). True and False are reserved words, not text. The third line of code looks like this:

```
Selection.Font.SmallCaps = True
```

This is a good time to check our progress by running the macro. Click the View Microsoft Word button to switch into Word, and select some text. Use the Windows Taskbar to switch back to the VB IDE and click the Run Sub button to run the procedure. Switch back to Word to verify that the selected text has been reformatted.

MASTERING TROUBLESHOOTING

Troubleshooting Simple Code Problems

What can go wrong? Visual Basic is expecting very specific kinds of information. In our example, if you don't enclose Tahoma in quotes, VB won't change the font—irritating, but not deadly. VB won't display an error message when that happens, either.

If you forget to put = True for the SmallCaps property, VB will stop executing in the middle of your code and open a message box.

Continued ▐▶

PART

VIII

Integration and
Automation

MASTERING TROUBLESHOOTING CONTINUED

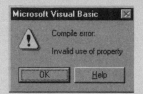

When you click the OK button, you'll switch to the VB IDE. The name of the faulty procedure will be highlighted, and the property that brought VB to a halt will be selected. Fix the problem, and then click the Run Sub button to try again.

This is a short and simple procedure, but there is still something you can do to improve it. All three lines of code refer to the same Font property of the `Selection` object. The code would run faster and be easier to read if you combined the three lines so that you're only referring to the `Selection.Font` property once. You can use a VB command called `With/End With` to frame the three property changes you want to make. Type `With` before the first `Selection.Font` and `End With` after the code that sets the SmallCaps property. Delete the redundant text to edit the procedure:

```
Public Sub FormatTitle1()
'Your comments go here
'

With Selection.Font
    .Name = "Tahoma"
    .Size = 14
    .SmallCaps = True
End With
End Sub
```

When you're finished editing, test the subroutine and save it. You can run this general procedure from the Macros dialog box, add it to a customized toolbar or menu bar, or use it in place of an event procedure, as you'll see in the next section.

Learning about Objects

Our procedure was written to format a title, but it requires the user to select the entire title first. We could improve the procedure by adding code to select the paragraph that the insertion point is placed in. A quick stop in the Object Browser is helpful. With Selection in the Class pane, scroll through the Members pane and you'll find

Paragraphs. Select Paragraphs and click the Help button for more information and examples. Paragraphs are a collection, and one of the code samples shows how to select the current paragraph in the collection:

```
Selection.Paragraphs(1).Range.Select
```

Paragraphs(1) means the first paragraph in the collection of paragraphs that make up the selection. Add this line of code above the With Selection.Font command line in your procedure to select the current paragraph before formatting.

There's a more devious way to learn about some of the objects, collections, and methods that are available: use the Macro Recorder. For example, you want to know how to insert a two-by-two table with code. Choose Tools ➤ Macro ➤ Record New Macro and enter a name. (The macro itself isn't going to be around long, so don't worry too much about its name.) After you click OK to start the recorder, use the Table menu or the Insert Table button to create the table. Then click the Stop Recording button. Open the VB IDE and activate the NewMacros module in either the current document (for a macro stored in the active document) or the project called NORMAL (which is where global macros are stored). Locate your macro, and you'll find the code that was generated to create a two-row, two-column table. You can copy (or cut) and paste this code to use it elsewhere in your code:

```
ActiveDocument.Tables.Add Range:=Selection.Range, NumRows:=2,
NumColumns:= 2, DefaultTableBehavior:=wdWord9TableBehavior,
AutoFitBehavior:= wdAutoFitFixed
```

At this point, you might wonder why we didn't determine how to select a paragraph by firing up the Macro Recorder and triple-clicking. The answer is simply that it doesn't work. In Word, turning on the Macro Recorder disables selecting with the mouse. When you select using the keyboard, only the relative movements of the cursor (up, down, left, right) are recorded. The code that's created doesn't tell Word how to select a paragraph, it tells Word how to select a block of text of a particular size and in a specific direction (up, down) from the initial position of the insertion point.

 MASTERING THE OPPORTUNITIES

Converting Access Macros to Visual Basic

Access clearly differentiates macros and VB procedures, which are stored in Access modules. Macros are easy to create, so many of us begin learning about Access development by writing macros. For a small application, macros may be enough. There are

Continued

MASTERING THE OPPORTUNITIES CONTINUED

two things you can only do with macros (the list gets a bit shorter with each version of Access): You can't run VB code when the database initially opens, but you can run startup code with the AutoExec macro; and if you want to make global key assignments, you must use macros.

For larger, multiuser applications, you'll probably want to turn some, if not all of your macros into VB procedures—and there are many reasons why VBA is superior to an Access macro:

- Macros can't be compiled, so they always run slowly compared to VB. The more macros, the worse the problem becomes, because macros also take up more room in memory.

- When you add a procedure to a form or report, the VB code is saved with the form or report. When you reuse the form in another database, the code's already there. With macros, you have to remember to copy the macro, too.

- With Visual Basic, you can manipulate other Office applications. For example, you can launch Word, open a mail merge main document, and merge letters using records in the Access database.

- You can trap errors with VB code and give users helpful messages that allow them to continue with their work. You can't trap errors with macros; if macros encounter an error, they just die.

To convert a macro to a VB procedure, select the macro in the Database window. Choose Tools ≻ Macro ≻ Convert Macros To Visual Basic to open the Convert Macro dialog box. You have two options during conversion: adding minimal error handling and adding remarks. Both choices are enabled by default. Click Convert and Access will create a new module with the name Converted Macro – *macro name* and convert a copy of the macro. The original macro remains, so you can delete it after you're sure you won't need it.

If the macro exists only in a form or report, open the form or report and choose Tools ≻ Macro ≻ Convert Form/Report Macros To Visual Basic.

Creating User Forms

We can't leave VBA without looking at one other component: the UserForm. Most of the programming done in VB (as opposed to VBA) is built on forms. Without the application interface provided by Office 2000, programmers have to use forms to develop an interface to hang their code on. You'll find uses for forms in VBA, too, when you want to collect information from users, provide structured choices, or give feedback. We've already worked with Word and Excel, so we'll switch to PowerPoint for the UserForm.

It isn't unusual for a company to specify standards for PowerPoint presentations used externally. A department or company may decide to assign specific templates to different product lines or types of presentations, as in this example from a consulting firm:

Topic of Presentation	Design Template
Connectivity	Radar
Viruses/Security	Lock and Key
Project Management	Strategic
Application Development	Neon Frame

We're going to create a custom dialog box that lets the user choose the type of presentation they're creating and applies the appropriate design template from the table above. To try this yourself, just open PowerPoint and create a blank presentation with one slide. Choose Tools ➢ Macros ➢ Visual Basic Editor to open the IDE. Choose Insert ➢ UserForm from the IDE menu to open a new form (see Figure 39.9).

PART

VIII

Integration and Automation

FIGURE 39.9

Choose UserForm from the Insert menu to open a new form.

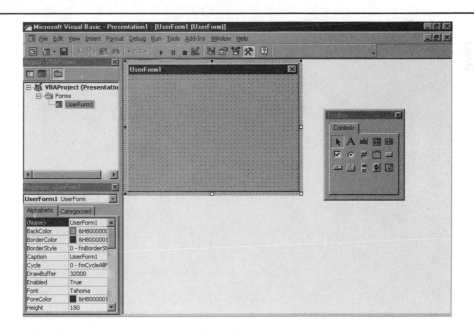

If the Toolbox isn't displayed, click the Toolbox button. Working with the form is similar to working with an Access form. See Chapter 31 if you want to review skills like sizing and moving form controls.

Choosing Controls for User Input

Our form will be used to collect three pieces of information from the user. First, they'll select a type of presentation. Second, they will let us know that they're finished selecting. Finally, users will confirm that they really want to change the design. This seems redundant, but this kind of interface is natural for Windows users. For example, when you use an Open dialog box, you can select one file and change your mind and select a different file before clicking the Open button. Clicking the Open button confirms that you're finished selecting a file—that this is the file you really want to open. If you decide you don't want to open the file, you click the Cancel button rather than the Open button.

We can begin work on the UserForm by placing two command buttons: one that applies a design template, and one that cancels the action by closing the UserForm. To place a command button, select the button in the Toolbox, and then click in the UserForm to place a button of the default size. Drag instead of clicking to create a larger or smaller button (or simply click to place the default button and then resize it).

To change the appearance of the button, you change the button's properties. Select the first button and look at the Properties window, shown here:

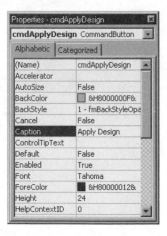

For more information about a property, click its name in the list and press F1. To change a property, click its name in the Properties window, and then type a value or choose a value from a drop-down list. For example, you would change the button's name by clicking on the Name property and typing text. The properties you'll want to change for the first button are listed here:

Property	Value	Description
(Name)	cmdApplyDesign	The name used to refer to the button in code; cmd is the prefix for a command button.
Caption	Apply Design	The text for the button face.
Control-TipText	Applies company-approved design to presentation.	The Help that appears when user hovers the mouse over the button.
Default	True	The user can "click" this button by pressing the Enter key.

Select the other button and change these properties to create a Cancel button:

Property	Value	Description
(Name)	cmdCancelDesign	The name used to refer to the button in code.
Cancel	True	The user can "click" this button by pressing Esc or closing the form.
Caption	Cancel	The text for the button face.

Then select the UserForm and change its properties:

Property	Value	Description
(Name)	dlgApplyDesign-Template	The name used to refer to the form; dlg is the prefix for a dialog box.
Caption	Apply Presentation Design	The text for the form's title bar.

Each form can have only one Default button and one Cancel button, but they can be the same button. You'll want to set the Cancel button as the Default button when *not* canceling results in an irreversible action like deleting a file.

Now we need to add controls to allow the user to select the presentation type. We could use command buttons again, but that would violate the Windows interface standards and make the form harder to use. Each control has a range of standard uses, and Windows users quickly learn what each type of control is used for. When you click a command button, something happens immediately: a form prints, a dialog box closes. Choosing a presentation type, however, is similar to choosing what to print in the Print dialog box. A user will choose only one item from a constrained list of mutually exclusive items. Selecting one presentation type should unselect any previously selected type of presentation, because we can only apply one design template. Just as in the Print What section of the Print dialog box, we'll use an *option group*.

If we were trying to squeeze this choice onto a form that was already crowded, we could use a list box control. One disadvantage of a list box is that you only see the current value. The advantage is that if you populate the list programmatically based on the records in a table (or any other list), you really don't care whether the list has five items or ten—the control takes up the same amount of space either way.

When you want users to select one item from a list or enter an item that doesn't appear on the list, use a *combo box*. Use check boxes if you want to allow users to select more than one option.

There are two ways to create an option group in VB: place option button controls in a frame, or write code to assign the same GroupName property to each option button control. The more controls you add to an application, the longer it takes to load and the less responsive it is, so some programmers avoid frames. Because we only have one dialog box, we'll definitely use a frame. Users are accustomed to frames, so frames make your form more understandable.

Select the Frame control in the Toolbox, and then click or drag in the UserForm to place the frame.

Once the frame is in place you can add option buttons. Select the Option Button control in the Toolbox and then click in the frame to place an option button. Add three more option buttons to the frame. Then change the Caption properties for the new controls. There are four different types of presentations, and the captions should appear in some discernible order. For example, they could be sorted alphabetically or listed by frequency of use. Use the Frame's Caption property to label the options. The form, with all controls placed, should look similar to Figure 39.10.

FIGURE 39.10

A UserForm with command buttons and a framed option group.

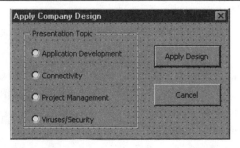

Name the four option buttons optTopic1, optTopic2, optTopic3, and optTopic4, and the frame fraTopics.

TIP You may be tempted to change the background of the UserForm or switch to an extremely conspicuous font for the option button labels. Don't. Users know what a good interface looks and acts like. For example, if the user changes the system colors in the Control Panel, the colors in your application should change, too. If you lock in a specific background, your users may not complain, but you've already planted the seeds of doubt. All experienced Windows users know, if only subconsciously, that "real" programs use the system colors.

Adding Code to the Form

The procedures you've written earlier in this chapter have been general procedures. Event procedures are attached to object events and run in response to an event. In this form, there are two events you care about: a user click on either of the two command buttons. You're probably asking: "But what about that beautifully constructed option group?" You really don't care when a user selects an option button; you just care which option is selected when they click the Apply Design button. And if the user clicks the Cancel button, it shouldn't matter if they've selected an option. But as soon as either command button is clicked, it's time for action.

The Cancel button doesn't need to do too much, so let's create that event code first. Select the Cancel button, right-click, and choose View Code to open the module attached to the UserForm. You won't find this module in the Project Explorer; it's only accessible through the form. You'll notice that the snippets for the command buttons have already been created. There's an underscore before Click in the subroutine names because the code is assigned to a button's Click event.

Before a form can be displayed, it must be loaded in memory with a command like Load *formname*. However, if you forget to load the form and just display it by invoking the form's Show method (*formname*.Show), VB will load the form and then display it, as you'll see shortly. When you don't want to display the form, you can hide it with its Hide method (*formname*.Hide), but the form is still in memory. To close the form, you must also unload it: Unload *formname*.

If the user clicks the Cancel button (or presses Esc), the appropriate response is to close the form. This code does the trick:

```
Private Sub cmdCancelDesign_Click()
    dlgApplyDesignTemplate.Hide
    Unload dlgApplyDesignTemplate
End Sub
```

PART

VIII

Integration and
Automation

You'll find your form `dlgApplyDesignTemplate` and all of its controls on the Objects list. To add the object name, just type enough unique letters of the name (such as `dlg`), hold Ctrl, and press the space bar to fill in the remainder.

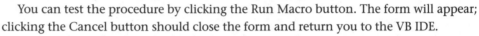 **NOTE** You don't have to use the form's name explicitly, as we have in these examples. If you prefer, you can use the pronoun `Me` to refer to the active object: `Me.Hide` will hide the object that currently has focus. Including the form name increases the amount of code, but it also provides documentation and makes debugging easier.

You can test the procedure by clicking the Run Macro button. The form will appear; clicking the Cancel button should close the form and return you to the VB IDE.

 Use the View Object and View Code buttons at the top of the Project Explorer to switch back and forth between the form and code windows.

When a user clicks the Apply Design button, you want to assign one of four possible templates depending on the selected presentation type. There are a number of ways to do this, but we'll use a series of simple `If...Then...Else` statements. After the appropriate template has been applied, we'll use the same code as the Cancel button to hide and unload the UserForm. Here's the procedure for the `cmdApplyDesign` button:

```
Private Sub cmdApplyDesign_Click()
If optTopic1.Value = True Then ActivePresentation.ApplyTemplate
FileName:="Neon Frame.pot" Else
If optTopic2.Value = True Then ActivePresentation.ApplyTemplate
FileName:="Radar.pot" Else
If optTopic3.Value = True Then ActivePresentation.ApplyTemplate
FileName:="Strategic.pot" Else
If optTopic4.Value = True Then ActivePresentation.ApplyTemplate
FileName:="Lock And Key.pot"
Me.Hide
Unload dlgApplyDesignTemplate
End Sub
```

Test the procedure to ensure that it works. There are a couple of errors you could make. For example, if you mistype the name of the template, you'll get an error at run time because PowerPoint can't find the template. This procedure also assumes that the templates are in the default Templates folder. For more information on error trapping and error messages, see the On Error statement in Visual Basic Help.

We still need one more procedure—a global procedure to open the UserForm. In the Project Explorer, activate Module1 and create the following code to display the UserForm:

```
Sub basShowdlgApplyDesign ()
    dlgApplyDesignTemplate.Show
End Sub
```

Saving Code in a Template

Earlier in the chapter, we noted that you can store global macros for Word (in NORMAL .DOT) and Excel (in the Personal Macro Workbook), but not for PowerPoint. However, in our example you'll want users to have access to the UserForm and procedure when they create new presentations. The easiest way to accomplish this is to save the presentation as a template. (Choose File ➢ Save As; in the Save As Type drop-down list, select Template.) See Chapter 38 for information on adding a custom command button or menu selection to run the procedure.

 NOTE Unlike Word, Excel, Access, and Outlook, PowerPoint doesn't have an event that fires when you open the application, so there's no place to attach an AutoExec macro or startup code.

Customizing the User Interface

As recently as the early 1990s, most personal computers and software used the text-driven DOS operating system even though Apple offered a slick, easy to use graphical interface. This does not mean, however, that an ugly interface is desirable or even acceptable today. The cost of an entry-level desktop hasn't changed in a decade, but more people purchase computers because the Windows interface has made computers "friendlier" and, therefore, more accessible. In the previous chapter, we showed you how to create customized toolbars, menus, and menu items. Now that you have some experience working with VBA, there are a few more tricks you can add to your interface design portfolio.

Mastering Command Bars

Office documents have two events that are great places to hang code that controls the user environment: Open and Before Close. For example, you have a custom toolbar named cmdCust1 that you want to display with a workbook. Open the workbook and move to the VB IDE. Select Workbook from the Object drop-down list in the Code window, and then choose Open from the Procedure list. Here's the procedure code to display the toolbar when the workbook is opened:

```
Private Sub Workbook_Open()
Application.CommandBars("cmdCust1").Visible = True
End Sub
```

This procedure runs just before the workbook closes; it hides the toolbar so it won't be visible after the workbook closes:

```
Private Sub Workbook_BeforeClose(Cancel As Boolean)
Application.CommandBars("cmdCust1").Visible = False
End Sub
```

One way to make a control easy to find is to plant it right in a document. You'll see this approach executed in Excel more often than the other Office applications. For example, the Expense Statement template includes command buttons and a two-button option group. Another control that's often overlooked but easy to implement is the ListBox control. Use a list box when you want to require users to choose from a list to keep entries consistent.

Before you can create the list box, you need to have the list of values that users will choose from. For example, we're going to use a list box to present sales regions: Canada, Mexico, Midwest, Northeast, Northwest, and South. If this list doesn't already exist somewhere in our workbook, we'll need to enter it, preferably in six contiguous cells.

To add the list box to the workbook, display the Forms toolbar and select the List-Box control. Click or drag in the workbook to place the control, right-click, and choose Format Control to open the Format Control dialog box. The Control page of the dialog box is shown in Figure 39.11. Specify the location of the values list in the Input Range text box. The Cell Link is the cell where the results of user choice appear. The result is the ordinal value of the list item selected. In our list, Canada is 1, Mexico 2, and so forth.

FIGURE 39.11

*Define the list box
properties on the
Control page of the
dialog box.*

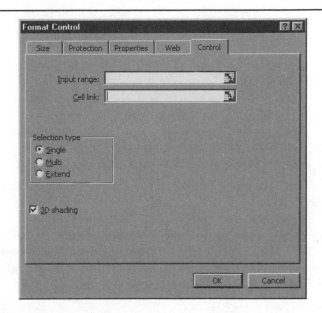

You can combine the ListBox control with Excel's Lookup functions to create a
very nice interface. For example, after a user picks the sales region you could fill in
shipping costs, the salesperson's name, or the address of the regional sales office from
a lookup table elsewhere in the workbook.

MASTERING THE OPPORTUNITIES

ActiveX and Forms Controls

Word and Excel each have two toolbars with nearly identical controls: the Forms toolbar and the Control Toolbox. The Control Toolbox uses the same ActiveX controls that
you've been using in the VB IDE. The controls on the Forms toolbar are not ActiveX controls, but controls that were created to support the macro capabilities of Word and
Excel. It's fine to use the Forms controls (discussed in Chapter 10 for Word and Chapter
26 for Excel) when you're just working in one application.

The ActiveX controls are more powerful tools, and they cross the application barrier. As
you've seen earlier in this chapter, the code behind an ActiveX control is stored in the
module, not in a macros workbook or a Word template, so you can copy a UserForm
and all its code to another application, modify it slightly (if at all) and reuse it. They're
Web ready, so with ActiveX controls, your applications can blow right past the desktop
to an intranet or Internet.

Creating an Access Switchboard

Access 2000 includes a Switchboard Manager that uses ActiveX controls and VB to create a unified interface that opens forms and tables, prints and previews reports, and runs queries. When you create a database with the Database Wizard, Access automatically generates a switchboard. To add a switchboard to your Access 2000 application, choose Tools ➤ Database Utilities ➤ Switchboard Manager. Access will either open an existing switchboard so you can edit it or prompt you to create a new switchboard before opening the Switchboard Manager dialog box. Initially there is one Main Switchboard page. Click the Edit button to edit the name of the main page. Click the New button to add pages. Two pages have been added to the switchboard shown in Figure 39.12.

FIGURE 39.12

Use the Switchboard Manager to create a user interface.

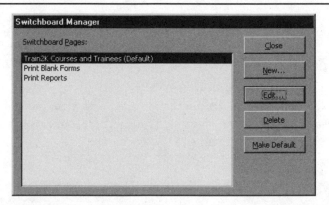

Select a page and click the Edit button to open the Edit Switchboard Page dialog box. Click the New button to add an item to the page:

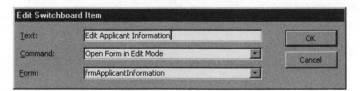

Enter a label for the switchboard item in the Text text box. Select the command that you want to execute from the Command box. If you select a command that requires an argument (such as Open Form), another text box will open. Choose the object that the argument requires; then click OK to close the dialog box and add the item to the switchboard page. When you're finished adding pages and items, close the Switchboard Manager dialog box.

To display the switchboard, open the form named switchboard. Open the form in Design view to change fonts or background colors. Don't delete any of the command buttons on the form, though. This simple-looking form is actually very sophisticated. The controls on the form are populated with code from records in a table called Switchboard Items.

To view the code, open the form in Design view and click the Code button on the toolbar.

TIP To automatically open the switchboard when the database is opened, choose Tools ➢ Startup. In the Startup dialog box, choose Switchboard from the Display Form/Page drop-down list.

More Fun with Clippit

The Office Assistant is a social interface—a largely successful attempt to get users to anthropomorphize their software so they'll treat it better. At first blush, this seems silly, but there is overwhelming research to indicate that users treat computers as if they were people. And it doesn't matter whether the users are novices or experienced programmers. Even when we know better, we treat our computer as we would treat other people.

NOTE For a fascinating look at the interface between people and technology, we suggest *The Media Equation: How People Treat Computers, Television, and New Media Like Real People and Places* by Byron Reed and Clifford Nass (Cambridge University Press, 1996). Reed and Nass have served as consultants at Microsoft for the past few years.

The Assistant is a programmable object, with properties like Animation and New-Balloon, used to create the Assistant's dialog space. We created the code below in Outlook 2000 to let users know that we've added the required company AutoSignature to their e-mail settings:

```
Private Sub Application_Startup()
Assistant.Animation = msoAnimationGetAttentionMajor
```

PART

VIII

Integration and Automation

```
With Assistant.NewBalloon
    .Heading = "Installation Update"
    .Text = "Outlook 2000 has been installed with the company AutoSignature.
Choose New Message from the New Object button to view your AutoSignature.
Call James at Ext. 1090 to request changes or corrections to your
AutoSignature."
    .Show
End With
Assistant.Animation = msoAnimationIdle
End Sub
```

This procedure is fired by Outlook's Startup event, so it runs each time the user launches Outlook. Event code for an application event is created in the application object. In Outlook 2000, you'll use the ThisOutlookSession component. Activate the component and then create the code. When you're finished, close Outlook. You'll be prompted to save the project if you haven't done so already.

When you launch Outlook, the Office Assistant appears with the balloon that you created, as shown in Figure 39.13. The code doesn't choose an Assistant; it simply controls the Assistant selected by the user. Remember this while you're creating text. Users will get confused if Rocky tells paper clip jokes or Clippit asks for tastier dog food.

FIGURE 39.13

You can program the Office Assistant's text and animations.

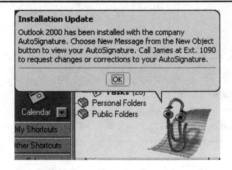

MASTERING THE OPPORTUNITIES

Mastering Visual Basic and VBA

If you want more help with Visual Basic, there are many sources of information. Don't overlook the Visual Basic Help files included with Office 2000. They're a vast improvement over the relatively skimpy development help provided with Office 97. For free technical help, visit the Visual Basic Technical Resources site at http://msdn .Microsoft.com/vbasic/technical/default.asp. Then move to the Visual Basic Web Directory at http://www.vb-web-directory.com for a list that includes non-Microsoft resources, as well.

Mastering Visual Basic 6 by Evangelos Petroutsos (Sybex, 1999) is an excellent, well-indexed VB reference that every VB and VBA programmer should have at hand. If you're just beginning to work with VBA but have experience with Office and with programming in another language, consider the Office 2000 version of Microsoft's CD-based tutorial, *Mastering Microsoft Office Development*.

Three very useful guides to VBA application development for individual Office components are *Excel 2000 Developer's Handbook,* by Marion Cottingham, *Word 2000 Developer's Handbook,* by Guy Hart-Davis, and *Access 2000 VBA Handbook*, by Susann Novalis and Jim Horbuss (all published by Sybex, 1999).

We also recommend the *Microsoft Office and Visual Basic for Applications Developer* magazine from Informant Communications group. Visit their Web site at http://www .informant.com.

PART

VIII

Integration and Automation

What's Next

In the final part of Mastering Office 2000, you'll learn about Web publishing with the Office 2000 applications. Many of the controls you've worked with in this chapter work equally well in HTML pages. As you're creating Web pages, consider adding the Office Assistant to help users navigate or get help with your Web documents.

PART IX

Publishing with Office

LEARN TO:

- *Design effective print and Web publications*

- *Publish documents to the Web*

- *Create print publications using Publisher 2000*

- *Develop Web sites with Publisher 2000*

- *Produce Web pages using Word, PowerPoint, Excel, and Access*

CHAPTER **40**

An Overview of Publishing and Design

FEATURING:

Elements of good design

Types of publications: print, Web, online publishing, and broadcasting

Office 2000 design tools

Web publishing with Office

Publishing and design tools abound in Office 2000. Whether you're producing a simple flyer or a full-fledged marketing campaign, everything you need is at your fingertips. Pick a design, and you can carry that design through your print publications to your on-screen presentations to a comprehensive Web site. The trick is in knowing how to make the most of the incredible array of tools at your disposal. In this chapter, we'll explore the elements of good design, how to choose the right media to communicate your message, and how to use Office 2000 to distribute your creations.

If you want to delve deeper into publishing with Office 2000, you'll find in-depth coverage of the publishing tools in the following chapters of this part. Chapters 41–43 guide you through print and Web publishing with Microsoft Publisher, and Chapters 44–46 focus on Web publishing using Word, Excel, Access, and PowerPoint.

Steps to Good Design

Once the purview of professional designers and print houses, effective communication in written media has become a part of many people's job descriptions. An increasing number of companies are relying on their employees to make them look good in all but the most high-end publications, such as magazines and books. And make no mistake, nothing surpasses the quality of a publication designed by professionals who have training in graphic arts and who possess natural artistic talent. However, even if you consider yourself artistically challenged, you can create attractive publications using Office 2000 and applying a few simple design rules.

It doesn't matter whether you are designing a print publication or a Web site. The key to good design can be summed up in three essential concepts: simplicity, consistency, and contrast:

- Keeping your publications simple helps readers focus on the content rather than the design. That doesn't mean you can't create lengthy publications—just keep them uncluttered, allow for plenty of white (open) space, and make sure your readers can easily find the content they need.

- Using consistent fonts and design elements such as colors and lines establishes a format that readers come to associate with your publication. Office 2000 makes it easy to be consistent by providing design templates that you can use from one type of publication to another.

- Contrast helps readers identify what is most important by making it stand out from the rest of the publication. Contrast draws your readers' eyes to those words and pictures you don't want them to miss. Once you have their attention, they are more likely to read the rest of what you have to say.

 TIP When presented with Office 2000's wealth of design tools, it is natural to want to try them all. Trying them is fine; actually using them in your publications should be done judiciously.

Before you jump right in and start picking out the clip art and fonts you are going to use, there are some preliminary steps that will help you avoid costly redesign as you go along. Spend some time making these decisions up front and you'll produce a higher-quality publication in less time and with less effort.

Understand Your Audience

Although the idea may seem obvious to some, it's amazing how many publications are produced with little or no consideration given to audience. Who is the publication intended to reach? Basic considerations such as age, sex, and educational level cannot be overlooked, and such factors as socioeconomic status, occupation, interests, political persuasion, religion, and the technical sophistication of your readers could all influence the type, style, and content of your publication. If you want to invite people to a social event, will they expect a formal invitation in two envelopes or will a flyer hung on the bulletin board by the coffee machine suffice? If you are trying to persuade a board to fund your proposal, can you provide them with a simple three-page document or do you need to wow them with a glitzy electronic presentation where charts and graphs dance across the screen? Careful consideration of your audience will help you decide what to prepare and what format(s) to use to communicate your message effectively.

Choose the Proper Media

Before we talk about choosing the proper medium (or media—Office lets you publish in more than one form) for your publication, it's important to understand the various options available in Office 2000. Of course, you can create superb printed documents using Word or Excel and a basic ink-jet or laser printer. Online documents, designed to be viewed electronically rather than in print, are gaining in popularity as a way to publish lengthy documents such as employee manuals and user guides. You can create electronic presentations and overheads and prepare 35mm slides using PowerPoint. With the addition of Microsoft Publisher to the Office 2000 suite, you

PART

IX

Publishing with Office

can easily produce flyers, newsletters, postcards, greeting cards, banners, calendars, advertisements, awards, programs, menus—you name it and you can probably develop it in Publisher. All the Office 2000 applications will let you save documents as Web pages for immediate posting to an intranet or external Web site. You can use PowerPoint and NetShow to broadcast presentations to other people on your network, adding both audio and video components to on-screen PowerPoint presentations. FrontPage (found in the Office 2000 Premium Edition) and Publisher let you create full-fledged Web sites with active content and all the latest bells and whistles. To create custom graphics, Microsoft Draw and the new full-featured PhotoDraw put powerful tools at your disposal to enhance any type of publication.

 NOTE   Although both online documents and Web documents are viewed electronically, online Office publications are viewed within a specific application such as Word, while Web documents are viewed in a browser such as Internet Explorer (IE).

With all these options available, deciding how to get your message across comes down to what you already know about your audience, how much time and what resources you have available to you, and what the purpose of the publication is. There is no point in creating a Web site with data access pages (see Chapter 45) to communicate information about your company's product lines to your sales reps if they don't have access to the intranet when they are on the road. On the other hand, it may make sense to create a printed catalog for your sales reps and then post an online catalog for consumers to access on your corporate World Wide Web site. Using a black-and-white version of the same design, you might produce flyers announcing special sale items that can be faxed to your customers the day before the sales rep arrives to visit them.

Office 2000 helps you think about creating publications that work together regardless of the vehicles you use. Figure 40.1 shows three types of publications—an invitation, a brochure, and a flyer—that were all created using the same Publisher design set to publicize a fundraising event. You could use elements from this set to create letterhead, design a Web site, and produce an electronic presentation with PowerPoint. The key is to not limit yourself—most people have to see something in three places in three different ways before they'll even remember they saw it!

PART

IX

Publishing with Office

FIGURE 40.1

All three publications in this set were created using a Publisher wizard.

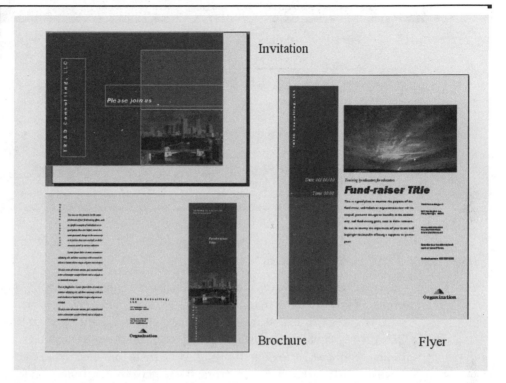

Invitation

Brochure

Flyer

Select the Right Tools

The vast majority of simple publications Office users produce can be created using Word. Does that mean you should use Word whenever possible? The answer is a resounding maybe. Word is a great tool for creating super-looking text, for presenting simple data in tables, and for creating documents that need only a graphic or two to spice them up. However, Excel is a better tool for laying out larger tables and creating beautiful charts. PowerPoint specializes in on-screen presentations, and Publisher's strength is in creating print and online publications that have a lot of graphic content. There is no definitive rule that says, "to produce X type of publication, use Office application Y and no other." Pick the tools that seem to be the most efficient and most conducive to the project you are undertaking. Don't worry if you find out later there is a better way—Office documents are generally easily converted to other formats using the Clipboard and other options (see Chapter 36 for more about converting, linking, and embedding in Office). Table 40.1 shows each of the Office applications and the types of publications you can create with them.

TABLE 40.1: CREATING PUBLICATIONS WITH OFFICE APPLICATIONS

Tool	Print	Online document	Electronic presentation	Online broadcast	Web page
Word	✔	✔			✔
Outlook	✔				✔
PowerPoint	✔	✔	✔	✔	✔
Publisher	✔				✔
Excel	✔	✔			✔
Access	✔				✔
FrontPage					✔

Lay Out the Publication

After you've decided who your publication (or set of publications) is for, what medium or media you are going to use to communicate your message, and what Office tools you are going to use, it's time to get an idea what you want your publication to look like. If you plan to use Publisher at any point, you may want to start by reviewing the design templates it provides. If you find one there that meets your needs, you may have just saved yourself a lot of work. If you need to start from scratch, however, there is no easier way than pulling out an old-fashioned paper and pencil. It may not be very high tech but it gets the job done quickly and efficiently.

 NOTE If the thought of reverting to paper and pencil leaves you cold, Publisher is an excellent tool to use to lay out a publication's design even if you actually plan to create the final product in Word or PowerPoint.

Your basic objective at this stage is to determine how much room you'll have for text, where you'll place standard design elements such as a company logo or masthead, and what other graphic elements you'll need to provide space for. You should create a model for every page of your publication so you know where you want page numbers to appear and how the left and right pages compliment or detract from each other. Figure 4.2 shows an example of a newsletter's cover page laid out in Publisher.

FIGURE 4.2

Laying out a publication's basic design elements helps you visualize the publication before you work with real content.

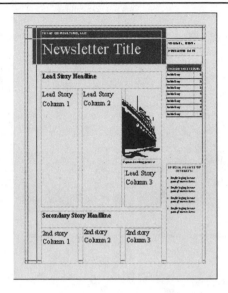

Identify and Create Content

Regardless of the type of publication you are creating, most of the content you present is probably text. Until the transmission of full-screen video over the Internet is perfected, even the multimedia-friendly World Wide Web is still primarily text. Therefore, it makes sense to spend some time preparing the text you plan to use in your publication. Generally speaking, most people write better when they focus on what they are writing rather than how the writing is going to look in its published version. If you are responsible for the content as well as the design of a publication, you may want to create the text first in Word. You can then import it or paste it into the final product. If others are providing you with content, ask them to send you Word documents that you can then incorporate into the design.

In addition to text, you have several options for how content is presented, depending on the type of publication you are creating. In a print publication you are limited to text and graphics, including clip art, photographs, charts, and tables. A Web site, on the other hand, opens the door to more active content such as scrolling text, animated images, audio, video, and dynamic database and spreadsheet pages. Table 40.2 shows options for presenting different types of data in Office 2000 publications.

PART

IX

Publishing with Office

TABLE 40.2: DIFFERENT WAYS TO PRESENT CONTENT

Content type	Print publication	Online document	Presentation	Online broadcast	Web page
Text	✔	✔	✔	✔	✔
Graphics	✔	✔	✔	✔	✔
Charts	✔	✔	✔	✔	✔
Tables	✔	✔	✔	✔	✔
Forms	✔	✔			✔
Audio		✔	✔	✔	✔
Video		✔	✔	✔	✔
Live data		✔	✔	✔	✔
Web scripts					✔

Adding Graphic Objects

Office 2000 offers several tools to assist you in creating and using graphic content:

Microsoft Clip Gallery is completely redesigned in Office 2000 to provide easier access to your favorite art, animation, and audio clips.

WordArt lets you create graphic images from text as shown in Figure 40.3. You can access WordArt from the Drawing toolbar.

Microsoft Draw provides you with drawing tools to create shapes, text boxes, and 3-D objects. To use Draw, turn on the Drawing toolbar or choose Insert ➢ Picture ➢ New Drawing from Word.

PhotoDraw, shown in Figure 40.4, is the latest addition to the Office family and offers a complete set of photo editing, drawing, and painting tools to create and edit your favorite graphics.

Design Gallery, found in Publisher, includes sidebars, boxes, logos, linear accents, marquees, and other objects that can be used in Publisher or pasted into other Office documents.

Microsoft Chart is an applet available in Office applications (Insert ➢ Picture ➢ Chart).

FIGURE 40.3

WordArt transforms simple headings into works of art.

FIGURE 40.4

PhotoDraw is a complete toolbox for creating and editing graphic objects.

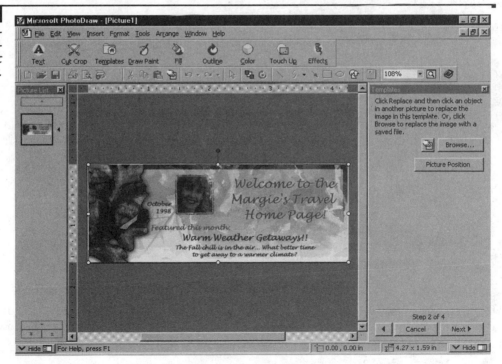

NOTE Two distinctly different versions of WordArt come with Office 2000, depending on the application you are accessing it from. You can launch the newest version from the Drawing toolbar in Word, Excel, or PowerPoint. Publisher offers a somewhat less dynamic version, so if you are working in Publisher, switch to Word, Excel, or PowerPoint and launch WordArt from the Drawing toolbar. Copy-and-paste the WordArt into Publisher. Most but not all of the enhanced features can be displayed in Publisher.

Inserting Other Objects

In each of the Office applications, you can insert objects created in other applications; for example, you can insert Excel charts into Word documents and Word tables into PowerPoint presentations. Refer to Chapter 36 for information about object linking and embedding.

 MASTERING THE OPPORTUNITIES

Adding Web Scripts to Office 2000 Documents

If you want to make Web pages come alive and don't mind dabbling in a little programming, you can add scripts to Web pages you create in any Office application. Scripts can be used for such things as counting the number of visitors to a Web site, replacing content based on a schedule, or managing banner ads. If you like the idea of using scripts but would rather let someone else develop them, you can add action to your pages with the Office WebBot components. If you are a developer, you can create your own scripts using VBScript or JavaScript and then insert them into your Office Web documents.

To create your own scripts, you first let the Microsoft Script Editor know which script language you are going to use to write the script. Choose Tools ➢ Macros ➢ Microsoft Script Editor and follow these steps (if the Script Editor is not installed, you may be prompted to install it):

1. Click the Source tab at the bottom of the Document (center) window.
2. Scroll through the Properties window and locate the `defaultClientScript` property. (If the window is not displayed, choose View ➢ Properties Window.)
3. Select VBScript or JavaScript from the drop-down menu.
4. Choose File ➢ Exit.

Continued

Next, you need to add script commands to the Tools menu. To do this, follow these steps:

1. Choose Tools ➢ Customize and click the Command tab.
2. Scroll down and select Tools in the Category column.
3. Scroll down the Commands column and drag Insert Script to the Tools menu. Wait for the Tools menu to open, and drag down to Macro. Wait for the Macro menu to open, and drop the command where you would like it to appear.
4. Repeat the process with Remove All Scripts and Show All Scripts.
5. Click the Close button.

Now you are ready to create a script. Click in the Web page and choose Tools ➢ Macro ➢ Insert Script. After you write the script (in your favorite scripting language and environment), you need to update the Web page you are developing by clicking the Refresh button on the Web toolbar.

Sample WebBots are available with the Microsoft Office 2000 Developer CD and can also be found on the Microsoft Office Update Web site, www.officeupdate .Microsoft.com.

Create the Final Product

After you have identified all the content for your publication, it's time to pull it all together into the finished product. If you are creating a print publication, be sure to check the Page Layout options and review the publication in Print Preview before sending it to the printer. If you are planning to publish your work on the Web, review the information in the next section about setting Web publishing options and publishing a Web page.

Setting Web Publishing Options

In each Office 2000 application, you can change the default settings for HTML publishing in the Web Options dialog box, although the available options differ slightly depending on the application you are using. Choose Tools ➢ Options. Click the Web Options button on the General tab to open the Web Options dialog box, like the one shown in Figure 40.5 for Word. Use the pages of this dialog box to set specific options for publishing.

FIGURE 40.5

Set options for your Web page in the Web Options dialog box.

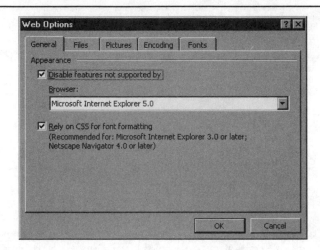

General Options

 The General options vary the most depending on the application. To find out about a specific option, click the What's This button in the title bar and choose the option you want to know about.

File Options

The settings on the Files page determine how the application saves files when you publish your document. Organize Supporting Files In A Folder is enabled by default; this option creates a separate folder for supporting files when the document is saved on a Web server. The folder's name will be the document's name with `files` appended. For example, the folder of supporting files for My Presentation will be named `My Presentation_files`. Disable the Use Long File Names option if you're saving your presentation on a network file server (rather than a Web server) and Windows 3.1 users on your network need to open your presentations.

Update Links On Save automatically checks to make sure the links to supporting files such as graphics, background textures, and bullets are updated when the Web page is saved.

Picture Options

Advanced browsers like IE 5 support Vector Markup Language (VML) and Portable Network Graphics (PNG). Displaying graphics in VML and allowing PNG as an output format results in smaller Web graphics, which download and save much more quickly. If you've ever waited while your low-speed modem slowly downloaded a dozen graphics, you know that VML and PNG are very good news. The bad news is that when you use VML, users with older browsers like IE 4 won't see any graphics at all—and IE 4 isn't all that old.

Screen Size

Unless you're creating a presentation for an intranet where you know the resolution of users' monitors exceeds the minimum 640 by 480, leave the default setting.

Encoding/Fonts

Encoding allows you to choose the language set you want to save with the Web page. The Fonts tab allows you to save the character set. If you are using another language from the Office Language Pack to create the Web page be sure to save the corresponding encoding with the Web page. You can also set the default font and font size on the Web page.

If a user opens the Web page and they have the default font on their system, that's the font the page will use. If they don't have the default font, Windows will substitute another font. It's a good idea to choose a common font that you can be confident most users will have available to them if you want your pages to display correctly.

MASTERING THE OPPORTUNITIES

Assigning a Hyperlink Base for a Document

If you are creating Web pages for a corporate intranet (or the rare Web site where all linked pages reside on the same domain), you can establish a hyperlink base for a document that provides a consistent path to where linked documents are located. This makes it easy to link to documents because you don't have to enter the entire path. It also means that if you change the location of the linked documents, all you have to do is change the hyperlink base and all the links in the document will still be viable. To set a hyperlink base for a document:

1. Open the document's Properties sheet (File ➤ Properties) and click the Summary page.

2. In the Hyperlink Base box, type the path you want to use for all the hyperlinks you create in this document.

If you want to override the hyperlink base and identify a fixed location for a particular link, just enter the full path to the link in the Insert Hyperlink dialog box.

Saving Documents as Web Pages

In some of the Office 2000 applications (except Access and Outlook), you can save documents as Web pages using the Save As Web Page option on the File menu. The Save As Web Page dialog box from Word is shown in Figure 40.6.

FIGURE 40.6

When you save as a Web page, you have the option of saving a page title that is different from the file name.

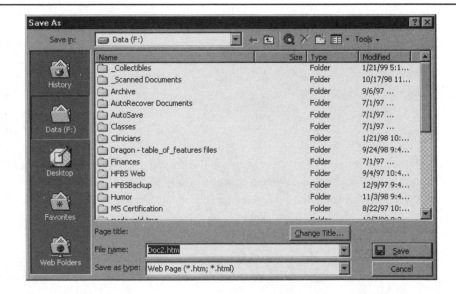

Click the Change Title button to open a dialog box where you can enter a title to appear in the browser's title bar when the page is displayed. (The file name is the default title.) In Word, you'll simply click Save to save an HTML version of the document. With PowerPoint and Excel, there are other options that you can set, and using Publisher you can create more than just Web pages—you can create an entire Web site. Chapters 43–46 provide application-specific information on Web publishing in Publisher, Word, Excel, Access, and PowerPoint.

NOTE Don't confuse saving a Web page with saving in a Web folder (see Chapter 37). A Web folder is a folder on a Web server, and files that you save in a Web folder do not have to be HTML files.

When you create an HTML document, you have several options for where you save it. You can save an HTML document to a

- Private folder where you can work with it just like any other Office document
- Shared folder where other users can open it in its original application
- Web folder where other users can open it in a browser
- Web server where it can become part of an intranet or Internet Web site

To save a document to a shared folder, a Web folder, or a Web server, you need appropriate permissions. Check with your server administrator if you want to save a document to one of these shared locations.

When you save a file as a Web page, all supporting files—such as those for bullets, background textures, and graphics—are saved in a separate subfolder. This subfolder is automatically named with the page name, followed by an underscore and the word files; for example, My Web Page_files.

 TIP Before you save a document as a Web page, create a folder in which to save the page and any related Web pages. This organizes the Web files and makes the supporting subfolders easy to find.

If you move or copy a Web page to another location, you must also move or copy the supporting folder in order to maintain all links to the Web page.

MASTERING TROUBLESHOOTING

Maintaining Formatting and Application Functionality

Even though Office 2000 applications can open HTML documents, saving a document as a Web page is not always a good idea. Browsers do not support all the features available in Office 2000, so saving a document as a Web page means that you lose some or much of the functionality available in the original application. Formatting that is not supported by HTML is not saved with the Web page. When you reopen the HTML Web page in Word or Excel, the formatting does not return.

To edit a Web page and maintain its formatting, you need to open the page in FrontPage 2000 or as a data access page in Design view in Microsoft Access 2000 (as discussed in Chapter 45, you can open any HTML page as a data access page in Access). If you want your colleagues to have full access to a document and retain all of its formatting and functionality, your best bet is to save it as an Office document in a shared folder.

Saving vs. Publishing

Office 2000 offers two choices for saving Web documents in Excel and PowerPoint:

- Saving as a Web page
- Publishing a Web page

 NOTE Office 2000 Help uses the terms *save* and *publish* interchangeably, but there are differences between them that are worth knowing about.

Saving a document as a Web page saves the document in HTML format and makes the page viewable in a browser. You may want to save a document first as an Office document and then save it again as a Web page. When you want to make changes to the Web page, open the Office document, make the changes there, and resave it as a Web page. This reduces the formatting losses you may experience if you open an HTML document in an Office application.

The option to publish a Web page is available in Excel, PowerPoint, and Publisher. Publishing a Web page automatically makes a copy of the page, requiring you to enter a different name or path for the file. It also provides you with options that are not available by simply saving. For example, publishing a PowerPoint presentation allows you to set additional options such as which slides are displayed and whether Speaker's Notes are available. Figure 40.7 shows PowerPoint's Publish As A Web Page dialog box.

FIGURE 40.7

Publishing a PowerPoint presentation as a Web page allows you to select additional options that aren't available by saving.

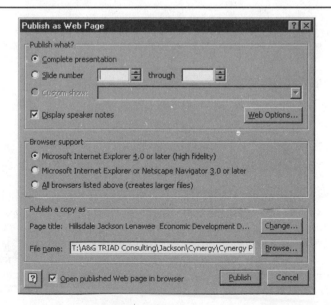

Excel allows you to publish individual worksheets, but you have to save a workbook as a Web page before you can access the entire book in a browser. So why would you want to publish? Publishing allows you to select a range of cells and allows you to append a worksheet or a range of cells to an existing Web page. If you'd like to find out more about publishing Excel pages, refer to Chapter 45.

Managing Published Web Pages

Managing Web pages you create in Office applications can be a bit tricky unless you have the Office Premium Edition, which includes FrontPage 2000. Once you publish a Web page to a Web server, you cannot make changes to it unless you have FrontPage available to open it in. That doesn't mean that all is lost, however. To make changes to a published Web page, open the copy of the Web page or original source document, make the changes you want to make, and republish the page to the same location. This will overwrite the existing page with the modified version.

A major part of managing a Web page is verifying that the hyperlinks work. When you don't have FrontPage, the best way to do this is to access the page just as any other user would and check the hyperlinks in your browser. If the links work there, they are fine. If they don't, correct the hyperlinks in your copy and republish the page to the Web server.

What's Next

The next six chapters walk you through the specifics of Office 2000 publishing. Chapters 41–43 cover print and Web publishing in Microsoft Publisher. Chapter 44 focuses on Web publishing in Word. In Chapter 45 you'll learn about the exciting new Web options in Excel and Access, and Chapter 46 covers Web publishing in PowerPoint.

PART

IX

Publishing with Office

CHAPTER <u>41</u>

Creating Electrifying Publications

FEATURING:

Elements of Publisher

The Publisher interface

Starting a publication from scratch

Saving your work

Setting Publisher options

Printing your publications

So you've just been handed the company newsletter to produce? Or perhaps it's the human resources employee manual. You have a project that requires that "extra-professional" touch, and you want it to look like it came off a printing press. When working with complex documents containing many graphic elements and text boxes, Publisher is the Office tool of choice.

Publisher is designed to handle multiple elements on a page. The focus, as you might expect, is on the overall appearance of the publication. Of course, you certainly can't ignore the formatting and content details of your document, and Publisher allows you to work well on that level, too; but the real power comes from the ease with which you arrange components on the page.

Flyers, newsletters, calendars, brochures, directories, and countless other publications will glide off your printer in no time. Let's take a look at just how easy it can be.

Elements of Publisher

If you are used to working in Word or another word processing program, you may have to learn to think differently about how to put together a document for publication. With this program you will quickly discover that it's not as simple as typing text on a page and letting it wrap at the margin. Before you place anything in a Publisher document, it needs to have space reserved for it.

The Object-Oriented Model

Publisher works from an object-oriented model. This simply means that everything on a page is an object of some kind and has to be in a frame. You can't just type text anywhere; you need a text box to house it.

Graphics such as ClipArt and WordArt behave much the same as they do in a Word document. However, you'll find that text is treated somewhat differently in Publisher. You can move an entire block of text (in a text box) anywhere on the page by clicking and dragging. It won't take you long to get used to the object-oriented model. Later in this chapter you will learn how to create text boxes using the text frame tool. In the next chapter we will explore other object tools so you can decide which to choose to create the type of object you need.

The Right Tool for the Job

Should you use Word or Publisher? The answer to that question depends largely on how comfortable you are with each tool and the design of the document you want to produce. There aren't many features available in one program that are unavailable in the other. So the question to ask yourself is this: "How easy is it to carry out the commands necessary to produce this document?"

The simpler the document, the more likely it becomes that Word is the better tool. No need for frames and fancy formatting if all you are producing is a one-page cover letter to accompany a sales brochure. But the brochure is likely to be a more complex document with an emphasis on graphics. In this case, you might want to switch to Publisher.

A related question is whether you expect readers to follow a single path through the document, as in a personal letter or a novel, or plan to provide multiple entry points, as in a magazine or Web site. If readers will have a choice about where to begin, you'll need to focus their attention on the main topic areas; and that implies a more complex, graphically rich document, for which Publisher is the better tool.

In the best of worlds, you make use of both tools to produce one publication. Since you can type text faster in Word (no need to create frames first), why not compose and edit at the text level in Word? You might even have someone else create the Word text you will eventually use. Design and create frames to house the text in Publisher; arrange graphic objects here as well, and import the text into the existing frames when you're ready for it.

The Publisher Interface

Unlike the Office 2000 applications that combine buttons from the Standard and Formatting toolbars into a single "personal" toolbar, Publisher shows the Standard toolbar by default. You can always recognize the Standard toolbar because its first button is the New button, shown at left. Buttons for common commands such as Print and Save also appear on this toolbar.

The Formatting toolbar is also on by default. However, you won't see it until you have created and selected an object. In Publisher 2000, the Formatting toolbar is dynamic. That is, it changes depending on what type of object is selected. If you have selected a graphic object, the Formatting toolbar displays the tools for wrapping, rotating, cropping, and flipping, among others. Selecting a text box causes the toolbar to display text-formatting tools: italics, alignment, and font size, to name a few.

It's the Object toolbar, however, where you will find yourself clicking each time you need to add another element to a page. Here is where you will begin. Using the Object toolbar, you will choose the tools to build text and graphics that give your publication that professional look.

Boundaries and Guides

Publisher equips you with everything you need to place and align objects precisely. You can choose to view the nonprinting boundaries and guides when needed and hide them when you're through.

The red outer line shows page margins, which default to 1" all around. The blue line appears 1/8" inside the outer margin boundary. Use the blue line as a guide to keep from placing objects directly on the margin.

 NOTE The term *boundary* implies that the program somehow prohibits you from working outside the designated area. This is not the case at all. There is nothing to prevent you from placing objects on Publisher's margin boundaries, or even outside them. Rely on your own judgement and design skills for proper object placement.

Adjust boundaries by choosing Layout Guides from the Arrange menu. Use the spin boxes or select and overtype the existing numbers to adjust left, right, top, and bottom margin boundaries. You may find it helpful to lay out your page in quadrants or other informal divisions. Use the grid guides for columns and rows to visually section off your publication as a professional layout artist might do.

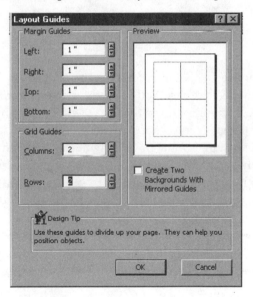

Rulers and Ruler Guides

The horizontal and vertical rulers are turned on by default in Publisher. Choosing View ➢ Rulers from the menu turns them off if you prefer. It is quite likely, however, that you will need rulers fairly frequently when creating documents with multiple objects. Click and drag either ruler to bring it onto the page of your document. Click the box at the intersection of the two rulers, as shown here, to drag both rulers at once. Measure distances from clip art to boundaries; measure text boxes and other objects to ensure design consistency. Simply drag the rulers away when you're through.

If you need a randomly placed guide to align objects, ruler guides are easy to place and move as necessary. You can insert as many horizontal and vertical ruler guides as you need. Simply point to the edge of either ruler, hold the Shift key, and drag the green ruler guide into your document.

Remove a ruler guide by holding the Shift key and dragging it back to the ruler from which it came. Since boundaries and guides can be distracting at times, you may wish to hide them by choosing View ➤ Hide Boundaries And Guides from the menu. Display them again by clicking View ➤ Show Boundaries And Guides.

 TIP Ctrl+Shift+O also hides and displays nonprinting boundaries and guides.

The Scratch Area

Think of the Publisher program window as a large table where you can place blank pages along with the text and objects that you will eventually display on them. When you are working at a table with all your text and art scattered about, you might arrange a picture in a particular location and then change your mind and place it on another page altogether. Later, you might decide you really want this picture on a page at the end of the document and set it aside for now.

In Publisher your table is the gray space surrounding the displayed page(s), called the scratch area. Use it to hold objects while you decide where to place them. If you're working on Page 3 and come across a piece of clip art you think you might need later, grab it now! Items you place in the scratch area are saved along with your publication.

Viewing Your Publication

Since the default zoom setting for blank documents is often too small to view text easily, you will find that you frequently need to enlarge text to proof it. When working with graphics, you'll probably want to zoom back out to determine whether the object is properly placed on the page. Zoom buttons really get a workout in Publisher. Click the plus sign to move closer to your document (that is, to enlarge it); click the minus (repeatedly, if necessary) to view from a distance.

Navigating between pages in Publisher 2000 is easier than ever. Page navigation buttons are displayed at the bottom left of the scratch area. Just click the page you wish to view. Adjacent pages may display two at a time. Zoom in as necessary to work more closely with one page or the other. You can also use the View menu to toggle on or off the two-page display and to zoom in or out.

Starting a Publication from Scratch

When you launch Publisher you will see the Catalog dialog box, shown in Figure 41.1. There are essentially three different ways you can begin creating a new publication: Publications By Wizard, Publications By Design, or Blank Publications.

You might be tempted to start your first publication using one of the many Quick Publication Wizards that walk you through steps to create cards, calendars, invitations, resumes, and other documents. (You'll learn more about Quick Publications in Chapter 43.) If you are happy with the results after the wizard finishes, this may not be a bad way to start. However, if you plan to edit any of the elements generated by the wizard, you'll need to recognize the different components used in a Publisher document and know what to do with them. That's why it is helpful to start from scratch when you are learning Publisher. Once you have built a document by placing, resizing, and formatting different objects, one at a time, it becomes easy to recognize and edit the various components produced by wizards.

From the Publisher Catalog dialog box select the Blank Publications tab. Several choices are available to you, as shown in Figure 41.2. You can select from the list on the left or scroll through the gallery on the right to see visual representations of the list items. Click the Custom Page button to enter specific page dimensions if you

PART

IX

Publishing with Office

don't see a style that suits your needs. Click the Custom Web Page button if you are designing for the World Wide Web.

FIGURE 41.1

The Catalog dialog box

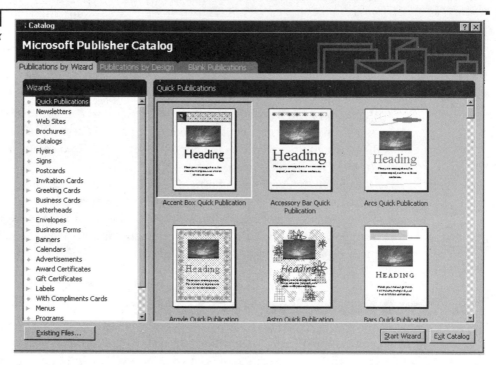

 NOTE See Chapter 43 for detailed information on using Publisher for Web Publishing.

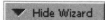 Choose one of the blank publication styles and click the Create button at the lower-right corner of the window. Your blank page will be displayed along with the Quick Publications Wizard on the left. To allow more working space, click the button to hide this wizard. Arrange boundaries and guides as desired, and you are ready to go!

Entering Text

 Since Publisher operates from an object-oriented model, you won't just start typing on the blank page. Instead, you will use the text frame tool to create a space to house your text.

PART

IX

Publishing with Office

FIGURE 41.2

Use the Blank Publications tab of the Catalog dialog box to start creating a publication from scratch.

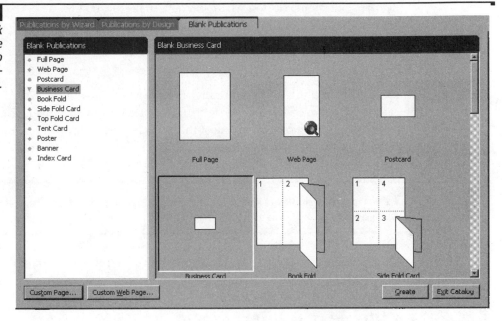

 TIP It's easy to forget about text frames and just start typing on a page. When you do this, Publisher will create one big text frame that fills the page. If you have only typed a word or two in the frame when you catch your error, you can quickly remove it and start again by clicking Edit ➤ Delete Object.

Click the text frame tool once to select it. Then move into your document and drag to create a frame of the approximate size and shape you need. Keep in mind that creating an object requires two separate actions. The first is to click the tool of choice; the second is to click and drag inside the document. Avoid dragging the button from the toolbar to your document since this won't allow you to create a frame.

 TIP If you forget to drag and only click the blank page, Publisher will create a text frame that measures 2" × 3". If Single Click Object Creation has been disabled, forgetting to drag creates nothing. (Publisher Options are discussed at length near the end of this chapter.)

Release your mouse button when you have dragged a text frame of the size and shape you want, and begin typing. The insertion point starts at the top-left corner of the frame, effectively left-aligning your text by default.

Resizing and Repositioning a Frame

At some point you will decide to change the size and/or position of your text frame. Select the object you wish to resize with a single click anywhere inside the frame. Then position your mouse over one of the resize handles until you see the resize pointer. Click and drag larger or smaller.

 TIP To resize an object and still maintain its original proportions, hold the Shift key while resizing.

Move an object by placing the mouse on the gray outline that frames it. When the mouse pointer changes to the moving van icon, click and drag to a new position.

Formatting Text in a Text Frame

Like Microsoft Word, Publisher offers two general types of text formatting: character and paragraph. Frequently, you can perform paragraph-editing functions by selecting just the text frame. To format characters, you usually have to select the text itself, rather than the frame that houses it. Figure 41.3 illustrates the difference between selecting a text frame and selecting text within a frame.

FIGURE 41.3

Selecting a text frame (left) is very different from selecting text within a frame (right).

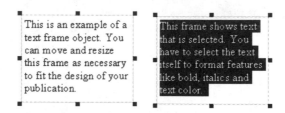

Formatting Characters and Words

Select a word, sentence, or paragraph within a text box and click the buttons on the Formatting toolbar to make them bold, italic, and/or underline. Basic text formatting works the same way as it does in Word. Change fonts and font sizes from the toolbar drop-down lists, or choose Format ➤ Font from the menu. Use the toolbar buttons to increase and decrease font size by two points.

Select text and click the Text Color button on the Formatting toolbar to see available color choices. Publisher 2000 provides built-in schemes to lend consistency to your creations. If you like the default scheme, simply click one of the color choices currently displayed to apply it to your text.

Click the More Color Schemes button to see additional scheme options. The More Colors choice takes you to the Colors dialog box where you can blend different colors to produce the exact shade you're looking for. Choose Fill Effects to explore different tints of a base color.

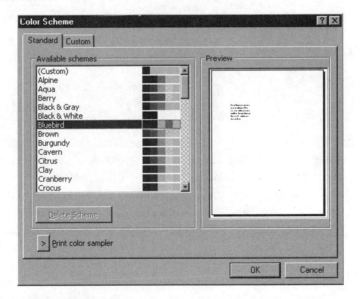

Paragraph Formatting

To apply formatting in a text box that contains one paragraph, you are only required to select the text frame before clicking the appropriate button. If the text box contains more than one paragraph, select all the text so formatting is applied to each

Publishing with Office

paragraph within the frame. Use the alignment buttons on the Formatting toolbar to change from left-aligned to centered, right-aligned, or fully justified.

Increase the indent of the paragraph with the toolbar button to move and align all the text in the frame one tab to the right. Decrease indent to move and align the text one tab to the left.

Bulleted and Numbered Lists Bullets and numbering now work much the same way they do in Word. Select the list of items you wish to bullet or number and click the appropriate toolbar button. The most recently used bullet or number format will be applied. If you wish to choose a custom format, select the list text and choose Indents and Lists from the Format menu.

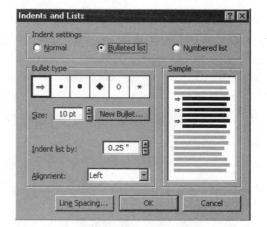

In the Indent Settings area, choose either Bulleted List or Numbered List, and the other options in the dialog box will reflect your choice. For a bulleted list, the most recently used bullet characters will be displayed. Click the one you like and change its size, if desired. (The size of the bullet character defaults to match the size of the text it precedes.) If you increase the number in the Indent List By field, the text moves farther away from the bullet character. Change the way the list aligns within its frame by selecting a different option from the Alignment drop-down list in this dialog box. Use the Line Spacing button to increase or decrease the space between your list items. Click the New Bullet button to see other choices for bullet characters.

If you choose the Numbered List option, there are three new settings to consider. First, choose a number or letter format from the list of available choices. Then choose the separator you prefer to use. Finally, adjust the Start At number if you are continuing from a previous list. You have the same options for changing the indent distance, alignment, and line spacing as you have with bulleted lists.

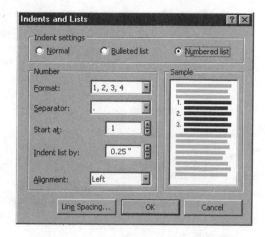

Drop Caps   Newsletter and magazine articles frequently begin with a *drop cap* to draw readers into the first paragraph:

Publisher offers numerous options for creating this eye-catching effect. Select the character you wish to format as a drop cap. Click Format ➤ Drop Cap from the menu. Scroll through the available drop caps, click the one you like, and click OK to apply it in your publication. If you don't see a drop cap style you like, try the Custom Drop Cap tab of this dialog box to choose the number of lines above and below the drop, as well as the the font, font style, and color of the drop cap.

PART

IX

Publishing with Office

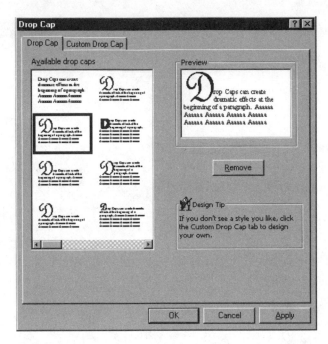

Change your mind later? Select the text frame with the drop cap you wish to remove. Click Format ➤ Change Drop Cap from the menu, and click the Remove button.

Inserting Pages

When it is time to place another page into your document, choose Page from the Insert menu to open the Insert Page dialog box. Choose where to insert the page and select whether you want a new page with one large text frame, duplicated background objects, or just a blank page. If you choose Insert Blank Pages, each page you add will have the layout guides you have already set.

Importing Text from Other Sources

When creating complex documents, it's best to separate the design process from the writing process. One way to do this is to compose and type the text for your publication in another program, most likely a word processor. As long as Publisher's converters are installed, you shouldn't have any problem bringing in text produced in another Windows-based program. There are essentially two ways to make this work.

Using the Clipboard to Bring in Text

Create an empty text frame in your Publisher document to house the text you wish to bring in. Open the text document in its native application and select the desired text. Click the Copy button to place the selected text on the Clipboard. (Use Ctrl+C on the keyboard if the application doesn't have a Copy button.) Switch back to the Publisher window, select the empty text frame, and click the Paste button or press Ctrl+V. Depending on the program used to create the pasted text, it may or may not retain its original formatting. If you have created a text frame that is too small to house the text you are pasting, Publisher will prompt you with a warning and options to create additional frames. Clicking Yes to these options will bring the text into a series of connected frames. (For more on this, see the section "Managing Text Frame Overflow.")

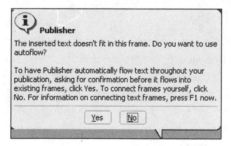

Using the Import Option

Create an empty text frame in Publisher, and make sure it is selected as you choose Insert ➤ Text File from the menu. The Insert Text dialog box opens to allow you to locate and select the desired file. Click OK. Publisher will import (and convert file formats, if necessary) to the selected text frame. You will see text overflow warnings if the receiving text frame is too small for the text you are importing.

NOTE If Publisher's converters are not installed and you attempt to import a file that requires them, you will be prompted to install this feature.

Managing Text Frame Overflow

When Publisher warns you about text frame overflow, you may want to ignore those warnings (click No to the overflow warning) and handle the problem manually. This method gives you better control over the placement and sizing of the text frames your additional text will flow into.

Resizing the Frame

 It is quite possible you won't want your imported text in multiple frames. And there may be times when you accidentally resize an existing frame too small to fit the text it contains. Any time you select a text frame that is too small to display its contents in total, the Text In Overflow Indicator appears at the bottom-right of the selected frame. One way to fix it is to place your mouse over one of the frame's object handles and drag to a larger size that allows all the text to be displayed. As soon as the frame is big enough, the Overflow Indicator disappears.

Selecting text and changing the font or font size might also give you more room in the frame. If you're double-spacing the text, consider using 1.5 instead. On the Format menu, click Line Spacing. Type the number of lines you want in the Between Lines field.

AutoFit Text

 In Publisher, you can use automatic copyfitting to resize text to fit into a designated amount of space. For example, if a title is too big to fit on one line, you can use copyfitting to reduce the font size of the text until it does fit.

Automatic copyfitting adjusts the text whenever you type or delete text, change formatting, or resize a frame. Using the copyfitting feature does not prohibit you from making manual adjustments, however. Try a little of both when creating and formatting your next publication.

Turn on automatic copyfitting using Format ➤ AutoFit Text. The Best Fit choice shrinks or expands text to fit in the text frame when you resize it. To reduce the font size of text until it no longer overflows, choose Shrink Text On Overflow.

To turn off automatic copyfitting, point to AutoFit Text on the Format menu and then click None. Now the font size will remain the same when you resize a text frame or insert additional text.

Connecting to Another Frame

Magazines, newspapers, and newsletters generally require layouts where articles begin on one page and continue on another. You can arrange and size the empty frames, and then bring in the text so that it automatically flows from frame to frame.

Create, size, and place the appropriate number of text frames where you want the text to appear in your publication. Type or import text into the first frame. If you are importing and Publisher prompts you to use AutoFlow, you can click Yes as long as the frames you want to use are the *only* empty ones in your document. Publisher will give you the option to automatically create additional frames if you haven't designated enough space for the text file you are importing. Give it a try in most cases. The worst that will happen is that you will have to resize or reset the properties on the new frames. (More on frame properties in the next chapter.)

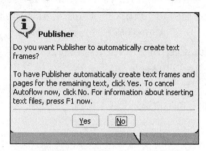

 Text imports gone awry can be fixed with a simple click of the Undo button. In Publisher 2000, you can now undo (and redo) multiple operations as in the other Office applications.

 As an alternative to AutoFlow, when the Text In Overflow indicator appears, you can choose Tools ➢ Connect Text Frames to turn on the Connect Frames toolbar. Click the Connect Text Frames button and move the mouse back into your document.

  The mouse icon now looks like a pitcher. When you place this icon inside any empty text frame, the pitcher tips to the right. Navigate to the text frame you want to use for your continued text and click once inside the frame to "pour" overflow contents. If the second frame overflows, click the Connect Text Frames button again and pour the overflow into another empty frame.

Follow your text forward and backward through a series of linked frames using the frame-navigation buttons. If you later wish to disconnect linked frames, select any of them and click the second button on the Connect Frames toolbar. You will disconnect all linked frames that follow the selected frame.

Inserting "Continued From" and "Continued On"

Help your readers follow an article through the publication with Continued notices at the top and/or bottom of linked text frames. Right-click a connected text frame, point to Change Frame, and click Text Frame Properties. Enable one or both Continued boxes.

PART

IX

Publishing with Office

By default, Continued messages appear in Times New Roman Italic in a font size somewhat smaller than the text in the frame. To change the appearance of one of these messages, select it and format as desired. You can change font, font size, alignment, and font color, and you can even reword the "continued" language, if you like. Rather than repeating this procedure multiple times, you can save all of your changes as a new or redefined style by choosing Text Style from the Format menu. Chapter 8 provides detailed information on creating and applying styles in Microsoft Word; the procedures in Publisher are similar.

You can remove Continued notices by right-clicking the linked text frame and choosing Change Frame ➢ Text Frame Properties. Disable one or both Continued boxes and repeat this procedure for each linked frame in the series.

Saving Your Work

The Open and Save dialog boxes in Publisher now match those found in the other Office applications. When opening files, you can choose to bring them in for editing or as read-only. The Save and Save As commands function as you would expect. (Chapter 2 covers opening and saving files in depth.) You also have other options for storing publications.

Save Options

Click the File menu to see the choices you have for saving Publisher documents. In addition to the usual Save and Save As commands, you have the option to Save The Current Publication As A Web Site or Use Pack And Go to prepare a document for use on another computer or with a commercial printing service.

Since the program only allows you to open one publication at a time, there's never a question of which document gets saved—it's always the one being displayed.

AutoConvert

Publisher 2000 allows users to convert content from existing publications into additional publications. That means you can use the text and graphics in your company's trifold brochure to create a Web site. And you can do it with only a couple of mouse clicks, without importing the content into another Publisher file. AutoConvert is a feature you can access when you create documents using wizards. See Chapter 43 for more information on Publisher wizards.

Setting Publisher Options

You can have as much or as little help from Publisher as you wish. Enable the settings that allow you to work most efficiently by choosing Options from the Tools menu.

General

The General tab of the Options dialog box offers miscellaneous options. You can change the default starting page number if you typically create a cover page in another application (PowerPoint, for example). In this case your Publisher documents should start page numbering with 2.

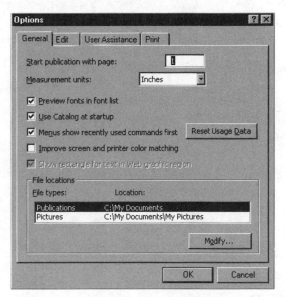

Select from the Measurement Units list to display other units of measurement on the rulers. If the Preview Fonts In Font List feature is enabled, the list of fonts on the Formatting toolbar and in the Format dialog box shows the name of the font in the typestyle of that font. In the case of symbol fonts, the list displays samples from that symbol set. If you prefer to load Publisher directly to a blank page, disable the Use Catalog At Startup feature. Improve Screen And Printer Color Matching allows you to get a better idea of how your colors will appear on the printed page. Ever wonder why your documents come off the printer in a lighter shade than they appear on screen? Try enabling this feature to see a more accurate screen view.

You can change the default locations for opening existing documents and inserting pictures by clicking the Modify button and selecting the folder you wish to default to. At any point if you decide to change the settings back to system defaults, click the Reset Usage Data button.

Editing

The Edit tab of the Options dialog box allows you to enable or disable Drag-And-Drop Text Editing. If you tend to accidentally drag your mouse over selected text, you might want to turn this off. Automatic selection of the entire word means that you can't select part of a word for formatting. Enabling this feature helps prevent you from accidentally missing parts of your text when you use the Format Painter.

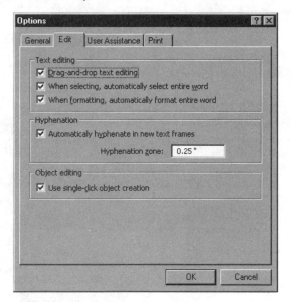

You will like the feature that allows you to automatically format the entire word where the insertion point currently rests. This means you don't have to double-click before you italicize a word in a sentence. Make sure the insertion point is somewhere in the word you wish to format and click the toolbar button(s) to apply desired changes. The Hyphenation Zone is the distance from the frame's right boundary within which Publisher will hyphenate words. You can change this distance or disable this option if you prefer not to hyphenate at all. Single-Click Object Creation allows you to click an object tool and click once in your document to create a 2"× 3" text frame, but you can still drag to create frames of other sizes.

User Assistance

The User Assistance tab of the Options dialog box offers you some control over how certain wizards behave. The Quick Publications Wizard is on by default when you select a blank page to begin. You can disable it here if you don't use it often.

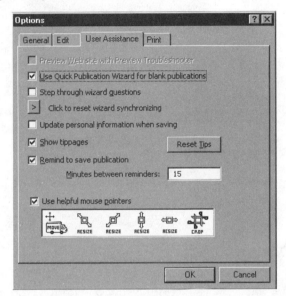

Step Through Wizard Questions allows you to proceed through a series of dialog boxes to produce a publication, rather than clicking the steps from a list. You can reenable smart coloring (covered at length in Chapter 42) by resetting wizard synchronization here. Disable tippages (a form of context-specific user assistance about Publisher's features) and save reminders if you prefer not to see these messages while you work. Helpful mouse pointers include the moving truck and arrows that say "Resize." Disabling these gives you a more typical set of pointer shapes.

Print Options

The Print options that are available to you depend on the type of printer(s) you have installed on your system. Enable the Print Troubleshooter to assist you with problems arising after you send publications to the printer. Enabling the Print Line-By-Line option may help if your DeskJet printer consistently mishandles objects and upside-down text. If you are connected to a printer designated for envelope printing, you'll see options for automatic formatting and print feed.

PART

IX

Publishing with Office

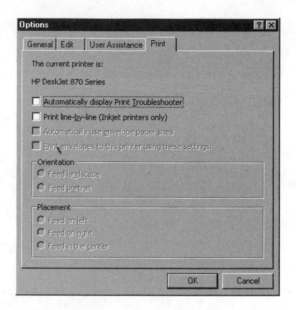

Printing Your Publications

Before you even begin creating your publication, you should give serious thought to how you are going to print the final product. Will you use your own printer or a commercial printing service? What type of paper will you print on? What color paper? Will you duplex? Staple? Fold? Collate?

It's a good idea to set up your publication for the type of printing you want before you place objects on the page. Otherwise you may be forced to make design changes just before the final printing.

Desktop Printing

If you are printing from a desktop printer, click File ➤ Print Setup for printer options. Select the size and location of the paper you will be using. (In Tray is the most common location; however, some printers have a sheet feeder as well.) Click the Properties button to set properties specific to your printer. Look for features like reverse order printing and collating. If your printer supports duplexing, booklet or banner printing, or stapling, you will also find these options under Properties.

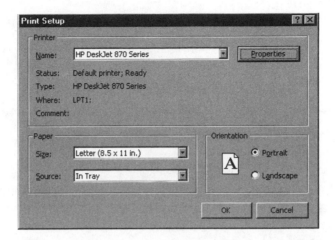

Click File ➢ Print to set options in the Print dialog box. Most options are similar to those in other Office applications: you can choose a printer, set a range of pages and a number of copies to print, and print to a file (for printing or further processing elsewhere). The Advanced Printing options are specific to Publisher. You can print at a lower resolution (it's a good idea to do this on drafts) and choose whether to let your printer substitute fonts. You can also choose to print crop marks and bleed marks. Bleeds are text and images that go beyond the trim edge of your publication (like those used in this book). If you want to print bleed marks, you have to select a paper size 1" larger than your document.

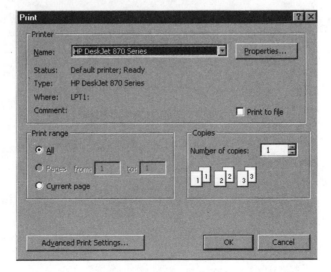

Working with a Commercial Printing Service

If you plan to print your final publication at a printing service, it is a good idea to set up your publication to do this right from the start. First you need to decide which type of printing service you will use: black-and-white printing, process color printing, or spot color printing. For either type of color printing, you also have the option of using the industry-standard Pantone Matching System.

NOTE If you're taking your publication in Publisher format to your printing service, use Pack And Go to save all the files your printing service will need.

Black-and-White Printing

In black-and-white printing, the printer uses only one color of ink (usually black, but most commercial printers will allow you to choose a different color if you want). Black-and-white printing uses grayscale to distinguish light and dark areas of your publication. Text and graphics can still produce dramatic effects in black-and-white. If you absolutely must have color and budget is a concern, considering printing on colored paper.

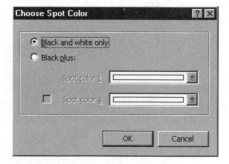

To set up for black-and-white printing, click Tools ➤ Commercial Printing Tools ➤ Color Printing to open the Color Printing dialog box shown in Figure 41.4.

Choose Spot Color(s) from the available options and then click Change Spot Color. In the Choose Spot Color dialog box, click Black And White Only. Click OK twice to close both dialog boxes.

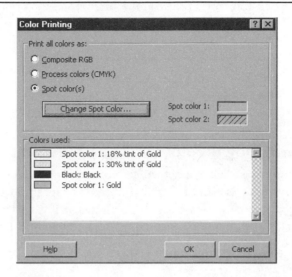

Process Color Printing

Use process color printing when your publication contains high-quality color photos
or if you need to print a wide range of colors. As you might expect, process color
printing costs more than other types because of the number of different colors you
use. If budget is a consideration, you might want to look at the other two commercial
printing options. To set up for process color printing, click the Tools menu, point to
Commercial Printing Tools, and click Color Printing to open the dialog box shown in
Figure 41.4. Click Process colors (CMYK) from the list of options. Selecting the Cyan
Magenta Yellow Black (CMYK) color model for a commercially printed publication is
important because not all colors you see on your monitor, which uses the Red Green
Blue (RGB) color model, can be printed using CMYK. To ensure that your printing service can match the colors on your screen, choose CMYK and then review the publication for color changes. If you see color changes you don't like, select the object and
recolor it in the publication.

Spot Color Printing

Spot color printing allows you to use color for lines and accents in your publication.
You can match up to two colors in a company logo or other artwork. Your publication
prints primarily in black, but you can choose up to two spot colors. Tints of the spot
colors can be used throughout the publication as well. Spot color printing is a nice
budget compromise between complete black-and-white and the more expensive
process color printing.

PART

IX

Publishing with
Office

Click Tools➤ Commercial Printing Services ➤ Color Printing. Select Spot Colors and click Change Spot Color. Select one or two spot colors and click OK.

 TIP If you choose black plus one spot color, all colors except black are converted to tints of the spot color.

Switching to Another Type of Printing

Change your mind about which type of printing to use? Click Tools ➤ Commercial Printing Tools ➤ Color Printing. Choose Composite RGB to switch back to desktop printing. Choose Process Colors or Spot Colors or, if you want to switch to black-and-white, click Spot Colors ➤ Change Spot Color and select the Black And White Only option.

Pantone Color Matching

When you work with a commercial printer, colors on your computer screen may not exactly match the colors that get printed in your publication. The colors in your Publisher file only tell your printing service *where* the color goes, not *what* the exact color will be.

Printing services support a number of different color-matching systems. It is best to ask your printer which colors and paper types would work best, before you design your publication. Most likely they will give you some numbered color swatches and suggestions for paper types. You can choose Publisher colors from process color-matching systems that your printing service supports and then specify colors from the swatches for use in your publication. Publisher provides the Pantone Matching System (PMS), which you can use to specify colors for a commercial printing service. Before you can use this color matching system, you have to decide whether to use spot color printing or process color printing.

Regardless of which type of printing you choose, navigate to the Color Printing dialog box shown earlier, in Figure 41.4. Choose the Spot Color Option and click Change Spot Color. Select More Colors from the Spot Color 1 drop-down list and click All Colors. Under Color Model, select Pantone from the list.

For spot color printing, make sure you are on the Pantone Solid tab. If you're opting for process color printing, use the Pantone Process tab. Under Color Type, choose whether your publication will be printed on Coated or Uncoated Paper. If you know the PMS number for the color you want, type it in the Find Color Name box and press Enter, or scroll to the color you want. Click OK four times to close all the dialog boxes.

You might design process color publications (like brochures or sales materials) that include spot color objects (like a company logo). In this case you need to convert each object's Pantone solid color to a process color that matches. Select the spot color object. Click Format ➤ Fill Color ➤ More Colors. Choose All Colors if it is not already selected. Under Color Model, choose Pantone. Make sure you select the Pantone Solid tab of the dialog box and choose Convert To Process under Color Type. Select the color and click OK twice to close both dialog boxes.

Font Embedding

Any time you plan to print your publication from a computer other than the one you used to create it, you should consider font embedding. Embedded fonts show up in printed material just as they appeared on your screen.

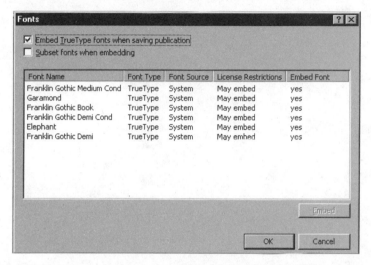

Click Tools ➤ Commercial Printing Tools ➤ Fonts to open the Fonts dialog box. If you choose Embed TrueType Fonts When Saving Publication, your fonts will appear as expected on most any computer and you will have the ability to edit using your own fonts whether the other machine has them installed or not. Choosing this first option causes your Publisher file to be larger because it saves the font sets along with it. The Subset option also embeds fonts but only saves the actual characters you've used in your publication. If the printing service needs to edit, they will be limited to those characters you have already included.

What's Next

As soon as you are comfortable creating and formatting text frames, you will want to look at the other object tools in Publisher. Pictures, ClipArt, WordArt, borders, shapes, and a myriad of other design elements are at your fingertips. In Chapter 42, you'll learn about placement, formatting, and editing of graphics.

CHAPTER <u>42</u>

Working with Graphic Objects

FEATURING:

Inserting Publisher graphic objects

Working with multiple objects

Recoloring objects

Modifying frame properties

Changing page setup options

Text frames can be put together in ways that create very professional-looking documents, as you saw in the last chapter. But certain types of business publications rely on exceptional graphics to interest the reader. What's a marketing brochure without illustrations? How can you sell products from a catalog without displaying pictures? Even text-heavy documents can benefit from the occasional sidebar (another type of graphic element).

In this chapter you will learn how to create, format, edit, and align different types of graphics for maximum "Wow!" factor.

Inserting Publisher Graphic Objects

There are so many object choices available in Publisher that it can be difficult to know where to begin. Some of the objects, like clip art, WordArt, and tables, may be familiar from other Office applications and are covered in greater depth elsewhere in the book. You will find that certain objects (like pictures and clip art) are easy to select and insert, while others (like WordArt) require that you spend some time on formatting. That's not to say you won't ever spend lots of time on the select-and-insert variety. Once you bring an object into your publication, you may decide to recolor, rotate, flip, or otherwise edit the piece. Your starting point for working with graphic objects is the Object toolbar:

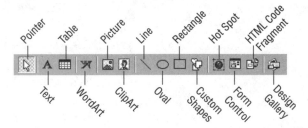

These Publisher frame tools work the same, in concept, as the text frame tool. One click on the object tool selects it. A click and drag in your document creates a space to house the object while you format and edit it. If Single-Click Object Creation is left enabled, you can create a 2" × 3" object frame with two clicks: one on the object tool and one in the document. As you would expect, you can move or resize an object at any time.

Tables

You may have heard it said that if you press Tab more than once on the same line, you should be working in a table. Use the Table frame tool to display data in columns and rows. By design, tables allow text to wrap within a cell so that there is a minimal amount of reformatting when text is inserted or deleted. Figure 42.1 shows an example of a publication that includes a table.

FIGURE 42.1

This publication shows several graphic design elements: WordArt, company logo, barbell design, drawn lines, and a table.

Ten Minute Trainer

Continuing computer education for students and former students of

Triad Consulting, LLC

Volume 1, Issue 1 February, 1999

TRIAD at a Glance

As a manager in today's business world, you know that having all of the information needed to make quality decisions is no easy task. Running an organization requires efficient and accurate data from a variety of sources. Computer technology makes collecting and communicating data easier-- but only for those who know how to use technology effectively. TRIAD Consulting can provide you with the knowledge you need to bring your organization into the information age. Whether it is designing data systems, training your employees, or helping you evaluate hardware and software to meet your needs, TRIAD can make technology work for you.

Installing powerful computers in your workplace will not make your organization more efficient unless your employees know how to make the best use of them. TRIAD offers customized training programs that are designed around the way your employees work and your organization's needs so employees can put what they learn into practice immediately when they return to their desks.

We provide training in Windows 3.1, Windows 95, NT Workstation, and Microsoft Office products: versions 4.2, 95, and 97. Our training teams also design and deliver specialized training your employees need, such as:

- Visual Basic for Applications
- Programming in Excel
- Impromptu (4 GL)
- Database theory

With the thousands of new computer products on the market today, deciding which ones will best meet your company's needs requires a dedicated information professional. TRIAD will research and answer your information management questions so you can decide how to make the most of your computer

Upcoming Training Classes

Class	Dates	Times
Beginning Word	12/3 and 12/10	4—7 PM
Beginning Excel	12/7 and 12/14	8—11 AM
NT Server	12/1—12/4	2—7 PM
Intermediate Word	12/11 and 12/18	4—7 PM

Quick System Maintenance

Illegal Operation Errors? Keyboard and Mouse freezing? Complete crashes without saving your documents? Yes, it can happen to you if you are not running proper system maintenance. Who would

(Continued on page 3)

1

As soon as you finish dragging the Table tool, the Create Table dialog box opens.

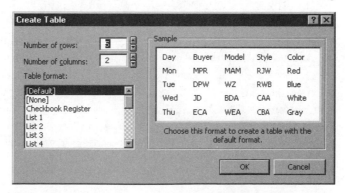

Enter the number of rows and columns for your table and choose a table format from the list on the left. Use the Sample window to view the borders, shading, and special text formatting included with each design. Select the one that's closest to what you have in mind; you can always modify formatting manually. When you click OK, Publisher throws a formatted empty grid onto your page.

Enter text and/or numbers into each cell, pressing Tab to move one cell to the right. You can also use the mouse or arrow keys to position your insertion point in a cell. Apply or remove formatting as you would in a Word table (see Chapter 6). Select rows or columns by clicking the gray header box (your pointer changes to a hand).

Class	Dates	Times
Beginning Word	12/3 and 12/10	4—7 PM
Beginning Excel	12/7 and 12/14	8—11 AM
NT Server	12/1—12/4	2—7 PM
Intermediate Word	12/11 and 12/18	4—7 PM

Select Cells

Select multiple rows or columns by dragging the headers. Select the entire table by clicking the gray box at the upper left of the table, where row and column headers intersect. Adjust column width and row height by dragging the Adjust tool between headers.

WordArt

Use the WordArt Frame tool to create dramatic shapes and patterns out of text. In Figure 42.1, the publication title and company logo are examples of WordArt. You can create letters that cascade up, ripple down, or wave like a flag, and you can add borders to the letters, fill them with patterns, or rotate them for different effects.

When you work in WordArt, the Publisher tools are not available to you. The toolbar displays only the WordArt tools, but you can get back to Publisher by clicking away from the object. Double-click an existing WordArt Object to edit it. Use the WordArt tool on the Object toolbar only when you want to create a new WordArt object. See Chapter 7 for more about working with WordArt.

You won't see ToolTips on the buttons in the WordArt toolbar, so you may have to experiment a bit at first. Or you can choose to edit using the Format menu from within WordArt. Choosing Format ➤ Border allows you to add or edit how your letters are outlined. Format ➤ Shading allows you to fill the interiors of letters with solid colors or patterns. If you want to shadow letters, choose a style and color by clicking

Format ➤ Shadow. You can rotate a WordArt object or "slide" the letters horizontally by choosing Format ➤ Rotation And Effects.

 TIP   Publisher 2000 uses a different version of WordArt than the other Office tools. To open the more robust WordArt through Microsoft Draw, click Insert ➤ Object. From the Insert dialog box, click Microsoft Draw 98 Drawing, and then click OK. Use the WordArt button on the Microsoft Drawing toolbar to create a new WordArt object. Chapter 7 describes editing this type of WordArt in detail.

Pictures and Clip Art

You will find frame tools for pictures and clip art on Publisher's Object toolbar. Publisher treats clip art and pictures much the same. Pictures usually look more like photographs while clip art has the flavor of a cartoon drawing. While it is true that you can insert clip art into a picture frame or insert a picture into a clip art frame, it's more efficient to start with the type of frame you need to produce the type of graphic you prefer.

When you drag a space using the Picture tool, a blank frame appears in your document. Insert a picture by double-clicking the empty frame (you can also select the frame and choose Insert ➤ Picture ➤ From File) to go to the Insert File dialog box. Navigate to the drive and folder where the picture is stored, select it, and click Insert. Double-click this object if you want to return to the Insert Picture dialog box and select a different picture to replace it.

The ClipArt tool behaves slightly differently. After you drag to create a space using the ClipArt frame tool, Publisher automatically takes you to the ClipArt Gallery, where you can browse the available art. Select one of the gallery objects to insert or, if you don't see one you like, you can cancel out of the gallery and insert a picture instead. Make sure the frame is selected and choose Insert ➤ Picture ➤ From File to select a picture stored on your local drive, a network drive, or a floppy disk. Chapters 7 and 15 both contain additional information on using the Clip Gallery.

Shapes

Publisher gives you the ability to draw lines of various weights and colors. You can also create ovals, rectangles, and a host of custom shapes like arrows, cubes, and triangles. The most commonly used shapes—lines, ovals, and rectangles—have their own buttons on the Object toolbar. Click a button to select the shape you like and drag the size you want in your document.

Select the frame that contains the shape and use the Fill button to select a color for its interior. The Border button allows you to select a plain black line to outline the frame, or you can click More Styles to select an alternate weight and color for the outline. If you want a border that is wider than 10 points, type the size you want in the field at the bottom-left of the Border dialog box.

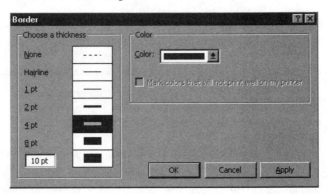

The Custom Shapes tool allows you to create hearts, stars, lightning bolts, triangles, and more. Once you have created a shape, Publisher 2000 gives you the ability to resize one or both object dimensions. The arrow shown below has been resized two ways: the width of the base has been narrowed, and the height of the tip has been shortened. To resize one dimension, place your pointer on the gray diamond and drag the Adjust tool. You still have the ability to resize the entire object using the regular handles.

Web Tools

There are three Web tools on the Object toolbar: Hot Spot, Form Control, and HTML Fragment. These and other powerful Web features are discussed at length in Chapter 43.

Design Gallery Objects

The Design Gallery contains roughly twenty categories of objects, such as mastheads, linear accents, calendars, and logos that you can add to your publication. You even have the ability to store objects that you create in a publication on a special tab of the

Design Gallery dialog box. That means you can store your company logo in the Design Gallery and easily use it again and again.

To display the Design Gallery, choose Insert ➤ Design Gallery Object. Figure 42.2 shows the Objects By Category tab of the Design Gallery.

FIGURE 42.2

The Design Gallery contains many categories of objects ready to be inserted into your publication.

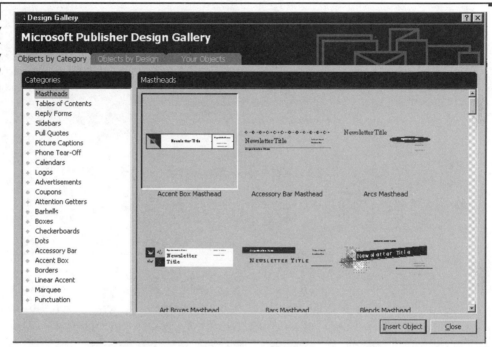

If you prefer, you can select a Design Gallery object based on a design set. Click the Objects By Design tab, shown in Figure 42.3, and select from the list on the left. You will see different types of objects with certain design elements in common. Using objects from the same set gives a consistent look and feel to your publication.

You can store the objects from your current publication on the Your Objects tab of the Design Gallery. (This is particularly helpful if you have edited or recolored objects and want to have them readily available for use in other publications.) When you first create a publication, its design set on the Your Objects tab is empty. You create a design set for your publication by creating categories and adding objects to the categories. Select the object you want to add and open the Design Gallery from the Objects toolbar.

PART

IX

Publishing with Office

FIGURE 42.3

The Objects By Design tab with the Tilt set selected

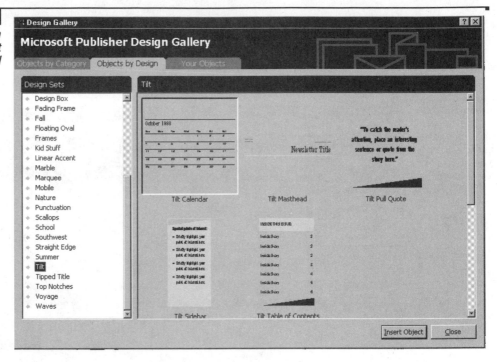

Choose the Your Objects tab and click the Options button in the lower-left corner. Click the Add Selection To Design Gallery menu option to open the Add Object dialog box. Under Object Name, type a name for the object; under Category enter a new category or select a category that you have already created. Click OK and then Close to return to your document. Changes that you make to the Design Gallery are saved when you save your publication.

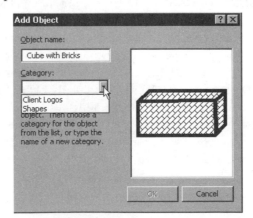

Essentials of Good Design

Knowing how to use Publisher's object tools won't guarantee good results. Before you put your first frame on a page, you should have an overall design in mind. And before you come up with your overall design, you should know the essentials of good design. Entire books have been written on this topic, and you would be wise to keep one handy for reference. At the absolute minimum, consider three elements when creating publications: simplicity, consistency, and contrast.

Simplicity means just that: Keep it simple! Use no more than two font families per publication. Use a sans serif font for headings and a serif font for body text. Avoid the tendency to include too many graphic objects. It should be obvious where you want your audience to glance when they first look at a page. Too many graphics can cause the reader's eye to wander all over the page with the likely result that they end up seeing nothing.

When a publication follows the consistency rule, every element seems to naturally belong there. The idea is to create a "personality" for your document. You may find this is easier to do with lengthy publications, but keep the rule in mind when you're designing a one-page flyer as well. Internally, use the same heading format for each section of your document. Choose a bullet character and stick with it throughout. Page numbers should appear in the same location on each page. Use an overall color scheme to create a unified look throughout. Work with the Objects By Design tab of the Design Gallery.

If you publish your document periodically, there are external consistency considerations as well. Certain graphic objects (borders, banners, and logos, for example) should remain the same from issue to issue. Illustrative graphics such as photographs will be different each time you publish, but text formatting and page setup should be consistent. Radical design changes between issues require notice to the reader, or they may not recognize your publication the next time they see it.

It is possible to overwhelm your audience with too much on a page. Be sure to incorporate contrast into your work. Leave plenty of white space around and between your objects. (It's called *white space* even if you print on blue paper.) The blank areas of your document are just as important as text and other objects in determining whether someone will want to pick up and read your publication.

You can add, rename, and delete categories in your design set by choosing Options ➤ Edit Categories at the bottom of the Your Objects tab of the Design Gallery. Choose the category you wish to edit and click the Rename button. Type the new category name and click OK. To remove a category, select it in the Edit Categories dialog box and click the Delete button. Click the Add button and type a name for the new category to add it to your design set.

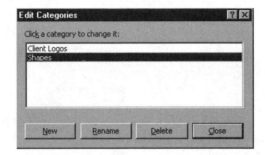

Delete an object from your design set by selecting it and choosing the Your Objects tab of the dialog box. Then click Options ➤ Delete This Object. Once again, these changes to the Design Gallery are saved when you save your publication.

The categories and objects you add are specific to the publication you added them from. However, if you want to insert an object from a design set you (or someone else) created in another publication, click Options on the Your Objects tab of the Design Gallery and choose Browse from the menu. Select the publication that has the object you want and click OK. The Your Objects tab now displays the design set for the publication you just selected. Choose the object you want and click Insert Object.

NOTE You can only rename and delete categories from the design set in the active publication. You cannot rename or delete categories from another publication's design set, and you cannot rename or delete Publisher's built-in object categories.

Working with Multiple Objects

Chapter 41 introduced Publisher's object-oriented model, in which every element of your publication is a separate object. Suppose you have a picture that goes with a particular section of your employee manual. If you change the placement of the section, you would want the picture to move with it, right? Or suppose you have two pieces of clip art that need to overlap slightly. Wouldn't you like to choose which piece is on top? Finally, suppose you're placing three objects at the left margin of your newsletter cover. You most certainly want them to line up, right?

These are some of the issues that come up when you work with many objects on a page.

Grouping Objects

  If a particular graphic will always appear next to a certain piece of text, it makes sense to group the two objects. Two or more objects with fixed positions relative to each other should be grouped, since grouped objects can be moved and resized as one unit. As shown here, a title should be grouped with the text or other object it describes so the two never become separated. Drag one and you're dragging the other as well:

Upcoming Training Classes

Class	Dates	Times
Beginning Word	12/3 and 12/10	4—7 PM
Beginning Excel	12/7 and 12/14	8—11 AM
NT Server	12/1—12/4	2—7 PM
Intermediate Word	12/11 and 12/18	4—7 PM

To group objects, select the first with a click. Hold Shift and click each additional object you wish to group. Click the Object Grouping icon at the bottom of the frame surrounding the selected objects. These objects are now "hooked" together so you can move and resize them as a group. Click the icon again to ungroup the objects. Now you can move and resize them separately—just click the one you want.

Layering Objects

There are times when you will want to place one object on top of another. The Bring To Front and Send To Back buttons make it easy to do that. Here is an example of a text box displayed on top of a piece of clip art. The objects are layered—clip art on the bottom, text on the top.

Insert and arrange the two objects you wish to layer. If you can't see the object that's currently on the bottom, select the one on the top and click the Send To Back button. If you can see at least part of the object that is underneath, select it and click the Bring To Front button.

Lining Up Objects

You can align selected objects to each other or a margin. The Snap To feature lets you easily align objects to a ruler guide as well. Select all objects to be aligned and click the Arrange menu. Then choose Align Objects to open the dialog box. (You can also right-click selected objects and choose Align from the shortcut menu.)

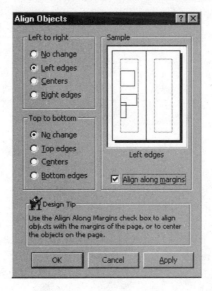

The titles of the option groups in this dialog box refer to the object frames themselves, so use the Left To Right options if you are aligning objects vertically. Use the options under Top To Bottom if you want to line up your objects horizontally across a page.

 TIP To center selected objects between the left and right margins, enable the Align Along Margins feature and then choose Left To Right Centers.

Snap To

The Snap To option makes it easy to align objects precisely. It creates an invisible grid on your page; objects are pulled to the imaginary grid lines or to nearby boundaries and ruler guides. You can also have objects snap to other objects.

You'll find the Snap To options on the Tools menu. Turn on Snap To Boundaries, and each time you drag an object near a boundary, it will "jump" to the edge of the boundary. Snap To Ruler Guides works the same way. If the boundaries and guides are hidden, objects will still Snap To. (Boundaries and guides were covered in more detail in Chapter 41.)

Rotating Objects

You can change the angle at which an object is displayed by rotating it any number of degrees. Click the Rotate tool on the Standard toolbar (or choose Arrange ➤ Rotate or Flip ➤ Custom Rotate) to open the dialog box. The rotation buttons in this dialog will change the display angle by 5 degrees per click. For larger rotations, you can simply type the degrees in the Angle box and click OK.

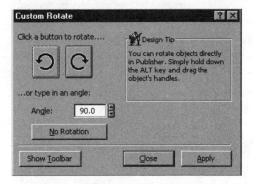

Click Show Toolbar to see the Measurement toolbar. You can change the size, spacing, display angle, or position of a selected object using the spin boxes shown here.

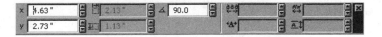

To rotate by 90 degrees, use the buttons on the toolbar or click Arrange ➤ Rotate or Flip ➤ Rotate Right (or Left).

TIP If you prefer working directly in Publisher, you can rotate any object by pressing Alt and dragging an object handle.

Flipping Objects

Publisher 2000 gives you the ability to "flip" a graphic from the Clip Gallery vertically or horizontally. Select the object and click the appropriate toolbar button. You can also choose Arrange ➤ Rotate or Flip ➤ Flip Horizontal (or Vertical).

Recoloring Objects

Frequently you will find a piece of clip art that looks great except for its color. Choose and insert it anyway because you have several options for changing object color(s) with a few clicks of the mouse. You can change all the colors in a picture to different shades of one color and leave the black lines untouched. Or you may prefer to have the black lines change with the new color as well. If these options don't work for you, you can bring the picture into Paint or Microsoft Draw and edit colors there.

TIP For an easy way to recolor clip art, copy the art into PowerPoint and click the Recolor button on the Picture toolbar. When you're finished, copy-and-paste back into your Publisher document.

To change all the colors in a picture to a single color, shade, or tint, select the picture and click Format ➤ Recolor Picture. You can also right-click the object and choose Change Object ➤ Recolor from the shortcut menu. Select a color from the drop-down list and choose whether to recolor the entire picture or leave the black lines as is. Unfortunately, recoloring an object using two or more colors is a much less efficient process in Publisher. The only easy way to do that is to automatically recolor clip art by applying a color scheme to the entire publication. Publisher will select colors for your objects that fit the scheme you select.

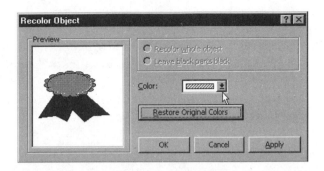

If you choose fill effects from the Color drop-down list, you have options for formatting tints and shades as well as gradients and patterns. *Tints* are a base color mixed with white; *shades* are a base color mixed with black. Tints and shades can be part of a custom color scheme.

 TIP To create a watermark, recolor pictures using tints or shades of a base color.

Patterns are simple repeating designs, and gradients use tints and shades to create vertical, horizontal, and other shading patterns. Here you can see the difference between a pattern and a gradient.

 TIP If you are planning to use a commercial printing service, it's probably best not to use patterns in your publication. Patterns can slow down the imaging time, thus increasing your costs.

Modifying Frame Properties

The shortcut menus for both text and graphic object frames give you access to properties you can modify for various purposes. For example, you can add a border so that the frame itself prints. You can add color, patterns, or other effects to an object's background. Changing frame properties also allows you to display text in multiple columns.

Text Frames

Right-click any text frame and point to Change Frame on the shortcut menu. Choose Fill Color to see a multitude of possibilities for background colors, with the current scheme's colors shown first. Choose More Schemes to choose another scheme of colors, or More Colors to see an entire palette. Fill Effects offers you options for tints, shades, patterns, and gradients.

The Line Color choice on the shortcut menu is unavailable if you have not previously applied a border to the frame. Use the Line/Border Style choice to apply a border of your chosen point size and color. The next time you wish to edit this object's border, you can do so under Line Color. Shadow Effects creates a gray shadow on the right and bottom borders of the text frame. Shadows look great with or without a border. Choosing Text Frame Properties from this shortcut menu brings you to a dialog box where you can adjust margins and change column settings.

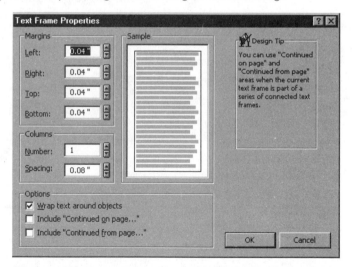

Change the distance from the text to the frame using the spin boxes for margin adjustment. Format text for two or more columns using the spin box on the Columns control. The spacing control adjusts space between columns.

Enable the Wrap Text Around Objects feature if you plan to place objects in the middle of text. The template shown here includes a text frame formatted for two columns with Text Wrapping enabled. The object and its caption are in two separate frames that have been grouped.

Graphic Frames

Select the object for which you wish to modify frame properties. Right-click and choose Change Frame or click the Format menu to see the same choices you get on the shortcut menu. You can format borders and add fills just as you would for a text frame. The Picture Frame Properties dialog box offers options for how closely you want text to wrap around the art. The margin controls in this dialog box control the distance from the picture to the frame.

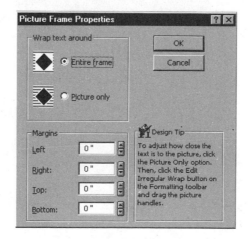

PART

IX

Publishing with Office

Cropping Art

 You can use just part of a picture or other graphic by selecting it and dragging the Crop tool over one of the resize handles. As you drag the frame border, instead of making the entire picture smaller, it removes the areas of the picture you drag over, leaving only the parts that remain inside the frame. Drag the Crop tool over as many of the resize handles as you need to use until your art is perfectly positioned. Click the Crop tool again to turn it off, or click anywhere else in your publication.

Modifying Page Setup Options

If you are printing on paper that is a different size than your publication, you may need to modify Page Setup. On the File Menu, click Page Setup. In the bottom-left corner of the dialog are settings for Portrait and Landscape. Choose the correct setting for your publication.

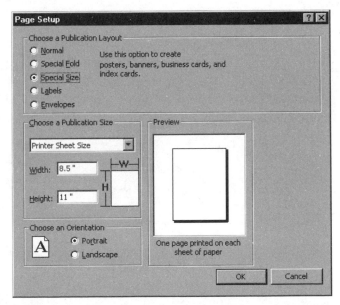

From the Publication Layout options, choose Normal if you want one printed page on each sheet of paper; choose this if you are duplexing on a manual-feed printer as well. The Special Fold option is for printing folded documents like cards or small booklets with two pages on a sheet. The Special Size option supports banners, index cards, and poster printing. The Special Fold, Special Size, Labels, and Envelopes options each display a list where you'll need to make further selections.

Margins

Publisher doesn't use page margins in the usual sense of the word. Instead, you get boundary lines that show a 1" margin by default. (Chapter 41 shows how to set up these lines the way you want them.) The boundary lines don't act like margins in Word; you can place objects on or outside them without having to adjust them. You can set margins for frames (see "Modifying Frame Properties" earlier in this chapter). Frame margins act more like the traditional margins you may be used to. They determine how far text or art appears from the edge of the frame.

Headers and Footers

Publisher also treats headers and footers differently than Word. Text and objects that appear on every page in a Publisher document are placed on a "background" layer. To display this layer, click View ➢ Go To Background. Any objects you may have already placed in the foreground become invisible as you work on the background, and the View menu now displays Go To Foreground as a choice.

Create a header by placing and formatting text and/or object frames outside the top margin boundary. Footers go just outside of the bottom boundary. Click the View menu and choose Go To Foreground to return to your regular document. You should still be able to see your background text and objects.

To hide a header or footer on the first page of your document, navigate to the first page of your publication. Hide all background objects using View ➢ Ignore Background. If there are other background objects besides the header or footer that you don't want to hide, drag a new text frame to cover just the header and/or footer. When you print, you won't see the empty text frame.

There may be times when you want to mirror header and footer setup. Booklets are a great example of when you might want to do this. Go to the background and create the header or footer as you normally would, but make sure you set it up to appear on every *right* page of your publication. Click Arrange ➢ Layout Guides. Enable the Create Two Backgrounds With Mirrored Guides feature and click OK. Switch back to the foreground and continue working.

What's Next

Now that you understand the elements that make up a publication, you might want to learn the shortcuts to creating quick, professional-looking documents. Publisher wizards offer dozens of templates for all types of documents, from corporate manuals to garage-sale flyers. Chapter 43 explores these wizards as well as other helpful features like design checking and personal information tracking.

PART

IX

Publishing with
Office

CHAPTER **43**

Publisher Wizards and Other Time-Saving Features

FEATURING:

Working with the Design Checker

Using personal information in publications

Organizing art with the Graphics Manager

Using wizards and shared designs to create publications

Creating mail merge documents

Creating and printing booklets

Producing Web publications

ow that you have a solid understanding of the text and graphic object components that make up a publication, you can use Publisher's time-saving features that allow you to put together eye-catching documents faster than ever! Publisher's redesigned wizards quickly guide you through the layout process. The Personal Information documentation feature allows you to insert your own company information into a publication with a couple of clicks.

Mail merge in Publisher works better than ever, and now you can use your Outlook address book as a data source to create a directory, mailing labels, or envelopes. If you're the person who puts together your company's employee manual or sales catalog, you'll want to take look at the features for creating directories and other booklet-type publications.

Working with the Design Checker

With lengthy publications, it's easy to overlook errors such as text that hides in the overflow area, or objects that overlap where they shouldn't. Publisher's Design Checker can help you find problem areas such as these. From the Tools menu, choose Design Checker to open the dialog box.

Choose whether to check all pages in your publication or a certain page range. Enable background checking if you have placed objects on the background. Publisher will check for potential design problems in several areas, although you can disable certain types of design checking under Options.

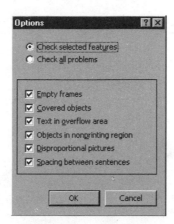

You may want to disable Covered Objects if you have intentionally overlapped objects in your publication. Disable the Disproportional Pictures check if you have deliberately resized a piece of art to change its original dimensions. (If Publisher spots a disproportional object problem, it gives you a Change button that will change the selected object back to its original proportions while keeping the same approximate size.) Click OK twice to close both dialog boxes and start the Design Checker. When Publisher notices a problem, it selects that frame in your document and displays a dialog box that describes the problem and gives you suggestions on how to handle it.

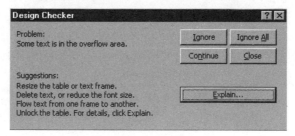

You can ignore the problem if it's something you want to leave as is, or if you prefer to go back and manually change it later. You can click Ignore All to have Publisher skip other problems like this. Or, you can fix the problem (following one of Publisher's suggestions); you don't have to close the dialog to make a fix. Simply click and edit in your document and then click Continue in the dialog box to finish design checking.

Using Personal Information in Publications

Publisher can store up to four sets of personal information. Each set contains fields such as name, address, job title, e-mail address, and logo. You can enter one set of data that reflects your business contact information and another for home information. If you are designing a publication for another organization, you can store that organization's information as well. Figure 43.1 shows the Personal Information dialog box, which you can open by clicking Edit ➤ Personal Information.

The Personal Information dialog box can store up to four sets of information for use in your publications.

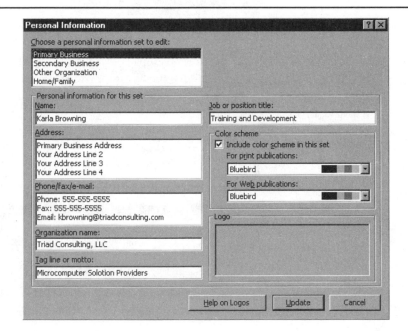

First, choose a personal information set from the list of four at the top of the dialog box. Then type information in each field as you want it to appear in your publication. (Don't worry about fonts and sizes here; plan to handle formatting when you insert this information later.) Enter data for as many sets as you wish. Click Update to save a set.

 TIP It's a good idea to choose a color scheme if you want to be consistent within the publications you create for each personal information set. Inserting personal information components will apply the selected color scheme to the current publication. If you update personal information by changing the scheme, the new scheme is applied to the current publication.

When you want to use any of the information you entered, take these steps:

1. Navigate to the page on which you wish to insert it.

2. Click Insert ➢ Personal Information.

3. Choose which field you want from the submenu and click it. Publisher inserts your data in its own text frame that you can arrange and format as you wish.

To insert additional fields (components) of data, go back to Insert ➢ Personal Information and select another field. You can include a field as many times as you wish throughout the publication. If you edit the information in a personal information set, all fields of that type will be updated in the current publication.

Organizing Art with the Graphics Manager

When you insert art into any Office 2000 application, you have the option to insert a link rather than embed the picture itself. This makes for much smaller file sizes in your Publisher documents. In the event you need to see details about links or edit links, you will need to use the Graphics Manager. You can also use the Graphics Manager to change an embedded object to a linked object.

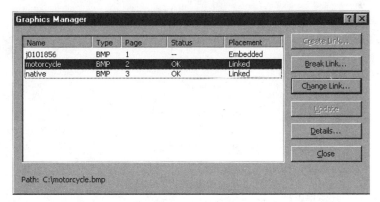

Click Tools ➢ Commercial Printing Services ➢ Graphics Manager to see a list of all the pictures or ClipArt in the active document. Select the name of the linked picture you wish to work with. Click Details to see information about the file such as its path, date last modified, and size.

To edit the link so that it points to a different picture, click Change Link. (You can do this from the Details screen or the Graphics Manager.) Change to the drive or folder where the new picture is stored, select it, and click Link To File.

In the event that Publisher can't follow a link to the original file (for instance, if the original file was renamed or on removable media like a CD that is no longer in the drive) the Update button becomes available for you to reestablish the link.

If you wish to break a link, you have two options for doing so: full resolution embedding or low resolution embedding. You can probably get by with low resolution until you print your final draft.

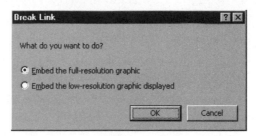

When you want to create a link for an object that is currently embedded, open the Graphics Manager and select the file. Choose Create Link and select one of the link options. If the embedded picture is already stored in a file you can browse to, choose the Browse To Locate option. If the embedded picture doesn't have an associated file, you can make one by selecting the second option and clicking OK. Choose a folder and file name for the picture and click Save. Now you can use the picture in other publications, as well.

Using Wizards and Shared Designs to Create Publications

How would you like to put together a design including color scheme, art, banners, sidebars, and text frames, all in a few minutes? Wizards and shared designs allow you to do just that! New and improved in Office 2000, Publisher's wizards and designs are easier to use than ever with more document types and new design themes for electrifying publications in minutes!

The Quick Publication Wizard

Publisher offers wizards for various types of publications, such as newsletters, flyers, brochures, calendars, and so on. For anything that doesn't fit one of these categories, the Quick Publication Wizard can get you rolling in a hurry. In the Microsoft Publisher Catalog (File ➤ New gets you there), choose Quick Publications from the list on the left. Browse the templates on the right, select the one you like, and click the Start Wizard button at the bottom of the screen. You will see your document on the right and the wizard on the left, as shown in Figure 43.2.

FIGURE 43.2

The Introduction step
of the Quick
Publications Wizard

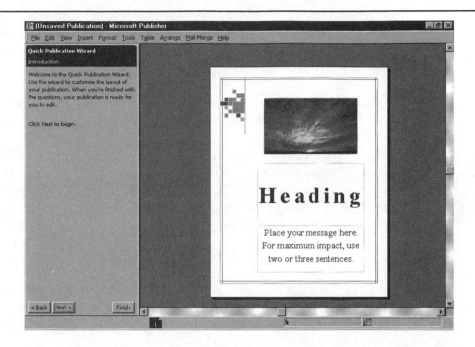

You're given a one-page document (to which you can add other pages as needed) and a series of steps to complete the design and layout of your publication. This wizard (and all others) starts with an Introduction step. Click Next to proceed. At the Color Scheme step, select from the list of schemes and click Next to move to the Layout step. Select from the list of layouts to determine the position of Publisher placeholders or choose No Layout if you want to add your own design elements.

Click Next to see the Personal Information step and add elements you want to include in your publication, or click Update to change the data in a personal information set. Be sure to select which of the four personal information sets you want to

PART

IX

Publishing with
Office

use before inserting or editing Personal Information components. You can click the Back button at any point in the wizard to return to a previous step. When you're through, click Finish to have Publisher create the publication based on the choices you made in the wizard.

Any time you wish to return to the wizard's original settings, navigate back to the Design step by choosing if from the list on the left and click the Reset Design button at the bottom of that page. You'll have options to delete text and/or graphics you've added since starting the wizard. You can also reset Page and Layout options. Hide the wizard at any time by clicking the Hide Wizard button at the bottom left of the screen.

In general, you can edit or replace the contents of graphic object frames with a double-click. Replace sample placeholder text by clicking on the appropriate text frame and overtyping it with your own message. Any pages, objects, and text frames you insert will have the settings you entered in the wizard.

Other Wizards

The Microsoft Publisher Catalog contains dozens of wizards to help you create many different types of documents. The catalog opens automatically when you launch Publisher (unless you have disabled that option). To see the catalog from within Publisher, click File ➢ New. Make sure you have selected the Publications By Wizard tab.

The Catalog Wizard

The Catalog Wizard should not be confused with the Publisher Catalog. The former is an item in the latter. The Catalog Wizard helps you create a publication that lists, for instance, products and services your company sells. When you start this wizard, you are given eight pages with frames ready for product descriptions, pictures, headings, and general information.

The Introduction, Color Scheme, and Personal Information steps work the same as with the Quick Publications Wizard. However, you'll be prompted at the third step to choose whether to include a placeholder for the customer's address. When you choose to include a customer's address, Publisher puts the text frame on the last page of the catalog, which is already formatted for mailing.

 TIP You can use Publisher's mail merge options to create address labels for mailing your catalog.

Once you finish the Catalog Wizard, you have options to set up inside page content, so you can quickly redesign how items and descriptions are displayed. Use the page navigators at the bottom-left of the workspace to select a set of inside pages. Click the Inside Page Content step from the list on the left and select from the list of layout options below it.

Insert new pages by choosing that option from the list and then clicking the Insert Page button. If you're inserting inside pages, you'll be given layout options for the new pages. There are separate option lists for the right and left pages, or you can click More Options to see the standard Insert Page dialog box.

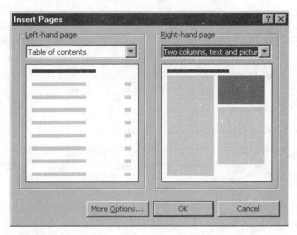

The Web Site Wizard

When you choose to create a Web site using the Publisher Wizard, you must first select a design, just as you would with any other wizard. The first three steps to creating a Web site are similar to what you have seen in other wizards, and the Web-specific steps are just as easy to use. Add sound, texture, or a customer order form with a few clicks. Preview animation using the Web Page Preview choice under the File menu.

NOTE The "Producing Web Publications" section at the end of this chapter provides detailed information about using Publisher as a Web tool.

The Pack and Go Wizard

Publisher file sizes tend to be much larger than regular word processed documents. Even if you link pictures, you may find that object formatting alone can cause your file to grow past floppy disk size in a hurry. If you need to take your file to another computer or to a commercial printer, or if you're concerned about storage space, make use of the Pack and Go Wizard.

Pack and Go only works if you have already saved the file in its regular (large) file format. Start the wizard by choosing File ➢ Pack and Go ➢ Take to Another Computer; then follow these steps:

1. The first step of Pack and Go tells you what the wizard will do for you. Click Next to move beyond this introductory screen.

2. Choose a location to put the packed file (the default is drive A, but you can browse to select another location). Click Next.

3. Choose whether to embed TrueType fonts, include linked graphics, or create links for embedded graphics. It's generally a good idea to select at least the first two if you're moving to a computer that might not have the same installed components as the system on which you created the publication. Click Next.

4. The last step of the wizard tells you what will happen to your file and how to unpack it when you need it again. Click Finish. The wizard will prompt you for additional disks if you're packing a large publication to floppy.

If you're packing for a commercial printing service, the wizard steps are mostly the same, but links are automatically created for embedded objects, and proof sets are printed for you as part of the process.

To open your packed publication, use the Windows Explorer to navigate to the drive or folder where it is stored and double-click unpack.exe. You will be prompted for an unpack location and warned about the possibility of overwriting files with the same name.

Using Shared Designs to Create a Publication

Let's say you have already created company letterhead using Publisher's Arcs design. Now it's time to create a company Web site. Or maybe you're trying to match design elements from the sales presentation you've developed in PowerPoint. For consistency's sake, you *should* use some of the same design elements in all publications and presentations. That's where Publisher's shared designs can be helpful. Figure 43.3 shows the Publications By Design tab of the catalog.

FIGURE 43.3

The Publications By Design tab of the catalog shows many types of documents using the same design sets.

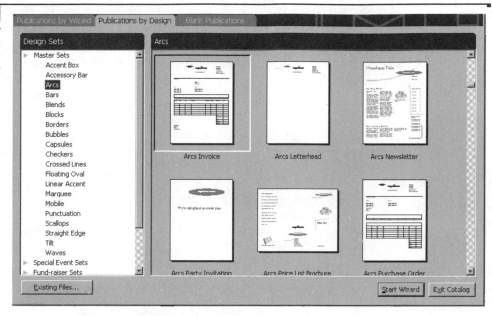

To create a document using shared designs, follow these steps:

1. Open the Publisher Catalog (File ➤ New).

2. Click the Publications By Design tab of the dialog box. The list on the left shows Publisher's design sets, many of which are shared across Office applications.

3. Select one of the designs on the left to see the various types of publications that use that design.

4. Select a document type from the right.

5. Click Start Wizard to begin making layout choices for that publication.

6. Proceed through the other steps as you would in any wizard.

Creating Mail Merge Documents

If you have created a publication with plans to mass-mail it to a long list of customers and other contacts, consider using Publisher's mail merge features. The Catalog Wizard and others allow you to include a placeholder for customer addresses. You can populate that placeholder with fields from an address list kept in Publisher or another Office application.

PART

IX

Publishing with Office

In general, the steps for mail merge are the same for Publisher as they are with Word. You open a data source (that's the file that has your names and addresses in it), and you insert the fields you need into a main merge document (that's the catalog or brochure you want to mail). You can also merge to mailing labels or envelopes rather than printing the address right on the publication you plan to mail.

 NOTE For additional information about all mail merge features, see Chapter 9.

Using Outlook as a Data Source

 In Publisher 2000, you can use an Outlook contact list as a data source for mail merge. To do this, select the text frame that will ultimately contain your mailing information. Click the Mail Merge menu, and choose Open Data Source.

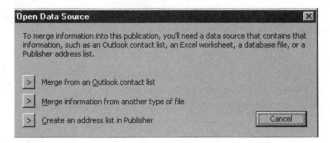

Notice that you have two other data source options besides using Outlook. If your address list is in Excel, Word, or Access, choose Merge Information From Another Type Of File. Click the third option if you don't have an electronic address list and want to create it now.

 NOTE Once you create an address list in Publisher or any other Office application, you can use it again and again to generate mail merge documents, envelopes, and labels.

To use Outlook, choose Merge From An Outlook Contact List. If your Outlook configuration contains multiple profiles, you will be prompted to choose which profile to use.

Select a profile from the drop-down list and click OK. Next, you will be prompted to choose which Outlook fields you want to use in your merge.

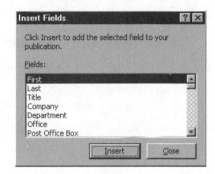

 WARNING If you forgot to select a text frame before starting the merge process, Publisher won't allow you to proceed with inserting fields. Click behind the dialog box to select (or create) a frame and try again.

Select the first field you need and click the Insert button. Continue selecting and inserting fields until you have finished; then click Close.

 NOTE Don't forget to type spaces and other punctuation between your merge codes in the main document. Publisher allows you to type with the Insert Fields dialog box open.

Once the correct fields are inserted, choose Merge from the Mail Merge menu. Preview your merged documents using the navigation buttons in the Preview Data dialog box. If you close the preview, you can retrieve it again by selecting Mail Merge ➤ Show Merge Results. The Mail Merge menu also lets you sort and/or filter as you would in a Word merge.

Printing Merged Publications

When it's time to print a document you have mail merged, click File ➢ Print Merge to set up options for printing.

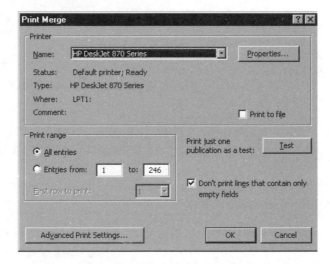

It's a good idea to proceed with caution, so always print a test copy of the merged document using the Test button in the Print Merge dialog box. This can help you spot errors with the document or with the merge before you have to throw away a hundred catalogs. Rather than printing a large number of entries at once, consider printing entries a few at a time. You don't want to come back to the printer in an hour only to find that you've printed 246 brochures using an ink cartridge that needed to be changed. Enable the Don't Print Lines That Contain Only Empty Fields feature so addresses won't have empty spaces in them where data fields are empty.

MASTERING TROUBLESHOOTING

Avoid Potential Merge Glitches

If you're having problems with an Excel data source in a Publisher Merge, open the Excel file and check two things. First, make a note of the sheet name that has the data you need for the merge. Then make sure Row 1 of that sheet contains the field names for your data, even if you have to delete a few rows to put them there. These precautions are necessary because Publisher prompts for a sheet name when opening a data source, and you won't get an option to use a named range, as you do in Word. Further, Publisher asks if you want to use Row 1 as the field names. If you say no, expecting Publisher to prompt you for another range, you may wind up in trouble. Rather than letting you choose a different row when you decline to use Row 1, Publisher automatically uses the Column A values as field names. This may not be helpful to you in every situation!

Problems can also arise using Outlook as a data source. If Personal Address Book isn't included as a service in the Outlook profile you select for your merge, Publisher won't even open it as a data source. (See "Managing Information Services or Accounts" in Chapter 21 to add an address book.)

Publisher also doesn't prompt you to use subfolders of the Contacts folder for any Outlook profile, so make sure the names and addresses you need for the merge are in the regular Contacts folder. Assign the merge contacts to a common Outlook category, and then filter on that category once the merge is complete.

Creating and Printing Booklets

With Publisher's improved wizards and designs, creating booklets is almost as easy as putting together any other document. However, there are a couple of additional issues you will need to address when creating booklets. Consider how your booklet will eventually be put together. Will you staple it? Will it be folded? Will it be bound? Will you print on both sides of the page? Answers to these questions determine how you should set up the publication to begin with.

Many of Publisher's wizards automatically set up the page appropriately for booklet printing. For instance, the Programs Wizard assumes you will print a four-page document on one 8.5" × 11" page, folded booklet style. (You can always insert additional pages, but be aware that you must add four at a time.) But what if you planned to print the program on 11" × 17" paper to make an 8.5" × 11" folded booklet? Simply change to the correct paper size in the Page Setup dialog box (discussed in Chapter 42) and choose the appropriate fold option.

Bound publications need an extra wide left margin, and if you're duplexing a bound publication, you should set up mirrored margin guides. Click Arrange ➤ Layout Guides to open the Layout Guides dialog box and enable this feature.

Printing Booklets

In general, you'll want to print booklet publications from the dialog box (File ➤ Print) rather than using the toolbar button. Just as with other Office applications, the toolbar button prints one copy of your entire document. This only works for booklets if you have a printer that supports automatic duplexing. If you don't, you'll have to feed pages through the printer twice: once for odd-numbered pages and again for even-numbered pages.

In the Print dialog box, if you choose Current Page, Publisher will ask whether this is a new booklet or part of a booklet already printed. Choose Yes or No depending on whether you're printing for the first time or you are just reprinting part of the document.

When you want to print an entire booklet on a printer that doesn't support automatic duplexing, you have to click the Options button in the Print dialog box to set it up for booklet printing. This will give you a prompt to feed the pages through the printer a second time to complete the back side. Publisher knows how to correctly paginate so that once you fold, the pages should be in the right order.

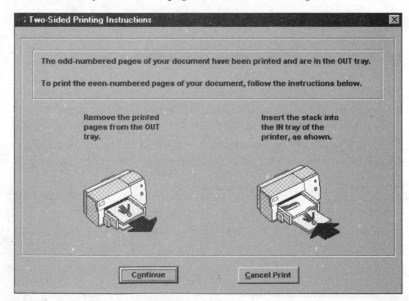

Producing Web Publications

Once you have learned the basics of putting together Publisher documents, creating a Web publication is a snap! You will find yourself using many of the features you already know how to use and then simply adding components to make your document Web-ready.

Setting up a page on the World Wide Web really involves two steps: creating the page and publishing the page. Publisher offers tools to guide you through the process from start to finish.

NOTE A Web publication can be either a single page or, more often, a collection of linked pages known as a Web. Once it's published to a Web server and assigned a URL, a Web can be considered a Web site.

Creating a Web Publication with a Wizard

One of the quickest ways to create an eye-catching Web document is to use the Publisher Web Page Wizard. From the Publisher Catalog (File ➤ New gets you there), select Web Sites from the list of wizards. Scroll through the choices on the right and click the design you want to use. Then click the Start Wizard button. You will be prompted to fill in your name and address, and the Personal Information dialog box will open. Click OK when you have finished entering (or editing) personal information.

Depending upon how your Publisher options are set, you may see the wizard steps one at a time, or arranged in a list (the default). Either way, you will make certain choices at each step.

1. If the wizard opens to the Welcome screen, click Next to continue.

2. At the Color Scheme step, select a color scheme from the list that displays. Click Next (if applicable).

3. At the Additional Pages step, enable the pages you want to include.

4. At the Form step, choose which forms, if any, you want to include. You may then see a message telling you where Publisher has placed your changes. Click OK, and then click Next.

5. Choose the type of Navigation Bar you want and proceed to the next step.

6. Choose whether or not you want a background sound.

7. Choose whether you want a texture applied.

8. Click Finish.

Once you finish the wizard, you will see a boilerplate for the Web with placeholder text and graphics. Select and replace this content with your own. The wizard automatically sets up hyperlinks to the pages you selected. You can return to previous wizard steps and make changes, or you can add pages. After you edit, your site is ready to post to the World Wide Web.

Creating a Web Publication from Scratch

If you prefer to start your Web with a blank slate, select the Blank Publications tab of the Catalog, choose the Web Page option, and click Create. You're given a blank page and a few additional tools on the Object toolbar.

Add text, graphics, and tables just as you would in regular print publications. Chapter 41 covers the basics of adding text, and Chapter 42 addresses adding other objects. You'll also find it necessary to incorporate Web-specific objects like navigation bars and hyperlinks.

Adding Design Objects from the Design Gallery

You can quickly spice up a blank page with Design Gallery objects such as Mastheads, Web Buttons, and Sidebars. Simply click the Design Gallery button on the Object toolbar and choose from the list of categories on the left. Click the object that appeals to you, and then click the Insert Object button. Position and resize the Web object as necessary.

Inserting Navigation Bars Navigation bars allow your Web site visitors to jump from one page to another. Insert one from the Design Gallery as you would any other Design Gallery object. Select the placeholder text and overwrite it with the navigation text you want Web viewers to see. Publisher creates the link automatically. Add new links as you insert new pages.

When you add new pages to your Web site, be sure to enable the option to Add New Hyperlink To Web Navigation Bar. That way, your Navigation Bar automatically grows with your site. You may also want to enable the option to Duplicate Objects on a particular page. When you do, the Navigation Bar appears on the inserted page.

TIP If you forget to enable the Duplicate Objects option, you can still insert the full Navigation Bar from the Design Gallery. Just make sure you select the same object you used before, and Publisher will insert the Navigation Bar with all the links you've created so far.

Working with Background Textures and Colors

Background enhancements help add that professionally designed flavor to your Web. Anything you place on the background appears on every page, lending continuity to the site. Textures are composed of one small picture tiled across the entire page. Adding color works just like the Fill feature for objects and frames, except that it fills the background on every page.

To add a texture to your Web pages, choose Format ➤ Color And Background Scheme. This opens the Color And Background Scheme dialog box.

On the Standard tab, enable the Texture check box to automatically bring up the Web Backgrounds dialog box. Select one of Publisher's backgrounds or navigate to your own folder and select the picture you want to use as a background texture. Click Open and you will return to the Color And Background Scheme dialog box, where you can preview the texture. Click OK to apply the texture to the Web, or click Browse to select another picture.

TIP To see a texture while you're still in the Web Backgrounds dialog box, switch to Preview view by clicking the View toolbar button's drop-down arrow.

Remove a background texture at any time by choosing Format ➤ Color And Background Scheme. Clear the Texture check box and click OK.

 WARNING If you choose a custom picture file for your background texture, it should be 20KB or smaller. Larger picture files require so much time to download that it may frustrate people attempting to view your site.

If you prefer to use a solid color background, shade, or tint, you can do so from within the Color And Background Scheme dialog box.

1. Click Format ➤ Color And Background Scheme.
2. Click the Standard tab.
3. In the Background section of the dialog box, click the arrow next to Solid color.
4. Choose the color you want from the palette or click More Colors to see additional color choices.
5. To use a shade or tint, click Fill Effects, and then choose the options you want.
6. Click OK.

Inserting a Hyperlink

Hyperlinks are text and objects on your site that readers click to jump from one location to another. Without hyperlinks, your site would appear as one long scrolling document that has no easy way to navigate through it. A hyperlink contains the address of another location on the World Wide Web. Clicking a text or graphic hyperlink takes the reader to that address. Publisher hyperlinks can point to another page within your site, a page within another Web site, a file on a local network drive, or an e-mail address.

Usually, text hyperlinks are identified by a specific color and/or underline. This color changes after a text hyperlink has been clicked or followed by the person viewing the site.

Take these steps to create a hyperlink from text:

1. Highlight the text you want to use for the hyperlink.
2. Click Insert ➤ Hyperlink to open the Hyperlink dialog box.

3. Choose the type of hyperlink you want to create.

4. Enter the URL, e-mail address, page from your Web site, or path to the file you want the hyperlink to point to.

5. Click OK. You will notice that the color of the hyperlinked text changes.

If you want to create a hyperlink from an object, follow the same steps, but select the object before opening the Hyperlink dialog box.

 TIP E-mail addresses and URLs are often so long that typing these character strings is tedious and prone to error. Instead, it's a good idea to open a browser or e-mail window, navigate to the URL or address you want to include in the hyperlink, and select and copy the hyperlink information. Then simply paste it into the Hyperlink Information field in Publisher's Hyperlink dialog box.

 Creating Multiple Hyperlinks on One Object   When you create hyperlinks from objects, the area of the object that contains the hyperlink is called a hot spot. Sometimes the entire object is a single hot spot, but often, you want different parts of the graphic to point to different hyperlinks. In that case, you need multiple hot spots on that graphic. On a company intranet, for example, each department might post a group picture. Creating multiple hot spots on the photo would allow the reader to click the person to whom they wished to send an e-mail message. Or each hot spot could point to a paragraph of biographical information about the employee.

Use the Hot Spot tool on the Object toolbar to create multiple hot spots on a single graphic. Click the tool, and then drag a box around the area of the object you want to make a hyperlink. When you release the mouse button, the Hyperlink dialog box opens. Enter the link information as you normally would. Use the tool as many times as you need to create the links you want on that object.

Testing Hyperlinks   It's important to follow all hyperlinks, making sure they work correctly, before you publish your Web. In fact, it's a good idea to test all links each time you make changes to your published Web site. Even if you haven't made changes to them, external hyperlinks should be tested on a regular basis. Your readers will become frustrated following dead links.

Publisher lets you test links by opening the Web in your default browser. You will see the page as if it were actually published on the World Wide Web. To open the page in your browser, click File ➤ Web Page Preview. Choose whether to view the entire site or just the current page. If you're testing links, you'll want to view the entire site, since your navigation bar can't link to pages that aren't open in the preview. Similarly, external links won't work unless you're online. That means you have to be plugged in to the Internet via modem or a network connection in order to follow external links.

To test each link, simply click it. If it takes you to the correct location, it's a good link. Click the Back button in the browser window to return to the original page and then test another link. Close the browser window when you're finished.

Modifying Hyperlinks   If a hyperlink isn't working the way you intended, you can modify or remove it by selecting the link and opening the Hyperlink dialog box.

1. Select the hot spot that contains the link you want to modify.

2. Click Insert ➤ Hyperlink to open the Hyperlink dialog box.

3. Under Hyperlink Information, specify a new address or page for the hyperlink, or click the Remove button if you want to completely delete the link.

4. Click OK.

You can also edit the text of a hyperlink by selecting it and overtyping with new text. As always, be sure to retest any links you've modified.

Creating Web-Based Forms for User Input

If you have spent any amount of time on the Net, you have probably seen some type of Web-based form. Ever ordered anything online? If you have, you probably entered information into a form. Companies often use forms, like the one shown on the facing page, to collect feedback from customers or potential customers. They also post order forms so customers can purchase products over the Net. Online forms allow readers to subscribe to publications or request materials.

Request for Systems Consultation

What's the best way to contact you?

○ Telephone

○ Fax

○ Email

For which problem areas are you seeking a solution?

☐ Employee training

☐ Upgrading hardware

☐ Upgrading software

☐ Other

Comments:

Address:

City: State/Prov:

Country: Zip/Post. code:

Phone:

E-mail:

Submit   Reset

Publisher's Design Gallery has several types of forms that you can customize to suit your own needs. Or, you may decide to create a form from scratch. Every online form contains *controls*—various types of places for the user to input data. Forms also contain labels and values associated with the controls that allow you to receive data sent by readers. For a complete description of how to create form controls and set labels and values, see Chapter 44.

NOTE If you plan to include a form in a Web site, be sure to talk with your system administrator or your Internet Service Provider to set up the additional server configuration and support files you will need to process and store data from the form.

Previewing a Web Site

While you're working in Publisher, it's hard to get an idea of what readers will see when they view your Web site. Hiding boundaries and guides helps, but you still can't view the whole thing unless you zoom way out, and then all you see is a long, rectangular document with text and graphics too small to see.

As mentioned in the "Testing Hyperlinks" section above, you can look at the site from your reader's viewpoint with just two clicks. Choose File ➤ Web Page Preview to have Publisher generate the document as a Web site and open it in your default

PART

IX

Publishing with Office

browser window. You can't edit from the browser window, but you can see potential problem areas and return to Publisher to fix them.

Checking a Web Site's Design

Earlier in this chapter, you learned how to use the Design Checker to spot potential problems with the layout of your printed publication. When you run the Design Checker for a Web publication, there are additional options Publisher can address. Click Tools ➤ Design Checker and choose the number of pages you wish to check. Then click the Options button to select the design elements you want Publisher to review.

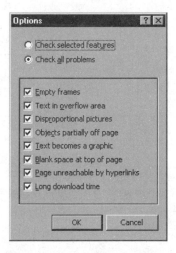

You'll notice this dialog box is similar to the regular Design Checker list. For instance, you can have Publisher notify you of text in the overflow area. But you can also check for pages that don't link back to the home page, and pages that might take too long to download. Choose the options you want Publisher to review, then click OK twice.

The Design Checker runs in the same way it does with print publications, pausing at each potential problem and offering suggestions on how to fix it. Remember that you can work outside this dialog box to fix problems, and then click Continue to move on. Choose Ignore to skip this occurrence of the problem or Ignore All to skip all similar problems. When you're finished with the Design Checker, click Close.

Saving and Publishing a Web Site

When you publish Web pages using the Save As A Web Page command on the File menu, Publisher creates a copy of the Web and posts that copy to the location you supply. You can publish a Web site to Web folders (see Chapter 37 for information about Web folders), to an FTP site, to a local network drive, to a folder on your hard drive, or to an Internet site using the Web Publishing Wizard.

When you use the Save As A Web Page command, Publisher does not ask you for a file name, only a folder location. The pages are given default names of `index.html`, `page 2.hmtl`, and so on. Do not rename the home page unless you receive instructions from your system administrator or Internet Service Provider to do so. However, you can change the file name and title of additional pages you add to the Web, using Web Properties (see the next section).

If you are saving a Web to a folder on your hard drive, be sure to create a new folder to house it. Because supporting files such as graphics and backgrounds are stored as individual files, you should make sure the related files are all grouped together in a specific folder.

 WARNING To save a Web to your company's intranet or to the Internet, you must know the exact name of the Web folder or site to which you want to publish and you must have access to it. Talk with your system administrator or your Internet Service Provider before attempting to publish a Web site.

Once you have published Web pages, you cannot edit them in Publisher. Instead, open the file you published from, make your editing changes there, and then republish the pages.

Changing Web Properties To rename Web pages and change other Web properties, click File ➢ Web Properties to open the Web Properties dialog box. You only need to set Site properties once, but Page properties have to be set for every page on the Web.

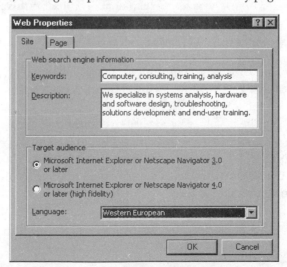

On the Site tab of the dialog box, enter the information you want the search engines to use for directing readers to your site by entering keywords. Separate keywords with a comma; you can keep typing even after you reach the end of the field. Enter a site description in paragraph form. This field also grows as you keep typing, but not all search engines store long text descriptions. Make sure you put the most important information first. Choose a target audience and language, and then click OK.

Before you set the properties on a page, navigate to that page in Publisher and open the Web Properties dialog box. Click the Page tab and rename the page, changing its extension and/or title.

TIP It's important to enter a descriptive name in the Page Title field on the Page tab because search engines use this text for indexing Web pages. The Page Title also appears in the title bar of a reader's browser window.

Adding a background sound that plays automatically when you open a Web page is easy. Just enter the name of the sound file in the File Name box on the Page tab, and indicate if you want it to Loop Forever or loop for a specific number of times. If you're going to publish this Web page, copy the sound file to the Web folder and then identify the path to it here. Otherwise, the Web page may not be able to locate the sound file when the page opens.

You have the choice of including a button for the current page on the Navigation Bar or leaving it off. Web designers disagree on this issue. Some say it's an unnecessary waste of space to include a link to the page you're currently viewing. Others prefer that the Navigation Bar appear consistent throughout the site, so all buttons are included on every page. You can enable or disable this feature as you prefer.

Creating a Web Site from an Existing Publication

You can easily convert documents like a company newsletter, sales brochure, or product catalog to a Web site. Publisher's AutoConvert feature allows you to do this with just a few clicks.

Open the document you wish to convert and choose File ➤ Create Web Site From Current Publication. You are prompted to run the Design Checker to identify design and performance problems that you may want to correct before publishing. After you run the Design Checker, make any corrections you want; then click the File menu, choose Save As Web Page, choose the folder you want, and click OK.

If you create a print publication such as a newsletter from a wizard, one of the steps may be Convert To Web Site. If that option is available, select it from the wizard and click Create. You'll then be prompted to choose whether to use the Web Site Wizard to create links or create them manually. Select one of the options and click OK.

If you haven't saved recent changes, you'll be prompted to do so before the conversion. Once the document is converted, edit, save, and print as applicable.

 TIP Converting a publication does not cause the file to be overwritten. During the conversion, Publisher makes a copy of the original Publisher file (.pub) and converts the copy to an HTML (.htm) file.

What's Next

By now, you're probably comfortable creating and editing many different types of Publisher documents, including Web sites. There may be times, however, when you want to publish Web materials generated from programs other than Publisher. The next few chapters address Web capabilities of the other Office 2000 applications.

PART

IX

Publishing with Office

CHAPTER 44

Creating Web Pages in Word

FEATURING:

Creating Web pages using the Web Page Wizard

Adding content to a Web page

Creating hyperlinks

Adding background sounds and movies

Adding scrolling text

Creating Web-based forms

Working with frames

Making a Web available for others to view

Your supervisor has just asked you to create a series of Web pages for your corporate intranet. If you haven't created Web pages but have heard the lunchroom rumors about HTML, this new assignment can be pretty intimidating. Fear no more. Office 2000 is designed to put your anxiety to rest. All you need to do is add a few new skills to your bag of tricks, and you'll be producing dazzling pages in no time.

Word 2000 provides three ways to create Web pages:

- Using the Web Page Wizard
- Applying a Web template
- Converting an existing Word document

The Web Page Wizard creates not only Web pages but full *Webs:* collections of pages with links between them. If the project you are undertaking involves multiple documents, the Web Page Wizard is generally the best choice because it creates links for you and gives your pages a consistent look and feel. If you are providing content to your corporate intranet and you've been given a template to use, you may want to apply the template directly or convert an existing document without going through the wizard. However, after you use the wizard, you'll find it's a great tool whatever your goal.

 NOTE What's the difference between a Web and a Web site? A Web becomes a Web site once it's published and assigned a URL.

Creating Web Pages Using the Web Page Wizard

The Web Page Wizard can create single pages or Webs that can be published entire as a Web site or appended to an existing site. If you want to create more than one page, it's a good idea to draw up the layout of your Web before you start the wizard (see Chapter 41 for more about designing a Web). You'll want to know the names of as many pages as possible so the wizard can create the links between them. If you have existing documents you want to include in the Web, be sure to know their names and where to locate them. The Wizard isn't included in the Typical Office installation, but it will be automatically installed on demand, so make sure you have access to the CD or network drive that Office was installed from.

When you are ready to create your Web pages, choose File ➤ New from the Word menu. Click the Web Pages tab in the New dialog box and select Web Page Wizard. Click OK to start the wizard and Next to move on to the first step.

The Title And Location page, as shown in Figure 44.1, determines the official title of your Web. Although it can be changed later, it's important to give your Web a descriptive title because the various Web search engines use the site's title when users search for a site on the Internet. A good title could mean the difference between someone finding your site or not.

By default, the wizard creates a new folder for your Web, so if you change the location be sure you change it to an empty folder. The wizard creates additional subfolders for storing graphics and other supporting files, but the main pages are stored in the folder you specify. If you don't designate a unique folder, your Web files will get mixed in with unrelated documents, making it difficult to manage the Web effectively. Enter the title and location and click Next.

FIGURE 44.1

Enter a descriptive title and folder location for your Web.

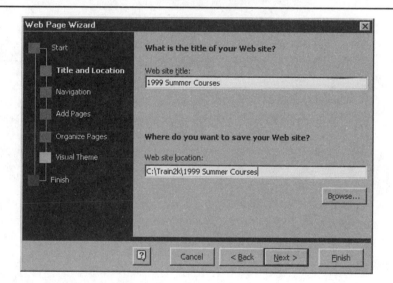

Using Frames for Navigation

The Web Page Wizard offers three choices for the layout of your pages, as shown in Figure 44.2:

- A Vertical Frame runs down the left side of the page and contains links to the other pages in the Web.

- A Horizontal Frame is positioned across the top of the page and contains links to the other pages in the Web.

- The Separate Page option doesn't use frames. Instead, each page opens in a full window. Forward and Back buttons and appropriate links are added to the pages.

Choose the Navigation option you prefer and click Next.

PART

IX

Publishing with Office

FIGURE 44.2

The Web Page Wizard
automatically creates
navigation links
between pages.

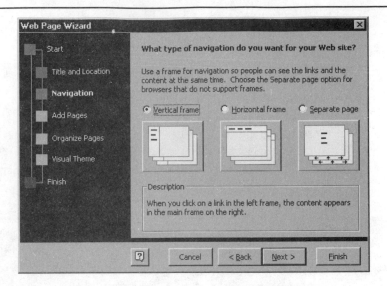

 WARNING Not all browsers support frames, and text readers (used by people with vision impairments) don't work well with frames. Many Web developers who use frames also offer visitors a no-frame alternative on the site's Welcome page, but if you can only choose one layout, choose the Separate Page option for the widest range of accessibility.

Differentiating Text Frames from Web Frames

You may already be familiar with text frames for positioning text on a page. Text frames are used extensively in PowerPoint and Publisher, and they can be used in Word and Excel to position a block of text outside of the normal paragraphs or cells. Web frames may contain text, but their primary purpose is to organize content on a Web page. Web frames typically appear on the top or left of a page and include navigational links that remain visible even when the visitor moves to a different page of your Web. See "Working with Frames" later in this chapter for more information.

Adding Pages

A Web created by the Web Page Wizard comes with three pages: a Personal Web Page and two blank pages. The Personal Web Page is a template that includes sections for work information, favorite links, contact information, current projects, biographical information, and personal interests. If you are not creating a personal Web with yourself as the focus, you can delete this page by selecting it and clicking Remove Page. The first blank page moves into position as the new home page for your Web.

 NOTE The home page is typically the first page visitors see when they visit a Web site, but it may be preceded by a Welcome page that gives visitors options such as no frames or no graphics.

If you want to add additional pages to your Web, now is the best time to do so. As shown in Figure 44.3, you can add a new blank page, add a page based on a template, or insert an existing document into the Web. To add a blank page, click the Add New Blank Page button, and the new page appears at the bottom of the list (you will be given the option to rename pages in the next step of the wizard).

FIGURE 44.3

Add a new blank page, a template page, or an existing file to your Web using the Add Pages step of the Web Page Wizard.

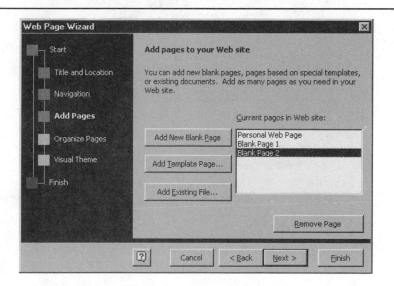

PART

IX

Publishing with Office

Using Templates

Word includes seven Web page templates. Some of these templates give you specific page layouts, such as the Left-Aligned Column and Right-Aligned Column templates. Others provide a structure for Web content, such as the Frequently Asked Questions and Table of Contents templates. To review each of the templates, in the Add Pages step, click the Add Template Page button. This opens the dialog box and preview window shown in Figure 44.4. Click any of the templates in the Web Page Template dialog box to see a full-page view of the template. When you have chosen the template you want to include in your Web, click OK. If you'd like to add another template page, click Add Template Page again and repeat the process.

FIGURE 44.4

A selected template is displayed as a full page behind the Web Page Template dialog box so you can see what elements it contains.

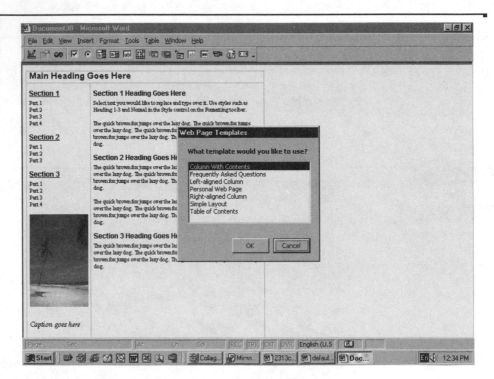

Adding Existing Documents

If you would like to convert any existing documents and add them to your Web, in the Add Pages step, click the Add Existing File button. Locate and double-click a file you would like to include. The Wizard saves a copy of the file as HTML and includes it in the Web folder. Repeat the process to add additional documents.

If you try to add an HTML page created in FrontPage 2000 or a page created in Excel or Access that uses the Office Web Components, it opens in its native application instead of being added in the wizard. When you have finished adding pages, click Next to move on to the Organize Pages step of the wizard.

 MASTERING THE OPPORTUNITIES

Creating Multiple HTML Pages

When you insert a file in the wizard, it is added as a single page, even if it's a multipage document. If you have a document that you want to include as several individual pages, use copy-and-paste to create and save a separate Word document for each page before launching the wizard, and then insert each document.

If you need to convert a number of Word documents to unlinked HTML pages, you can use the Batch Conversion Wizard. Create a new folder, then move or copy all the Word documents to the folder. Choose File ➢ New. In the New dialog box, click the Other Documents tab and double-click the Batch Conversion Wizard. (If the wizard isn't listed in the dialog box, you need to install it from the Office 2000 CD or your network.) The wizard is also used to convert files to Word from formats used in applications like WordPerfect, Works, Windows Write, Excel, or Outlook, and to recover corrupt documents.

Organizing the Links

Now that you have the pages in your Web, you can rename them and change their relative order as shown in Figure 44.5. This order determines the order of the links. Use the Move Up and Move Down buttons to rearrange the pages and the Rename button to change a page's name. Click Next to move on to the next step.

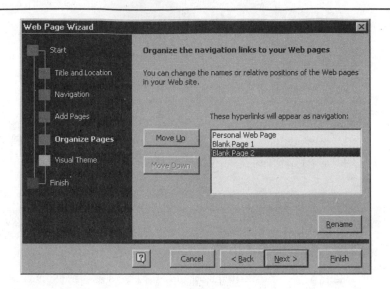

Applying Themes

Themes were first introduced in FrontPage 98 and are now included in several Office 2000 applications. A theme is a collection of colors, fonts, graphics, backgrounds, bullet characters, and styles that fit together. Office includes over 60 themes that can be applied to print publications, online documents, and Web pages. To select a theme, click the Browse Themes button in the Visual Theme step of the Web Page Wizard.

The Theme dialog box, shown in Figure 44.6, displays a preview of each theme listed on the left. Options for Active Graphics (typically appearing as animated bullets and horizontal lines) and Background Image are on by default. If you would also like to use Vivid Colors, click the check box. You can see the results of turning these options on or off in the preview window on the right, although you won't see active graphics actually move.

Once you decide on a theme (you can also choose No Theme from the top of the list), click OK. If you decide to use a theme, make sure Add Λ Visual Theme is selected in the Visual Theme step of the wizard.

Click Next to move to the last step of the wizard and click Finish. The wizard will create your Web pages, add the links you specified, and save the pages to the folder you chose.

FIGURE 44.6

FIGURE 44.6

You can apply Web themes to Web and print documents to create a consistent look and feel for all your publications.

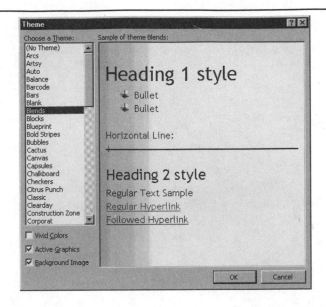

Exploring Your Web

After the Web Page Wizard finishes its job, it opens the home page in Word. If you used frames in your Web site, the Frames toolbar opens (see more about frames in "Working with Frames" later in this chapter). The home page contains navigation links to other pages in the Web, either in frames, as shown in Figure 44.7, or at the top of the page if you choose the Separate Page option.

FIGURE 44.7

The Web Page Wizard creates your Web pages and opens the home page.

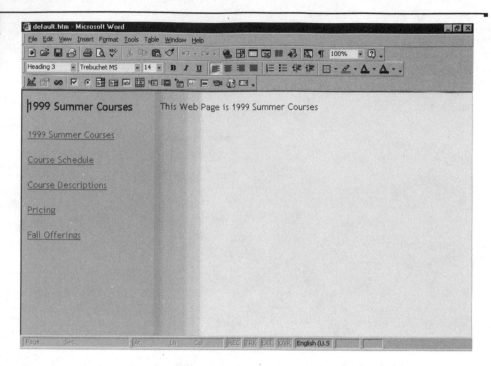

To view the other pages of the Web, point to any of the navigation links. The pointer changes to a hand and provides a screen tip about the file location of the hyperlink. Click the hyperlink to open the page. When the page opens, the Web toolbar, shown in Figure 44.8, also opens.

FIGURE 44.8

The Web toolbar

The Web toolbar is the standard Internet Explorer browser toolbar. Click the Back button to return to the home page.

Exploring Web Files

To see the files the Web Page Wizard creates, open the folder in My Computer or Windows Explorer.

You may notice a number of subfolders and files that you aren't familiar with. `Default.htm` is the file name the wizard automatically assigns to the first or home page of the Web. The wizard creates a subfolder for each page and uses it to house graphics and other objects related to the page. For example, when you insert a graphic on a page and save the page, Word automatically saves the graphic to the page's corresponding subfolder. Graphics and other objects are not saved as part of a Web page but rather are saved separately and linked to the page. This is standard Web design protocol and helps keep the myriad of individual files streamlined and organized.

Adding Content to a Web Page

Editing Web pages in Word is not much different than editing other Word documents. You have access to all of Word's formatting and editing tools, including fonts, paragraph formatting, bullets, tables, and borders and shading. Web pages also include features that are not typically used in print documents: hyperlinks, frames, form controls, active graphics such as scrolling textboxes, and other special multimedia features. If you learn to use these tools effectively, you'll be able to design Web pages that are dynamic, attractive, and effective.

Saving and Reopening a Web

If you create a Web using the Web Page Wizard, the wizard automatically saves the Web pages and associated files. After you make changes to any of the pages, click the Save button or choose File ➢ Save to resave the files just as you would any other document.

When you reopen a Web, you can choose to open individual pages for editing or the entire Web. The frame at the left or top of your Web pages is actually a separate page, so it will not open when you open individual pages. To make changes to the frames page, open the file `TOC Frame.htm`. To open the home page with the frame giving you access to the entire Web, open the file called `default.htm`.

Creating Hyperlinks

Hyperlinks are what make the World Wide Web what it is. When Tim Berners-Lee, CERN researcher, developed HTML, his primary interest was in being able to access related documents easily, without regard to computer platform or operating system, by connecting the documents through a series of links. Hyperlinks allow readers to pursue their areas of interest without having to wade through tons of material searching for specific topics. And hyperlinks take readers down paths they might never have traveled without the ease of clicking a mouse. Adding hyperlinks to your documents moves information down off the shelf, dusts it off, and makes it a living, breathing instrument that people can really use.

Creating a hyperlink in an existing Web page is easy. Just follow these steps:

1. Enter or select some descriptive text in the page to define the link; for example, you could type **Click here to view new courses** or select the existing text that says New Courses.

2. Select the text, right-click within it, and choose Hyperlink to open the Insert Hyperlink dialog box, as shown in Figure 44.9.

3. Type a file or Web page name or click the File or Web Page buttons to browse for the file. Click the Place In This Document button to create a link to another location in the same document, or click the E-mail Address button to create a link to an e-mail message form.

4. If you want to change the hyperlink text, enter new text in the Text To Display box.

5. Add a screen tip to the hyperlink by clicking the Screen Tip button and entering the text you want to appear in a screen tip.

6. Click OK to create the link.

For more about creating hyperlinks and bookmarks in Word documents, refer to Chapter 11.

FIGURE 44.9

Create hyperlinks to other documents, Web pages, e-mail addresses, and other places in the same document using the Insert Hyperlink dialog box.

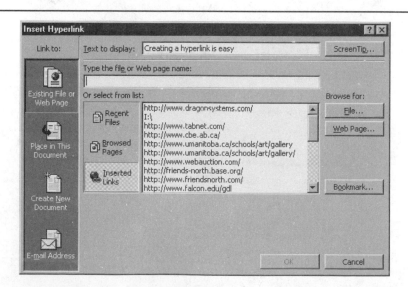

NOTE Word automatically creates a hyperlink when you type an address it recognizes as an Internet or file path address. If, for example, you type **www.train2k.com**, Word will create a hyperlink to that address. To turn hyperlink automatic formatting on or off, choose Tools ➢ AutoCorrect. Click AutoFormat As You Type and check or clear the Internet and Network Paths With Hyperlinks check box. Check or clear the same box on the AutoFormat tab.

MASTERING TROUBLESHOOTING

Troubleshooting Hyperlinks

A hyperlink's effectiveness depends on its being able to locate the file or Internet address it is linked to. If the file has moved or been renamed, or the Web address no longer exists, clicking the hyperlink will return an error message. It's important to regularly verify hyperlinks you've included in your site. If a link does not work, check the following:

1. Do you currently have access to the Internet or intranet site the link is calling? If not, check the link again when access has been restored.
2. Has the site or file moved? If so, right-click on the link and choose Edit ➢ Hyperlink. Update the location of the linked file.
3. Does the file still exist? If not, right-click on the link and choose Edit ➢ Hyperlink. Click Remove Link.

If the link still does not work after you have followed these steps, make sure the address is spelled correctly and there are no syntax errors in the address (for example, a comma instead of a dot).

If Edit Hyperlink does not appear on the shortcut menu when you right-click, it could be because the text contains a spelling or grammar error. Word will display the Spelling shortcut menu until the error is corrected.

Inserting Graphics

Visitors to a Web site expect to see more than just text. Graphics add impact to your Web pages, as long as they are fast-loading. The trick is to use small, attention-grabbing graphics on main pages and give visitors the option to view larger, more elaborate graphics by clicking to another page.

Inserting a graphic into a Web page is no different than placing one in a Word document. The Clip Gallery is available from the Insert menu; from the gallery you can choose art or any other clip art or photos you want to use (for more about inserting graphics, see Chapter 7).

PART IX

Publishing with Office

Web browsers don't support all the graphics features available in Word. To ensure that your Web pages look as good when viewed by a browser as they do in Word, features that are unsupported have been disabled. Only some of the wrapping styles available in Word documents, for example, are available for use in Web pages. As a result, you may find that once you've inserted a graphic, you have difficulty positioning it where you want it. To change how text wraps around the picture so you can more easily place the graphic where you want it, right-click on the graphic and choose Format Picture or choose Format ➤ Picture from the menu. Click the Layout tab and change the Wrapping Style, as shown in Figure 44.10.

A number of other options are available in the Format Picture dialog box. Because not all browsers can display graphics and some people don't want to wait for graphics to appear on Web pages, it's possible to insert alternative text that describes the graphic. When the Web page opens, the alternative text appears while the page is loading, allowing visitors to click when they find the text they want without waiting for the graphic. To specify alternative text, click the Web tab of the Format Picture dialog box.

MASTERING TROUBLESHOOTING

Troubleshooting Graphics

If you are having trouble positioning graphics on a Web page, you might want to try a Web designer's trick. Insert a table into the page. Three columns are usually sufficient, but add more columns if you want to line up a series of graphics. Then, position the graphic inside a cell of the table and change the table properties so the table expands to fill the size of the screen:

1. Click inside the table and choose Table ➤ Table Properties.

2. Click the Table tab and changed Preferred Width to 100% Measured In Percent (Although this step is not necessary, it makes it easier if you aren't sure about precise placement and sizing). Click OK.

3. Now place the graphic inside the cell of the table that corresponds to the position you would like for the graphic. Click the Center button on the Formatting toolbar to center the graphic in the cell.

Before publishing the Web page, you can change the table's borders to No Borders. To do this, select the table, choose Format ➤ Borders And Shading, click the Borders tab, and click None. Your table won't be visible on the page, but the graphics will stay where you put them.

The Web Tools Toolbar

Word comes equipped with a Web Tools toolbar, as shown in Figure 44.11, to help you add sounds and video, create forms, and add scrolling text. To turn on the Web Tools toolbar, choose View ➤ Toolbar and click Web Tools (not Web).

FIGURE 44.11

The Web Tools toolbar can help you add sounds, video, forms, and scrolling text.

PART

IX

Publishing with
Office

Adding Background Sounds and Movies Even though we don't seem to mind being constantly barraged by sounds from radio and television, most of us have not yet developed a fondness for sounds from the Web. Only occasionally will you happen upon a Web site that opens with background music drawing you in (or turning you away). However, if you'd like to add background sounds to your site, Word makes it easy for you to do.

Although you can add a sound or movie to a Web page in Web Layout view, it's helpful to be in Design mode so you know where the Sound or Movie icon is in case you want to remove it later. Open the Web Tools toolbar and click the Design Mode button to go into Design mode. Before inserting the Sound or Movie button, move the insertion point to an obvious position at the top of the page. This is where the icon representing the sound or movie file will appear.

TIP You can move into Design mode from any view, not just Web Layout view, but if you're working on a Web page, it's best to begin in Web Layout view so you know what your finished product will look like.

When you're all set, click the Sound button on the Web toolbar. Enter the name of a .wav file or click Browse and locate the file. Click the Loop down-arrow to choose the number of times you want the sound to play, either 1–5 or Infinite. Click OK. Click the Design Mode button to return to your previous view. The sound file should begin playing immediately and will play whenever you open the page, as many times as you instructed it to.

TIP A user's browser (along with add-ins like RealPlayer) determines the types of sound files they can play. MIDI and WAV files are common, but MP3 (MPEG audio) files are becoming the most common. After you insert the file, test it in your browser.

To add a movie file, click the Movie button on the Web toolbar (remember to click the Design Mode button and position the insertion point first). Enter the settings in the Movie Clip dialog box, as shown in Figure 44.12. It's a good idea to include an alternative image to display in browsers that do not support movie clips, or put the clip on a page so that users can choose whether or not to download it. However, even if a browser does support movie clips, the image will be small and difficult to see on most systems. If possible, test the display on several machines with different browsers to see how the movie file looks before making it a permanent part of your Web page.

PART

IX

Publishing with
Office

FIGURE 44.12

*To display a movie clip
on a Web page, enter
the settings for the clip
you want to play and
an alternative graphic
for those browsers that
do not support clips.*

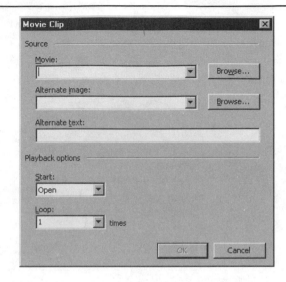

Removing Sound or a Movie from a Web Page   To remove a sound or movie clip, move into Design mode. Locate the Sound or Movie icon, as shown here. Select the icon and choose Edit ➤ Clear.

Adding Scrolling Text   Scrolling text is a way to grab your visitors' attention with a special announcement or notice. If you've used the Windows Scrolling Marquee screen saver, you're already familiar with the concept. To add scrolling text, follow these steps:

1. Click the Design Mode button on the Web Tools toolbar.
2. Position the insertion point where you want the scrolling text to appear.
3. Click the Scrolling Text button on the Web Tools toolbar.
4. Enter the text in the text box, as shown in Figure 44.13.
5. Set the options for Behavior, Direction, Background Color, Loop, and Speed.
6. Click OK to insert the scrolling text box.
7. Click the Design Mode button to exit Design Mode; the text box doesn't scroll in Design mode.

FIGURE 44.13

*Catch your visitors'
attention with
scrolling text.*

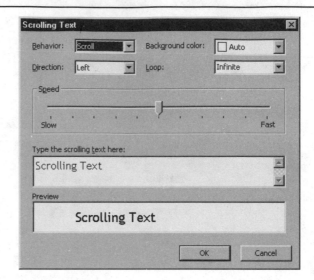

You can resize or move the scrolling text box in Design mode as you would any text box in Word. To delete a scrolling text box, switch to Design mode, click the box to select it, and choose Edit ➤ Clear.

Creating Web-Based Forms

To make the Web truly interactive, information has to go in both directions. Web users need the ability to send information to the site owners, and Web owners need to know about who their visitors are and what they are looking for. Web forms provide a way for visitors to respond to surveys, register with a site, voice their opinions about issues, search your site, or submit feedback.

You can add a form to any Web page. When you add a form control from the Web Tools toolbar, Word automatically adds Top of Form and Bottom of Form boundaries to the form, as shown here:

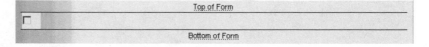

Word comes equipped with 11 built-in controls for you to use on forms. Here's a quick look at each one.

Check Boxes

 Use check boxes when users are allowed to select more than one option within a group. For example, you could have your check box say something like "Send me more information about:" and then list various choices for the user to select from.

Option Buttons

 Option buttons indicate that a user can select only one item from a group of options, such as receiving information Daily, Weekly, or Monthly.

Drop-Down Boxes

 Drop-down boxes give users a list of specific options from which they can choose one. For example, from a drop-down list of cities you can pick yours to see its weather report.

List Boxes

 List boxes are similar to drop-down boxes in that they give users a list of options to choose from. However, instead of clicking an arrow to open a list, users use scroll buttons to scroll through the list. List boxes allow users to select multiple choices by using Shift or Ctrl while clicking.

Text Boxes

 Text boxes are fields where users can enter text, such as a name, address, or other specific information.

Text Areas

 Text areas are open text boxes with scroll bars where users can write a paragraph or more to give feedback, describe a problem, or provide other information.

Submit Buttons

 Submit buttons are essential elements on a form, because a user must click the Submit button so that the data they entered will be sent to the Web server for processing.

Submit With Image

 The Submit With Image control lets you substitute an image for the standard Submit button. Make sure users know they have to click this button to submit their data—and that clicking the button submits the data. For example, don't use the same image for a Next Page button and a Submit button.

PART

IX

Publishing with Office

Reset

Reset is a form control that clears the data in the current form so the user can start over.

Hidden

Hidden is a form field, invisible to the user, that passes data to the Web server. For example, a hidden control could pass information about the user's operating system or Web browser.

Password

Password replaces typed text with asterisks so users can type passwords confidentially.

Laying Out a Form

Tables are a big help in laying out a form so it looks organized. Create the table so it has twice the number of columns you would want to display in a single row. For example, in Figure 44.14, the third row contains three fields, so the table contains six columns. After you have inserted all the field names and form controls, save the page and open it in Internet Explorer or another browser to see how it looks.

FIGURE 44.14

Using a table to lay out form fields helps to align them in organized columns.

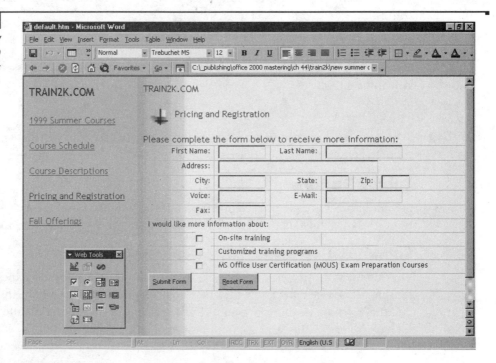

To open a Word Web page in a browser, follow these steps:

1. Start the browser.

2. Click File ➤ Open and locate the `default.htm` for the Web site you want to view. Click OK.

3. Use navigation links to move from the home page of the Web site to the page you are working on.

4. After you have viewed the page, minimize the browser and return to Word.

5. Make any additional changes and save the Word Web page again.

6. Maximize the browser and click the Refresh button on the browser toolbar.

 NOTE Because of the way different browsers display form fields, it is difficult to make every field line up perfectly with the fields above it unless you use tables.

Setting Form Field Properties

All form controls have properties that determine how they behave. Some form controls require that you set the properties before the control can be used. For example, you must enter the values that you want to appear in a drop-down list so the user has options to choose from. To set or edit a control's properties, double-click on the control to open the Properties dialog box, as shown in Figure 44.15.

FIGURE 44.15

Set or edit form field properties in the Properties dialog box.

To enter options for a drop-down list or a list box, type the first value in the DisplayValues property. Enter a semicolon and no space before entering the next value. The values you type will each appear on a separate line in the list. To test the drop-down list box, exit Design mode and click the down arrow on the form control.

It's helpful to any programmers who might work on your Web site if you change the name of a control from the default name to a name that describes the field, for example, change HTMLText1 to FirstName. Control names cannot contain spaces, but they can contain numbers and uppercase and lowercase letters.

For more information about form control properties, refer to the Word Help topic *Form controls you can use on a Web page.*

NOTE Data submitted by Web forms is processed by the Web server and stored as a comma-delimited text file, an Access table, or other database format. The Web server has to be set up to accept and process the data. Talk with your Web server administrator before publishing a form on a Web site.

Working with Frames

A frame is a structure that displays a Web page on every other page of the Web site. The page that displays the frames is called a frames page. Although the Web Page Wizard is the easiest way to create a simple navigational frame, Word offers you the option of adding and deleting frames manually, if you prefer.

TIP There's a Frames toolbar that you can use to add, delete, and set the properties of frames. Right-click on any toolbar and choose Frames to display the toolbar.

To add a frame, click Format ➤ Frames. If you only want to add a table of contents to the existing document, choose Table Of Contents In Frame. This option creates a table of contents for the displayed document based on heading styles used in the document. Figure 44.16 shows an example of a table of contents frame for this chapter. A link is created for each heading formatted using a heading style (for more about using heading styles, see Chapter 8).

FIGURE 44.16

The Table of Contents in Frame option creates a table of contents for the displayed document based on the heading styles.

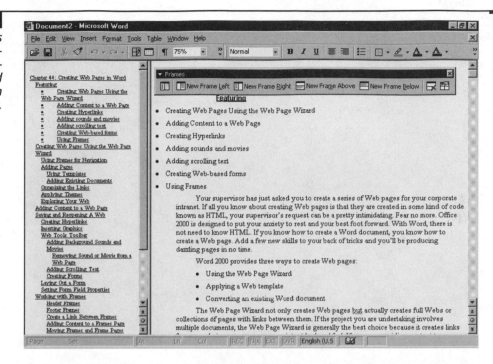

To create a page that you can add frames to, choose New Frames Page to create the frames page. Choose Format ➤ Frames again to choose the position of the frame you would like to add. You have several frame options, as shown here:

New Frame Above creates a header frame, and New Frame Below creates a footer frame. If you plan to add horizontal and vertical frames, add header and footer frames first so they extend the width of the page, as shown in Figure 44.17. Resize frames by dragging the frame border in the direction you want.

PART

IX

Publishing with Office

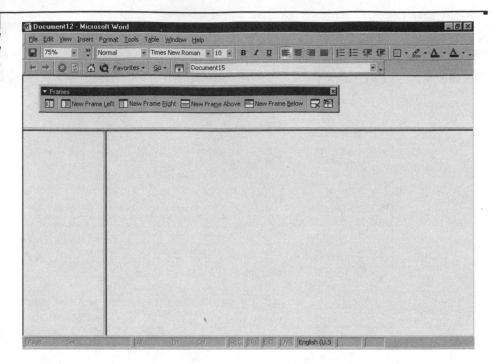

Add content to each frame. When you save the frames page, each page will be saved separately as M, M1, M2, and so on. Before saving a frames page, create a folder to save it in. Word will automatically save the frames as individual pages in that folder. If you add graphics or other objects, Word creates subfolders to house them in. Give the frames page a name that will remind you it's a frames page. If it is the home page of the Web you are creating, however, save it as `default.htm`.

Setting Frame Properties

Right-click on any frame or select the frame and click the Frame Properties button on the Frames toolbar to open the Frame Properties dialog box, shown in Figure 44.18. The initial page should be set to the frame that is open. However, you can change the page that opens in a frames page by selecting a different initial page. Give the frame a name by selecting or entering one in the Name box. Adjust the size of the frame by adjusting the size controls. By default, frames are set to a relative size. You can change the relative size to a specific pixel size or a percentage of the screen display by changing the Measure In option.

FIGURE 44.18

Change Frame properties to adjust the size of frames, borders, and other frame settings.

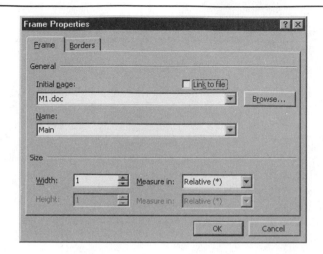

On the Borders tab of the Frame Properties dialog, set whether you want to display frame borders and, if you do, what size and color you want them to be. You can determine if you want users to be able to adjust the frame size by clearing or checking the Frame Is Resizable In Browser check box. Turn scroll bars on or off using the Show Scrollbars In Browsers setting.

WARNING If you move a frames page to a different folder or drive location, you must copy all of the related frames documents to the same location.

Removing a Frame from a Frames Page

If you decide you want to remove a frame from a frames page, click in the frame and choose Format ➤ Frames ➤ Delete Frame or click the Delete Frame button on the Frames toolbar. You may want to save the frame under a different name before you delete it in case you decide you want to use it at a later time. To save the frame under a different name, right-click in the frame and choose Save Current Frame As.

MASTERING THE OPPORTUNITIES

Viewing the HTML Source of a Web Page

Although Word 2000 provides some exciting Web page design options, creating a complex Web site requires some knowledge of HTML and other Web programming tools. While you are creating Web pages in Word, Word is writing the HTML code behind the scenes. You can view this code and even edit it directly by choosing View ≻ HTML Source. This opens the Microsoft Development Environment design window where you can edit HTML and active server page (.asp) files. If you are not a programmer, this is a good place to take a look at what it takes to produce the content you are creating and see HTML in actual application. If you are a programmer, you can edit the HTML file and add Microsoft Visual Basic, JScript, and VBScript to your files.

Making a Web Available for Others to View

When you have your Web looking just the way you want, it's time to put it "out there" for others to use. In today's environment, you have two primary places to publish a Web: your company's intranet or the World Wide Web. If your company has an intranet, contact the Web administrator to see how to proceed from here. It may be as simple as saving the files to a Web folder (see Chapter 37 for more about Web folders).

If you want your Web pages to be available for the whole world to see, you need to either identify an Internet Service Provider who can host your Web site or set up a computer to run as a Web server. The cost of having a Web site hosted by an ISP has come down dramatically, so unless you have a burning desire to run your own server, the smartest choice is to let a specialist do it. ISPs are sure to have fast equipment, T1 lines for fast connections, and multiple phone lines to handle the heavy traffic generated by your site.

What's Next

Excel and Access 2000 offer exciting new ways to bring active and passive data to the Web. If your goal is to create Web pages that contain searchable databases of your products or even just an up-to-date staff directory, you'll love the way you can use Excel and Access to enliven your Web pages.

CHAPTER 45

Creating Web Pages with Excel and Access

As you've probably noticed, a significant number of the improvements in Office 2000 are Web features. Some of the slickest changes are in Excel and Access, and they range from improved HTML support to entirely new tools for Web-based desktop reporting from your Office data applications. We'll first look at the tools Excel provides for Web publishing.

Publishing Excel Documents on the Web

Some of the Office 2000 Web improvements aren't easy to spot. You know, for example, that you can save an Excel worksheet as HTML, just as you could in Office 97. Well, the new functionality in Office 2000 is that you can open that worksheet again in Excel and all the formulas and functions still work because HTML is an Excel *companion format*, supported at the same level as the application's native format. You can also open HTML files directly from Excel and drag and drop HTML tables from your browser directly into Excel worksheets. The more you work with the new features in this chapter, the more you'll appreciate how much easier Web publishing is when you don't have to convert files between the XLS and HMTL formats.

Saving and Publishing HTML Documents

When you save or publish Excel 2000 worksheets as Web pages, the pages you create are either *interactive* or *noninteractive*. Noninteractive pages are simply static pages that users can look at to examine data, like those you could publish in prior versions of Excel. With the interactive opportunities made available by using the *Office Web Components*, users can work with the data via the browser using some of the same tools they would in Excel 2000.

 TIP There are differences between saving and publishing in Office 2000—for example, saving always creates noninteractive pages. See Chapter 40 for more information about Web publishing in Office.

There are three Office Web Components: the Spreadsheet component, the Charting component, and the PivotTable component. Each one supports specific kinds of interactivity. With the Spreadsheet component, users can add formulas, sort and filter data, and format the worksheet. The Charting component is linked to data in a Spreadsheet component so that the chart display will change when the data in the spreadsheet changes. The PivotTable component lets your users analyze database information using most of the sorting, filtering, grouping, and subtotaling features of PivotTable reports.

 MASTERING THE OPPORTUNITIES

Mastering the Opportunities: Understanding Office Web Components

The Office Web Components are based on *COM*, the *Component Object Model*. With these components, you don't need to learn Java to create the slick interactive interface your users are asking for. The COM standard defines groups of functions called *interfaces*. Interfaces like the Office Web Components are grouped into component categories, which are in turn supported by applications like Excel, Access, and Internet Explorer 4 and 5. COM objects used in Office 2000 are only interactive if the user's browser supports COM. If a user has an older browser, they'll still see the spreadsheet, chart, or pivot table, but they will not be able to manipulate it in their browser.

To create a Web page, either interactive or noninteractive, open the spreadsheet you want to save to the Web. Then choose File ➤ Save As Web Page from the menu bar to open the Save As Web Page dialog box. In the Selection area of the dialog box, choose the sheet(s) or range(s) you want to save or publish. To create interactive pages, enable the Add Interactivity check box to add Office Web Components to your page:

You can save an entire workbook as a Web page, complete with sheet tabs; however, the page cannot be interactive. To save an entire workbook, don't click Publish. Simply click the Save button to create the Web page and close the dialog box. Change any other settings you wish, and then click the Publish button to open the Publish As Web Page dialog box, as shown in Figure 45.1.

If you have enabled interactivity, choose the component you wish to use from the drop-down list by selecting the kind of functionality you want browser users to have. Click the Publish button, and Excel creates the Web page, including any interactivity you have specified. A Web page that includes the Spreadsheet component is shown in Figure 45.2. The same cells, published without interactivity, were published above the Web component; the end of this noninteractive list appears at the top of the browser window.

PART

IX

Publishing with Office

FIGURE 45.1

By specifying functionality, you choose an Office Web Component.

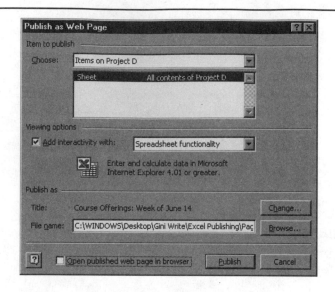

FIGURE 45.2

An interactive Excel Web page that includes the Spreadsheet component

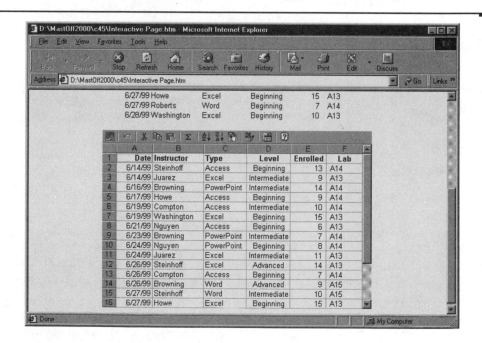

Most of the toolbar buttons are familiar Excel buttons. There are two additions, the Export To Excel button and the Properties button. The Export To Excel button recreates the Excel worksheet at a user-specified location. The Properties button opens additional user tools, as shown in Figure 45.3.

FIGURE 45.3

Users can change the properties of selected cells.

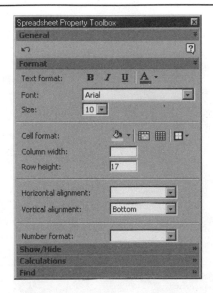

To place a second component on a page, choose File ➤ Save As Web Page and then click Publish to reopen the Publish As Web Page dialog box. Enter the existing HTML file in the File Name text box (see Figure 45.1). You'll be prompted to replace or add to the page:

In Figure 45.4, we've published the same data using the PivotTable component. The COM object works like the Excel PivotTable report with areas for row data, column data, and page data (filter data). See Chapter 26 for more information on PivotTable reports.

The Chart component displays both the chart and the underlying data (see Figure 45.5). Users manipulate the data to change the chart, just as they would in Excel. They can't change the chart type or other chart features, so make sure you create a chart that's useful before saving it as an interactive page.

PART

IX

Publishing with Office

FIGURE 45.4

The PivotTable component lets users interactively analyze data.

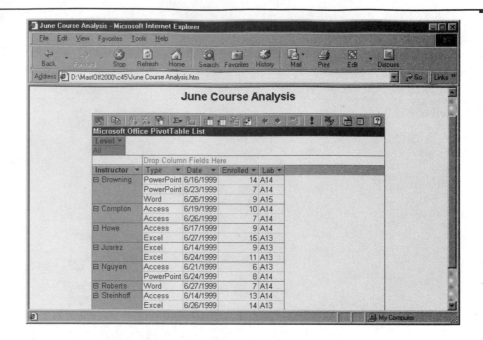

FIGURE 45.5

The Chart component reflects changes in the underlying data.

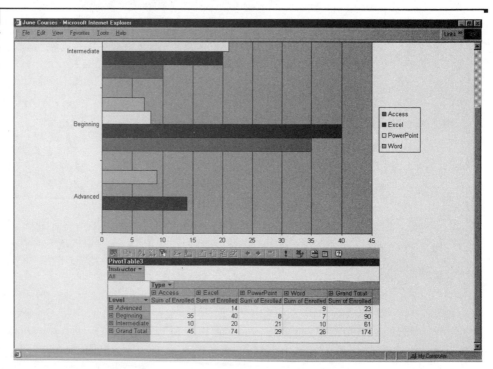

Creating Web Pages in Access

You can create three very different kinds of Web pages with Access 2000: dynamic Data Access Pages, server-generated HTML pages, and static Web pages. You use different tools to create the different types of pages. There are advantages and disadvantages to each type.

Data Access Pages, created with the Data Access Page Wizard, are DHTML (Dynamic HTML) pages that can include Office Web Components. Data Access Pages are interactive. You can allow users to edit and enter database data from a browser, but they must have Office 2000 and Internet Explorer 5 or higher. Therefore, make sure to create Data Access Pages in a relatively closed environment, like an intranet, where users need to work interactively with up-to-the-minute data and you know they have the required client-side software.

Server-generated HTML pages let you present live data, but the data will not be updatable. Microsoft Internet Information Server is required on the server side to generate the HTML pages, so these are not generic "publish anywhere" pages, but they work with a variety of browsers. Server-generated HTML pages are useful in a heterogeneous environment like the Internet when you need to display current read-only data to a variety of client browsers.

You'll create static pages when you want users to view—but not change or manipulate—data, and significant data changes are infrequent. Static pages are purely HTML, so you can publish them on a Web server that doesn't include Internet Information Server.

Creating Data Access Pages

Data Access Pages can be posted on a Web site or your company intranet or sent via e-mail to someone off your network. Data Access Pages aren't saved as objects in your database; rather, they're saved as separate files on your hard drive. They are dynamic Web pages bound directly to the data in your database. Data Access Pages are designed for Internet Explorer 5; earlier versions of Internet Explorer don't support them.

To create a Data Access Page from your data, choose Pages in the Objects bar of the Access Database window. On the Pages page, click Create Data Access Page By Using Wizard. The Page Wizard starts, as shown in Figure 45.6. It's very similar to the Report Wizard, and your Data Access Page will resemble an Access report. In the first wizard dialog box, the Tables/Queries drop-down list, select a table to base your page on, and then double-click fields in the table that you want to include in the page.

FIGURE 45.6

Select fields for your page in the Data Access Page Wizard.

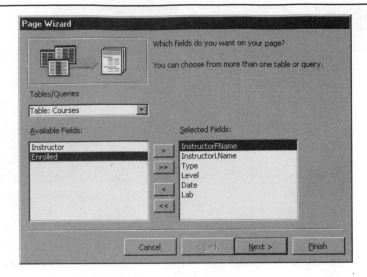

If you want to create a page in which users can drill down for related records in another table, select the related table in the Tables/Queries drop-down list, and double-click fields you want to add from that table. Then click Next. In the next step (if you've chosen related tables), you can group your data as you would in an Access report.

 NOTE Adding grouping levels makes the data displayed in the page read-only.

When you've set your grouping levels, click Next. The next wizard dialog box lets you set sorting options for the data in the related records. In the last step of the wizard, name your page. To open the finished page, select the Open The Page option. To add text to the page such as a title, select Modify The Page's Design. Enable the Apply A Theme check box to select an Office 2000 theme for your Web page. When you've finished setting options, click Finish to create the Web page. Access creates a folder named *page name*_files within the folder that houses the Access database. For example, if you name your page Courses, the folder for the page will be called Courses_files. Data Access Pages are stored as HTML files and graphic files in the new folder. Figure 45.7 shows a Data Access Page displayed in Access 2000 Form view. Choose File ➢ Web Page Preview to display a Data Access Page in your browser.

FIGURE 45.7

Data access pages are bound to your database.

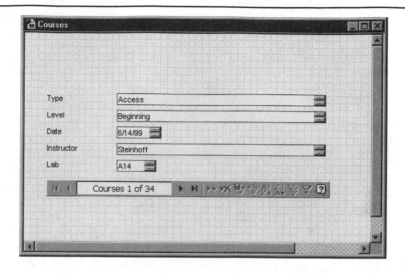

 TIP To delete the page, select the Pages group in the Database window, select the Data Access Page, and click the Delete button. When you delete a page, you'll be given the choice to delete just the link and keep the page (the unlinked page will be a static snapshot of the data when the page was created), or delete all the page files.

Figure 45.8 shows a Data Access Page created from the same data in Internet Explorer 5. In this case, we chose to group based on Instructor in the wizard. The result in the browser is a *Grouped Data Access Page*. This grouped list is read-only, but if you want a slick way to present large quantities of categorized data, grouping is the answer. Users can show or hide details by clicking Expand indicators on the left side of the page. When a user prints the contents of the browser window, only the data that is displayed is printed. Combine the power of grouping with the sorting and filtering toolbar buttons, and you have the tools you need to create a fast and friendly reporting tool for end users. For information on adding titles and other objects to your page, see "Working with Pages in Design View" later in this section.

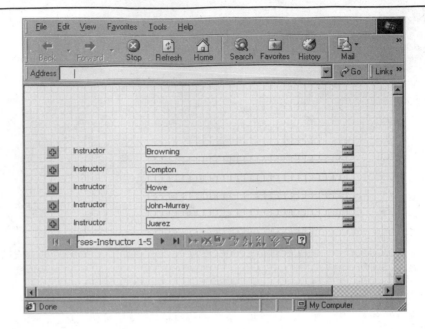

Using Data Access Pages

After you've created a Data Access Page, users with a Microsoft Office 2000 license can open the page using the Internet Explorer browser (version 5 or higher). To test an interactive Data Access Page in its intended environment, open it in IE. The page has a toolbar at the bottom that viewers can use to navigate, sort, or filter the records (see Figure 45.8). Navigating, sorting, and filtering records works here just as it does in Access database forms.

If the Data Access Page was created from an editable recordset and you didn't group the data on the page, users can edit and enter records in the page as they would in a form. If a viewer makes changes to the data, they must save the changes by clicking the Save button on the Page toolbar, or they can undo changes by clicking the Undo button on the toolbar.

 WARNING Any changes a user makes and saves are made directly to the data in your database, so be careful who has access to your Data Access Pages.

Working with Pages in Design View

To modify the design of the Data Access object on a Web page, open the page in Design view by clicking the Design View button. Figure 45.9 shows the Courses Grouped by Instructor page from Figure 45.8 in Design view. At the top of the page are text boxes in which you can enter a title (Click Here And Type Title Text) and description (Click Here And Type Body Text). The Data Access object has, at minimum, a header and a navigation section. The lowest-level header is equivalent to the Details section in a form or report. A new header and navigation section is added for each grouping level, so there are two sets of headers/navigation sections used in Figure 45.9: one for the details (Courses) and another for the grouping level (Courses–Instructor).

FIGURE 45.9

Open the page in Design view to modify its design.

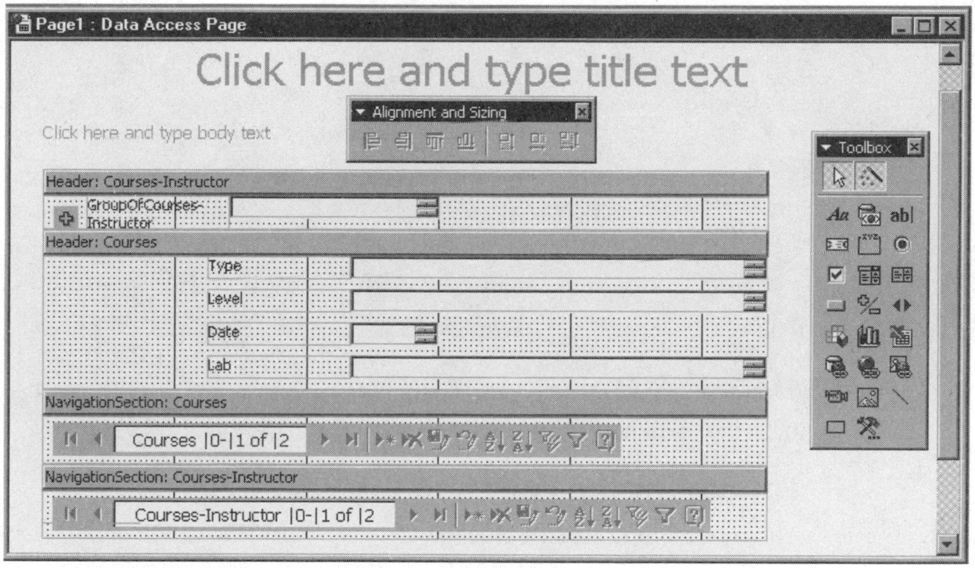

TIP Even if you don't have FrontPage (which is included in the Premium edition of Office 2000), you can still design professional Web pages with Access 2000. You can open any Web page in Design view and edit the page even if the page wasn't created in Office. Click the Pages tab in the Database window and choose Edit An Existing Page.

PART

IX

Publishing with Office

Adding Fields to the Page

You add fields to the Data Access Page just as you would add a field to a report or form, but you use a beefier version of the Field List. You can select fields from any table in the database. Click the Field List button to open the Field List dialog box, shown in Figure 45.10. Choose fields to add to the page from the Database page of the dialog box. Click the Add To Page button to add the selected field to the Data Access object within the page.

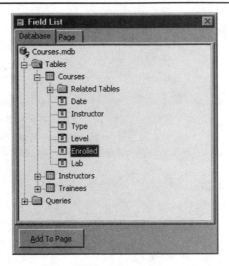

The Page page displays the fields already used in the Data Access Page. Right-click a field to delete it or change its data source.

Formatting the Page and Controls

The themes in Access are shared with the other Office 2000 applications, so this is an easy way to make sure your Data Access Page has the same look and feel as the rest of your Web site. To change the theme, choose Format ➤ Theme from the menu. In the Theme dialog box, preview the different backgrounds, choose other graphical options, and click OK.

Move and resize controls as you would in forms or reports. When you move a control, its label moves with it. Aligning and sizing controls is more tedious here than in a form, so this is a good place to leave Snap to Grid (on the Format menu) enabled.

Use the Alignment and Sizing toolbar (refer back to Figure 45.9) to align or size controls relative to another control. Alignment does not work in the same way as the alignment options in form or report design, because you can't select multiple controls on a Data Access Page. To right-align two controls, select the first control, click the Align Right button on the toolbar, and then click the second control.

Changing, Sorting, and Grouping

The sections of the Data Access object function like an outline. The header for the primary grouping is at the top of the page. If you have two levels of grouping, the secondary grouping header appears next, followed by the third header for the detail. If you have one grouping level (like Courses-Instructor in Figure 45.9), you can create a second level by promoting a field from the Courses section.

  Select the field you want to group by; then either click the Promote button on the toolbar or right-click and choose Promote from the shortcut menu. Likewise, when you want to remove a grouping level, select a field in a group header, and then either click the Demote button or right-click and choose Demote from the shortcut menu.

 Many of the Data Access object's properties are tied to the grouping levels. To change group properties, open the Sorting And Grouping dialog box, as shown in Figure 45.11, by clicking the Sorting And Grouping button. Select the group you want to change and then, in the bottom pane, change the property value. Table 45.1 describes the group properties.

FIGURE 45.11

Open the Sorting and Grouping dialog box to set section options.

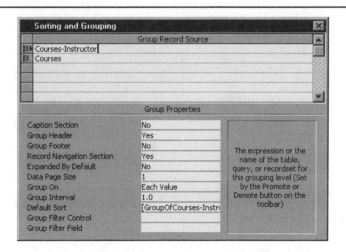

TABLE 45.1: DATA ACCESS PAGE GROUP PROPERTIES

Property	Default	Description
Caption Section	No	Display/hide a section for a title above the group header.
Group Header	Yes	Display/hide the group header containing the field control.
Group Footer	No	Display/hide the group footer.
Record Navigation Section	Yes	Display/hide the Navigation buttons for the group, including the New Record button.
Expanded by Default	No	Display/hide records in the level below this level when the page opens.
Data Page Size	Varies	Default is All in lowest-level group, 1 in higher-level groups. Change this setting to All to display all values in a group.
Group On and Group Interval	Varies	Number of characters (text fields), date ranges, or numeric ranges used to group data.
Default Sort		Name of the field you want to sort the grouping level on, or a list of field names separated by commas.
Group Filter On		Name of list box or combo box with value used to filter records.
Group Filter Field		Name of a field in the group's record source that contains the values you want to filter from.

The group properties make it easy to change the Data Access Page layout to make it more useful. Figure 45.12 shows the wizard-created page from Figure 45.9 with just a few changes:

- A title and body text were added in the default locations.
- The controls in the Courses group were rearranged to be listed horizontally.
- In the Courses–Instructor and Courses groups, the Data Page Size property was set to All. In both groups, the Record Navigation Section was turned off. All records are now displayed and, since this isn't an updatable record set, there's no need for the New Record button.
- All text boxes were bolded.
- A theme (Blends) was applied to the page.

FIGURE 45.12

*A few simple property
changes make the
page more useful.*

Courses by Instructor

Click the Expand button to view the courses offered by the instructor in June and July.

    ⊞   Browning

    ⊟   Compton

Courses currently offered by this instructor include:

Access	Beginning	Date	6/26/99	Lab	A14
Access	Beginning	Date	7/6/99	Lab	A14
Access	Intermediate	Date	6/19/99	Lab	A14
PowerPoint	Intermediate	Date	7/17/99	Lab	A14

    ⊞   Howe

    ⊞   John-Murray

    ⊞   Juarez

    ⊞   Nguyen

    ⊞   Roberts

    ⊞   Steinhoff

Using the Data Access Page Toolbox

The Data Access Page toolbox includes a number of tools you're familiar with if you've designed Access forms or reports (see Figure 45.1) or if you've created forms using Visual Basic. However, there are other controls that are specifically for use on Web pages, including the three Office Web Components you saw at the start of this chapter. You already know how to use the components in Excel. We'll use the Pivot-Table component as an example of how to work with the components in an Access Web page.

PivotTable   Spreadsheet
component   component

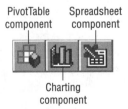

Charting
component

To add an Office Web Component to the active Web page, click the Component's toolbox button, and then click on the page to place the Component.

Right-click on the component and choose Property Toolbox or click the Property Toolbox button on the component's toolbar. Whether you work in Excel or Access, the Property toolbox is the same. In Excel, however, you usually select a range of cells that serves as the data source for the component before placing the component. In Access, you have to place the component first and then select a data source. Open the Data Source section of the Property toolbox and choose Data Source Control. To summarize data in a table or query in the active database, leave MSODSC as the Data Source Control in the Get To Data Using section. Then select from the tables, queries, and data sets that are already used in the page in the Use Data From drop-down list. As soon as you select a data source, the row, column, and data areas appear in the PivotTable component.

NOTE If you've used the L/R naming standard, it really pays off in the Use Data From drop-down list. You used the tbl and qry prefixes for tables and queries, so all the other list items are data sets used in other objects on the Web page.

Click the Field List button on the component's toolbar to open the list of fields in the data source. (Make sure you don't click the Field List button on the Access toolbar—it won't do you much good here.) Drag fields from the list to the row, column, data, and page areas of the PivotTable component. When you've added the fields to the table, spend a moment browsing the Advanced properties, which allow you to lock in filters and sort order and to hide or display the Property toolbox when the user opens the page in their browser. Figure 45.13 shows a pivot table illustrating current course enrollments in our Courses By Application page. You can use all three of the Web components to create solid intranet reporting tools; this pivot table, for example, lets any Office 2000 user view total enrollment by course and by instructor without ever opening Access or Excel.

Detailed information about all of the intrinsic HTML and COM controls in the Data Access Pages Toolbox is beyond the scope of this book, but that shouldn't discourage you from trying those that you haven't used before. Data Access Pages support Visual Basic Script and JavaScript, so they have a lot of flexibility. For more specific information about Data Access Page features, we recommend *Mastering Access 2000* by Alan Simpson and Celeste Robinson (Sybex, 1999).

FIGURE 45.13

You can add the Office Web Components to any page.

Courses Query					
Drop Filter Fields Here					
	Type ▼				
	⊞ Access	⊞ Excel	⊞ PowerPoint	⊞ Word	⊞ Grand Total
Instructor ▼	Sum of Enrolled	Sum of Enrolled	Sum of Enrolled	Sum of Enrolled	Sum of Enrolled
⊞ Browning	7	15	30	9	61
⊞ Compton	26		11		37
⊞ Howe	33	15			48
⊞ John-Murray		39	10		49
⊞ Juarez		20		15	35
⊞ Nguyen	6	15	8		29
⊞ Roberts		10		7	17
⊞ Steinhoff	20	27		25	72
⊞ Grand Total	92	141	59	56	348

Creating Server-Generated HTML Pages

Server-generated HTML pages are the active pages you're used to seeing on the Web exported from forms, tables, or queries. They're not updatable in a browser, but they are live data. There are two flavors of server-generated pages: ASP and IDC/HTX. ASP (Active Server Pages) is a better format, but the pages contain ActiveX components so they require a Web server with Internet Information Server (IIS) version 3 or higher. The IDC/HTX format supported by earlier versions of IIS generates two files: a text file with instructions for connecting to the database and an HTML template for the Web page. With both formats, you have to publish the page on a Web server, which creates the HTML page on demand. Ask your system administrator which version of IIS is installed on your Web server.

 NOTE When you create a server-generated page, you'll be asked to specify a data source: an ODBC connection to your database. For more information on creating data sources, see Chapter 35.

To create a server-generated page, first select the form, table, or query you want to use for the page in the Database window. Then choose File ➢ Export from the menu. In the Save As Type drop-down list, choose either Microsoft IIS 1-2 to create IDC/HTX pages or Microsoft Active Server Pages. Select a file location, enter a file name, and click Save. The IDC/HTX Output Options dialog box shown in Figure 45.14 opens so you can enter additional information.

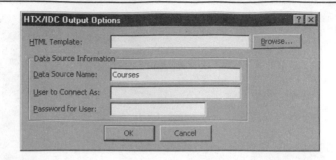

An HTML Template is an HMTL file that contains formatting and tags for Access. If you don't select a template, the server applies default formatting. The Data Source Name is the ODBC data source that connects to your database. In the User To Connect As and Password For User boxes, enter the username and password for the data source. If you don't enter usernames and passwords, the defaults are used (for example, Admin with no password for an Access database). Click OK to create the page.

 TIP   After you've created a server-generated page, you must publish the page before you can view it because the server generates the page. To do that, you'll need to consult your system or Web administrator.

Creating Static HTML Pages

Static HTML pages are snapshots of the data at the time you create the page. There's nothing interactive, dynamic, or even linked here. However, don't overlook their usefulness for data that changes infrequently. Static pages load quickly and are exceptionally egalitarian. If your browser will let you view anything on the Web, it will let you view a static HMTL page. To create a static page, choose the form, table, or query that you want to place on the page from the Database window. Choose File ➤ Export to open the Export As dialog box. Choose HTML files as the Save As Type, select a file location, and click Export to create the page. A static HTML page created by exporting the Courses table is shown in Figure 45.15.

FIGURE 45.15

Any browser can display static pages like this one.

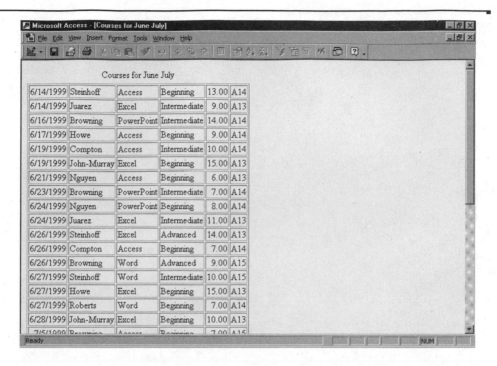

		Courses for June July			
6/14/1999	Steinhoff	Access	Beginning	13.00	A14
6/14/1999	Juarez	Excel	Intermediate	9.00	A13
6/16/1999	Browning	PowerPoint	Intermediate	14.00	A14
6/17/1999	Howe	Access	Beginning	9.00	A14
6/19/1999	Compton	Access	Intermediate	10.00	A14
6/19/1999	John-Murray	Excel	Beginning	15.00	A13
6/21/1999	Nguyen	Access	Beginning	6.00	A13
6/23/1999	Browning	PowerPoint	Intermediate	7.00	A14
6/24/1999	Nguyen	PowerPoint	Beginning	8.00	A14
6/24/1999	Juarez	Excel	Intermediate	11.00	A13
6/26/1999	Steinhoff	Excel	Advanced	14.00	A13
6/26/1999	Compton	Access	Beginning	7.00	A14
6/26/1999	Browning	Word	Advanced	9.00	A15
6/27/1999	Steinhoff	Word	Intermediate	10.00	A15
6/27/1999	Howe	Excel	Beginning	15.00	A13
6/27/1999	Roberts	Word	Beginning	7.00	A14
6/28/1999	John-Murray	Excel	Beginning	10.00	A13
7/5/1999	Browning	Access	Beginning	7.00	A15

Open the HTML page in Design view to apply a theme or add a title, scrolling marquee, or other elements. Remember, you can add Office Web Components if your intended users have IE 5 and Office 2000.

What's Next

In the next chapter, you'll find out how to use PowerPoint to deliver Web-based presentations. You can deliver the presentations in real time with Presentation Broadcast, but any presentation can be saved for later use on the Internet or an intranet, adding another type of interactivity to your Web site.

PART

IX

Publishing with Office

CHAPTER 46

Creating Online Presentations with PowerPoint

FEATURING:

Saving Web presentations

Publishing Web presentations

Setting PowerPoint Web options

Setting up and broadcasting presentations

With PowerPoint 2000, you can save or publish presentations for individuals to use online at their convenience, or you can deliver a real-time presentation on the Internet or an intranet for an audience of one or one thousand.

Preparing Presentations for the Web

There are two different methods you'll use to make PowerPoint 2000 presentations available for browsing on the Internet or your company's intranet: saving and publishing. When you save a presentation, other PowerPoint 2000 users connected to your network can access the HTML document, which allows them to edit the presentation. A published presentation, however, is like a published Web site: other users can view it and follow its links, but they cannot edit it. You'll save a presentation to a network file server while you and any colleagues are working on it; then, once it's ready to "go live," you'll publish it to a Web server.

Before saving or publishing your presentation, it's a good idea to preview (File ➤ Web Page Preview) the way the presentation will look in your default browser. Then, choose File ➤ Save As Web Page from the menu bar to open the Save As dialog box shown in Figure 46.1.

FIGURE 46.1

Use the Save As dialog box to save or publish presentations.

Saving a Presentation as a Web Page

The page title for the presentation is displayed near the bottom of the Save As dialog box. The title will appear in the title bar of the user's browser; the default title is the presentation's title (choose File ➢ Properties to see this) or its file name. To change the page title, click the Change Title button (see Figure 46.1) and enter a new title in the Change Title dialog box, then click OK to return to the Save As dialog box. Click the Save button to save the presentation and close the dialog box.

Publishing a Web Presentation

With PowerPoint 2000, you can publish an entire presentation, selected slides, or even a single PowerPoint slide. The first page of a PowerPoint publication, displayed in Internet Explorer 5, is shown in Figure 46.2.

FIGURE 46.2

The published presentation includes navigation controls browser users expect to see.

Collapsible outline

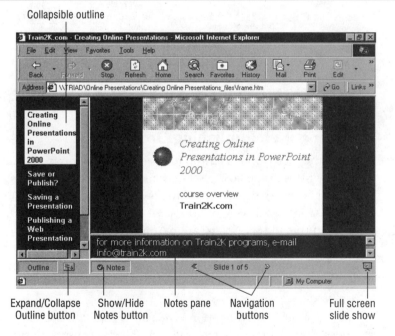

Expand/Collapse   Show/Hide   Notes pane   Navigation   Full screen
Outline button   Notes button   buttons   slide show

To publish your presentation, first choose File ➢ Save As Web Page, then click the Publish button in the Save As dialog box (see Figure 46.1) to open the Publish As Web Page dialog box, shown in Figure 46.3.

Set options for your Web presentation in the Publish As Web Page dialog box.

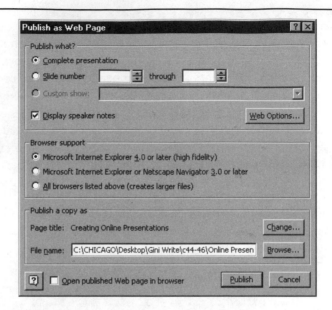

In the Publish What section, choose to publish the entire presentation, a range of slides, or a custom show you created using the Slide Show ➤ Custom Shows command. Enable the Display Speaker Notes check box if your presentation includes speaker's notes that you want users to see in a separate Notes pane.

Setting Web Publishing Options

Click the Web Options button to open the Web Options dialog box. Use the four pages of this dialog box to set options for publishing the current presentation. The General options available only in PowerPoint are detailed here; see Chapter 40 for information about Web options used in all the Office applications.

With the Add Slide Navigation Controls option enabled on the General page of the Web Options dialog box, your presentation will include an Outline pane with a collapsible outline (see Figure 46.2) in the color scheme you select, a Notes pane, and navigation buttons below the presentation. Turn this option off if you're publishing a single slide.

The Show Slide Animation While Browsing option displays animations within slides. If animations are manually advanced, the user will click the navigation buttons to switch slides and click the slides to move through the animations. There are no instructions to tell the user to do this, so we suggest you set automatic timings for all animations if you enable this check box.

The Resize Graphics To Fit Browser Window option is enabled by default. When you publish your presentation, this option automatically resizes graphics so they'll display best in the Screen Size setting specified in the Picture options.

When you've finished setting Web options, click OK to close the Web Options dialog box and return to the Publish As Web Page dialog box.

Selecting Browsers to Support

Choose the browsers you wish to support based on the intended distribution of your presentation. If you're publishing a presentation for your company's intranet, all you have to do is select your company's browser standard. For wider distribution (as with the Internet), there are additional issues to consider:

- Pages that link to your presentation serve as gatekeepers. If users need Internet Explorer 4 or higher to effectively view your home page, you may as well choose IE 4 support for your presentation that's accessed via the home page.

- The newer the browser, the more bells and whistles it will support. For example, IE 4 supports multimedia, including PowerPoint sound effects and movies. However, choosing the latest and most powerful browsers means that users may have to download a newer version of a browser to view your presentation. Even if you put a link to the browser's download page on your Web site, some users won't take the time to do this; they'll just browse elsewhere.

- The best browser format for WebTV is not the newest; it is the IE/Netscape 3 standard. With the number of WebTV users increasing, you may wish to choose this older standard to maintain a broader user base.

- Choosing to support all browsers is the egalitarian approach and guarantees the widest possible access to your publication. However, it results in larger files, which means that everyone who wants to view your presentation will need more time to download it.

In the Publish A Copy As section, change (or leave the default) page title. Click the Browse button to select a destination for the presentation. (To save to a Web folder, select Web Folders from the Places pane.) If you wish to preview the presentation as soon as it is published, enable the check box at the bottom of the dialog box. Click Publish to publish a copy of the active PowerPoint presentation. If you change the presentation, you'll need to publish it again if you want the published copy to reflect your changes.

PART

IX

Publishing with Office

MASTERING TROUBLESHOOTING

Troubleshooting Web Presentations

After you publish a presentation, you may notice that the slide show (in PowerPoint) and the same presentation viewed as pages in your browser behave differently. Functionality that comes from PowerPoint isn't available in your browser. For example, when you right-click during a Web presentation, the presentation shortcut menu does not appear. This makes sense—your browser probably doesn't have a PowerPoint shortcut menu the rest of the time, either!

There are a number of PowerPoint features that don't work on a Web page, regardless of the browser support you select when you publish your presentation. Features that do not have Web support include:

- Embossed and shadow effects for fonts
- OLE multimedia objects
- Multislide sound effects (moving to another slide stops sound)
- Text animated by letter or by word rather than by paragraph
- Chart effects
- Spiral, stretch, swivel, and zoom effects

The browser you're using (or the browser you chose to support when you published) also affects the published product. Internet Explorer 3, for example, doesn't support sound and video playback.

Broadcasting Presentations

You can broadcast a PowerPoint presentation over the Internet or an intranet. Presentation Broadcasting is often used in place of a face-to-face meeting or conference call when you have participants at remote locations, reducing the time and expense of traveling. Unlike a published presentation that users browse at their leisure, a broadcast occurs in real time, so you schedule the broadcast and invite participants in advance using Outlook (or another e-mail program). However, you can also record the broadcast and save it so that participants who could not attend or wish to review the presentation can do so.

Broadcasts come in two sizes: 1 to 15 participants and 16 or more participants. (This assumes that participants need their own Internet connections. If two people are sitting in front of the same monitor, count them as one participant.) You can use Internet Explorer 4 or 5 to broadcast to up to 15 people. For 16 participants or more, you'll need access to a NetShow server, so talk to your Web administrator. A NetShow server is also required if you include live video, regardless of audience size.

There are three steps required to get ready for the actual broadcast:

- Selecting the broadcast options
- Selecting a shared folder and server
- Scheduling the broadcast

 TIP Presentation Broadcasting uses Office automation to create appointments and invitations to the presentation in Outlook 2000. You can create and broadcast presentations regardless of your e-mail client, but if you intend to broadcast on a regular basis, you'll want to use Outlook and speak to your network or Web administrator about installing a NetShow server.

Setting Up Your Broadcast

With the presentation you wish to broadcast open and active, choose Slide Show ➢ Online Broadcast ➢ Setup and Schedule to open the Broadcast Schedule dialog box, shown here:

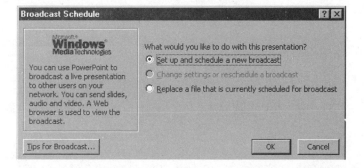

 TIP Online Broadcast is an install-on-demand feature in the standard Office installation. The first time you use this feature, you may be prompted to install it.

Selecting Broadcast Options

Select whether you want to set up a new broadcast or change an existing broadcast, and then click OK to open the appropriate dialog box. A Description page used when scheduling a new broadcast is shown in Figure 46.4. Enter a title and (optional) description for the presentation. In the Contact text box enter (or click the Address Book button and select) the e-mail address that participants should use to send e-mail questions or responses to during the broadcast.

 TIP You can schedule and broadcast a presentation on different computers. It's easiest to schedule the broadcast on the computer of the person who's hosting the presentation so PowerPoint will pick up their default description information.

FIGURE 46.4

Information from the Description page is used to create a lobby page for the broadcast.

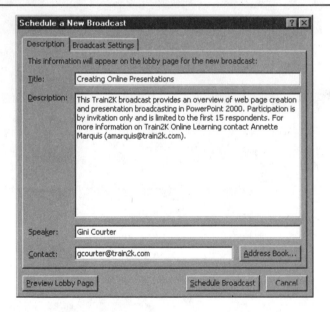

Set the options you want to use for the broadcast on the Broadcast Settings page, shown in Figure 46.5. Table 46.1 describes each of the options.

FIGURE 46.5

Specify broadcast options on the Broadcast Settings page.

TABLE 46.1: PRESENTATION BROADCAST SETTINGS

Setting	Description
Send Audio	Broadcasts live audio during the presentation.
Send Video	Broadcasts live video; requires a NetShow server.
Camera/Microphone Is Connected To Another Computer	If a different computer will be used for audio/video feed, specify its name here.
Viewers Can E-Mail	Address for e-mail feedback during the broadcast.
Enable Chat	Enables Microsoft Chat; requires a Chat server.
Record The Broadcast And Save It	Records a copy of the broadcast for later viewing in the specified location.
Viewers Can Access Speaker Notes	Gives access to all speaker notes.

PART

IX

Publishing with Office

Selecting a Shared Folder and Server

Click the Server Options button to select a location from which your presentation will be broadcast to display the Server Options dialog box, as shown in Figure 46.6. You must specify a shared folder and you can optionally specify a NetShow server. If a participant does not have permission to access the shared folder you specify, they will not be able to participate, so you may want to talk with your network administrator about creating a folder with very broad permissions for broadcasting presentations. After you specify a shared folder, you can select a NetShow server.

Select a shared folder for the broadcast.

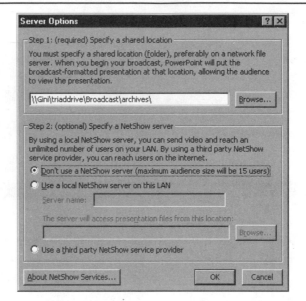

TIP   For the shared folder and the location where you save a recording of the broadcast, you must enter a server and folder with the file URL, \\server\\sharedfolder; don't use network path syntax such as c:\My Documents\Broadcasts. (See Figures 46.5 and 46.6.) Ideally, the shared folder's URL and the PowerPoint presentation's file name should not contain spaces; if they do, you'll have to double-check how the URL appears whenever it is referenced because the spaces will be represented by the characters %20. If the shared folder you want to use is on your computer or a mapped drive, click the Browse button and locate the folder through the Network Neighborhood to have the correct syntax automatically entered in the dialog box.

Previewing the Lobby Page   Click the Preview Lobby Page button to view the first page participants will see when they join the presentation. Figure 46.7 shows the Lobby page created from the settings shown in Figures 46.4 and 46.5. A Lobby page with typographical errors or other mistakes can set a poor tone for your broadcast, so examine the page carefully before continuing.

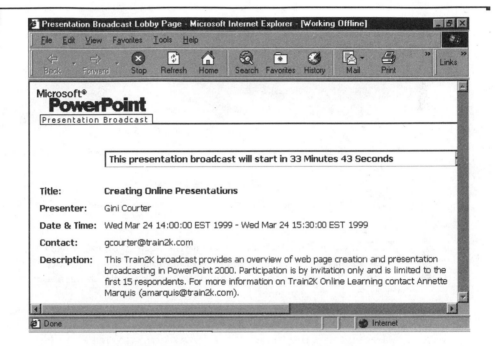

FIGURE 46.7

The Lobby page greets participants prior to the broadcast.

Scheduling the Broadcast

After you set all your other options, click the Schedule Broadcast button to schedule the presentation broadcast. PowerPoint will validate your settings to make sure, for example, that the folder you selected exists. If you did not select a NetShow server, you'll be reminded that you are limited to 15 participants. Then, PowerPoint will open an Outlook appointment form so you can set a time and date for the meeting and invite participants, as shown in Figure 46.8. The Subject will appear as the subject of the e-mail invitations to potential participants, so feel free to change it. While you're entering information, check the Event Address text box—it's the location of your shared folder. If the address (which now includes the presentation file name) contains spaces, you'll need to edit the Event Address so it refers to the correct folder and file.

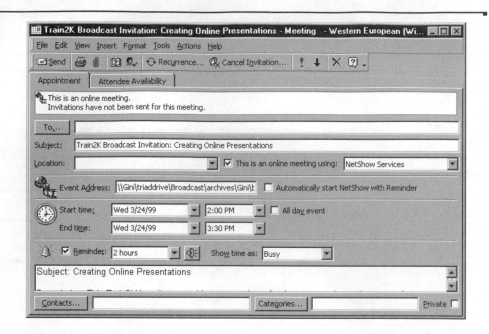

 TIP If you're the person presenting the broadcast, you might want to set a reminder at least 30 minutes in advance and have Outlook automatically launch NetShow when the reminder occurs. For other information about completing the appointment form, see "Scheduling Appointments" in Chapter 20.

After you send the appointment, PowerPoint will create and send e-mail invitations to the attendees. If you don't use Outlook as your e-mail client, you'll need to enter the broadcast date and time in the message; PowerPoint will automatically include a hyperlink to the broadcast location that the participants can click to join the broadcast. PowerPoint then saves the broadcast version of the presentation. This can take several minutes for a lengthy presentation, but PowerPoint will let you know when the presentation is ready:

You'll receive e-mail responses from participants who use Outlook to let you know whether or not they will be attending the broadcast. After you read an e-mail response, the list of attendees on the second page of the Outlook appointment item will be automatically updated. The presentation appointment appears on your Outlook calendar. If you need to change broadcast times or cancel the broadcast, right-click the appointment and use the shortcut menu in Outlook, or open the PowerPoint presentation and choose Slide Show ➢ Online Broadcast ➢ Setup And Schedule.

 TIP It's a good idea to rehearse your presentation between the time you send the invitations and the scheduled broadcast time. Chapter 16 shows how to use PowerPoint's rehearsal tools.

Broadcasting the Presentation

You'll want to start preparing a few minutes before the advertised broadcast time. Open the presentation in PowerPoint and choose Slide Show ➢ Online Broadcast ➢ Begin Broadcast to open the Broadcast Presentation dialog box, shown in Figure 46.9. PowerPoint will launch the NetShow service or connect to the NetShow server.

FIGURE 46.9

The Broadcast Presentation dialog box is used to set up the server, audio, and video.

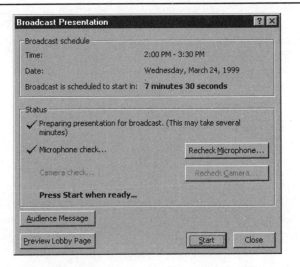

PART

IX

Publishing with Office

You'll be prompted to check your microphone (and camera if you're using video) to make sure both are operational. If the check is not satisfactory, make adjustments, and then click the Recheck button to test again.

This is a good time to click the Preview Lobby Page button so you can see the participants' view, as shown in Figure 46.7 earlier in the chapter. As the time to broadcast approaches, your participants will begin to log in. They'll see their own version of the lobby page with the clock counting down to show time. The clocks are not synchronized: they simply subtract the system clock time from the scheduled broadcast time. Make sure your system clock isn't set ahead a few minutes, or you could begin the broadcast before all your participants have a chance to join.

If you have last-minute information for participants, click the Audience Message button in the Broadcast Presentation dialog box to display a text box. Information you enter in the text box will be posted in place of the timer in the participants' browsers:

At the end of the broadcast, remain on line for a Q&A with the speaker!

When you're ready to begin broadcasting, click the Start button in the Broadcast Presentation dialog box. The Lobby page will be replaced with the first slide in your presentation. Advance slides and animated objects just as you would in a live electronic presentation. The presentation will end with a black slide. When you click the last slide, the broadcast ends, and participants are returned to the Lobby page. If you recorded the presentation, participants can click the Replay Presentation button in their browser to view the presentation again.

 NOTE There is a significant lag after you click before slides change or animations appear. Monitor your browser window; it reflects what your participants are actually seeing. Participants can't easily remind you to slow down or speak more clearly, so take your time as you move through the presentation.

Participating in a Broadcast

 You must have IE 4 or 5 to participate in a PowerPoint broadcast. To participate, you need an e-mail invitation. If you are using Outlook, you will see a reminder 15 minutes before the broadcast begins, with a View NetShow button. Click the button to launch IE and see the Lobby Page for the broadcast. When the broadcast begins, it will appear in the IE window. Adjust your audio volume so that the sound is clear. To view the entire presentation at your own pace, click the View Previous Slides link in your browser. In many presentations, you'll be allowed to e-mail questions or responses from your browser during the presentation. Some presentations also let you use Microsoft Chat to have a dialog with other participants.

What's Next

You've reached the end of the book, but not the end of learning about Microsoft Office Professional 2000. If you'd like to learn more about a particular Office application, we recommend the individual Mastering books published by Sybex. *Mastering Word 2000* (by Ron Mansfield and J.W. Olsen), *Mastering Excel 2000* (by Mindy C. Martin, Steven M. Hansen, and Beth Klingher), *Mastering Access 2000* (by Alan Simpson and Celeste Robinson), and our own *Mastering Outlook 2000*, for example, are each the length of this book, but each is devoted to a single Office product. Each book will take you farther into the application than we can here.

If you were intrigued by topics in the last few chapters, we'd recommend *Mastering Microsoft FrontPage 2000* (by Daniel A. Tauber and Brenda Kienan with Molly E. Holzschlag) for more help with Web publishing. To increase your macro and VBA expertise (Chapter 39), spend some time in *Mastering Visual Basic 6* (by Evangelos Petroutsos), and then return to Office 2000 and work with the Visual Basic Help files. The VB files included with Office 2000 are an excellent resource.

Finally, don't forget to check the Microsoft Web site frequently: http://www.microsoft .com. Like all Microsoft products, Office 2000 will continually evolve. Look in the Office Update and Developers' areas of the Web site for patches, add-ins, graphics, and sample files, as well as the latest news about unique uses for Office 2000 programs.

PART

IX

Publishing with Office

APPENDICES

APPENDIX **A**

Installing
Microsoft
Office 2000

nstalling Microsoft Office 2000 is relatively easy if you do the necessary preparation. Before you put the Office 2000 CD in your drive, you'll want to make sure
you have enough memory and hard drive capacity to use Office. Table A.1 lists
Microsoft's minimum and recommended hardware requirements and our comments. If you don't have enough hard drive space, consider removing files or folders
you don't use.

TABLE A.1: MINIMUM AND RECOMMENDED HARDWARE REQUIREMENTS FOR OFFICE 2000

Requirement	Microsoft Recommendation	Comments
32 bit Windows OS	NT 4.0 with Service Pack 3 or Windows 95 or 98	Windows 95 does not support some Outlook functionality.
Compatible PC	Pentium 90 or faster	We suggest at least a Pentium 200 unless you only want to run one or two programs at a time.
Memory	32MB or more	We tested Office 2000 at 40, 48, 64, 96, and 128MB. With less than 64MB, we noted performance differences—the more memory, the better.
Hard drive	250MB or more free; if you want to support more than one language, add 50MB for each language	If you don't have at least 500MB free, it's time to add another hard drive.
Registry (Windows NT only)	4MB or more free	
CD-ROM	Not indicated	At least 8X; the Office CDs would not run on the 4X drive we tested.

There are a number of versions of Office 2000; the differences are outlined in
Chapter 1, but each is supplied on one or more CDs. To begin installation, close any
open applications, and then insert CD 1 in your CD-ROM drive. The CD should run
automatically. If you've disabled the Windows AutoRun feature, open My Computer
or Explorer; then locate and double-click the setup.exe file on the CD-ROM to begin
installation. The Windows Installer will load and check your computer system, and
the message "Preparing to Install..." will appear in the Microsoft Office 2000 Setup
dialog box on the screen. In the first step of Office 2000 setup, shown in Figure A.1,

verify your name. Setup gets your name from your computer system; if it is incorrect, select and type over your name. Enter your initials and the 25-character CD key for the Office 2000 CD. Generally, you'll find the key on the CD case, but it may be included on a separate license packaged with your CD. Click Next to continue.

FIGURE A.1

Enter your name, initials, and CD Key to begin installation.

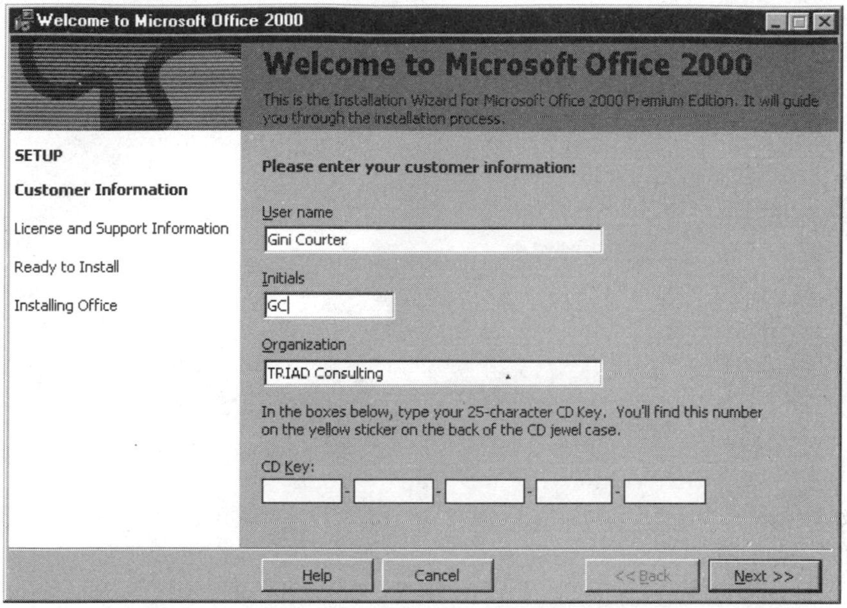

The EULA (end user license agreement) appears on the second page. You didn't really buy Office 2000 from Microsoft—you're licensing it. Take a minute and scroll through the terms of the agreement so you understand your rights and responsibilities with the software. (If you don't indicate that you agree with the terms, you cannot install Office 2000.) When you've finished reading, click the I Accept The Terms In The License Agreement option and click Next.

The third step of installation is to choose the Typical installation (or Upgrade Now if you have a prior version of Office) or indicate that you wish to customize the installation. We suggest that you choose Customize even if you don't want to make any changes to the Typical installation. Customizing is the only way you can see what features you are installing. Click Next.

In the fourth step (see Figure A.2), choose a location for the Office 2000 files. The default location is the Program Files directory on your boot drive (the hard drive that also has Windows installed). Office 2000 installs about 100MB of files on your boot drive, even if you choose to install on another hard drive; the remaining 150MB of files will be put in the drive and folder you designate here. Click Next to continue.

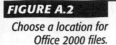

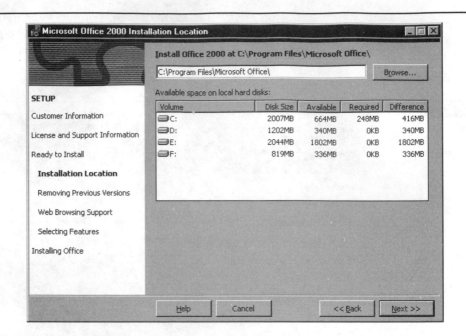

The Windows Installer searches your computer to see if you have any previous versions of Office programs installed. The applications will be listed, and you can choose to retain or remove them when Office 2000 is installed. If you are not sure you want to remove the programs right away, you can retain them. You can always remove the Office 95 or 97 applications later using Add/Remove Programs in the Windows Control Panel. Click Next to continue.

The Office 2000 CDs include Internet Explorer 5. You can install Office 2000 without installing IE 5, but there are some high-end Office features (like Presentation Broadcasting in PowerPoint) that use IE 5. Choose a Typical or Complete IE 5 upgrade or elect to retain your prior version of Internet Explorer, and then click Next.

If you chose a Custom installation, you'll now have an opportunity to review the optional application components that will be installed. The Office 2000 programs are listed in an Explorer-like tree. Click on a feature to see its description below the list. To see the options for an application, click the Expand button (the plus sign in front of the icon) to expand the view. In Figure A.3, Word has been expanded.

FIGURE A.3

*Click the plus sign to
view options for an
application.*

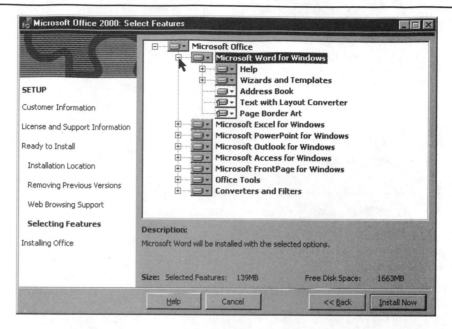

The Installer shows you the features that would have been installed if you had chosen Typical installation. With earlier versions of Office, you had an unappealing choice: either waste drive space on components you might not use or rerun Setup to add components you did not install initially. With Office 2000, you don't have to waste drive space or reinstall. A new feature called *Installation on Demand* lets you choose to install a component or feature the first time you try to use it. If there are features that you think might be needed at some point, you can make them available in the Setup program's Select Features window. Click on a feature's icon and select how, where, and when you want the feature installed from the menu:

Run From My Computer: Installs the feature on your computer now.

Run All From My Computer: Installs the feature and any related "subfeatures" on your computer now.

Run From Network: Installs the feature on your network.

Run All From Network: Installs the feature and any related "subfeatures" on your network.

Installed on First Use: Opens a message box to verify that you wish to install the feature on your computer the first time you attempt to use it in the application. This option is the default on some but not all features. For example, additional templates are by default installed on first use.

Not Available: The feature is not installed; to install the feature, you must run Office 2000 Setup again.

The required disk space and total free space available on the drive you selected earlier are displayed at the bottom of the dialog box (see Figure A.3); as you add or remove features from the installation list, these numbers change. You won't be allowed to select additional features after you exceed the free drive space. If you only have one hard drive and are installing features on your computer, make sure you still have 50–100 MB free after all the features are selected or you'll create problems for the Windows virtual memory manager.

 TIP If you work in a mixed-platform office with colleagues who use other computers and other application programs, pay particular attention to the Office Tools and Converters and Filters features. If you don't know what programs your colleagues use, you can hedge by installing all the filters and converters, or indicating they should be installed on demand.

When you have finished specifying which features should be installed, click the Install Now button to begin installing Office 2000. Depending on the features you selected and your computer's system speed, installation may take up to 50 minutes. A progress meter appears in the Setup dialog box to indicate how much of the installation is completed. At times, the meter may stop completely for several minutes. Don't assume this is a problem. If installation stops for more than 10 minutes with no drive activity, press Ctrl+Alt+Del to open the Close Program dialog box to see if Setup is shown as Not Responding. If it is, select Setup and click End Task (you may have to do this two or three times) to exit Setup. Exit Windows completely, restart Windows, and then launch Office 2000 Setup again from the CD.

When the first CD is finished, the Installer will prompt you to reboot your computer; click Yes.

 WARNING Although Microsoft's installation instructions indicate that you do not have to reboot until you have installed all of the Office 2000 CDs, we recommend rebooting after each CD to avoid problems with the installation process.

After you reboot your computer, the Installer requires a few more minutes to complete the installation before you are ready to use your new Office 2000 applications.

INDEX

Note to the Reader: Throughout this index **boldfaced** page numbers indicate primary discussions of a topic. *Italicized* page numbers indicate illustrations.

Symbols

' (apostrophes) in Visual Basic, 913
* (asterisks)
   in Access, 766
   in Excel, 549, 637, 646
   in Word, 102, 143
@ (at signs) in Excel, 637
\ (backslashes) in Excel, 637
^ (carets) in Excel, 549
, (commas) in Excel
   in format codes, 633
   for function arguments, 590
   in range names, 586
   for unions, 558
$ (dollar signs) in Excel, 594–595
= (equal signs)
   in Access, 736, 806
   in Excel, 549, 590
   in Word, 143
! (exclamation points) in Access, 766
> (greater than signs)
   in Access, 736, 806
   in Excel, 549
< (less than signs)
   in Access, 736, 806
   in Excel, 549
– (minus signs)
   in Access, 766
   in Excel, 549, 633
   in Word, 143
(number signs)
   in Access, 766
   in Excel
      for column overflow, 685
      in format codes, 632

() (parentheses) in Excel, 549, 552–553, 633
+ (plus signs)
   in Excel, 549
   in Word, 143
? (question marks)
   in Access, 766
   in Excel, 633
" (quotation marks) in Excel format codes, 633
/ (slashes)
   in Excel, 549, 633
   in Word, 143
[] (square brackets)
   in Access, 766, 810
   in Excel, 633
_ (underscores) in Excel, 586

A

absolute cell references, **593–595**, *594*
Accept option, 272
Accept All option, 272
Accept button, 506
Accept Change button, 272
Accept Labels In Formulas option, 551
Accept Or Reject Changes dialog box, 272–273, *273*
Access application
   Data Access Pages in, 7, **1063**
      controls for, **1068–1069**
      creating, **1063–1065**, *1064–1066*
      Design view for, **1067**, *1067*
      fields for, **1060**, **1068**, *1068*
      toolbox for, **1071–1072**
   databases in. *See* databases
   file formats for, 31–32, *32*
   formatting in

R

radar charts, 603
raised borders, 774
Range Finder, **557–558**
Range Of Recurrence option, 484
ranges
    for charts, 608, *609*
    in formulas, **557–558**
    names for, **585–588**, *587–588*, 685
    for pivot tables, 660, *661*
    printing, 576
    selecting, **548–549**
RATE function, 596
Read message icon, 465
read-only files, 261
Read-Only Recommended option, 279
Reapply The Formatting Of The Style To The
    Selection option, 179
receiving task assignments, **486–487**
Recently Used Files option, 698
Recolor Object option, 869
Recolor Picture dialog box, 333–334, *333*
Reconfigure Mail Support button, 380, 442, 522
Record Macro dialog box, 900–901, *901*, 914
Record Narration dialog box, 370, *370*
Record Navigation Section property, 1070
Record The Broadcast And Save It setting, 1085
recording
    Journal events, **431–434**, *431–434*
    macros, **900–901**, *901*
    slide show narrations, **369–371**, *370*
records
    in Access, 713
        adding hyperlinks to, **747–748**
        adding objects to, **746–747**, *747*
        deleting, **733**
        filtering, **735–737**, *735–736*
        sorting, **734–735**
        validating entries in, 744
    in Excel
        adding and deleting, **658**
        in databases, 640
        searching for, **658–659**

    for mail merge sources, 199–201
        editing, **202–205**, *204–205*
        entering, **202**
        sorting, 221
        specifying, **219–221**, *220*
Records ➤ Filter/Advanced Filter/Sort com-
    mand, 734
Records ➤ Remove Filter/Sort command,
    734–735
rectangles
    in Drawing, 151–152
    in Publisher, 987
Recurrence Pattern button, 484
recurring appointments, **497**, *497*
recurring tasks, **483–485**, *483*
Red Green Blue (RGB) color model, 979
redefining Word styles, **178–180**, *179*, *181*
Redo button, 35
Redraw button, 675
Reenter Password To Open (or Modify) box, 279
#REF value, 685
references, **593–595**, *594*
    circular, **686–687**, *687*
    in conditional formatting, **630–631**
    errors in, 685
    external and 3-D, 587
    in formulas, **557–558**, **593–595**, *594*
    for linking, 679, **681–682**, *682*
    in macros, **904**
    names as, **589**, *589*
referential integrity, **754–757**, *755*
Refresh Data button, 838
Refresh Data On File Open option, 840
Refresh Every X Minutes option, 839
refreshable text importing, **657**
refreshing. *See* updating
regular text in mail merge, 209
Rehearsal dialog box, 365
Rehearse Timings button, 365
Reject option, 272
Reject All option, 272
related tables, 719, 767
relating contacts, **408**

X

Y

Learn Proven Techniques from the Experts

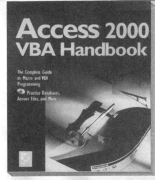

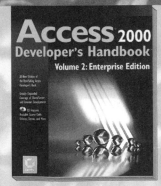